Shakespeare, Co-Author

A Historical Study of Five Collaborative Plays

Shakespeare, Co-Author

A Historical Study of
Five Collaborative Plays

BRIAN VICKERS

OXFORD
UNIVERSITY PRESS

OXFORD
UNIVERSITY PRESS

Great Clarendon Street, Oxford OX2 6DP

Oxford University Press is a department of the University of Oxford.
It furthers the University's objective of excellence in research, scholarship,
and education by publishing worldwide in

Oxford New York

Auckland Bangkok Buenos Aires Cape Town Chennai
Dar es Salaam Delhi Hong Kong Istanbul Karachi Kolkata
Kuala Lumpur Madrid Melbourne Mexico City Mumbai Nairobi
São Paulo Shanghai Taipei Tokyo Toronto

Oxford is a registered trade mark of Oxford University Press
in the UK and in certain other countries

Published in the United States
by Oxford University Press Inc., New York

First published 2002

First published in paperback 2004

British Library Cataloguing in Publication Data

Data available

Library of Congress Cataloging in Publication Data

Vickers, Brian.
Shakespeare, co-author : a historical study of five collaborative plays / Brian Vickers.
p. cm.
Includes bibliographical references (p.) and index.
1. Shakespeare, William, 1564–1616–Authorship. 2. Shakespeare, William,
1564–1616. Two gentlemen of Verona. 3. Shakespeare, William, 1564–1616. Titus
Andronicus. 4. Shakespeare, William, 1564–1616. Timon of Athens. 5. Shakespeare,
William, 1564–1616. King Henry VIII. 6. Shakespeare, William, 1564–1616. Pericles. 7.
Playwriting–Collaboration–History. I. Title.

PR2937 .V53 2002 822.3'3–dc21 2002031262

ISBN 0-19-925653-5
ISBN 0-19-926916-5 (pbk.)

1 3 5 7 9 10 8 6 4 2

Typeset in Sabon
by SNP Best-set Typesetter Ltd., Hong Kong
Printed in Great Britain
on acid-free paper by
T.J. International Ltd., Padstow, Cornwall

For

WARD ELLIOTT
JONATHAN HOPE
MACDONALD JACKSON
DAVID LAKE

Preface

THIS BOOK ASKS the question, 'How much do we know about Shakespeare's collaborations with other dramatists?', and attempts to extend that knowledge. Given that collaboration was very common in the Elizabethan, Jacobean, and Caroline theatre, and that every major and most minor dramatists shared in the writing of plays, it would be highly unusual if Shakespeare had not done so. Indeed, since the early nineteenth century scholars have been accumulating many kinds of evidence identifying at least four co-authors: George Peele on *Titus Andronicus*, Thomas Middleton on *Timon of Athens*, George Wilkins on *Pericles*, John Fletcher on *Henry VIII* and *The Two Noble Kinsmen*. The case for those co-authors seems to me sufficiently strong to warrant a detailed evaluation of the claims made, and the methodologies used. I mention in passing *1 Henry VI* and *Edward III*, where the identity of the sharer(s) is still shadowy, and also discuss 'The Booke of Sir Thomas More', where Shakespeare contributed one scene and an additional speech for the revision of a play which seems never to have been produced. *More* is an anomaly in many respects, but the intensive study of this theatre manuscript since the 1920s has yielded several important insights into the nature of collaborative composition in those days, and into the practice of authorship studies today.

When I planned this study I imagined that it would be a relatively straightforward matter to trace the emergence of a coherent methodology in Shakespeare authorship studies. I found, in fact, that there were many types of method, some fully worked out in the mid- and late nineteenth century, others only emerging since the 1960s. I also realized that some of these earlier approaches, although valuable, had been either never properly noticed or else forgotten, so that their findings had to be rediscovered one or more generations later. Tracing the history of this development turned out to be more complex, and far more rewarding, than I had expected. In any discipline it is inevitable that the historical tradition will not be passed on intact, due to the restricted availability of some texts (published in foreign languages, or in obscure journals) and to general changes in taste. But I discovered that many of these essays arguing for Shakespeare's co-authorship had been consistently overlooked or misrepresented by otherwise rational scholars, who seemed determined to cling at all costs to the post-Romantic image of him as a solitary genius having no need of aid from lesser mortals. The Shakespeare 'conservators' ignored or rejected large parts of the scholarly record, and no doubt influenced many readers unacquainted with the scholarship, and who lacked either the training or the access to learned libraries that would enable them to judge for themselves. But even more influential—in a bad way, as I have come to see—were the editions of individual plays in the Arden, New Penguin, and new Oxford and Cambridge series, which are read by successive generations of college students and increasingly used by theatre directors. To anyone who thinks that knowledge automatically advances it is sobering to realize that the four editions of *Titus Andronicus* that have recently appeared in these deservedly popular series—by Eugene Waith (Oxford, 1984), Alan Hughes (Cambridge, 1994), Jonathan Bate (Arden, 1995), Jacques Berthoud and Sonia Massai (Penguin, 2001)—all deny the very detailed case made over the last eighty years for Peele's authorship of at least three scenes in that play (1.1, 2.1, 4.1—several scholars would add 2.2). Similarly conservative attitudes, unwilling to accept the evidence for a co-author, have been enshrined in recent editions of *Timon of Athens*, *Pericles*, and *Henry VIII*, and it seems a matter of some importance to try to put the record straight.

My opening chapter discusses the standard processes of collaboration as they can be reconstructed from the plays themselves and from documents connected with the Elizabethan stage, such as the surviving correspondence and other dealings between the impresario Philip Henslowe and the group of script-writers to whom he fed sums of money in return for acts of a play. I summarize the huge discussion of *Sir Thomas More* in order to introduce the methods used in authorship studies, a topic pursued in more detail in Chapter 2. Here I review the range of tests used since the early nineteenth century, some of which have fallen into disuse or ill-repute—much the same thing. Whoever reads any of the five plays discussed here will often notice distinct differences in the verse style between one scene and that following. As the early pioneers showed—Charles Lamb (1808), Henry Weber (1812), Charles Knight (1842–9), Samuel Hickson (1847), James Spedding (1850), F. G. Fleay (1874)—these differences can be isolated and counted, involving such objectively measurable features of verse style as the use of eleven-syllable lines (the so-called 'feminine endings'), the placing of internal pauses, and the use of run-on lines (enjambement). The authorship divisions made by such methods in the nineteenth century were remarkably accurate, and have been confirmed by quite different linguistic tests. Although fashions changed, and verse tests went out of favour for a while, their validity was confirmed by the introduction of far more rigorous metrical procedures by Ants Oras (1960) and Marina Tarlinskaja (1987). The latter's methods, based on the quantitative metrics of the modern Russian school, can seem forbiddingly technical at times, but it is worth persevering with them for the great precision with which they can identify an author's characteristic metrical preferences.

Another method that went out of favour, due to its having been abused, was the identification of anonymous authors on the basis of verbal parallels. J. M. Robertson, in particular, who stigmatized any passage in Shakespeare which seemed to his aesthetic sense unworthy of the bard, and cast around to find likely co-authors or revisers, heaped up piles of verbal parallels without any scholarly consideration for accidental resemblances or commonplace poetic diction. He and others discredited the method, but they provoked two scholars in the 1930s (Muriel St Clare Byrne and A. M. Sampley) to redefine the criteria by which parallel passages could be validly used in authorship studies. As I show, all the leading authorities on the two most fruitfully studied dramatic canons, those of John Fletcher and Thomas Middleton, have admitted verbal parallels as relevant supporting evidence: E. H. C. Oliphant, R. H. Barker, Cyrus Hoy, David J. Lake, and MacDonald P. Jackson.

These scholars have used other newer, linguistic, approaches, such as identifying an author's preferred vocabulary (Latinate or Anglo-Saxon, learned or popular), habits of word-formation, choice of oaths or expletives, variant grammatical forms (*has* or *hath*, *whiles* or *while*), and even the frequency with which they use such apparently insignificant 'function words' as *and* or *of*. The whole trend of authorship studies in the last half-century has been towards more intense computation, using statistical methods and electronic data-processing. The advantages of such approaches are great, but so are the risks, and for this reason I have given a separate discussion of statistics and stylometry (as this quantifying approach is sometimes known). Here, to begin with, I document some recent misuses of literary statistics, both to provide a cautionary tale and to address the situation diagnosed by MacDonald Jackson, in which

Most literary scholars unduly distrust statistics, tending to suppose that one 'can prove anything' by them. The truth is, however, that the greater your understanding of statistical tests of significance the less likely you are to be duped by a mere show of statistical argument. They simply allow a just assessment of the strength of the evidence presented, and of the probabilities in favour of a particular conclusion.[1]

That said, it remains true that the quantifying of stylistic features is an essential tool in authorship studies, and has often been used to great effect. My text includes dozens of statistical tables, some from published work, others of my own devising. Readers are urged to treat these as an integral part of the argument.

The bulk of this book consists of a detailed evaluation of the claims made for Shakespeare's co-authorship of the five plays discussed here. I have included every study that I could find which made a notable contribution to the discussion, for or against. Since I am by nature and conviction a historian of ideas, concerned with the ways in which knowledge has come into being, I have not felt it unusual to be discussing work written in 1812 by an editor of

---

[1] M. P. Jackson, *Studies in Attribution: Middleton and Shakespeare*, Jacobean Drama Studies, vol. 79 (Salzburg, 1979), pp. 5–6.

Beaumont and Fletcher (Henry Weber), or by a distinguished German editor and translator such as Nikolaus Delius in the 1860s. It is a naïve but all too common assumption these days that work produced more than twenty years ago is no longer worth reading, as the citation of authors in current periodical articles will show. However, in authorship studies we must be prepared to recognize that valuable contributions have been made in every generation since the early 1800s, and that their findings have been frequently repeated by later scholars. Although approaching the topic historically, I have not attempted to write a history of Shakespeare authorship studies, which would have involved a great deal of summarizing, and tracing many false paths. Here I am only interested in the pertinent arguments that scholars have made, addressing the concrete evidence of an author's style or thought, and using valid methodologies. I have selected the arguments and examples quoted, as my own understanding of the issues has developed, so that the evaluations made here are personal—but also, I hope, rationally argued and persuasive.

Much of my discussion addresses the co-authored plays' language and style, where differences of authorship are most visible, and can best be differentiated using quantitative methods. But I have consciously avoided the error, as I see it, of some recent studies, which treat stylistic evidence as a thing in itself, a pool of statistics having an autonomous significance. I believe that stylistic and linguistic evidence should be interpreted in the context of a whole play, or a writer's whole oeuvre, as can be seen from my treatment of Peele's share in *Titus Andronicus*, where I draw on many of his other poems and plays to show the identity of style, on several levels, between them and the four scenes he contributed to that play. In the concluding chapter (7) I return to the whole text, showing that co-authorship can be seen just as clearly in the treatment of character and motive as in language. Aaron as treated by Peele is very different from what he becomes when Shakespeare takes over the writing; Middleton's characterization of Timon, the Steward, and Alcibiades differs greatly from Shakespeare's; while in the two plays shared with Fletcher the differences are even more striking: Wolsey in *Henry VIII*, or Emilia in *The Two Noble Kinsmen*, as treated by the two co-authors, might be characters from two different plays.

In preparing this book I have contracted a number of debts, the greatest being to the four scholars to whom it is dedicated. Like everyone else working in this field, I have learned a great deal from their published work, which demonstrates a remarkably sustained attention to linguistic detail, a readiness to bring many areas of knowledge to bear on the problem in hand, and a willingness to redefine a hypothesis in the light of new evidence. In a period which has seen the fragmentation and disintegration of literary criticism in many areas it is heartening to see scholarship of this quality going from strength to strength. In addition to this general indebtedness, I have been fortunate in that all four have generously exchanged information and sent me their work in progress. David Lake allowed me to quote from an unpublished essay, as did MacDonald Jackson, who also—along with Jonathan Hope— read the penultimate version and made many fruitful suggestions. They are all, in a way, co-authors of this book, and I hope it is worthy of them.

My old friend Richard Gordon generously shared his vast knowledge of Roman history with me when I was attempting to strengthen the argument for Peele's co-authorship of *Titus Andronicus* by differentiating his Latinity from Shakespeare's.

Over several years of research and writing I have been very fortunate to have the help of my assistant Katherine Hahn, whose skills in understanding my meaning were matched by the good-humoured resilience with which she endured its constant revisions. My former assistant, Dr Margrit Soland, kindly helped check both the typescript and the proofs. Annette Baertschi was highly competent in doing bibliographical work, helping with the typing, and preparing the index. Stefan Keller applied his expertise to converting the illustrations into electronic form. I have been privileged to enjoy near ideal working conditions at the ETH, and I thank the current Vice-President for Research, Professor Ulrich Suter, in the name of all who have administered its resources in the quarter-century I have been working here.

At Oxford University Press I wish to thank my editor, Sophie Goldsworthy, for her encouragement and support, Frances Whistler for co-ordinating production, and Pat Lawrence for her meticulous copy-editing.

Last, and most, I thank Sabine, Helen, and Philip for putting up with an author who all too often grumbled about the task he had undertaken.

B. V.

Contents

List of Plates

List of Figures

List of Tables

References and Abbreviations

The first time the title of a book or journal article is cited in each chapter it is given in full in the text or notes, and subsequently cited in the short form, e.g. 'Greg 1955'. Those titles referred to most often are listed in the Bibliography. Frequently cited journal titles are always abbreviated, as are some books, as follows.

ABBREVIATIONS OF JOURNALS AND BOOKS

ALLC Bulletin	*Association of Linguistic and Literary Computing Bulletin*
CahiersE	*Cahiers Elisabéthains*
CHS	*Shakespeare: The Critical Heritage*: see Vickers 1974–81
CHum	*Computers and the Humanities*
Eliz. S	*The Elizabethan Stage*: see Chambers 1923
ELR	*English Literary Renaissance*
ES	*English Studies*
GM	*Gentleman's Magazine*
JCS	*Jacobean and Caroline Stage*: see Bentley 1941–68
JEGP	*Journal of English and Germanic Philology*
LLC	*Literary and Linguistic Computing*
MLR	*Modern Language Review*
MP	*Modern Philology*
MRDE	*Medieval and Renaissance Drama in English*
MSR	*Malone Society Reprints*
NQ	*Notes and Queries*
PBA	*Proceedings of the British Academy*
PBSA	*Papers of the Bibliographical Society of America*
PMLA	*Publications of the Modern Language Association of America*
RES	*Review of English Studies*
RORD	*Research Opportunities in Renaissance Drama*
SB	*Studies in Bibliography*
ShJb	*Shakespeare Jahrbuch*
ShN	*Shakespeare Newsletter*
ShQ	*Shakespeare Quarterly*
ShS	*Shakespeare Survey*
ShStud	*Shakespeare Studies*
SP	*Studies in Philology*
TLS	*Times Literary Supplement*
TNSS	*Transactions of the New Shakspere Society*
TxC	*A Textual Companion*: see Wells *et al.* 1987

PART I

Elizabethan Drama and the Methodology of Authorship Studies

I

Authorship in English Renaissance Drama

No issue in Shakespeare studies is more important than determining what he wrote. We cannot form any reliable impression of his work as a dramatist unless we can distinguish his authentic plays from those spuriously ascribed to him, whether by publishers in his own age or by scholars in the four centuries intervening, and unless we can identify those parts of collaborative plays that were written by him together with one or more fellow dramatists.

AUTHORSHIP AND AUTHENTICITY

Most modern readers accept the canon of Shakespeare's works as if it had come together by some innate self-justifying force. Their one-volume editions include as entirely his work the five plays I shall be studying here—*Titus Andronicus*, *Timon of Athens*, *Pericles*, *King Henry VIII*, and *The Two Noble Kinsmen*—indeed, many recent specialist editions of those plays ascribe them wholly to Shakespeare, dismissing all evidence of another hand at work. It is a curious fact that the theatrical and publishing tradition which established the authenticity of the plays ascribed to Shakespeare also managed to suppress—or perhaps just obscure—any sign that he ever worked together with other dramatists. How did this erosion of his co-authors come about? Was it accidental, or deliberate? To answer these questions we need to know how that authenticating tradition established itself.

The first substantial evidence of Shakespeare's output as a dramatist was a list given by Francis Meres in his *Palladis Tamia: Wits Treasury* (1598). A graduate of Pembroke College, Cambridge, and subsequently rector and schoolmaster in Wing, Rutland, Meres published an essay 'Of Poetrie', or 'A comparative discourse of our English Poets with the Greeke, Latine, and Italian Poets', which contains the following tribute:

As the soule of *Euphorbus* was thought to live in *Pythagoras*: so the sweete wittie soule of *Ovid* lives in mellifluous & hony-tongued *Shakespeare*, witnes his *Venus* and *Adonis*, his *Lucrece*, his sugred Sonnets among his private friends, &c.

As *Plautus* and *Seneca* are accounted the best for Comedy and Tragedy among the Latines: so *Shakespeare* among the English is the most excellent in both kinds for the stage; for Comedy, witnes his *Gentlemen of Verona*, his *Errors*, his *Love labors lost*, his *Love labours wonne*, his *Midsummers night dreame*, & his *Merchant of Venice*: for Tragedy his *Richard the 2. Richard the 3. Henry the 4. King Iohn, Titus Andronicus* and his *Romeo and Iuliet*.

As *Epius Stolo* said, that the Muses would speake with *Plautus* tongue, if they would speak Latin: so I say that the Muses would speake with Shakespeares fine filed phrase, if they would speake English. . . .[1]

Any belief that Meres might have been making some original judgement was dashed by Don Cameron Allen's demonstration that Meres had modelled himself on a popular work by the neo-Latin writer, J. Ravisius Textor, *Officina* (1520; seven editions by 1595), simply inserting English names for the original catalogue of Latin authors.[2] (Meres also plagiarized from English authors: Ascham, Webbe, Puttenham, Sidney.) Although completely derivative as a critic, Meres at least testifies to the fact that by 1598 Shakespeare was known to have written his two narrative poems (published in 1593 and 1594 respectively), some sonnets, which were circulating in manuscript copies, six comedies (including the enigmatic *Love's Labour's Won*), four history plays—although no such genre was then recognized—and two tragedies. Meres's silence on Shakespeare's earlier plays, such as the three parts of *Henry VI* and *The Taming of the Shrew*, may reflect the fact that they were no longer in the London repertory. Certainly popularity was an element in his works becoming known, as we see from Gabriel Harvey's note (*c.*1598–1601) that 'The younger sort takes much delight in Shakespeares Venus, & Adonis, but his Lucrece, & his tragedie of Hamlet, Prince of Denmarke, have it in them, to please the wiser sort' (Chambers 1930, ii. 197). Soon several Shakespearian characters were famous enough to be alluded to frequently, notably Falstaff, Hamlet, Romeo, Richard III, and Julius Caesar (pp. 199 ff.).

Shakespeare's activity as a poet and dramatist was gradually documented by the works which got into print. His two narrative poems were the first of his writings to be published, *Venus and Adonis* (1593), *The Rape of Lucrece* (1594). Neither of them included his name on the title-page, but both contained a dedication signed 'William Shakespeare'. *Venus and Adonis* was reprinted ten times by 1617, *Lucrece* five times (Chambers 1930, i. 543–7). Shakespeare's name also appeared on a spuriously published collection of twenty short poems, *The Passionate Pilgrime*, an octavo brought out by William Jaggard in 1599 (reprinted twice: n.d., 1612), which included

---

[1] E. K. Chambers, *William Shakespeare: A Study of Facts and Problems*, 2 vols. (Oxford, 1930), ii. 193–4.
[2] See D. C. Allen (ed.), *Francis Meres's Treatise 'Of Poetrie'* (Urbana, Ill., 1933), pp. 31–50.

versions of two sonnets (nos. 138, 144), and three poems extracted from *Love's Labour's Lost*. In 1601 Edward Blount published *The Phoenix and the Turtle*, a collection of poems by Robert Chester celebrating the wedded love of his patron, one of which was a *Threnos*, signed 'William Shakespeare'. In 1609 Thomas Thorpe published *Shake-speares Sonnets*.

The first of Shakespeare's plays to be printed were *Henry VI*, Parts 2 and 3, or, as they were then called, *The First part of the Contention betwixt the two famous Houses of Yorke and Lancaster* (1594), and *The true Tragedie of Richard Duke of Yorke* (1595), both 'Bad quartos'. This term describes versions of plays put together by actors from the memory of actual performances, the texts sometimes eked out with written material, such as an actor's 'part' or role, gaps being filled with material of their own invention.[3] Shakespeare's name occasionally appears on these early quartos, whether memorial reconstructions or legitimate texts passed on to the printer by the acting company, which effectively owned the copyright. Thus it appears not on the first (1597) but on the second quarto (1598) of *Richard III*, and on the four subsequent quarto editions (1602, 1605, 1612, 1622) published by 1623. Shakespeare's name appears on the first quarto (1598) of *Love's Labour's Lost*; not on the first (1597) of *Richard II*, but on all the subsequent quartos (1598—twice, 1608, 1615); not on the first quarto (1600) of *A Midsummer Night's Dream* but on Thomas Pavier's 1619 reprint, falsely dated '1600'; on both quartos (1600, 1619) of *The Merchant of Venice*; not on the first quarto (1598) but on the second and subsequent quartos of *1 Henry IV* (1599, 1604, 1608, 1613, 1622). Shakespeare's name appeared for the first time in the register kept by the Stationers' Company, the association of printers who licensed publishing (mostly in London), on 23 August 1600

---

[3] In recent years some scholars have contested the distinction between 'Good' and 'Bad' Quartos, but without eliciting universal agreement. Their arguments seem to me insufficient, and it is symptomatic that they have failed to give a fair account of the evidence and arguments produced by G. I. Duthie, *The 'Bad' Quarto of Hamlet: A Critical Study* (Cambridge, 1941), and Alfred Hart, *Stolne and Surreptitious Copies: A Comparative Study of Shakespeare's Bad Quartos* (Melbourne and London, 1942). For the disastrous effects of this scepticism, which must now take the 1603 quarto of *Hamlet* to be Shakespeare's first draft of the play, see Brian Vickers, 'Hamlet by Dogberry: A perverse reading of the Bad Quarto', *TLS*, 24 Dec. 1993, pp. 5–6. This is a review of the edition of the 1603 quarto of *Hamlet* by Graham Holderness and Bryan Loughrey, *The Tragicall Historie of Hamlet Prince of Denmark* (Hemel Hempstead, 1992), a remarkably confused attempt to mix the traditional role of an editor with some postmodern ideas about the indeterminacy of editing and the non-existence of the author, claiming that this 'Bad' Quarto deserves to be included in a series called 'Shakespearean originals' as being somehow an 'authentic' theatrical text. A more heartening contribution has been made by Kathleen O. Irace, who decided to test the theory of these texts having been produced by memory, and 'designed a computer-assisted analysis in order to measure the degree of correspondence—if any—between the six short quartos and the alternative familiar versions, in lines spoken and heard by every character in each of the twelve texts. Rather than overturning the theory of memorial reconstruction, to my surprise I found that it provided strong evidence confirming the hypothesis': Irace (ed.), *The First Quarto of Hamlet* (Cambridge, 1998), pp. 6–7, with literature cited there.

for 'Two bookes, the one called Much a Doo about nothinge. Thother the second parte of the history of Kinge Henry the IIIJth with the humours of Sir John Falstaff: Wrytten by master Shakespere' (Chambers 1930, i. 377, 384). A 'booke' was the term used to describe a playhouse manuscript or prompt-book, prepared by or for the 'book holder', who acted as stage manager and prompter. Both 2 *Henry IV* and *Much Ado* were issued in a single quarto edition (1600), each verified as being 'Written by William Shakespeare'. That Shakespeare's name already had some drawing power for the book-buying public is shown by the fact that his name appeared on the title-page of both quartos of *Hamlet*, the spurious 1603 text, produced by actors eking out their memory of the play with the script of one or two roles (only 2,154 lines long, it contains over 400 lines not by Shakespeare), and the authentic one issued by his own company 'according to the true and perfect Coppie', and now 3,723 lines long (1604, 1611). Shakespeare's name appeared on both quartos (1602, 1619) of *The Merry Wives of Windsor*; on the single quarto (1609)— both issues—of *Troilus and Cressida*; and on the first quarto of *Othello* (1622). The Stationers' Register for 26 November 1607 included an entry for 'A booke called Master William Shakespeare his historye of King Lear, as yt was played before the Kinges maiestie at Whitehall uppon Sainct Stephens night at Christmas Last, by his maiesties servantes playinge vsually at the Globe on the Bankesyde' (Chambers 1930, i. 463), an unusually full record, reflecting the privileged position that he and his company now enjoyed. The respectful title 'Master' appeared in abbreviated form as 'M. William Shakespeare' on both the 1608 quarto of *Lear* and on Pavier's 1619 reprint, misdated as '1608'. Shakespeare's name does not appear on the title-pages of the quarto editions of two plays written solely by him, *Romeo and Juliet* (1597, 1599, 1609), and *Henry V* (1600, 1602, 1619), nor on the play which he wrote jointly with George Peele, *Titus Andronicus* (1594, 1600, 1611). His name, alone, appears on the title-page of *Pericles* (1609), which he wrote jointly with George Wilkins, and when Pavier reissued the two parts of *The Whole Contention* in 1619, after the dramatist's death, he described them as 'Written by William Shakespeare, Gent.'.

No great significance should be attached to the presence or absence of Shakespeare's name in the early quarto editions, for the theatre company selling texts to a printer for its own gain (often in times of hardship) was not obliged to communicate the authors' names. But these simple publishing details do establish that Shakespeare's fame as a dramatist soon spread to the booksellers and the reading public. His name appears (by my count) on a total of forty-nine quarto and octavo editions of plays and poems published between 1598 and 1622, far more frequently than any other poet or drama-tist, indeed, more often than most professional writers.

The legitimacy of these quarto editions was established by the single authoritative document establishing the canon of Shakespeare's authentic plays, the first collected edition, a large folio volume, *Mr. William Shakespeares Comedies, Histories, & Tragedies. Published according to the True Originall Copies* (London, printed by Isaac Jaggard and Ed. Blount, 1623).[4] This volume was edited by John Heminge (d. 1630) and Henry Condell (d. 1627), whose names also appear in the folio among 'The Names of the Principall Actors in all these Playes', along with Shakespeare himself, Richard Burbage, William Kempe, Robert Armin, and twenty others. Heminge (together with Shakespeare, Burbage, Augustine Phillips, William Kempe, George Bryan, Thomas Pope, and Richard Cowley) had been one of the eight 'sharers' in the acting profits of the Chamberlain's Men, the acting troupe founded in the summer of 1594, which performed at the Curtain until they built the Globe in 1599. With the accession of James I in 1603 they were able to acquire the monarch as their patron, being renamed the King's Men. Condell probably joined the Chamberlain's Men in 1594, although not at first as a sharer. Heminge (with Shakespeare again) was also one of the five 'housekeepers' of the Globe, entitled to a share of the takings, and he and Condell enjoyed that privilege when the company opened the Blackfriars, their indoor (winter) playhouse, in 1608. In his will Shakespeare left both Heminge and Condell 26s. 8d. to buy a ring in his memory. The involvement of two actors who had worked with Shakespeare for nearly twenty years guarantees the authenticity of all the plays included in their edition, although of course it does not mean that Shakespeare was the sole author of those plays.

When Heminge and Condell were collecting Shakespeare's works for publication they had to negotiate with those printers who owned the copyright of plays already published, some of whom set up a syndicate with Jaggard and Blount; between them they had a clear title to twenty-two plays. All of these quarto editions were used, in one way or another, sometimes by collation (not always systematic) with surviving manuscripts in order to produce the printed texts of the folio, with the exception of *Pericles* (to which I shall return). Jaggard and his colleagues also secured from the King's Men the printing rights for sixteen hitherto unpublished plays, of which the company owned the manuscripts. These manuscripts were either Shakespeare's original draughts or some version prepared for acting by the 'book-keeper' or prompter, as we would call him today. The plays published for the first time in the 1623 folio were *The Tempest, Two Gentlemen of Verona, Measure for Measure, The Comedy of Errors, As You Like It, All's Well That Ends Well, Twelfth Night, The Winter's Tale, Henry VI*, three parts, *Henry VIII*,

---

[4] The best modern edition is the Norton Facsimile, prepared by Charlton Hinman, *The First Folio of Shakespeare*, in its second edition, with a new introduction by P. W. M. Blayney (New York and London, 1996).

Coriolanus, Timon of Athens, Julius Caesar, Macbeth, Anthony and Cleopatra, and *Cymbeline*. The thirty-six folio plays formed the accepted canon of Shakespeare's works in 1623, together with the narrative poems *Venus and Adonis* (1593) and *The Rape of Lucrece* (1594), *Phoenix and the Turtle* (1601), and the *Sonnets* (1609). The folio was successful enough to be reprinted in 1632, with no additions, although with some printing alterations, of varying value.

The importance of the First Folio in authenticating Shakespeare's plays cannot be emphasized too highly. But by the same token it established the image of Shakespeare as the sole author of all the plays it contained, an image which persists to the present day and has allowed many scholars to dismiss out of hand any arguments for co-authorship. I shall present below abundant evidence that one of the quartos reprinted in the folio, *Titus Andronicus*, was the joint work of Shakespeare and Peele, and that two of the plays published for the first time in the folio, *Timon of Athens* and *Henry VIII*, were jointly written with Middleton and Fletcher, respectively. Evidence that Shakespeare had worked with a co-author emerged not long after the Second Folio was published, for the Stationers' Register for 8 April 1634 included an entry for John Waterson: 'Entred for his Copy under the hands of Sir Henry Herbert and master Apsley Warden a Tragi Comedy called the two noble kinsmen by John ffletcher and William Shakespeare' (Chambers 1930, i. 528), and later that year Waterson duly published a quarto edition of *The Two Noble Kinsmen . . . Written by the memorable Worthies of their Time, Mr John Fletcher, and Mr William Shakespeare.* This collaborative play did not appear in the first edition of the plays of Beaumont, Fletcher, Massinger, and others (1647), but it was included in the Second Folio, *Fifty Comedies and Tragedies. Written by Francis Beaumont and John Fletcher, Gentlemen. All in One Volume. Published by the Authors Original Copies, the Songs to each Play being added* (1679), but without any mention of Shakespeare's authorship, and it never appeared in any of the folio editions of Shakespeare's works. This is the more surprising, since the Third Folio, printed for Philip Chetwinde in 1663, was reissued in 1664, and now included 'seven Playes, never before Printed in folio, viz. Pericles, Prince of Tyre. The London Prodigall, The History of Thomas Ld. Cromwell. Sir John Oldcastle, Lord Cobham. The Puritan Widow. A Yorkshire Tragedy. The Tragedy of Locrine'. With the exception of *Pericles*, these ascriptions were spurious, constituting what is now known as 'The Shakespeare Apocrypha'. The Fourth Folio (1685), the last published in the seventeenth century, reprinted the contents of the Third, with additional errors and corrections.

The process of authenticating Shakespeare's plays, then, seems to have been one that could not accommodate, at the same time, the recognition that he sometimes wrote collaboratively. Heminge and Condell may not have known that Shakespeare was only part author of *Titus Andronicus*, since the 1594 Quarto records that 'it was Plaide by the Right Honourable the Earle of Darbie, Earle of Pembrooke, and Earl of Sussex their Servants' (Chambers 1930, i. 312). Heminge joined Strange's Men in May 1593 (a company known after September 1593 as the Earl of Derby's),[5] but the play may be earlier than this. However, as sharers of the King's Men, and lessees of the Globe and Blackfriars, it is hard to imagine that Heminge and Condell did not know that Thomas Middleton was the co-author of *Timon of Athens* (which they included in the Folio)—if it was ever performed. They surely knew that Shakespeare was part author both of *Pericles* (with George Wilkins) and *The Two Noble Kinsmen* (with Fletcher), since these plays had been performed by the King's Men, but they included neither of them in the 1623 Folio. They (or Shakespeare) may have felt that the 1609 quarto of *Pericles* (printed for Henry Gosson) was corrupt, produced by some unauthorized means, although the title-page announces it as 'By William Shakespeare'. The Stationers' Register records that 'A booke called The booke of Pericles prynce of Tyre' was entered to Edward Blount on 20 May 1608 (Chambers 1930, i. 518), and Blount ultimately became one of the syndicate who printed the 1623 Folio, so that there is no prima-facie reason why the play could not have been included. The Stationers' Register also records that the copyright was transferred by the widow of Thomas Pavier in 1626 to E. Brewster and R. Bird, and again in 1630 from Bird to Richard Cotes, but none of these reprinted the play. As for *The Two Noble Kinsmen*, written *c*.1613–14 and performed at court in 1619, since Fletcher wrote regularly for the King's Men, especially for their indoor theatre, the Blackfriars (opened in 1609), it remains equally mysterious why this play never appeared among Shakespeare's works, when *Henry VIII*, their first collaboration, had done so. Another play apparently written by Shakespeare and Fletcher, *Cardenio*, has perished altogether. John Heminge, who acted as the company's treasurer, was the payee on 20 May 1613 for court performances of 'six several playes . . . One other Cardenno', and received further payment for a performance on 8 June 1613 'before the Duke of Savoyes Embassadour'. In 1653 Humphrey Moseley, a stationer and manuscript collector, registered 'The History of Cardennio, by Mr. Fletcher & Shakespeare', the last record of the play. When we consider that surviving plays in the period 1579–1642 total 620, with at least 1,500 titles lost,[6] its disappearance is not unusual. There is a doubtful tradition that Lewis Theobald acquired the manuscript, adapting it for his

[5] E. K. Chambers, *The Elizabethan Stage*, 4 vols. (Oxford, 1923), ii. 118–27, 321; hereafter referred to as *Eliz. S.*

[6] See Gertrude M. Sibley, *The Lost Plays and Masques (1500–1642)* (Ithaca, NY, 1933) for an annotated checklist of the titles of works known but lost. Some scholars estimate the total number of plays produced in this period to be around 3,000.

own play *The Double Falsehood* (1727), but the arguments claiming that Theobald's text preserves something of Shakespeare and Fletcher's original seem to me unconvincing.[7]

Perhaps the most sensible interpretation of the activities of Heminge and Condell in bringing together the thirty-six plays contained in the First Folio was their desire to preserve all the plays for which they could secure the printing rights in whose composition Shakespeare had been involved, whether as whole or part author. We can perhaps get a better perspective on their treatment of the authorship question by reviewing the publishing history of co-authored plays between 1580 and 1642. In general, the main priority of most title-pages of quarto play-texts published in this period was to identify the theatre company which owned the play, and was allowing it to be published: *The Tragedie of King Richard the Second. As it hath been publikely acted by the right Honourable the Lord Chamberlaine his Servants.* Secondarily, the theatre may be specified: *The Tragœdy of Othello, The Moore of Venice. As it hath been diverse times acted at the Globe, and at the Black-Friers, by his Maiesties Servants,* or a royal connection advertised, *The Merry Wives of Windsor* having been '*divers times Acted . . . Both before her Maiestie and else-where*'. The author's name was an optional extra, and was often not divulged. Sometimes only the dramatist's initials were revealed: 'R.G.' for Robert Greene, 'I.M.' for Marston, 'G.P.' for Peele, 'T.M.' for Middleton, 'P.M.' for Massinger, 'W.R.' for Rowley, or their name abbreviated: 'Ch. Marl.' for Christopher Marlowe. John Ford(e) identified himself to those in the know with the anagram 'Fide Honor', which appears on several title-pages (but the dedications are frequently signed with his name).

Given the low priority then attached to naming the dramatist, it is hardly surprising that many of the plays now known to be collaborations were published anonymously. Yet a number of them did identify the dramatists concerned (sometimes erroneously[8]), and if we arrange these instances chronologically we will discover what seems to be an increasing readiness to acknowledge joint creations.[9] In some cases individual dramatists may have

---

[7] For a recent discussion see Jonathan Hope, *The Authorship of Shakespeare's Plays: A Socio-Linguistic Study* (Cambridge, 1994), pp. 89–100. MacDonald Jackson believes that 'the case for supposing *The Double Falsehood* to preserve something of the Shakespare–Fletcher *Cardenio* is quite strong' (personal communication).

[8] In 1639 *The Ball: A Comedy* was published, apparently '*Written by George Chapman and James Shirly*', but the ascription to Chapman is now rejected. In 1652 appeared *The Widdow . . . Written by Ben: Johnson. John Fletcher. Tho: Middleton Gent.*, all three supposed authors being deceased (Jonson in 1637, Fletcher in 1625, Middleton in 1627); modern scholarship assigns it to Middleton. The following year saw publication of *The Spanish Gipsie . . . Written by Thomas Midleton and William Rowley. Gent.*, but this was largely the work of John Ford: see Brian Vickers, '*Counterfeiting*' *Shakespeare* (Cambridge, 2002), Appendix III.

[9] My source for this survey is W. W. Greg, *A Bibliography of English Printed Drama to the Restoration*, 4 vols. (London, 1939–57).

been instrumental in getting their contribution recognized. Before 1600 only two collaborations were publicly acknowledged, *The Tragedie of Dido Queene of Carthage* (1594), 'Written by Christopher Marlowe, and *Thomas Nash. Gent.*' (see Plate 1), and *A Looking Glasse for London and England* (1594), 'Made by Thomas Lodge Gentleman and Robert Greene In Artibus Magister'. In the 1600s several plays disclosed their co-authors. In 1604 the third edition of *The Malcontent* appeared, 'Augmented by *Marston*. With the Additions . . . Written by *Ihon Webster*', followed in 1605 by*Eastward Hoe . . . Made by Geo: Chapman. Ben: Jonson. Ioh: Marston* (see Plate 2).[10] In 1607 no fewer than three of Dekker's co-authored plays were published: *North-ward Hoe . . . by Thomas Decker, and John Webster*; *The famous history of Sir Thomas Wyat . . . written by Thomas Dickers, and John Webster*; and *West-ward hoe . . . written by Tho: Decker, and John Webster*. Also in 1607 appeared *The Travels of the Three English Brothers*, without any indication of authorship; however, three copies exist in which a leaf has been inserted with a dedication to the Sherley family signed by the authors, 'Iohn Day. William Rowley. George Wilkins' (see Plate 3).[11]

The second decade saw the publication of another collaboration by the prolific Dekker, *The Roaring Girle. Or Moll Cut-Purse . . . Written by T. Middleton and T. Dekkar* (1611). Middleton's name reappeared on the title-page of *A Faire Quarrell . . . Written By Thomas Midleton, and William Rowley Gent.* (1617). This decade also saw the first published acknowledgement of the numerous collaborations in which John Fletcher was involved, *The Scornful Ladie . . . written by Fra. Beaumont and Jo. Fletcher, Gent.* (1616), and *A King and no King . . . written by Francis Beaumont, and John Flecher* (1619). The third decade began with the publication of another of their most popular plays, *Phylaster: Or, Love lyes a Bleeding . . . Written by Francis Baymont and John Fletcher. Gent.* (1620), and *A Courtly Masque: The Device Called, The World tost at Tennis . . . Invented and set downe, By Tho: Middleton & William Rowley Gent.* (1620). These two collaborations were shortly followed by the first public witness to the many co-authored plays in which Philip Massinger took part, *The Virgin Martyr . . . Written by Philip Messenger and Thomas Deker* (1622). The same year brought forth a Red Bull play, *The true Tragedy of Herod and Antipater . . . Written by Gervase Markham, And William Sampson. Gentlemen.* The following decade brought to light another Massinger collaboration, *The Fatall Dowry . . . Written by P.M. and N.F.* (1632), the second set of initials referring to Nathan Field. In the 1630s several re-editions of collaborative plays previously ascribed to Fletcher alone now disclosed his co-author. *Cupids Revenge*

---

[10] R. W. Van Fossen, in his edition for the Revels Plays (Manchester, 1979), gives a judicious account of the authorship allocation, pp. 1–11 and Appendix 3, p. 226.

[11] See Greg 1939–57, entry 248 (i. 381).

THE
Tragedie of Dido
Queene of Carthage:
Played by the Children of her
Maiesties Chappell.

Written by Christopher Marlowe, and
Thomas Nash. Gent.

Actors

Iupiter.	*Ascanius.*
Ganimed.	*Dido.*
Venus.	*Anna.*
Cupid.	*Achates.*
Iano.	*Ilionens.*
Mercurie.	*Iarbas.*
Hermes.	*Cloanthes.*
Æneas.	*Sergestus.*

At LONDON,
Printed, by the Widdowe *Orwin,* for *Thomas Woodcocke,* and
are to be solde at his shop, in Paules Church-yeard, at
the signe of the blacke Beare. 1594.

PL. 1. Title-page to *Dido, Queene of Carthage,* 1594 Quarto

EASTVVARD
HOE.

As

It was playd in the
Black-friers.

By

The Children of her Maiefties Reuels.

Made by

GEO: CHAPMAN. BEN: IONSON. IOH: MARSTON.

AT LONDON
Printed for *William Aſpley.*
1 6 0 5.

PL. 2. Title-page to *Eastward Hoe!*, 1605 Quarto

To honours fauourites, and the
intire *friends* to the *familie*
of the SHERLEYS,
health.

T is a cuftome amongst friends , (and fure a friendly cuftome) if the obftacles of Fortune the impediments of Nature, the barre of time , the diftance of place do hinder, nay if death it felfe doth make that long feperation amongst friends, the fhadow or picture of a friend, is kept as a deuoted ceremonie : In that kinde to all well willers to thofe worthy fubiects (of our worthleffe Pennes) wee dedicate this Idea and fhape of honor. Being vnable to prefent the fubftances, wee haue epitomiz'd their large volume in a compendious abftract , which wee wifh all to perufe , and yet none but friends, becaufe wee wifh all fhould be friends to worth and defert , and wee our felues fhould haue a fafe harbor and vmbrage for our well willing , yet weake labours: If wee haue not lim'd to the life the true portrait of their deferts, (our wills being fealed with our endeuours , and peiz'd by an able cenfurer) we goe (with the Prouerbe to a willing execution, Leniter, ex merito quicquid patiare, ferendum eft.

Cælo beat Mufa.

In our beft indeuours,
yours,

IOHN DAY.
WILLIAM ROVVLEY.
GEORGE WILKINS.

PL. 3. Cancelled Dedication to *The Travels of the Three English Brothers* (1607).
By permission of the British Library

appeared in 1615 as the sole work of Fletcher, but the second edition (1630) declared it to have been *'written by Fran. Beaumont and Jo. Fletcher Gentlemen'*. *The Maides Tragedy* had appeared in 1619 and in 1622 with no author named, but the Third Quarto (1630) acknowledged *'written by Francis Beaumont, and John Fletcher Gentlemen'*, a retrospective admission repeated for the second quarto of *The Knight of the Burning Pestle* (1635), the first (1613) having been anonymous. Both authors' names appeared on the first quarto of *Wit With-out Money* (1639), while in 1634 Fletcher's name had figured with Shakespeare's on the quarto of *The Two Noble Kinsmen* (see Plate 4). In the same year appeared *The late Lancashire witches . . . Written by Thom. Heywood and Richard Broome*, and 1639 saw the publication of *The tragedie of Chabot Admirall of France . . . Written by George Chapman, and James Shirly*, although this was not a simultaneous collaboration but Shirley's revision of a play written by Chapman in about 1613.

The 1640s continued the retrospective documentation of Beaumont's collaborative activities. *The tragedy of Thierry King of France, and his Brother Theodoret* was published anonymously in 1621; the 1648 Quarto described it as 'written by John Fletcher', the Third edition (1649) adding Beaumont's name. *The Elder Brother* was ascribed to Fletcher alone in 1637, the Third Quarto (1651) belatedly acknowledging Beaumont's contribution. The closing of the theatres in 1642 killed off Renaissance drama, but it ultimately released for publication in the 1650s several notable collaborative plays performed two or three decades earlier: *The Wild-Goose Chase . . . Being the Noble, Last, and only Remaines of those Incomparable Dramatists Francis Beaumont, and John Fletcher, Gent.* (1652); *The Changeling . . . Written by Thomas Midelton, and William Rowley. Gent.* (1653); *The Excellent Comedy called The Old Law . . . by Phil. Massinger. Tho. Middleton. William Rowley* (1656); *The Sun's-Darling. A Moral Masque . . . Written by John Foard and Tho. Decker Gent.* (1656); and *The Witch of Edmonton: A known true Story. Composed into A Tragi-comedy By divers well-esteemed poets; William Rowley, Thomas Dekker, John Ford, etc.* (1658)—scholars could have done without the 'etc.'.

In this brief survey I have documented only the first publication of acknowledged co-authored plays, not their reprintings (often considerable). Nor have I attempted to list the many collaborations of which we have evidence in Henslowe's Diary, the Stationers' Register, the licensing records of Sir Henry Herbert, and other contemporary sources, most of which are documented in those magnificent reference works, E. K. Chambers, *The Elizabethan Stage*, and G. E. Bentley, *The Jacobean and Caroline Stage*. My aim has been simply to survey the public evidence of drama texts being openly acknowledged as the work of two or more dramatists. In Table 1.1 I have listed declarations of authorship on quarto texts of both

THE
TWO
NOBLE
KINSMEN:

Prefented at the Blackfriers
by the Kings Maiefties fervants,
with great applaufe:

Written by the memorable Worthies
of their time·
{ Mr. *John Fletcher*, and } Gent.
{ Mr. *William Shakfpeare*. }

Printed at *London* by *Tho. Cotes*, for *Iohn Waterſon*:
and are to be fold at the figne of the *Crowne*
in *Pauls* Church-yard. 1 6 3 4.

PL. 4. Title-page to *The Two Noble Kinsmen*, 1634 Quarto

TABLE 1.1. *Acknowledgement of authorship in published play-texts, 1570–1659*

Decade	Single-authored plays	Co-authored
1570	19	
1580	21	1
1590	34	2
1600	79	5
1610	55	4
1620	28	5
1630	129	8
1640	70	1
1650	62	6
Totals	497	32

single and co-authored plays in the period 1570–1659, drawing on Greg's *Bibliography*.[12] The total of published co-authored texts is not inconsiderable, although much lower than that for single-authored plays. It may well be that co-authors, having a smaller vested interest in a playscript than if they had been solely responsible, were less concerned to get collaborative work published (if, indeed, authors ever took the initiative in these matters). It remains a puzzle why so relatively few collaborative plays got into print—perhaps the theatre companies, or the stationers, thought them to be less vendible than plays of single authorship. Such questions may not be answerable, but the fact remains that acknowledgement of collaborative authorship had been common for over twenty-five years when the First Folio was published, and became even more frequent in the thirty years following its publication—continuing, indeed, into the 1660s. Having reconstructed this context, we can now see that Heminge and Condell would have had plenty of precedents for acknowledging Shakespeare's co-authorship. Perhaps they felt that to do so would be out of place in a project dedicated to preserving the plays which had been liked so much 'when they were acted', as they put it in their dedication of the folio to the Earls of Pembroke and Montgomery:

---

[12] I have excluded material from play-lists and collected editions (Jonson, Shakespeare, Beaumont and Fletcher, Shirley). I have included all play-texts published with an author's name or initials on the title-pages, including masques and pageants, whether or not they had been performed in the public theatre. In *From Playhouse to Printing House. Drama and Authorship in Early Modern England* (Cambridge, 2000), pp. 173–6, D. A. Brooks analysed the titles listed in the Harbage–Schoenbaum *Annals of English Drama* for the period 1580–1604, including Henslowe's records. His totals of 868 single-authored, 138 co-authored plays—as against those published, 497 and 32—confirms that collaborative plays were less likely to reach print.

We have but collected them, and done an office to the dead, to procure his Orphanes, Guardians; without ambition either of selfe-profit, or fame: onely to keepe the memory of so worthy a Friend, & Fellow alive, as was our Shakespeare . . . (Sig. A₂ᵛ)

Loyalty to the dead might have been diluted by acknowledging the contributions of (probably) Nashe and others to *1 Henry VI*, Peele to *Titus Andronicus*, Middleton to *Timon of Athens*, and Fletcher to *Henry VIII*.

Heminge and Condell were not the only editors and publishers who failed to disclose co-authorship, even when they knew of it. Those responsible for publishing the folio containing thirty-four *Comedies and tragedies written by Francis Beaumont and John Fletcher, gentlemen, never printed before* (1647) did not reveal the massive contributions made to that canon by Massinger, Webster, Jonson, Chapman, Shakespeare, Field, Rowley, Ford, and Shirley, names equally absent in its expanded reissue (1679).[13] Neither in this case, nor in the 1623 Shakespeare folio, can we accuse the publishers of acting in bad faith, or with a deliberate intention to deceive. But the evidence I have collected of the frequent acknowledgement of co-authorship on title-pages between the 1590s and 1650s opens up the possibility that Heminge and Condell's failure to disclose Shakespeare's co-authors was an act of conscious omission, and one which was in its own time anachronistic. There were ample precedents for such acknowledgements, but they chose not to follow them. I would not want to make too much of this point, but the corollary of the fact that a tradition did exist in which collaborative plays were publicly acknowledged is that scholars today who rely on the folio editors' silence on these matters to bolster their own belief that Shakespeare never ever collaborated[14] are being even more anachronistic. Whether consciously or not, the folio editors placed Shakespeare outside the common and accepted practice of co-authorship in Elizabethan, Jacobean, and Caroline drama. Unknowingly, they laid the way for a quasi-bardolatrous belief in Shakespeare as the special case, the Romantic genius who needed no adjutants. The aim of this book is to show that belief to be a myth whose exposure is long overdue.

DRAMATISTS AS COLLABORATORS

My survey of publicly acknowledged co-authorship also revealed the many major and minor dramatists involved: Marlowe, Nashe, Chapman, Jonson, Dekker, Webster, Day, Rowley, Wilkins, Middleton, Fletcher, Beaumont, Massinger, Field, Heywood, Brome, Shirley, Ford. Given that co-authorship was so common, it would have been remarkable had Shakespeare not

---

[13] C. Hoy, 'The Shares of Fletcher and his Collaborators in the Beaumont and Fletcher Canon (VII)' *SB* 15 (1962): 71–90.

[14] 'What, *never*?'—'Hardly ever!': W. S. Gilbert, *HMS Pinafore* (1878), Act 1.

sometimes worked like this: the evidence presented here suggests that he did
so in at least seven surviving plays. To establish how common the collaborative process was, and how it worked, I shall use some well-known sources,
including Henslowe's Diary,[15] together with Neil Carson's *Companion* to it,[16]
and the useful survey[17] provided by G. E. Bentley, compiler of *The Jacobean
and Caroline Stage*, that marvellous record of English drama from 1616 to
1642.[18] Bentley pointed out that collaboration was already common in the
amateur drama of the early Elizabethan period. *Gorboduc* (1562)[19] was
described on the title-page of the First Quarto (1565) as a play 'Where of
three Actes were written by Thomas Nortone, and the two laste by Thomas
Sackvyle'. *Jocasta* (1566) was 'digested into Acte by George Gascoygne and
Francis Kinwelmershe of Grayes Inne'; *Gismond of Salerne* (1566) was
produced by 'the Gentlemen of the Inner Temple', the 1591 Quarto (renamed
Tancred and Gismunda) recording that each act had a different author: Rod.
Stafford, Henry Noel, 'G. Al.', Christopher Hatton, and Robert Wilmot
respectively.[20] No fewer than eight 'Gentlemen of Grayes-Inne' collaborated
on *The Misfortunes of Arthur* (1588), 'reduced into Tragicall notes
by Thomas Hughes', a palimpsest of Senecan tragedy using elaborate
dumbshows.[21]

Turning to the professional theatre, Bentley pointed out that although the
authors of most plays before 1590 are unknown, for the period 1590–1642

We know the titles (often no more) of about 1,500 plays. . . . For about 370 we know
nothing at all about authorship. For the remaining 1,100 or so, we have the evidence
that between 1/5 and 1/6 contained the work of more than one man as either collaborator, reviser, or provider of additional matter. (Bentley 1986, pp. 198–9)

Setting aside over 200 amateur plays, which were seldom collaborated,
Bentley guessed

that as many as half of the plays by professional dramatists in the period incorporated
the writing at some date of more than one man. In the case of the 282 plays mentioned

---

[15] *Henslowe's Diary*, ed. R. A. Foakes and R. T. Rickert (Cambridge, 1961); page references
included in the text, spelling modernized.

[16] Neil Carson, *A Companion to Henslowe's Diary* (Cambridge, 1988).

[17] *The Professions of Dramatist and Player in Shakespeare's Time 1590–1642* (Princeton,
1986), pp. 197–234.

[18] G. E. Bentley, *The Jacobean and Caroline Stage*, 7 vols. (Oxford, 1941–68); hereafter
referred to as *JCS*.

[19] All dates for plays refer to their first known performance, as estimated in A. Harbage, rev.
S. Schoenbaum, *Annals of English Drama 975–1642* (London, 1964); supplements: 1966, 1970.
I have not consulted the 'third edition' of this invaluable reference tool, ed. S. S. Wagonheim
(London, 1989), which has numerous errors: see the critical review by Anne Lancashire in *ShQ*
42 (1991): 225–30.

[20] All four of these academic plays were well edited by John W. Cunliffe in *Early English
Classical Tragedies* (Oxford, 1912).

[21] Cf. Greg 1939–57, no. 89 (i. 167–8).

TABLE 1.2. *Collaborative plays at the Rose Theatre, 1597–1600*

Season	F	O	I	A	Total	C	%	FT	FC	%
Autumn–Winter 1597/8	5	2	3	—	8	2	25	5	2	40
Spring–Summer 1598	11	5	5	—	16	10	62	11	9	82
Autumn–Winter 1598/9	15	3	9	2	24	10	41	15	9	60
Spring–Summer 1599	6	—	10	—	16	5	31	6	3	50
Autumn–Winter 1599/60	8	—	8	1	16	6	37	8	3	37
Spring–Summer 1600	7	—	4	—	11	4	36	7	4	57

Note: F: 'In Full'; I: 'In Earnest'; O: 'Old'; A: 'Alterations'; C: 'Collaborated Plays'; FT: 'Finished Plays'; FC: 'Finished Collaborated Plays'.
Source: Carson 1988, p. 58.

in Henslowe's diary (far and away the most detailed record of authorship that has come down to us) nearly two-thirds are the work of more than one man. (p. 199)

Neil Carson made a closer analysis of Henslowe's records, which revealed 'the very high incidence of multiple authorship' at the Rose Theatre. Table 1.2 classifies the plays bought between the autumn–winter season 1597/8 and the summer season of 1600. The proportions of 60 and 82 per cent in two seasons are indeed astonishing, but they are probably untypical. As Carson showed, whereas the Admiral's Men under Edward Alleyn had spent relatively little of the money they borrowed on playscripts, once the principal actors from the Admiral's and Pembroke's Men combined in the summer of 1597 to form a reorganized company under Robert Shaa, they 'spent almost three-quarters of the money they borrowed on new plays' (Carson 1988, p. 47). An average season 'might include ten new plays and perhaps some twenty old works' (p. 37), and normally 'the players mounted new plays at the rate of about two a month but acquired them somewhat faster', thus building up 'a surplus of scripts' (p. 50). The seasons following the amalgamation, which saw this frantic purchasing of plays, between sixteen and twenty-four over four seasons, were indeed unusual, the players 'struggling to build up their stock' of playbooks again (ibid.).

Most of our knowledge concerning the process by which dramatists placed their work with theatrical companies derives from records kept by the impresario Philip Henslowe (c.1566–1616), who in 1587 built the Rose, the first Bankside theatre; owned the theatre at Newington Butts (by 1594); and was associated with his son-in-law, Edward Alleyn, in both the Fortune Theatre (built 1600) and the Hope (rebuilt 1613). The document known as 'Henslowe's Diary' was in fact a business record, kept from 1592 to 1604, in which Henslowe at first merely recorded the companies performing at his theatre (probably the Rose), the plays performed, and his takings. After 1597, when the Admiral's Men were reorganized, Henslowe began to record the money he advanced to the company for purchasing plays, properties, costumes, play licences, and payments to the actors. These fuller records transform the picture of dramatists working collaboratively. As G. E. Bentley pointed out, 'for 1597 *The Annals of English Drama* lists 23 plays, six with single authors, one collaboration, and 16 of unknown authorship'. But for 1598, when Henslowe's accounts begin, the *Annals* 'lists 46 plays, 16 by single named playwrights, 20 collaborations by two or more, and only ten' plays of unknown authorship. Bentley deduced that 'theatres and writers did not change in 1598; the proportion of records preserved changed' (Bentley 1986, p. 200).

A crucial document in the preliminary negotiations for writing and performing a play was its 'plot'. Elizabethan and Jacobean dramatists used the word 'plot' in two senses, distinguishing between 'theatre plots' and 'author plots'. The first type described 'the skeleton outlines of plays scene by scene, written on large boards for the use of actors and others in the playhouse'.[22] These theatre plots consisted mainly of the characters' entrances and exits, listing the actors' names, and providing 'occasional notes of the action and of the properties and noises required'.[23] Seven such plots are extant, two dating from about 1590, connected either with Lord Strange's or the Lord Admiral's Company, the remaining five from 1597–1602, prepared for the later Admiral's Men. They were reprinted in facsimile with a wonderfully rich commentary by W. W. Greg. The other sense of 'plot' referred to the scenario which the dramatists worked out in advance, partly for their own convenience, partly to secure advance payment from the playhouse proprietors. A play called *The Faithful Friends* (*c.*1614) was entered in the Stationers' Register in 1660 as being by Beaumont and Fletcher (Daborne, Massinger, and Field have been proposed as the real authors), and its text survives in a manuscript which includes an inserted leaf in different handwriting. Originally the scribe had written 'the text of several scenes between a set of clownish characters, but when he came to the end of Act 4, where such a scene was apparently called for, instead of furnishing the text he merely entered what he described as "The Plott of a Scene of mirth" describing the action required' (Greg 1921, i. 326). But the quarto leaf inserted at this point contains the text of this scene. The original authorial manuscript may have been defective, the lost scene subsequently recovered; or the scene may have been originally left to be acted extempore, and later written out in full (ibid. 326–7). Either way, this chance survival gives us a unique glimpse of the

---

[22] W. W. Greg, *Dramatic Documents from the Elizabethan Playhouses*, 2 vols. (Oxford, 1921), i. ix.

[23] W. W. Greg, *The Shakespeare First Folio: Its Bibliographic and Textual History* (Oxford, 1955), p. 163.

amount of detail with which Elizabethan authors conceived the play yet to be written:

The Plott of a Scene of mirth to conclude this fourth Acte.

Enter Sr Pergamus the foolish knight like a Bridegroome leading Flauia his Bride, Bellario the singing Soldier, Black Snout the Smith, Snipp Snapp the Tayler and Cauleskin [*sic*] the Shomaker.

An Alter to be sett forth with the Image of Mars Dindinus [*sic*] the Dwarfe bearing Sr Per: Launce and sheild wch are hung vp for trophees and Sr Perg Vowes for the loue of Flauia neuer to beare Armes agen, the like dos Bla: snout who hangs vp his Sword and takes his hammer vowing to God Vulcan neuer to Vse other Weapon, The Taylor and the Shoomaker to vowe the like to God Mercury Then Bellario [to] Sings a songe how they will fall to there old Trades, a clapp of Thunder and all run of |

finis 4 Act

(Greg 1921, i. 2 n.)

The only complete example of an author-plot (dated post-1627), now in the Folger Shakespeare Library, was printed by J. Q. Adams.[24] It involves King Philander of Thrace and his sister Suavina, who is in love with Aristocles. Their court includes Euphrastes, 'supposed father of Aristocles', and Phonops, 'a begging cavalier'. The author has outlined four of the five acts, and given plot summaries for each scene (spelling and punctuation modernized):

Act 1, scene 1. Philander and his sister Suavina walk and confer; she grieves for the war.
Scene 2. Philander telleth Euphrastes the cause why he will not marry Suavina to any but a present King.
Scene 3. Aristocles and Suavina discover their passion and are discovered by Phonops.
Scene 4. Philander doth banish Aristocles.
Scene 5. Euphrastes doth counsel Aristocles to go to the wars between the Epirot and Achaian. (Adams 1945, pp. 24–5)

(To judge from his preference for the *-th* ending, the author may have been a provincial dramatist, like Shakespeare, unaffected by the newer linguistic modes.) In Act 2, Aristocles duly goes to the wars as an unknown soldier, wins a victory, but is banished by Salochin, King of Macedon, whose daughter Corintha intercedes for him, thereby arousing Suavina's jealousy . . . and so on. As the plot develops it is interesting to see how the author sketches in quite elaborate sequences of stage business, with the appropriate emotions:

Act 3, scene 5. Aristocles and Suavina exceed for joy at meeting; recounting their weal and woe. Corintha weeps to sympathize with their free passions, and vows an emulous

---

[24] J. Q. Adams, 'The Author-Plot of an Early Seventeenth-Century Play', *Library*, 4th ser., 25 (1945): 17–27.

but fond [?] love to Aristocles. Suavina declares the promise made to Salochin, they all conspire to defeat him. The manage whereof is left to Aristocles, but charged to be bloodless. (ibid. 26)

The dramatist also sketches in suitable details of gesture ('Phonops begs mercy on his knees . . . Aristocles kicks him away') and vivid action, conceived in theatrical terms:

Act 4, scene 10. Ascania meditating in the private walks of her garden, Phonops with the pass key and Philocles enter, cast a hood over her and carry her away. Phonops bids him gag and bind her. He warrants her and leads her by the two thumbs; leads her off the stage and brings her on again. (pp. 26–7)

The dramatist also made notes on Greek geography ('Mountains: Olympus, crowned with box and laurel'), philosophy, and 'national properties' (social customs and politics). It is impossible to tell whether this writer was being unusually conscientious about his homework, but such attempted fidelity to the historical actuality being represented is a feature of many Elizabethan plays.

A brief look at Henslowe's records for the Admiral's Men will establish some of the basic processes by which plays came to be written. It was vitally important for the company to 'secure a continual supply of new scripts', indeed 'none of the activities reflected in Henslowe's diary . . . would have been possible without the contribution of the dramatists who supplied the plays' (Carson 1988, pp. 41, 54). Where some modern critics, for ideological reasons, try to play down—or as they call it—'decentre' the author, the historical fact is that the playscript was the single most important element in mounting a play. Dramatists working on a play (often their major source of income) regularly secured an advance payment from Henslowe, who recorded the amount paid, the authors involved, and the play title (when known). 'Lent unto the company the 18 of August 1598 to buy a book called *Hot Anger Soon Cold* of Mr. Porter, Mr. Chettle, and Benjamin Jonson in full payment the sum of £6' (Foakes and Rickert 1961, p. 96). That sum may have been divided equally among the three dramatists, if they had had an equal share in the writing. At other times an unequal payment recognized greater and lesser responsibilities: 'Lent unto the company the 19 of August 1598 to pay unto Mr. Wilson, Munday, and Dekker in part of payment of a book called *Chance Medley* the sum of £4 5s in this manner Wilson 30 shillings, Chettle 30 shillings, Munday 25 shillings. I say £4 5s' (ibid.). But a further writer was involved, as we discover from an entry five days later: 'Paid unto Mr. Drayton the 24 of August 1598 in full payment of a book called *Chance Medley* or *Worse Afeared Than Hurt* the sum of 35s' (p. 97). The play had now acquired a subtitle, which may express the collaborators' developing conception of their work. Both of these plays have perished, and were it not for Henslowe's account-keeping we would be ignorant that Jonson was a co-author both of *Hot Anger Soon Cold*, and of *Robert II*, or *The Scot's Tragedy*, for which Henslowe loaned 40s. on 3 September 1599 to 'Thomas Dekker, Benjamin Jonson, Harry Chettle and other gentleman' (p. 124). Whoever the 'other gentleman' was, Henslowe advanced a further 20s. on 15 September, 10s. on the 16th, and 20s. on the 27th (ibid.).

The financial rewards may have been piecemeal, but once a dramatist had established himself as a dependable co-author he could earn a respectable wage. Henslowe's usual fee for a whole play was £6, although beginners might earn less. John Day, who sold his first play to Henslowe's company in 1598, earned £8 in the spring and summer of 1600, and subsequently wrote for both the Admiral's and Worcester's company, earning nearly £14 per year from both sources (Carson 1988, pp. 60–1). During the late sixteenth century it has been estimated that a workman would earn about £12 for a six-day week over a full year, and a schoolmaster between £12 and £20 annually, not including 'other perquisites such as board or lodging' (p. 66). By these standards, Henry Chettle, who in the summer season of 1598 'suddenly became the most prolific and highly paid of the dramatists working for Shaa and Downton', his income amounting to £18. 15s. in that season, and reaching £25. 5s. in 1601–2, was earning well—if only he could have avoided running up debts to Henslowe (pp. 61–6). Chettle had the necessary qualities of a professional dramatist, 'speed and flexibility', being 'apparently able to alternate or combine projects, interrupting one to work on another' (p. 62). The acting companies 'tried to bind their dramatists to them from time to time, eliciting promises from both Porter and Chettle to write for no other company, but such schemes seem to have been fruitless' (p. 63). In fact, Carson's analysis of Henslowe's records shows that 'the majority of the playwrights mentioned in the diary were independent agents selling their talents wherever they could' (p. 64). Between November 1602 and March 1603 the team of co-authors Day, Hathway, and Smith 'moved freely from one theatre to another', selling two plays to Downton and Juby at the Fortune Theatre, three plays to Beeston and Pallant of Worcester's Men, and two plays to Henslowe, Duke, and Lowin at the Rose (p. 64). A similar 'fluidity of relations' can be traced in the shifting allegiances of Thomas Heywood, who by 1602 was a sharer in Lord Worcester's Men at the Rose, writing two plays of his own, collaborating on five others, and providing additions for an old play. Yet, despite being both a sharer and playwright there, Heywood continued to write for the Admiral's Company (p. 65). The demand for playscripts was so great that writers could serve two or more masters.

G. E. Bentley showed that the majority of the plays Henslowe bought for both the Lord Admiral's Company and for the Earl of Worcester's Men were not individual compositions but collaborations, and he argued that this pattern applied to other troupes whose records have not survived (Bentley 1986, p. 205). However, Henslowe may have been exceptional in the extent to which he kept a number of playwrights closely linked to the company, using his skills as a moneylender to provide them with a regular source of income; not every theatre manager may have been ready to take such risks. Neil Carson's analysis of the playwrights' income (1988, Table V, pp. 139–40) showed that Henslowe's writers often operated on the same seasonal basis as the players, a group coming together to work on several projects during a season and then breaking up. Dekker and Drayton were co-authors of seven plays in the spring and summer of 1599, after which Drayton left, perhaps to work for one of the new boys' companies.

> Sometimes the groupings appear to have been fluid, at others fairly static. In Fall–Winter 1599–1600 seven playwrights—Chettle, Dekker, Drayton, Hathway, Haughton, Day and Munday (with the assistance in one play of Wilson)—among them did all the writing for the entire season. The dramatists appear to have been grouped into two 'syndicates'. Drayton and Munday collaborated with Hathway and Wilson; Chettle and Dekker worked with Day and Haughton, who seem to have formed some sort of a partnership. The groups functioned independently—Hathway always collaborating with Drayton and Munday, Haughton only writing with Chettle, Dekker, or Day. (Carson, 1988, p. 59)

Whether other theatre companies were able to form and sustain such a 'stable' of dramatists may be doubted.

Every major playwright in this period worked collaboratively at some point in his career. Jonson took part in at least five collaborations, including *The Isle of Dogs*, *Page of Plymouth*, and *The Spanish Tragedy* (for which he wrote additions, now lost, in 1602). Jonson's experiences in collaborative writing were not always happy; indeed, on two occasions he ended up in gaol. In 1597 Jonson seems to have been employed to finish the fragment of a satiric comedy, *The Isle of Dogs*, which Nashe had begun. On 28 July the Privy Council was informed of 'a lewd plaie that was plaied in one of the plaie houses on the Bancke Side, contaynynge very seditious and sclandrous matter'. They promptly had 'some of the Players' locked up in the Marshalsea, 'wherof one . . . was not only an Actor, but a maker of parte of the said Plaie'. Nashe had fled to Great Yarmouth, but the two players, Gabriel Spencer and Robert Shaa, stayed in prison until 8 October, along with 'Benjamin Jonson', the offending co-author.[25] Jonson got into trouble again for his involvement in *Eastward Hoe!*, a city comedy, 'playd in the Blackfriers' theatre, 'By The Children of her Majestie Revells', a collaboration between Chapman, Jonson, and Marston which was published in 1605. Among its satiric targets were the 'thirty-pound knights' created in such abundance by James I, the standard fee for obtaining a knighthood, which opened the door of social advancement to both deserving and undeserving

---

[25] C. H. Herford, P. and E. Simpson (eds.), *Ben Jonson*, 11 vols. (Oxford, 1925–52), i. 15–16.

alike. One of the knights in the play, Sir Petronel Flash, said to be living on the Isle of Dogs (just opposite the king's summer residence at Greenwich Palace), may have been presented on stage by an actor mimicking James's Scots accent.[26] Whatever the offence, all three dramatists were imprisoned for having aroused 'his Majesty's high displeasure'. Several letters are extant from Chapman and Jonson seeking their release, one of which, from the latter to the Earl of Salisbury, conveys the dramatist's sense of indignity by its reluctance to divulge the cause of the offence:

I am here, my most honoured Lord, unexamined or unheard, committed to a vile prison, and with me a gentleman (whose name may perhaps have come to your Lordship), one Mr. George Chapman, a learned and honest man. The cause (would I could name some worthier, though I wish we had known none worthy our imprisonment), is (the word irks me that our fortune hath necessitated us to so despised a course), a play, my Lord . . . (cit. Petter 1973, p. 129)

Jonson now makes the satirist's standard apologia,[27] that he had lashed the vice but spared the person, having 'so attempered my style . . . since my first error, which yet is punished in me more with my shame than it was then with my bondage'. (The 'first error' was his collaboration with Nashe, for which Jonson had been tried by Salisbury, then Sir Robert Cecil.) The dramatists were soon released, but they may not have been pleased to find the play published so speedily, with their authorship acknowledged.

In another of his collaborations, *Sejanus, His Fall*, performed in 1603 by the King's Company at the Globe, with Shakespeare in the cast, we know that Jonson did not wish to print his co-author's contribution. When he published the play Jonson rewrote it, removing all the scenes contributed by the 'second pen' (probably George Chapman). As he notified readers of the 1605 Quarto,

Lastly I would inform you that this book, in all its numbers, is not the same with that which was acted on the public stage, wherein a second pen had good show: in place of which I have rather chosen to put weaker (and no doubt less pleasing) of mine own, than to defraud so happy a genius of his own right by my loathed usurpation. (cit. Bentley 1986, p. 207)

As Bentley says, 'only Jonson, with his growing preoccupation with posterity, would have gone so far as painstakingly to weed out of the text all the words of his collaborator . . .' (ibid.). When Jonson published *Volpone* in 1607 the Prologue defiantly announced that

> five weeks fully penned it
> From his own hand, without a coadjutor,
> Novice, journeyman, or tutor.

---

[26] *Eastward Hoe!*, ed. C. G. Petter (London, 1973), pp. xxiii–xxix.
[27] Indeed, actually paraphrasing Martial's preface to his *Epigrams*, as Herford and Simpson noted (i. 195–6).

Neil Carson suggested that Jonson's four categories—'coadjutor, | Novice, journeyman, or tutor'—might 'imply a chain of command in the theatre', and he found some evidence in Henslowe's Diary that a young playwright joining the company as a 'novice' may have been apprenticed to a 'tutor' (Carson 1988, pp. 60–3).

For other dramatists in this period, not so concerned to claim the status of literature for play-texts, collaboration was a normal way of sharing the burden of composition, producing a script more quickly, and taking part in a collective enterprise. At any one time in Jacobean London up to thirty dramatists may have been involved in group composition, several occupied with more than one play, changing partners according to the project in hand. Between about 1606 and 1614 John Fletcher and Francis Beaumont wrote some ten plays for the King's Men. In 1612–13 Fletcher wrote three plays together with Shakespeare for the same company, and after Beaumont married an heiress in 1613–14 and gave up playwrighting, Fletcher continued actively collaborating until his death in 1625, producing at least nineteen plays together with Massinger. Thomas Heywood described his play *The English Traveller* (1633) as 'one reserved amongst two hundred and twenty, in which I have had either an entire hand, or at the least a main finger' in (*Eliz. S*, iii. 339). If this figure can be believed, the majority of these plays must have been collaborations.

Given that multi-authorship was so common, we would like to know how dramatists divided up the writing, once they had jointly sketched out the plot as a whole. One common method was to assign individual acts to one or more writers. Writers of Inns of Court plays in the Elizabethan period, we recall, each wrote one act (Bentley 1986, p. 228). Nashe left a self-exculpating account of the *Isle of Dogs* affair, dismissing his creation as

An imperfect Embrion . . . for I having begun but the induction and the first act of it, the other four acts without my consent, or the least guess of my drift or scope, by the players were supplied, which bred both their trouble and mine too. (cit. ibid., 229)

The unit of composition (and payment), as Nashe witnesses, was often one or more acts. From his Diary we can see that on 3 December 1597 Henslowe loaned Jonson 20s. 'upon a book which he was to write for us before Christmas next after the date hereof which he showed the plot unto the company' (Foakes and Rickert 1961, p. 73). As we have seen, these 'plots' were often very detailed, and another dramatist could easily write a play based on the drafted scenario. When Jonson failed to deliver this play as promised, on 23 October 1598 Henslowe advanced £3 to 'Mr. Chapman on his play book and two acts of a tragedy on Benjamin's plot' (ibid. 100). In this instance Jonson had invented the story, but Chapman supplied the treatment—to use the terminology of Hollywood. On 4 January 1599 Chapman received another £3 'upon three acts of a tragedy' (p. 103), although it is not clear whether these three loans refer to the same play. The dramatic companies were evidently used to receiving plays in instalments, the 'act' forming a unit of composition and payment, alternating with the sheet(s) of paper that the dramatist had covered with writing. Scribes usually wrote on folio paper (*c.*12 × 7¾ inches), 'on separately folded sheets, in units that is of four pages . . .' (Greg 1921, i. 205). Samuel Rowley writes to Henslowe on 4 April 1601 reporting that the authors (John Day and William Haughton) have read out to him excerpts from their latest venture: 'I have heard five sheets of a play of *The Conquest of the [West] Indies* and I do not doubt but it will be a very good play. Therefore I pray ye deliver them forty shillings in earnest of it, and take the papers into your own hands, and on Easter eve they promise to make an end of all the rest.'[28]

The Henslowe Papers in the Dulwich College Library contain several revealing letters from Robert Daborne to Henslowe in 1613–14, concerning plays in the process of being written, alongside the dramatist's continuing debts. On 17 April 1613 Daborne contracts to deliver to Henslowe by the end of the Easter term (31 May) a play called *Machiavelli and the Devil* for a payment of £20, of which he receives £6 now, 'and must have other £4 upon delivery in of three Acts, and other £10 upon delivery in of the last scene, perfected' (Greg 1907, p. 67). On Monday, 3 May, Daborne asks for more money, but promises that 'on Friday night I will deliver in the three Acts fair written, . . . and if you please to have some papers now you shall' (p. 69). By Saturday, 8 May, Daborne has not delivered the three acts as promised, only 'some papers I have sent you, though not so fair written all as I could wish', and he asks Henslowe 'to appoint any hour to read Mr. Alleyn' what he has so far written (p. 69). On Sunday, 16 May, Daborne arranges to read some of the play to Henslowe and Alleyn alone the following Tuesday, 'for I am unwilling to read to the general company until all be finished' (p. 70), and on Wednesday, 19 May, he receives more money, agreeing that 'this play is to be delivered in to Mr. Henslowe with all speed' (p. 71). On 5 June, however, *Machiavelli and the Devil* is still not finished, but Daborne sends another instalment and announces progress on his next project:

I have not only laboured my own play . . . but given Cyril Tourneur an Act of *The Arraignment* [*of London*] to write, that we may have it likewise ready for [the company] . . . I have sent you two sheets more, fair written. (p. 72)

The need to keep the theatrical companies supplied with material must have been one reason for co-authorship, with the main mover farming out acts to

---

[28] W. W. Greg, *Henslowe Papers: Being Documents Supplementary to Henslowe's Diary* (London, 1907), p. 56; Foakes and Rickert 1961, p. 294. The progress of this play's composition and performance can be followed there, pp. 167, 168, 169, 170, 178, 179, 180, 181, 182, 198, 295.

willing helpers. Presumably Daborne had drafted the plot of this play—which Greg thought to be a dramatization of Dekker's tract, *The Bellman of London* (p. 75 n.)—before calling in Tourneur.

Despite all his promises, Daborne had still not finished *Machiavelli* by 10 June, protesting 'I can this week deliver in the last word, and will that night [the company] play their new play read this; whereof I have sent you a sheet and more fair written. You may easily know there is not much behind and I intend no other thing, God is my judge, till this be finished' (p. 72). Daborne receives a further loan at this point, but on 18 June we find him assuring Henslowe, 'Sir, I sat up last night till past 12 to write out this sheet', claiming that he would have finished the play that morning if he had not had to appear in court. A week later he has still not finished the play, but the company are evidently already rehearsing it, for he has been forced to make alterations at the actors' request, and the playhouse scribe has started to copy out the actors' parts: 'for their good and mine own I have took extraordinary pains with the end, and altered one other scene in the third Act, which they now have in parts' (p. 73). Modern readers may wonder how Daborne managed to retain his sense of the play's unity over this protracted composition period, pursued by his debtors on the one side and Henslowe's messenger on the other. Unity is indeed a rare commodity in co-authored plays. Working on *The Araygnment of London* later that year, on 23 August Daborne and Tourneur agree with Henslowe about their payment (p. 75), and on 14 October Daborne promises 'to bring in the whole play next week', asks for a further advance, and mentions that he could also sell it to the King's Men (p. 76). A fortnight later he sends Henslowe 'two sheets more, so that you have ten sheets' in all, asks for more money, and claims that the King's Men 'have given out that they shall have it'; Henslowe advances another 20s. (pp. 76–7). On 13 November Daborne is still at work, assuring Henslowe that 'your man was with me, who found me writing the last scene, which I had thought to have brought you tonight, but it will be late ere I can do it, and being Saturday night my occasion urges me to request you spare me ten shillings more . . .' (p. 78). Henslowe must have refused the advance and taunted Daborne with not fulfilling his contract, for in another letter dated that day Daborne protests:

Mr. Henslowe, you accuse me with the breach of promise: true it is, I promised to bring you the last scene, which, that you may see finished, I sent you the foule sheet, and the fair I was writing, as your man can testify—which, if great business had not prevented, I had this night finished . . . I will not fail to write this fair, and perfect the book, which shall not lie on your hands. (p. 78)

On 27 November Daborne receives a further loan (pp. 78–9), finally delivering 'all my papers' on 9 December (p. 70), and on the following day signs a new contract for a play called *The Owl*, 'which I will undertake shall make as good a play for the public house as ever was played', the completed book to be delivered 'at or upon the tenth day of February next ensuing . . .' (p. 80). And the same story starts again: broken deadlines, piecemeal delivery, final completion.

Daborne's correspondence with Henslowe reveals the hand-to-mouth existence of many Elizabethan and Jacobean dramatists. In June 1613 he, Nathan Field, Massinger, and Fletcher contracted with Henslowe to deliver a play by 1 August (Greg 1907, pp. 65–7, 74–5). At some point that summer Field and his co-authors got into trouble with the law, and ended up in a debtors' prison. (How they managed to do so is a mystery: perhaps they collectively owed rent, or tavern debts.) Field, who was also an actor, wrote a desperate letter to Henslowe on their behalf (Plate 5), his co-authors adding their voices:

Mr. Henslowe,
You understand our unfortunate extremity, and I do not think you so void of Christianity but that you would rather throw so much money into the Thames as we request now of you, rather than endanger so many innocent lives. You know there is £10 more, at least, to be received of you for the play: we desire you to lend us £5 of that (which shall be allowed to you), without which we cannot be bailed, nor I play [act] any more. Till this be despatched it will lose you £20 ere the end of the next week, beside the hindrance of the new play. Pray sir, consider our cases with humanity, and now give us cause to acknowledge you our true friend in time of need. We have entreated Mr. Davison to deliver this note, as well to witness your love as our promises, and always acknowledgement to be ever your most thankful and loving friends,

Nat: Field

The money shall be abated out of the money remains for the play of Mr. Fletcher and ours.

Rob: Daborne

I have ever found you a true loving friend to me, and in so small a suit, it being honest, I hope you will not fail us.

Philip Massinger

Henslowe duly advanced the £5 they asked for, releasing them from gaol, so that they could return to being playwrights (pp. 65–6). Field and Massinger continued in their profession, but after many attempts Daborne finally gained preferment, taking holy orders shortly after 1614 and moving to Ireland, becoming Chancellor of Waterford in 1619, Dean of Lismore in 1621, a post he held until his death in March 1628. Writing sermons was a more secure, less anguished activity than writing plays.

Documents such as this letter from Field, Daborne, and Massinger, one of the few written records of co-authorship, bring home the tenuous existence of dramatists for whom a play represented the chance to cover the necessities of life. The companies' need for constant new material put the dramatists

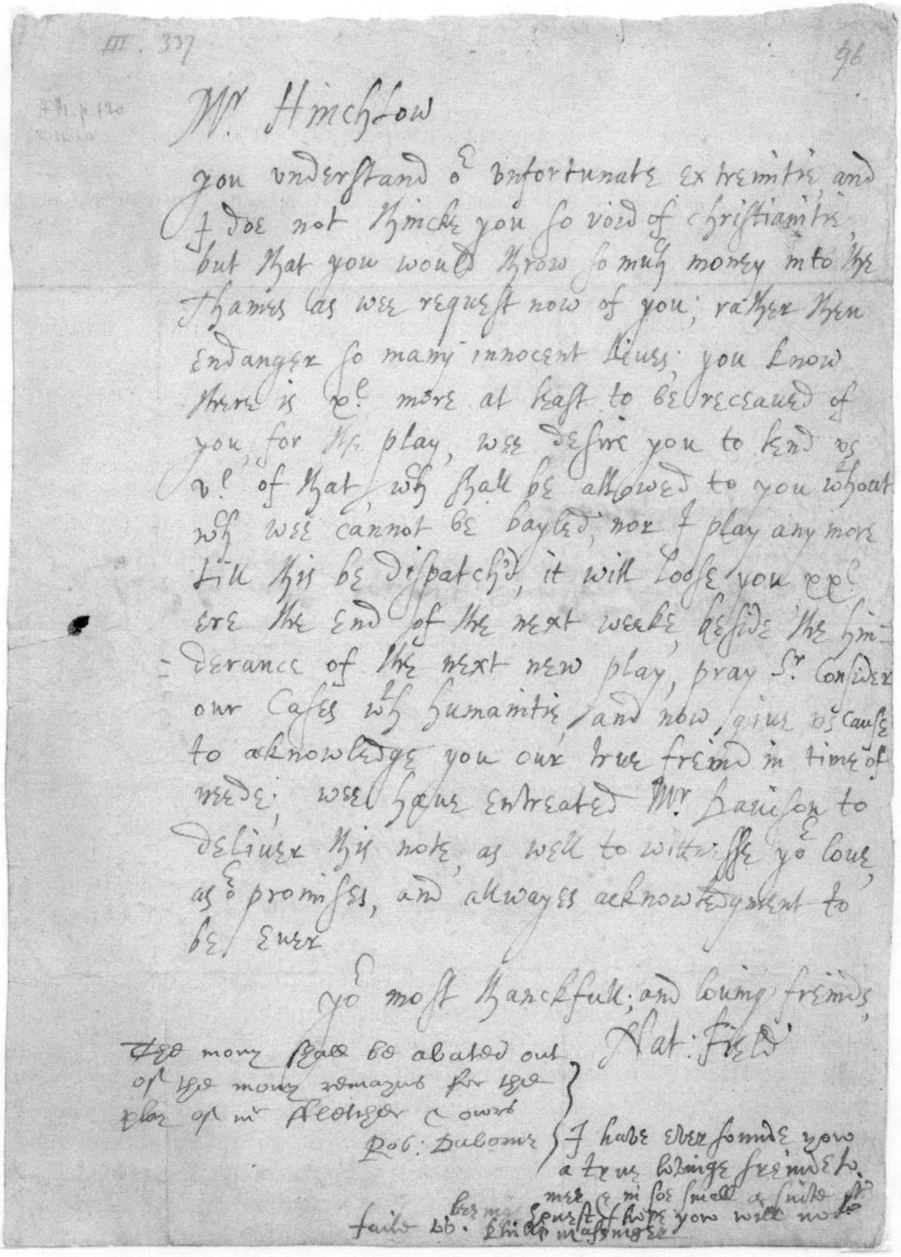
Mr Hinchlow
you understand our unfortunate extremitie, and
I doe not thincke you so void of christianitie
but that you would throw so much money into the
Thames as wee request now of you; rather then
endanger so many innocent lives; you know
there is xl more at least to be receaved of
you for the play, wee desire you to lend us
vl of that, wch shall be allowed to you wthout
wch wee cannot be bayled, nor I play any more
till this be dispatch'd, it will loose you xxl
ere the end of the next weeke beside the hin-
derance of the next new play, pray Sr consider
our cases wth humanitie, and now give us cause
to acknowledge you our true freind in time of
neede; wee have entreated Mr Davison to
deliver this note, as well to witnesse yor love
as our promises, and alwayes acknowledgment to
be ever
yor most thanckfull; and loving freinds,
Nat: Field

The mony shall be abated out of the mony remayns for the play of mr Fletcher & ours
Rob: Daborne

I have ever founde you a true lovinge freinde to mee & in soe small a suite, it beeinge honest, I hope you will not faile us. Philip Massinger

Pl. 5. Letter to Philip Henslowe from Nathan Field, Robert Daborne, and Philip Massinger. By permission of the Governors of Dulwich College

under great pressure, and carried with it further risks. If Daborne had to break off writing a play because 'necessity enforced me to the common pleas bar this morning, to acknowledge a final recovery' (p. 73), other dramatists found themselves in court once their play had been put on stage. One of the most revealing documents concerning joint authorship also derives from a brush with the law. A Star Chamber case in February 1625, recovered by C. J. Sisson, concerned a play called *The Late Murder in Whitechapel, or Keep the Widow Waking*, which Sir Henry Herbert, Master of the Revels, had licensed in mid-September 1624. This play, performed at the Red Bull Theatre in Clerkenwell (a converted inn, which specialized in raucous and sensational productions), united in one plot two recent scandals, tragic and comic. The tragic story told how Nathaniel Tindall killed his mother, Joan, pleaded guilty, and on 3 September 1624 was sentenced to be hanged near the house in Whitechapel where he had committed the murder.[29] The comic one recounted another true story, how an unscrupulous suitor kept a rich old widow (Mrs Anne Elsden) in a state of drunkenness and sleeplessness until she went through a ceremony of marriage with him in a London tavern, at which point he robbed her of all that he could lay hands on. These events took place between April and August 1624, and by September a play was put on at the Red Bull, written at great speed by Dekker, Webster, Rowley, and Ford. They were working in competition with another theatrical company, for in a contemporary copy of Sir Henry Herbert's licence for 'A new Trag: call: a Late Murther of the sonn upon the mother writt: by M[r] Forde & Webster this   Sept. 1624. £2'—double the sum usual at this time for licensing a new play—that entry is followed by this one:

The same Trag: writt: M[r]. Drew & allowed for the day after theirs because they had all manner of reason.

As G. E. Bentley suggested, the second licence indicates 'that two different companies prepared plays on this topical subject at the same time; that Herbert, after hearing arguments, allowed both plays so that they could be acted in competition; that for unspecified reasons he allowed that Dekker, Rowley, Ford, and Webster play a one-day advantage'.[30]

At the same time a ballad on the widow's duping, 'composed by one Richard Hodgkins', was printed and sung in public around London, also advertising the play, for the ballad-monger was hired by Aaron Holland (who built the Red Bull Theatre and helped run it) to perform under Mrs Elsden's window. At this point the widow's son-in-law started a legal action against the authors of the ballad and the play. In the course of his deposition in the

---

[29] C. J. Sisson, *Lost Plays of Shakespeare's Age* (Cambridge, 1936), pp. 94–7.

[30] *JCS* iii. 253. Thomas Drew or Drue is credited with other plays for the Palsgrave's Men at the Fortune theatre in 1623–4: ibid. iii. 280–6.

Star Chamber, 'The answer of Thomas Dekker one of the Defendants' (3 February 1625), the dramatist admitted that he and his fellows 'did make and contrive . . . the said play . . . upon the instructions given them by one Ralph Savage'—presumably factual information about the events—and declared

> that true it is, he wrote two sheets of paper containing the first Act of a play called *The Late Murder in Whitechapel, or Keep the Widow Waking* and a speech in the last scene of the last Act of the boy who had killed his mother. Which play (as all others are) was licensed by Sir Henry Herbert Master of His Majesty's Revels authorizing thereby both the writing and acting of the said play. (Sisson 1936, pp. 110–12)

By declaring that the play had been officially licensed Dekker was evidently hoping to give their composition some respectability.

Dekker's account of his part in the composition helps us to understand how collaboration worked. He testified to having contributed 'two sheets of paper', that is, four leaves or eight pages, containing the first act and a speech in the fifth act by the boy who had killed his mother, presumably his repentance speech before execution. Sisson computed the lengths of separate acts in surviving manuscript plays to be from five to twelve pages (pp. 111–12), and deduced that Dekker 'wrote the first act on the first six pages, and the separate speech on the last leaf which could be detached and inserted in its proper place, when the play was assembled' by the theatre's book-keeper or editor, who would prepare the prompt-copy and the individual actors' parts. These facts also indicate that 'the play was jobbed out to the four authors in detached acts, with one important passage at least reserved for special treatment' (p. 112).[31] The key factor involved was the company's haste to cash in on these sensational events, for since the play was licensed in September 1624 and the 'marriage' took place at the end of July, the authors had at the most one month to get the play written. This haste 'precluded anything in the shape of close continuous collaboration between all four dramatists', Sisson argued, suggesting that 'Dekker and Rowley, the original defendants, worked out the plot together, then called Webster and Ford into consultation, and apportioned the acts'. Dekker would probably have 'completed the first act, and so introduced the persons of the play and given them their characters'. He then read this to the others and provided them with a complete scenario, 'with sufficient summaries of the action of each act' for the other authors to get on with their work separately. Responsibility for continuity presumably remained with the initiator, but could also be shifted on to the book-keeper.

---

[31] Bentley agrees that 'Evidently Rowley, Ford, and Webster each wrote the second or third or fourth act and one part of the fifth. Dekker and Rowley had had much experience of this sort of thing, but it has surprised the more literary admirers of Ford and Webster to find those poets of tragic genius lending themselves to this vulgar phase of the show business in 1624': *JCS* iii. 255. Despite Bentley's disparaging comments, co-authorship was an economic necessity for professional dramatists, and not without artistic satisfaction.

This legal document suggests two further points. The fact that Dekker wrote both the first act, probably the comic plot, and the key speech in the tragic plot, 'opposes the common assumption that in collaboration the comic part was assigned to one author and the tragic to another' (p. 113). Dramatists could work equally well on both, as Shakespeare did in *The Two Noble Kinsmen*, contributing not only the heroic eloquence of the play's opening and closing episodes but also a scene for the serio-comic subplot involving the lovesick Jailer's Daughter.[32] Much would depend on which of the collaborators had taken the initiative in suggesting or plotting the play. In the case of *Keep the Widow Waking*, Sisson concluded, 'it seems probable that Dekker, who wrote the first act and so introduced the stories and characters, who reserved for himself the outstanding opportunity offered by the murder plot, and who alone appeared before the Court, was the principal agent in the making of the play and was entrusted with its execution' (p. 114). At this point Dekker was a freelance, while Rowley was a member of Prince Charles's Company.

After Sisson's lively reconstruction of the controversial circumstances surrounding *Keep the Widow Waking*, it is a matter of great regret that its text has not survived. One other co-authored play also dogged by legal difficulties which fortunately has survived is the famous British Library manuscript Harleian MS 7368, entitled 'The Booke of Sir Thomas More'[33]—'booke' implying a playhouse manuscript. This play is unusual in several respects. First, it seems never to have been performed. The manuscript bears signs of having been edited, at least in part, for theatrical purposes, but the editing was not completed. Secondly, its composition apparently took place in two distinct phases, separated by a number of years, as if an abortive first attempt to get the play on the boards had failed, the second attempt also failing. Five or six dramatists were involved, Shakespeare's contributions being made at the second stage, which may be datable from internal evidence. In all the other plays I discuss here, Shakespeare was the co-author during a single period of composition, resulting in a play which was then performed by the theatre company (*Timon of Athens* may be an exception). Here, though,

---

[32] See Chapter 6.

[33] I draw on Greg's edition for the Malone Society (Oxford, 1911), reissued with a supplement to the introduction by Harold Jenkins (Oxford, 1961), here referred to as *MSR*. Quotations, however, are from the modernized edition, *Sir Thomas More*, ed. V. Gabrieli and G. Melchiori for the Revels Plays (Manchester, 1990), cited as Gabrieli and Melchiori 1990. For helpful discussions of the whole issue see A. W. Pollard (ed.), *Shakespeare's Hand in The Play of Sir Thomas More* (Cambridge, 1923); Chambers 1930, i. 499–515; R. C. Bald, 'The Booke of Sir Thomas More and its Problems', *ShS* 2 (1949): 44–65; and T. H. Howard-Hill (ed.), *Shakespeare and 'Sir Thomas More': Essays on the Play and its Shakespearian Interest* (Cambridge, 1989). A valuable research tool is Thomas Clayton, *The 'Shakespearean' Addition in the Booke of Sir Thomas Moore: Some Aids to Scholarly and Critical Shakespearean Studies* (Dubuque, Ia., 1969; Shakespeare Studies Monograph Series, 1), which includes orthographical indexes and concordances.

the contributions he made failed to turn *Sir Thomas More* into a viable theatrical vehicle. But although anomalous in these respects, the manuscript has attracted a great deal of scholarly attention, being (almost certainly) the only surviving holograph by Shakespeare. This intense scrutiny has stimulated authorship studies, although scholarly opinions have diverged.

The manuscript is a thin folio volume, the pages measuring $11\frac{1}{2} \times 8\frac{1}{4}$ inches, and consists of thirteen leaves of the original version, which Greg estimates may have consisted of eight sheets. As C. J. Sisson described the manuscript, 'the whole play in its original version was first written out in one hand (which scholars refer to as S) and then five others (A–E) contributed additions or revisions. Leaves which were entirely superseded were then removed from the MS. and have not survived. The revisions left the text in a chaotic state . . .'.[34] A scholarly consensus now agrees that the original manuscript is in the hand(s) of Anthony Munday, consisting of seventeen scenes, totalling 1,986 lines. Into the dramatic sequence are inserted six additions, in the following hands (I have added act, scene, and line references, as in the Revels edition):

I	Hand A [Henry Chettle]: revision of scene xiii. 1–71, incorrectly placed (cf. 4. 4. 19–98)
II	Hand B [Thomas Heywood]: rev. iv. 1–65 (2. 1. 1–76)
	Hand C [Playhouse scribe]: rev. iv. 66–120 (2. 2. 1–43)
	Hand D [Shakespeare]: vi. 123–270 (2. 3. 1–159)
III	Hand C [?transcribing Shakespeare]: insertion to rev. viii. 2–22 (3. 1. 1–21)
IV	Hand C: rev. viii. 1–210 (3. 1. 1–249)
	Hand E [Thomas Dekker]: rev. viii. 212–42 (3. 1. 250–81)
V	Hand C: rev. viii^a. 1–17 (3. 2. 1–22)
VI	Hand B: rev. ix^a. 1–67 (with 21–36 deleted: 3. 2. 305–55) and rough draft of viii^a. 2–6 (3. 2. 1–5)

Hand C, presumably that of the playhouse scribe, who also wrote the plot of *The Seven Deadly Sins* and a fragmentary plot in the British Museum (*MSR*, p. xxxv), seems to have begun editing the manuscript, correcting inconsistencies in the speech headings and stage directions. He has also added the names of several actors, a detail which suggests that the play was being cast for performance, although no record survives of it ever having been performed.[35] (But of course we only know a fraction of the drama performed between 1576 and 1642.)

---

[34] C. J. Sisson (ed.), *William Shakespeare: The Complete Works* (London, 1954), p. 1235.

[35] Cf. Greg, *MSR*, p. xv; Chambers 1930, i. 512; Bald 1949, p. 49; H. Jenkins, *MSR*, p. xliii; and S. McMillin, *The Elizabethan Theatre and 'The Book of Sir Thomas More'* (Ithaca, NY, 1987), ch. 2, 'Parts for Actors: Casting the Play' (pp. 34–52).

The Booke of Sir Thomas More raises many difficult and perhaps insoluble questions. When was the play originally written, and for which theatrical company? When were the additions written, and for which company? How was the collaboration divided up? Were some of the writers involved in revising the play also responsible for its original composition? Each of these questions has received widely varying answers, on bewilderingly diverse grounds. First exposure to the *Sir Thomas More* controversy can be very confusing; after a while one begins to evaluate arguments and form an individual judgement. Without citing every author *pro* and *contra*,[36] what follows is my reading of the evidence.

The original play seems to have been written in 1592–3, when it would have had an immediate social and political resonance. In these years resentment among London tradesmen about the commercial prosperity of foreign shopkeepers led to an outburst of xenophobia so threatening that the Privy Council issued a proclamation, warning of severe measures to be used if people or property were damaged.[37] These events were an uncanny echo of similar unrest in 1517, climaxing in the so-called 'Ill May-Day' riots, an event which is used in the play (against the historical record) to show More quelling the riot, being rewarded by King Henry VIII with a knighthood and place on the Privy Council. Several topical allusions support a date of 1592–3, although some of these would have been relevant over the next decade. After a careful reconstruction of the theatrical implications of the play's large cast (it calls for twenty-two speaking characters in the first 472 lines alone) Scott McMillin suggested that only two Elizabethan companies were large enough to mount so demanding a play, 'the Queen's men in the 1580s, followed by Strange's men in the early 1590s'. McMillin concludes that it was 'originally written for Strange's men between the summer of 1592 and the summer of 1593 and that the representation of the Ill May-Day uprising was intended to reflect the crisis over aliens that was troubling the City during those months' (McMillin 1987, pp. 58, 73).

One other indication of the play's topicality survives, in that 'the original parts of the manuscript—and only those—bear several marginal notes, corrections, crossings out and marks for omission of whole passages in the hand of Edmund Tilney, the Master of the Revels from 1579 to 1610' (Gabrieli and Melchiori 1990, pp. 17–18). On the manuscript's first page, partly obliterating a number of speech headings, Tilney wrote (spelling modernized):

---

[36] For a useful survey of the secondary literature (although evidently biased against a late dating of Shakespeare's additions) see G. Harold Metz, ' "Voice and credyt": The Scholars and *Sir Thomas More*', in Howard-Hill 1989, pp. 11–44.

[37] Cf. Chambers 1930, i. 510–11; Bald 1949, pp. 52–3; and Gabrieli and Melchiori 1990, pp. 18–19.

Leave out ... the insurrection wholly, with the cause thereof, & begin with Sir Thomas More at the mayor's sessions, with a report afterwards of his good service done being Shrieve of London upon a mutiny against the Lombards—only by a short report and not otherwise, at your perils. E. Tilney.

Tilney crossed out single speeches in the first scene that he found offensive, and finally marked the whole scene for deletion. Later in Act 1 he wrote against one speech: '*Mend this*'; the word 'English', used to describe English resentment at what they thought were the abuses of foreigners, is replaced with the noncommittal 'man', while the words 'stranger' and 'Frenchman' are crossed out and replaced with 'Lombard'. In Act 4, against a scene dealing with questions of conscience and religion, he wrote '*all alter*'.

Tilney's drastic interventions, which would have effectively killed the play stone dead,[38] are fascinating evidence of the Elizabethan authorities' sensitivity to controversial issues. Yet, strikingly enough, as Greg first pointed out,[39] the revisers ignored Tilney's instructions, indeed the scene contributed by Shakespeare represents the citizens on the verge of a riot, before More restores order with an eloquent defence of law and tolerance. The revisers' collective disregard of the censor suggests that the revisions might date from a later period, such as after June 1603, when the appointment of Sir George Buc redefined responsibilities within the office,[40] or—I suggest—when the actors thought that they had a powerful patron who had more influence with the authorities than the Master of the Revels. The main motives for the revisions that were made in the manuscript were not in fact political but theatrical, and McMillin has ably shown that they were aimed at cutting the play, both in the number of scenes and in the total speaking parts. In addition, a new role was added for a clown, scenes were reorganized both to create better transitions and to allow time for costume changes in roles that were doubled. Several other theatrical factors suggest that the play was revised with a view to its revival in 1603–4 by the Admiral's Men, probably at the Fortune Theatre.[41] The additions have also been dated by the internal, stylistic evidence, as we shall see.

[38] Greg wrote: 'it was quite impossible to comply with the demands of the censor without eviscerating the play in a manner fatal to its success on the stage' (*MSR*, p. xv); Bald computed that 'Tilney's order would have involved the omission of a total of 666 lines, or over a quarter of the play' (1949, p. 50).

[39] *MSR*, pp. xiii–xv.

[40] Chambers 1930, i. 511–12; McMillin 1987, pp. 94–5. Gary Taylor commented: 'I suspect they hoped to deceive Tilney, not persuade him': Taylor, 'The Date and Auspices of the Additions to *Sir Thomas More*', in Howard-Hill 1989, pp. 101–30, at pp. 123–4, 129 n. 62.

[41] McMillin 1987, pp. 74–134. Taylor has attacked McMillin's argument, finding no evidence that the play's revision was intended for the Admiral's Men, and urging that it could equally well have been taken over by the Chamberlain's/King's Men, Shakespeare's company. The two companies came into being on the demise of Strange's Men, and one of their unperformed scripts 'might have become the property of either company, depending upon the exact division of the spoils' (Taylor 1989, p. 107).

As for the original division of labours, they may have corresponded to the play's three-part structure. E. K. Chambers observed that the seventeen scenes

can be grouped into three sections, dealing respectively with the Rise, Greatness, and Fall of More. The first section (Scc. i–vii) was devoted, except for the description of an isolated early prank of More in Sc. ii, to the events of 'Ill May-Day', 1517. More was represented as taking a leading part (Sc. vi) in quelling the riot against the Lombard and French aliens in London. The second section (Scc. viii and ix) was mainly occupied with a visit of Erasmus to More, and with a play, in which More took an impromptu part. The third gave the closing episodes of his life, from his resignation of the Chancellorship (Sc. x) to his execution (Sc. xvii).[42]

In the original play the senior partner seems to have been Anthony Munday, who spent some time at the English College of Rome, where he would have had access to the play's less readily available source material.[43] Munday made a fair copy of the whole play, which he would hardly have done had he not been involved in writing it, and in one instance made 'a fundamental revision which he added after transcribing his copy: the second version he supplied of the play's final lines'.[44] He seems to have been assisted by Chettle and perhaps one other dramatist, although it has not proved easy to assign authorship of individual scenes. In 1919 E. H. C. Oliphant[45] identified three verse styles in the play: one 'somewhat old-fashioned', namely Munday, to whom he assigned scenes i–vii and part of viii; a second, 'much jerkier and less regular, with a partiality for an anapaestic foot here and there', perhaps Heywood, to whom he provisionally assigned scenes ix and xiv–xvii; and a third, 'the master of a much finer and impressive verse', Henry Chettle, to whom he gave scenes x to xiii (Oliphant 1919, pp. 228–9). John Jowett found it 'possible that, as Oliphant proposed, Chettle wrote scenes x–xiii in their entirety', but claimed several other scenes for him (Jowett 1989). Two younger writers took part in the revisions: Heywood (born *c.*1573/5) added a substantial role for a clown, while Dekker (born *c.*1572) provided a conclusion to scene viii, allowing more time for necessary doubling (McMillin 1987, pp. 80–1, 47). Munday collaborated with one or both of these dramatists on up to ten plays between 1597 and 1602.[46] As we know from Henslowe's Diary, between

---

[42] Chambers 1930, i. 501. McMillin (1987, pp. 20–31) follows Chambers in recognizing a three-part structure, giving more detail about the alterations made.

[43] G. Melchiori, '*The Book of Sir Thomas More*: Dramatic Unity', in Howard-Hill 1989, pp. 77–100, at p. 78.

[44] J. Jowett, 'Henry Chettle and the Original Text of *Sir Thomas More*', in Howard-Hill 1989, pp. 131–49, at p. 132.

[45] E. H. C. Oliphant, 'Sir Thomas More', *JEGP* 18 (1919): 226–35, at pp. 228–9.

[46] Cf. J. M. Nosworthy, 'Shakespeare and *Sir Thomas More*', *RES*, NS 6 (1955), at pp. 13–14. L. L. Schücking, in 'Shakespeare and *Sir Thomas More*', *RES* 1 (1925): 40–59, an essay virtually ignored by subsequent commentators (perhaps because he expressed scepticism about Shakespeare's identification with Hand D), made an illuminating comparison (pp. 49–53)

1598 and 1602 Dekker 'was engaged in the composition of forty-four plays for Henslowe, and at least one—*Satiromastix*—for other companies'.[47]

Inevitably, interest in *Sir Thomas More* has been mostly fuelled by the excitement of discovering the only existing playhouse manuscript containing scenes written by Shakespeare. In 1871 Richard Simpson suggested that the three pages (fos. 8[a], 8[b], 9[a]) were Shakespeare's autograph, and Sir Edward Maunde Thompson, a distinguished handwriting scholar, confirmed the identification. There have been some sceptics, but it is now generally agreed that it is more likely Shakespeare's autograph than not.[48] One peculiarity of the handwriting on these three pages is the amount of space that Shakespeare allowed himself. As John Dover Wilson pointed out, whereas 'Munday averages 79 lines to a page, Hand A 71 lines, Hand B 66, and Hand C 60', Shakespeare's three pages contain 45, 50, and 52 lines respectively, an ' "unusually expensive way" ' of using paper, as A. W. Pollard put it.[49] According to Peter Blayney, this makes Shakespeare 'not only the most uneconomical user of paper in the MS, but fairly exceptional for the period'. Whereas Hand C, 'a professional theatre scribe whose business is clarity', gets more lines on the page, 'Shakespeare's letter-forms are not appreciably larger than the scribe's: the difference lies in the line-separation'[50]—as if he were allowing himself ample space for interlinear additions and corrections. Shakespeare also left spaces between some words for punctuation marks to be added later, perhaps when he had decided what degree of emphasis was needed. Giorgio Melchiori has drawn attention to Shakespeare's 'extremely sparing use of punctuation, marking the end of a sentence in the middle of a line simply by leaving a wider space between its last word and the first word of the next sentence'.[51] The playhouse scribe, attempting to regularize the text, failed to understand Shakespeare's meaning and intentions. At one point More tells the rioting citizens to

---

between *Sir Thomas More* and some other plays on English historical themes, the two-part *Sir John Oldcastle* by Munday, Drayton, Hathway, and Wilson (1599, 1600)—which received additions by Dekker in 1602; *Thomas Lord Cromwell* (1600), by 'W.S.', and two lost plays, *The Life of Cardinal Wolsey* (1601) by Chettle, and its sequel *The Rising of Cardinal Wolsey* (1601) by Chettle, Munday, Drayton, and Wentworth Smith. Apart from *Thomas Lord Cromwell*, which was produced by Shakespeare's company, the rest of these titles were all written—like many other historical and 'pseudo-historical' plays in these years—for the Admiral's Men.

[47] Bentley, *JCS* iii. 242. Dekker's attack on Jonson in *Satiromastix* was written for the Lord Chamberlain's Men.

[48] See E. M. Thompson, *Shakespeare's Handwriting: A Study* (Oxford, 1916); *MSR*, pp. xxxvi–vii; Dawson 1990. For a sceptical view, see Michael L. Hays, 'Shakespeare's Hand in *Sir Thomas More*: Some Aspects of the Paleographic Argument', *ShStud* 8 (1972): 241–53.

[49] Wilson, 'Bibliographical Links between the Three Pages and the Good Quartos', in Pollard 1923, pp. 113–41, at p. 116, citing Pollard in *TLS*, 21 Oct. 1920.

[50] P. Blayney, '*The Booke of Sir Thomas Moore* Re-Examined', *SP* 69 (1972): 167–91.

[51] G. Melchiori, 'Hand D in *Sir Thomas More*: An Essay in Misinterpretation', *ShS* 38 (1985): 101–14, at p. 104. Melchiori noted that other instances of the use of a space for punctuation appear to survive in texts set from Shakespeare's 'foul papers', such as the 1600 quarto of 2

> Wash your foul minds with tears, and those same hands
> That you like rebels lift against the peace,
> Lift up for peace, and your unreverent knees
> Make them your feet.   To kneel to be forgiven
> Is safer wars than ever you can make
> Whose discipline is riot.
> In, in to your obedience: even the hurly
> Cannot proceed but by obedience.
> What rebel captain,
> As mutinies are incident, by his name
> Can still the riot? Who will obey a traitor?

(Addition IIc, 231–9; 2.3.116–26)

In the fourth line of that excerpt, after 'feet', Shakespeare left a gap, intending to add punctuation. Not realizing this, the playhouse scribe treated that line as a self-contained semantic unit, albeit ridiculous:

> and your unreverent knees,
> Make them your feet to kneel to be forgiven.

(The Prologue to *Pyramus and Thisbe* is too close for comfort!) Unable to make sense of the four lines following, the scribe simply crossed them out and added four words of his own to bridge the gap until the next bit he could understand:

> [Tell me but this,] what rebel captain . . .

(If the mistaking of a single punctuation mark can create such confusion, it is chastening to reflect what other errors may have come down to us in early printed books.) Another type of lacuna that Shakespeare, like other dramatists, left in his theatrical manuscripts was that of speech headings, which he would add only after completion of the text. Towards the end of his contribution he seems to have been hurried and become careless, misplacing a speech heading and assigning to the crowd 'a speech which was surely meant for only one speaker' (Melchiori 1985, p. 107).

If the handwriting and punctuation of these pages point to Shakespeare's authorship of Addition IIc, so does their spelling. Dover Wilson, whose extensive studies of the evidence for Shakespeare's handwriting preserved by the spellings in the original quarto texts were to culminate in his important work on the manuscript of *Hamlet*,[52] pointed out that many spellings in the Addition were typical of Shakespeare's practice elsewhere (Wilson 1923, pp. 122–41). For instance, although printers may have regularized his spelling,

---

Henry IV, Induction, 15: 'And no such matter [ ] Rumour is a pipe': the Folio adds a question mark after 'matter' (Melchiori 1985, p. 104).

[52] *The Manuscript of Shakespeare's 'Hamlet' and the Problems of its Transmission*, 2 vols. (Cambridge, 1934).

there is some evidence that Shakespeare omitted the *e* after *c* in words like 'insolence', 'obedience'. Some quarto misprints 'can best be explained by Shakespeare's habit of omitting *e* after *c*', such as 'pallat' for 'palace' (*RJ* 5.3.107), which 'strongly suggests that here Shakespeare spelt the word "palac", forming his *c* like a *t*, as might easily happen in English script' (p. 124). Wilson showed that 'out of the twenty-eight occurrences of words which we should now end with -*ce* the writer of the addition omits the final e in [six] instances', namely 'insolenc', 'obedienc' (three times), 'obedyenc', and 'ffraunc' (p. 133). Wilson noted other instances where Shakespeare omitted the mute *e*, after *g* ('charg', 'straing'), and after *n* ('ymagin', 'doon', on' = one), among others. He also showed that by writing 'mas', 'trespas', 'stilnes' Shakespeare preferred the older spelling, with -*s* endings, rather than -*ss* ('*s* had come in early in the 16th century and was going out at the end of it': p. 135). He also used *c* and *t* interchangeably, before -*ion*, -*ient*, -*ial* ('*c* was the early form, which *t* was superseding . . .'), such as 'adicion', 'infeccion' (ibid.).

Dover Wilson's work on characteristic Shakespearian spellings in Addition IIc was updated in 1964 by A. C. Partridge,[53] who pointed to other idiosyncrasies: while '*i* and *y* were interchangeable in Elizabethan spellings', in these three pages the choice of *y*-spellings is abnormally high, 'unless compared with those of the earlier half of the sixteenth century, in such works as *The Prayer Book*' (p. 58). In the following three lines, for instance, there are thirteen *y* spellings:

> and that yo^u syth as kings in your desyres
> aucthoryty quyte syelenct by yor braule
> and yo^u in ruff of yor opynions clothd

> (200-2)

Partridge endorsed Dover Wilson's argument that, despite the printer's tendency to standardize spelling, Shakespearian idiosyncrasies did survive, such as omitting the mute terminal *e*, and giving the full vowel spellings for *shoold* and *woold*. But, he warned, although an awareness of idiosyncratic spellings can help us to identify individual authors it needs to be based on a wide sample. Of the spellings which Dover Wilson took to be abnormal, for example, Partridge showed that several of them occur in *The First Prayer Book of Edward VI* (1549), such as -*cc*- for (ksh) in 136 *infeccion*, *affliccion*, *benediccion*, *unccion*, and others. The *Prayer Book* has several *ea* spellings, which printers would have simplified to *e*; so Shakespeare's 208 *sealfe* is matched by

---

[53] 'The Manuscript Play *Sir Thomas More*: List of Contractions in Dramatic Use by 1600', in Partridge 1964, pp. 43–66 (line references are to the transcription of lines 123–270 in *MSR*, pp. 73–8). Partridge's Appendix IV (pp. 169–71) discusses 'The Hands in *Sir Thomas More*', that is, handwriting as an indication of authorship.

mealte, *shead*, *leat*, and *read* for red (p. 61). Shakespeare's phonetic spellings
130 *straing* and 251 *Iarman* (= German) have comparable orthographies in
Heywood (pp. 48, 61), while *on* for *one* occurs in Jonson and other contemporaries. Some of Shakespeare's spellings, which seem odd to us, turn out to
be quite coherent. Partridge observed that 'the notation of preterite and past-
participle endings of weak verbs' in Addition IIc is orthographically consistent, whether in verse or prose: 'after voiced stem-finals -*d* is used, e.g. 202
clothd; after unvoiced stem-finals -*t*, e.g. 201 *sylenct*. The full orthography
-*ed* is always syllabic, e.g. 134 *infected*. Precisely the same system obtains in
Shakespeare's *Richard II* (Q1), *Thomas of Woodstock*, and in the manuscripts of Antony Munday' (pp. 57–8). The recognition of a system here may
counteract the widespread view that Elizabethan spelling was simply chaotic.

While agreeing with Dover Wilson that 'Shakespeare's spelling was old-
fashioned', Partridge was able to correct his and other scholars' belief that the
idiosyncratic spelling 173 *scilens*, also found eighteen times in the speech
headings for the character Silence in *2 Henry IV*, was unique,[54] having located
'*scylens*' in Rastell's 1533 edition of Heywood's *The Pardoner and the Frere*,
and '*scilence*' in *Thomas of Woodstock*, almost contemporary with *More* (p.
62). A much rarer spelling was 244 *liom*, rather than the usual *lyam* (or
'leash'): when Shakespeare reused the word in *King Lear*, he must have
spelled it differently ('Hounde or Spaniell, Brache, or Lym': 3.6.67), for the
Quarto compositor read it as 'him', the Folio printer as 'Hym'. Another
nonce-word in the *More* Addition is 138 *pumpion*, which Shakespeare also
used in *The Merry Wives of Windsor* (3.3.34; F1). But while accepting
Partridge's corrections, the significant point is surely that this cluster of
idiosyncratic spellings—*Iarman*, *infeccion*, *scilens*, *liom*, *pumpion*—is not
found together in any other writer, and must be strong supporting proof of
Shakespeare's authorship.

Valuable though this small-scale evidence is, the main case for
Shakespeare's authorship of this scene in *Sir Thomas More* involves larger
verbal parallels. Studies by R. W. Chambers (1923, 1931,[55] and 1939[56]), by
Caroline Spurgeon (1930),[57] and by Karl Wentersdorf (1973),[58] all provided
convincing documentation of the close identity between this scene and at least
twenty passages in ten of Shakespeare's acknowledged plays. In the first part
of the scene (2.3.1–55), before More addresses them, the mob displays many

---

[54] The Revels editors still believe that this spelling is 'found . . . nowhere else in Elizabethan
texts' (Gabrieli and Melchiori 1990, p. 98).
[55] 'Some Sequences of Thought in Shakespeare and in the 147 lines of *Sir Thomas More*', *MLR*
26 (1931): 251–80.
[56] 'Shakespeare and the Play of *More*', in Chambers, *Man's Unconquerable Mind* (London,
1939), pp. 204–49, 407–8; repr. 1952.
[57] 'Imagery in the *Sir Thomas More* Fragment', *RES* 6 (1930): 257–70.
[58] 'Linkages of Thought and Imagery in Shakespeare and *More*', *MLQ* 34 (1973): 384–405.

of the characteristics Shakespeare had given them for the Jack Cade scenes in 2 *Henry VI* (4.2–4.10), and which he repeated in *Julius Caesar* and *Coriolanus*. Summarizing the similarities between *More* and 2 *Henry VI*, Chambers listed a complex of parallels: '(*a*) the entry of the mob leader, *talking amid clamour*, (*b*) the false economics of the *halfpenny loaf*, (*c*) the logic-chopping with *argo*'—a perversion of the logician's *ergo*[59]—'(*d*) the *undoing* of the poor by parsnips (or writing, as the case may be), (*e*) the *infection* [in 2 *Henry VI*, 'corruption'] spreading therefrom, (*f*) the murderous outburst, and (*g*) the instability of the mob'. These parallels do indeed 'make the few lines in *More* read like a summary of the Jack Cade scenes in *Henry VI*', the two plays sharing 'an effect of mingled humour and horror, quite unlike anything else in Elizabethan drama . . .' (Chambers 1939, pp. 220–1).[60] Anyone who compares the two scenes will not doubt Shakespeare's authorship of both. As the following chapter will show, modern scholarship has applied a wide range of methods to investigating the authorship shares in 'Sir Thomas More', including verse tests, parallel passages, vocabulary, and linguistic preferences. Studies of Shakespeare's chronology have produced more accurate methods for dating his contributions. And in the final chapter I shall consider this collaboration in terms of the problems faced by co-authors in achieving unity of character and design. Although problems remain, the scholarly tradition identifying Shakespeare's contribution to *Sir Thomas More* provides an excellent demonstration of the power of modern attribution studies.

In this chapter I have reconstructed something of the material context within which collaboration took place. The writing process was a speedy one, for Henslowe's accounts show that plays were normally finished in four to six weeks (Carson 1988, p. 59). On 13 March 1598 Henslowe recorded that Chettle and Day 'have promised to deliver [*Henry I*] by the twentieth next day following'; on 9 August, concerning another project, he noted that 'Mr Drayton hath given his word for the booke to be done within one fortnight' (Foakes and Rickert 1961, pp. 88, 96). Plays were vehicles of entertainment, no doubt often ephemeral. But many great works have survived, and some extant masterpieces were produced by two or more co-authors. It seems only fair to try to identify which playwrights contributed which parts, if only—four hundred years after the event—to give each the recognition they deserve.

---

[59] Chambers thought that the clown's perversion of *ergo* was unique to Shakespeare, but MacDonald Jackson found another instance of it in Middleton's *The Phoenix* (4.3.16), a parallel which, he judged, does not weaken 'the immensely strong case for Shakespeare's authorship of Hand D': 'A Non-Shakespearian Parallel to the Comic Mispronunciation of *ergo* in Hand D of *Sir Thomas More*', *NQ* 216 (1971): 139.

[60] In a rather diffuse essay, '*Sir Thomas More* and the Shakespeare Canon: Two Approaches', in Howard-Hill 1989, pp. 171–95, at 171–4, John Velz has pointed out further parallels with 2 *Henry VI*.

Identifying Co-Authors

Scholarly research identifying the authors involved in co-authored plays dates back to the early nineteenth century, to the fruitful attempts by Lamb, Weber, Spalding, Hickson, and Spedding to distinguish Shakespeare and Fletcher's shares of *The Two Noble Kinsmen* and *Henry VIII* (see Chapter 6 below). Improbable though it may seem to those unacquainted with the history of authorship studies, these pioneers used sound methods and produced results that are still accepted. In this present discussion I want to review some of the methods currently used, focusing on the canon of two dramatists who frequently took part in collaborations, John Fletcher and Thomas Middleton. Their work is especially relevant since they both collaborated with Shakespeare. I was tempted to add John Ford, for some interesting work has been done on his co-authored plays, but the general knowledge among scholars of seventeenth-century drama concerning his canon is so fragmented that much preparatory work would be needed. However, I occasionally cite some evidence for his authorship of the *Funerall Elegye* for William Peter.[1]

The many problems connected with the canon ascribed to 'Beaumont and Fletcher', the most celebrated of all collaborations, were investigated by F. G. Fleay in the 1870s, by Robert Boyle in the 1880s, and by E. H. C. Oliphant in a series of studies carried out in the 1890s and revised in the 1920s. His classic survey of the Beaumont and Fletcher canon[2] synthesized the consensus of scholarship concerning the various partnerships which could be discerned in the plays first collected in a folio edition as *Comedies and Tragedies Written by Francis Beaumont and John Fletcher Gentlemen. Never printed before, And now published by the Authours Originall Copies* (1647). This volume collected 34 plays and a masque; the Second Folio (1679) added another 18, making 52 in all. After five hundred pages of analysis, Oliphant's summary of the authorship allocations was as follows: Fletcher was involved in no fewer than 50 of the plays, Massinger in 18, Beaumont in 17, Field in 5, Jonson in 3, Middleton in 2, Ford in 2, Webster in 2, Shirley in 2, Shakespeare, Rowley, and Tourneur in 1 each (Oliphant 1927, pp. 15–16, 513). Thirty years later

---

[1] See Brian Vickers, *'Counterfeiting' Shakespeare: Evidence, Authorship, and John Ford's* Funerall Elegye (Cambridge, 2002), Appendix III, and 'Defining the Ford Canon', forthcoming.

[2] *The Plays of Beaumont and Fletcher: An Attempt to Determine their Respective Shares and the Shares of Others* (New Haven, 1927; repr. New York, 1970).

Cyrus Hoy began work on Beaumont and Fletcher with a doctoral dissertation, supervised by Fredson Bowers, and published his findings in the journal *Studies in Bibliography* in seven annual instalments (Hoy 1956–62).[3] Hoy investigated 54 plays, reaching the conclusion that Fletcher 'is the sole or partial author of fifty-one. Massinger . . . is present as reviser or collaborator in nineteen plays. Beaumont is the sole or partial author of fourteen, Field the partial author of four. Jonson, Middleton, Rowley, and Ford are each present in two plays; Shirley and Webster are each present in one. Shakespeare is present in one of the plays of the Beaumont and Fletcher canon, and Fletcher is present in one of the plays of the Shakespeare canon' (Hoy 1962, p. 86). Readers will notice that, by comparison with Oliphant's results, Fletcher's share has gone up by one play, as has Rowley's, while Beaumont's has gone down by three plays, Jonson's by two, and Field, Middleton, Webster, and Shirley by one each; Tourneur has disappeared. Behind these changes lie many detailed scholarly arguments, of course, but the general picture of multiple collaboration has not changed.

The study of Middleton's canon had been pursued sporadically by scholars in the earlier twentieth century, but the two major contributions, by David J. Lake and MacDonald P. Jackson, appeared almost simultaneously in the 1970s. Lake, working in Australia, published his book in 1975;[4] Jackson, working in New Zealand, had started work on Middleton in the late 1960s, but did not publish until 1979, although he reviewed Lake's book (favourably) in 1976.[5] Jackson decided to publish his researches 'as the independent findings which they are, without incorporating references [to Lake's work] or altering my book in the light of it', so that it could 'stand as a check upon his, and vice versa'.[6] Jackson recorded the remarkable fact that Lake and himself had 'independently reached virtually identical conclusions about every disputed and collaborate play associated with Middleton . . .'. As he commented, this surely constitutes 'a vindication of these methods, or at least a guarantee of their objectivity and of the accuracy with which they have been applied'. The two approaches turned out to be complementary in terms of method and scope, for while 'in studying linguistic forms and expletives we have uncovered much the same group of words and spellings as characteristic of Middleton, each has noted some that the other has overlooked or ignored' (Jackson 1979, p. vi). Lake studied Middleton's plays in conjunction with 132 plays by 'all the major dramatists writing during Middleton's career' (Lake 1975, pp. 18–19), while Jackson studied his corpus by

---

[3] C. Hoy, 'The Shares of Fletcher and his Collaborators in the Beaumont and Fletcher Canon (I)', *SB* 8 (1956): 129–46; II, *SB* 9 (1957): 143–62; III, *SB* 11 (1958): 85–106; IV, *SB* 12 (1959): 91–116; V, *SB* 13 (1960): 77–108; VI, *SB* 14 (1961): 45–67; VII, *SB* 15 (1962): 71–90.

[4] *The Canon of Thomas Middleton's Plays* (Cambridge, 1975).

[5] *JEGP* 75 (1976): 414–17.

[6] M. P. Jackson, *Studies in Attribution: Middleton and Shakespeare* (Salzburg, 1979), p. vii.

comparison with 100 non-Middleton plays, 43 of which were not in Lake's sample, 'so that our inferences about Middleton's peculiarities are based, to a considerable extent, upon different comparative material' (Jackson 1979, p. vi). Cyrus Hoy included in his seven instalments meticulously collected and tabulated data of linguistic forms in some 71 Jacobean plays, so that between the three scholars we can be sure that few significant documents have been overlooked.

Lake includes a huge amount of tabulated data in his book, in the text, in a comprehensive table, spreading across forty—unfortunately, unnumbered—pages, and in appendices (Lake 1975, pp. 244–56, etc.), as does Jackson (1979, pp. 179–212, etc.). Their joint findings must carry considerable weight. In addition to the plays traditionally ascribed to Middleton, they have confidently assigned to him *The Revenger's Tragedy*—joining at least half a dozen scholars in the wake of Oliphant's pioneering essay[7]—*The Second Maiden's Tragedy*, *A Yorkshire Tragedy*, and *The Puritan*. They differ over some plays—Lake claimed Middleton as co-author (with Dekker and Barry) of *The Family of Love*, which Jackson denied,[8] while claiming that Middleton wrote the first scene of *A Yorkshire Tragedy*, which Lake denied—but their overall agreement, on both general and specific issues, is indeed impressive. There is all the more reason, then, for Shakespearians to take seriously their independent findings that Middleton was the co-author of *Timon of Athens*, a claim to be discussed in Chapter 4. But of course some students of Shakespeare, including highly qualified scholars and even editors, continue to dismiss any notion that he collaborated with other dramatists. Such resistance may be expected, indeed Jackson has suggested that a general principle governs 'the success of attribution studies: the more important the play or the proposed author, the greater the degree of scepticism a case for authorship will attract' (1979, p. 161). Three of the four plays on which Shakespeare collaborated—*Titus Andronicus*, *Timon of Athens*, *Henry VIII*—were included in the 1623 First Folio, and some scholars take refuge in this fact as guaranteeing that they were wholly by Shakespeare. But the correct position is surely that Heminge and Condell, while verifying Shakespeare's major responsibility for all the plays in that volume, were not claiming that he had never collaborated, for as actors and sharers with theatrical careers dating back to the 1590s they knew that collaboration was very common. To rest on the authority of the Folio is to commit the fault that David Lake has described as a 'staunch belief in all external evidence' and which he labels ' "doxolatry", a coinage which might be defined as "unreasonable veneration for assertions that lack credentials" ' (1975, p. 5). The internal evidence, if properly studied,

---

[7] E. H. C. Oliphant, 'The Authorship of *The Revenger's Tragedy*', SP 23 (1926): 157–68.
[8] For the definitive ascription to Lording Barry, see now G. Taylor, P. Mulholland, and M. P. Jackson, 'Thomas Middleton, Lording Barry, and *The Family of Love*', PBSA 93 (1999): 213–41.

as these scholars have shown only too well, allows us to assign authorship with a high degree of probability.

I open this survey of the techniques used for identifying co-authors with the oldest method, which takes its origin when a reader familiar with the verse styles used in Elizabethan drama recognizes two or more different styles in a play. This immediate reaction responds to a whole range of elements which give verse style an individual voice, and it depends on the complex workings of an attentive reader's memory, a reaction which (so far) no computer can emulate. It is initially 'subjective', in the sense that all knowledge of the world is mediated through individual perceiving agents, but it can be formulated and tested objectively, once adequate methods have been evolved. Scholars of Elizabethan drama began an intensive investigation of such methods in the 1870s: one pioneer described 'the great step we have to take':

> our analysis, which has hitherto been qualitative, must become quantitative; we must cease to be empirical, and become scientific: in criticism as in other matters, the test that decides between science and empiricism is this: 'Can you say, not only of what kind, but how much? If you cannot weigh, measure, number your results, however you may be convinced yourself, you must not hope to convince others, or claim the position of an investigator; you are merely a guesser, a propounder of hypotheses.'[9]

With these words, the Revd F. G. Fleay (1831–1909) addressed the New Shakspere Society on the value of 'metrical tests as applied to dramatic poetry', urging the need for a quantitative, empirical approach which is still being echoed today. Fleay's work on Shakespeare will be considered in subsequent chapters, but he also used his method to differentiate the verse styles of other dramatists. Often criticized for his undoubted weaknesses (conflicting totals, mislaid data, frequent self-corrections), Fleay was a talented, many-sided scholar with a sensitive ear for verse, as he showed in a brilliant pastiche, taking a ten-line speech from Dryden's *All for Love* and rewriting it in the metre of Fletcher, Beaumont, Massinger, Greene, and Rowley '(at his worst, doing job-work)' (Fleay 1874*a*, pp. 3–6). His second paper addressed the Beaumont and Fletcher canon, and explained that he had begun his analyses with the plays that Alexander Dyce declared to be Fletcher's unaided work, examining 'their peculiarities in rhythm'. Fletcher's plays, Fleay argued, can be distinguished by no fewer than six different criteria:

---

[9] F. G. Fleay, 'On Metrical Tests as applied to Dramatic Poetry. Part I. Shakespeare', *TNSS* I (1874): 1–16, 38–9 (a 'Postscript' correcting 'a numerical blunder'), at p. 2; this study repr. in F. G. Fleay, *Shakespeare Manual* (London, 1876), pp. 121–38.

(1)   By number of double or female endings; these are more numerous in Fletcher than in any other writer in the language, and are sufficient of themselves to distinguish his works.

(2)   By frequent pauses at the end of the lines; this union of 'the stopped line' with the double ending is peculiar to Fletcher: Massinger has many double endings, but few stopped lines.

(3)   By moderate use of rhymes; this distinguishes him from Beaumont, who has more rhymes than Fletcher or Massinger, and who in serious passages has few double endings.

(4)   By moderate use of lines of less than five measures: he has more than Massinger, however.

(5)   By using no prose whatever. Massinger also admits none: there are two little bits in his works; both, I think, intercalated.

(6)   By admitting abundance of tri-syllabic feet, so that his (Fletcher's) lines have to be felt rather than scanned; it is almost impossible to tell when Alexandrines are intended.[10]

Fleay provided tables for Fletcher (17 plays) and Massinger (15), listing the incidence of double endings, rhyming lines, alexandrines, and lines of less than five measures. As he rightly saw, the rhyme test alone 'would not be safe' as a means of distinguishing authors, but 'the double endings would be conclusive. Fletcher's range [per play] is from 1500 to 2000, in round numbers, with an average of 1775; while Massinger's ranges from 900 to 1200, with an average of 1000' (pp. 54–5). Fleay then applied these criteria to the joint plays of Fletcher and Massinger, taking eight plays and assigning acts and scenes to each. In addition to the four criteria used for Fletcher alone, he added 'the weak-ending test', showing that 'Massinger often ends his lines with words that cannot be grammatically separated from the next line; articles, prepositions, auxiliaries &c., *am*, *be*, *of*, *in*, *the*, *this*, &c. Fletcher used the stopped line, usually' (p. 57). As we shall see in later chapters, the detailed analytical techniques evolved by modern scholars have validated Fleay's insights.

Fleay demonstrated his method on *The Little French Lawyer* (1619), arguing that 'a simple reading of the text shows the existence of two authors, from the frequent changes of style and treatment: a marking of the unstopped line makes the division', as follows:

Fletcher: Act 2, Sc. 1, 2, 3; 3. 2, 4, 5; 4. 1, 2, 3, 4, 6*b*, 7; 5. 1*a*, 2, 3*a*
Massinger: Act 1, Sc. 1, 2, 3; 3. 1, 3; 4. 5, 6*a*, 7*a*; 5. 1*b*, 3*b*

This division corresponds to the plot-structure, for, 'of the three stories contained in this play, namely that of La Writ, and that of Annabella, were assigned to Fletcher; the third, that of Lamira, being given to Massinger'. Fleay cited a further piece of evidence for two authors being involved, the fact

---

[10] F. G. Fleay, 'On Metrical Tests as applied to Dramatic Poetry. Part II. Fletcher, Beaumont, Massinger', *TNSS* 1 (1874): 51–72, at p. 53; this study repr. in Fleay 1876*b*, pp. 151–70.

that 'in every place where Dinant's name occurs in the scenes assigned to Fletcher, it is pronounced Dínant, paroxyton: but in the Massinger scenes it is oxyton, Dinànt' (p. 58). When Cyrus Hoy discussed the authorship of this play some eighty years later, using a quite different range of linguistic evidence (the collaborators' preferences for such variant forms as *ye*, *hath*, *'em*), he made substantially the same division:

Fletcher: 2.1, 2, 3; 3.1–2, 4; 4.1–4, 6*b*; 5.1*a*, 2
Massinger: 1.1, 2, 3; 3.3; 4.5, 6*a*, 7; 5.1*b*, 3 (Hoy 1957, pp. 150–1)

Several of Fleay's other divisions of joint-authored plays show a considerable overlap with Hoy's, establishing the general reliability of his method.

Fleay's claim that collaborating dramatists could be identified by the characteristics of their verse styles was endorsed by E. H. C. Oliphant fifty years later. Paying a guarded tribute to Fleay's 'industry and cleverness', while acknowledging that he 'mixes up fact and theory in a very perplexing manner', jumping to conclusions on inadequate grounds, Oliphant judged that verse tests provided confirmatory, rather than primary evidence (Oliphant 1927, pp. 4–6). As he drily observed,

I cannot believe that, because a scene contains 20 per cent run-on lines, 5 per cent double endings, and 3 per cent weak endings, therefore it must belong to the writer whose figures approximate most nearly to those figures, for, in point of fact, verse-statistics are frequently misleading; but, on the other hand, when one finds the verse of some scenes in a play showing certain marked characteristics, and that of other scenes wanting in all those characteristics, it seems to me the height of foolishness to deny that there we have tolerably good evidence of a dual authorship. (p. 5)

Accordingly, Oliphant attempted to define for each dramatist discussed the typical 'facture of the verse' (p. 30). Fletcher, he judged, 'has the most distinctive and individual style', marked 'by his excessive use of double endings, of which he usually has about seventy in every one hundred lines . . . more than half as much again as Massinger's' (p. 32). In 4.3 of *The Loyal Subject*, for instance, Fletcher wrote one sequence of 39 lines which includes 35 double endings, 3 triple, and 1 single; 'a few lines further on in the same scene there occur 38 successive lines of which 31 are double endings, six triple endings', and but one single, the word 'power', which could also be read as a double ending (p. 32 n.). Fletcher obviously intended this effect, for he often obtained it 'by means of some conventional and wholly unnecessary end word (such as "still" or "else" or "too")', thrown in for no other purpose', also 'sir' or 'lady' (p. 33). The second distinctive feature of Fletcher's verse is his avoidance of 'run-on verse . . . indeed he pauses at the end of about 90 per cent of his lines'. As Oliphant put it, Fletcher 'threw off the monotonous succession of iambic after iambic' but 'remained bound by . . . the curse of final pauses' (pp. 34–5). Nevertheless, he 'gained the appearance of careless ease that he desired', making his verse seem 'as unobtrusive as possible', scarcely ever using rhyme (p. 36).

As Oliphant showed, Fletcher's verse style is so distinctive that it can be easily distinguished from his other collaborators. (As we shall see in Chapter 6, the striking differences between Fletcher's style and Shakespeare's have long enabled scholars to distinguish their shares in *Henry VIII* and *The Two Noble Kinsmen*.) As for Francis Beaumont, his verse differs from Fletcher's 'in nearly every respect. Instead of stopt, he uses run-on lines; instead of double, single endings; instead of slurring over several syllables in order to end the line where the speaker naturally takes breath, as Fletcher does, he is apt to conclude his verse with any tenth syllable that comes handy, whether it be adjective, preposition, or conjunction. The extra emphatic syllable', so common in Fletcher, 'is scarcely to be found in Beaumont' (p. 50).[11] Oliphant had the gift of being able to describe and differentiate verse styles, but it was more than mere impressionism. He provided statistics, sometimes in an informal manner—Beaumont's 'double ending percentage is usually about 20, and his unstopt line percentage about 30' (ibid.)—at other times in more detail. Thus he argued that Massinger's verse shows a 'greater evenness' than either Beaumont or Fletcher's, avoiding their 'jolting changes from iambic to trochee', regularly emphasizing 'a light syllable, such as "of", "you", "in"', and frequently employing double endings, as much as 'from 40 to 50 per cent, while his percentage of run-on lines is usually 35 or 40' (pp. 58–9). Oliphant was the first to devise a 'middle-ending speech test', showing that in Massinger the 'percentage of speeches that end where the verses end is ordinarily as low as 15, while Beaumont's is over 55, and Fletcher's about 45' (p. 60). This is indeed a useful method of 'distinguishing Massinger from his colleagues in long scenes of verse', and Oliphant used it well in discussing individual plays. Oliphant also used detailed statistical evidence to differentiate the work of Nathan Field, applying twenty-two tests, eighteen of which yielded positive results (pp. 79–80).

Oliphant's observation that Massinger 'cared not how great an emphasis he threw on a light syllable, such as "of", "you", "in"' (p. 58), was statistically confirmed a few years later in an independent study by F. L. Jones.[12] Having noticed 'the frequency with which [Massinger] terminates his lines with the insignificant words *of* and *to*', Jones 'examined 172 plays by thirty-three (plus several anonymous) playwrights' (Jones 1932, p. 727). He found that Massinger's predecessors 'exhibited a strong distaste for *of* and *to* at the end of a line', and especially disliked 'split-phrases', such as this:

---

[11] Yet Oliphant subsequently judged that detailed verse tests, valuable for other dramatists, would have 'comparatively little' point for Beaumont, 'because he seems, during his brief career, to have attained no stability of style' (p. 80). This is certainly Cyrus Hoy's view, who found Beaumont particularly hard to distinguish (Hoy 1958, pp. 85–7).

[12] F. L. Jones, 'An Experiment with Massinger's Verse', *PMLA* 47 (1932): 727–40.

Deform'd and crooked in the features *of*
Thy body, as the manners of thy mind

Having read through his large sample, Jones computed averages for each dramatist by adding the total instances and dividing by the number of plays. Massinger used *of* and *to* at line-endings more than 300 times in the form of a split phrase, his averages for these two prepositions being 20 and 14 respectively. The figures for other dramatists are: Dekker, $^3/_4$ and 0; Fletcher, 2 and 0; Jonson, 3 and 0; Webster, 2 and 0; Field, 6 and 1; Ford, 3 and 1. Jones found the averages to be 'on the whole, reliable; for the playwrights are surprisingly consistent in the regularity with which they use these words from play to play' (p. 729). Further, 'among the playwrights who make a pronounced use of these words it is possible to distinguish one from another, for each has his own peculiarities . . .'. However, Jones warned that 'the *of* and *to* count cannot be applied successfully to an anonymous play . . . , for in this respect the ways of a later Elizabethan dramatist are incalculable; the play may belong to a writer not included in the table' (p. 732). In authorship studies, as in other activities, we have to start with the known. Jones's readiness to admit the limitations of his database and method is rare in this discipline, but within the data assembled he was highly successful in distinguishing scenes written by Massinger, even on a blind test (pp. 732–6).

The validity of verse tests is undeniable, and even though their popularity has waned—due in part to the hostility expressed both by E. K. Chambers and G. E. Bentley—scholars continue to find them useful. E. H. C. Oliphant, in his pioneering essay ascribing *The Revenger's Tragedy* to Middleton, found in it

almost all the characteristics of Middleton's verse, the prevalence of rhyme, including a fair percentage of double-ending rhyme, varying lengths of line, an extraordinary fondness for triple endings, a slurring of syllables so as to crowd fourteen or fifteen or even more into the limits of a pentameter . . . , the use of words with a contracted 'it' (such as 'in't') to make double-endings, the use of the Fletcherian extra emphatic syllable, and an occasional resort to a trochaic line after a double-ending. (Oliphant 1926, p. 159)

That remarkably detailed description was evidently the product of wide reading and intensive study yet, curiously enough, Oliphant believed that evidence from the verse style was 'incapable of proof. In matters of the ear every one must judge for himself—at least, every one to whom God has given an ear' (p. 160). But verse style, like all other forms of linguistic utterance, is capable of analysis, and had Oliphant not despaired of 'the hopeless task of proving my case in that way', he could have counted the incidence in *The Revenger's Tragedy* of each metrical feature he had noticed, similarly for other Middleton plays of the same date, and then compared the results. That step was taken by R. H. Barker, in the second seminal essay on the authorship

TABLE 2.1. *Feminine endings in Middleton and others*

Play	Number of lines tested	Number of feminine endings	Percentage of feminine endings
Chaste Maid in Cheapside	400	185	46.3
No Wit	500	226	45.2
Second Maiden's Tragedy	500	210	42
Revenger's Tragedy	400	110	27.5
Phoenix	250	67	26.8
Michaelmas Term	150	36	24
Atheist's Tragedy	500	37	7.4

Source: Barker 1945, pp. 56, 127.

of *The Second Maiden's Tragedy* and *The Revenger's Tragedy*.[13] Taking samples of between 400 and 500 lines (approximately a quarter of a play's total length), Barker counted the number of feminine endings in both plays, comparing the data with those for other relevant plays by Middleton, and by Tourneur, to whom *The Atheist's Tragedy* had been ascribed. Combining his two tables into Table 2.1, we notice a distinct difference.

Barker laconically described these figures as providing 'a kind of rough check' (1945, p. 55), but they clearly place *The Revenger's Tragedy* within the norms for Middleton's verse, while just as clearly differentiating it from Tourneur's *Atheist's Tragedy*. Like Oliphant, perhaps, Barker seems to have been diffident about citing statistics, for they do not appear in the admirable book on Middleton that he subsequently wrote.[14] There he drew briefly on verse tests when discussing plays in which Middleton collaborated. In *Wit at Several Weapons* he noted that in several scenes 'the percentage of feminine endings is high . . . and there are parallels with Middleton's work'; in *The Old Law* he noted the same high incidence of feminine endings in 'scenes that on other grounds I have assigned to Middleton' (Barker 1958, pp. 179, 186). Despite Oliphant's scepticism and Barker's diffidence, other Middleton scholars have used metrical evidence without any misgivings. David Lake, reporting the received view that Middleton's oeuvre 'falls into two very distinct halves, with a lacuna of perhaps four or five years between the early (pre-1608) comedies and the later (post-1612) comedies, tragi-comedies and tragedies' (Lake 1975, p. 34), showed that Middleton's style changed considerably over these years. His 'verse, from his earliest undoubted play (*Phoenix*,

---

[13] R. H. Barker, 'The Authorship of *The Second Maiden's Tragedy* and *The Revenger's Tragedy*', *Shakespeare Association Bulletin*, 20 (1945): 51–62, 121–33.
[14] R. H. Barker, *Thomas Middleton* (New York, 1958).

1603–04) onwards, is largely end-stopped, with considerable use of feminine endings and rhyme; between the earlier and the later plays the percentage of feminine endings increases from about 25 per cent to about 45 per cent while the frequency of rhyme decreases' (pp. 34–5). Lake himself relied on Barker's verse statistics when advocating Middleton's authorship of *The Revenger's Tragedy*, a case also argued by F. L. Jones in his work on 'split phrases' in Massinger and elsewhere.[15] In a detailed appendix, Lake drew on the work of both scholars to devise a new verse test, computing the 'grades of run-on lines' in that play, which turned out to correspond much more to Middleton's known style than to Tourneur's (pp. 257–69).

MacDonald Jackson also used Barker's account of Middleton's early verse style—'predominantly end-stopped, with a liberal use of rhyme and of feminine endings'—to support Middleton's authorship of *A Yorkshire Tragedy*. Tucker Brooke, in his collection of the apocryphal Shakespeare plays, had argued that 'the verse of the *Yorkshire Tragedy* has few, if any, of the characteristics of Shakespeare's later verse. The end-stopped lines amount to about 88 per cent., an exceedingly high proportion for late work, while as many as 20 per cent. of the verse lines—two in every ten—are in rhyme. This large number of rhyming lines is not to be found in any but the earliest of the genuine plays . . .'.[16] Building on these figures, Jackson estimated that 'about a quarter of the blank verse lines have feminine endings' (Jackson 1979, p. 50). Two additional details involving verse form point to Middleton, one being the large amount of grammatical inversion found in this play.

Arguing that the verse is thoroughly unlike Shakespeare's around 1605, Brooke notes that 'the rhymes, moreover, are frequently obtained by means of a distortion in the word order, such as Shakespeare was not reduced to even in his apprentice work'. (ibid.)

R. H. Barker had made the same point about the early Middleton, who was always in a hurry, 'satisfied with almost any rhyme that comes to hand. Inverting the normal order or otherwise doing violence to idiom, distorting the niceties of meter or relying on inferior imagery—these things seem to mean nothing to him so long as the rhyme-words come' (Barker 1958, p. 74). The second stylistic feature, 'even more characteristic of Middleton', as Jackson observed, are '*A Yorkshire Tragedy*'s sudden, and often arbitrary, transitions between prose, blank verse, and rhyme; nearly all editors and commentators remark upon this feature of Middleton's style' (Jackson 1979, p. 50)—one to be remembered when we come to examine *Timon of Athens*.

A new and more rigorous approach to metrical studies was opened up in

---

[15] Jones 1932, pp. 728–9 n. 2, and 'Cyril Tourneur', *TLS*, 18 June 1931.

[16] C. F. T. Brooke (ed.), *The Shakespeare Apocrypha: Being a Collection of Fourteen Plays which have been Ascribed to Shakespeare* (Oxford, 1908), p. xxxv.

1960 by Ants Oras, who studied the positions at which pauses occur within a blank verse line, and 'in what ratios compared with other positions in the line'. Oras computed 'the incidence of internal pauses in each of the nine positions possible within an iambic pentameter line in relation to the totals of such pauses, regardless of the amounts represented by such totals'.[17] Whether a play has 'only a hundred internal pauses indicated by punctuation', or a thousand, is irrelevant, since this method allows us to draw a profile for each play and to chart a verse dramatist's changing practices. Oras started from the principle that 'authors may deliberately choose to use little or much pausation in their verse, but they will generally be less aware of the positions in the line in which they pause. It is these less conscious pause patterns that I have attempted to find and analyze'. Although deliberate variations will be recorded, he argued that 'the total patterns are likely to reveal much over which the person concerned has little or no control, almost as people are unable to control their cardiograms' (ibid.). Oras compiled three types of table and graph to record (1) the 'pattern formed by all the pauses indicated by internal punctuation (*A-patterns*)'; (2) the 'pattern of "strong pauses", i.e. pauses shown by punctuation marks other than commas (*B-patterns*)'; and (3) 'a pattern of "splits" or "line splits", i.e. breaks within the pentameter line dividing speeches by different characters—by far the heaviest type of pause, rarely found before 1600 (*C-patterns*)' (p. 3). Oras described the A-pattern as 'the most inclusive one, [showing] the greatest continuity' in Shakespeare (p. 13). His presentation of statistical data was exemplary. The tables at the end of his book (pp. 61–88) give the raw figures for the internal pauses in every play studied, together with the percentages for each position, these figures bringing out a marked shift in metrical emphasis over Shakespeare's career. Finally, Oras converted these percentage figures into a graph (known to statisticians as a frequency polygon[18]), showing in visual form the percentage figures on the vertical axis, the horizontal axis representing the pause position within the five-stress, ten-syllable line. Decimal points below 5 are rounded down, those above are counted as a full unit; the figures at the top of each graph indicate the total number of internal pauses in each work (pp. 5–6). Oras supplied over 700 individual graphs, which allow us to see at a glance the pause profile for every Shakespeare play, and for groups of his plays according to periods and genres.

Oras's work has many important implications for Shakespeare studies. But he also discussed the metrical practices of several Jacobean dramatists, including Jonson (pp. 17–18), Fletcher (pp. 21–6), Massinger and Middleton (pp. 23–4), Heywood (pp. 24–5), Webster (pp. 27–8), Tourneur (pp. 28, 58),

---

[17] A. Oras, *Pause Patterns in Elizabethan and Jacobean Drama: An Experiment in Prosody*, University of Florida Monographs, no. 3 (Gainesville, Fla., 1960), p. 2.
[18] See C. S. Butler, *Statistics in Linguistics* (Oxford, 1985), pp. 20–2.

Dekker and Marston (pp. 28–9). More important, Oras showed that his methodology could be applied to authorship studies by analysing separately those parts of a play reliably ascribed to co-authors. Such exercises are particularly valuable, for the later test in effect checks the validity of earlier ones, made on quite different principles. Oras was able to define the 'special physiognomy', as he put it (p. 23), of a great many Elizabethan and Jacobean plays, presenting 'C-graphs' (pentameter lines split between different characters) for 9 plays by dramatists from the 1590s, 8 plays by Chapman, 5 by Marston, 18 by Jonson, 8 by Dekker, 19 by Heywood, 4 by Day, 21 by Shakespeare, 15 by Massinger, 7 by Beaumont, 15 by Middleton, 7 by Webster, 1 by Tourneur, 7 by Ford, 7 by Brome, 4 by Shirley, and 10 by D'Avenant (pp. 52–9). This is a remarkably rich digest of most careful research, of enormous value to authorship studies, and practically unknown to scholars of English Renaissance drama. Oras also made computations for co-authored plays, from which we can see that the graph for Dekker's share of *The Sun's Darling* (1624) corresponds closely to that for plays of which he was sole author, while the very different graph for Ford's share of that play closely matches that for *'Tis Pity She's a Whore* (?1632). The graphs which Oras provided vividly distinguish Shakespeare's share of *Henry VIII* and *The Two Noble Kinsmen* from Fletcher's, and differentiate Fletcher and Massinger's shares in nine plays that they wrote together. Middleton's authorship of *The Second Maiden's Tragedy* (1611) is instantly recognizable, closely resembling the contours of *The Witch* (c.1609–16), *Women beware Women* (1621), and Middleton's share of *The Changeling* (1622). As for *The Revenger's Tragedy* (1606), its pausation profile approximates very closely to the graphs for two other Middleton works produced at this time, *A Trick to Catch the Old One* (1605) and *Your Five Gallants* (1607): the stylistic profile for all three plays is wholly unlike that of *The Atheist's Tragedy* (1609). I have included some of these graphs in Appendix 1, so that readers can see these distinct physiognomies for themselves.

The meticulous computation of pause patterns made by Ants Oras allowed MacDonald Jackson, the most inventive of attribution scholars, to make a fresh approach to Shakespeare's canon and chronology.[19] Jackson took Oras's inclusive count of pauses in Shakespeare's thirty-eight plays (Oras 1960, pp. 66–8), and used a computer statistical programme to create a matrix in which 'each play or part-play [was] correlated with every other' (Jackson 2002, p. 38). He arranged the plays according to the dates and chronology assigned by the Oxford *Textual Companion*, and listed for each work the five highest correlations with other Shakespeare plays. His results revealed a remarkably close correlation between plays of roughly the same

---

[19] M. P. Jackson, 'Pause Patterns in Shakespeare's Verse: Canon and Chronology', *LLC* 16 (2002): 37–46.

TABLE 2.2. *Pause patterns and Shakespeare's chronology*

Play title	Date	The five highest correlations with other plays				
R3	1592–3	*Err* 9977	*R2* 9906	*Tit* 9982	*Rom* 9860	*2H4* 9844
Err	1594	*R3* 9977	*R2* 9924	*2H4* 9908	*Rom* 9856	*Jn* 9840
LLL	1594–5	*Rom* 9965	*R2* 9928	*Shr* 9921	*Jn* 9870	*Tit* 9853
MND	1595	*Jn* 9957	*Rom* 9820	*LLL* 9774	*1H6* 9746	*Err* 9721
Rom	1595	*LLL* 9965	*R2* 9947	*Shr* 9911	*Jn* 9872	*R3* 9860
R2	1595	*Rom* 9947	*LLL* 9928	*Err* 9924	*R3* 9906	*2H4* 9898
Jn	1596	*MND* 9957	*Rom* 9872	*LLL* 9870	*Err* 9840	*R2* 9814

Source: Jackson 2002, p. 39.

date, the highest correlation coefficients (0.9977) being scored by *Richard III* and *The Comedy of Errors*. As a whole, Jackson commented, his recalculation of Oras's data showed 'the extraordinary consistency of Shakespeare's metrical development, which resembles organic growth' (p. 40). In Table 2.2 I select some data from Jackson's table for the plays written between 1592–3 and 1596. (Decimal points have been omitted from the correlation coefficients.) As well as showing the close interrelations between the metrical profiles of plays dating from the same period, that excerpt from Jackson's data draws attention to the firm placing of *King John* in this chronological sequence. Recent attempts to redate the play to 1590–1 (so as to make it precede *The Troublesome Reign of John, King of England*, published anonymously in 1591) now seem even less convincing, for it would also imply that 'the accepted datings of the first dozen Shakespeare plays are all several years too late'. As for *Pericles*, Jackson's application of Oras's pausation analyses show clear differences between Acts 1–2, attributable to George Wilkins, and Acts 3–5, undoubtedly by Shakespeare (see Chapter 5).

The study of metrics has developed enormously since the time of F. G. Fleay, and has been applied to Shakespeare in many fruitful ways, as we shall see. The pioneering treatment of Shakespeare's verse by Marina Tarlinskaja,[20] applying the quantified metrics of the Russian school, is especially promising. Abandoning the Greco-Latin system, based on quantitative verse, which classified metres as 'iambic', 'trochaic', and so on, Tarlinskaja treated the typical ten-syllable line of English verse as a unit alternating weak (W) and strong (S) syllables:

1	2	3	4	5	6	7	8	9	10
W	S	W	S	W	S	W	S	W	S

[20] M. Tarlinskaja, *Shakespeare's Verse: Iambic Pentameter and the Poet's Idiosyncrasies* (New York, 1987).

In Tarlinskaja's system the even positions are 'ictic' or strong (from *ictus*, a rhythmical or metrical stress), the odd ones non-ictic or weak, but of course the metrical norm recognizes both a loss of stress in the 'S' position and stressed syllables in the 'W' position (Tarlinskaja 1987, pp. 6, 332). Tarlinskaja then analysed the complete corpus of Shakespeare's verse, over 800,000 lines, calculating the ictic stresses and establishing 'metrical profiles' for each play, act by act. By so doing she was able to trace a smooth evolution over the course of Shakespeare's writing career 'from a more rigid to a looser verse form', the result of 'both conscious and unconscious effort' on his part, which provides 'yet another proof' of the integrity of the canon: 'Only one author could have written 37 plays in which the rhythmical evolution is displayed so consistently over the course of 25 years' (pp. 63, 65). Tarlinskaja also defined several other metrical phenomena which both characterized Shakespeare's verse style and differentiated it from that of contemporary dramatists, notably 'proclitic and enclitic microphrases' (pp. 204–14). Like Ants Oras, whose work she praised for its sensitivity and rigour (p. 199), Tarlinskaja's results are meticulously documented, her statistics providing detailed evidence of Shakespeare's metrical practice from year to year, enabling other scholars to test the accepted chronology.[21] The value of her work for authorship studies is that, having established the metrical norm for every point in Shakespeare's career, in the co-authored plays it instantly reveals the presence of another writer, whose metrical practices can be shown to be either quite different or corresponding to an earlier stage of Shakespeare's development. As succeeding chapters will show, Tarlinskaja has documented the presence of distinctly different verse styles in *Titus Andronicus*, *Timon of Athens*, *Pericles*, and both *Henry VIII* and *The Two Noble Kinsmen*.

Yet, while welcoming these new and more accurate approaches to Shakespeare's verse, we must regret that, as yet, they have not been applied to other Elizabethan, Jacobean, and Caroline dramatists. The prominence thrust upon him by posterity has been damaging to others, as well as to him.

PARALLEL PASSAGES

The second approach to authorship studies that I wish to discuss derives, like the first, from the familiar experience of reading or seeing a play and being reminded of some other work. One scene of *The Critic or, A Tragedy Rehearsed* (1771), Sheridan's sprightly satire on contemporary drama, takes place in the theatre. The author, Puff, is rehearsing his new play, *The Spanish*

---

[21] See MacDonald P. Jackson, 'Another Metrical Index for Shakespeare's Plays: Evidence for Chronology and Authorship', *Neuphilologische Mitteilungen* 95 (1994): 453–8.

Armada, accompanied by his friends Sneer and Dangle, who comment on the rehearsal. When Puff's 'mysterious yeoman' enters, the following exchange takes place:

> *Enter* A BEEFEATER
> BEEFEATER. 'Perdition catch my soul but *I* do love thee'
> SNEER. Haven't I heard that line before?
> PUFF. No, I fancy not—Where pray?
> DANGLE. Yes, I think there is something like it in *Othello*.
> PUFF. Gad! now you put me in mind on't, I believe there is, but that's of no consequence—all that can be said is, that two people happened to hit on the same thought—And Shakespeare made use of it first, that's all.
> SNEER. Very true.[22]

Puff's disingenuous response is exactly what we would expect of a plagiarist, but Sneer's question—'Haven't I heard that line before?'—is the more important one in this context, for it typifies the instinctive reaction of readers or theatregoers who find that one text reminds them of another. If the reader can properly document his or her reaction, by citing appropriate linguistic evidence, then a convincing case can be made. But all too often verbal parallels are seized on without any reflection on their potentially deceptive nature. As Muriel St Clare Byrne showed, in a classic essay, in order to establish valid parallels scholars must take account of several basic points:

(1) Parallels may be susceptible of at least three explanations: (*a*) unsuspected identity of authorship, (*b*) plagiarism, either deliberate or unconscious, (*c*) coincidence;
(2) *Quality* is all-important, and parallels demand very careful grading—e. g. mere verbal parallelism is of almost no value in comparison with parallelism of thought coupled with some verbal parallelism;
(3) mere accumulation of ungraded parallels does not prove anything;
(4) in accumulating parallels for the sake of cumulative effect we may logically proceed from the known to the collaborate, or from the known to the anonymous play, but not from the collaborate to the anonymous;
(5) in order to express ourselves as certain of attributions we must prove exhaustively that we cannot parallel words, images, and phrases as a body from other acknowledged plays of the period; in other words, the negative check must always be applied.[23]

Anyone who has worked on attribution studies will surely accept all five points. I would emphasize the importance of Byrne's second criterion, the value of being able to cite a 'parallelism of thought coupled with some verbal parallelism', and her fifth, the need to apply a negative check, in order to show

---

[22] Sheridan, *Plays*, ed. Cecil Price (Oxford, 1975), p. 378.
[23] M. St Clare Byrne, 'Bibliographic Clues in Collaborate Plays', *Library*, 4th ser. 13 (1932): 21–48, at p. 24.

that 'words, images, and phrases' occur throughout the work of one author but not in that of his contemporaries.

Byrne illustrated the truth of her fourth principle by studying the work of Henry Chettle at three clearly distinguished levels: an 'A class, of acknowledged plays' solely by him; a 'B class of collaborate acknowledged plays'; and a C class, 'anonymous plays in which Chettle might have had a hand'. The methodological principle involved is clear:

Unless the parallels *within* class A are numerically overwhelming, and aesthetically striking, additional parallels from class B will prove nothing. If they are, however, then comparison between classes A and C will be just as instructive as that between A and B. (p. 25)

Failure to observe this principle, Byrne pointed out, led H. Dugdale Sykes into an 'inherent fallacy' concerning Chettle: '*on impression* he groups A, B, and C together as Chettle's work, and *then* proceeds to gather parallels from B and C regardless of the essential A reference' (ibid.). Parallels between two plays in class B will prove nothing, while 'B and C parallels are logically not admissible to begin with' (p. 29). Byrne then examined the list of fifteen words that Sykes had claimed to be characteristic of Chettle, grouping occurrences into her three classes, and finding insufficient class A results to 'justify any decided opinion' (pp. 25–7). Sceptical that these words were in any way unusual, Byrne checked in Bartlett's *Shakespeare Concordance*, finding 'no less than 58 Shakespearian uses of *bright*, 66 of *shine*, and 34 of *beams*', allegedly Chettle's individual imagery, '29 of *aspect*, 18 of *vex*, and 14 of *vexed*, 47 of *honored*, 28 of *livery*, 12 of *cloudy*, 10 of *crystal*, 6 of *icy*, 5 of *milk-white*, 3 of *muffle*, and 9 of *purple* used in connection with blood', not to mention more than 200 Shakespearian uses of *comfort*. As she rightly concluded, 'it is obviously ludicrous to take as *characteristic* of Chettle words which appear in these numbers in any other dramatist, and in such very scanty numbers in his acknowledged work' (p. 27). Byrne easily showed that such phrases as 'civil/uncivil', or '*lights* used for *eyes*' are 'fairly commonplace in character'. Taking 'Sykes's parallels one by one they are either cancelled by the negative test, or else their significance is so whittled away as to make them practically valueless' (p. 28).

Muriel St Clare Byrne's essay remains an important caveat for all engaged on authorship studies. Another highly effective demonstration of the errors liable to occur if these criteria are not met was given by Arthur M. Sampley, objecting to the undisciplined attribution of plays to George Peele by J. M. Robertson and H. Dugdale Sykes (elsewhere a much more reliable scholar). To counter their claims, Sampley assembled 'a list of 133 words and phrases which have been called characteristic of Peele',[24] and then checked their

---

[24] A. M. Sampley, ' "Verbal Tests" for Peele's Plays', *SP* 30 (1933): 473–96, at p. 473.

occurrences in the works of Shakespeare, Kyd, Marlowe, Spenser, Greene, Nashe, and the *OED*. References to classical mythology, said to be unique to Peele, occurred in many other texts: Aetna (19 other instances), Ate (18), Phoebe (15), Styx (13), Prometheus (6). Sampley found that words or phrases claimed as characteristic of Peele were widely used in other Elizabethan texts: 'coal-black' (26 occurrences), 'counterpoise' (26), 'daunt' (52), 'doom' (155), 'empery' (34), 'entrail' (46), 'flatly' (25), 'glistering' (32), 'gratulates' (20), 'manly' (61), 'massacre' (40), 'meanwhile' (37), 'policy' (90), 'progeny' (29), 'reproachful' (21), 'ruthless' (27), 'sacred' (185), 'sacrifice' (55), 'solemnize' (29), 'suspect' as a noun (20), 'wreakful' (16), and 'youngling' (20). The claimants for Peele's authorship had also cited a number of phrases which were easily shown to be commonplace: 'to arms' (7 occurrences), 'in the cause' (6), 'damned deed' (5), 'kill . . . heart' (13), 'men of war' (7), 'mourning weeds' (6), 'for the nonce' (19), 'now or never' (5), 'private . . . public' (6), 'sheep before wolves' (12), 'short tale to make' (4), 'sink or swim' (4), 'suck . . . bane' (5), 'suck . . . blood' (6), 'thrice-happy' (23), 'trust me' (33), and 'work . . . woes' (8). In this way Sampley showed that 'about ninety percent . . . of the words and phrases' said to characterize Peele occur in the work of those contemporary writers whose vocabulary had been analysed, this in turn forming 'only a small proportion of the actual instances of those words in Elizabethan literature', most of which 'probably occur twenty times as frequently' as in his list (pp. 493–4). Sampley was certainly justified in expressing doubt concerning the validity of basing authorship claims solely, or largely, on the evidence of 'words and phrases' (pp. 474, 496).

The papers by Byrne and Sampley demonstrating the weakness of the undisciplined use of parallels based on single words or short phrases were both published in the early 1930s, and many readers might charitably expect that they had discredited it altogether. Yet equally naïve and unreflective methods were still being used by Gary Taylor in 1985–6, in his assertions that Shakespeare wrote the lyric 'Shall I die?', and by Donald Foster in 1985–96, claiming Shakespeare's authorship of an anonymous *Funerall Elegye*.[25] But, while discrediting the methods of Robertson and others, Sampley's honesty in presenting all his evidence resulted in his listing sixteen words and phrases found in Peele for which he had discovered no parallel anywhere else, evidence that could be important for further research. He also recorded the fact that 'twelve of these words and phrases do occur in *Titus Andronicus*' (p. 496), without subjecting that fact to further reflection—a point to which we shall return in Chapter 3.

For many years writers on authorship issues have warned against the dangers of relying on verbal parallels, while continuing to use them. As Rupert Taylor observed, 'the very words *parallel passage* provoke controversy. The

---

[25] See Vickers 2002.

truth, cynically stated, is that everybody uses parallel passages but mistrusts them in the hand of others.'[26] E. H. C. Oliphant described parallel passages as 'a method capable of much abuse and one to be used with great caution, but nevertheless . . . of no little value' (Oliphant 1926, p. 160). He then compiled eight pages of parallels between *The Revenger's Tragedy* and Middleton, of which I select two (pp. 161–2). The Duchess's bitter reflection here,

> O what a grief 'tis, that a man should live
> But once i'th' world, and then to live a bastard,
>
> .   .   .   .
>
> Begot against the seventh commandment,
> Half-damn'd in the conception . . .
>
> (1.2.160–3)

echoes, in form and content, the Lord Cardinal's observation in *Women Beware Women*:

> What a grief it is to a religious feeling
> To think a man should have a friend so goodly,
> So wise, so noble, nay a duke, a brother,
> And all this certainly damn'd!
>
> (4.1.186–9)

And in comic vein, the clownish servant Dondolo in this play is rebuked by his mistress Castiza, and told to 'cut off a great deal of dirty way' (*RT*, 2.1.17–18): just so, in *A Mad World my Masters* a humorous servant, also called Dondolo, announces his intention 'to be short, and cut off a great deal of dirty way' (1.1.75). These two striking parallels are only a fraction of the links that Oliphant demonstrated between *The Revenger's Tragedy* and Middleton. They clearly transcend the categories of coincidence or imitation.

Following Oliphant's lead, by 1945 R. H. Barker could record that 'parallels are not perhaps at the moment a fashionable form of evidence', but he still used them with good effect to list resemblances between *The Second Maiden's Tragedy* and *The Revenger's Tragedy*, 'some of them first noticed by Fleay[27] more than fifty years ago' (1945, pp. 61–2). Barker himself accumulated five pages of parallels between other Middleton plays and *The Second Maiden's Tragedy* (pp. 56–60), and another five pages of Middleton parallels that he had noticed with *The Revenger's Tragedy* (pp. 127–32), in addition to 'the many parallels pointed out by Oliphant and other scholars'. For both plays Barker quoted further similarities in attitude (especially the use of irony), dramatic situation, characterization, and style (pp. 53–5, 122–6). In his

---

[26] R. Taylor, 'A Tentative Chronology of Marlowe's and Some Other Elizabethan Plays', *PMLA* 51 (1936): 643–88, at p. 643.

[27] Cf. F. G. Fleay, *A Biographical Chronicle of the English Drama, 1559–1642* (London, 1891), ii. 264, 272, 330–1.

subsequent monograph on Middleton, returning to *The Revenger's Tragedy*, Barker defended the work of E. H. C. Oliphant, 'the distinguished scholar who first presented the case for Middleton' as the author of that play, in terms that reveal the continuity of method within authorship studies, despite changes of fashion:

> He was right after all, and the scholars who for a generation now have ignored or sneered at his evidence, sometimes—when they have condescended to mention it— printing the word *evidence* itself between inverted commas, have not turned out to be our most reliable guides. But scholarship seldom divorces itself entirely from fashion, and what appeals to one generation—parallel passages, for example—is sometimes completely rejected by the next one. I should perhaps apologize for putting more parallels here, but I am putting them in. (Barker 1958, p. 166)

Some of these parallels were new, others Barker defiantly repeated, even though Samuel Schoenbaum (notoriously opposed to the use of any internal linguistic evidence in authorship studies) had branded them 'suspect' (pp. 166–9). Barker also made good use of verbal parallels in distinguishing Dekker's share of *The Roaring Girl* from Middleton's (pp. 170–6), Middleton's share of *Wit at Several Weapons* (pp. 177–80), the respective shares of Middleton and Rowley in *The Old Law* (pp. 184–9) and *The World Tossed at Tennis* (pp. 190–1), and those of Middleton and Webster in *Anything for a Quiet Life* (pp. 191–2).

Identification of parallel passages continues to be a major weapon in authorship studies, and scholars continue to issue warnings about their value. In 1959 Cyrus Hoy described them as 'of course, notoriously untrustworthy aids to determining authorship' (1959*a*, p. 100), but he none the less made judicious use of them. David Lake stated that 'this type of evidence has been grievously abused in the past', rightly observing that the average 'parallel passage' cited 'has been (1) undefined as to objective points of similarity, (2) hence uncountable for statistical purposes, (3) striking in thought and diction and hence open to imitation, (4) not subjected to the negative check', thus defeating four of the main desiderata for valid internal evidence (Lake 1975, p. 9). Yet, Lake added, all these faults are avoidable, for 'if the parallel is defined, counted, fairly unobtrusive, and searched for through a whole corpus of comparison plays', so as to establish 'a recurrence of identical elements', then it may legitimately be used (p. 10). And MacDonald Jackson independently agreed: 'I think that the best "parallels" are good enough to require some explanation beyond pure chance' (Jackson 1979, p. 62). Lake suggested that verbal parallels (which he called 'collocations') should be delimited to clearly defined categories, including 'combinations of more than one word . . . co-occurring in the same sentence', the combination being care-fully defined and its occurrence counted 'through the entire corpus'; 'some particular grammatical or semantic pattern'; and 'single words in special senses', that sense being 'always established by the context' (Lake 1975, p. 14). As he observed, collocations often 'have the advantage . . . of high distinctiveness, but usually the disadvantage of low-frequency', and are best used 'in combination with colloquialisms and contractions to show that such items do not signify a mere transcript or superficial revision, but true author-ship' (ibid.). They are not always susceptible to statistical analysis, being in the nature of highly individual verbal combinations. Here again the 'negative check' is important: collocations can be admitted when examining 'collab-orate play scenes whose authorship can be proved by other means; especially when the item in question does not occur in the undoubted works of the other collaborator' (p. 18). Many scholars would agree with Lake that verbal parallels form contributory, rather than primary evidence, and 'should never be relied on to prove a case alone; but the lack of parallels is a suspicious circumstance in any authorship case, and therefore parallels should be cited as "defensive" evidence' (p. 77 n.), to be used in parallel with 'probative evidence', such as the distinctive use of contractions and other linguistic habits (pp. 168–9).

Lake gave several valuable instances of how to use collocations, as when denying Middleton's responsibility for *Blurt, Master Constable*, and ascrib-ing it to Dekker (pp. 66–90). In addition to the major differences between the two dramatists in their use of synonyms, contractions, oaths, and expletives, he showed that 'every scene [of the play] is marked by Dekker parallels and/or linguistic practices' (p. 88). These parallels include such distinctive phrases as 'besides himselfe', found in *Blurt* and in Dekker's part in *Northward Hoe!*, there being no instance of that phrase in Middleton: 'I am a servitor to God Mars' (*Blurt*), and 'a follower of god Mars' (*Northward Hoe!*); 'because He be sure he shall not start [i.e. "escape"]' (*Blurt*), and 'because you shal be sure ile not start [i. e. "escape"]' (*Old Fortunatus*), for which Lake found no par-allel elsewhere. As he pointed out, 'the likeness between these collocations is very striking, but the collocations themselves are so unremarkable that imita-tion is very unlikely' (p. 85). Lake cited another thirty instances in *Blurt* of collocations which are 'curious' or 'uniquely Dekker's', and for which no instance exists in Middleton. Lake also used collocations as contributory evi-dence for Middleton's authorship of *The Puritan* (pp. 113–17) and *The Second Maiden's Tragedy*.

Verbal parallels, including 'single words in special senses', have formed a strong element in the case for Middleton's authorship of *The Revenger's Tragedy*. E. H. C. Oliphant had pointed to several unusual words in that play which all recur in Middleton, such as *shine* as a noun, *pleasure* as a verb (meaning 'oblige'), *unbribèd*, *hereafter* (used as an adjective), and *sasara* for *certiorari* (Oliphant 1926, pp. 160–5). R. H. Barker added an even rarer word, *luxur*, used twice in the play (1.1.12, 2.2.129), for which *OED* gives only two other occurrences, both in pamphlets by Middleton (*The Black*

Book and *Father Hubbard's Tales*), suggesting that Middleton coined it
(Barker 1945, p. 126). In addition to rare words the frequency with which an
author repeats common or widely used words can become a hallmark of his
style. The word *slave*, used as a term of abuse 26 times in *The Revenger's
Tragedy*, was a favourite of Middleton (12 instances in *Your Five Gallants*, 12
in *The Phoenix*, 8 in *Michaelmas Term*): 'it does not appear at all in *The
Atheist's Tragedy*' (ibid.). Middleton was equally fond of the word *comfort*,
which appears 17 times in this play, and frequently in other Middleton plays,
with typical scores of 19, 18, 17, 15, 13, and 11 instances (Lake 1975, table
1.1, segment 3); the word *comfort* appears only twice in *The Atheist's
Tragedy* (Barker 1945, p. 126). Of many other verbal parallels I select the
most striking, first pointed out by R. H. Barker. In *The Revenger's Tragedy*[28]
Vindice 'boasts about his virtuosity and describes himself as an instrument of
retribution', struck by the brilliance of his latest idea:

> But I have found it;
> 'Twill hold, 'tis sure; thanks, thanks to any spirit
> That mingled it 'mongst my inventions.

> (4.2.200–2)

And he reassures his brother:

> Nay, doubt not, 'tis in graine;
> I warrant it hold colour.

> (223–4)

In exactly the same way, Follywit in *A Mad World, My Masters*, another
'clever man who is blinded by his own cleverness' (Barker 1958, pp. 70–1),
admires his virtuosity, soon shown as illusory:

> Peace, 'tis mine own, i'faith; I ha't!
>
> .   .   .   .
>
> Thanks, thanks to any spirit
> That mingled it 'mongst my inventions!

> (3.3.68–71)

He, too, assures his companions that there will be no delay:

> And thou shalt see't quickly, i'faith: nay, 'tis in grain; I warrant it hold colour.

> (81–2)

As David Lake commented, 'this double parallel to exactly the same two sentences in the same sequence . . . has no counterpart in any other play', and the
way that 'these two sentences occur, in close proximity, in a single scene in
each play, is very strong evidence that one mind is responsible for both, for

---

[28] Quotations are from R. A. Foakes (ed.), *The Revenger's Tragedy* (London, 1966).

what we observe here is a sequence of verbal ideas retrieved intact by the memory of an author' (Lake 1975, p. 147). The only other explanation would be plagiarism, but the passage has no striking beauties that another author would envy, and all the other verbal parallels to Middleton within this play make plagiarism (a popular theory with those who wish to discredit such evidence in authorship studies) highly unlikely.

The use of verbal parallels by R. H. Barker and David Lake was exemplary in applying safeguards to a type of evidence often prematurely dismissed as unreliable. Cyrus Hoy also used parallels cautiously but effectively, as when discussing *The Queen of Corinth*, a play written by Massinger, Fletcher, and Field. Having distinguished each author's contribution on the basis of their well-established linguistic preferences, Hoy added further strong evidence linking the Field scenes to his other known plays. These include grammatical inversions, his use of the 'fairly uncommon verb "exquire" ("to search out, seek for")', his habit of heading speeches *All*, and three extensive parallel passages, between six and seven lines long (Hoy 1959a, pp. 99–100). In *The Honest Man's Fortune*, similarly, Hoy pointed to Fletcher's repeated use of rhetorical questions,[29] and Massinger's tendency to echo the same words and phrases over and over (pp. 105–6). Massinger's self-borrowings, indeed, constitute a subcategory of collocations or verbal parallels which deserve special notice, since the phenomenon recurs in other dramatists. They formed the basis of Robert Boyle's pioneering work on the Beaumont and Fletcher canon in the 1880s,[30] and Hoy himself gave a convincing account of the 'verbal formulae' in his plays. Hoy argued that Massinger's favourite turns of phrase, so frequently repeated, are 'but the outward and visible signs of the more inward stereotypes of feeling and thought, of situation and incident that are the very stuff of Jacobean drama'. A recurring dramatic situation elicits 'a corresponding verbal formula' in an automatic response that itself becomes stereotyped.[31] Massinger repeatedly contrasts 'the extremes of asceticism and sensuality, and the effect of one upon the other' by juxtaposing such terms as 'cold' and 'fire', 'heat' and 'thaw', regularly associating the terms 'youth/heat/blood' (Hoy 1959b, pp. 603–4). As we know from Eugene Waith's pioneering study,[32] Jacobean tragicomedy thrived on juxtaposing extreme states, or reversing them. So Massinger frequently opposes absolute

---

[29] E. H. C. Oliphant also itemized Fletcher's 'continual employment of a few stock words, phrases and expressions': Oliphant 1927, pp. 45–6. Alfred Hart documented Fletcher's paucity of invention when comparing his vocabulary to Shakespeare's: see my discussion of *The Two Noble Kinsmen* in Chapter 6.

[30] Boyle summed up these researches in 'Beaumont, Fletcher, and Massinger', *TNSS* 11 (1886): 579–628, claiming that, in essays published in *Englische Studien* between 1882 and 1887, he would have 'collected about 1000 parallel passages from all his works' (p. 585).

[31] C. Hoy, 'Verbal Formulae in the Plays of Philip Massinger', *SP* 56 (1959): 600–18, at p. 601.

[32] E. M. Waith, *The Pattern of Tragicomedy in Beaumont and Fletcher* (New Haven, 1952; repr. Hamden, Conn., 1969).

values, one of which is accepted, the other found wanting, with a set of verbal formulae appropriate to each (Hoy 1959*b*, pp. 614–16). This striving for absolute states naturally runs to hyperbole, and results in dramatic situations where characters declare 'the situation of the moment to "transcend" all that has gone before by way of example': Hoy could cite no less than 21 instances of Massinger using this verb in this situation (pp. 611–12). The many reversals in his plays each have their own formulae—indeed, in one case the absence of the verbal stereotype when the situation occurs is proof that Massinger did not write that particular scene (pp. 604–7). Pitched to a highly emotional state, his characters constantly declare that they 'are "rapt" beyond themselves' (15 instances cited), or ' "transported" ' (22 instances); they are ' "overwhelmed with wonder" ' (8 instances), or suffer an ' "excess of joy" that . . . can also "ravish" ' (11 instances). 'Characters in Massinger are regularly "amazed" ' (7 instances), 'they are "thunderstruck" ' (5 times), ' "stand rooted" in surprise' (4 times), or else 'amazement, often touched with horror, turns them into statues' (5 times), like the Gorgon's head (5 times). Hoy's thorough survey ended with the rather disillusioned conclusion that in Massinger's plays 'emotional developments of stunning impact are rendered through what amount to little more than verbal posturings' (pp. 616–18). Whatever our evaluation of the stereotyping, such self-borrowing—also found in Dekker, Fletcher, and Ford, among others—amounts to a stylistic habit which can be of great value in authorship studies.

In a recent essay, establishing beyond question that Middleton wrote *A Yorkshire Tragedy*, R. V. Holdsworth described Middleton, also, as 'a highly self-imitative writer, capable of detailed retrieval of material across gaps of twenty years or more'.[33] Holdsworth's case rested on a multitude of verbal parallels, often minute details of language. At one point in *A Yorkshire Tragedy* the Husband is 'reduced to agitated mumbling': 'Hum, um, um' (iv. 17). Holdsworth showed that 'three-part exclamations involving the loss of an aspirate after the first syllable', such as 'Ha, a, a', or 'Oh-o-o', are common in Middleton's plays (Holdsworth 1994, pp. 3–4; six instances cited). Earlier the Husband had exclaimed 'Ime damnd, Ime damnd . . . hee's gon, hee's gon' (ii. 27–9): Holdsworth noted that 'Middleton likes to mark distress with these doubled cries', each of these exclamations reappearing elsewhere (p. 12; four instances). In this play, as in *The Revenger's Tragedy*, Middleton used several expressions with highly idiosyncratic connotations, as *OED* testifies. For the Husband's assertion, 'I will not bate | A whit in humour' (ii. 81–2), *OED*'s only example of the expression *bate in* comes from *The Revenger's Tragedy*, 'I bate in courage' (p. 13). The Husband's sarcastic question, 'Is the rubbish sold, those wiseakers your lands?' (iii. 37–8), provides *OED*'s only

<hr />

[33] R. V. Holdsworth, 'Middleton's Authorship of *A Yorkshire Tragedy*', *RES* 45 (1994): 1–25, at p. 21. Scene and line references are to the edition in Brooke 1908, pp. 249–62.

seventeenth-century 'example of *wiseacre* as including an allusion to "acres",
i.e. land', but Middleton used the expression twice elsewhere, while 'the use
of "rubbish" for land, which is not recognized by *OED*', also occurs in two
other works by Middleton (p. 16). The Husband's complaint, ''tis our bloude
to love what we are forbidden' (iv. 73–4), is echoed by Lussurio in *The
Revenger's Tragedy*: 'It is our bloud to erre, tho hell gapte lowde' (1.3.72).
Holdsworth could not 'parallel this use of *blood* with the infinitive, in *OED*
or elsewhere' (p. 17). No fewer than eight of these close verbal parallels
between *A Yorkshire Tragedy* and Middleton's plays and prose works occur
in one scene, iv. 65–87 (pp. 17–19). Altogether Holdsworth cited 202 passages from Middleton paralleling *A Yorkshire Tragedy* (probably written in
the second half of 1605), 116 of which date before mid-1606, 63 of these
coming from plays written between 1605 and that date (p. 22). *Timon of
Athens* was probably written by Shakespeare and Middleton in 1605, and
Holdsworth itemized twenty parallels between *A Yorkshire Tragedy* and
Middleton's scenes for *Timon*, to be considered in Chapter 4. As Holdsworth
justly observed, the parallels he cited 'are too distinctive to explain in terms of
commonplace idioms' (p. 21).

Verbal parallels have proved useful in identifying the co-authors of *Sir
Thomas More*. The case for Shakespeare's authorship of Addition IIc derived
initially from the similarities between its handwriting and Shakespeare's
other autographs, an identification which generated a wide range of supporting stylistic and linguistic evidence. One other passage in 'The Booke of Sir
Thomas More' has been ascribed to Shakespeare on internal evidence alone,
Addition III, written in the hand of the playhouse scribe. This is a soliloquy
for More, inserted in the manuscript just before the revised version of the
scene where Erasmus visits More (scene viii). In it More meditates on the
relationship between fortune, God's design, and the instability of success:

> It is in heaven that I am thus and thus,
> And that which we profanely term our fortunes
> Is the provision of the power above,
> Fitted and shaped just to that strength of nature
> Which we are born [withal]. Good God, good God,   5
> That I from such an humble bench of birth,
> Should step as 'twere up to my country's head,
> And give the law out there—I, in my father's life,
> To take prerogative and tithe of knees
> From elder kinsmen, and him bind by my place   10
> To give the smooth and dexter way to me,
> That owe it him by nature. Sure, these things,
> Not physicked by respect, might turn our blood
> To much corruption. But More, the more thou hast,
> Either of honour, office, wealth and calling,   15

> Which might accite thee to embrace and hug them,
> The more do thou in serpents' natures think them,
> Fear their gay skins with thought of their sharp state,
> And let this be thy maxim: to be great
> Is, when the thread of hazard is once spun,   20
> A bottom great wound up, greatly undone.
>
> (3.1.1–21)

Arguments for Shakespeare's authorship of this speech were presented by E. K. Chambers,[34] R. C. Bald (1931),[35] and J. M. Nosworthy,[36] partly in terms of parallels of phrasing with plays that Shakespeare had written between 1598 and 1605, partly in terms of deeper stylistic resemblances. I summarize their arguments without further acknowledgement.

The opening line resembles Iago's words, ''tis in ourselves that we are thus or thus' (*Oth.*, 1.3.322–3). More's remarkable ascent from a 'humble bench of birth' to his 'country's head' (6–7), echoes Leontes's description of Camillo, 'whom I from meaner form | Have bench'd and rear'd to worship' (*WT*, 1.2.313–14). More's sense of the threat to established hierarchy that his sudden rise represents, that he should 'take prerogative and tithe of knees | From elder kinsmen' (9–10), echoes in content Ulysses' reference to a hierarchy already disturbed, affecting

> The primogenity and due of birth,
> Prerogative of age
>
> (*TC*, 1.3.106–7)

And, in sound and rhythm, it recalls Parolles' evocation of

> The great prerogative and rite of love
>
> (*AWW*, 2.4.41)

More's rise has unsettled hierarchy further in that his 'elder kinsmen', who are owed precedence, must now 'give the smooth and dexter way to me' (11–12)—that is, as the Revels editors explain, 'give me the place of honour by letting me walk where the ground is less uneven (smooth) and on their right (dexter)'. The coupling into a semantic unit of two words having a distinct meaning is an instance of the rhetorical figure *hendiadys*, which Shakespeare used with remarkable frequency.[37] Commentators cite 'their huge and proper life' (*H5*, 5 Chorus 5), 'their steep and thorny way' (*Ham.*, 1.3.47), and 'smooth and welcome news' (*1H4*, 1.1.66). Shakespeare uses

---

[34] E. K. Chambers, *William Shakespeare: A Study of Facts and Problems*, 2 vols. (Oxford, 1930), i. 514–15.

[35] R. C. Bald, 'Addition III of *Sir Thomas More*', *RES* 7 (1931): 67–9.

[36] J. M. Nosworthy, 'Shakespeare and *Sir Thomas More*', *RES*, NS 6 (1955): 12–25.

[37] See George T. Wright, 'Hendiadys and *Hamlet*', *PMLA* 96 (1981): 168–93, and Vickers 2002, pp. 163–88.

'dexter' elsewhere only in *Troilus and Cressida*: 'my mother's blood | Runs on the dexter cheek' (4.5.127–8).

Other verbal parallels include the verb 'physic' (13), often used by Shakespeare: 'The labour we delight in physics pain' (*Mac.*, 2.3.55), 'that will physic the great Myrmidon' (*Tro.*, 1.3.378); and the verb 'accite' (16), which occurs twice in *2 Henry IV* (2.2.64–5, 5.2.141–2), the second time in Henry's announcement that after the coronation 'we will accite . . . all our state', where the word is also 'associated with the idea of office or state' (Nosworthy 1955, p. 20). The noun 'maxim' (19) is one of several words or phrases linking Addition III with *Troilus and Cressida*, the only other Shakespearian use of this term: 'Therefore this maxim out of love I teach' (1.2.318). More's awareness that the more glory he possesses,

> Either of honour, office, wealth and calling,

the more enemies he may have, echoes several Shakespearian passages in which 'the notion of government . . . prompts such agglomeration' (Nosworthy 1955, p. 20). This technique is actually an instance of the rhetorical figure *articulus* (*brachylogia*), which heaps up single words with no conjunctions intervening:

> throw away respect,
> Tradition, form and ceremonious duty
>> (*R2*, 3.2.172–3)

> As honour, love, obedience, troops of friends
>> (*Mac.*, 5.3.25)

> Insisture, course, proportion, season, form,
> Office and custom
>> (*Tro.*, 1.3.87–8)

> For to the king God hath his office lent
> Of dread, of justice, power and command
>> (*More*, Addition IIc, ll. 221–2)

More's sense that his achievements, if not 'physicked by respect, might turn our blood | To much corruption' (13–14), uses an idea of corrupt blood found also in *King John*, *2 Henry IV*, *Twelfth Night*, *King Lear*, and—significantly—*Troilus and Cressida*, in Hector's speech:

> If this law
> Of nature be corrupted through affection
>> (2.2.176–7)

a passage which also refers to 'distemper'd blood' (169), and to 'adders' (172). So More reminds himself to regard his potential enemies as 'serpents', having a 'sharp state': we recall Lear's discovery, 'How sharper than a

serpent's tooth it is | To have a thankless child' (1.4.310–11). As Nosworthy
pointed out (1955, p. 20), More's concluding maxim,

> to be great
> Is, when the thread of hazard is once spun,
> A bottom great wound up, greatly undone
>
> (19–21)

is identical in syntax—'adjective, adverb, and "the self-same tune and
words"' to Hamlet's similar discovery of a moral principle in the course of a
soliloquy reviewing his past and future life:

> Rightly to be great
> Is not to stir without great argument
> But greatly to find quarrel in a straw
> When honour's at the stake
>
> (4.4.53–6)

Finally, More's metaphor of 'the thread . . . once spun' echoes one of the Jack
Cade scenes in *2 Henry VI*, another rebellion by the London proletariat:
'Argo, their thread of life is spun' (4.2.31), and his collocation of 'thread' and
'bottom' occurs in *Two Gentlemen*, *Taming of the Shrew*, and *A Midsummer
Night's Dream*.

   The arguments from parallels of vocabulary, phrasing, syntax, and rhetoric
make Shakespeare's authorship of Addition III as certain as it could ever be
from internal evidence. It has undeniable links with Addition IIc, a connection which reciprocally strengthens the ascription to Shakespeare, and both
scenes share many links with the discussions of law and order in *Troilus and
Cressida*: the two works are cut from the same cloth.

   Evidence from verbal parallels has also proved valuable in identifying other
co-authors of *Sir Thomas More*. One of the contributors to this manuscript
was the playwright Henry Chettle, sole or co-author of at least forty-eight
plays for Henslowe between (probably) the early 1590s and his death, some
time between 1603 and 1607. As Muriel St Clare Byrne showed in a classic
essay, 'hack-work for Henslowe was a business matter for his halfpenny-a-
liners like Munday and Chettle', who seldom achieved anything like an
individual style, and are for that reason extremely difficult to identify (Byrne
1932, p. 22). None the less, by studying Chettle's Addition 1 to *Sir Thomas
More* (fo. 6a), Byrne was able to recognize some individuality. This scene, a
revision of scene xiii (*MSR*, pp. 49–50), has been misplaced in the manuscript
'Booke' (*MSR*, pp. 66–8). In it Chettle rehandled 'what was either his own,
Munday's, or some one else's original draft' of a rather dull scene in which
'More, having broken the news of his fall to his wife and family, is listening to
his wife's laments, and philosophizing on the position in which they find
themselves' (Byrne 1932, p. 34). Byrne argued that Chettle's rehandling

makes the scene 'more personal, dramatic, and moving', humanizing More's character, and preparing the audience for his doom. Yet the actual writing is full of deletions and corrections, as Chettle 'keeps changing his mind, cancelling and finally cutting some nine rather satiric and not good lines, and leaving only a dignified and compassionate conclusion' (p. 35). Byrne conceded that some of Chettle's writing was indistinguishable from Munday's, both using the same conventional range of epithets, and both moving unpredictably from blank verse to couplets and back (a habit that, as we shall see, also characterized Thomas Middleton and George Wilkins, in their sole-authored works as well as in their collaborations with Shakespeare). But Byrne also identified personal features in Chettle's writing, such as 'a leaning towards irregular blank verse' (p. 38), and the use of unusual words, including 'clouds | that *ouerdreep* thy beautie' (Add. 1, l. 11), an idiosyncrasy also found in *The Death of Robert Earle of Huntington* (a collaboration with Munday) in the form 'dreepes' (p. 41); and the spelling *tortur* (l. 21), which occurs twice in Chettle's *The Tragedy of Hoffman* (*c*.1602–3) in the form *tortor* (p. 35).

As we saw in Chapter 1, E. H. C. Oliphant claimed that Chettle contributed not only to the revision of *Sir Thomas More* but to the original play. John Jowett has recently argued that case in detail, using several different kinds of evidence. One linguistic detail typical of Chettle, unlike Munday, is a preference for the contractions *twixt, nere, yond, for to*.[38] Chettle's liking for the words *hurt* and *remedy* may also discriminate between his scenes and Munday's (pp. 135–6). Chettle's favourite asseverations include *God save*, *yfaith*, and *Oh God*; Munday preferred *God blesse*, *bir Lady*, and *in faith* (pp. 136–7). In their plays of sole authorship, Chettle preferred *you* to *ye* by a ratio of 'well over three to one', while Munday used *ye* slightly more often than *you*: the contrasting usage recurs in *More*, six scenes of that play showing 'an overwhelming preference for *you* which is most unlikely to originate with Munday' (pp. 140–1). The dramatists can also be clearly distinguished according to the rhymes that they favoured. In Addition 1 Chettle used two rhymes found also in *Hoffman*, 'death/breath' and 'fall/all' (p. 138), while a study of the rhymes throughout *Sir Thomas More* shows strong convergences with *Hoffman* in five scenes, which provide no less than 38 links with *More* (pp. 139–40).

Jowett then listed a large number of verbal parallels between the two plays, rightly observing that such parallels 'are of the greatest value where they combine two or more factors such as vocabulary, image-patterns, and dramatic situation' (p. 141). Since *Hoffman* also contains an insurrection episode, it might seem that the parallels merely derive from the common subject-matter,

---

[38] J. Jowett, 'Henry Chettle and the Original Text of *Sir Thomas More*', in T. H. Howard-Hill (ed.), *Shakespeare and 'Sir Thomas More'* (Cambridge, 1989), pp. 131–49, at p. 134.

but Jowett argued that 'the detailed correspondences suggest the creative habits of an individual mind and are therefore not so easily dismissed' (p. 142). Jowett was able to demonstrate 'a wider association of words and ideas' between the two plays (pp. 142–6), suggesting that *Hoffman* is the later play, adding a 'consistent ironic dimension' to the narrative, which 'represents a move to a more complex mode' (p. 144). Of the many correspondences he listed I pick out the 'euphemistic sense of *tickle*' in the insurrection episode of both plays, in both of which the citizens 'revolt against *strangers*': 'their *saucie presumption* (l. 33) in *More* compares with their *presumptuous hearts* (l. 1234) in *Hoffman*' (p. 142). In the dramatic context the phrase 'And these embraces serve' (*More*, l. 239) 'is close to "And this one sentence serves" (*Hoffman*, l. 2185). The embraces facilitate crime; the sentence extenuates it' (ibid.). In *More* 'Doll speaks figuratively of death by poisoning', using the distinctive word *begin*, meaning 'toast':

> heere I beginne this cuppe of death to thee
>
> (666)

In *Hoffman* Jerom offers Hoffman a cup and asks 'Heere cozen, will you begin to my father?' (l. 1533): 'again, with the idea that both the beginner and the person toasted who next drinks from the *cup* will be poisoned' (p. 144). In *More* we find the couplet

> Hees great in studie, thats the statists grace,
> that gaines more reverence than the outward place
>
> (772–3)

In *Hoffman* the same rhyme recurs, with a very similar syntactic 'surround':

> In vowes of combination, ther's a grace
> That shewes the intention in the outward face.
>
> (590–1)

Jowett also analysed vocabulary parallels between the two plays, showing distinctive identities between *Hoffman* and scenes i, vi, and vii of *Sir Thomas More* (p. 146). Weighing all the evidence, Jowett made a strong claim for Chettle's authorship of those scenes, together with ii, x, xii, and xiii. Jowett's study of the case for Chettle's co-authorship of the original *Sir Thomas More* is exemplary for the way in which it applies a number of quite different approaches, discovering a 'general pattern . . . of impressive consistency between the different kinds of evidence, "objective" and impressionistic, dense and dispersed, alike' (p. 147). That convergence of evidence shows the strength of modern authorship studies, and suggests that many more discoveries have yet to be made.

The whole methodology of using verbal parallels as a guide to authorship took on a new dimension in 1995, when the Chadwyck-Healey firm issued two large electronic databases, 'English Poetry' and 'English Verse Drama'. These were soon enlarged and incorporated into an online database, 'Literature Online' (or LION), of potentially great importance to attribution studies, as MacDonald Jackson has shown.[39] Although it omitted some works,[40] the drama section of the database includes the full texts of 663 plays for the period 1580–1660, in the original spelling of the quarto editions (mostly), errors and all. Using this resource, Jackson was able to add more evidence supporting the Middleton ascriptions that he and David Lake had made in the 1970s. Among the expletives they identified as characteristic of Middleton are *puh* and *my life for yours*, both of which occur in *The Puritan* and *The Revenger's Tragedy*. Checking the LION database, and adding Middleton texts not included there (among them the MS holograph of *A Game at Chess* in the library of Trinity College, Cambridge, which contains some characteristic Middleton spellings), Jackson found that 'eight out of the nine plays containing both *puh* and *my life for yours* are associated with Middleton, and 45 of the 47 instances in plays containing both expletives are his' (Jackson 1998, p. 3). *The Revenger's Tragedy* and *The Puritan* also use the expletives *la you/why la*, as do only four other plays in the electronic database, three of them by Middleton, the other (*Wit at Several Weapons*) being almost certainly a collaboration between Middleton and Rowley (pp. 3–4). The asseveration *a my troth* occurs in only six of these 663 plays, all but one by Middleton, while the oath *cuds me* appears in the Rowley collaboration just mentioned, in five other plays by Middleton, and in *The Second Maiden's Tragedy*, which has repeatedly been claimed for Middleton (p. 4). Using the LION database, Jackson discovered that the 'Middletonism *alate* (printed as a singe word, meaning "of late")' appears in *The Second Maiden's Tragedy* and in thirteen plays or entertainments, all but three by Middleton (pp. 4–5). *The Revenger's Tragedy* shares with Middleton's holograph of *A Game at Chess* several unusual spellings, which the LION database now proves to be extremely rare indeed outside the Middleton canon (here taken to include *The Second Maiden's Tragedy* and several scenes in *Timon of Athens*): the spellings *reuennewe* for *revenue* (unique), *closse* for *close*, *dambd* for *damned*, and *froath* for *froth* (p. 5).

The practice of citing verbal parallels has often, and justly, been criticized for its one-sidedness. Scholars have regularly cited only the positive features linking a disputed play with their authorship candidate and have neglected

---

[39] Jackson, 'Editing, Attribution Studies, and "Literature Online": A New Resource for Research in Renaissance Drama', *RORD* 37 (1998): 1–15. See also his wry note on some of the problems involved in using this resource: '*Titus Andronicus* and Electronic Databases: A Correction and a Warning', *NQ* 244 (1999): 209–10.

[40] Jackson noted that 'three early Middleton comedies have been accidentally left out: *The Phoenix*, *A Trick to Catch the Old One*, and *Michaelmas Term*' (Jackson 1998, p. 3). Many poets were omitted from the 'English Poetry 900 to 1900' database: *caveat lector*.

'negative checks', so failing 'to establish the absence of these features from the work of other dramatists'. As Jackson puts it, 'there is no longer any excuse for this kind of failure' (p. 6). The virtual completeness of this electronic database means that both criteria can now be satisfied, and ascriptions verified and rejected with some confidence.[41] For instance, Jackson records that he and David Lake were both 'non-committal about E. H. C. Oliphant's claim that Middleton was (with Dekker) part-author of *The Bloody Banquet*, published in a quarto of 1639 as by "T.D.", though we each appreciated Oliphant's uncanny ability to recognize Middleton's style and found some evidence to link the play with Middleton. It is clear to me now that those links are so strong as to constitute virtual proof that Oliphant was right' (p. 4). *The Bloody Banquet* contains two of the eleven most distinctive Middleton exclamations, *puh* and *why la you now*, the latter (combining *why la* and *la you*) being 'an especially rare Middleton marker', occurring in only four other seventeenth-century plays, all by Middleton. This detail, added to the other evidence adduced by Lake and Jackson, 'tips the balance in favour of the probability' that Middleton was co-author of the play.

In my own study of *A Funerall Elegye*, a poem published in 1612 as by 'W.S.', and once attributed to Shakespeare,[42] these new electronic resources helped me identify the real author as the dramatist John Ford. Among many other types of evidence supporting this thesis I discovered that a number of words in that short poem were only used elsewhere by Ford.[43] According to the Chadwyck-Healey databases, the word *flote* ('float'), used not as a verb but as a noun meaning 'flood', and often contrasted with 'ebb' (used metaphorically to describe high and low fortunes), which occurs in the *Elegye* (98–9), is found in his prose work *The Golden Meane*, in Ford's scenes for *The Spanish Gypsy*—and in four other plays by Ford. It occurs nowhere else in English drama between 1578 and 1642. (An apparent exception is Ariel's report that Alonso's other ships 'are upon the Mediterranean Flote' (F1 *Tempest*, TLN 353). But reliable authorities gloss 'float' here as 'wave, billow; (hence) sea' or 'afloat'.) Similarly, the rare word *partage*, used

---

[41] Jackson records some verbal characteristics in the anonymously published play *Edmond Ironside* which weaken still further the case made by Eric Sams for Shakespeare's authorship. The expression '*whenas*, usually printed as two words and meaning simply "when"', is found eleven times in *Edmond Ironside*, according to the LION database, a total only matched by Robert Greene's '*Alphonsus King of Aragon* with twelve instances'. Furthermore, 'plays wholly or partly by Greene are easily the most prominent among those in which *when as* appears. The use of *when as* eight times in the anonymous *King Leir* is worth noting' (Jackson 1998, p. 7). Jackson also pointed out that Greene was 'conspicuously fond of metrical fillers', such as *like to* (meaning 'like'), found frequently in his plays but also in *Edmond Ironside* and *King Leir*, and *for to* (69 times in *Alphonsus King of Aragon*, 45 times in *King Leir*, and more than 10 times in several Greene plays). The question of Greene's authorship of *Edmond Ironside* looks to be worth pursuing.

[42] See D. Foster, *Elegy by W.S.: A Study in Attribution* (Newark and London, 1989), and Vickers 2002.   [43] See Vickers 2002, pp. 387–8, 407, 415–16.

metaphorically to refer to the sharing of an experience, is used in the *Elegye* (543), in *The Golden Meane*, in one of the scenes Ford wrote for the collaborative play *The Fair Maid of the Inn*, and three times elsewhere in Jacobean or Caroline drama, each time in a play by Ford. Taken together with other abundant forms of evidence, these unique verbal links add greatly to the case for Ford's authorship of the anonymous *Elegye*. Attribution studies will undoubtedly benefit from these new resources.

VOCABULARY

While verbal parallels, including rare words or words used in special senses, remain a valid tool in authorship studies, much help can be derived from large-scale studies of a writer's vocabulary. One relevant approach concerns what we might call a writer's global vocabulary, and in particular the relative presence of native and imported words. Linguists have long been aware that the English language is a unique fusion of Anglo-Saxon (or Germanic) with Latinate (or Romance) elements, thanks to a borrowing and integration process that has been going on for nearly a thousand years. These two main families resist any neat separation within English, and their fusion should be conceived as a continuum. At one end of this scale are the many short, mono-syllabic words which recur so often in anyone's vocabulary (the ten most frequently used words in Shakespeare are *the, and, I, to, of, a, you, my, that, and, in*). At the other are Latinate polysyllabic compounds, led by the prize specimen, *honorificabilitudinatibus*, noted in Erasmus's *Adagia*, and which Shakespeare aptly borrowed to characterize the pedants in *Love's Labour's Lost* (5.1.40). Along this continuum we can place Shakespeare's ordinary people, clowns who commonly misuse hard words, servants, rulers, generals, scholars. None of these groups uses either pure Anglo-Saxonisms or pure Latinisms (since many English words in common use derive from Romance sources), but we may reasonably expect that educated people will use a higher percentage of Latinate words, whether they are poets, dramatists, or characters in plays.

Analysing a writer's vocabulary according to its proportion of Anglo-Saxon or Germanic elements is potentially useful in authorship studies, as F. E. Pierce demonstrated in 1909.[44] Attempting to discriminate the relative shares of Dekker and Webster, who had collaborated on several plays, Pierce discovered distinct differences in their vocabulary and prose rhythm, 'largely due to the use of words of Greek or Latin derivation which contain three or more syllables; such words, for example, as *confusion, opinion, politic, immediately, satisfy, remember, misery*. Dekker almost always uses these

---

[44] F. E. Pierce, *The Collaboration of Webster and Dekker* (New Haven, 1909; repr. Hamden, Conn., 1972).

words sparingly, whereas Webster steadily employs a great number of them' (Pierce 1909, p. 5). Both writers are so consistent in their preferences that Pierce was able to use this characteristic of style to distinguish their work. Pierce wished to put this test on a scientific basis by computing the percentage of Latinate words (which he defined as having three or more syllables), but he faced the problem that many scenes in their collaborative plays were written in prose and—as anyone knows who has ever tried to collate prose passages in different editions of Shakespeare—whereas verse lines are constant in all editions, the layout and lineation of prose on the page varies according to a book's format and design. To provide a common unit of measure Pierce reduced each whole scene 'to solid prose lines', calculating 'how many lines it would contain if it were printed as one solid block of prose, without breaks at the ends of metrical lines, without gaps between speeches, and without stage-directions. Then the whole number of three-syllable words (of Greek or Latin derivation) divided by the number of solid prose lines equals the ratio of these words to a line' (p. 6). In a scene of 100 'solid lines', having 22 Greco-Latin words, the word-average would be 0.22, such words occurring about every five lines.

Pierce's method was completely rational, but it unfortunately needed a degree of manual computation that few scholars have been willing to under-take. Samuel Schoenbaum mocked Pierce for 'a fine display of pointless effort' and for displaying 'impressionism rationalized'.[45] But the identifica-tion of Latinate and Germanic vocabularies is anything but impressionistic, as users of etymological dictionaries can confirm, and the enquiry as such is legitimate. While it may be true that Pierce did not take all relevant factors into consideration, his test certainly produced valid results on its own terms. The average figures he calculated for the two dramatists (Table 2.3) proved as much. Although these global statistics clearly show the vocabulary differ-ences between the two dramatists, with Dekker never attaining Webster's degree of Latinity, Pierce recognized that for analytical purposes the relevant unit must be the scene, so he provided detailed figures for every scene in their plays (pp. 9–28). On this basis he was able to identify their respective con-tributions to *Westward Hoe!* and *Northward Hoe!*, showing that in each play the vocabulary of major characters—Birdlime and Justiniano in the former, Bellamont and Mayberry in the latter—differs in style according to which dramatist is at work (pp. 26–8).

Pierce performed the same experiment for Ford's collaboration with Dekker, reminding his readers that 'a large number of new Latin derivatives had come into English during or shortly before the Elizabethan period. Such new additions are always appropriated first by the cosmopolitan aristocracy

---

[45] S. Schoenbaum, *Internal Evidence and Elizabethan Dramatic Authorship: An Essay in Literary History and Method* (London, 1966), pp. 75–6.

TABLE 2.3. *Latinate vocabulary in Webster and Dekker*

Webster		
	Duchess of Malfi	0.349
	The White Devil	0.342
Dekker	*The Whore of Babylon*	0.252
	Old Fortunatus	0.247
	Satiromastix	0.213
	II The Honest Whore	0.153
	Shoemaker's Holiday	0.116

Source: Pierce 1909, p. 8.

and the learned professions'. Ford, educated at Oxford and the Inner Temple, 'would naturally be expected to use more than Dekker the bohemian, the child of the people'.[46] This uncanny anticipation of socio-historical linguistics as used by Jonathan Hope (see below) proves that Pierce had indeed identified a relevant stylistic marker, and that he deserves respect, not derision. When Pierce applied his 'Three-Syllable Latin Word Test' to Ford, the averages of complete plays show that his vocabulary was even more Latinate than Webster's, and far more so than Dekker's. Dekker's average score for whole plays ranged from 0.252 to 0.116, while Ford's scores were a whole class higher, from 0.419 to 0.313—the single exception being *'Tis Pity She's a Whore*, which scored only 0.193 (Pierce 1912*a*, p. 147). Pierce used his method successfully to differentiate both dramatists' contribution to *The Sun's Darling* (ibid., 146–8), but found it unable to separate the work of Rowley and Dekker on *The Witch of Edmonton*, although both had distinctly lower levels of Latinity than did Ford.[47] Pierce's pioneering work on the dual inheritance of English vocabulary as a means of differentiating authorship was taken up in 1928 by Matthew Baird, in an unpublished Oxford dissertation, whose findings were further refined by MacDonald Jackson.[48] Endorsing Pierce's demonstration that 'Dekker customarily used polysyllables of Greek or Latin origin more sparingly than did Webster or

[46] F. E. Pierce, 'The Collaboration of Dekker and Ford (I). The Authorship of *The Sun's Darling*', *Anglia*, n. F. 34 (1912): 141–68, at pp. 150–1.

[47] F. E. Pierce, 'The Collaboration of Dekker and Ford (II). The Authorship of *The Witch of Edmonton*', *Anglia*, n. F. 34 (1912): 289–312, at pp. 290–2.

[48] Baird, 'Collaboration of Thomas Dekker and Thomas Middleton', B.Litt. Diss., Oxford, 1928; as reported in Jackson 1979, pp. 99–101, 106, 111. Jackson also judged Schoenbaum to be 'quite wrong to dismiss Pierce's test as "impressionism rationalised"', for Pierce's 'three-syllabic Latin word test . . . gives precisely the same results for *Westward Ho* and *Northward Ho* as Murray's compelling analysis of the linguistic evidence' (Jackson 1979, p. 117 n. 11). See P. B. Murray, 'The Collaboration of Dekker and Webster in *Northward Ho* and *Westward Ho*', *PBSA* 56 (1962): 482–6.

TABLE 2.4. *Latinate and polysyllabic words in the* Funerall Elegye *and in late Shakespeare*

Work	Number of lines	Latinisms	Frequency: per line	Polysyllabic words	Frequency: every x lines
Funerall Elegye	578	870	1.51	78	7.4
Cymbeline	555	538	0.97	19	29.2
Winter's Tale	472	503	1.07	13	36.3
Tempest	502	552	1.09	17	29.5

Source: Vickers 2002, tables 8.1, 8.2.

Ford', Jackson drew on Baird's more sensible handling of the data (simply totalling the number of words in each scene or play and dividing it by the number of polysyllabic words), to show with new clarity the distinct difference between the two dramatists' use of these 'three-syllable Latin words'. Using Baird's data, Jackson was able to establish the proportion of Latinate words in whole plays, where the average rate for ten plays by Middleton was one every 61.3 words; for seven plays by Dekker the proportion was one every 93.2 words (Jackson 1979, p. 209). Jackson then applied the Pierce–Baird method to *The Roaring Girl*, showing that 'in Dekker's share of the play one out of every 90 words is a "three-syllable Latin word"; in Middleton's share the proportion is one in 65' (p. 101).

While not applicable in every attribution study, this method has distinct uses. For instance, it used to be argued that Shakespeare was the 'W.S.' listed on the title-page as author of *A Funerall Elegye* (1612) to the memory of William Peter (Foster 1989). Among many linguistic details in the *Elegye* that seemed to me uncharacteristic of Shakespeare were its propensity for polysyllabic words, especially those of Latinate origin. To test this observation at Pierce's three-syllable level would have produced an unwieldy amount of data, so I restricted my count to words of four or five syllables, making a separate computation of Latinate words. To provide a sample from Shakespeare matched for date, I selected scenes from three late plays, *Cymbeline*, *A Winter's Tale*, and *The Tempest*, which date from c.1609 to 1612. I also matched for sample length (the *Elegye* extending to 578 lines) and for subject-matter.[49] The results of both enquiries are summarized in Table 2.4. For polysyllabic words I counted not 'types' (individual words) but 'tokens', the total number of words, with repetitions. As my table shows, the author of the *Elegye* used Latinate words about 50 per cent more frequently than Shakespeare, while he used four- and five-syllable words between four and five times more frequently than Shakespeare did in a comparable sample at

[49] For fuller details see Vickers 2002, pp. 227–31.

the same point in time. These results make it unlikely that Shakespeare would have adopted such an academic vocabulary, replete with abstractions, had he been writing a consolatory elegy on the death of a personal friend.

Vocabulary computations for attribution purposes are, by necessity, global, treating all the words in a literary text irrespective of which characters use them, or for which purposes. The working assumption behind this approach is that an author's whole vocabulary will display stable character-istics, independent of a play's genre or individual physiognomy. A literary critic will of course prefer a contextual approach, looking at vocabulary in the unfolding dramatic situations, as words are applied to specific purposes in individual speech contexts. This was the approach used by Jürgen Schäfer in an outstanding study of Shakespeare's 'Germanic and Romance vocabu-lary',[50] unfortunately never issued in translation. Schäfer computed the pro-portion of Latinate vocabulary in a play scene by scene, responding even to changes within a scene. In the colossal opening confrontation of *King Lear*, for instance, he showed that the Latinate element in Lear's speeches announc-ing his 'darker purpose' and expressing his anger at Cordelia and banishment of Kent (1.1.36–119, 143–79) amount to more than 20 per cent of his total (Schäfer 1973, pp. 88–9). When Lear redefines his contract with Cornwall and Albany (1.1.132–41), the percentage of Latinate words rises to 28 per cent, the highest level in the play. But when he offers Cordelia to France and Burgundy (1.1.189–213) his language is almost devoid of Romance words— I suggest, as if he thought it not worth expending any linguistic energy on 'my sometime daughter'.

Schäfer's study is a model of uniting linguistics and literary criticism, but it is unfortunately not applicable to authorship studies. More helpful are studies which attempt to define changes in an author's vocabulary over time. The German scholar Gregor Sarrazin pioneered the computation of 'vocabu-lary links' between Shakespeare's plays, showing that many of the words he used tend to recur most often in plays written close together in time. As we shall see in a later part of this chapter, his work has a valuable application in establishing the chronology of Shakespeare's plays, and hence allowing us to test any claimed attribution by checking its word links to authentic plays of a known date.

Another pioneering scholar, the Australian Alfred Hart, devised a method of charting new words as they occur across Shakespeare's career.[51] Using Alexander Schmidt's *Shakespeare Lexicon*,[52] Hart first counted the number

---

[50] See Jürgen Schäfer, *Shakespeares Stil. Germanisches und romanisches Vokabular* (Frankfurt, 1973).

[51] Alfred Hart, 'The Vocabularies of Shakespeare's Plays', *RES* 19 (1943): 128–40, and 'The Growth of Shakespeare's Vocabulary', *RES* 19 (1943): 242–54.

[52] Schmidt, *Shakespeare Lexicon: A Complete Dictionary of all the English Words, Phrases and Constructions in the Works of the Poet*, 3rd edn., revised and enlarged by Gregor Sarrazin, 2 vols. (Berlin, 1902; New York, 1971). Sarrazin added a 'Supplement' (ii. 1453–85).

of words in each play, and the number of words peculiar to each play or poem (Hart 1943*a*, 129–32). He then divided the forty plays and poems into four groups of ten, and computed the percentage of peculiar words in the vocabulary of each (132–8), showing that Shakespeare's vocabulary was far larger than that of any other contemporary dramatist. In a second essay Hart then systematically computed the number of words occurring in one play only, in two plays, three plays, up to ten (Hart 1943*b*, 242–7). Unfortunately, he was unaware that Gregor Sarrazin had already treated this issue, from a slightly different perspective. This new arrangement of his data allowed Hart to compute the 'inflow of fresh words into Shakespeare's vocabulary' (247–54), with results which proved to be of great value to authorship studies. For by treating separately those sections of *Timon of Athens*, *Pericles*, and *Henry VIII* long thought to be by a co-author, he was able to show that the degree of vocabulary innovation found there was far below Shakespeare's normal rate. I shall draw on Hart's findings in the chapters devoted to those plays, together with his earlier study of the vocabulary of *The Two Noble Kinsmen*.[53] While greeting Hart's pioneering work, which has still to be improved on, I remain puzzled that his parallel study of the vocabulary of *Edward III*[54] failed to distinguish two hands in the play, as other studies suggest. This deficiency may remind us that in authorship studies no single method is absolutely reliable, and that there is safety in numbers.

LINGUISTIC PREFERENCES

Whether consciously or not, writers tend to reveal distinct preferences in the type of words that they use, and the frequency with which they draw on them. Comparable preferences, patterns of choice and avoidance, can be traced at less significant verbal levels, such as a seventeenth-century writer's liking for *ye* rather than *you*, *has* or *does* rather than *hath* or *doth*, *whiles* rather than *while* or *whilst*. This unglamorous line of research has turned out to be a most valuable resource in authorship studies, subject to certain methodological cautions. Cyrus Hoy made the basic point that

> in evaluating linguistic criteria as a test of authorship . . . no linguistic form can be regarded as distinctive of a particular dramatist in any absolute sense; the extent to which he employs a given form may distinguish sharply enough his practice from that of two other dramatists, but not necessarily from that of a third. Thus emerges the necessity, in determining linguistic criteria for the work of any one dramatist, of singling out forms which are at once representative of his language preferences, while

---

[53] 'Shakespeare and the Vocabulary of *The Two Noble Kinsmen*', *RES* 10 (1934): 278–87, repr. in Hart, *Shakespeare and the Homilies: And Other Pieces of Research into the Elizabethan Drama* (Melbourne, 1934; New York, 1970, 1977), pp. 242–56.
[54] 'The Vocabulary of *Edward III*', in Hart 1934, pp. 219–41.

serving to differentiate his work from the maximum number of his known or supposed collaborators. The value to be attached to any piece of linguistic criteria is, in the end, completely relative: all depends upon the degree of divergence between the linguistic patterns that are to be distinguished. (Hoy 1956, p. 134)

Since external evidence for authorship and collaboration is often unreliable, David Lake argued, work based on internal linguistic evidence must achieve reliability by using only items that are

(1) objective: unambiguously defined features, recognition of which is not a matter of opinion;
(2) quantifiable (since differences between authors are in most features matters of greater or lesser frequency, not on invariable use or non-use). (Lake 1975, p. 6)

MacDonald Jackson also emphasized that the pattern of research should be first to identify linguistic habits in an author's 'unaided and undoubted works', in order to discover criteria which can be applied to plays of disputed authorship. In this process 'stylistic and sub-stylistic minutiae' are often more useful in identifying an author than are 'elements of greater aesthetic or human significance', 'for the minutiae can be counted and the distinctiveness of the pattern they form . . . numerically assessed', unlike the larger issues. It follows that

for demonstration in matters of attribution, as opposed to the formulating of hypotheses, the making of assertions, or the deployment of forensic skill in an attempt to persuade, quantification is necessary, and some sophistication in the statistical analysis of one's data is highly desirable. Most literary scholars unduly distrust statistics, tending to suppose that one 'can prove anything' by them. The truth is, however, that the greater your understanding of statistical tests of significance the less likely you are to be duped by a mere show of statistical argument. They simply allow a just assessment of the evidence presented, and of the probabilities in favour of a particular conclusion. (Jackson 1979, pp. 5–6)

Jackson's comment on the danger of literary scholars being 'duped by a mere show of statistical argument' is of permanent relevance.

One of the earliest identifications of a linguistic form 'distinctive of a particular dramatist', as Hoy put it, has proved to be one of the most reliable. In 1905 R. B. McKerrow contributed an edition of *The Spanish Curate* to A. H. Bullen's short-lived 'Variorum Edition' of the Beaumont and Fletcher plays (planned in eleven volumes, only four were issued between 1904 and 1911, when it expired).[55] McKerrow treated this play as 'the joint-work of Fletcher and Massinger. There are certainly two well-marked styles to be noticed—that of the tragic part and that of the comic' (McKerrow 1905,

---

[55] R. B. McKerrow, edition of *The Spanish Curate* in A. H. Bullen (ed.), *The Works of Francis Beaumont and John Fletcher*, Variorum edition (London, 1905), vol. ii.

p. 104). McKerrow accepted the authorship ascription made by F. G. Fleay on the basis of verse tests (Fleay 1874*b*, p. 56), giving the following division:

Massinger: Act 1 (all); 3.3; 4.1, 4.4; 5.1, 5.3
Fletcher: Act 2 (all); 3.1, 3.2, 3.4; 4.2, 4.3, 4.5, 4.6, 4.7; 5.2

McKerrow drew attention to a linguistic difference that confirmed the verse tests' validity, involving

the words *you* and *ye* in the play. As may be seen by reference to other works of the two dramatists, Massinger rarely makes use of the more colloquial form *ye*, Fletcher very frequently. Now in this play we find that *ye* occurs 275 times, 271 times in the scenes attributed to Fletcher, and only four in those attributed to Massinger. Or to look at the matter from another point of view, for every *ye* in Massinger's part we find 50 *you*'s; for every *ye* in Fletcher's part only 0.65 *you*'s. Further, of the scenes attributed to Fletcher there are only three, namely 2.3, 3.1, and 4.2, in which *ye* does not occur more frequently than *you*. In one of these, namely 2.3, the *you*'s and *ye*'s are equal: in the others, 3.1 and 4.2, the *you*'s predominate, but all these scenes are very short. (McKerrow 1905, p. 104)

McKerrow's colleague, W. W. Greg, applied the same test to the play that he edited, *The Elder Brother*,[56] for which 'the results are striking, though the application is somewhat complicated'. Greg found it

necessary further to distinguish *you*, *ye*, and *y'* (i.e. *ye* combined with another word, as *y'are*, *t'e*, or itself reduced to *'e*). Furthermore, *you* is the more emphatic form and also the more respectful, though this is not always strictly observed. There are thus a certain number of cases in which *ye* could not be used, while there are no cases in which *you* could not, though it is rare in combination. Consequently an increase in the number of *ye*'s represents a stronger tendency towards the form than is apparent from the actual percentage. The use of unelided *ye* is particularly important. In the present play the figures appear as follows:

	TOTALS			PERCENTAGE		
	you	*ye*	*y'*	*you*	*ye*	*y'*
Massinger	129	3	12	89.5	2.1	8.4
		15			10.5	
Fletcher	189	45	26	72.7	17.3	10
		71			27.3	

---

[56] W. W. Greg., edition of *The Elder Brother* in A. H. Bullen (ed.), *The Works of Francis Beaumont and John Fletcher*, Variorum edition (London, 1905), vol. ii.

In [Massinger's] *Maid of Honour* the figures are sufficiently striking:

you	ye	y'
384	0	1

(Greg 1905, p. 4)

When Cyrus Hoy performed his long series of studies into the shares of Fletcher and his collaborators, between 1956 and 1962, he found *ye* the single most important stylistic marker for identifying Fletcher's hand. It appears very prominently in fourteen plays in the Beaumont and Fletcher canon, the minimum incidence being 133 times (in *The Woman's Prize*), the maximum a dizzying 543 times (in *The Wild Goose Chase*). Since *ye* recurs with a steady frequency throughout all fourteen plays, Hoy concluded that they represent Fletcher's unaided work (Hoy 1956, pp. 132–3). In other plays in the canon, such as *The Spanish Curate* and *The Prophetess*, the pronoun 'is to be found only within single acts, or within individual scenes within acts, at the end of which it is abruptly broken off'. Hoy showed that the remaining parts of these plays, lacking this pronoun, were written by Massinger, in whose fifteen unaided plays '*ye* occurs but twice', his preferred pronominal form being *you*. When Massinger revised scenes written by Fletcher he eliminated *ye*, and imposed his own idioms (Hoy 1957, pp. 144–5).

Another important linguistic habit identified in these early studies of Beaumont and Fletcher concerned the co-authors' preferences in the use of word-contractions. Ashley H. Thorndike, studying *The Influence of Beaumont and Fletcher on Shakespere*,[57] outlined 'a new test' for determining Fletcher's hand, namely 'the great frequency with which he uses "'em" instead of "them"—"kill 'em", "with 'em", etc.' (Thorndike 1901, p. 24). Thorndike estimated the proportion of *'em* to *them* in Fletcher's *The Woman's Prize* to be 60 to 41, in *Bonduca* 83 to 6, a ratio of preferences quite unlike Shakespeare's. For *Cymbeline* the figures are 3 to 64, for *The Winter's Tale* 8 to 37, and for *The Tempest* 13 to 38 (pp. 25–6). The value of colloquial contractions in distinguishing collaborators was taken further in 1916 by W. E. Farnham,[58] later known for his work on Shakespeare and medieval tragedy. Farnham distinguished three groups of elision, what he called 't-contractions . . . formed by the clipping of the *i* from the word *it* and the connecting of the remaining *t* by an apostrophe to the preceding word', such as *in't* for *in it*, *to't*,

---

[57] Thorndike, *The Influence of Beaumont and Fletcher on Shakespere* (Worcester, Mass., 1901; repr. New York, 1966).
[58] W. E. Farnham, 'Colloquial Contractions in Beaumont, Fletcher, Massinger, and Shakespeare as a Test of Authorship', *PMLA* 31 (1916): 326–58.

on't; 'the-contractions', combining the definite article 'with a preceding preposition, which . . . drops its last letter', as in *i'th*, or *i'th'* for *in the*, *o'th* or *o'th'* for *of the*; and 's-contractions', formed by combining the words *his* or *us* with a preceding word, keeping only the *s*, as in *on's* for *on us* or *on his*, *in's*, *make's*, *cram's*, and so forth (Farnham 1916, pp. 328–9). Farnham used this indicator to distinguish Fletcher from Beaumont and to argue for Davenport as a co-author of *The Captain* (pp. 332–41). Cyrus Hoy adopted earlier work on contractions to increase the number of stylistic markers with which he analysed the differing preferences of Fletcher and Massinger. As MacDonald Jackson summarized these differences, Fletcher 'strongly preferred *'em* to *them*, avoided the third person singular verb forms *hath* and *doth*, and regularly employed such contractions as *i'th'*, *o'th'*, *ha's* [for *he has*], and *'s* for *his*. Massinger avoided *ye*, used *'em* less frequently than Fletcher, made liberal use of *hath*, and employed *i'th* and *'s* seldom, *h'as* only once, and *o'th'* never' (Jackson 1979, p. 11). Hoy's analyses clearly differentiated the two dramatists, with a mass of linguistic detail (Hoy 1956, pp. 142–6), concluding that 'the linguistic patterns of the two are as nearly opposite as they could well be'.

Hoy could not differentiate the other collaborators in the canon with this degree of clarity, but he was able to classify enough distinct preferences to produce a positive identification in virtually every one of the fifty-four plays. Beaumont, whose work is present in twelve plays of the canon, proved hardest to identify, having fewer distinct preferences, so that Hoy had to draw on additional evidence, 'linguistic, metrical, syntactical' (Hoy 1958, pp. 89, 91). In his unaided plays Nathaniel Field used *ye* steadily, far less frequently than Fletcher but more often than Massinger; he used *hath* far more often than Fletcher, and *doth* far more often than Massinger; and he liked the contraction *'ee* (for *ye*), used 'in combination with the preceding auxiliary *do* (contracted to *d'*), or the preceding prepositions *to* and *with* (contracted to *t'* and *w'* respectively)' (Hoy 1959a, pp. 92–3). Shirley also liked *d'ee* and *w'ee*, preferred to write *shalt* and *wilt* as *shat* and *wot*, their negative forms as *shannot* and *wonnot* (pp. 108–9). Middleton made negligible use of *ye*, preferring the *y'* form, used *'em* rather than *them*, spelled *o'th'* as *a'th'*, and had a distinctive form *sh'as* for *she has* (Hoy 1960, pp. 79–81). Rowley preferred *'um* to *'em* (pp. 82–8), while John Ford frequently used *'ee* forms, employed *ye* and *'em* infrequently, and preferred not to use the forms *'i'th'*, *o'th'*, and *'s* for *his* (pp. 100–1). It is perhaps unkind to summarize Hoy's work with such brevity, but readers can easily verify both the rich amount of detail presented, and the meticulous analyses. He was certainly justified in concluding that 'the most signal achievement of this study' had been to show that we can distinguish the work of the five or six main dramatists involved in the Beaumont and Fletcher plays 'on the basis of fundamentally different language practices', and that linguistic evidence 'will serve to [decisively] differentiate their work in collaboration' (Hoy 1962, p. 87).

David Lake and MacDonald Jackson independently applied the same methods to the Middleton canon in great detail, indeed few writers have had their most minute linguistic preferences examined so closely. Lake made good use of synonym preferences to distinguish Dekker's work from Middleton's: 'Middleton clearly prefers *beside* (adverb or preposition) to *besides*; Dekker even more clearly prefers *besides*. Middleton's use of *while* and *whilst* is variable, but Dekker nearly always writes *whilst*' (Lake 1975, p. 50). This finding is one of several indicating that Middleton had no hand in *Blurt, Master Constable*, for in four out of five synonym tests his usage differs from that found there (pp. 72–3). As Lake judged, 'synonym ratios have great virtues for authorship work: they do not require a knowledge of text-length'—since we are dealing with ratios, not relative frequencies—'and they are not much affected by content—in the case of synonyms like *between* and *betwixt*, they are probably not affected by anything except personal preference' (p. 127).

Lake also used evidence from contractions to identify and distinguish writers at work:

Middleton is outstanding among Jacobean dramatists in his considerable use of *I've*, *t'as*, and *we're*, which Dekker does not use at all. Middleton's frequencies of *y'ave*, *they're*, and *on't* are all much higher than Dekker's. On the other hand, Dekker's frequency of *it's* is equalled only by Jonson among the major dramatists, whereas Middleton in his early period uses *it's* only three times in five plays, and never more than once per play. (pp. 50–1)

Given Middleton's preference for *on't*, which appears at least thirteen times in any one of his plays, its absence from *Blurt*, along with 'the non-appearance of Middleton's favourite *'em* and *I'm*', are further signs of Dekker's authorship (p. 80). Jackson also catalogued Middleton's preferences and avoidances, collecting them into 'bundles' for easier computation. He showed that Middleton rarely uses three variant forms, *hath*, *doth*, and *ye*, while he is very fond of six contractions, *I'm*, *I'd*, *I've*, *on't*, *ne'er*, *e'en*. Middleton's consistent avoidance of the first group 'distinguishes almost all his plays from the bulk of Jacobean drama, as sampled by Hoy. In only three of over one hundred non-Middleton plays dealt with by Hoy does the combined total of *hath*, *doth*, and *ye* fall below 12, whereas in only three' of Middleton's eighteen dramatic works does it rise above that figure (Jackson 1979, p. 20). As for the six contractions he grouped together, Jackson found that in Middleton's thirteen unaided plays the total instances range from 43–144, with an average of 90. In one hundred plays by thirty other dramatists the range was from 0–55, the average 16 (pp. 20–1).

We can already see how modern authorship studies, using stringently conducted computations, have evolved powerful discriminating tools. Jackson applied his two bundles of features to the anonymous play *The Second Maiden's Tragedy* (*SMT*) with striking results. Since its proposed authors include Tourneur, Jackson analysed his *Atheist's Tragedy*, together with representative tragedies by Middleton, Massinger, and Chapman. His results

TABLE 2.5. *Verbal contractions in Middleton and other dramatists*

	The Second Maiden's Tragedy	The Atheist's Tragedy	Middleton	Massinger	Chapman
'em	33	18	30–45	7–52	0
ye/y'	3:20	1:17	4–6:20–5		18:9
hath	2	14	0–5	27	37–67
doth	0	10	0–7		
ha's	8	7	3–12 (av. 6)	1	0
ha' (*have*)	9	37	2–33	0	0

Source: Jackson 1979, pp. 13–17.

(slightly abridged in Table 2.5) give the actual total of instances for each contraction in the two tragedies, and the normal range of usage for the four dramatists. From these data it is immediately evident that Massinger and Chapman can be ruled out completely. So can Tourneur, for in only one item (*ha's*) does his play show similar figures to *The Second Maiden's Tragedy*. All other features point consistently to Middleton's authorship, and Jackson added several other supporting markers. The 'contraction *'tas* for *it has* occurs 3 times in *The Second Maiden's Tragedy*' and is found in eight of Middleton's unaided plays (p. 15). In *SMT* the combined total of *hath*, *doth*, and *ye* is only 5: in eleven of Middleton's plays the range is 0–5, which is very low, seeing that in only two of seventy-one plays by eleven major Jacobean dramatists is the total less than 12. Another relevant marker consists of 'contractions in *'t* following a preposition or verb', such as *on't*, *for't*, or *in't*: there are 95 of these in *SMT*, while Middleton's range in thirteen unaided plays is 41 to 156, five of his plays averaging over 100. Of many other markers that Jackson identified I select the total for Middleton's six favourite contractions, which average 90 in his plays, but only 16 in the base sample of 100 plays: in *The Second Maiden's Tragedy* they total 112, a highly significant correlation statistically. Jackson felt 'justified in declaring that there will never be found a Jacobean play which is undoubtedly by a dramatist other than Middleton' in which these six contractions occur so frequently, the bundle '*hath-doth-ye*' occur so infrequently, and in which 'the overall linguistic pattern is as Middletonian' as that of *The Second Maiden's Tragedy* (p. 22). Many readers will agree.

Earlier I described research into the minutiae of linguistic preferences as 'unglamorous'. That term can also be ascribed to the study of dramatists' preferred swear words, another helpful indicator in authorship studies. Arguing that Middleton had written both *The Second Maiden's Tragedy* and *The*

TABLE 2.6. *Oaths and ejaculations in Middleton*

Play	Total number of oaths	Number of *faith*
A Chaste Maid in Cheapside	106	58
Michaelmas Term	102	58
No Wit	101	54
The Revenger's Tragedy	98	44
The Phoenix	83	35
The Second Maiden's Tragedy	70	25
The Atheist's Tragedy	45	9

Source: Barker 1945, pp. 56, 127.

Revenger's Tragedy, R. H. Barker computed the number of times that 'the oath *in faith* (or *faith* or *by my faith*—there are several variations)' appeared in each play, in other Middleton plays, and in Tourneur's *Atheist's Tragedy*. The results (combined in Table 2.6) were illuminating. D. J. Lake also tabulated Middleton's favourite oaths and exclamations (Lake 1975, tables following p. 252, table 1.1, segment 1). Among these some, such as *cuds me*, and *push*, are rather distinctive, and both occur in *The Second Maiden's Tragedy* (p. 187). MacDonald Jackson went to the extraordinary length of checking every instance of 39 expletives in thirteen plays by Middleton and 100 by thirty other dramatists (Jackson 1979, pp. 67–79). Of these 39 expletives, 'eleven are proportionately at least ten times more frequent in Middleton's plays' than in any other, such as *puh*, which is used 29 times in his canon, only 4 times elsewhere, *push* (27:5), *a my troth* (15:1), and *life* (35:5). Jackson then analysed the occurrence of the other 28 expletives in Middleton and the 100-play sample, showing that both sets of data make it 'almost certain' that Middleton wrote *The Puritan*, *The Revenger's Tragedy*, and *The Second Maiden's Tragedy*, and strengthen his case for the authorship of *A Yorkshire Tragedy* (p. 78).

The study of linguistic preferences, such as word-contractions and variant verb forms, has also proved fruitful in dating Shakespeare's contributions to *Sir Thomas More*. A. C. Partridge drew attention to a significant detail in Addition IIc, the fact that Shakespeare used the modern form *has* once (134), the older-fashioned *hath*, four times (196, 221, 223, 225).[59] Partridge observed that '*has* first appears in a Shakespearian Good Quarto, though rarely, in 2 *Henry IV*, probably written *c.*1597. *Hamlet* (Q2) is the first play in which Shakespeare relaxed his preference for *hath*', and while *has* is found

[59] Partridge, *Orthography in Shakespeare and Elizabethan Drama: A Study of Colloquial Contractions, Elision, Prosody and Punctuation* (London, 1964), 57.

in such early plays as *Henry VI* and *Two Gentlemen of Verona* this is 'because they are First Folio texts, probably re-edited after *c.*1600' (pp. 62–3). Partridge showed that in these three pages Shakespeare abbreviated the definite article, both at the beginning of a word (proclitic), as in 140 *th*ipp (= the hip), 217 *th*appostle, and at the ending (enclitic): 180 by*th*,[60] 199 too*th*, and regularly contracted the beginning (*aphesis* or *aphaeresis*) of prepositions: 218, 228, 229 *gainst* (all verse passages), and their ending (*apocope*): 217 *oft*. He abbreviated *he* to the colloquial *a* three times (165*a* twice, 264), and used other common abbreviations of pronouns—181 *th*art, 132 and 21 *t*is, 152 and 165 letts (p. 57). Looking at Shakespeare's linguistic development, Partridge suggested that at first he spelled out pronoun and verb combinations in full (*they are, thou art*), only beginning to abbreviate the pronoun around the turn of the century, one of several details that led him to choose 'a date soon after 1600' for Shakespeare's Addition to *Sir Thomas More* (p. 63).

D. J. Lake brought other linguistic evidence to bear on this problem. Lake first studied Dekker's autograph section of Addition IV, ll. 212–42 (Hand E; *MSR*, pp. 87–8), drawing on Peter B. Murray's demonstration that 'Dekker began using the colloquial *has* and *does* (rather than *hath* and *doth*) and the contractions *I'm* and *ha'* (for "have") rather precisely about 1600', for the two plays he wrote before this date are without colloquialisms, while those written between 1601 and *c.*1611–20 use them abundantly.[61] In his *More* scene Dekker used *ha', I'm*, and *does*, allowing the strong inference 'that the Addition [IV] must be later than 1599. Indeed, it is probably later than 1601, since in that year Dekker was still very seldom using *I'm*' (Lake 1977, p. 115). MacDonald Jackson extended Lake's argument from the use of colloquial forms to Shakespeare, drawing on some valuable research by Frederick O. Waller.[62] Isolating ten forms of contraction—(in modern spelling) *does, has, i'th', o'th', th', 't* (excluding *'tis*), *let's, in's, -ll* (excluding *I'll*), and *-em*, Waller showed that Shakespeare's orthographical tendency was towards an increased use of the more colloquial forms. Jackson systematized Waller's computation into a useful table, which revealed a 'clear and substantial change . . . around 1600' (just the year when Dekker's spelling habits also changed), *Twelfth Night* containing 'more than three times as many colloquial forms as the immediately preceding *As You Like It*' (Jackson 1978, p. 155). Jackson then showed that Shakespeare's scene in *Sir Thomas More* has 5 instances of *let's*, 4 of *we'll*, 3 of *th'*, 2 of *you'll*, and 1 each of *has, by'th*,

---

[60] Partridge found *byth* first used in a printed play-text in Q2 *Romeo and Juliet* (1599), and in the manuscript play *Thomas of Woodstock*, suggesting a 'post-1600 theatrical revision' for that text (p. 35).

[61] Lake, 'The Date of the "Sir Thomas More" Additions by Dekker and Shakespeare', *NQ* 222 (1977), p. 114, citing Murray, 'The Collaboration of Dekker and Webster in "Northward Ho" and "Westward Ho" ', *PBSA* 56 (1962): 482–6.

[62] F. O. Waller, 'The Use of Linguistic Criteria in Determining the Copy and Dates for Shakespeare's Plays', in W. F. McNeir and T. N. Greenfield (eds.), *Pacific Coast Studies in Shakespeare* (Eugene, Ore., 1966), pp. 1–19.

to'th, *'twere*, *what's*, *that's*, and *there's*. 'This gives a total of 21 such forms in 147 lines, or one for every 7 lines, a ratio of occurrence which unequivocally associates Hand D of *Sir Thomas More* with the post-1600 Shakespeare plays' (p. 156). Although it might seem obvious that a mob scene would include colloquialisms, Jackson showed that in More's formal address to them (2.3.67–159) 'there are 6 colloquial forms . . . in 79 lines, giving a rate of one for every 13 lines, which is not matched by any pre-1600 play'. Unaware (like many who write on *More*) of A. C. Partridge's discussion,[63] Jackson observed that the low proportion of *hath* to *has* (4 : 1) 'is not found in any play before *Twelfth Night*', and also noted that 'Hand D uses no *-eth* verb endings, which are fairly common in almost all Shakespeare's plays written before 1598'. Unknowingly echoing another observation by Partridge, that 181 *thart* 'appears in no Good Quarto at all, only in First Folio texts' (Partridge 1964a, p. 63), Jackson found this 'significant contraction' occurring once in *King John* (1596–7; F1), the other nineteen Shakespearian instances belonging to the period 1600–12. The evidence, then, consistently points to a date for Shakespeare's additional scene not before 1600, and perhaps 'several years later' (p. 156). Jackson subsequently strengthened this conclusion,[64] drawing on the findings by Estelle W. Taylor of Shakespeare's increasing preference for the *-es* over the *-eth* verb ending.[65] Dividing the canon into two groups, the twenty plays up to *As You Like It* (A), and the fourteen plays after *Twelfth Night* (B), Jackson produced the figures reproduced in Table 2.7. Jackson pointed out that hand D uses no *-th* endings at all, and 'seven *-s* endings for third person singular verbs other than *has* and *does*', three of them in More's formal address to the mob, further evidence that Shakespeare's addition must date from after 1600.[66]

In authorship studies, when differing approaches point in the same

[63] S. McMillin, *The Elizabethan Theatre and 'The Book of Sir Thomas More'* (Ithaca, NY, 1987), might have been glad to know that Partridge (1964a, p. 64) also observed that the play had been cast; the Riverside and Revels editors could have benefited from his close scrutiny of spelling and vocabulary.

[64] M. P. Jackson, 'Hand D of *Sir Thomas More*', NQ 226 (1981): 146.

[65] E. W. Taylor, 'Shakespeare's Use of *ETH* and *ES* Ending of Verbs in the First Folio', *CLA Journal*, 19 (1976): 437–57; repr. in V. Salmon and E. Burness (eds.), *Reader in the Language of Shakespearean Drama* (Amsterdam and Philadelphia, 1987), pp. 349–69. However, the thorough study of this topic by Dieter Stein, a historian of the English language, gives slightly different figures. In an essay, 'At the Crossroads of Philology, Linguistics and Semiotics: Notes on the Replacement of *th* by *s* in the Third Person Singular in English' (ES 68 (1987): 406–31), drawing on his earlier study, *Grammatik und Variation von Flexionsformen in der Sprache des Shakespeare Corpus* (Munich, 1974), Stein also divided Shakespeare's plays into two groups, A (the twenty up to *As You Like It*), and B (the fourteen on from *Twelfth Night*), with the following results: Group A: *-eth* endings 75, *-es* endings 73; Group B: *-eth* endings 15, *-es* endings 168 (Stein 1987, p. 413). Although differing, Stein's results certainly support Jackson's diagnosis of a 'cusp' in Shakespeare's usage around 1600. His figures for the auxiliary verbs (*doth*, *does*; *hath*, *has*) for AYLI are 25:1; 52:3; for TN 13:4; 35:20 (p. 414).

[66] Gary Taylor, using a 'colloquialism-in-verse test' of his own devising, based on 20 colloquial abbreviations, placed the *More* scene 'after *Twelfth Night* and *Troilus* (1601–2) but before *Measure for Measure* (late 1603–4)'. Cf. Taylor 1989, pp. 120–2.

TABLE 2.7. *Variant verb endings in Shakespeare*

Group A	*-eth* 239	*-es* 68
Group B	*-eth* 29	*-es* 185

Source: Jackson 1981, p. 146.

direction, it shows that the hypothesis was sound, the methodology viable. All the recent investigations into the date of Shakespeare's contributions to *Sir Thomas More* locate it in a time-span between 1600 and 1605. As later chapters will show, these modern techniques of dating texts using linguistic and stylistic criteria have proved helpful in distinguishing those parts of *Titus Andronicus* and *Pericles* written by Shakespeare from those which we must assign to a co-author.

FUNCTION WORDS

The reader's naked eye can perceive all the linguistic preferences we have looked at so far, and—once alerted to the fact—can also notice that 'Middleton normally tended to avoid parentheses, whereas Dekker used them liberally', another detail that helps to differentiate their shares in *The Roaring Girl* (Jackson 1979, pp. 95–101). But some authorship tests evade the normal reading experience, demanding special notation and statistical analysis. One such is the analysis of 'function words', those parts of speech which perform essential grammatical functions so unobtrusively that compilers of concordances regularly omit them. These include the definite and indefinite articles, conjunctions, prepositions, pronouns, auxiliary verbs, all elements that recur frequently in any piece of verse or prose and which are used by many writers with distinct preferences. In a classic study, Mosteller and Wallace were able to assign the authorship of the *Federalist* papers (published in 1787–8) by studying the incidence of 165 different function words in the work of the three writers involved. One used *upon* eighteen times more frequently than the others, and showed a strong preference for *also*, *by*, and *on*, while one of his colleagues made proportionally greater use of the function words *an*, *of*, and *there*.[67] In a pioneering study MacDonald P. Jackson applied this method to Jacobean drama, analysing samples from twenty dramatists and charting the incidence of thirteen function words: *a/an*, *and*, *but*, *by*, *for*, *from*, *in*, *it*, *of*, *that*, *to*, and *with* (Jackson 1979, pp. 82–93). The

---

[67] Frederick Mosteller and David L. Wallace, *Inference and Disputed Authorship: The Federalist* (Reading, Mass., 1964); cf. Jackson 1979, pp. 81–2.

resulting computations use elementary statistics—assessing probability distribution by establishing the arithmetic mean, measuring the standard deviations, and using the chi-square 'goodness-of-fit' test (pp. 84–9)—which need not concern us here. Jackson's work used samples, not complete texts, and he acknowledged that a test based on these thirteen function words alone did not possess 'enough discriminatory power [to] demonstrate Middleton's authorship of any one of the disputed plays regarded singly' (p. 87).

But his results certainly strengthened the case for Middleton's authorship of *The Revenger's Tragedy*, as can be seen from the chi-square test, in which he juxtaposed results from *The Revenger's Tragedy*, *The Atheist's Tragedy*, and thirteen Middleton plays. In this test 'the greater the value of chi-square obtained, the greater the degree of dissimilarity between the two plays'. *The Revenger's Tragedy* shows a correlation with Middleton's plays ranging from 20.6 to 44.0, while the figure for *The Atheist's Tragedy* is 80.7, a striking discrepancy. 'Each of the thirteen Middleton plays is closer to *The Revenger's Tragedy* in its use of the thirteen selected function words than is *The Atheist's Tragedy*.' Considering that both plays 'were written within a few years of one another and belong to the same genre', this is a further sign that Tourneur wrote the one play, Middleton the other (p. 88). As Jackson argued, this test 'shows a good deal of promise as a possible means to the solution of authorship problems', once sufficient data have been collected and analysed. He concluded that only four of the thirteen words he had considered could reliably discriminate between Middleton's work and that of his fellow dramatists: *a/an* and *it*, which he used considerably more frequently than most other writers, while making much less use of *and* and *with*. But 'more than one hundred other such words . . . might also be investigated', and several of these could turn out to have the same degree of 'potency as discriminators between Middleton and his fellows' as have these four markers (p. 90): this is a new method with considerable promise. In a series of tables (pp. 202–7) Jackson presented data for the thirteen function words from 26 Middleton play samples, and for 59 further plays by 20 other dramatists, opening up several areas of study. As we shall see when discussing *Timon of Athens* (Chapter 4), a study of function words does differentiate Middleton's share of the play from Shakespeare's.

As MacDonald Jackson demonstrated, the function word test can be used for both positive and negative discrimination, identifying the work of one author and excluding that of others. But it is only from the actual reading experience of the texts in question that one can discover which function words will prove to be reliable markers. In my own reading of the *Funerall Elegye* for William Peter published in 1612 as by 'W. S.', I was struck by the frequency with which the word *of* occurred, some 144 times in a poem of only 578 lines, 30 of these instances at the beginning of a verse line. Moreover, many of these occurrences—107 in my count—took the form

TABLE 2.8. *The function word* of *in the* Funerall Elegye *and in Shakespeare*

A Work	B Total deca-syllabic lines	C Total *of*	D Frequency per 1,000 lines	E *Of* beginning verse line	F Every *x* lines	G ⟨noun + *of* + noun⟩	H G as percentage of C
Funerall Elegye	578	144	249.1	30	19.3	107	74.3
Venus and Adonis	1,194	122	102.1	5	238.8	61	50.0
Rape of Lucrece	1,855	242	130.5	17	109.1	149	61.6
Sonnets	2,154	368	170.8	20	107.7	113	30.7
Cymbeline	2,695	414	153.6	46	58.6	207	50.0
Winter's Tale	2,046	295	144.2	48	42.6	168	56.9
The Tempest	1,524	219	145.1	26	58.6	100	45.7

Source: Vickers 2002, pp. 235–6.

⟨noun + *of* + noun⟩, sometimes as a normal genitive, as in 'the tide of this surrounding age'. More unusually, the author of this poem regularly used this construction for a partitive genitive, expressing the relation of part to whole, as in 'tale of woe', or 'act of friendship'. Since the *Elegye* had been ascribed to Shakespeare, I counted the frequency of occurrence for *of* in Shakespeare's poems and late plays, to permit a comparison with the *Funerall Elegye*. The results, collected in Table 2.8, show a clear difference between the two authors. The author of the *Elegye* begins a verse line with *of* between five and twelve times more frequently than did Shakespeare in his poems, and between two-and-a-half and three times more often than Shakespeare did in the late plays. The proportion of ⟨noun + *of* + noun⟩ constructions within the total instances of *of* in Shakespeare's poems ranges from 30.7 to 61.6 per cent, and in the late plays from 45.7 to 56.9 per cent (Vickers 2002, pp. 232–8). In the *Elegye* it is 74.3 per cent. These discrepancies ruled out Shakespeare as a candidate for the *Elegye*'s authorship,[68] as did many other tests.

Since a substantial body of evidence suggested that John Ford had written the *Elegye*, perhaps under commission from a friend of Peter's family, I performed the same computation on Ford's early poems, *Fame's Memoriall* (1606) and *Christes Bloodie Sweat* (1613), together with his two prose works, *The Golden Meane* (1613–14) and *The Line of Life* (1620). As Table 2.9 shows, the correlation between the three poems for both the frequency of *of* and its occurrence at the beginning of verse lines is remarkably high. Although the prose works naturally provided no data for verse lines, the proportion of the ⟨noun + *of* + noun⟩ construction in terms of the total instances of the preposition *of* is remarkably constant, 74.6 and 76.3 per cent, as

[68] See also Colin Burrow (ed.), Shakespeare, *The Complete Sonnets and Poems* (Oxford, 2002), pp. 152–8.

TABLE 2.9. *The function word* of *in the* Funerall Elegye, *and in Ford's poems and prose works*

A	B	C	D	E	F	G	H
Work	Total deca-syllabic lines	Total *of*	Frequency per 1,000 lines	*Of* beginning verse line	Every *x* lines	⟨noun + *of* + noun⟩	G as percentage of C
Funerall Elegye	578	144	249.1	30	19.3	107	74.3
Fames Memoriall	1,176	433	372.6	53	22.2	393	90.7
Christes Bloodie Sweat	1,908	465	243.7	75	25.4	368	79.1
Golden Meane	—	740				552	74.6
Line of Life	—	503				384	76.3

Source: Vickers 2002, p. 331.

against the *Elegye*'s 74.3 per cent. I also investigated this linguistic feature in Ford's nine sole-authored plays, together with the five co-authored works (Vickers 2002, pp. 329–38). Even though his dramatic writings date from the 1620s and 1630s, long after the *Funerall Elegye*, the consistency with which Ford favoured the function word *of*, whether to begin a verse line or in the formula ⟨noun + *of* + noun⟩, was impressive. As Robert Davril also observed, 'there are few authors in English literature (was there ever one?) who used *of* to such a prodigious extent . . .'.[69] On both counts Ford could be clearly distinguished from his co-authors, Dekker, Rowley, Massinger, and Webster.

These examples from the Middleton and Ford canons show that function words can reliably function as both positive and negative indicators, identifying a probable author while eliminating other candidates. Being a potentially useful weapon in Shakespearian authorship studies, readers interested in such matters approached Gary Taylor's long essay on Shakespeare's canon and chronology in the Oxford *Textual Companion*[70] with high expectations. Taylor indeed discussed function words at length, including seven tables of data (*TxC*, pp. 80–9), but his treatment of the topic had several failings, minor and major. Thomas Merriam drew attention to some typographical and computational errors, and pointed out that in table 2 (*TxC*, p. 82) 'the percentages of the ten individual function words use their count sum as a base, while the figures marked TOTAL use the entire word count for each play/poem as a base'.[71] Then in table 3, where Taylor 'tests' the canon of

[69] Robert Davril, *Le Drame de John Ford* (Paris, 1954), p. 440; my translation.

[70] Taylor, 'The Canon and Chronology of Shakespeare's Plays', S. Wells and G. Taylor, with J. Jowett and W. Montgomery, *William Shakespeare: A Textual Companion* (Oxford, 1987), pp. 69–144, double columns. This work will be referred to as *TxC*.

[71] T. Merriam, 'Taylor's Statistics in *A Textual Companion*', NQ 234 (1989): 341–2, at p. 341.

Marlowe against Shakespeare's, he expressed the value for each word no longer as percentages but as proportions, given as decimal fractions (0.07 for *but* in the first column, compared to 6.28 per cent in the first column of table 2); but he still retained percentages in the column marked TOTAL. As Merriam noted, while Taylor retained the second method for tables 3 to 7, in table 7 he reverted to the percentage system for the play *Edmund Ironside*, combining two heterogeneous systems in one table. This unannounced shift of method is confusing, to say the least, and shows signs of haste or inadequate co-ordination between the various sources of data presented here. The student of Shakespeare, faced with new material of such complexity, deserved a more careful exposition.

Yet, once this statistical information has been absorbed, what value should we set on it? Taylor believed it to have severe limitations. The function word test, he wrote, 'is more useful in establishing that a work does *not* belong in the Shakespeare canon than in establishing' that it does. The fact that 'other writers do sometimes use these words in frequencies which overlap with Shakespearian norms' (p. 81) reduces its value as a criterion for identifying authorship. It may distinguish between the Marlowe canon and the Shakespeare canon as a whole, although even this is not sure, but if using it for individual works 'you could not prove, on the basis of this test alone, that Shakespeare did *not* write them' (p. 83). If true, this would be a damaging weakness, for we shall seldom want to use the function word test to investigate the whole canon of a writer's work, since in most cases this is not in doubt: it is precisely for individual works, or for parts of works, that we need a reliable criterion. Taylor produced function word tables for fifteen Elizabethan works, but to him the results simply confirmed that the test 'rules works out more reliably than it rules them in' (p. 85). The 'primary interest' of the function word test, Taylor finally declared, 'is its possible value in arbitrating on Shakespeare's share in works of collaborative or disputed authorship' (p. 86). But he instantly described it as inadequate even for this task: 'because it deals in statistical possibilities, it cannot be applied straightforwardly to very small samples, like the 1,387 words attributed to Shakespeare in *Sir Thomas More*, or the two brief Hecate passages allegedly interpolated into *Macbeth* (303 words, not counting the songs)'. All the same, he believed, it should work for 'large chunks of full-length plays' (the reader may smile at the unscientific word 'chunks', after all this striving for accuracy to within two decimal points), and so, with assistance, he analysed function words in eleven works in which another hand was suspected. The results of this computation are set out in table 6 (*TxC*, p. 87), but in his discussion Taylor described some of the results as inconclusive; others were said to confirm a hypothesis of joint authorship; and others were simply over-interpreted. The totals for *The Taming of the Shrew*, *2 Henry VI*, and *3 Henry VI* 'contain no figure in excess of two deviations': however, Taylor warned, these results 'cannot rule out the possibility of dual authorship in those works', for the 'collaborator's preferences' might easily have overlapped with Shakespeare's, and in any case it is difficult to tell them apart in such a small sample. In plain English, the test as Taylor applied it proved nothing either way.

It is strange, to say the least, that Taylor should give so much prominence to the function word test, making it appear the most important tool in Shakespearian authorship studies, but then express so many doubts about its efficiency. After all, he himself recorded that it had worked extremely well in Mosteller and Wallace's 'classic study of the Federalist Papers', allowing them to distinguish the contributions of Alexander Hamilton and James Madison (*TxC*, p. 80). MacDonald Jackson's use of this tool for the Middleton canon, Taylor added, 'showed that such tests are *potentially* of great value' (my italics). In fact, Jackson proved their value beyond question, as we have seen, for they provided strong confirmatory evidence for Middleton's authorship of *The Revenger's Tragedy*, *The Second Maiden's Tragedy*, *The Puritan*, and *A Yorkshire Tragedy*. If correctly designed and executed, the function word test functions well.

The fact that Taylor achieved such disappointing results, leading him to doubt the test's efficacy, may be due to his having designed it badly. And indeed, M. W. A. Smith, the doyen of stylometry as applied to Elizabethan drama, having praised Taylor's 'bravery' for laying so much weight on statistical evidence, discovered several 'fundamental flaws' in his work.[72] Taylor's discussion of function words was skewed from the outset, for having initially announced that he had chosen 25 common words in Shakespeare in order to establish typical patterns of usage (the list given on page 80 actually includes 39 words), he subsequently reduced the list to 10: *but*, *by*, *for*, *no*, *not*, *so*, *that*, *the*, *to*, and *with*. As Smith observed, it is strange that Taylor should have omitted 'one of the most typical, the indefinite article *a/an*', and also left out all contractions, such as *for't* and *i'th'*, which would certainly have affected his results.[73] But the real problems began when Taylor processed his data, choosing thirty-one core plays in the Shakespeare canon (omitting co-authored works) and calculating the percentage in each play of the ten selected words, rather than the frequency of occurrence. Smith pointed out that 'a percentage rate of use of words is not an accepted starting point from which to embark on a statistical description: a regularity of use is implied which is not reflected in the plays themselves. This is a fundamental deficiency which permeates all Taylor's investigation . . .' (Smith 1991*b*, p. 73). Taylor's second table gives values for each word, but not for its independent occurrence in the text. Instead, he gives one figure representing 'its

---

[72] M. W. A. Smith, 'Statistical Inference in *A Textual Companion* to the Oxford Shakespeare', *NQ* 236 (1991): 73–8, at p. 73.

[73] MacDonald Jackson included contractions in his studies of Middleton's use of function words: Jackson 1979, pp. 83–4.

percentage of the total number of occurrences of all ten words', and a total figure recording 'the proportion of the total vocabulary of the play which these ten function words represent' (*TxC*, p. 80). Smith objected that the number of readings taken is 'far too few to determine if the distributions are normal', but also, and more seriously, that the 'essential prerequisite for Taylor's approach, that all eleven items of data for each work be independent, is . . . not satisfied'. The details supporting this charge are statistically complex (Smith 1991*b*, pp. 73–4), indeed Smith acknowledged that two colleagues had to help him reconstruct the procedures by which Taylor had obtained his figures, but his judgement was unequivocal: 'Such an approach is devoid of both theoretical foundation and statistical meaning' (p. 74). Taylor's procedure distorted the outcome of his tests from the outset.

As a professional statistician, Smith found that Taylor's interpretation of his results was 'equally naïve', for he took data already used for one purpose and applied it to 'subsequent steps of the procedure', so compromising the integrity of the method. Having pointed out errors in Taylor's own data for *Macbeth* and Middleton's *Game at Chess* (p. 75), Smith re-computed the whole of Taylor's data 'as far as possible', providing four corrected tables (pp. 76–7). He then evaluated their ability to perform the role expected of them by this whole exercise, namely to discriminate authorship. His 'inescapable conclusion', however, was that 'the revised procedure is no more able to provide reliable information on authorship than Taylor's original flawed approach. Certainly none of Taylor's confident assertions based on his statistical study were adequately underpinned . . .' (p. 75). The point at issue is the dubious value of function words when expressed as percentages. For, 'while function words can distinguish authors, their occurrences in texts are frequently more erratic than the statistical description of a random variable would allow. The use of percentages can disguise such behaviour' (ibid.). Taylor obviously lacked the necessary knowledge and experience in using statistics to make proper use of these methods. Smith ended by warning that 'numerous apparently obscure and arcane pitfalls await an intrepid Shakespearian who ventures into interdisciplinary regions by invoking well-known statistical procedures without first examining their appropriateness to the intended application . . .'. Yet he hoped that his critique would not deter 'literary scholars . . . from embarking on statistical studies' (p. 78).

Gary Taylor's handling of statistical evidence, with its various defects, inevitably affected his evaluation of individual plays. Many users of the *Textual Companion* will have been surprised to notice that table 6, 'Function words in disputed works' (p. 87), includes not only *Pericles*, *Titus Andronicus*, *Timon of Athens*, *Henry VIII*, and *The Two Noble Kinsmen*, as we would expect, but also *Macbeth*. What is that play doing there? It has long been known that two songs from Middleton's *The Witch* (*c*.1613) were inserted into the text of *Macbeth* as printed in the First Folio, and the Oxford editors follow many of their predecessors in assigning to Middleton the two scenes of rather uninspired verse (3.5, 4.1), in which Hecate appears (*TxC*, 20–2, 73, 129, 543). Taylor duly omitted this material from his function word computations, but all the same, he claimed, the figures he had calculated for *Macbeth* 'arouse some anxiety': the 'high deviance for the word *by* suggests that the remainder of the play [that is, not just the Hecate scenes, ascribed to Middleton] may also have been affected verbally by adaptation. Only three figures out of 341 in the core canon have a deviance higher than this 2.82 registered in *Macbeth*' (p. 86). The statistical principle involved is that in a normal frequency distribution '95 per cent of the individual figures will fall within two standard deviations of the arithmetic mean'. Taylor treated any figures in excess of two standard deviations as potentially abnormal, and hence un-Shakespearian, but he did admit that the highest figure of deviations from the arithmetic mean in his table 2 was 3.17, the score (according to his method) for *The Rape of Lucrece*. 'This does not mean', he hastened to inform readers, 'that *Lucrece* was written by someone other than Shakespeare; it means that, in a homogeneous population, it should not surprise us' to find one item of the 341 values he has computed should reach this score, which is only 0.29 per cent of his population (p. 81). Should so much importance be attached to a single item? What, then, of the score of 2.82 for the word *but* in *Macbeth*? Unfortunately, if the reader who wishes to check this figure turns back to table 2, giving the figures for the core canon, he will find them expressed in percentages, charting 'their frequency relative to one another', not in decimal fractions, so that it is impossible to make any comparison. The value of 2.82 may define the upper range of standard deviations in Shakespeare, but it is also explicable on internal evidence, being affected by other factors: after all, patterns of action, consequence, and causation are especially likely in a play involving witchcraft and violence. In any case, since we are dealing with the forty-eight uses of *by* in *Macbeth* listed in Spevack's *Concordance* (six of them in prose), it seems unwise, on the basis of one statistic for one word, to disseminate doubts about the authenticity of a whole play. Taylor earlier castigated critics who, capitalizing on the absence of Shakespearian manuscripts or of 'publications overseen by the author personally', have endorsed 'the hypothesis of massive corruption in transmission' (p. 19)—but have not he and the Oxford editors done the same thing with their newer tools? Our doubts about this procedure are exacerbated by the arbitrary way in which Taylor uses his statistical evidence, as he does with other forms of argument. The 'suspect scenes' in *Titus Andronicus* yield a figure of 2.55 standard deviations for *but*, yet—unlike for the figure of 2.82 for *by* in *Macbeth*—Taylor now pronounces this result not 'statistically significant', nor does it 'discriminate very usefully between different parts of the play' (p. 86). Similarly in *The Two Noble Kinsmen*, where the part ascribed to Shakespeare scores a 2.28 for *by*, that by Fletcher has a 2.49 *total*:

the reader is left wondering whether these figures are strictly comparable. Taylor found the figures for *Henry VIII* 'even more confusing', those for *1 Henry VI* 'equally confusing', and he could 'only conclude that, in its present state, the [one should read, 'my'] function word test can discriminate successfully with some collaborations, but not others' (p. 88).

It seems to me that the function-word test is a perfectly reliable tool, if used properly. Taylor suggested that it 'can eliminate some individual works decisively; about other works it can only create suspicion' (p. 83), but any methodology which created, but could not resolve suspicion, would be a distinct liability. We must hope that a competent statistician will one day apply the function word test not only to whole plays by Shakespeare but to those portions in which a co-author's hand has been detected. Until then, this approach can still be regarded as a potentially valuable tool.

STATISTICS AND STYLOMETRY

The methods that I have been describing are all generally accepted, subject to the usual cautions about their proper use. I have arranged them in roughly chronological order, from the verse tests and parallel passages used in the nineteenth century up to the close study of linguistic preferences and function words intensively used in the last fifty years. Within that progression we can see a steady move towards the quantification of data, and it was a natural step to call in high speed electronic calculators to perform more elaborate statistical analyses, a method now known as stylometry. The terms 'stylometric' and 'stylometry' actually antedate the computer, for the *OED Supplement* (1986) records them in 1935 and 1945, respectively, both terms being used by classicists working on Plato. The word may be recent, but the activity dates back to the nineteenth century, to the work of Augustus de Morgan (1851) and T. C. Mendenhall (1887) on word length as an index of authorship, to that of W. Lutoslawski (1897), who distinguished no fewer than 500 different stylistic markers in Plato, and to the pioneers involved with The New Shakspere Society (1874 onwards).[74] The discipline has produced two classic studies, Alvar Ellegård's identification of the author of the *Junius* letters,[75] and Mosteller and Wallace's work on the *Federalist* papers. There have been other valuable studies in recent times, such as those by Anthony Kenny and

---

[74] For brief histories of the discipline see C. B. Williams, *Style and Vocabulary: Numerical Studies* (London, 1970); A. Kenny, *The Computation of Style: An Introduction to Statistics for Students of Literature and Humanities* (Oxford, 1982), pp. 1–14.

[75] Ellegård, *A Statistical Method for Determining Authorship: The 'Junius' Letters, 1769–1772* (Gothenburg, 1962), and *Who was Junius?* (Stockholm, 1962); Mosteller and Wallace 1964.

Gerard R. Ledger.[76] Anyone familiar with these works will agree that stylometry is a serious scholarly discipline. But it is also subject to wide variations, both in the claims made for it and in its results. Its optimistic users claim that it can provide a 'fingerprint' or even 'a DNA identification', yet a recent, and extremely careful exponent acknowledges 'the uncertain nature of stylometric investigation' (Ledger 1989, p. 15). Some scholars ascribe to the computer a superiority over the naked eye. Barbara Stevenson, for instance, states that 'when reading a text, a person sees thousands of words, seemingly without a pattern. In stylometry, a computer counts linguistic features, and statistical tests establish general traits of the writer's language that the unaided human eye cannot discern.'[77] But the attentive reader does notice patterns, and can also choose the most fruitful linguistic features to analyse with the help of electronic devices. Conversely, statistical computation based on poorly chosen, or even irrelevant, linguistic detail can be futile. Calculations produced by computers will vary in value according to the intelligence, experience, and perceptiveness of the brains who have devised them.

Anthony Kenny, in a thoughtful review of stylometry's claim to be an infallible science, declared it 'wrong to suggest that each author has a stylistic fingerprint, and to compare the computer to a microscope which reveals fine details' imperceptible to 'the naked eye of the literary scholar'. If we must invoke scientific disciplines, Kenny suggested,

the appropriate comparison is with the camera of an aerial photographer. Photography from the sky can enable patterns to be detected which are obscured when one is too close to the ground: it enables us to see the wood despite the trees. So the statistical study of a text can reveal broad patterns, macroscopic uniformities in a writer's work which can escape notice as one reads word by word and sentence by sentence.[78]

But of course an experienced student of style can notice both regularities and irregularities. Indeed, some of the best stylometric studies deal with phenomena which have been observed in an attentive reading, and have then been subjected to quantified analysis. As more texts become available in electronic form, the illusion may spread that scholars in computer laboratories will be able to process (or 'crunch') linguistic data derived from texts that they need not bother to read. However, experience suggests that to run elaborate tests on some linguistic detail is not enough: you must also be able to show why it might be relevant, what meaning it could have in terms of a writer's style, or in a literary work produced by collaboration.

[76] Kenny, *The Aristotelian Ethics* (Oxford, 1977), and *A Stylometric Study of the New Testament* (Oxford, 1986); Ledger, *Re-counting Plato: A Computer Analysis of Plato's Style* (Oxford, 1989).

[77] B. Stevenson, 'Adapting Hypothesis Testing to a Literary Problem', in R. G. Potter (ed.), *Literary Computing and Literary Criticism* (Philadelphia, 1989), pp. 63–74, at p. 70.

[78] A. Kenny, *A Stylometric Study of the New Testament* (Oxford, 1986), p. 116.

Although these methods are less than twenty years old it is already clear that some of their early users, seduced by advanced technology and the ease of computation, have carried out tests having no proper rationale, and violating basic principles in statistics. Of course, distrust of statistics is ancient, and widespread: as F. J. Furnivall noted in 1874, 'it has been often said that statistics can be made to prove anything'.[79] But the proper reaction to this distrust is to learn to use statistics properly. Beginners may well be discouraged by such apparently recondite terminology as the Bell curve, standard deviations, chi-square tests, goodness-of-fit, Bayes's formula, the binomial and the Poisson probability distribution, probability vectors, and so forth. However, several helpful handbooks exist,[80] and it does not take a great deal of time to understand what statisticians are talking about, even though non-mathematicians will be unable to replicate the computations. The application of mathematical methods to problems involving natural language is obviously fraught with difficulties, once we go beyond the basic stage of computing the number of times that a particular word, metrical variant, or grammatical feature occurs per thousand lines of text, say. Languages form autonomous systems, in which words are combined according to linguistic rules, not according to the free or random patterns that may be observed in other forms of behaviour treated by statistical computation. Since statistics always involves interpretation, the evaluations that qualified statisticians make of each other's work is of great importance to laymen who depend on their technical knowledge.

Within the chronological development I have sketched, the move from performing statistical calculations by hand to using computers ought to have been unproblematic. Unfortunately, some of the first practitioners of stylometry as applied to Shakespeare came up with astonishing, and indeed improbable, results. Since the early 1980s newspapers have regularly carried sensational stories according to which 'the computer'—as if a higher agent, enjoying magical powers, without human interference—'has proved that Shakespeare wrote the whole of *Sir Thomas More*', or the whole of *Titus Andronicus*, or the whole of *Pericles*. These findings challenged a long accumulated scholarly tradition, and indeed offended against common sense. After all, the manuscript of *Sir Thomas More* in the British Library is in the handwriting of five different dramatists, together with a playhouse scribe, and three of those writers—Chettle, Munday, Shakespeare—can be seen in the act of composition, scratching out what they have just written as a fresh thought came to them. How could this play possibly be the work of one author?

[79] 'Discussion. Mr. Furnivall on the Ryme Test', *TNSS* 1 (1874): 31–5, at p. 35.
[80] I have benefited from Derek Rowntree, *Statistics Without Tears: A Primer for Non-mathematicians* (Harmondsworth, 1981); Frederick Williams, *Reasoning with Statistics: How to Read Quantitative Research* (Orlando, Fla., 1968; 4th edn., 1992); Butler 1985.

From such beginnings stylometry as applied to Shakespeare has aroused suspicion, fuelling the distrust of statistics already present. It has become a source of controversy, both between those who practise it, and between them and the general scholarly public, who are naturally confused when one group of experts tells them that Acts 1 and 2 of *Pericles* were written by Shakespeare, and are promptly contradicted by another group telling them the opposite. Who should we believe? It then becomes necessary to evaluate the rival claims, since both cannot be right. In this process we have to judge the statistical methods used, and the assumptions behind them, for if the rationale is misguided, the result—however meticulously calculated—will be worthless.

The three sensational claims concerning 'Shakespeare's sole authorship' that I have quoted all derive from the work of a theological scholar, Revd A. Q. Morton, who developed his version of stylometry when studying ancient Greek prose, and in particular the letters of St Paul contained in the New Testament. The authenticity of the Pauline Epistles has been vigorously discussed over the last two centuries, using a large range of criteria, theological, linguistic, and literary or rhetorical (considering the Epistle as a literary form).[81] Morton, however, chose to revive a thesis proposed by the Tübingen biblical scholar F. C. Baur in 1845,[82] according to which only the four major Epistles—Romans, 1 and 2 Corinthians, Galatians—are genuine, the remaining spurious. Arguing this case,[83] Morton relied on three stylometric methods, computing sentence lengths, word frequencies, and what he called 'positional stylometry', which involves studying the frequency of a word placed first in a sentence, the last word, the last but one, and so on.[84] These might seem reasonable methods to the layman, but for over twenty years biblical scholars and statisticians have severely criticized Morton's methodology. A paper which Morton gave to the Royal Statistical Society (Morton 1965) aroused several serious objections (pp. 224–31), which I shall summarize here, since they will prove relevant to Morton's later work on Shakespeare. One critic pointed out that Morton had, without warning, shifted from computing the number of instances of the function word *kai* ('and') per thousand

---

[81] See *The Oxford Companion to the Bible*, ed. Bruce M. Metzger and Michael D. Coogan (New York and Oxford, 1993), under the title of each Epistle.

[82] F. C. Baur, *Paulus, der Apostel Christi* (Tübingen, 1845; Engl. trans. 1873–5).

[83] See A. Q. Morton, 'The Authorship of Greek Prose', *Journal of the Royal Statistical Society*, Series A, 128 (1965): 169–224; followed by a discussion, pp. 224–31; *Paul, the Man and the Myth: A Study in the Authorship of Greek Prose* (London, 1966), with J. J. McLeman; *Literary Detection: How to Prove Authorship and Fraud in Literary Documents* (London, 1978).

[84] See e.g. S. Michaelson and A. Q. Morton, 'The New Stylometry: A One-word Test of Authorship', *Classical Quarterly*, 22 (1972): 89–102; S. Michaelson and A. Q. Morton, 'Last Words: A Test of Authorship for Greek Writers', *New Testament Studies*, 17 (1971): 192–208; A. Q. Morton, 'Once: A Test of Authorship Based on Words which are not Repeated in the Sample', *LLC* 1 (1986): 1–8.

words, to the number per sentence (pp. 224–5). Another critic objected that Morton's thesis rested upon 'direct comparisons made between Epistles of widely different length using constants which have not been rendered independent of Epistle length', so violating an important statistical principle (p. 228). A third drew attention to the crucial fact that many manuscripts of Greek texts contain no marks of punctuation. Where a system was used, it varies greatly from one manuscript to another and bears 'little relation to those inserted by modern editors in the printed versions'. Since Morton 'merely followed the punctuation of the printed texts', his 'positional stylometry', together with his use of sentence length as a stylistic criterion, must be judged methodologically 'suspect' (p. 229).

The most searching criticisms of Morton's methods in this symposium were made by Gustav Herdan, a specialist in statistical linguistics, praised by C. B. Williams and others for his substantial 'studies of the structure of many different languages'.[85] Herdan agreed that the absence or uneven nature of original punctuation in early Greek texts makes 'work on sentence length impossible', and in fact renders any test based on it *'the most unsuitable of all available tests'*. If applied to classical Greek texts this criterion would prove that the works of Xenophon and Aristotle were written by the same author. Further, Morton failed to define what he understood by sentence length (p. 230), and when variables are not defined, computation is valueless. Herdan showed that Morton's choice of sentence length as a stylistic marker was dubious in theory and severely flawed in practice (pp. 229–31), and that his results contradicted all other 'extra-linguistic, historical and theological evidence'. To base authorship arguments purely on stylometric evidence, we can already judge, is a hazardous step, especially if that evidence proves to be self-contradictory. Symptomatically, when Morton 'records a "few significant differences"' between the Epistles he regards as genuine he immediately excuses them on literary grounds, even though he began his paper by denigrating literary criticism as unscientific, compared to stylometry. As Herdan observed, this evasiveness 'means nothing else but that the significance tests only partly support his hypothesis', and that 'the linguistic criteria chosen by the author are conspicuous for lacking discriminating power' (p. 231). Herdan concluded that Morton's paper 'can only serve to discredit the method of literary statistics'. Yet Morton's was taken to be the unquestionable model for Shakespearian stylometry in the 1980s and beyond.

Other New Testament scholars made equally severe criticisms. P. F. Johnson, responding to a paper by Michaelson and Morton which analysed

---

[85] Williams 1970, p. 10. See ibid. 154–5, for details of twenty books and articles published by Herdan between 1953 and 1966, including *Type-Token Mathematics: A Text-book of Mathematical Linguistics* (The Hague, 1960), *Quantitative Linguistics* (London, 1961), *The Calculus of Linguistic Observations* (The Hague, 1962), and *The Advanced Theory of Language as Choice and Chance* (Berlin, 1966).

the frequency of the occurrence of the last words in sentences according to grammatical categories (nouns, aorist verbs, and so on), drew attention to several 'dubious assumptions, inconsistencies and errors' in the paper's statistics, including the authors' extrapolation of 'expectations'[86] from samples, not from the entire 'population' of Pauline writing, and their invoking different criteria when faced with discordant results.[87] Johnson concluded that 'the sentence may not after all be a satisfactory unit' for stylometric analysis, and complained that Morton's methodology ignored fundamental literary considerations:

the manner of Paul's writing may be such that the category of word appearing at the end of a sentence is often determined by the context or considerations of style and rhetoric. Hence a change in style during the course of a letter would cause a variation in the frequency of word-categories; and similarly there would be no reason to expect a consistent frequency of last-word categories as between two separate pieces of writing. (Johnson 1974, p. 99)

Johnson dismissed Morton's 'hypothesis that the last words of [Paul's] sentences bear the alleged significance' as 'a psychological improbability' (p. 100). That Morton ignored such fundamental issues should warn all who read stylometric studies to be ever alert, asking themselves what significance may be attached to a given method, and what discriminatory powers it has. Anthony Kenny, in his stylometric study of the New Testament, also criticized Morton's theories,[88] pointing out that they had not changed between 1965 and 1978, when Morton published *Literary Detection*—in which none of his critics is even mentioned, confirming Herdan's judgement, twenty years earlier, that Morton was 'impervious to any objective criticism of the method he uses' (Herdan 1965, p. 230). Kenny showed, however, that Morton's figures

[86] Norman Thomson, in a cautionary note with the engaging title 'How to Read Articles which Depend on Statistics', *LLC* 4 (1989): 6–11, warned non-statistical readers that the terms 'expectation' or 'expected result' carry a special meaning in statistics, being 'an extension of that of "average". The reason for using another word is that averages can be calculated only when there is a finite population for which some numerical attribute can be totalled and divided by the number of items. Where an infinite population is present such a calculation is impossible, yet the idea of there being an overall average of all possible numbers drawn from say a Normal distribution is so intuitively reasonable that the idea demands to be carried over from the finite to the infinite case. This is what lies behind the idea "expected" in statistics' (Thomson 1989, p. 8), as in such statements as 'the statistically expected number of children per family is 2.7'.

[87] P. F. Johnson, 'The Use of Statistics in the Analysis of the Characteristics of Pauline Writing', *New Testament Studies*, 20 (1974): 92–100, at pp. 93–9.

[88] Kenny concluded that Morton's identification of four major Epistles as forming 'a uniquely homogeneous corpus within the Pauline writings is a claim that evaporates on close investigation' (p. 114). Kenny showed that, if applied to the Aristotelian corpus, 'to use the last-word test as a criterion of authorship would lead to absurd results' (p. 115). Norman Thomson added more statistical evidence showing that neither 'the purportedly genuine Pauline Epistles' nor the 'supposedly non-Pauline ones' have the homogeneity that Morton claimed (Thomson 1989, pp. 8–10), concluding that 'Morton's submission that he has a powerful test for distinguishing some of the Epistles from the rest begins to look decidedly weak' (p. 10).

for sentence length distributions had changed considerably, being based on a more recent edition of the New Testament, although Morton kept silent about this. The discrepancies between the earlier and later figures are so great as to disprove Morton's claim that the variations in sentence length in different modern editions of a Greek text are statistically insignificant (Kenny 1986, p. 108). As for the undoubted variation in sentence lengths between the Pauline Epistles, Kenny argued that 'many alternative hypotheses would explain the data, including an absurdly simple chronological one', namely that, 'as he grew older, Paul grew fonder of longer sentences' (p. 110). Kenny did not argue this, but he showed that such a case could be made, 'merely to illustrate the kind of alternative hypothesis that is no less consistent with the data than variation in authorship' (p. 111). Those who use statistical stylistics in literary studies must always be ready to revise hypotheses, and beware of using 'statistically significant differences as a rigid criterion for variation in authorship' (p. 113).

The deficiencies of Morton's methodology emerged even more clearly from Kenneth Neumann's study of the Pauline Epistles,[89] which showed that Morton used inappropriate statistical models, and applied indices of style in isolation from other indices (Neumann 1990, p. 14). He based some arguments on the incidence of *hapax legomena*, generally deemed an unreliable criterion (pp. 24–5); his use of *kai* as a stylistic marker aroused much criticism, his statistics proving 'of little value' since he failed to differentiate between the various uses of the word (pp. 39–41); another common conjunction said to be a reliable index, the word *dē*, turned out to be useless (p. 42); the proportion of nouns with/without a definite article was also proved to be non-significant (p. 75). In sum, the indices Morton used 'are among the weakest and most ineffective stylistic criteria' (p. 214). As this brief survey shows, since 1965 New Testament scholars have delivered devastating criticisms of A. Q. Morton's methodology. Unmoved by their objections, Morton widened his scope, and in a book optimistically called *Literary Detection: How to Prove Authorship and Fraud in Literary Documents*, applied his methods to writers ranging from Shakespeare to Walter Scott and John Fowles. This book attracted the attention of scholars specializing in the statistical analysis of literature, whose criticisms exactly echoed those made of his New Testament studies: Morton's 'tests' simply do not work. In one of his case studies Morton decided to investigate whether the strokes that Sir Walter Scott suffered between 1823 and 1832 left any mark on his prose style, noting in passing Scott's journal entry recording that he had paid a considerable sum of money to his publisher, Robert Cadell, for 'emendations to the text . . . [of] "these

---

[89] Kenneth J. Neumann, *The Authenticity of the Pauline Epistles in the Light of Stylostatistical Analysis* (Atlanta, Ga., 1990). For commentary on Morton's work see pp. 2–4, 14–15, 38–44, 51–2, 61–2, 74–5, 77, 105, 214–16 (the book has no index).

apoplectic books"' (Morton 1978, p. 134). In other words, if his publisher corrected the later novels, Scott cannot even be held responsible for their language or style. Morton seems not to have realized the significance of this fact, still claiming that he could detect any stylistic change simply by taking twenty samples each from *The Antiquary* (1816) and *Castle Dangerous* (1831), and computing the frequency with which Scott used the word *but* as the initial word in a sentence (pp. 134–6). To the student of literature it will seem bizarre to take such a stylistic detail as evidence of anything, but the important point, as Barbara Stevenson showed, is that Morton's own tests were inadequate, failing to meet accepted statistical criteria, since seven of the twenty-six tests he ran (nearly 25 per cent) showed inconsistencies, whereas he claimed a significance level of 5 per cent (Stevenson 1989, p. 68). Morton, always flexible, disregarded his own statistical results, asserting that Scott's style had been unaffected by time and disease—indeed 'a leap in logic', as Stevenson put it (p. 69). Further, because the samples Morton took were so small, and his hypothesis so grand, even a tiny change in the data would transform his results.[90] Stevenson ran the chi-square test again on *Castle Dangerous*, supposing that the initial *but* appeared eighteen times, instead of the twenty recorded in Morton's sample, and 'got a result opposite to Morton's', one which would suggest that Scott's style did in fact change (p. 70). Morton has claimed that 'stylometry is a science and a powerful one' (Morton 1978, p. 39), and even that 'Stylometry is already *the most widely tested critical system ever devised* . . .':[91] Morton's self-confidence is unshakeable, but it should now be transparently clear that his method is unable to perform what it undertakes. The gap between promise and performance proved equally large when Morton attempted to analyse three novels by John Fowles, each written in a radically different style from the others, to prove that stylometry can detect consistent features of which the author is unaware. Morton attempted this task by studying the placing of ten common words (*and, as, at*, etc.) 'in eleven preferred positions and in 27 collocations' (pp. 143–6). However, as Stevenson showed, he 'was unable to uncover linguistic habits common to all these works, but that did not deter him from advancing stylometry as a valid

---

[90] Another instance of Morton having based large conclusions on small samples is his essay, 'Authorship: The Nature of the Habit', *TLS*, 17–23 Feb. 1989, pp. 164, 174. Here Morton blithely describes the 'advances in stylometric methods' that he had pioneered, again ignoring criticism of his methods. For this exercise he combined two techniques, counting both 'the total number of words in each sentence' and 'the number of nouns in the same sentence', without citing any evidence that these techniques could reliably identify or differentiate authorship. Having analysed a mere 'twenty-five successive sentences' from *The Revenger's Tragedy* and *The Atheist's Tragedy*, he confidently pronounced that 'Middleton did not write *The Revenger's Tragedy*' (p. 174). Morton assured readers that his 'new technique . . . can be taught, learnt and used within an hour or two', and 'stands on a firm foundation'. But his results here run counter to a great number of other studies of this topic, which use far larger samples, and with a much greater methodological awareness.

[91] 'Stylometry vs. "Stylometry"', *ShN*, 34 (1984): 5; author's italics.

test' (Stevenson 1989, p. 69)—indeed, Morton claimed to have confirmed 'the startling hypothesis that, for writers in an uninflected language, the placing of words in preferred positions or in collocations offers a range of tests of authorship' (Morton 1978, p. 146). M. W. A. Smith, having made a rigorous analysis of Morton's work, came to the opposite conclusion, that there is 'no evidence that once-occurring words in prescribed positions of sentences can discriminate between authors'.[92]

In *Literary Detection*, Morton applied his methods to Shakespeare, starting with *Pericles* (Morton 1978, pp. 184–8). Here Morton studied twelve common words (*a, and, as* . . .) occurring as the first word of a sentence, some frequent collocations (*and* followed by *a* or *the*, *by* followed by *the*, *to* followed by a verb, and so on), and proportionate pairs of words (*a* plus *an*, *no* plus *not*). He reported that in all the comparisons he had made between the two sections of the play (Acts 1 and 2, Acts 3–5) he could find 'no statistically significant difference' (p. 188). Morton's method, now taken up by his Edinburgh colleagues,[93] was soon applied to *Titus Andronicus*, thanks to the intervention of G. Harold Metz, who hailed Morton's work as if it marked a scholarly watershed: 'Shakespearean authenticity studies may have entered a new era with the advent of computer-assisted methods of stylometric analysis recently applied to English texts for the first time.'[94] Ominously introducing himself as 'one of the team of scholars preparing the projected New Variorum edition of *Titus Andronicus*', Metz gave an enthusiastic but woefully uninformed account of *Literary Detection*, trustingly informing fellow Shakespearians that the methods of 'Morton and his associates' had 'proved valid for Greek authenticity studies' (Metz 1985, pp. 149–50). Wishing to know what their approach could tell him about a play in which many scholars had attributed the whole of Act 1, and three other scenes (2.1, 2.2, and 4.1) to Peele, Metz, 'in an effort to preserve a "laboratory" setting', as he hopefully described it, had communicated the text of *Titus* to the Edinburgh group with the mere information that 'a question of authenticity existed' concerning Act 1. In response to his query Morton 'identified . . . seventeen compositional habits . . . in the two parts of *Titus*', and made comparisons which 'demonstrated that no statistically significant differences in [linguistic] habits occurred between the two parts of the play', so confirming the 'hypothesis of the unity of the play' (Metz 1985, p. 153). But, Metz added, since the 'doubters' of Shakespeare's authorship 'have . . . put forth a litany of

[92] M. W. A. Smith, 'Hapax Legomena in Prescribed Positions: An Investigation of Recent Proposals to Resolve Problems of Authorship', *LLC* 2 (1987): 145–52, at p. 150.

[93] See A. Q. Morton, S. Michaelson, and N. Hamilton-Smith, 'To Couple is the Custom: A General Stylometric Theory of Writers in English', Internal Report CSR-2278 (Edinburgh University, Dept. of Computer Science, 1978).

[94] Metz, 'Disputed Shakespearean Texts and Stylometric Analysis', *Text*, 2 (1985): 149–71 —its title should really be: 'Shakespearean Texts and Disputed Stylometric Analysis'—at p. 149. Metz had published an earlier version of this essay in *ShN* 29 (Dec. 1979), p. 42.

Elizabethan dramatists as candidates for his collaborator', giving special consideration to George Peele (p. 154), he had asked Morton to apply his methods to Peele's *Araygnement of Paris* (entire) and *David and Bethsabe* (three scenes). Then, like the Delphic oracle, Morton gave the hoped-for ruling:

c) All of *Titus Andronicus* is the work of a single playwright . . .

e) There may be surface similarities between Shakespeare's and Peele's writing, but stylometric analysis demonstrates that Peele's habits are radically different from Shakespeare's.

f) Peele was neither the collaborator nor the predecessor of Shakespeare in the writing of *Titus Andronicus*. (p. 155)

In addition, Metz reported, Morton had declared that 'the probability that the works of Peele belong to the same [statistical] population as the three plays of Shakespeare'—he had considered *Titus*, *Pericles*, and *Julius Caesar*—'is less than one in ten thousand million', so that Peele cannot have written any of them. Yet, Morton magnanimously conceded, 'the two writers resemble each other in many habits and so, from a literary point of view, to argue that they are similar is theoretically possible'. The literary critic should therefore take note 'that stylometrical resemblance proves nothing and only differences matter', otherwise he may 'easily mislead himself' (ibid.).

At some point in the communication between Metz and Morton, we can see, fundamental misunderstandings have occurred, which totally vitiated the 'laboratory setting'. The whole point about Peele's presence in this discussion is not that his style has 'superficial similarities' with Shakespeare's, but that it is strikingly different, and different in just the same way that 1.1, 2.1, 2.2, and 4.1 of *Titus* differ from the rest of the play. Literary critics noticed this eighty years earlier, and hardly need to be put in their place by 'stylometricians' who have misunderstood the issue. However, to Shakespearians unwilling to confront the abundant evidence that Shakespeare collaborated with other dramatists on seven plays in his canon, Morton's astronomical figure denying co-authorship in this play proved irresistible. Jonathan Bate, in his recent edition of *Titus Andronicus* for the Arden Shakespeare (Third Series), cited Metz's 1985 essay as proving that 'computer analysis' had confirmed 'that the whole of *Titus* is by a single hand. . . . According to Andrew Q. Morton, who undertook the analysis, the statistical probability of Peele's involvement is less than one in ten thousand million'.[95] To rest on such authorities, without checking their credentials, is a risky business.

Morton subsequently published a paper describing one of the stylistic markers he had used in pronouncing Shakespeare's sole authorship of *Titus*, its use of *hapax legomena*, words which occur only once in a text, arguing that 'while the number of once occurring words varies in a complex manner,

---

[95] *Titus Andronicus*, ed. Jonathan Bate (London, 1995), p. 83.

the number placed in different positions is characteristic of the writer'
(Morton 1986, p. 1). Morton first examined some writers of Greek prose and
the Pauline Epistles, looking at the first and last words of each sentence—
although he once again failed to disclose that Greek manuscripts have either
no punctuation or only vestiges of it—his survey purportedly proving that
'the occurrence of words not repeated in the sample, *when recorded in positions defined by punctuation*, makes a reliable and fairly sensitive test of
authorship . . .' (p. 5; my italics)—punctuation, we remind ourselves, having
been supplied by various modern editors, according to their own criteria. For
his analysis of Elizabethan drama, however, without explanation, Morton
abandoned this test and substituted another, examining the once-occurring
words in terms of 'the most frequent words in the text', postulating that 'these
words have the same number of occurrences to left and right of them and it
must be rarely that literary form, or any other influence, changes within the
compass of three successive words of a text' (ibid.). But Morton failed to give
good reason for thinking that studying such a phenomenon could throw any
light on authorship, and the basic principle remains, that although computers
can carry out such checks there must be some coherent rationale for using
them. Morton reported that he had applied his test to three Shakespeare
plays, *Titus Andronicus*, *Julius Caesar*, and *Pericles*, giving a total of 3,897
once-occurring words, which were examined to see how many of the eight
frequent words Morton had chosen (*a*, *and*, *in*, *it*, *of*, *the*, *to*, *I*) occurred to
their left or right. But if the methodology is the first crucial element in style
studies, equally important is the choice of sample texts, and it is completely
mysterious why Morton should include among his three chosen plays two
(*Titus*, *Pericles*) long known to be collaborations. Having assumed that all
three are wholly by Shakespeare, and basing his analysis on the punctuation
of the plays (p. 5, table 7)—which, like his Greek texts, was provided by
modern editors (not identified)—Morton compared them with two plays by
Peele, producing elaborate statistical tables with chi-squared data. His conclusion was that 'Shakespeare is entirely consistent in his habits of placing
once occurring words before and after these mark words', while the figures
for Peele, 'held by some scholars to resemble Shakespeare so closely that he
has been nominated as the writer of parts of *Titus Andronicus*', in fact show
that 'the probability that Peele wrote a play of Shakespeare is less than one in
forty million' (p. 8). The already astronomical figure of 'less than one in ten
thousand million' has been silently scaled down by a factor of 250, but it
remains meaningless. Once again we see that Morton had failed to grasp that
Peele's style is known to be very different from Shakespeare's, and that his
conclusion is as unreliable as the methodology and the text samples used.

Anyone familiar with the large literature on *Pericles* and *Titus Andronicus*,
which has used many different linguistic and literary approaches and reached
the opposite conclusion, may suspect that Morton's methods are fundamen-

tally unreliable. M. W. A. Smith, a mathematician who has done valuable work in applying statistical analysis to Elizabethan and Jacobean drama, confirmed that suspicion in a trenchant series of articles published between 1984 and 1989. Metz, the naïve layman, hopefully imagined that 'Scientific stylometry purposefully reduces the element of human judgment in determining questions of style, thereby bringing the adverse effects of human error within limited confines so that they too can be quantified . . .' (Metz 1985, p. 156— did he really mean to say that stylometry quantifies errors?). Smith showed that Morton's samples were too small, his presentation of data fragmentary, failing to document crucial stages in his findings, which made it 'difficult to deduce any reliable information'.[96] Morton's method is unreliable, to begin with, because it depends on stylistic features which occur infrequently.[97] It is also inconsistent, because Morton arbitrarily changes his method when it suits him. His figures for *to* followed by a verb in the two parts of *Pericles* did not quote the chi-square value (as he had done for every other collocation examined), which would have revealed an obvious difference between them. Instead, he simply proclaimed: 'Poisson distribution, no significant difference' (Morton 1978, p. 186). Morton several times 'changed the method for determining significance in the light of knowledge of the data', so violating good statistical practice, in which 'rules for deciding which method is most appropriate [should be] derived in advance of such knowledge' (Smith 1985*a*, pp. 4–5). Smith judged Morton's work to illustrate the general law that 'once the subjectivity of the experimentalist enters, the advantage of the objectivity of statistical interpretation departs' (Smith 1985*b*, p. 347), and he showed that Morton introduced several 'unquantifiable' elements which actually increased 'the likelihood of error' (pp. 349, 351). Having corrected some of Morton's errors and recalculated his figures, Smith declared his claim of Shakespeare's sole authorship of *Pericles* to be 'unwarranted'. In a further essay on *Pericles*,[98] Smith pointed out once again that Morton's presentation of his material has huge gaps, insufficient or missing documentation, major errors of computation, inconsistent methodology, 'haphazard methods for selecting data', and uses a 'limited and incomplete . . . test for establishing the accuracy of the method' (pp. 343–55). Having recalculated many of Morton's statistics, Smith concluded: 'when so many comparisons of samples by two or more authors' by testing typical features 'fail to reveal differences, the effectiveness of the method itself does become suspect' (p. 355). Smith's well-founded verdicts were that stylometry, 'as Morton himself applies it, appears to lack powers of discrimination'; that 'the criterion he uses for

[96] M. W. A. Smith, 'An Investigation of the Basis of Morton's Method for the Determination of Authorship', *Style*, 19 (1985): 341–68, at pp. 343–7.
[97] M. W. A. Smith, 'An Investigation of Morton's Method to Distinguish Elizabethan Playwrights', *CHum*, 19 (1985): 3–21, at p. 4.
[98] 'The Authorship of *Pericles*: New Evidence for Wilkins', *LLC* 2 (1987): 221–30.

distinguishing authors is unreliable'; that his method 'does not distinguish authors at all', and that it can lump together works by different authors, or ascribe to different authors two works by the same hand.[99] That devastating judgement of a professional statistician should serve as a caution to literary scholars.

The third play to which Morton's methods were applied was *Sir Thomas More*. Here again the scholarly consensus, that Shakespeare wrote Additions IIc and III, was rudely challenged when Thomas Merriam published an essay in 1982[100] suggesting that about 90 per cent of the play was by Shakespeare. Merriam adopted Morton's method (Morton even provided him with figures for *Julius Caesar* and *Titus Andronicus*), and he fully endorsed his findings: 'Dr. Morton has shown by stylometry that [*Titus Andronicus*] is homogeneous. His conclusion has been accepted by the New Variorum edition of the play' (Merriam 1982, p. 2); 'Dr. Morton has tested [*Pericles*] with stylometry and has found there to be no statistically significant difference between the first two acts . . . and the rest of the play . . . I have confirmed this' (pp. 2–3). Turning to *Sir Thomas More*, Merriam reported that he had performed twelve tests on 'proportional pairs, in which counts of selected word pairs as *a* and *an* are compared statistically', and thirteen tests on 'collocations, habits which involve a test word immediately followed by (*fb*) or preceded by (*pb*) another word' (p. 1), such as 'and *fb* to', or 'been *pb* have'. His conclusion was that 'the control for Shakespeare and the sample for More belong to the same population. This indicates a common author' (p. 2).

Once again M. W. A. Smith came to the rescue of Shakespeare scholars lacking the technical knowledge to evaluate Merriam's claims. Smith showed that Merriam's work on *Pericles* had contained 'very many errors', which also affect his work on *Sir Thomas More* (Smith 1985*a*, p. 6). Many readers will have been astonished by Merriam's decision to treat *More* as a unified artefact, given the long-established identification of additional scenes in the handwriting of Munday, Shakespeare, Heywood, Dekker, and Chettle. Smith, using C. J. Sisson's modernized edition (1954), performed the obvious step of removing their lines from the sample and testing it again. The result, on 'a rigid application of Morton's and Merriam's criterion for different authorship would indicate that Shakespeare was not responsible for most of *Sir Thomas More*'. Merriam's evidence was shown to be 'insubstantial', offering no 'grounds for advocating a revolutionary overthrow of a great weight of scholarship' (p. 6). Unsurprisingly, Merriam published an objection, which, Smith replied, showed that he had failed to understand the

[99] Smith 1985*a*, pp. 4, 5, 10, 144; Smith, 'Pseudoscience: A Comedy of Statistical Errors', *Style*, 22 (1988): 650–3; Smith, 'Forensic Stylometry: A Theoretical Basis for Further Developments of Practical Methods', *Journal of the Forensic Science Society*, 29 (1989): 15–33, at p. 25.
[100] 'The Authorship of Sir Thomas More', *ALLC Bulletin*, 10 (1982): 1–7.

point at issue. The journal editor then closed the discussion with the telling comment: 'Readers are at liberty to verify the theoretical soundness of the method used by Merriam for themselves.'[101]

Long-running controversies are usually of more interest to the participants than to anyone else, but the continuing exchanges between Merriam[102] and Smith do illuminate some issues relevant to the Shakespeare authorship question. Reiterating his demonstration that Morton's 'claims for the efficacy of [his] method were based on sparse and incomplete evidence', and that it was fundamentally 'insensitive to differences of authorship',[103] Smith drew attention to a basic misunderstanding in Merriam's application of a statistical measure commonly used to test a hypothesis about authorship—Merriam's hypothesis being that Shakespeare was the sole author of *More*. In using the chi-square measure, when values produced by testing word samples exceed a prescribed value, a hypothesis is disproved. However, Smith pointed out, 'the test works one way only', for 'when the chi-square is less than the prescribed value, the outcome is that no evidence is acquired. In Merriam's test of *More*, chi-square did not reach the prescribed value, so, far from confirming the initial assumption, his test obtained no evidence whatever to suggest that Shakespeare was the author.' Merriam presented his conclusions with a contorted double negative—' "I had discovered a remarkable absence of reason to believe that the play was not Shakespearean" ', but Smith commented that there is nothing remarkable about the result, giving the inherent limitations of the test (Smith 1992*a*, p. 438). Merriam's other defences of his thesis and attacks on his critics violated standard statistical practice in several ways: by 'subjectively [selecting] specific tests in full knowledge of the relevant data in the disputed text' (p. 440); failing to devise 'a procedure planned so that the investigator cannot influence the result' (p. 441); and making comparisons with works of uncertain authorship, when 'only works whose authenticity is virtually certain are appropriate for purposes of comparison' (p. 442). Smith's paper may be said to have 'resolved the conflict between scholarship and stylometry about the authorship of *Sir Thomas More* by demonstrating that the latter was inept' (p. 444).

M. W. A. Smith not only corrected the errors of Morton and his followers, but made valuable contributions of his own to Shakespearian stylometry. He evolved a much more stringent series of tests, which he applied to *Pericles*.[104]

---

[101] 'The Authorship Controversy of Sir Thomas More', *LLC* 1 (1986): 104–8.

[102] T. Merriam, 'Was Munday the Author of *Sir Thomas More*?', *Moreana*, 24 (1987): 25–30; 'Did Munday Compose *Sir Thomas More*?', *NQ* 235 (1990): 175–8; 'Chettle, Munday, Shakespeare and *Sir Thomas More*', *NQ* 237 (1992): 336–41; 'Invalidation reappraised', *CHum*, 30 (1997): 417–31.

[103] M. W. A. Smith, 'Shakespeare, Stylometry and *Sir Thomas More*', *SP* 89 (1992): 434–44, at p. 437.

[104] I limit this listing of Smith's contributions to works published after 1987 in the major journals on literary computing. Smith published earlier versions in *The Bard* and *Shakespeare Newsletter*, but they have now been superseded. See Smith 1987*b*; Smith, 'The Authorship of

His approach studied in turn the first words of speeches (Smith 1988), frequently recurring words from the remainder of the play (Smith 1987*b*), and consecutive pairs of words (Smith 1989*b*). In each case his procedure was the same, first selecting a pool of words which could serve to discriminate between authors. The frequency of occurrence of these words formed the basis for a series of tests in which both parts of *Pericles* (Acts 1–2, 3–5) were compared with two plays each by Shakespeare, Webster, and Chapman, four by Middleton, three by Jonson, one by Tourneur, the Shakespeare part of *Sir Thomas More*, and Gorge Wilkins's *The Miseries of Enforced Marriage*. Smith was careful to describe in advance his methodology, using contingency tables and the chi-square test, omitting certain classes of words (proper names, verbs, and pronouns), and specifying a minimum rate of occurrence of a word, at least three times per thousand, which would show 'whether or not a difference in its usage makes it a potential discriminator' (Smith 1988, p. 29; 1987*b*, p. 222). Smith set in advance an arbitrary value of 3.841 for a component of chi-square, in order to 'avoid any suggestion of subjectivity'. That arbitrarily chosen figure, he noted, 'could be replaced by any other value found to be more suitable', but any such change 'should not be made in the light of data obtained for the investigation itself' (Smith 1987*b*, p. 225)— a methodological error that Morton failed to avoid.

Smith then took the words which were found to distinguish a pair of authors and divided them into two groups, Group A for those appearing most frequently in one author, Group B for the other. In order to validate his method, Smith performed a simulation test in which Webster's *The Duchess of Malfi* and Ben Jonson's *The Alchemist* were 'assumed to be anonymous, with Chapman, Jonson, Middleton, Shakespeare and Webster as possible authors'. Once the ten possible comparisons were carried out, a clear affinity was shown between *The Duchess of Malfi* and *The White Devil*, making Webster the much more likely author than any of the other four dramatists. Similarly, Smith's test correctly identified Jonson as the author of *The Alchemist*, which showed clear affinities with *Epicoene* and *Volpone* (Smith 1988, pp. 32–4; Smith 1987*b*, pp. 222–8; Smith 1989*b*, pp. 114–19). It is most encouraging that these two independent tests validated the methodology. Smith then compared the last three acts of *Pericles* with the work of Chapman, Middleton, Jonson, Webster, Tourneur, and Wilkins, in each case showing that part of the play to be more akin to Shakespeare than any of the

Acts I and II of *Pericles*: A New Approach Using First Words of Speeches', *CHum*, 22 (1988): 23–41; 'A Procedure to Determine Authorship Using Pairs of Consecutive Words: More Evidence for Wilkins's Participation in *Pericles*', *CHum*, 23 (1989): 113–29; 'Function Words and the Authorship of *Pericles*', *NQ* 234 (1989): 333–6; 'A Note on the Authorship of *Pericles*', *CHum*, 24 (1990): 295–300. One non-Shakespearian investigation by Smith is important for its methodology: '*The Revenger's Tragedy*: The Derivation and Interpretation of Statistical Results for Resolving Disputed Authorship', *CHum*, 21 (1987): 21–55, 267.

other five dramatists. For the first two acts, the same tests showed that Wilkins's authorship was much more likely than Shakespeare's (Smith 1988, pp. 35–7; Smith 1987*b*, pp. 228–9; Smith 1989*b*, pp. 119–23). In a later note Smith reported the result of applying twelve new tests to the play: eleven of them showed that Acts 1 and 2 of *Pericles* were more akin to Wilkins than to Shakespeare or the other five dramatists tested (Smith 1990).

Throughout his work Smith drew attention to possible inconsistencies in his method, and was careful not to claim too much for it. Given the uneven nature of Elizabethan dramatic texts, he warned, 'any method for identification of writers of this period should . . . be robust, and accordingly, interpretation of results should be conservative' (1987*b*, p. 227). Another reason for caution, he suggested, 'is that, even in well-defined cases, numerical studies may not be totally objective by virtue of the vagaries of natural language' (p. 229). 'Identifying the author of an anonymous text by a statistical method', he repeated, 'is a tentative process; the findings are perturbed by the difference between literature on the one hand and, on the other, by the output of an imaginary random generator of words governed only by statistical laws' (1988, p. 36). It follows that 'infallibility should not be expected from purely mechanical models; they either suggest possible candidates for further investigation or complement existing literary or other arguments' (1989*b*, p. 122). Smith's lack of dogmatism, his readiness to unite 'purely mechanical' approaches with literary and linguistic analysis, and above all the rigorous and self-critical manner in which he applies his wide statistical expertise, makes his version of stylometry one in which other scholars can have complete confidence. As the later discussion of *Pericles* will show, widely experienced scholars in authorship studies have been able to build on and extend his methods.

Morton, Metz, and Merriam were not the only first-generation exponents of computer-driven stylometry to misapply these methods. Barron Brainerd, a professor of mathematical linguistics, published two statistical studies of Shakespeare which exemplify several faults. In one Brainerd set out to explore the relation between a tiny part of speech, the personal pronoun, and the three major genres within which Shakespeare worked, since he believed that pronouns are 'sensitive to genre'.[105] I cannot see any rationale for this belief, and the conduct of Brainerd's essay failed to produce one. In order to prove his point, Brainerd embarked on a dazzling series of computations. Along the way he performed a 'discriminant analysis'—'to objectify quantitatively a subjective classification' (Brainerd 1979, p. 9: that is, to assign the thirty-eight plays to their genres according to 'pronominal variables'), but discovered that his data did not clearly distinguish genres, which can only

---

[105] B. Brainerd, 'Pronouns and Genre in Shakespeare's Drama', *CHum*, 13 (1979): 3–16, at p. 5.

mean that behind each play must lie a 'second genre'. So he suggested the following 'subgenres': Tragical Comedy, Historical Comedy, Romantic Comedy, Tragical History, Comical Tragedy (which includes *Hamlet* and *Othello*), Historical Tragedy, Romantic Tragedy, Tragical Romance, and Indeterminate (p. 11)—Polonius lives!—but there is no trace of parody here. For each group of plays Brainerd averaged out his data to discover the 'genre centroid' in each case (p. 14)—which proves that anything may be computed, whether it is meaningful or not—and concluded with a justification for future research programmes which sounds unmistakably like one of the 'projectors' satirized by Swift in *Gulliver's Travels*:

> If the work started in this paper leads to the development of generally accepted objective keys to global genre, then it should ultimately be possible by assigning individual characters objectively to one or another genre, to arrive at such results as that X and Y are comic characters, while U, V and W are tragic and so on. Were this program carried to its logical conclusion in other areas as well as genre, we could possess a critical precision undreamed of in the past. (p. 15)

But one could also just read the plays.

In a second essay Brainerd attempted to use computer-generated data to establish the chronology of Shakespeare's plays. Anyone familiar with previous scholarship on Shakespeare's chronology will know how many different types of evidence need to be brought to bear on each other—bibliographical, biographical, historical, stylistic (using several criteria). Brainerd, however, thought he could do so simply by identifying 'lexical variates covarying with date of composition'.[106] Using Spevack's *Concordance*, although aware that it 'does not distinguish the various possible word-forms it concords' (Brainerd 1980, p. 222)—so that *might* can be either a noun or a modal auxiliary—Brainerd chose such variates as *could* (*couldst*, *couldest*), *have* (in 21 forms), *who* (8 forms), and plotted them against 'date of composition' (which he took from the Riverside edition) to yield a 'correlation coefficient' (pp. 222–3). Brainerd proposed to solve the problem of chronology by finding 'a test or calibrating set' of plays with established dates of composition, locating the 'predicator-variables' in these plays, and then obtaining 'predicated dates' for the remainder. This all sounds reassuringly scientific, and the statistical techniques are certainly very complex, but the study was vitiated by the author's reliance on antiquated theories about the composition and revision of Shakespeare's plays. He believed that *Two Gentlemen* may have been 'written in two parts in 1592 and 1593'; quoted Dover Wilson's theory that *Much Ado* 'has been revised', and Chambers's rejection of it (p. 225); cited Malone's theory that—presumably because it contains praise of the future Queen—*Henry VIII* was 'first acted in the reign of Elizabeth I' (p. 229). No

---

[106] B. Brainerd, 'The Chronology of Shakespeare's Plays: A Statistical Study', *CHum*, 14 (1980): 221–30, at p. 221.

scholar today takes any of these claims seriously. This union of outdated scholarship and up-to-date computing expertise produced disconcerting results: on Brainerd's findings *Richard III* would be moved from 1592 to 1596; *Love's Labour's Lost* from 1594 to 1601; *Hamlet* from 1599 to 1604—despite the fact that it already existed at least by 1603, when the Bad Quarto appeared; and so on. The drastic rearrangement of Shakespeare's chronology involved—in 1607 he supposedly wrote *All's Well that Ends Well*, *Henry VIII*, and *The Two Noble Kinsmen*—contradicts all the other evidence, and allows us to dismiss Brainerd's method, despite its technical sophistication, as wholly unreliable.

Yet, despite its obvious faults, in his long essay on 'Canon and Chronology' for the Oxford *Textual Companion*, Gary Taylor praised Brainerd's essay as 'statistically, the most sophisticated analysis of Shakespeare's vocabulary in relation to chronology', having 'tested 120 lemmata'—a technical term for the main entries in a dictionary—against 'what we know of the sequence of composition' and found that twenty of them 'had chronological correlations with an absolute value greater than 0.4' (*TxC*, p. 101). That generous evaluation typifies the bias within Taylor's survey of authorship studies, which gives a brief and uneven coverage of the varied criteria used over the last two centuries (verse tests; parallel passages; linguistic markers) while enthusiastically endorsing the newest numerical approaches. Elsewhere, in his survey of individual plays, he provided an excellent, detailed account of the many forms of evidence used to identify Middleton's hand in *Timon of Athens* (pp. 127–8), well-informed notes on the co-authors involved in *Pericles* (pp. 130–1) and *Henry VIII* (pp. 133–4), and a helpful (if tentative) discussion of the types of evidence pointing to Peele's share of *Titus Andronicus* (pp. 113–15). But in this essay on the canon Taylor placed greatest emphasis on quantitative methods, assembling a huge amount of statistics, including ten tables, seven of them computing function words, the eighth computing the percentage of rhyme and prose in each play, the ninth listing 'colloquialisms' in verse, the last summarizing four verse tests. Taylor's energy and enterprise in assembling all this material are commendable, but the data do not all satisfy the same criteria of empirical accuracy as the basis for quantitative computation. The range of material may seem impressive, but in stylometry, as in other disciplines, it is not the case that more is automatically better, since any amount of data will not be able to correct a false hypothesis. As Gerard Ledger has said, it is not always true that 'the greater the number of variables the greater will be one's success in discriminating between styles', for 'what really counts is the level of correlation between each variable and the differences in style which interest us' (Ledger 1989, p. 10). In other words, readers of stylometric criticism must evaluate the explanatory power of each stylistic marker chosen, and acquire enough knowledge to be able to judge both a methodology and its results. The more evidence we find that scholars analysing literature statistically have invested energy and self-criticism in the exercise, the greater confidence we may feel in their conclusions.

A valuable example of a long-term stylometric project applied to Shakespeare is the collaboration of Ward Elliott and Robert Valenza, the former a professor of politics, the latter a mathematician and statistician, at Claremont McKenna College, California. Over an eight year period (1987–90, 1992–4) Elliott and Valenza ran a 'Shakespeare Authorship Clinic', in which undergraduate students under their supervision developed a total of 51 computer tests of Shakespeare play authorship, 14 of poem authorship, and applied them to the 37 plays normally ascribed to Shakespeare. They also tested 27 plays sometimes ascribed to Shakespeare, and several poems of unknown or disputed authorship. Their detailed summary of years of work,[107] a long laborious process of trial, error, and self-correction, is an impressive document, both for its description of the methods used (Elliott and Valenza 1996, pp. 192–210) and the tabulated results (pp. 211–42). Taking the acknowledged works of Shakespeare as their baseline, Elliott and Valenza used and rejected 'something like 300 tests which did not show a sharp enough distinction between Shakespeare and other' dramatists, or which studied stylistic features more attributable to editors, such as exclamations and parentheses (p. 203).

These 51 tests, producing 1,785 trials, were organized into three rounds. The first round of tests included one checking what they call 'Shakespeare badges' or preferred words, against 'flukes' or non-preferred words, run as groups ('Bundle of Badges') (p. 196), and three 'Thisted-Efron tests', which measure 'vocabulary richness and author partiality to some rare words, but not to others' (p. 197). First-round tests also included hyphenated compound words, a typographical feature where the researchers recognized the influence of printers and editors, and run-on lines, where they did not, simply using modernized editions (p. 198). Among the second-round tests Elliott and Valenza studied contractions, confirming the observations by MacDonald Jackson (1979) and David Lake (1975) of Middleton's higher use of contractions. Their sample of nine Middleton plays, amounting to about a tenth of their collection, has three-quarters of the total uses of *I'm* and *you're*, and 95 per cent of the total instances of *we're*, *I've*, and *you've* (p. 199). Their independent tests supported Lake and Jackson's ascription to Middleton of *The Second Maiden's Tragedy*, *The Revenger's Tragedy*, *The Puritan*, and *A Yorkshire Tragedy* (pp. 199, 204). Given the high quality of the work performed by those two Middleton scholars, the agreement between their conclusions and those of Elliott and Valenza is reassuring, suggesting that

---

[107] W. E. Y. Elliott and R. J. Valenza, 'And Then There Were None: Winnowing the Shakespeare Claimants', *CHum*, 30 (1996): 191–245.

the independent findings of the Claremont group are based on a reliable methodology.

Their third-round tests included counts for six prefixes and six suffixes per 20,000 words, tested against several contemporary dramatists, the results offering some new tools for comparative analysis. 'Shakespeare used *ex-* words more frequently than Beaumont, Dekker, Greene, Peele, and Porter', and '*where-* and *there-* words—that is, *wherein / therein . . .*' more frequently than six contemporary dramatists, if less frequently than Daniel and Kyd (p. 200). These details, when combined with other known preferences, such as one for words beginning with *un-*, or ending with *-less, -able, -ful, -ly*, and so forth, could produce valuable stylistic markers. It may prove useful to know that 'Shakespeare's characters frequently used adversions, such as *look, look you, do you see?, hark / list, mark*, or *hear me*—to draw someone's attention to something', only Jonson rivalling him in this respect (p. 201).[108] It could be helpful to know that 'Shakespeare used some intensifiers, such as *most* (with adjective or adverb, as in "most noble") and *very*, more frequently' than his contemporaries (p. 201), partly for what it tells us about his characters' evaluation of events and states of mind, partly as another potential stylistic marker. The more such reliable signs we have, the better our chances of being able to recognize, and discriminate authors.

The wide range of tests used by Elliott and Valenza, even in this brief summary, evinces confidence that they have not applied some idiosyncratic and inappropriate methodology. They show an admirable open-minded readiness to adopt new approaches and learn new tricks, mastering Marina Tarlinskaja's quantified metrics, which included counts of 'leaning microphrases', that is, phrases having a 'clinging monosyllable' which loses stress by virtue of its metric position, divided into *proclitic* (to the left of the stressed word) and *enclitic* (to the right) (Tarlinskaja 1987, pp. 215–16). Commendably, Elliott applied this meticulous test to 3,000-word samples taken from Shakespeare's poems and plays, both early (the narrative poems and *Richard II*) and late (the *Sonnets* and *The Tempest*), in order to establish a normal range of usages for Shakespeare, carefully observing several methodological complications (Elliott and Valenza 1996, pp. 201–2, 243–4 n. 16, and Appendixes 4–6, pp. 236–42). Scholarly initiative of this kind, a pragmatic readiness to consider many different options, has been one of the strongest features of the Elliott–Valenza research programme.

Their overall results were also reassuring, inasmuch as 'the core Shakespeare plays had 1598 (98 per cent) passes out of 1632 test runs' (p. 194)—that is, they were consistent with one another within statistically acceptable limits, establishing a common authorship. Of the 34 rejected runs, a quarter were caused by *Titus Andronicus* and *3 Henry VI* (pp. 194, 211), a

---

[108] See also Mark Eccles, 'Shakespeare's Use of "Look How" and Similar Idioms', *JEGP* 42 (1943): 386–400.

result confirming doubts concerning the former text, at least. In their analysis Shakespeare's Addition IIc to *Sir Thomas More* scored many rejections, no doubt because small samples show more variability than large ones (their norm being 20,000 words). But if compared with a small set of 3,000 word samples 'its rejections would drop from 21 out of 51 tests to two out of 14 tests' (p. 195). That is a more comforting result, but the sample is still too small for reliable results. On whole works their results supported long-expressed doubts concerning several other plays, which were found not to match Shakespeare, including *1 Henry VI* (10 rejections), *Pericles*, Acts 1–2 (15), *Timon of Athens* (15), and Fletcher's portions of *The Two Noble Kinsmen* (19) and *Henry VIII* (16). More surprising, perhaps, is that Shakespeare's parts of those Fletcherian plays also attracted rejections (4 and 11, respectively), as did his ascribed portion of *Titus Andronicus* (8 rejections). Elliott and Valenza concede that these rejections may be explicable due to the smallness of the sample size (p. 195). Whereas their results 'are standardized for sample size, normally to 20,000 words' (p. 193), the average length of an Elizabethan play, their samples for Shakespeare's share in those three plays were much smaller (14,528, 11,953, and 7,789 words respectively). Another factor which could explain the uncharacteristic results for Shakespeare's parts of these plays is the well-known phenomenon by which writers collaborating on a play tend to adopt some elements of their partner's style. But it would be interesting to see what results emerged if this range of tests were applied not to samples, but to complete play texts.

The Elliott–Valenza tests are characterized by three basic principles: first, a 'clean baseline', that is, texts as thoroughly purged of dubious material as possible; secondly, a 'block and profile' method, comparing like-sized blocks to each other in order to establish an author's 'profile', his characteristic linguistic preferences; and thirdly, what they call the 'silver bullet' approach, relying on negative evidence to disprove common authorship, rather than on shared unique quirks purporting to prove it. Their results seem to me, and to others working in this field,[109] accurate and reliable examples of literary statistics, or 'word-crunching' as it is sometimes called. Of course, they do not settle the issue of Shakespeare's co-authored plays once and for all. Anthony Kenny concluded his stylometric examination of the Pauline Epistles by acknowledging that 'what is to be said [of their] authorship . . . is in the end a matter for the Scripture scholar, not the stylometrist' (Kenny 1986, p. 100).

---

[109] MacDonald Jackson has welcomed the results of their 'battery of tests', and commented: 'the failure of *Titus Andronicus* to meet the Shakespearean norms is particularly marked', especially the 'stratum that is labelled (probably misleadingly) "early", that includes Act 1', frequently ascribed to Peele (see Chapter 3 below). This stratum 'is largely responsible for the anomalous results: it is rejected by no fewer than seven tests, while the other stratum is rejected by only two' (M. P. Jackson, 'Stage Directions and Speech Headings in Act 1 of *Titus Andronicus* Q (1594): Shakespeare or Peele?', *SB* 49 (1996): 134–48, p. 148 n. 28).

Similarly, Elliott and Valenza concede that it is 'possible that people who read these plays, instead of just crunching them, can think of special reasons' why *The Merry Wives of Windsor*, *Love's Labour's Lost*, and *As You Like It* 'score so unusually high in Shakespeare-rare and Shakespeare-new words' (p. 204). I cannot think of any quick answer to that question, but I gladly agree that 'pure', or 'technical' stylometry, as we may call it, needs to be supplemented by a wide range of literary and linguistic analyses. To quote Kenny again,

> In the context of authorship attribution stylometric evidence should not be regarded as superseding or trumping external and internal evidence of a more traditional kind. The stylometrist simply brings his contribution of new evidence, of a less familiar kind, to be weighed in the balance along with indicators to which we have been long accustomed. (Kenny 1986, pp. 116–17)

In authorship studies it is essential to bring together as many different methods as possible. If they all point in the same direction, that can establish with high probability the presence, and sometimes even the identity, of a co-author. If the tests do not confirm each other, a scholar must revise his hypothesis or produce a convincing explanation for the discordance.

LANGUAGE CHANGE AND SOCIAL CLASS

All the methods in attribution studies so far discussed treat the words of the text as linguistic counters whose significance resides in the frequency with which they are used, or the collocations in which they occur. Such approaches are not necessarily unhistorical, since they do in practice recognize the meanings which these words had in Shakespeare's age. But attribution studies have so far made little use of the history of the English language, in particular the recognition that language change has a social dimension. The key point is that linguistic innnovations are mostly made by an educated class, responsive to outside influences and to social change. F. E. Pierce made several pioneering attempts to differentiate the language of Renaissance dramatists according to their use of Latinate word forms. In 1912 he showed that John Ford, educated at Oxford and the Middle Temple, used such words far more frequently than did the popular dramatist Thomas Dekker, and reminded his readers that

> a large number of new Latin derivatives had come into English during or shortly before the Elizabethan period. Such new additions are always appropriated first by the cosmopolitan aristocracy and the learned professions. Ford, the aristocrat and lawyer, would naturally be expected to use more than Dekker, the bohemian, the child of the people.[110]

[110] Pierce 1912*a*, pp. 141–68, at pp. 150–1.

No doubt other scholars produced similar insights into the relation between linguistic change, education, and social class, but it was not until much later in the twentieth century that these topics received systematic study. The new discipline of sociolinguistics, developed by William Labov and others,[111] has studied linguistic behaviour as it is affected by class, income, residence, education, and other social markers. In a pioneering study,[112] Suzanne Romaine applied this approach historically, showing that the same criteria could be applied to linguistic material from the past. The changes studied by historical linguistics, such as the shift within verb inflections from *hath* and *doth* to *has* and *does*, or the complex use of *thou* and *you* forms, can now be reinterpreted in sociological terms. Not surprisingly, urban English, especially in London (the only really large city in Shakespeare's age), was the leader in linguistic change, reflecting a high degree of self-consciousness about new fashions, foreign imports, technical jargon, and much else. In the intensely language-conscious 1590s any deviations from the norm, as defined by writers living in London, could soon be represented on stage, sometimes satirically, as Arthur H. King showed in his classic study of Ben Jonson.[113]

The value of socio-historical linguistics for clarifying disputed issues in authorship studies has recently been shown by Jonathan Hope, who examined five plays in which Shakespeare collaborated, and a further eleven attributed to him.[114] I shall draw on Hope's specific findings when I discuss these plays in the following chapters; here I want to introduce the methodological issues. In general, Hope argued, linguistic usage reflects social status, generational differences, and residence. Thus it is likely that 'in-coming prestige variants like "you" instead of "thou" are used more frequently by younger, more educated, more urban members of the speech community', while older, less educated, provincial writers will preserve traditional habits (Hope 1994, p. 7). So a dramatist like Fletcher, born in 1579, whose father became Bishop of London in 1594, whose uncle was a distinguished diplomat, and who probably went to Cambridge, can be expected to use more of these 'in-coming prestige variants' than Shakespeare, born in 1564 'in the rural south-west midlands', with his 'lower class status, and lack of higher education' (p. 8). Not all of these criteria have equal value, I would say. Going to university, for instance, may have translated some to a higher social status, but for others it rather confirmed the status they already enjoyed, and certainly did not privilege many poor scholars. Such reservation apart, Hope's use of sociohistorical linguistics convincingly differentiated several authors, and is the

---

[111] See e.g. William Labov, *Sociolinguistic Patterns* (Philadelphia, 1972); Jean Aitchison, *Language Change: Progress or Decay?* (Cambridge, 1991).

[112] *Socio-Historical Linguistics* (Cambridge, 1982).

[113] *The Language of Satirized Characters in 'Poëtaster', a Socio-Stylistic Analysis 1597–1602* (Lund, 1941).

[114] J. Hope, *The Authorship of Shakespeare's Plays: A Socio-Linguistic Study* (Cambridge, 1994).

first such study which arouses confidence in its methodology. Briefly put, he applied three grammatical criteria: the auxiliary *do* (pp. 11–26), relativization markers (pp. 27–53), and *thou* as against *you* (pp. 54–64). These are all well documented as subject to change in the period *c.*1590–1625, even though linguistic historians still disagree as to why and how changes occurred.[115]

For the *do* auxiliary, in present-day Standard English we recognize two norm or 'regulated' usages, in the formation of questions ('Did you go home?'), negatives ('I didn't go home'), and positive declarative sentences ('I did go home'), where the auxiliary automatically adds emphasis. In Early Modern English, however, the auxiliary was optional in such unregulated forms as 'went you (not) home?' and 'I went not home', while positive declaratives did not imply emphasis. These 'unregulated' forms were deemed non-standard by 1700, and already in Shakespeare's lifetime those conscious of changing usage may have avoided them (pp. 11–12). Taking texts of single authorship, and computing the proportion of regulated and unregulated forms in Shakespeare and six other dramatists, Hope reached the striking conclusion that at no point did Shakespeare's usage overlap with that of any other author. The regulation rate for his plays never exceeds 84 per cent, and remains constant throughout his career, while that of the others never falls below 85 per cent (p. 17). Here is a new and powerful authorship tool, which clearly differentiates Shakespeare from Marlowe, also born in 1564 but coming from a different sociocultural and geographic milieu (pp. 19–20). Date of birth, Hope suggested, is less important than a writer's birthplace and education: 'Shakespeare's south-western upbringing . . . makes him a highly unregulated writer; while Fletcher's more urban birth and childhood push him to the fore of this innovation' (p. 20). Indeed, this is one linguistic feature in Shakespeare which might have struck his contemporaries as old-fashioned.

Hope admitted that his second grammatical category, the use of relative pronouns, is not quite as revealing as the auxiliary *do*. First, relative choice cannot be reduced to a 'regulated'/'unregulated' dichotomy, as with auxiliary *do*; secondly, a writer might use one marker rather than another as a deliberate stylistic choice, as when writing in a formal mode (p. 31). The markers studied here (omitting *the which* and *whose*) are *who(m)*, *which*, *that*, and 'zero' (or 'deletion'). Dr Hope classified clauses 'according to three intersecting criteria: whether they were restrictive or non-restrictive; whether the antecedent was personal or non-personal; whether the relative functioned as subject or object of its clause' (pp. 31–2). Relativization in present-day English covers three forms: 'the man that I know', 'the man who I know', and 'the man (o) I know', the so-called zero-position. As we have seen, in Early Modern English this distinction was not obligatory, for a fourth form was

---

[115] For some of the many conflicting theories on the causes of these linguistic changes see e.g. Hope 1994, pp. 12–18, 38–9, 56–9.

accepted, 'The man which I know', freely used with both animate and non-animate antecedents (pp. 27–8). Two examples from Shakespeare show *which* being used with a personal antecedent:

> Where is that slave
> Which told me they had beat you to your trenches?
>
> (*Cor.*, 1.6.39–40),

and *who(m)* with a non-personal antecedent:

> the elements
> Of whom your swords are temper'd
>
> (*Temp.*, 3.3.62).

Two further quotations illustrate Shakespeare's use of *that* in non-restrictive relative clauses ('a relative clause delimits the range of reference of the antecedent'):

> I chiefly,
> That set thee on to this desert, am bound
> To load thy merit
>
> (*Cym.*, 1.6.72–4),

and zero in a subject position:

> I have a mind [o] presages me such thrift,
> That I should questionless be fortunate
>
> (*MV*, 1.1.175–6)

where we might have expected 'a mind that presages'.

Well aware that some elements of language were liable to alteration in the printing-shop (since printers in the sixteenth and seventeenth centuries not only regularized spelling and punctuation but enforced distinct spelling preferences), Hope checked all the plays which exist in both folio and quarto, finding 'no evidence that the editors or compositors of the first folio modernised the relative markers', with the exception of *Richard III*, in any case a problematic text (p. 33). His careful computation again revealed a consistent distinction between Shakespeare and his younger co-author. Fletcher's use of *who* and *which* in respect of the animateness of their antecedents is more 'modern' than Shakespeare's, since the sample analysed gives the following results: Fletcher used *who* with a personal antecedent 94 per cent of the time, Shakespeare 88 per cent; Fletcher used *which* with a non-personal antecedent 96 per cent, Shakespeare 92 per cent; Fletcher used *that* in relative clauses 91 per cent, Shakespeare 88 per cent; and Fletcher used *which* in non-restrictive clauses 74 per cent, Shakespeare 47 per cent (pp. 35–6). Having computed these differences, Hope candidly admitted that they 'are not great enough to allow their use as an authorship tool' (p. 36). However, compiling the percentages for the overall use of relative markers did reveal significant differences, although they were not explicable in sociolinguistic terms (p. 37). Where that theory predicts that the more urban, higher-status Fletcher would use *who* forms more often than Shakespeare, the unexpected result of Hope's analysis was that 'Fletcher avoids *who* and *which* forms in favour of *that*, and particularly zero forms', seemingly striving for the informality of speech (p. 38). While able to marry the insights of socio-historical linguistics with a rigorous statistical method, Hope could still attend to the particular qualities of drama texts. Although exemplary in his expertise with statistics, he was well aware that in many areas of language study statistical methods cannot be used: relativization strategies cannot be reduced to a simple binary pattern, since they involve several related variables.

His third category, the distinction between the formal *you* and the informal *thou*, is amenable to binary treatment, subject to some qualifications. Hope showed that Fletcher used a higher proportion of *you* forms than Shakespeare, another expectedly modern trend, but that both dramatists' usage was much less consistent than the auxiliary *do*, with far larger internal variations, making it an unreliable tool for quantitative treatment (pp. 58–60). The problem once again is the large number of social and psychological variables governing the use of *thou* in Renaissance English, which created a complex system, or rather 'a series of intersecting and competing systems giving different implications to the forms' (p. 57). A further difficulty, which Hope frankly acknowledged, is that the purely linguistic evidence here is complicated by the question of style. That is, many features of language in drama reveal the playwright's deliberate choices, depending on genre, characterization, and the constantly changing contexts in which the represented people can switch from *thou* to *you* and back in order to express intimacy, distance, anger, dismissiveness, and so forth.[116]

On authorship issues, as in other areas of Shakespeare studies, it has often proved tempting to combine literary critical and linguistic approaches in an undisciplined manner. As we have seen, in the Oxford *Textual Companion* Gary Taylor argued that several scenes in *Macbeth* had been supplied by Middleton, indeed he even made the blanket assertion that 'Middleton was

---

[116] The many linguists who have shed light on the complex principles governing the use of second-person pronouns in Shakespeare will be puzzled by Donald Foster's recent claim that 'Shakespeare, relative to his contemporaries, prefers the formal "you" to the informal "thou". Even Shakespeare's lovers prefer "you" to "thou" in their stage dialogue. Shakespeare generally reserves the informal "thou" for close male–male friendships, as between Mercutio and Romeo or between Prince Hal and Falstaff (that is, until the final scene of *1 Henry IV*, when the bond is broken, and Falstaff suddenly stops "thou"-ing Hal)': 'Response to Elliott and Valenza, "And Then There Were None" ', *CHum*, 30 (1996): 247–55, at p. 251. For more reliable accounts of this issue see essays reprinted in V. Salmon and E. Burness (eds.), *A Reader in the Language of Shakespearean Drama* (Amsterdam and Philadelphia, 1987), pp. 7–9, 142, 153–61, 163–79.

responsible for *whatever alterations and additions were made to the play*' (*TxC*, p. 543): my italics draw attention to the begged question. Taylor backed up this suggestion partly with literary–critical arguments of his own,[117] partly with statistical evidence derived from Roger Holdsworth's unpublished 1982 doctoral dissertation on Middleton and Shakespeare. This thesis was inaccessible to me, but Jonathan Hope consulted it, and reported on Holdsworth's suggestion that Shakespeare (born in 1564) was more likely to use the *thou* pronoun than Middleton (born in 1580). Taking twenty plays by Shakespeare, twelve by Middleton, Holdsworth found that Shakespeare uses *thou* and its contractions on average 135 times in each play, as against Middleton's average of sixty-four times, and that in Shakespeare's share of *Timon of Athens*, as he estimated it, ' "*thou* is almost three times more common" ' than in Middleton's share (Hope 1994, p. 55). These figures look impressive, but Hope pointed out that Holdsworth's collection of data for the 'T/V choice' was incomplete: 'his figures do not include forms such as *thee* and *thy*, and offer no indication of the ratio of T forms to V. He assumes implicitly that *thee* and *thy* forms will be proportional to *thou* forms, but this is not always the case.' Holdsworth counted only forty-three *thou* forms in *Macbeth*, compared with over 100 in any other Shakespeare tragedy, part of his claim that he could detect Middleton's hand in that play. However, Hope showed that Holdsworth's argument from these statistics was seriously flawed, in two respects: 'not only does this total exclude *thee* and *thy* forms, it makes no allowance for length, which is an important factor in the case of *Macbeth*. When all T forms are included, and allowance is made for length, the play does not, in fact, look anomalous at all' (pp. 55–6). Hope then compiled a 'T index' for Shakespeare's plays, counting all *thou* forms, dividing them by the number of lines in the play, and multiplying by 100. The '*thou* index' for *Macbeth* is 9, the same value as for *All's Well* and *Othello*, compared to 8 for *Julius Caesar* and *Measure for Measure*, 7 for *Hamlet* and

----

[117] For Taylor the 'likeliest candidate for extended writing' by Middleton is 1.2, which includes the captain's description of Macbeth's battle with Macdonald, and Ross's account of 'Bellona's bridegroom'. In his New Arden edition (London, 1951), Kenneth Muir briefly defended the authenticity of 1.2, against Dover Wilson's theory that it must have been written soon after the Hecuba speeches in *Hamlet*, arguing that 'the resemblance can better be explained as a deliberate attempt on Shakespeare's part to adopt a style suitable for "epic" narrative . . .' (p. xxii). Taylor criticized Muir for not discussing the possibility of Middleton's presence in this scene (why should he?) and for suggesting that Shakespeare used 'an uncharacteristic "epic style" ' (*TxC*, p. 129). However, Taylor foisted the term 'uncharacteristic' on to Muir, having seemingly forgotten the Player's speech in *Hamlet*, Exeter's narrative of the death of York at Agincourt (*Henry V*, 4.6), and several similar speeches in the early histories. Taylor went on to suggest that Banquo's account of the weird sisters (1.3.37–45)—'What are these, | So wither'd and so wild in their attire . . . ?'—'might be an addition, or a substitution for a Shakespearian original'. Where is the slightest evidence for this? None was given, but Taylor could still conclude, ominously, that 'the whole issue of adaptation requires further investigation, based in part upon a more thorough examination of the links between *Macbeth* and the Middleton canon' (p. 129). The word 'links' once again begs the question.

Coriolanus (pp. 62–3). Hope subsequently performed analyses of *Macbeth* in terms of two other sociolinguistic criteria, the use of auxiliary *do*, and relative markers, each giving results entirely within Shakespeare's normal range (pp. 104–5). It is most gratifying when ungrounded authorship attributions can be refuted by cogent argument and the proper use of statistics.

The ultimate address in socio-historical linguistics is obviously the author, the whole methodology postulating observable distinctions between writers according to generational differences and cultural environment. As Hope implicitly admitted when dealing with the *you/thou* form in *Henry VIII* (see Chapter 6), this approach needs to be complemented by others which consider linguistic effects as resulting from conscious authorial decisions. It is perfectly possible that Shakespeare deliberately individualized characters by their grammatical preferences for old-fashioned forms, such as Polonius advising Laertes to 'Give no unproportion'd thought his act' (*Hamlet*, 1.3.60), or Gonzalo's complaint that 'My old bones akes' (*The Tempest*, 3.3.2). Even Ferdinand's reference to Miranda as 'The Mistris which I serve' (*The Tempest*, 3.1.6) may express a respect form appropriate to a courtly lover's subservient position. Certainly status affects usage: Hope showed that the high frequency of *thou* forms in *The Tempest* is partly due to 'Prospero's holding all of the other characters prisoner', but also to the presence of Ariel, since Shakespeare prefers the second-person form for spirits (pp. 61–2). Almost the only factor that Hope failed to consider is the source-material used. Just as we know that Shakespeare's vocabulary was affected by the historical chronicles that he drew on, it may be that the various grammatical anomalies that Hope identified in *The Comedy of Errors* (pp. 40–2) are due to Shakespeare having boldly conflated two comedies by Plautus, *Menaechmi* and *Amphitruo*: working from Latin may have a distinct effect on one's English. Sociolinguistic theory assumes that linguistic habits formed by social and regional influences, being below the level of conscious awareness, will be constant in time. Hope's discovery that Shakespeare's regulation rate for the auxiliary *do* remains constant throughout his career 'confirms that writers are likely to be consistent in their usages across their careers, and that we do not have to take chronology into account' (p. 22). But at the level of style an author's conscious choice can blur the influence of biographical factors, reducing the value of the T/V distinction for authorship studies (p. 64).

Hope assembled and evaluated a vast amount of data, showing commendable tact in its application. Where some players in this game often use a single test, with monomaniacal reiteration, he argued that authorship studies should be 'cumulative, with cases to be built on a variety of independent tests, rather than just one type of evidence' (pp. 108–9). Hope frankly conceded that his chosen grammatical categories work for some writers but not others, a readiness to acknowledge the limitations of one's method which is rare in authorship studies, and arouses confidence in this book's findings. Many of the approaches evolved in attribution studies that I have described here continue to be used, having a proven validity, but Hope's application of socio-historical linguistics created a new tool which has already yielded valuable results for Shakespeare's co-authored plays, as the following chapters will show.

DATING AND CHRONOLOGY

It is a familiar phenomenon in all the arts that an artist's modes of expression change over time. Studies of composers or painters regularly divide their work into early, middle, and late periods. Anyone who listens in sequence to the string quartets of Beethoven will perceive enormous changes between the first set (opus 18), the 'Rasoumovsky Quartets' (opus 59), and the five late works (opus 127, 130, 131, 132, and 135). These changes can be described in technical detail by musicologists,[118] but are instantly recognized by an experienced listener. Similarly the paintings of Rembrandt, or Picasso, studied in chronological order, will reveal all kinds of change, from techniques of applying paint to overall design, which can evolve from simplicity to complexity (and back), including self-quotation and ironic commentary.

For any writer who worked over an extended period of time, we may expect that changes will be visible at many levels of language and style. In attribution studies, the value of being able to date individual plays, and so establish the chronological sequence of composition is that works of anonymous or composite authorship can be tested against the established development of the authors in question. In Renaissance English drama Shakespeare's chronology has been the focus of detailed investigation since the editions of Capell and Malone,[119] and in this section most of my examples will come from Shakespeare. Modern studies of his chronology[120] have synthesized several different types of evidence: the entry of a play in the Stationers' Register; its publication date; any historical references it contains; allusions in contemporary letters or other documents to its theatrical performance or existence in manuscript; and stylistic or linguistic features. Evidence from these latter sources are of secondary value, of course, but they can play an important role in confirming or questioning a date established on other

---

[118] See e.g. Joseph Kerman, *The Beethoven Quartets* (London, 1967), and Charles Rosen, *The Classical Style: Haydn, Mozart, Beethoven*, new edition (London 1997), especially part VII, on Beethoven (pp. 379–512).

[119] See Brian Vickers (ed.), *Shakespeare: The Critical Heritage*, vi. *1774–1801* (London and Boston, 1981), pp. 251–3 (Capell), 189–91 and 531–3 (Malone). This work will be referred to as *CHS*.

[120] Cf. Chambers 1930, i. 243–74, 'The Problem of Chronology'; J. G. McManaway, 'Recent Studies in Shakespeare's Chronology', *ShS* 3 (1950): 22–33; G. Taylor, 'The Canon and Chronology of Shakespeare's Plays', in *TxC*, pp. 69–144. For some reservations about Taylor's methods see my comments in *RES* 40 (1989): 402–11.

grounds. I should like to review some of the linguistic and stylistic approaches, with special reference to the dating of Shakespeare's contributions to *Sir Thomas More*.

Verse tests were the staple of chronology studies from the 1870s onwards, the most reliable data being brought together by E. K. Chambers in his two-volume survey, *William Shakespeare* (1930). Chambers summarized the work of a number of nineteenth-century scholars in a series of 'Metrical Tables' (ii. 397–408), Fleay ('corrected'), Boyle, König, Conrad, Pulling, Hertzberg, and Ingram, adding his own computations. This material was resurveyed by Karl P. Wentersdorf,[121] who used it to emphasize the regularity of Shakespeare's metrical development. But applying this data to co-authored and undated plays can be problematic, as the case of *Sir Thomas More* shows. In 1925 G. B. Harrison took More's speech to the mob (2.3.105–51) and counted its use of the 'internal stop'—that is, 'a line of verse within which a new sentence is begun', finding 10 such stops in 41 lines (*sic*), or a ratio of 1 in 4. Briefly analysing three other speeches of comparable length he concluded that the *More* fragment was closest to *Troilus and Cressida* (1602).[122] Unfortunately, in performing this calculation Harrison modernized both the spelling and punctuation of the passage, allowing the telling riposte of Alfred W. Pollard that the same procedure, as tested on *The Merchant of Venice* (1595–6), would place *More* closer to that play.[123] Chambers himself produced a more reliable analysis, observing that 'More's long speech shows a good deal of internal pausation and other variation from the early blank-verse norm'. Chambers computed that 'the 77 lines of More's speech, not quite continuous, from "Look what you do offend" to "momtanish inhumanyty" [2.3.66–151] ... yield 22 double endings (including runs of 5 and 4), 4 extra mid-line syllables, 16 trochees in the first foot, 6 in the third, 3 in the fourth, 8 tri-syllabic feet (of which one is harsh), 6 run-on lines, 16 strong internal pauses. This, for what it is worth, does not suggest the earliest Shakespeare' (Chambers 1930, i. 509).

Such precise analysis is welcome, but Chambers provided no chronological framework, perhaps expecting readers to consult his digest of metrical tables. D. J. Lake did so in 1977, suggesting that 'the verse style of More's speeches in Hand D . . . belongs clearly to the period of *Hamlet* and after. The whole rhythm of the verse—the frequency of anapaestic resolutions and

---

[121] Karl Wentersdorf, 'Shakespearean Chronology and the Metrical Tests', in W. Fischer and K. Wentersdorf (eds.), *Shakespeare-Studien. Festschrift für Heinrich Mutschmann* (Marburg, 1951), pp. 161–93. However, this essay is vitiated by several outmoded approaches to Shakespeare, both biographical (*Coriolanus* and *Antony and Cleopatra* are 'free from the pessimistic gloom of the preceding works', and show 'no signs of the sex nausea that pervades . . . the tragedies and comedies of the "pessimistic period" ': p. 179), and aesthetic (*Cymbeline* has 'poor—even faulty—dramatic construction': p. 190).

[122] 'The Date of *Sir Thomas More*', *RES* 1 (1925): 337–9.

[123] 'Verse Tests and the Date of *Sir Thomas More*', ibid. 441–3.

heavy interior pauses, and the lack of rhyme—should make this obvious . . .'
(Lake 1977, p. 115). Lake cited three 'objective features' to substantiate this
impression: feminine endings, alexandrines, and half-line conclusions of
speeches (or 'broken ends', as they are sometimes called). In More's nine
speeches Lake counted 'eighty full lines of verse; of these full lines, twenty-
two (27 per cent) have feminine endings; three lines (4 per cent) are alexandrines (*MSR*, 251, 259, 269); seven out of the nine speeches (78 per cent)
conclude with a half line'. Consulting Sir Edmund's metrical tables, Lake
showed that the first play to average 27 per cent feminine endings is *The
Merry Wives of Windsor*, with *Hamlet* a little lower; the first play with anything like 4 per cent alexandrines is *Measure for Measure*; and a 78 per cent
proportion of 'broken ends' is equalled by no play before *Macbeth* or *Antony
and Cleopatra*. The range of dates for *Sir Thomas More* on this verse evidence, then, would be between 1599 and 1606. Well aware that sceptics
would object that 'the shortness of the *More* text—eighty lines, only nine
speeches—renders these comparisons a little suspect', Lake then 'checked
every play by Shakespeare which is likely to have been written by 1599', looking for a passage which might exhibit these features of versification: but he
found none. 'Only one sequence of nine verse speeches in the pre-1600 plays
contains seven broken ends, and that is the deliberately structured set piece'
in *The Merchant of Venice*, that is, the night scene between Lorenzo and
Jessica—'The moon shines bright. In such a night as this . . .' (5.1.1–32). But
whoever looks at that scene will notice that whereas More's half-lines result
in dramatic pauses, deliberately created (I suggest) to show the mob slowly
responding to his words, the half-lines ending these lovers' speeches are
promptly filled with the next refrain of 'In such a night' (six times in all).
Otherwise, Lake showed, this scene, with only one feminine ending and no
alexandrine, is obviously much earlier than the *More* scene. Even the Forum
scene in *Julius Caesar* (3.2), taking verse speeches of Brutus and Antony
longer than one line, is demonstrably earlier in Shakespeare's development,
for of 144 lines 20 (14 per cent) have feminine endings, 4 (28 per cent) are
alexandrines, and 2 (17 per cent) have broken ends. It is not until *Coriolanus*
(1607–9) that we find 'a crowd scene with the verse characteristics of
Shakespeare's *More* addition' (Lake 1977, p. 115).

If verse tests from the Victorian era still have validity, so do citations of
parallel passages, a method widely used down to the late twentieth century
and beyond. For *Sir Thomas More*, the studies that I cited in Chapter 1 which
identified Shakespeare as the author of Addition IIc on the grounds of
parallels of language, especially thematic imagery, indirectly helped to date
Shakespeare's contribution to the late 1590s or early 1600s. The three closest
plays with thematic parallels, R. W. Chambers argued,[124] were *Richard II*

---

[124] 'Shakespeare and the Play of *More*', in R. W. Chambers, *Man's Unconquerable Mind*
(London, 1939), pp. 238–9.

(1595), *Troilus and Cressida* (1602), and *Coriolanus* (1608). The expanded range of parallels cited by Wentersdorf[125] run from *King John* (1596) to *Macbeth* (1606)—to give the dates preferred by the Oxford *Textual Companion*. Apart from a structural resemblance to the treatment of the mob in 2 *Henry VI* (1591–2), nothing in Shakespeare's scene for *Sir Thomas More* fits the date of 1592–3 which some scholars proposed for the play's original composition. J. M. Nosworthy subsequently studied the scene's vocabulary, taking twenty-six words from the three pages, and identifying their occurrence elsewhere in Shakespeare. To give some examples:

howskeeper. This first appears in *Twelfth Night*.
topt. Found only in *Hamlet* and *Pericles*.
removing (sb.). Found only in *Othello*.
shark (vb.). Found only in *Hamlet*.
ynnovation. Found only in *1 Henry IV*, *Hamlet*, and *Othello*. The phrase 'hurlyburly innovation' in the first-named is interesting in view of the cancelled phrase 'yoᵣ (warrs) hurly' in the three pages.
gospell. Used only in *Twelfth Night* and, as a verb, in *Macbeth*.
adheres. First appears in the middle period in *Twelfth Night*, *Hamlet*, and *The Merry Wives*. There are two isolated late examples.
Charterd. The only instance of 'charter' as a verb is in *Henry V*. (Nosworthy 1955, pp. 14–17)

Nosworthy made no absolute claims for this evidence, but since 'the majority of these words make their strongest, and sometimes their only, contact with plays of the middle period, . . . it may legitimately be claimed that the vocabulary of the three pages is entirely characteristic of Shakespeare's verbal habits for, roughly, the period 1598–1602' (Nosworthy 1955, p. 16). I have simplified Nosworthy's case, which provides a useful example of how vocabulary links can be used to establish a date of composition within a chronological range.

A much more systematic approach to vocabulary linkages was invented by that pioneering German scholar, Gregor Sarrazin,[126] who rightly described it as 'the first attempt to use vocabulary statistics to determine the chronology of poetic compositions' (Sarrazin 1897, p. 121). Sarrazin recorded what other readers must have noticed, that in his early works Shakespeare uses many words which do not recur later, and conversely introduces new words in his late work (pp. 121–2). Further, in each play there are words which recur once only, and are never reused. In *King Lear*, for instance, the words 'conjunct', 'dowerless', 'houseless', 'machination', and 'suspend' are used only in

[125] K. Wentersdorf, 'Linkages of Thought and Imagery in Shakespeare and *More*', *Modern Language Quarterly* 34 (1973): 402.
[126] 'Wortechos bei Shakespeare', *ShJb* 33 (1897): 121–65; 34 (1898): 119–69; all translations are mine.

TABLE 2.10. *Rare words and Shakespeare's chronology*

Play	Correlations with the four main periods			
Richard III	I. 38.	II. 30.	III. 14.	IV. 14.
Merchant	I. 15.	II. 24.	III. 16.	IV. 21.
Othello	I. 21.	II. 31.	III. 36.	IV. 26.
Tempest	I. 21.	II. 28.	III. 21.	IV. 32.

Source: Sarrazin 1898, p. 125.

that play. Sarrazin set out to identify all the words that Shakespeare used only twice (which he dubbed 'dislegomena') or three times ('trislegomena'). Using Alexander Schmidt's *Shakespeare Lexicon* as his source, Sarrazin compiled extensive lists of these rare words (1897, pp. 128–65; 1898, pp. 120–63), and tabulated his data in chronological form, dividing Shakespeare's work into four main periods, the first from *Henry VI* to *A Midsummer Night's Dream*, 'ca. 1588–94'; the second from *The Taming of the Shrew* to *Henry V*, 'ca. 1594–99'; the third from *Hamlet to Macbeth*, 'ca. 1600–1606'; and the fourth from *Coriolanus* to *Henry VIII*, 'ca. 1606–1612' (p. 124). Sarrazin then disposed his count of rare words across the four periods, showing a striking correlation between the vocabulary instances and the chronological group into which each play could be assigned. In Table 2.10 I have selected four specimen plays, one from each group, to illustrate Sarrazin's results. Sarrazin was aware of some limitations in his method: that a low number of instances could yield irregular, hence unrepresentative statistics; and that some word links could be due to similarities of plot or genre. But his methodology was sound, and much weight must be given to his conclusions that neither *Timon of Athens* nor *Pericles* was the work of Shakespeare alone (1898, pp. 119, 168).

The value of rare word links for checking questions of chronology was proved by Elliott Slater[127] and MacDonald Jackson, who showed that 'Sarrazin's data may be reworked in more sophisticated ways' (Jackson 1979, p. 149). Having recomputed Sarrazin's data into four groups, using a different chronology (pp. 149, 211), Jackson devised a 'vocabulary index' for each play 'by simply working out the percentage of links . . . with the third and fourth groups', plays belonging to the second half of Shakespeare's career, setting out his results in a table (pp. 149–50, 212). Jackson demonstrated the relevance of this approach to attribution studies by discovering two strata of composition in *Titus Andronicus* (pp. 151–4), his results clearly pointing to the presence of Peele as Shakespeare's co-author (see Chapter 3).

[127] See a series of articles by Slater in *NQ* 220 (1975): 157–63, 169–71; 222 (1977): 109–12; 223 (1978): 147–9, and E. Slater, *The Problem of 'The Reign of King Edward III': A Statistical Approach* (Cambridge, 1988). Despite his advocacy of the method, Slater concluded that it could not, on its own, establish Shakespeare's chronology.

TABLE 2.11. *Percentage of punctuation-marked pauses in Shakespeare*

Pause position after syllable	1	2	3	4	5	6	7	8	9
Shakespeare average for *Julius Caesar* to *Timon*	3	7	4	26	15	27	11	6	1
'Shakespearian' additions to *More*	6	2	2	26	15	24	19	6	0

Source: Jackson unpubl., pp. 5, 7.

MacDonald Jackson has recently used both vocabulary links and metrical evidence to test the hypothesis that Shakespeare's contributions to *Sir Thomas More* date from the early seventeenth century (Jackson unpublished). Using the data provided by Ants Oras recording the pause patterns of each Shakespeare play, in chronological sequence (Oras 1960, p. 68), Jackson concentrated on nine plays, from *Julius Caesar* (1599) to *Timon of Athens* (c.1604–5), calculating the average percentages for pauses after each position in the verse line. He then made the same calculation for More's speeches in Hand D's Addition IIc, and his soliloquy in Hand C, Addition III, using the punctuation of G. B. Evans in his 1974 Riverside edition (calculations performed using the manuscript punctuation, he reported, gave 'similar results, with the low figures slightly lower and the high figures slightly higher'). The results are presented in Table 2.11. Those figures clearly show that Addition D dates from the early seventeenth century. Jackson then performed a vocabulary test on More's soliloquy ('It is in heaven that I am thus and thus'), listing all the words in the speech that occur ten or fewer times in the Shakespeare corpus. Entering the number of links with each play on a chronological table of Shakespeare's plays, he found that 'the ten plays from *Tit.* to *MND* yield 19 links, the ten plays from *Rom* to *JC* yield 22, the eight plays from *AYL* to *Tim.* yield 34, and the nine plays from *Lr* to *H8* yield 20. The four groups are roughly equivalent in total vocabulary size.' Jackson then computed 'the figures to be expected on the assumption that vocabulary links are distributed by chance proportionally to the size of the four groups', and juxtaposed them with the actual figures (see Table 2.12). As Jackson commented, 'the excess of links with Group III plays is statistically significant—it is most unlikely to have occurred fortuitously. So the vocabulary of this speech solidly connects it with Shakespeare plays of the period 1599–1600 to 1604–1605.' As Jackson wrote elsewhere, 'the stylistic and sub-stylistic evidence associating the Hand D addition with the middle-to-late phase of Shakespeare's playwriting career is so strong' that we cannot reject this 'dating without also rejecting Shakespeare's authorship'.[128] In recent years authorship studies have developed far more detailed methods for determining linguistic pre-

[128] *ShS* 43 (1991), p. 263, reviewing Howard-Hill 1989.

TABLE 2.12. *Word links between* Sir Thomas More *and Shakespeare*

	I	II	III	IV
Expected links	26.5	23.5	21.9	23.0
Obtained links	19	22	34	20

Source: Jackson unpubl., p. 6.

ference, and with a comparable increase in methodological awareness. But, rather than overturning the authorship identification made by R. W. Chambers and Karl Wentersdorf on the basis of iterative imagery, recent research by Partridge, Lake, and Jackson has confirmed them. The *Sir Thomas More* Additions show how the varying approaches in authorship studies can and do converge, mutually reinforcing each other.

The stylistic markers that I have described in this chapter—verse tests, parallel passages, distinct vocabulary, linguistic preferences, contractions, expletives, function words—add up to a powerful group of tools for the identification of writers involved in collaborative plays. As we have seen, allowing for occasional errors and misjudgements, there is an impressive continuity of method over a long period, from F. G. Fleay in the 1870s, to H. D. Sykes and E. H. C. Oliphant in the 1920s, down to Cyrus Hoy, David Lake, and MacDonald Jackson since the 1960s and 1970s. The intensive study of linguistic detail accumulated by modern authorship studies has given that discipline a real scholarly solidity and reliability. Its validity, however, was called in question by Samuel Schoenbaum in a book often cited by scholars who do not wish to be bothered by arguments for co-authorship. This study of *Internal Evidence and Elizabethan Dramatic Authorship* established from the outset a cautionary note: ' Internal evidence is a limited but essential instrument of literary scholarship; our task is to recognize the nature of the limitations and to profit from the benefits it is able to confer when properly employed' (Schoenbaum 1966, p. xx). At several points Schoenbaum asserted the superior value of external evidence, even denying internal evidence any independent validity: 'External evidence may and often does provide incontestable proof; internal evidence can only support hypotheses or corroborate external evidence', and is primarily justified in Renaissance drama when the available outward evidence is inadequate (p. 150). But Schoenbaum's survey of the main sources of external evidence—title-pages, the Stationers' Register, the Revels Office-book, play catalogues, and other records (pp. 151–9)—candidly admitted that their frequent lacunae and errors make them unreliable witnesses. It follows—or should have followed—that internal evidence must often play a major role in attribution studies. But Schoenbaum's history of these studies from Edward Ravenscroft's adaptation of *Titus Andronicus* in 1687 to the mid-1960s (pp. 7–143) abounded with sarcastic dismissals or ironic praise of attempts to establish the co-authorship of Elizabethan plays, tendentiously described as 'disintegration',[129] and pouring special scorn on the scholars who cite parallel passages,[130] the 'parallelographic school', as W. W. Greg once called it. Schoenbaum criticized many of the legitimate methods used in authorship study, such as verse tests (pp. 4, 35–7, 41–3, 47–8, 52–3, 76, 184–6), although he was himself unaware of the important studies by P. W. Timberlake (1931) and Ants Oras (1960). Sometimes Schoenbaum endorsed the validity of a scholarly method, praising Willard Farnham's essay on colloquial contractions as a test of authorship (1916) as 'the most elaborate and carefully considered attempt up to that time to employ linguistic criteria of authorship' (p. 97). However, Schoenbaum ignored Farnham's result, which confirmed Fletcher's substantial contributions to *Henry VIII* and *The Two Noble Kinsmen*. Schoenbaum found fault with several other important methods in attribution studies, seeking to reduce or deny their validity. He expressed considerable scepticism about the value of iterative imagery (pp. 123–5, 186–9), 'stylistic evidence' in general (pp. 36–7, 119), and even statistics (pp. 68, 72, 76), actually praising scholars who 'disdained metrical and other quantitative tests' (p. 78). Schoenbaum seemed to want to disarm attribution studies of their whole methodology, dismissing many studies as 'impressionistic' (e.g. pp. 74, 75, 102, 116, 205) or 'subjective' (pp. 102, 218). But Schoenbaum's own judgements were equally subjective. He accepted very few ascriptions,[131] and rejected out of hand all the evidence amassed for Middleton's share in *Timon of Athens* (pp. 90, 94, 162, 206), preferring to think of it as an unfinished play by Shakespeare alone (pp. 61, 76, 135–6). He dismissed without discussion the case made for Peele's co-authorship of *Titus Andronicus* (pp. xviii, 113–14, 117, 134, 162), Wilkins's part in *Pericles* (pp. 44, 55, 89), and seemed to have reluctantly conceded Fletcher as the co-author of two plays, although he refrained from saying so outright.

---

[129] Cf. pp. 5, 10, 17, 27, 44, 85, 90, 101 n., 115, 123, 134, 162, 189–93.

[130] Cf. pp. 52, 56, 67, 75, 89, 91, 95, 120, 140, 189–95, 211–12.

[131] Of the plays he considered, the only authorship attribution based on internal evidence that Schoenbaum admitted was Shakespeare's hand in *Sir Thomas More* (pp. xix, 86, 104–6, 124–5, 134). He accepted, purely on external evidence, Chapman's authorship of *Sir Giles Goosecap* (pp. 69–72, 78) and Ford's authorship of *The Queen* (pp. 78, 84, 90, 194, 197, 201, 218). However, he rejected the strong case made for Ford's sole responsibility for *The Laws of Candy* (pp. 131, 132) and *The Spanish Gipsy* (pp. 90, 163–4, 171), and for his part-authorship of *The Fair Maid of the Inn* (pp. 92, 131–2, 165): see Vickers 2002, Appendix III, for a brief survey of Ford's involvement in all three plays. Having earlier accepted the case made for Middleton, rather than Tourneur, having written *The Revenger's Tragedy*, Schoenbaum recanted at length (pp. 199–217), conceding that the 'internal . . . stylistic and substylistic evidence for Middleton is extensive and varied' (p. 216), yet still denying its validity.

Schoenbaum's book emphasized the 'limitations' of internal evidence for authorship to the point where he virtually disqualified it. A typical sequence is his rejection of the case made by several careful scholars that Middleton and Rowley did not write *The Spanish Gypsy* (as the 1653 and 1661 Quartos declared), in which he effectively denied the value of quantified linguistic analysis, concluding: 'the play cannot be dislodged from the Middleton canon on the basis of subjective critical impressions' (Schoenbaum 1966, pp. 163–5). Defending this approach, MacDonald Jackson declared it 'an empirical fact that some linguistic features of the unaided plays of Middleton appear with such consistency in the early texts as to distinguish these Middleton plays from plays by other dramatists of the period' (Jackson 1979, p. 21). As for Schoenbaum's sarcastic dismissal of 'subjective critical impressions', Jackson retorted that 'the absence from *The Spanish Gypsy* of linguistic evidence for Middleton's participation is an objective fact of some weight' (p. 135). Anyone predisposed to share Schoenbaum's scepticism may be shocked to discover that, although he cited the essay by H. Dugdale Sykes ascribing the play to Ford, he did not deign to discuss the considerable linguistic evidence that Sykes produced. By such evasions scholars insulate themselves from recognizing that an area of knowledge has been opened up, with undoubted results. Authorship studies in the last forty years, I believe, have in many respects realized Fleay's call in 1874 for a scholarly approach that would be both quantitative and reliable.

PART II

Shakespeare as Co-Author

Introduction

Since collaborative authorship was standard practice in Elizabethan, Jacobean, and Caroline drama, it would be extremely surprising if Shakespeare had not shared this form of composition. The realization that he probably did so on eight surviving plays—*1 Henry VI*, *Edward III*, 'The Booke of Sir Thomas More', *Titus Andronicus*, *Timon of Athens*, *Pericles*, *Henry VIII*, *The Two Noble Kinsmen*, and perhaps one now lost—*Cardenio*—means that to enquire which parts he contributed to plays of joint authorship is not only legitimate but essential. Scholars who pursue authorship studies are still liable to be given the contemptuous label of 'disintegrators', harking back to a period of unbridled and unhistorical speculation, in which critics like J. M. Robertson attributed any part of any play that they felt to be beneath Shakespeare's superhumanly high standards to the intervention of inferior dramatists tampering with his texts. The follies of this school were clinically exposed by E. K. Chambers in a famous lecture on 'The Disintegration of Shakespeare',[1] and there is not much danger of them being repeated. But, of course, the very term 'disintegration' begs the question to be discussed. If critics attempt to deny the authenticity of some parts of a play known to be wholly Shakespeare's, on the grounds of alleged stylistic incompatibility—such as the Player's speech in *Hamlet*, which has been ascribed to Kyd, Peele, and Marlowe, among others—we can rightly label their work 'disintegration' and dismiss it without more ado. But if scholars analyse plays in which readers have long noticed major discrepancies with Shakespeare's language and dramaturgy, such as the opening act of *Titus Andronicus*, or the first two acts of *Pericles*, they are not 'disintegrating' Shakespeare's solely authored text but reclaiming the appropriate parts for their original authors. This is a work of elementary justice, to begin with, which will also sharpen our awareness of how Shakespeare normally wrote, and what effect the process of collaboration had on him and his fellow dramatists. As Peele put it in *Titus Andronicus*, '*Suum cuique* is our Roman justice' (1.1.280): that is Justinian's well-known definition of justice, *suum cuique tribuere*, to give to each man what belongs

---

[1] The British Academy Shakespeare lecture for 1924, reprinted in J. W. Mackail (ed.), *Aspects of Shakespeare* (Oxford, 1933), pp. 23–48, and in Chambers, *Shakespearean Gleanings* (Oxford, 1944), pp. 1–21.

to him. Such a study should properly be called not 'disintegration' but 'restitution'.

The study of Shakespeare as co-author poses a number of problems, beginning with the prestige that posterity has thrust on him. As Ashley Thorndike wrote in 1901, scholars 'have found it difficult to think of Shakspere condescending to write a play in company with another dramatist, especially when, as in *Henry VIII*, his part is somewhat the less important'.[2] But, he went on,

> This objection is simply another exhibition of the common fallacy of always regarding Shakspere as a world genius and never as an Elizabethan dramatist. Shakspere's own practices and the general practice of Elizabethan dramatists, show that his collaboration with Fletcher would be no cause for wonder. (pp. 35–6)

The unhistorical nature of this overestimating Shakespeare must be obvious to all, but such prejudices are among the hardest to uproot. Half a century later Marco Mincoff was making the same complaint:

> Anyone attempting to ascribe non-canonical plays or parts of plays to Shakespeare is faced with an even more difficult task than in other cases of doubtful authorship. Not so much because of the difficulty of recognizing his style but because of the tremendous body of prejudice one has to overcome. The canon of Shakespeare's works has been conned so religiously and invested with such an odour of divinity that conditioned aesthetic reflexes have been established in most critics which place him in a very special position—his beauties have received an additional glamour both through familiarity from childhood and through a constant chorus of praise.[3]

Writing fifty years after Mincoff, I can only echo his diagnosis of the ingrained resistance that still exists whenever the question of Shakespeare's co-authorship arises.

Shakespeare, like every other dramatist we know of writing between 1579 and 1642, would have regarded co-authorship as a perfectly normal way to produce a play. He, like them, would recognize the advantages for a young dramatist in working with someone more knowledgeable or more experienced, and for an older partner in having an energetic junior helper, more in touch with newer modes. As we saw from the general survey in Chapter 1, the chief writer planning a play would often co-opt other dramatists according to their special gifts, in comedy or tragedy, in plotting, or in writing set speeches. Each of Shakespeare's known collaborators, so far as we can tell, brought special aptitudes to their collaboration. George Peele (1556–96), his co-author for *Titus Andronicus*, was born into an academic environment, and

---

[2] A. H. Thorndike, *The Influence of Beaumont and Fletcher on Shakspere* (Worcester, Mass.; repr. New York, 1966), p. 35.

[3] M. Mincoff, 'The Authorship of *The Two Noble Kinsmen*', ES 33 (1952): 97–115, at p. 97.

distinguished himself in the world of university Latin drama.[4] His father, James Peele, was from 1562 to 1585 Clerk of Christ's Hospital, a London grammar school (then in Newgate Street) which gave scholarships to boys from poor families (as it still does). James Peele was well known as a teacher and practicer of bookkeeping, on which he wrote two pioneering books; he also taught writing and arithmetic and wrote City pageants (Horne 1952, pp. 6–17). George naturally attended Christ's Hospital for the standard nine years of a petty- and grammar-school education, and entered Christ Church, Oxford, in 1572, taking his BA in 1577, his MA in 1579, and continuing in residence until 1581. We know that Peele was active in university drama, for he translated one of Euripides' *Iphigeneia* plays (presumably from Latin into English, since only exceptional scholars in the Renaissance knew enough Greek to tackle such a difficult text), and he associated with three other Oxford neo-Latin dramatists, Richard Edes, Leonard Hutton, and William Gager. Gager (also of Christ Church), author of two well-received Latin plays, *Meleager* and *Ulysses redux*, addressed a laudatory Latin epistle to Peele on his translation of *Iphigeneia*, urging him to 'Go on binding the ancient poets to you', and reminding him that 'each of these languages [Latin and Greek] is beyond a great number of men' (pp. 31–56).[5] Peele took up residence in London, but maintained his connections with Oxford, being paid £20 in 1583 for helping to produce the plays at Christ Church (pp. 57–64).

One consequence of Peele's university education was a rise in social status. As David Horne observed, 'Peele went to the University as the son of a merchant and member of the London middle class. When he returned in 1581 to begin fifteen years as a writer of court poetry, pageants, and plays, he could call himself gentleman and join a group which regarded itself as inferior only to the nobility' (p. 65). Living near the Inns of Court in Holborn, Peele associated with a group of Oxford graduates also trying to make careers in poetry and drama, including Thomas Watson, John Lyly, and Matthew Roydon. Richard Stapleton's Inner Temple compilation, *The Phoenix Nest* (1593), included poems by Peele, Watson, and Roydon. Peele's first play, *The Arraignment of Paris*, was presented before the Queen by the Children of the Chapel between 1581/2 and 1583/4, and as a City Poet he wrote several pageants for Lord Mayor's shows, two of which survive (1585, 1591). Peele made the transition from the private to the public theatre with *The Battle of Alcazar* (c.1588), written for Henslowe and performed by the Lord Admiral's Company. Three other plays survive (*The Old Wife's Tale*, *Edward I*, and *David and Bethsabe*), and at least two are known to be lost (*The Hunting of*

---

[4] See David H. Horne, *The Life and Minor Works of George Peele* (New Haven, 1952): this is volume i of C. T. Prouty (ed.), *The Life and Works of George Peele*, 3 vols. (New Haven, 1952–70).
[5] For Gager and neo-Latin university drama see J. W. Binns, *Intellectual Culture in Elizabethan and Jacobean England: The Latin Writings of the Age* (Leeds, 1990), pp. 120–40.

Cupid; The Turkish Mahomet and Hiren the Fair Greek). Although limited, Peele's output covered several different genres: pastoral, melodrama, folk play, chronicle, tragedy. Some sources claim that he became an actor, but Horne's sceptical review of the evidence concluded that 'Peele, in common with the rest of his scholarly set, never lowered himself by treading the boards of the public stage' (pp. 83–7). Peele did publish several occasional poems addressed to noble patrons, suggesting that his ambitions were not confined to the public theatres, and he certainly enjoyed the respect of many well-read contemporaries.

In his preface to Greene's *Menaphon* (1589) Nashe hailed Peele as 'the *Atlas* of Poetrie, *and primus verborum Artifex*', praising his 'pregnant dexterity of wit, and manifold varietie of invention' (pp. 128–9). In Robert Greene's supposed deathbed pamphlet, *Greene's Groats-worth of witte, bought with a million of Repentance* (1592; entered in the Stationers' Register on 20 September), Peele is linked with Marlowe and Nashe, three 'Gentlemen, his Quondam acquaintance, that spend their wits in making plaies'.[6] The three dramatists are individually addressed, Peele being 'no less deserving than the other two, in some things rarer, in nothing inferior', but all three are warned not to continue writing for the common actors, who 'gette by schollers their whole living', and are now daring to usurp the roles of gentlemen and scholars by writing plays themselves—a clear attack on Shakespeare. This pamphlet was seen through the press by Henry Chettle, but recent studies of the two writers' styles have convincingly argued that Chettle actually wrote it.[7] At all events, a few weeks later Chettle reverted to this attack in a letter 'To the Gentlemen Readers' prefacing his own pamphlet, *Kind-Harts Dreame* (no date; Stationers' Register, 8 December 1592), in which he recorded that 'one or two' of the 'divers play-makers' attacked in it have taken offence (Chambers 1930, ii. 189). Chettle, claiming that through-out his writing career he has 'hindred the bitter inveying against schollars', apologized to one of these offended dramatists:

I am as sory as if the originall fault had beene my fault, because my selfe have seene his demeanor no less civill than he exelent in the qualitie he professes: Besides, divers of

---

[6] E. K. Chambers, *William Shakespeare: A Study of Facts and Problems*, 2 vols. (Oxford, 1930), ii. 188.

[7] See W. B. Austin, *A Computer-Aided Technique for Stylistic Discrimination: The Authorship of 'Greene's Groatsworth of Wit'* (Washington, 1969), and D. A. Carroll (ed.), *Greene's Groatsworth of Wit* (Binghamton, NY, 1994), pp. 1–31, 105–6 (summarizing Austin's work), and 131–45. John Jowett, in 'Johannes Factotum: Henry Chettle and *Greene's Groatsworth of Wit*', *PBSA* 87 (1993), 453–86, endorsed Austin's analysis (pp. 455–61) and added fresh arguments, concluding: 'On the basis of internal evidence, and taking into account the materials available to Chettle and the absence of any independent testimony to Greene's authorship, the *Groatsworth* must, to all intents and purposes, have been written by him' (p. 466). Jowett described the *Groatsworth* as a forgery (pp. 453, 477), and Chettle as a 'fabricator' (p. 473).

worship have reported his uprightness of dealing, which argues his honesty, and his facetious grace in writing, that approoves his Art.

From Malone to Samuel Schoenbaum,[8] biographers of Shakespeare have happily identified him as the writer so soothingly conciliated. But Lukas Erne has recently read these texts more carefully, showing that Chettle's pamphlet is in fact addressed to one of the three 'Gentlemen' writers singled out in *Greene's Groatsworth*,[9] and that these words were actually directed at Peele. As Erne argues, the *Groatsworth* opposed two rival groups, the gentlemen playwrights and the actors. Shakespeare is counted among the latter, whereas the pamphlet is addressed to the former, a distinction that 'excludes Shakespeare as a possible candidate' (Erne 1998, p. 432). Marlowe and Nashe were graduates of Cambridge, Peele of Oxford; Peele and Marlowe were able to translate from Latin; all three had a right to be called 'a scholar and a gentleman', indeed Peele signed some of his works 'George Peele, Maister of Arts in Oxford'. Erne points out that the anonymous *Parnassus* plays, written and acted at Cambridge around 1600, make the same distinction between 'the university' dramatists, or 'schollars' and Shakespeare, one of 'these mimick apes' (p. 433). As for Chettle's reference to 'the qualitie he professes', Erne reminds us that the word 'quality' did not necessarily refer to the acting profession, and suggests that it signified Peele's 'occupation as a writer and producer of pageants, particularly as a city poet, a reading which may be given further weight by Greene's preceding adjective "civill" ' (p. 438). In this connection it is worth noting that the Henslowe papers at Dulwich contain a letter from one W.P. to Edward Alleyn concerning a theatrical wager, and affirming that 'my meaninge was not to prejudice Peeles credit'. W. W. Greg commented that 'there is no clear evidence' that Peele was an actor, and had 'little doubt that it was of Peele's credit as an author that Alleyn had shown himself careful'.[10] Erne's thesis, that Chettle's remarks were not addressed to Shakespeare but to Peele, had been argued earlier by two considerable scholars, F. G. Fleay and Gregor Sarrazin. There seems to be little doubt that Chettle was praising Peele, not Shakespeare, for 'his facetious grace in writing, that approves his Art' (Erne 1998, pp. 434–8). In choosing to collaborate with Peele, then, Shakespeare was hardly 'condescending'.

Shakespeare's second co-author, the evidence suggests, was Thomas Middleton (1580–1627). Son of a prosperous London bricklayer, who owned land adjoining the Curtain Theatre, Middleton was matriculated at Queen's College, Oxford, in April 1598. He does not seem to have taken a degree, and

---

[8] Samuel Schoenbaum, *William Shakespeare: A Documentary Life* (Oxford, 1975), pp. 117–18.

[9] Lukas Erne, 'Biography and Mythography: Rereading Chettle's Alleged Apology to Shakespeare', *ES* 79 (1998): 430–40.

[10] W. W. Greg, *Henslowe Papers: Being Documents Supplementary to Henslowe's Diary* (London, 1907), p. 32.

a witness in a long-running family lawsuit recorded in February 1601 that 'nowe [Middleton] remayneth heare in London daylie accompaninge the players', a tantalizingly vague phrase.[11] Middleton published three poems when he came down from Oxford, and by 1602 he was writing for the stage. Philip Henslowe paid him for two plays put on by the Admiral's Men, first, *The Two Shapes* (or *Caesar's Fall*), which he worked on with Dekker, Drayton, Webster, and Munday, receiving a final payment on 29 May 1602; secondly, *The Chester Tragedy*, all his own work, for which he was paid in November. Also in 1602, it seems, Middleton had written *The Family of Love* for one of the children's companies, and went on to write *The Phoenix* (beween March 1603 and April 1604) for the Children of Paul's, the company for which he wrote at least three comedies between 1604 and 1607 (*Michaelmas Term*; *A Mad World, My Masters*; *A Trick to Catch the Old One*). In 1606 he wrote *The Viper and Her Brood* (now lost) for the Children of the Chapel, and when the Children of Paul's collapsed in 1606 some of his plays were published.

In his twenties Middleton had been one of the principal playwrights of the children's companies, and he soon reached a similar position with the adult troupes. In about 1604 he helped Dekker with *The Honest Whore* for the Admiral's Men—now renamed Prince Henry's—and between 1606 and 1608 he shifted permanently to the adult players, writing *The Revenger's Tragedy* (*c.*1606–7) for the King's Men, *The Roaring Girl* (*c.*1604–8, with Dekker) for Prince Henry's Men, and *A Chaste Maid in Cheapside* (*c.*1611) for the Lady Elizabeth's. Middleton was one of the leading dramatists of the new city comedies,[12] and also excelled in tragedy. In 1611 he wrote *The Second Maiden's Tragedy* for the King's Men, 'and for a decade thereafter he seems to have worked chiefly for this company, the most distinguished and most successful one in London, the company of Shakespeare and Fletcher. Several of his King's plays—*The Witch* [*c.*1610–16] and *The Widow* [*c.*1616], for example—are rather more in Fletcher's manner than his own, but from his point of view this can scarcely have been a fault. He was deliberately adapting himself to changing tastes . . .' (Barker 1958, p. 13). When Shakespeare came to write *Timon of Athens* in about 1606, a tragedy with a strong satirical element, Middleton was a most appropriate writing partner.

Shakespeare's next co-author, as far as we can tell, was George Wilkins (*c.*1578–1618), about whom little is known.[13] He was probably the son of

    [11] R. H. Barker, *Thomas Middleton* (New York, 1958), p. 8.
    [12] See Brian Gibbons, *Jacobean City Comedy* (rev. edn., London, 1980); A. Covatta, *Thomas Middleton's City Comedies* (Lewisburg, Pa., 1973).
    [13] The main information about Wilkins's life was assembled by Roger Prior: R. Prior, 'The Life of George Wilkins', *ShS* 25 (1972): 137–52; and 'George Wilkins and the Young Heir', *ShS* 29 (1976): 33–9. See also Mark Eccles, 'George Wilkins', *NQ* 220 (1975): 250–2, and 'Brief Lives: Tudor and Stuart Authors', *SP* 79 (1982), 'Texts and Studies', p. 131. In 1612 Wilkins was described as 'of the Age of thirtye Syxe yeres or th[r] aboutes' (Prior 1972, p. 138); in 1614 he was said to be 'aged 40 yeres or thereaboutes' (Prior 1976, p. 37).

'George Wilkins, the Poet', who died in 1603. Wilkins kept a tavern (or was it a brothel?) in Turmill Street, Clerkenwell, an area notorious for whores and thieves, and he led a disreputable existence, being involved in several law-suits. In 1602 he was charged with keeping the peace, and between 1610 and 1618 he is mentioned in the Middlesex sessions records in no fewer than eighteen cases, accused of assault on women (twice), and associating with whores, who were also charged with theft. One of the few law cases where Wilkins appeared not in the dock, but as a witness, was in 1612, in the quarrel between Stephen Belott and Christopher Mountjoy, two French Protestant wig-makers, for non-payment of a dowry. 'Both Shakespeare and George Wilkins gave depositions. Shakespeare had lived in Mountjoy's house, and testified that he had known Belott and Mountjoy for ten years "or thereabouts". Wilkins had known them for seven years' (Prior 1972, p. 138).

Wilkins emerged as a writer in 1606, with an English version of Justinian, *The Historie of Iustine*, most of which is copied from an earlier translation by Arthur Golding. Wilkins published a pamphlet, *The Three Miseries of Barbary* (c.1606–7), and one play of his own composition, *The Miseries of Enforced Marriage* (1607). With Dekker he wrote part of a jest-book, *Jests to Make You Merrie* (1607), and he contributed some scenes to *The Travels of The Three English Brothers* (1607), a play written in collaboration with Day and Rowley. In 1608 Wilkins published *The Painful Adventures of Pericles Prince of Tyre*, a novel based partly on Laurence Twine, *The Patterne of Paineful Adventures* (c.1594; 1607), and partly on the play *Pericles*, which was written and performed c.1607–8, but not published until 1609. Many commentators have wondered why Shakespeare should have chosen Wilkins as a co-author, and it seems to me that Ernst Honigmann provided a convinc-ing explanation when defending the ascription to Wilkins of *The Historie of Justine*, made by the editors of the *Short Title Catalogue*. As Honigmann pointed out,[14] *Justine* is 'a narrative dealing with the same historical period as the unhistorical *Pericles*', Antiochus the Great figuring largely in both works, and it shares with the play 'the same geographical centre (the eastern Mediterranean), the same literary atmosphere (the history specializes in tales of violence, shipwrecks, incest, brothels, sudden reversals, etc.), and some names not found in the *Apollonius* sources of the story . . . such as Pericles and Lysimachus' (Honigmann 1965, p. 196). Adding *Justine* to his canon helps to define 'Wilkins's special interest in Mediterranean histories: *Three Miseries of Barbary*, *The Travels of the Three English Brothers*, *Pericles* (the novel) and *Justine* all being located in the same area, it becomes more likely that *Pericles* the play originated with Wilkins too—rather than that he fin-ished a draft by Shakespeare' (pp. 196–7). Honigmann's indication of this 'special interest' may explain Shakespeare's choice of Wilkins as a co-author. Since Shakespeare at this time was evidently returning to themes drawn from

[14] E. A. J. Honigmann, *The Stability of Shakespeare's Text* (London, 1965).

Greek and post-classical romance, which had figured in his earlier work—shipwrecks, separation, danger, loss, family reunion—it may be that Wilkins, as the current specialist in 'the eastern Mediterranean' and its adventures, seemed the most suitable dramatist to work with.

No mystery surrounds Shakespeare's choice of John Fletcher (1579–1625), who, in 1613, by the time they worked together on *Henry VIII* and *The Two Noble Kinsmen*, 'was one of the most prominent dramatists' of the younger generation (Thorndike 1901, p. 35). His father, Richard Fletcher, had been successively Master of Bene't College (now Corpus Christi), Cambridge, chaplain-in-ordinary to Queen Elizabeth, Bishop of Bristol, Worcester, and then London (1595). But soon after this prestigious appointment he fell into the Queen's disfavour for remarrying after his first wife died (widowers in high ecclesiastical office were supposed to set a good example by remaining celibate). He was suspended from office and died in debt.[15] It had long been assumed that Fletcher attended his father's college in Cambridge, but recently Nina Taunton has shown that no documentary evidence of his matriculation or graduation exists.[16] Wherever Fletcher was educated, he acquired a thorough knowledge of rhetoric,[17] and learned enough Latin to be able to make use of the Senecan *controversiae* for the plots of many plays.[18] Fletcher's first theatre experience came when he worked with Francis Beaumont on *The Woman Hater* (*c*.1606–7), written for the Children of St Paul's, Fletcher apparently revising Beaumont's work.[19] Together Beaumont and Fletcher produced *Cupid's Revenge* (*c*.1608) and *The Scornful Lady* for the Queen's Revels, who performed at the Blackfriars Theatre. For The King's Men they wrote a whole series of successful plays, including *Philaster* (1609), *The Maid's Tragedy* (1610), and *A King and No King* (1611). Fletcher published *The Faithful Shepherdess*, a tragicomedy (performed by the Queen's Revels) in about 1608, and several other plays of his sole composition before and after Beaumont's withdrawal from the theatre in 1613: *Monsieur Thomas* (*c*.1611), *The Night Walker* (*c*.1611), *The Woman's Prize* (*c*.1611), *The Captain* (1612), *Bonduca* (*c*.1613), *Valentinian* (*c*.1614), and *Wit Without Money* (*c*.1614). As G. E. Bentley pointed out, Shakespeare's company seems to have secured exclusive rights to Fletcher's services when they began acting

---

[15] G. McMullan, *The Politics of Unease in the Plays of John Fletcher* (Amherst, Mass., 1994), pp. 7–10.

[16] 'Did John Fletcher the Playwright Go to University?', *NQ* 235 (1990): 170–2. McMullan (1994, p. 277 n. 21) says that Taunton 'attempts (unconvincingly) to show that the evidence for Fletcher's matriculation at Bene't college is inadequate': if he has any better evidence he should cite it.

[17] C. Hoy, 'The Language of Fletcherian Tragicomedy', in J. C. Gray (ed.), *Mirror up to Shakespeare* (Toronto and London, 1984), pp. 99–113.

[18] E. M. Waith, *The Pattern of Tragicomedy in Beaumont and Fletcher* (New Haven, 1952; repr. Hamden, Conn., 1969).

[19] C. Hoy, 'The Shares of Fletcher and his Collaborators in the Beaumont and Fletcher Canon (III),' *SB* 11 (1958): 85–106, at pp. 98–9.

at the Blackfriars Theatre, late in 1609 or early in 1610.[20] Fletcher belonged to the social class that frequented the more exclusive indoor theatres, and he was a leading figure in the evolution of tragicomedy, a new genre that shared certain features with romance. As Bentley argued, writing for the private theatres affected both dramatists' work (Bentley 1948, pp. 47–8), and may have been a decisive stimulus on Shakespeare's three late Romances. Fletcher had been working for the King's Men since 1608, and his credentials as co-author in 1612–13, when they worked together on *Henry VIII*, *The Two Noble Kinsmen*, and (perhaps) *Cardenio*, could hardly have been better.

This brief account of the dramatists who have been identified as Shakespeare's co-authors shows that each had practical experience of writing for the theatre, in a range of genres and for a variety of companies, and that each had specific capabilities. We know frustratingly little about Peele's career, but the other three had all taken part in collaborations before working with Shakespeare. In this book I focus on the five plays he wrote with them, between about 1593 and 1613, since each dramatist produced enough work independently of Shakespeare to provide adequate points of comparison. If we can show what their language, characterization, and dramaturgy was like working without Shakespeare, we can identify with more certainty those parts of plays that they produced jointly.

As for two other plays in which Shakespeare was involved as co-author, *1 Henry VI* and *Edward III*, scholarship has yet to produce convincing candidates for his partners. For *Edward III*, I agree with the scholars who have attributed to Shakespeare three scenes from the romantic subplot, involving the King's abortive love for the Countess of Salisbury (1.2, 2.1, 2.2), and one from the martial main plot (4.4).[21] But the co-author's identity remains a mystery: he made diligent use of the sources, but his verse style lacks the flexibility, expressiveness, and wit that we find in Shakespeare's. *1 Henry VI* has been a text of suspect authorship ever since 1787, when Edmond Malone published *A Dissertation on the Three Parts of 'Henry VI', tending to show that those plays were not written originally by Shakespeare* (CHS, vi. 521). Scholars soon reclaimed Parts 2 and 3 as authentically Shakespearian, but Part 1 has long been doubted. A recent study by Gary Taylor has made a fresh evaluation,[22] using a number of linguistic markers—the spellings 'O' or 'Oh',

---

[20] G. E. Bentley, 'Shakespeare and the Blackfriars Theatre', *ShS* 1 (1948): 38–50.

[21] For Shakespeare's part in *Edward III*, Kenneth Muir's two essays in *Shakespeare as Collaborator* (London, 1960), pp. 10–55, are still a useful starting-point, followed by Giorgio Melchiori's edition, *King Edward III* (Cambridge, 1998), subject to some criticisms I expressed in *Yearbook of English Studies*, 30 (1999), pp. 301–2. One of Shakespeare's scenes, giving a demonstration of how to write love-poetry, is treated as a practical exercise in literary criticism and included in Vickers 1999, pp. 325–32.

[22] G. Taylor, 'Shakespeare and Others: The Authorship of *Henry the Sixth, Part One*', *MRDE* 7 (1995): 145–205.

Pucell or *Puzell*; stage directions (especially those using the direction 'here'); the obsolete *-eth* inflection; the use of *ye*; the contraction *ne'er*; the presence of round brackets; the variant forms *among* and *amongst*, *betwixt* and *between*; the use of compound adjectives; feminine endings and medial pauses; and the pronunciation of *Orleans* and *Henry* as disyllabic or trisyllabic (Taylor 1995, pp. 153–69). Taylor concluded that Part 1 is not 'linguistically . . . of one piece', but that four distinct styles can be distinguished: 'Z'—whom he subsequently identified with Thomas Nashe—wrote Act 1; Shakespeare wrote Act 2, scene 4, and 4.2–4.7.32. According to Taylor, two unidentified dramatists completed the play: 'W' wrote 2.1–2.3, 2.5, and 4.1; 'Y' wrote Acts 3 and 5. For the ascriptions, Taylor made additional use of parallel passages and specific linguistic evidence in order to identify Nashe (pp. 174–7), and Shakespeare (pp. 182–6, 189–94). Obviously, more work is needed to check these ascriptions, but Taylor's essay may provide a firm base for future studies.[23]

   One of the striking discoveries in my work on the five co-authored plays discussed here is how often recent approaches, using new methods, have confirmed authorship divisions originally made on stylistic evidence, supplemented by verse tests. These identifications were made by experienced readers of Renaissance drama: Taylor rightly praised the 'critical acumen' of F. G. Fleay, who in 1876 attributed 2.4 and Talbot's death sequence (4.2–4.7) to Shakespeare (p. 173), and also recorded that Marco Mincoff[24] had ascribed the same sequence to Shakespeare in 1976 'through stylistic analysis alone' (p. 164). Taylor noted, further, that in 1935 Archibald Slater had attributed Act 1 to Nashe, after 'an analysis of the characteristics (chiefly the faults) of Nashe's verse'. The great Nashe editor, R. B. McKerrow, in the introduction to the unpublished first volume of his projected Oxford edition of Shakespeare's *Complete Works* (now in the Bodleian Library), endorsed the attribution. As Taylor observed, 'McKerrow's endorsement of [Slater's] judgment of Nashe's verse style provides a comforting confirmation that the statistics are compatible with the intuitions of a practiced and perceptive reader' (p. 177). My own discussion of these co-authored plays aims to unite many different approaches. As the following pages will show, authorship studies have had a long history but are continuously evolving, producing new and more varied methods, and future researchers may yet identify the dramatists who shared the writing of these two plays with Shakespeare.

---

[23] However, Taylor's claimed list of parallels between *1 Henry VI* and the anonymous *Edmund Ironside* (pp. 180–1) is rather naïve. Many other parallels can be found in Elizabethan drama, as the Chadwyck–Healey database will prove, for such phrases as 'true subject', 'base . . . peasant', 'loss of . . . life', 'to thy cost', 'laughest thou', 'of force', 'plighted faith', 'lawful king', 'with your patience', and 'conclude a peace'. The dozens of instances that can be found include many from anonymous plays.

[24] Marco Mincoff, *Shakespeare: The First Steps* (Sofia, 1976), a sensitive study of 'the development of Shakespeare's craftsmanship both as dramatist and poet' (p. 7).

In each of the chapters that follow, my discussion will be largely chronological, documenting the first recognition of anomalous elements in the five plays concerned, and the forms taken by the debate over Shakespeare's possible co-authors. This arrangement has two advantages: first, it allows us to trace the development of knowledge, as each generation of scholars builds on their predecessors' work, correcting and extending it. In this relatively modest area of scholarship the wish that Francis Bacon expressed for the course of the physical sciences, 'that the art of discovery may advance as discoveries advance', has certainly come true.[25] Secondly, a chronological arrangement reveals almost the contrary phenomenon, the extent to which those wishing to preserve their belief in Shakespeare's sole authorship have ignored, misunderstood, or misrepresented the scholarly tradition identifying the presence of a different hand at various points in each of these five plays. These differences are primarily linguistic, involving vocabulary, grammar, syntax, verse style, and rhetoric. But they are also visible at the level of plotting and characterization, both areas in which co-authorship often led to problems of coordination and consistency. The final chapter will move from verbal analysis to literary criticism in order to look at the plays' larger form.

---

[25] The closing sentence of Bacon's *Novum Organum*, Book I: '*Artem inveniendi cum inventis adolescere posse, statuere debemus*'; J. Spedding *et al.* (eds.), *The Works of Francis Bacon*, 7 vols. (London, 1857–9), i. 223, iv. 115.

3

Titus Andronicus with George Peele

The external evidence for the genesis of *Titus Andronicus* is meagre, and has become even smaller of late. Like W. K. C. Guthrie, the distinguished historian of Greek philosophy, who began a book on the Orphic religion with the words 'I used to know a great deal about Orpheus'—subsequent scholarship having distinguished real from mythical knowledge—we now have even fewer certainties about *Titus*. The play was entered in the Stationers' Register on 6 February 1594 as 'a book intituled a Noble Roman Historye of Titus Andronicus', and the First Quarto, published that year, described it as

The Most Lamentable Romaine Tragedie of Titus Andronicus: As it was Plaide by the Right Honourable the Earle of Darbie, Earle of Pembroke, and Earle of Sussex their Seruants [Danter's device] London, printed by John Danter . . .[1]

The only copy of this First Quarto was found in Sweden in 1905, and was purchased by Henry Clay Folger for his library; subsequent quarto editions—none of which disclose authorship—appeared in 1600 and 1611, the latter providing the copy-text for the 1623 Folio, which added a scene (3.2) not found in the Quartos. The only other evidence for the play's existence in 1594 was provided by an entry made by Philip Henslowe in his receipts for the period beginning 27 December 1593, from 'the earle of susex his men':

ne—Rd at titus & ondronicus the 23 of Jeneware . . . iijⁱⁱjviijs

The date is usually corrected to read '24th', since it is the fourth performance recorded by Henslowe that week, and plays were not usually performed on Sundays. Henslowe noted further performances on 28 January and 4 February. In the summer season of 1594, 'beginninge at newington my Lord Admeralle men & my Lorde chamberlen men' performed 'andronicous' on 5 June and 12 June.[2]

For many years it was assumed that the abbreviation 'ne', which Henslowe prefixed to that and other entries, meant 'new', newly revised, or newly

---

[1] E. K. Chambers, *William Shakespeare: A Study of Facts and Problems*, 2 vols. (Oxford, 1930), i. 312.
[2] R. A. Foakes and R. T. Rickert (eds.), *Henslowe's Diary* (Cambridge, 1961), 21–2.

licensed, which would establish a play's first performance on that date. But recently Winifred Frazer has challenged such assumptions.[3] For one thing, she pointed out, Henslowe marked one play 'ne' on 28 April 1592 and again on 11 June 1596; another received that annotation on 14 January but also on 11 February 1597 (Frazer 1991, p. 34). Secondly, the entries identifying 'newington', such as that quoted above for June 1594, undoubtedly refer to the theatre at Newington Butts, situated in the Surrey village of Newington (where the archery butts were), about a mile south-west of London Bridge, which Henslowe may have owned. But, unlike all other such headings, they do not specify the date of the first performance there. Frazer argued that 'ne' must be an abbreviation for Newington Butts, and that since Henslowe included no date he meant 'beginning at Newington on sundry days'. She quoted further documents (*Eliz. S* ii. 404–5) according to which theatre companies were enjoined to perform at the Newington Butts theatre from time to time, perhaps when theatres on the south bank were contracted out for some other purpose (Frazer 1991, p. 35). These convincing arguments remove any ground for concluding that *Titus Andronicus* was indeed a new play in January 1594,[4] and leave the question of its date wide open.

Another early document connected with the play that has been recently revalued is the pen-and-ink drawing (now at Longleat House) made by Henry Peacham on a folio sheet, beneath which are copied some forty lines of text from *Titus Andronicus* (a composite version, with abridgements, of 1.1.104–20, 121–6, 5.1.125–44). The drawing represents seven figures: on the left two armed soldiers and a man wearing a laurel crown and holding a tasselled ceremonial spear, are confronted by three kneeling figures (a queen, and two young men, unarmed) and a blackamoor, standing and holding a sword (Chambers 1930, i. 312). The text quoted below, in a different hand, begins with an interpolated stage direction, '*Enter Tamora pleadinge for her sonnes going to execution*', but all attempts to relate the drawing directly to the play *Titus Andronicus* have had to acknowledge several incompatibilities, and could only describe it as vaguely 'emblematic'. Recently June Schlueter has provided a fresh and convincing reinterpretation,[5] showing that it depicts a sequence from a play performed in Germany by English actors which survives in German only, *Eine sehr klägliche Tragoedia von Tito Andronico und der hoffertigen Käyserin* (1620). This play, in which Titus' son Vespasian has a prominent role, is perhaps a translation of the lost '*tittus & vespacia*' recorded in Henslowe's diary in 1592 (Schlueter 1999, pp. 172–3). Her summary of the German play's action at the end of Act 1 shows that it

---

[3] Winifred Frazer, 'Henslowe's "ne" ', *NQ* 236 (1991): 34–5.
[4] Neither of the play's most recent editors noticed Frazer's definitive correction: see A. Hughes (ed.), Shakespeare, *Titus Andronicus* (Cambridge, 1994), pp. 1–6, J. Bate (ed.), Shakespeare, *Titus Andronicus* (London, 1995), pp. 69–70.
[5] June Schlueter, 'Rereading the Peacham Drawing', *ShQ* 50 (1999): 171–84.

corresponds in every point to Peacham's drawing (pp. 174–6), removing any possible link with the play ascribed to Shakespeare in the First Folio. Since the drawing is dated 1594, Peacham may well have seen *Titus and Vespasian* in the London theatres.

These two recent revaluations of the scholarly tradition concerning *Titus Andronicus* leave us knowing less than we thought we did, but of course our knowledge of so many areas of Elizabethan and Jacobean drama is patchy in the extreme. In 1598 Francis Meres recorded *Titus Andronicus* among Shakespeare's plays (Chambers 1930, ii. 194), and it appeared as his in the 1623 Folio. We have no external evidence as to Shakespeare having shared the writing with another dramatist, indeed for many years a majority of the play's commentators doubted the testimony of Heminge and Condell, the Folio editors, and Shakespeare's colleagues of twenty years' standing, that he was at least partly responsible for it. These doubts about Shakespeare's authorship had no scholarly basis, external or internal, but expressed an aesthetico-ethical dislike for the violence and corporeal mutilations that take place both on and off stage. Any attentive and unprejudiced reading of the play could show that the violence is in no way gratuitous, but part of a closely organized depiction of several cycles of harm and counter-harm, in which Titus is both agent and victim. The first of these cycles arises from the sacrifice of Alarbus, Tamora's son, done to appease the spirits of Titus' two sons, killed in battle with the Goths (1.1.35,[6] 95–129). Titus ignores Tamora's appeals for pity, and she is left helplessly exclaiming against this 'cruel, irreligious piety'. But her son Demetrius invokes the memory of Hecuba (who avenged her son Polydorus by killing the sons of Polymnestor, his murderer— an action described with sickening power in Euripides' *Hecuba*[7]), hoping that Tamora will obtain the same 'opportunity of sharp revenge' on Titus (135–41). When Tamora unexpectedly becomes Roman Empress she initially begs the Emperor Saturninus to dissemble with Titus, in order to gain time to prepare her revenge (1.1.442–55). She duly achieves it through her sons, and when Demetrius and Chiron are about to rape and mutilate Lavinia, Titus' daughter, Tamora brushes aside her appeals and reminds her (2.3.158–65) how ruthlessly Titus rejected her pleas for pity when Alarbus was slain.

If Titus is the agent in this cycle of retribution, his sacrifice of Alarbus bringing down disaster on his own head, in the other revenge-cycles generated in the play's opening scene he is the victim. Titus generously ceded to Saturninus the Emperorship of Rome, which the people had offered him (1.1.179–233), and happily accepted the Emperor's return gesture of taking

---

[6] The First Quarto (1594) contains three and a half lines at this point, announcing the imminent sacrifice, which were omitted in Q2 (1600), Q3 (1611), and F1 (1623). Editors have taken the omission as a sign of confusion or revision in the text—mistakenly, as I shall argue in Chapter 7.

[7] See Brian Vickers, *Towards Greek Tragedy* (London, 1973), pp. 81–3, 281–2.

Lavinia for his bride (234–43), a satisfying gift exchange. So Titus is duly appalled when his brother, Marcus, and two of his sons (Lucius, Quintus) support Bassianus, Saturninus' brother, who forcibly insists on his prior claim to Lavinia (1.1.51–2), and abducts her (276–86). When Mutius, his remaining son, tries to protect the abductors, Titus kills him (287–91). Having thus twice sacrificed his own interests for the Emperor's sake, Titus is deeply hurt when Saturninus announces that he has suddenly fallen in love with Tamora, and publicly rejects Lavinia, along with Titus' 'lawless' family (296–340). As already mentioned, Tamora seems to play the peacemaker here (428–81), but subsequently, with the connivance of her lover, Aaron the Moor, she encourages her sons to carry out their dreadful revenge, involving the rape and mutilation of Lavinia (her tongue cut out, her hands chopped off so that she may not reveal the identity of her rapists). These events, like the subsequent execution of Titus' sons, Titus' self-mutilation brought about by Aaron's evil, and the crowning multiple revenge, are the organic consequence of the discord and division generated by this opening scene. Rather than descending to the level of a 'video nasty', as one up-to-date detractor puts it,[8] Shakespeare responded to the dreadful violence inflicted on Lavinia and Titus with full recognition of their sufferings, and an insistent call for sympathy. The difficulty that earlier critics had with Shakespeare's use of verbal conceit and word-play is explicable, given their insensitivity to the stylistic conventions of early Elizabethan drama, conventions which Shakespeare drew on and helped to reinforce. But it is disappointing to find contemporary scholars continuing to dismiss the play on unexamined aesthetico-ethical grounds.

The first suggestion that the play is not of sole authorship was made by Edward Ravenscroft, one of the Restoration dramatists who adapted Shakespeare for a new sensibility. In the Preface to his *Titus Andronicus, or The Rape of Lavinia. A Tragedy, Alter'd from Mr. Shakespeare's Works*, performed and published in 1678, he assured his readers that

I Think it a greater theft to Rob the dead of their Praise than the Living of their Money. That I may not appear Guilty of such a Crime, 'tis necessary I should acquaint you, that there is a Play in Mr. *Shakespeare*'s Volume under the name of *Titus Andronicus*, from whence I drew part of this. I have been told by some anciently conversant with the Stage, that it was not Originally his, but brought by a private Author to be Acted, and he only gave some Master-touches to one or two of the Principal Parts or Characters; this I am apt to believe, because 'tis the most incorrect and undigested piece in all his Works; It seems rather a heap of Rubbish than a Structure.

Ravenscroft was certainly guilty of misrepresentation, for although he claimed that if we were to 'Compare the Old Play with this, you'l finde that none in all that Authors Works ever receiv'd greater Alterations or Additions,

---

[8] Harriett Hawkins, *The Devil's Party: Critical Counter-interpretations of Shakespearian Drama* (Oxford, 1985).

the Language not only refin'd, but many Scenes entirely New: Besides most of
the principal Characters heighten'd, and the Plot much encreas'd', in fact he
made few alterations until the final scene.[9] We may well believe, with J. C.
Maxwell, that Ravenscroft had no evidence for the story and that 'his chief
motive may well have been to justify his own rewriting of the play'.[10] Still,
Ravenscroft's allegation proved surprisingly influential over the next 200
years, as many readers, ignorant of, or unsympathetic to, the Elizabethan
'tragedy of blood', expressed their distaste for the play by doubting its
authenticity.

Charles Gildon, in 1710, found it 'so very shocking' that he could 'easily
believe what has been said, that this is none of *Shakespeare*'s Play, that he only
introduc'd it and gave it some few Touches', an opinion echoed in 1725 by
Alexander Pope, and in 1730 by Lewis Theobald, who found 'something so
barbarous and unnatural in the fable, and so much trash in the diction' that
Shakespeare can only have given it 'some of his masterly touches' (*CHS*, ii.
253, 413, 460). The conviction that Shakespeare could not have written such
a 'barbarous' play was expressed by many subsequent critics.[11] The two most
influential editors in the late eighteenth century, Edmond Malone and George
Steevens, shared this distaste. Malone dismissed *Titus* as a 'spurious piece', of
which Shakespeare merely 'wrote a few lines', while Steevens argued that
some other dramatist wrote it, since it contained 'a greater number of classical allusions &c. than are scattered over all the rest' of Shakespeare's
undoubted plays.[12] Many nineteenth-century critics continued to dismiss
Titus Andronicus as too shocking to be Shakespeare's. 'I beg to be allowed to
reject the whole of this play', wrote Charles Bathurst in 1857: 'I wish I had
never read it',[13] while another Victorian called it 'the play of the shambles'. In
such reactions we can see with remarkable clarity how discussions of a work's
authenticity can be affected by completely external considerations, here a distaste for its subject-matter. These critics simply rationalized their distaste for
the play's offences against 'taste' and decorum by denying its authenticity.

Yet some of the detractors recognized Shakespeare's hand. Despite dismissing 'the fable [as] at the same time shocking and puerile', Benjamin Heath
recognized, 'scattered here and there, many strokes resembling his peculiar
manner, though not his best', the play being perhaps 'his most juvenile per-

---

[9] *CHS*, i. 238–9; the two final scenes are excerpted at pp. 239–48.

[10] J. C. Maxwell (ed.), *Titus Andronicus* (London, 1961), p. xxi.

[11] Representative opinions rejecting Shakespeare's authorship of *Titus Andronicus* include
William Guthrie in 1747 and John Upton in 1748 (*CHS*, iii. 204, 307); Benjamin Heath and
Samuel Johnson in 1765, Richard Farmer in 1766—who was convinced that 'this *horrible* piece
was originally written by the Author of the Lines thrown into the mouth of the Player in *Hamlet*'
(*CHS*, iv. 560; v. 142, 277); John Pinkerton and John Monck Mason in 1785 (*CHS*, vi. 397, 404).

[12] For Malone's verdicts (*Titus* being described as 'A Tragedy Erroneously Ascribed to
Shakespeare') cf. *CHS*, vi. 46, 190, 527, 555); for Steevens's, cf. ibid. 196–7, 303, 577.

[13] *Remarks on Shakespeare's Versification* (London, 1857), p. 11.

formance' (*CHS*, iv. 560). Francis Gentleman (in 1774) found the 'characters and incidents . . . totally offensive', human nature represented as unbelievably depraved, so that 'this play must be horrid in representation' as it is 'disgustful in perusal'. Still, Gentleman conceded that 'in different parts *Titus Andronicus* bears strong, nay evident, marks of Shakespeare's pen', and in 1775 Elizabeth Griffiths supposed 'the intire piece to be his . . . because the whole of the fable as well as the conduct of it is so very *barbarous*' that Shakespeare could hardly have adopted it from anyone else. 'Besides, he would never have strewed such sweet flowers upon a *caput mortuum* if some child of his own had not lain entombed underneath.' These were intuitive responses from writers having a wide knowledge of Shakespeare and other Elizabethan dramatists, but they had no greater authority than that. However, scholarly arguments defending the play's authenticity were soon forthcoming. In 1766 Thomas Tyrwhitt pointed out that it was included in the authentic works of Shakespeare listed by Francis Meres in *Palladis Tamia* (1598), a fact which constituted 'a decisive . . . authority for ascribing it to *Shakespeare*'. Dr Johnson simply dismissed this argument (*CHS*, v. 240, 532–3), but Edward Capell, a far greater scholar and editor, soon provided evidence that could not be brushed aside. In the introduction to his ten-volume edition of 1768, Capell showed that the play was included in the First Folio, in a text based on the 1611 Quarto, and he included *Titus* among the Folio plays whose authenticity he defended (the others being *The Three Parts of Henry VI*, *Love's Labour's Lost*, and *The Taming of the Shrew*). As Capell observed at the end of his introduction, those who doubt their authenticity ought to have recalled that

all these contested plays are in the Folio, which is dedicated to the Poet's patrons and friend, the earls of *Pembroke* and *Montgomery*, by editors who are seemingly honest men, and profess themselves dependant upon those noblemen. To whom, therefore, they would hardly have had the confidence to present forgeries and pieces supposititious; in which, too, they were liable to be detected by those identical noble persons themselves, as well as by a very great part of their other readers and auditors. (*CHS*, v. 304–5)

As for *Titus Andronicus*, Capell accepted the general description of it 'as a very bundle of horrors . . . unlike the Poet's manner and even the style of his other pieces', but he set an example of a truly historical approach by relating both features to the history of the Elizabethan theatre. Dating the play *c*.1589, Capell placed it in the vogue for violence shown by dramatists between 1585 and 1595, who, 'falling in with that innate love of blood which has often been objected to *British* audiences, and choosing fables of horror which they made horrider still by their manner of handling them . . . produc'd a set of monsters that are not to be parallel'd in all the annals of play-writing'. Instancing *The Wars of Cyrus*, Marlowe's *Tamburlaine*, Kyd's

Spanish Tragedy, *Soliman and Perseda*, and *Selimus*, Capell argued that Shakespeare, who 'wrote certainly for profit', adapted himself to these models in both content and form, 'this *Proteus*' even copying their use of a regular decasyllabic line (p. 316).

However, Capell added, his judgement of the play's authenticity was not formed on historical grounds.

For though a work of imitation, and conforming itself to models truly execrable throughout, yet the genius of its Author breaks forth in some places, and to the editor's eye Shakespeare stands confess'd. The third act in particular may be read with admiration even by the most delicate, who, if they are not without feelings may chance to find themselves touch'd by it with such passions as tragedy should excite—that is, terror, and pity. (*CHS*, v. 319–21)

It is commendable that Capell should have singled out as authentically Shakespearian the sequence beginning with Marcus Andronicus leading the violated Lavinia to her father, for my later discussion will show that in this sequence Shakespeare's dramaturgy can be distinguished for the first time from Peele's, who was responsible for the whole of Act 1 and the first two scenes in Act 2 (see Chapter 7). In his *Notes and Various Readings*, announced with the 1768 edition but unfortunately not published until 1780, Capell repeated his reasons for accepting it as an authentic early work, its 'classical quotations and classical images' coming from a beginning writer, 'his school learning hanging about him fresh'. The versification, also, he judged (most perceptively), is that of the early 1590s, 'the numbers' being 'too constrain'd and too regular, and wanting that rich variety which his ripen'd judgment and experience' introduced. Capell was evidently not among those critics whom he had mocked as being 'without feelings', as we can see from one of the play's tragic climaxes. When Titus is confronted in swift succession by his daughter, raped and mutilated, and the severed heads of his two sons, his brother Marcus exclaims 'Alas, poor heart, that kiss is comfortless' (3.1.249). Most modern editors add a stage direction, 'Lavinia kisses Titus',[14] but Capell was more perceptive:

'*To* Lavinia, *seeing her kiss the Heads of her Brothers*', had follow'd these words as a direction, would the place have admitted it. The behaviour of all these personages upon this dreadful occasion is singularly proper, and the horrid '*laugh*' of the father has something great in it, even for Shakespeare. (*CHS*, vi. 244–5)

Capell refers to Titus' reactions to these catastrophes, first numbed then breaking out, 'Ha, ha, ha!'. Marcus asks 'Why dost thou laugh? It fits not

---

[14] This stage direction is found in the editions by J. D. Wilson (1948), J. C. Maxwell (1953, 1961), G. B. Evans (1974, 1997), D. Bevington (1980), E. M. Waith (1984), and A. Hughes (1994). To his credit, J. Bate (1995), following Capell, gives '*Lavinia kisses the heads*'.

with this hour', and Titus replies: 'Why, I have not another tear to shed' (3.1.263–5).

Capell's appreciation of the play's merits was shared by some nineteenth-century critics, notably Charles Knight. In his preface to the play for his 'Pictorial Edition' of Shakespeare (8 vols., 1838–43), repeated in his 'Library Edition' (12 vols., 1842–4), and collected in his *Studies of Shakspeare* (1849), Knight quoted Henry Hallam's opinion[15] that ' "*Titus Andronicus* is now, by common consent, denied to be, in *any* sense, a production of Shakespeare" ', before vigorously combating it. This 'common consent', he objected, was that of one school of critics only, the eighteenth-century tradition summed up by Malone, whereas 'the German critics, from W. Schlegel to Ulrici, agree to reject' it (Knight 1849, p. 42). Knight conceded that the play does not affect us to the degree that *King Lear* does (ibid.), but pointed to the characterization of Tamora, who as the action develops embodies 'that wonderful conception of the union of powerful intellect and moral depravity which Shakespeare was afterwards to make manifest with such consummate wisdom' in the character of Lady Macbeth (p. 46). Aaron, too, his villainy mitigated by the touch of humanity in his affection for his child, is a Shakespearian creation (p. 47). As to the play's style, it is significant that Knight exempted Act 1, in which the verse is set out with 'the stately pace of [its] time', from the general comment that 'we are very soon carried away, by the power of the language, the variety of the pause, and the special freedom with which trochees are used at the ends of lines . . .' (p. 49). Even in the later scenes of intense suffering, Knight observed, 'there is much poetry but no raving. When woe upon woe is heaped upon Titus, we have no imprecations', and when Marcus urges Titus, having been tricked into amputating his hand, that he should 'speak with possibility / And do not break into these deep extremes' (3.1.215), Knight pointed out that, far from 'deep extremes . . . The unhappy man has scarcely risen into metaphor, much less into braggardism' (pp. 49–50). Where one critic had compared Aaron to another theatrical Moor, Eleazar in *Lust's Dominion*, Knight invited readers to 'trace the cool, determined, sarcastic, remorseless villain, Aaron, through these blood-spilling scenes, and see if he speaks in "King Cambyses' vein", as Eleazar speaks' (p. 50). An autodidact and populist educationalist, Charles Knight possessed both perception and independence of judgement, qualities which he admirably displayed, as we shall see, in arguing divided authorship in *Timon of Athens*.

Despite Knight's advocacy, disbelief that Shakespeare could have written such a shocking play persisted into the twentieth century. In 1929 John

---

[15] Hallam, *An Introduction to the Literature of Europe in the Fifteenth, Sixteenth, and Seventeenth Centuries*, 4 vols. (London, 1839–40), ii. 385.

Bailey could remark: 'Of *Titus Andronicus* I need say nothing, as scarcely anyone thinks Shakespeare wrote it.'[16] Luckily, a growing number of scholars were beginning to challenge this received idea, which had persisted for two and a half centuries. However, at the same time that arguments for the play's authenticity were being made, a newer and for some scholars more disturbing argument emerged, that Shakespeare was only responsible for part of the play. The pioneer in this school of thought was T. M. Parrott, who in 1919 published an essay arguing that in *Titus* Shakespeare had revised the work of some unidentified predecessor.[17] Although we can ignore his purely speculative account of 'an old, pre-Shakespearean play', dating apparently from between 1584 and 1589 (for which no evidence exists), Parrott did provide the first detailed analysis of the play's diction and verse, which indicated the presence of a co-author. Parrott argued that Shakespeare could be differentiated from his predecessors by 'the combined ease and power with which he handles their common medium, blank verse', his 'increasing mastery' of that medium being shown by his 'steadily increasing use of the feminine ending', an additional syllable overflowing the normal decasyllabic line. Shakespeare did not invent this metrical variant, but 'he quite outranked all his predecessors in the frequency with which he employed it' (Parrott 1919, p. 24). Parrott made calculations showing that Greene and Kyd hardly ever used the feminine ending, Peele slightly (according to Parrott's figures, from 0.03 per cent in one play to 2.2 per cent in another), Marlowe more so (from 2 to 3.8 per cent). The average figures for whole plays that Parrott quoted for Shakespeare (derived from earlier scholars, Goswin König and H. D. Gray) were: *King John* 6.3 per cent, *Richard 3* 15.5 per cent, *Romeo and Juliet* 8.2 per cent, *Richard 2* 11 per cent, and *Titus Andronicus* 8 per cent (p. 24). But his closer inspection of individual scenes revealed a great variation in the use of feminine endings in *Titus*: 'half the scenes show a low percentage running from about 2.3 to about 6.5 per cent, the other half a high percentage running from about 8 to nearly 21 per cent', figures corresponding quite closely to Shakespeare's range (p. 25).

Parrott then performed a detailed analysis of the whole play, 'using the test of parallels in thought and diction' to confirm his hypothesis of two separate authors. The long opening scene of Act 1 (470 lines in his text) 'has about 3.6 per cent feminine endings', and resembles structurally the opening scene of George Peele's *Edward I* (1591), as several critics had pointed out. Parrott declared this act to be 'written throughout in verse of a deadly monotony rising at best to a somewhat stilted rhetoric', but 'sinking again and again to utter bathos', as in this sequence:

[16] Cit. J. D. Wilson in his edition of *Titus Andronicus* (Cambridge, 1948), p. xvi.
[17] T. M. Parrott, 'Shakespeare's Revision of *Titus Andronicus*', *MLR* 14 (1919): 16–37.

Ascend, fair Queen, Pantheon. Lords, accompany
Your noble emperor and his lovely bride,
Sent by the heavens for Prince Saturnine,
Whose wisdom hath her fortune conquerèd:
There shall we consummate our spousal rites

(1.1.333–7)

As he put it, 'though one rose from the dead to persuade us, no ear trained to
the music of Shakespeare's verse could accept such lines as his', indeed Parrott
could not find 'a single trace of Shakespeare's hand in the whole act'.[18] The
language of this scene, Parrott stated, 'contains numerous clear parallels to
the known works of Peele . . . ; per contra it does not contain a single clear
and convincing parallel to any of Shakespeare's plays' (pp. 25–6). Many of
these parallels had been pointed out by Robertson, reapplying evidence provided by Charles Crawford in claiming that Shakespeare wrote the whole
play.[19] The truly striking parallel, as scholars admit to this day, concerns that
passage where Marcus asks Titus to accept a white toga,

This palliament of white and spotless hue
And name thee in election for the empire
. . . .
Be *candidatus* then, and put it on.

This invitation echoes two passages from Peele's poem, *The Honour of the
Garter* (1593),[20] the first (ll. 91–2) describing Edward III, founder of the
Order, as

A goodly King in robes most richly dight,
The upper like a Roman palliament.

The second passage (ll. 313–16) is an apostrophe to 'sacred loyalty':

thy weeds of spotless white,
Like those that stood for Rome's great offices,
Make thee renown'd, glorious in innocency.

George Steevens had noted in 1773 the unusual use of the word '*palliament*
for *robe*, a Latinism which I have not met with elsewhere in any English writer,
ancient or modern; though it must have originated from the mint of a scholar'
(*CHS*, vi. 197). That scholar was George Peele, who coined the word himself,
and to whom Parrott and others attributed the two classical allusions in this

---

[18] The first line of that quotation seems to me especially revealing of the difficulties the poet
found himself in, being forced to omit the definite article before 'Pantheon' in order to make the
line scan. Earlier, he had managed to reconcile grammar and metrics: 'And in the sacred Pantheon
her espouse' (242)—although both the Quarto and Folio compositors printed the meaningless
word 'Pathan'.

[19] C. Crawford, 'The Date and Authenticity of *Titus Andronicus*', *ShJb* 36 (1900): 109–21.

[20] Quoted from Wilson 1948, p. xlvi.

scene, one to Hecuba's murder of Polymestor (ll. 136–8), the other to the burial of Ajax (l. 379). These allusions 'are drawn directly from plays by Euripides and Sophocles presumably known to Peele, but as Root has shown[21] . . . apparently outside Shakespeare's range of reading' (p. 25). Shakespeare's reading knowledge has often been underestimated, but it is certainly true that Peele had a much fuller classical education. Parrott ascribed to Peele two other scenes where the percentage of feminine endings was unusually low, 2.1 and 4.1 (2.3 and 2.5 per cent, respectively), and pointed out that they each contain quotations from Seneca's *Hippolytus* (2.1.136, 4.1.81–2).

As for the Shakespearian scenes, with their much higher percentage of feminine endings, Parrott indicated several 'unmistakable parallels' to Shakespeare's narrative poems, *Venus and Adonis* (Stationers' Register, 18 April 1593; Q1, 1593) and *The Rape of Lucrece* (Stationers' Register, 9 May 1594; Q1, 1594). The description of the hunt, for instance:

> And, whilst the babbling echo mocks the hounds,
> Replying shrilly to the well-tuned horns,
> As if a double hunt were heard at once
>
> (2.3.17–19)

echoes the account in *Venus and Adonis* of how the hounds

> spend their mouths: Echo replies,
> As if another chase were in the skies
>
> (*VA*, 695–6)

The later passage from the play,

> Whilst hounds and horns and sweet melodious birds
> Be unto us as in a nurse's song
> Of lullaby to bring her babe a sleep
>
> (2.3.27–9)

again echoes the poem:

> By this, far off she hears some huntsman hollo
> A nurse's song ne'er pleased her babe so well.
>
> (*VA*, 973–4)

The early Ovidian poem also provides a parallel for the sinister moment later in this scene where Quintus and Martius find the pit into which Demetrius has thrown the dead body of Bassianus, a 'subtle hole'

> Whose mouth is covered with rude-growing briars,
> Upon whose leaves are drops of new-shed blood
> As fresh as morning dew distill'd on flowers
>
> (199–201)

[21] Cf. R. K. Root, *Classical Mythology in Shakespeare* (New York, 1903), pp. 5–6.

Parrott cited a passage from the poem depicting 'the blood of a newly slain victim staining the plants near by':

> Whose blood upon the fresh flowers being shed,
> Doth make them droop with grief
>
> (*VA*, 665–6)

but, as Dover Wilson pointed out (1948, p. 321), 'even closer in diction' is the line 'So they were dewed with such distilling showers' (*VA*, 66). We can certainly agree that these and other parallels[22] with *Venus and Adonis* 'can hardly be accidental' (Parrott 1919, p. 29). The same must be said of this parallel between the play

> Sorrow concealèd, like an oven stopp'd,
> Doth burn the heart to cinders where it is
>
> (2.4.36–7)

and the poem:

> An oven that is stopp'd, or river stay'd,
> Burneth more hotly, swelleth with more rage:
> So of concealed sorrow may be said.
>
> (*VA*, 331–3)

Another series of parallels links *Titus Andronicus* with *The Rape of Lucrece*. 'In the poem Lucrece pleads with her would-be ravisher', and

> his unhallow'd haste her words delays,
> And moody Pluto winks [sleeps] while Orpheus plays.
>
> (*Lucr.*, 552–3)

In the play Marcus says that if Lavinia's ravisher had heard 'the heavenly harmony' of her tongue,

> He would have dropped his knife and fell asleep,
> As Cerberus at the Thracian poet's feet.
>
> (2.4.48–51)

'The situation is identical: a brutal ravisher stayed by the charm of his victim's voice' (Wilson 1948, p. 126). These are deeper associations of ideas, 'more convincing than mere verbal parallels' (Parrott 1919, p. 29). Parrott also compared Marcus's anguished description of Lavinia's amputated tongue:

> Alas, a crimson river of warm blood,
> Like to a bubbling fountain stirr'd with wind,
> Doth rise and fall between thy rosed lips
>
> (2.4.22–4)

---

[22] Cf. 'Titan's blushing face' (2.4.31–2) and 'Titan's burning eye' (*VA*, 177–8); 'engine of her thoughts' applied to a woman's tongue (3.1.82), and 'engine of her thoughts' (*VA*, 367).

to the poem's description of how Brutus drew 'the murderous knife' from his wife's death-wound, at which a 'purple fountain' of blood issued out,

> And bubbling from her breast, it doth divide
> In two slow rivers, that the crimson blood
> Circles her body
>
> (*Lucr.*, 1734–8)

As Parrott described it, Marcus's 'whole speech . . . is a sort of epitome of *Lucrece*, a poeticizing and decorating with picturesque conceits of the brutal fact of bodily outrage' (p. 30). Again, when Titus addresses the 'villains, Chiron and Demetrius':

> Here stands the spring whom you have stained with mud
>
> (5.2.170)

his words echo the poem:

> Mud not the fountain that gave drink to thee
>
> (*Lucr.*, 577)

'In the play the words are spoken to the ravishers of Lavinia; in the poem it is Lucretia's plea to Sextus; in each case the lady is the spring, or fountain, stained, or threatened with the stain of mud. No parallel could be closer' (p. 35).

T. M. Parrott's essay of 1919 may stand as the first attempt to establish the authenticity of *Titus Andronicus* by using the methods of modern authorship studies, combining quantitative analysis of the play's verse styles with the citation of enough close parallel passages to make the case for the separate presence of Peele and Shakespeare beyond the possibility of coincidence or imitation. Parrott found it 'indisputable . . . that there are at least two hands in the play, writing two quite different styles, and that one of these is Shakespeare's . . .' (p. 36). Although many readers have agreed with him, it is a historical fact that every attempt to identify Shakespeare as a co-author of a play has been answered by others claiming him as sole author. Only rarely, however, do such counter-claims actually address the linguistic evidence cited in the original claim.

In drawing attention to the many parallels between the play and the two narrative poems, Parrott was a precursor of an important shift in scholarly attitudes, the recognition that *Titus Andronicus* owes as much to Ovid as to Senecan tragedy. This insight was properly formulated by Howard Baker in his study of three early tragedies, *Gorboduc*, *The Spanish Tragedy*, and *Titus Andronicus*.[23] Earlier scholars had assumed that the play's climax, where

---

[23] H. Baker, *Induction to Tragedy: A Study in a Development of Form in 'Gorboduc', 'The Spanish Tragedy' and 'Titus Andronicus'* (Baton Rouge, La., 1939; New York, 1965), pp. 119–39.

Titus entertains Tamora to a banquet at which she eats a pie made from the flesh of her rapist sons, derives from Seneca's *Thyestes*. Baker showed that it is in many respects closer to Ovid's story of Philomela (*Metamorphoses*, Book 6), a popular text in Elizabethan grammar schools well known in the original Latin, given wider circulation both by Arthur Golding's translation and in its retellings by Gower in *Confessio Amantis*, Chaucer in *The Legend of Good Women*, and several Elizabethan writers. In Shakespeare, as in Ovid, the banquet is specifically in revenge for a rape followed by the cutting out of the victim's tongue, and the victim takes part in its preparation (in Ovid, Philomela is helped by her sister, Progne; Lavinia by her father, Titus). Baker also showed that the much-admired set-piece description in *Titus*, the 'barren detested vale' where the rape takes place (2.3.94 ff.), is explicitly identified with the play's Ovidian model, as Titus says:

> Lavinia, wert thou thus surpris'd, sweet girl,
> Ravish'd and wrong'd, as Philomela was,
> Forc'd in the ruthless, vast, and gloomy woods?
>
> .   .   .   .   .   .
>
> O! had we never, never hunted there,
> Pattern'd by that the poet here describes,
> By nature made for murders and for rapes.
>
> (4.1.51 ff.)

(Since this scene was probably written by Peele, we see that both dramatists had shared the planning of the whole play, an argument that they collaborated, rather than Shakespeare revising an earlier piece by Peele.)

Taking stock of all the classical allusions in the play, Baker counted: 'Ovid, sixteen (excluding the repeated references to Philomel); Virgil, fifteen; Livy-Painter, four; Horace, two (from Lyly's grammar); Seneca, two (both are short Latin tags from *Hippolytus*)', and a scattering of lesser references (Baker 1939, p. 139). In other words, far from the play containing an unusual number of scholarly allusions, as Steevens thought, and therefore being far beyond Shakespeare's capacity, it drew on the standard authors of the Elizabethan grammar-school curriculum. This point helps to place *Titus Andronicus* within the known extent of Shakespeare's classical learning, a body of knowledge that T. W. Baldwin was soon to expound with extraordinary detail in his reconstruction of the Elizabethan grammar school, *William Shakspere's 'Small Latine and Lesse Greeke'*.[24]

---

[24] T. W. Baldwin, *William Shakspere's 'Small Latine and Lesse Greeke'*, 2 vols. (Urbana, Ill., 1944; repr. 1966). Baldwin naturally quoted the passage where Demetrius reads from a scroll the well-known lines in Horace, '*Integer vitae, scelerisque purus . . .*', and Chiron comments, 'O, 'tis a verse in Horace; I know it well: | I read it in the grammar long ago' (4.2.20–3), referring to Lily's Latin grammar, the standard text in all Elizabethan grammar schools. Baldwin showed that Shakespeare quotes several times from the grammar's second part, the *Brevissima Institutio*, and 'not mere scraps selected at random': 'each quotation is specially fitted to its context' in the play

Howard Baker also pointed out structural and other similarities between *Titus*, *Hamlet*, and *King Lear*, so helping to rehabilitate the play as an integral part of Shakespeare's development in tragedy. Other scholars in this period took the rehabilitation process further, but as so often the wish to validate a play as authentically Shakespearian seems to exclude acknowledging the presence of another author. As we have seen, in 1933 A. M. Sampley made a vigorous attack on the unscholarly practices of J. M. Robertson in claiming George Peele's authorship of several plays on the slender basis of single words or commonplace phrases. Sampley succeeded in discrediting most of these identifications, but honestly recorded that, having whittled down their list of 133 'typical' Peele expressions to sixteen that were indeed characteristic of him, he discovered that 'twelve of these words and phrases do occur in *Titus Andronicus*'. However, he added, 'of these twelve, six (*architect*, *'joy*, *men of war*, *sacred*, *Styx*, *'tice*) are nearly as common in other writers as in Peele'.[25] Bent on discrediting Robertson and H. D. Sykes, Sampley failed to disclose the other six words, and even omitted to mention that the otherwise unknown noun 'palliament' occurs in Peele (p. 486), but also in *Titus Andronicus*. As we shall see, that point was left to rest for sixty years until Brian Boyd took it up, strengthening the case for Peele's hand in the play. Sampley's silence shows how the authorship issue in *Titus Andronicus* could have been pursued in the 1930s, by pulling together findings from different approaches—if only Shakespearian scholars had followed the example of their colleagues working on Beaumont, Fletcher, Massinger, Middleton, and Ford.

One of the great dangers of Shakespeare criticism is isolation, leading to ignorance of methodologies being practised in neighbouring disciplines, or even by scholars working on Elizabethan and Jacobean drama. The works of Shakespeare, and all the attendant secondary literature, are rich enough to keep any student fully occupied, but unless we also look in other directions we will miss new evidence and new methods. Studying the evolving discussion of the authenticity of Shakespeare's plays it is striking how often relevant

---

(Baldwin 1944, i. 578–9). Baldwin devoted a long chapter to Shakespeare's knowledge of Ovid (ii. 417–55), and specifically reviewed the Ovidian borrowings in *Venus and Adonis* and *Titus Andronicus*, concluding that the play was written after the poem, 'hence not earlier than 1593' (ii. 433–6). Some recent scholarship would support that date. Alan H. Nelson, in 'George Buc, William Shakespeare, and the Folger *George a Greene*', *ShQ* 49 (1998): 74–83, dates *Titus* to Dec. 1593 (pp. 82–3), while Jina Politi, ' "The Gibbet-Maker" ' *NQ* 236 (1991): 54–5, draws a parallel between the Clown's answer to Titus' question, 'Shall I have justice? What says Jupiter?'—'Ho, the gibbet-maker? He says that he hath taken them down again, for the man must not be hang'd till the next week' (4.3.80–3), and the execution of Henry Barrow and John Greenwood. On 24 Mar. 1593 they were brought out of prison, but were reprieved at the last minute. They received another last-minute reprieve a week later, on 31 Mar., but were duly 'hang'd . . . the next week', on 6 Apr. 1593—which provides a *terminus ab quem* for the play's composition.

[25] A. M. Sampley ' "Verbal Tests" for Peele's Plays', *SP* 30 (1933), 496.

TABLE 3.1. *Feminine endings in* Titus Andronicus

Act, scene	Full lines	All feminine endings	Proper names	Feminine endings, strict count	Total percentage	Strict percentage
1.1	470	13	4	9	2.7	1.9
2.1	124	3	0	3	2.4	2.4
2.2	24	1	0	1	4.1	4.1
2.3	295	33	2	28	11.1	9.4
2.4	53	3	0	3	5.6	5.6
3.1	291	23	3	15	7.9	5.1
3.2	79	10	0	8	12.6	10.0
4.1	123	3	0	2	2.4	1.5
4.2	169	20	0	20	11.8	11.8
4.3	84	11	2	9	13.0	10.7
4.4	104	9	0	8	8.6	7.6
5.1	153	31	3	28	20.2	18.3
5.2	201	13	1	11	6.4	5.4
5.3	172	25	3	20	14.5	11.5
Total	2,342	198	18	165	8.4	7.0

Source: Timberlake 1931, p. 114.

contributions have been simply passed over by later scholars. A highly significant contribution to the study of Shakespeare's verse was made by Philip Timberlake in 1931, studying the eleven-syllable line, or so-called 'feminine ending' in English blank verse drama.[26] Timberlake discussed *Titus Andronicus* in connection with the claims made by Robertson, H. D. Gray, and T. M. Parrott, pointing out that the figures they gave varied greatly, deriving from different definitions of what constitutes a feminine ending. His own meticulous count[27] corrected this fault, as can be seen from Table 3.1. Accepting a date of 1593 for the play, Timberlake argued that 'if Shakespeare's hand is present, it must be of that year; if not, the play should agree in its use of feminine endings with the work of men writing before that year' (Timberlake 1931, p. 115). His figures for Greene's range of feminine endings were 0.1–1.6 per cent; for Marlowe, 0.4–3.7; for Kyd, ranging from 1.2 per cent in *The Spanish Tragedy* to 9.5 per cent for his translation of

[26] P. W. Timberlake, *The Feminine Ending in English Blank Verse: A Study of its Use by Early Writers in the Measure and its Development in the Drama up to the Year 1595* (Menasha, Wis., 1931).
[27] The length of scenes as given by Timberlake derives from W. A. Neilson (ed.), *The Complete Works of Shakespeare*, Student's Cambridge edition (Cambridge, Mass., n.d.), and differs from modern editions.

TABLE 3.2. *Feminine endings in* Titus Andronicus *by author*

Group	Total lines	Feminine endings (strict)	Average (percentage)
A (Peele)	741	13	1.75
B (Shakes.)	1,601	150	9.36

Garnier's *Cornelia*. For Peele, Timberlake's figures for the plays closest in subject-matter to *Titus Andronicus*—that is, serious blank verse plays presenting armed conflict—were 1.5 (*The Battle of Alcazar*) and 1.8 per cent (*Edward I*) (pp. 18–24). In striking contrast, the proportion of feminine endings in Shakespeare's early plays ranges from 10.4 (*2 Henry VI*), 10.7 (*3 Henry VI*), 16.8 (*Richard III*), to 8.2 per cent (*Richard II*)—to stay in the historical-tragical mode (pp. 86–94, 101–4, 107–8). Readers will instantly notice that the figures for three scenes in *Titus Andronicus*, 1.1 (1.9 per cent), 2.1 (2.4 per cent), and 4.1 (1.5 per cent) are far too low for Shakespeare, as Parrott had also pointed out. Timberlake thought that 2.2 was so short that 'no safe conclusion can be drawn from metrical figures', but there is other stylistic evidence pointing to Peele's hand. Timberlake was so methodical in the presentation of his data that we may recalculate the averages for this suggested authorship division, assigning the Group A scenes (1.1, 2.1, 2.2, 4.1) to Peele, Group B to Shakespeare (see Table 3.2). These figures clearly distinguish two different dramatists, and correlate well with the norms for comparable plays by Peele (1.5–1.8 per cent) and Shakespeare (8.2–16.8 per cent). Timberlake concluded that 'the percentages of feminine endings quite agree with other tests' in showing that Peele may have had a part in *Titus*, but 'they show further that a considerable part of the existing text was written by someone whose employment of feminine endings was far beyond that of Peele, Greene, Lodge, Nashe, or Marlowe . . . It is, in fact, beyond the work of any writer except Shakespeare, whose plays of that period amply verify his practice' (p. 118). This double conclusion was extremely important, both validating Shakespeare's hand in the greater part of the play and identifying the presence of another dramatist, for whom the most likely candidate so far suggested was George Peele. Yet Timberlake's meticulous work made little impact on the scholarly discussion of *Titus Andronicus*.

The undeserved obscurity which Timberlake's study received was caused in some degree by Hereward T. Price, who discussed the play's authorship in 1943 'with the idea of subjecting as many tests of authorship as possible to as severe a criticism as possible'.[28] Challenging criticism is always welcome, of course, since a well-argued and properly illustrated thesis will stand up to any

[28] H. T. Price, 'The Authorship of *Titus Andronicus*', *JEGP* 42 (1943): 55–81, at p. 55.

onslaught. But Price, in his desire to claim Shakespeare's sole authorship, mis-represented the counter-arguments so completely that no one took any notice of Timberlake's contribution until 1979, when MacDonald Jackson validated its worth.[29] Price attacked metrical tests as obeying what he polemically called 'the law of variation', namely that 'if a play shows variation of any kind, say as . . . in the percentage of the feminine endings from one scene to another, then, such variation is proof either of multiple authorship or that different stages of revision are embedded in the text . . .'. But, Price argued, Shakespeare's early work has 'a curious unevenness in quality', so that 'some scenes turn out to be better written than others. A purely mechanical application of statistics will never explain these variations in excellence or make clear to us the processes of a poet's mind' (Price 1943, p. 64). Here, though, Price shifted the grounds of discussion, introducing irrelevant aesthetic criteria— 'better written', 'variations in excellence'. None of the scholars using metrical tests has ever tried to discuss such issues, let alone clarify 'the processes of a poet's mind'. Their goal is simply to identify characteristic metrical practices, and to quantify the range within which variations occur. It is not the fact of variation which matters, since every writer will inevitably vary his style from one scene to another, but the degree of variation, which can be informative.

Price either never realized this point, or deliberately suppressed it, giving an utterly misleading account of Timberlake's work, which, he claimed, was 'vitiated by the underlying assumption that the percentage of feminine endings in a play ought to be fairly uniform'. But Timberlake never made such a claim, only that different writers had characteristically different rates, a fact he demonstrated beyond question by meticulous analyses of dozens of Elizabethan plays. Price failed to mention the strikingly low rates of feminine endings in the work of Greene, Peele, and many of their contemporaries, and the equally striking high rates in Shakespeare, telling his readers that 'it is normal for the use of this ending to vary from scene to scene', and that in '*The Two Gentlemen* the figures vary between 2.6 per cent and 22.1 per cent . . .' (p. 65). But anyone able to check Price's account against Timberlake's will notice how distorted it is: the figure of 2.6 per cent comes from 1.1, a short scene (75 lines), and therefore likely to be untypical, and it is by far the lowest figure for the whole play. Only two other scenes have rates below 10 per cent, while the average for the whole play is 15.7 per cent, a rate comparable with Shakespeare's other plays of this period, and up to ten times greater than many plays produced in the 1580s and 1590s. Price dismissed the issue by saying that '*Titus* has just about the number of feminine endings that one would predict for a play by Shakespeare. They are unevenly distributed, as usual in Shakespeare' (p. 65), a confident-sounding but vacuous and false

---

[29] M. P. Jackson, *Studies in Attribution: Middleton and Shakespeare* (Salzburg, 1979), pp. 151–2.

judgement. Price must be found wanting in a scholar's duty to represent the arguments of his predecessors fairly, whether one agrees with them or not. Trying to deny any difference between Act 1 and most of the rest of the play, he declared that 'its rhetoric is too complex and its construction too masterly for anybody but Shakespeare'. Many readers before and after Price have given detailed accounts of the deficiencies of this act, in terms of its repetitiveness, stereotyping, and dramaturgical awkwardness, but the defender of Shakespeare can always ignore such responses. Price performed a valuable service in analysing the play's overall structure and characterization, drawing useful parallels with *King Lear* (pp. 70–7), but his dismissal of all authorship tests showed conservatism in its worst light.

The first detailed evaluation of Peele's share in *Titus Andronicus* since J. M. Robertson was made by John Dover Wilson, who cited much of the earlier literature in his edition, praising Parrott's 1919 essay as 'at once the most systematic and the most suggestive'. The parallels that Parrott drew between the play and *Venus and Adonis* might be dismissed as imitation, Wilson pointed out, but those with *Lucrece* prove either 'a Shakespearian authorship or revision of *Titus*' (Wilson 1948, p. xix). Agreeing with Muriel St Clare Byrne's classic essay on the importance of 'quality' in the evidence from parallels— that is, the superior value of parallelisms existing in both thought and language—Wilson claimed 'parallelism of situation or theme' as an extension of this category, and stated a principle which my survey of authorship studies since the nineteenth century certainly supports, namely that 'once parallels of high quality have been found in sufficient number to establish identity of authorship, parallels of lower quality become interesting too' (pp. xix–xx). Wilson then cited twenty-four 'high quality' parallels between *Titus* and Shakespeare's early plays and poems, most of them exhibiting 'identity of cadence, as well as similarity of situation, thought, image or phrase' (pp. xx–xxiii). He added a dozen common Shakespearian 'turns of speech' which he had noted in *Titus*, not individual to Shakespeare, but all occurring in that play. These include such habits as a 'cumulative succession of phrases or epithets beginning with "this" or "that"', 'sentences beginning "Now will I"', the emphatic use of 'even' at the beginning of a line, and the expression 'As who should (would) say', meaning 'as if to say'. For these 'turns of speech' Wilson cited about forty instances from Shakespeare's early plays, and included many more in his notes (pp. xxiii–xxiv). He was fully justified in concluding that 'the external evidence for Shakespeare's hand in the play has been corroborated by the internal' (p. xxv).

Yet, although Wilson could 'not find a single convincing trace of Shakespeare in the whole of Act 1', like 'Parrott and many other critics' he did discover there ample traces of George Peele (pp. xxv–xxxiv). To begin with, Wilson argued, the verse of Act 1 lacks several distinct qualities found in Shakespeare's verse, especially 'its vital dramatic quality'. In Shakespeare's authentic work 'the form and movement of the verse is determined by the individuality of the character speaking it; it *sounds* like the utterance of a human voice', and expresses an individual energy of thought (p. xxvi). In the first act of *Titus*, by contrast, the verse has a 'deadly monotony' and 'metrical flatness'. But the verse

is dramatically flat also, since all the characters speak with the same voice, frame their sentences after similar patterns, and even borrow words and phrases from each other. Almost every speech, for instance, during the first half of the act, i.e. for some 240 lines, begins with a vocative and continues with a verb in the imperative mood. Saturninus opens the play with

> Noble patricians. Patrons of my right.

And when Bassianus follows on, seven lines later, like this:

> Romans, friends, followers, favourers of my right,

he seems an auctioneer, outbidding his rival by one alliterative word. The speech he then delivers is, moreover, a bag of tricks, some of which are used several times in other parts of the act. (p. xxvii)

The words 'of my right', for instance, are repeated from line 1, and the word 'right' recurs as a terminal word on no fewer than three subsequent occasions, at lines 41, 56, 279. In that speech Bassianus also uses 'the tiresome rhetorical device' of referring to himself in the third person, which 'occurs more than a dozen times elsewhere in this act'. The lines of Bassianus vowing to

> consecrate
> To justice, continence and nobility
>
> (1.1.14–15)

are echoed in idiom and structure shortly afterwards, in lines given to Titus:

> consecrate
> My sword, my chariot, and my prisoners
>
> (1.1.248–9)

The most striking repetition, Wilson observed, involved a speech by Bassianus earlier in the scene, where he begins with a vocative referring to himself:

> *If ever* Bassianus, Caesar's son
> *Were gracious in* the *eyes* of *royal* Rome,
> Keep *then* this passage to the Capitol
> ·   ·   ·   ·   ·   ·   ·   ·
> *And*, Romans, fight for freedom in your choice.
>
> (1.1.10–17)

At lines 428–31 'Tamora in a briefer speech reproduces the very structure of Bassianus' nine lines and in part his words, even concluding, as he does, with a line commencing "And", and reiterating the vocative with which the speech opens':

> My worthy lord, *if ever* Tamora
> *Were gracious in* those *princely eyes* of thine,
> *Then* hear me speak indifferently for all;
> *And* at my suit, sweet, pardon what is past.

As Wilson rightly observed,

Once we begin noting the echoes and repetitions in Act 1, there is no end to them. For a sample: the words 'gracious' and 'return' become obsessions, and are used half a dozen times or more in the first 170 lines; 'in arms' or 'with arms' occurs at the end of ll. 2, 30, 32, 38 and 196; the Goths are three times described as having been 'yoked' by Titus (ll. 30, 69, 111), and his sons twice as 'alive and dead' (ll. 81, 123); 'appeasing' the 'shadows' of the dead is also twice spoken of (ll. 100, 126); and the tomb to which they are consigned is called 'sweet cell of virtue' in l. 93 and 'virtue's nest' in l. 376. Among other recurrences are three lines (ll. 294, 300, 344) beginning 'Nor thou nor he', 'Nor her nor thee', 'Nor thou, nor these' respectively; the odd word 're-salute' (ll. 75, 326) which is not found elsewhere in the canon; echoes like 'live in fame' (l. 158), 'sleep in fame' (l. 173), 'lives in fame' (l. 390), and 'repose in fame' (l. 353); a strained use of 'humbled' (ll. 51, 252, 472). In a word, Act 1, the product of a mind working mechanically, is a tissue of clichés in metre, sentence structure and phrasing. (pp. xxviii–xxix)

Earlier critics had described Peele's verse as prone to 'diffuseness and tautology',[30] but Wilson was the first to document the density of self-repetition found in Act 1 of this play.

Wilson described 'most of the clichés and tricks' he itemized as 'indubitably Peele's . . . No dramatist of the age is so apt to repeat himself, or so much given to odd or strained phrases, which once coined, or borrowed from some one else, he will reproduce time after time . . .' (pp. xxix–xxx). Wilson quoted several passages from Peele's earlier plays to demonstrate the continuity of his style, particularly 'his trick of falling into the vocative line' opening a speech, complete with imperatives, and reference to oneself in the third person. This complex of stylistic traits 'became in Peele's years of decline almost a spasmodic reaction', and account for the mechanical way these mannerisms occur in *Titus Andronicus* (pp. xxx–xxxi).

One of the most valuable features of Dover Wilson's edition remains his

---

[30] H. Dugdale Sykes, for instance, judged that 'Diffuseness and tautology are perhaps the most conspicuous defects of Peele's versification. In particular no dramatist of the period shows so absolute a lack of compunction in using two words of the same meaning simply to fill out a line', such 'to *yield* and to *surrender up*': *Sidelights on Shakespeare* (Stratford-upon-Auon, 1919), p. 134.

citing of parallel passages in Peele's poems and plays. Since readers will find it difficult to track down an edition more than fifty years old, and since none of the mainline editions published since then—by E. M. Waith (1984),[31] Alan Hughes (1994),[32] Jonathan Bate (1995)[33]—has included this material, I should like to quote some of it. Wilson arranged it in the sequence of the play's action, but I group it according to the works being echoed, to show how many of his own writings Peele recalled. I shall also add some parallels of language and style that I have myself noticed.

To begin with the poem having the closest link to *Titus Andronicus*, *The Honour of the Garter. Displaied in a Poem gratulatorie*. This, 'the noblest of [Peele's] court poems', as David Horne describes it, was written to celebrate the Earl of Northumberland's installation as a Knight of the Garter: the ceremony took place on 26 June 1593, the Earl having paid Peele £3 for it three days earlier.[34] The poem begins as a dream-vision, the poet having fallen asleep near Windsor Castle, being surprised by the noise of a cannon greeting a 'hoste of aerie armed men':

> Anon I saw
> Under a Canapie of Crymsin bysse,
> Spangled with gold and set with silver bels
> That sweetlie chimed, and luld me halfe a sleepe,
> A goodly king in robes most richly dight.
> The upper, like a Romaine Palliament,
> In deede a Chapperon, for such it was;
> And looking neerer, loe upon his legge,
> An auncient badge of honor I espyed,
> A Garter brightly glistring in mine eye . . .
>
> (86–96)

Peele continues in this courtly style, a mixture of Chaucer and Spenser's *Shepheardes Calender*, to describe the history of the founding of the Garter order, celebrating English heroes, who are freely mixed with those of ancient Greek, Roman, and biblical sources—

> For in the house of Fame what famous man,
> What Prince but hath his Trophie and his place?
>
> (252–3)

All these heroes, naturally enough, embody the chivalric virtues, and Peele appropriately introduces an apostrophe to the highest of these virtues:

---

[31] E. M. Waith (ed.), Shakespeare, *Titus Andronicus* (Oxford 1984).
[32] A. Hughes (ed.), Shakespeare, *Titus Andronicus* (Cambridge, 1994).
[33] J. Bate (ed.), Shakespeare, *Titus Andronicus*, New Arden Shakespeare, third series (London, 1995).
[34] D. H. Horne, *The Life and Minor Works of George Peele* (New Haven, 1952), p. 173.

> O sacred loyaltie, in purest harts
> Thou buildst thy bowre: thy weedes of spotlesse white;
> Like those that stood for Romes great offices,
> Makes thee renownd, glorious in innocencie.

(313–16)

For his opening scene in *Titus* Peele drew on the same associations of words and ideas, as Marcus informs Titus that 'the people of Rome' have decided to reward him for his 'justice' and send

> This palliament of white and spotless hue,
> And name thee in election for the empire.
> Be *candidatus*, then, and put it on . . .
>
> (1.1.179–85)

The *Garter* poem echoes—or is echoed by—*Titus* in several other ways. The poem contains many celebrations of martial virtue, regularly pairing two or more abstract ideals: one hero is

> renowned
For arms, for honour, and religious love
(285–6)

another performed 'deedes to fame and virtue consecrate' (1.384). In the play the same verbal groupings reappear. Bassianus describes the Roman Capitol as being

> to virtue consecrate,
To justice, continence, and nobility
(1.1.14–15)

while Titus offers obeisance to Saturninus, to whom

> I consecrate
My sword, my chariot, and my prisoners.
(1.1.248–9)

In the *Garter* poem Bouche and Bedford are 'renowned for armes' (209, 285–6): in the play we meet 'Renownèd Titus, flourishing in arms' (1.1.38). Marcus entreats Titus 'by honour of his name' (1.1.39), a formula that occurs in the *Garter* poem, 'in honour of that name' (212)—and, as Wilson noted (p. 104), recurs in Peele's *Edward 1*, *The Araygnment of Paris*, and *The Battle of Alcazar*. In the *Garter* poem, immediately following, Peele addresses Wriothesley, 'To whom my thoughts are humble and devote' (213): twelve lines later in *Titus* Bassianus addresses 'her to whom my thoughts are humbled all' (1.1.51). In the *Garter* poem Borough is hailed as 'Patrone of Musicke and of Chivalrie' (386), in *Titus* Saturninus describes the patricians as 'patrons of my right' (1.1.1), and Titus is called 'patron of virtue' (1.1.65). Titus' opening lines,

> Hail, Rome, victorious in thy mourning weeds!
> Lo, as the bark that hath discharged his fraught
> Returns with precious lading to the bay
> From whence at first she weighed her anchorage,
> Cometh Andronicus, bound with laurel boughs,
> To re-salute his country with his tears
>
> (1.1.70–5)

echo an autobiographical sequence in the *Garter* poem:

> Haile Windsore, where I sometimes tooke delight
> To hawke and hunt
>
> . . . .
>
> And where in Princely pleasure I reposde
> In my returne fro Fraunce
>
> . . . .
>
> Loe from the house of Fame, with Princely traines
>
> . . . .
>
> I resalute thee heere, and gratulate . . .
>
> (347–8, 350, 369, 372)

The rare word 're-salute', found nowhere in Shakespeare, recurs later in the opening scene, in Saturninus' vow: 'I will not re-salute the streets of Rome . . .' (326).

In the *Garter* poem Peele salutes one of his virtuous knights: 'long maist thou live, | And dye in fame' (398–9), and assures them all that they will 'survive, and triumph in eternitie' (410). Similarly, Lavinia hopes that her father will 'live in fame' (1.1.158), and Marcus welcomes his nephews, 'You that survive, and you that sleep in fame', to this 'funeral pomp' which 'triumphs over chance in honour's bed' (1.1.73, 176–8). The choric epitaph over Mutius, slain by his father, is 'He lives in fame, that died in virtue's cause (1.1.390): in the *Garter* poem Peele enjoins one of his heroes 'to follow vertues cause' (389). Readers will have observed how many of these parallels with *The Honour of the Garter* occur in the passage addressing individual knights and celebrating their virtue, a process that takes up much of the action in the opening scene of *Titus Andronicus*. Peele echoed the *Garter* poem in the scene following, where Aaron describes Tamora as 'Safe out of fortune's shot . . . Advanced beyond pale envy's threatning reach' (2.1.2–4). The heroes celebrated in the poem will 'triumph in eternitie, | Out of Oblivions reach, or Envies shot' (410–11). Like many practitioners of epideictic rhetoric, Peele is conscious that while virtue deserves to be celebrated, envy and malice will attack her, warning readers of his *Garter* poem that 'the Carle [Churl] Oblivion' and 'Envy' can blemish or obscure deserved merit:

> Yet in the house of Fame and Courtes of Kings,
> Envy will bite, or snarle and barke at least
>
> (336–40)

So, in *Titus*, Aaron warns Chiron and Demetrius that

> The Emperor's court is like the house of fame,
> The palace full of tongues, of eyes and ears
>
> (2.1.127–8)

Wilson noted that allusions to Chaucer's *House of Fame* were 'a constant theme of Peele's', citing four other instances from the poems and plays. In vowing revenge Titus promises: 'I will go get a leaf of brass, | And with a gad of steel will write these words' (4.1.101–2): so Peele assures the 'Lordly Peeres' honoured by the Garter that

> Your names are in this Register of Fame,
> Written in leaves and characters of golde.
>
> (407–8)

Peele's other poems provide fewer parallels, but some significant ones. From *An Eclogue Gratulatory* (1589), welcoming Essex's return from Portugal—to 'gratulate' was a favourite Peele verb—the poet recalled two phrases. Essex returned 'laden with Honors spoile' (87), just as 'laden with honour's spoils, | Returns the good Andronicus to Rome' (1.1.36–7); Essex should have received a hero's welcome: 'Laurell bowes . . . adorne his browes' (94–5) as Titus did, 'bound with laurel boughs' (1.1.75). In *Polyhymnia* (1590), a poem celebrating thirteen pairs of noblemen jousting in honour of the Queen, Peele also used the formulaic 'To Virtue or to Vesta consecrate' (280), and he may have recalled his (admittedly commonplace) praise there of 'A liberal Hand, badge of nobilitie' (190) for Tamora's appeal to Titus to be 'merciful; | Sweet mercy is nobility's true badge' (1.1.118–19)— in *Descensus Astraeae* (1591) he had written 'Sweet mercy sways her sword' (30). From this jousting poem he echoed the description of his heroes on horseback, 'Swift as the Swallow' (169) in Titus' boast that he has 'horse will follow where the game . . . runs like swallows o'er the plain' (2.2.23–4)—presumably he meant 'as swift as swallows'; in *Edward I* a servant is told to 'hie away as swift as swallow flies' (1433). In *Descensus Astraeae* Peele revealed again his fondness for the verb 'to gratulate', using it twice in a poem of only 146 lines. The Presenter offers his 'Emblem' to the citizens of London, their 'honor and [their] oath to gratulate' (12), while the final speaker assures the Lord Mayor that here 'Are come these strangers lovingly inflamde | To gratulate to you my lovely Lord | This gladsome day wherein your honors spring' (125–7). From *Anglorum Feriae* (1595), another poem praising Queen Elizabeth, Peele recalled a passage he had written describing the 'Loyall

English knightes in armes' (159), ready with their swords 'To wounde his crest whatever foe he bee | That any way in hir dishonor braves' (168–9). In exactly the same chivalric terms Titus complains, 'Marcus, even thou hast struck upon my crest, | And with these boys mine honour hast thou wounded' (1.1.364–5). In the poem Peele described how

> the rising sune
> gallops the Zodiack in his fierie wayne.
>
> (23–4)

In the play Aaron uses the same association of ideas to describe Tamora's sudden rise:

> As when the golden sun salutes the morn,
> And having gilt the ocean with his beams,
> Gallops the zodiac in his glistering coach.
>
> (2.1.5–7)

Indeed, Peele was so pleased with this phrase that he repeated it in *Descensus Astraeae*, where time makes 'heavens bright eie | Gallop the Zodiacke' (3–4).

Peele's earliest surviving poem (written between 1579 and 1581) was *The Tale of Troy*, a reworking of the fall of Troy in under 500 lines which derived less from the *Iliad* than from Ovid's *Metamorphoses* (Book 13) and *Heroides* (Epistles 5, 16, 17), and from the English medieval versions by Caxton and Lydgate.[35] Peele echoed his Troy poem several times in the play, most appropriately for Titus' proud boast that, in the service of Rome, he has

> buried one-and-twenty valiant sons,
> Knighted in field, slain manfully in arms
> In right and service of their noble country
>
> (1.1.195–7)

Peele used the same chivalric diction in the first edition (1589) of his poem (some details are changed in the 1604 Quarto)[36] to describe Hecuba, who 'did enrich' Priam 'With twenty sonnes', who were

> All Knights at Armes, gay, gallant, brave and bolde,
> Of wit and manhood such as might suffice,
> To venter on the highest peece of service.
>
> (15, 20–2)

In the poem Peele described Hecuba, 'this thrice-wretched lady', as being pursued by 'Fortunes spight and mallice' until breaking-point, 'And worne with sorrows, waxen fell and mad' (460–2). In the play young Lucius has often heard Titus Andronicus say that

---

[35] C. T. Prouty (ed.), *The Life and Works of George Peele*, 3 vols. (New Haven, 1952–70), i. 149–50 and iii. 12–24.

[36] Cf. Prouty 1952–70, i. 183.

Extremity of griefs would make men mad.
And I have heard that Hecuba of Troy
Ran mad for sorrow.

(4.1.18–20)

In *Titus Andronicus* Saturninus scornfully describes Lavinia as 'that changing piece' (1.1.309)—or 'fickle wench' as Waith glosses the phrase: in *The Tale of Troy* (1589 Quarto), needless to say, Cressida is described as 'that chaunging peece' (289), while Helen is 'this reprochfull peece' (196)—that is, one deserving reproach. In *Titus* Marcus, begging Titus to give Mutius proper burial, recalls how 'wise Laertes' sonne | Did graciously plead for his funerals' (1.1.380–1): in the *Troy* poem we find the same combination, 'wise Laertes' sonne' (360). At the end of the opening scene Titus invites everyone 'To hunt the panther' (1.1.493), a non-Shakespearian beast, but one referred to in the *Troy* poem, where Hector is 'like the untam'd Panther' (303). In *The Praise of Chastity*, 'by G. P. Master of Arts' from *The Phoenix Nest* (1593), we read of heroes able 'To tame wilde Panthers but by strength of hand' (42).

Some of Peele's words and phrases may be distinctive, but the many parallels between *Titus* and his poems and plays show that his diction was basically unadventurous, the same limited range of words and phrases doing duty in many different contexts. Peele had a generalized vocabulary, in which military and heroic terms used for the Earl of Essex could be reused for a Roman hero without any sense of incongruity. It is no surprise, then, to find passages from *Titus Andronicus* echoing the language of *Edward I*, a play set in medieval England.[37] Marcus celebrates Titus for having 'yoked a nation strong, trained up in arms' (1.1.30): Helinor, the Queen Mother, celebrates England as 'a warlike nation traind in feates of armes' (*Edward I*, l. 16). Marcus entreats Titus 'by honour of his name: | Whom worthily you would have now succeed' (1.1.39–40): Helinor urges the Scottish king to 'Shake thy speres in honour of his name, | Under whose roialtie thou wearst the same' (699–700). Titus' first speech, in which he offers 'to re-salute his country with his tears, | Tears of true joy for his return to Rome' (1.1.75–6) echoes Helinor's welcome to her sons: 'With teares of joye salutes your sweet returne' (51). Titus presents 'the poor remains' of his sons (1.1.81), Helinor describes 'The poor remainder of the royall Fleete' (5). Titus urges Tamora to 'patient yourself' (1.1.121): Glocester tells Helinor to 'Pacient your highnes' (44). Titus buries his sons with the wish

In peace and honour rest you here, my sons
. . . repose you here in rest

(1.1.150–1)

---

[37] My quotations are from the edition by Frank S. Hook, in Prouty 1952–70, ii (1961), pp. 1–212. The play consists of 23 scenes, lines being through-numbered.

Edward I addresses his nobles: 'Now then let us repose and rest us heere' (636). Lavinia catches up the concluding line of Titus' valedictory speech:

Titus. In peace and honour rest you here, my sons!
Lavinia. In peace and honour live Lord Titus long!

(156–7)

Peele used this repetition of a complete line three times in *Edward I*:

Edward. And wil our Coronation be solemnized,
　　Upon the fourteenth of December next.
Q. Eli. Upon the fourteenth of December next?

(195–7)

Versses. I tooke the chaine and gave your Grace the rope.
Balioll. You tooke the chaine and give my Grace the rope.

(2058–9; also 1003–5)

Titus hopes that Lavinia will 'outlive thy father's days | And fame's eternal date, for virtue's praise!' (1.1.167–8): Edward celebrates his 'worthie men at armes, | For chivalrie and worthie wisdoms praise' (673–4). Saturninus assures Tamora that 'he comforts you | Can make you greater than the queen of Goths' (1.1.268–9): Lluellen welcomes Meredeth as 'the man, | Must make us great' (768–9)—both are instances of what grammarians call the 'zero relative' form, the word 'who' being omitted. Saturninus announces 'I'll trust by leisure him that mocks me once' (1.1.301): the Queen Mother is sure that something wished for 'wil come by leisure' (219). Titus laments: 'The dismall'st day is this that e'er I saw' (1.1.384): David welcomes 'The sweetest sunne that ere I saw to shine' (1002). Saturninus promises Tamora that 'This day shall be a love-day' (1.1.490): Mortimer urges himself to 'make their love holidaies' (1244). Titus, a Roman general, promises Saturninus that tomorrow morning 'we'll give your grace *bonjour*' (1.1.494): King Edward 'bids his Souldiers *Bien veneu*' (111). We expect to find a Capitol in ancient Rome (*Tit.*, 1.1.12, 41, 77), but may be surprised to find a medieval English king apostrophizing 'O glorious Capitoll, beautious Senate house' (102). In his soliloquy Aaron urges himself to capitalize on the dominance he has achieved over Tamora,

　　　　　Fettered in amorous chains,
　And faster bound to Aaron's charming eyes
　Than is Prometheus tied to Caucasus

(2.1.15–17)

Peele remembered here two passages from *Edward I*, one where Lluellen vows that he will recapture his love:

> the Chaines that Mulciber erst made,
> To tie Prometheus lims to Caucasus,
> Nor furies phanges shal hold me long from her
>
> (787–9)

and Edward I's declaration of his love for Queen Helinor:

> Fast to those lookes are all my fancies tide.
>
> (1629)

Demetrius calls his brother 'youngling' (2.1.73), a word found in *Edward I* (1063), and *Alcazar* (256). Other Peele word-favourites found both in *Titus* and *Edward I* include 'gratulate': 'And gratulate his safe return to Rome' (*Tit.*, 1.1.221), 'Friends gratulate to me my joyfull hopes' (*Ed. I*, 826), and 'remunerate': 'and will nobly him remunerate' (*Tit.*, 1.1.398), 'Nobles strive who shall remunerate' (*Ed. I*, 140), 'We will remunerate his resolution' (2036).—Although, as reference to the Chadwyck-Healey database will show, other writers in this period may have used one of these words, Peele was the only author to use *remunerate*, *gratulate*, and *resalute*.

The unity of diction in Peele's plays and poems, an amalgam of Greco-Latin military and ethical terms with native post-medieval English stock, is seen again in *The Battle of Alcazar*, a play based on recent European history, the defeat in 1578 of the army led by Sebastian, the young King of Portugal, leaving a power vacuum which Spain swiftly occupied. English interest in the play was increased by the subplot, concerning Captain Thomas Stukley, the adventurer who called himself 'Marquis of Ireland'. Many parallels link this story of violence and revenge with *Titus*. In both plays Peele prefers the word 'brethren' to 'brothers', a usage that scholars have singled out as a stylistic marker differentiating his hand from Shakespeare's (see below), in at least one instance in the trisyllabic form 'bretheren'.[38] In both plays we find the word 'successful' (used by Shakespeare only four times outside this play) being applied to victory in battle, with a further idiosyncrasy, its combination with the preposition *in*.[39] The word 'successful' occurs three times in the first scene of *Titus Andronicus*, four times in *The Battle of Alcazar*. Titus is 'successful in the battles that he fights', his sons are welcomed 'from successful wars', and Titus recalls how he 'led my country's strength successfully' (1.1.66, 172, 194). In *Alcazar* 'souldiers [having] rightfull quarrels ayde | Successful are', a general's wife is confident that 'this battell [will] succesfull be', another warrior's widow wishes the general to be 'successfull in thy

---

[38] Cf. *Titus*, 1.1.89, 104, 122, 123, 146, 160, 348, 357; *Alc.*, 26 and stage direction following, 27, 33, 48, 133, 139, 297.

[39] This usage seems to be unique to Peele: I find it nowhere in the Chadwyck–Healey databases; Shakespeare combines 'successful to' (*Winter's Tale*, 3.1.12). Peele also writes of 'successe in love' (*Araygnement of Paris*), and 'successe in our enterprize' (*Edward I*), although this usage is less distinctive: cf. 'success in arms' (*1 Henry VI*, 4.7.62).

worke thou undertakes', while the victorious Muly Mahamet proclaims that 'the God of kings | Hath made thy warre successfull by thy right' (110–11, 185, 188, 1381–2). The Emperor Saturninus consoles Tamora:

> Clear up, fair queen, that cloudy countenance
>
> (1.1.263)

Abdelemec comforts some 'distressed ladies':

> Now cleere your waterie eies, wipe teares away
>
> (105)

Marcus Andronicus refers to 'the woeful fere' (husband) in the story of Lucretia (*Tit.*, 4.1.88), a word only occurring once elsewhere in the Shakespeare canon (*TNK*, 5.1.116); it is found in *Alcazar* (112). The word 'remunerate' recurs twice here: 'To gratifie and to remunerate | Thy love', and 'to remunerate | Thy worthines and magnanimitie' (*Alc.*, 77–8, 352–3). The trick of echoing a whole verse line, used by Lavinia catching up Titus' speech, recurs three times in *Alcazar*:

> *Sebast.* To aide Mahamet king of Barbarie?
> *Bish.* To aide Mahamet king of Barbarie
>
> (716–7)
> *Sebast.* To propagate the fame of Portugall.
> *Embas.* To propagate the fame of Portugall
>
> (765–6; also 363–4)

Many other parallels of language and thought link these two plays. Bassianus describes the corpses that he brings 'unto their latest home' (*Tit.*, 1.1.83), an unShakespearian expression used by the Presenter in *Alcazar*, describing the victims whom Muly Mahomet 'hales to their longest home' (*Alc.*, 25). The Roman Lucius feeds Alarbus' entrails to 'the sacrificing fire | Whose smoke like incense doth perfume the sky' (*Tit.*, 1.1.144–5), and the pagan Muly pays 'thankes to heaven with sacrificing fire' (*Alc.*, 1375), a phrase echoing an earlier one, 'sacrifice . . . | Not with sweet smoake of fire, or sweet perfume' (361–2).

Despite the contemporary story and exotic setting, *The Battle of Alcazar* has the same generalized chivalric-ethical colouring that we find through-out Peele's poetry and plays, not least in the 'Romaine Tragedie' of *Titus Andronicus*. The phrase 'by honour of his name' (*Tit.*, 1.1.39) is shared with *Alcazar*, 'in honor of thy name' (908), as is the phrase 'in mourning weeds' (*Tit.*, 1.1.70; *Alc.*, 205). Marcus' dead kinsmen sleep 'in honour's bed' (*Tit.*, 1.1.178), while Stukley is sure that he is about to die 'in that bed of honour' where Sebastian lies (*Alc.*, 1369–70). These chivalric value terms suffuse the Roman play, as in Lavinia's obedient reply to Saturninus' hope that she is 'not displeased' with his 'Princely . . . usage' of Tamora (2.1.266–70):

Not I, my lord, sith true nobility
Warrants these words in princely courtesy.

(271–2)

'Princely' must have been one of Peele's favourite epithets, for the
Chadwyck–Healey database of English Renaissance drama records him using
it over thirty times (it also fits easily into iambic verse). It occurs twelve times
in *The Battle of Alcazar*, once echoing Lavinia's coupling of it with the
specifically chivalric term 'courtesy': Abdelmelec gives thanks to Bassa 'In
honour and princely curtesie', and is in turn greeted as 'courteous and
honourable' (72–3). Subsequently Peele describes the Portugese King's 'wel-
comes . . . to strangers' as being 'Princely and honourable as his state
becomes' (445–6), and in general attaches the term 'princely' to any suitable
noun: 'princely grace', 'princely heart', 'princely mind', 'princely coarse', and
many more. As for the other chivalric epithet that Lavinia uses, 'true' (*trewe*,
treuthe or loyalty, is arguably the key concept in the medieval chivalric
romance), Peele uses that term even more frequently (nearly fifty times), most
often in *Alcazar* ('The true office of right and roialtie', 'True unfained faith'),
and *Edward I* ('true liegemen', 'true allegeance'). In *Titus Andronicus*
Tamora swears that she will massacre the Andronici, 'And make them know
what 'tis to [harm] a queen' (1.1.454): Abdelmelec vows to defeat Sebastian,
'And make him know and rue' his aggression (*Alc.*, 1062). Titus orders his
sons 'To attend the Emperor's person carefully' (2.2.8); Abdelmelec has a
'trustie band of men | That carefully attend us in our camp' (*Alc.*, 66–7).

Peelean diction also links *Titus* to his early 'Pastorall', *The Araygnment of
Paris*, itself a reworking of his *Tale of Troy*. In the Prologue Ate arrives from
hell, prophesying that the choice Paris is to make between the three goddesses
will cause 'Proude Troy' to fall,

King Priams pallace waste with flaming fire,
Whose thicke and foggie smoake peircing the skie,
Must serve for messenger of sacrifice
T'appeaze the anger of the angrie heavens

(11–15)

Peele recalled this passage in *Titus Andronicus*, dramatizing the Romans'
wish to exact retribution from the Goths for 'their brethren slain':

Religiously they ask a sacrifice
.   .   .   .
T'appease the groaning shadows that are gone
.   .   .   .
And entrails feed the sacrificing fire,
Whose smoke like incense doth perfume the sky.

(1.1.124, 126, 144–5)

Having killed the disobedient Mutius, Titus tells Lucius that 'Nor thou, nor he, are any sons of mine' (1.1.294–5), a construction repeated three times in this scene (ll. 300, 344, 425): in his oration to the gods' council Paris realizes how limited his pleas can be, 'sith nor that, nor this may doe me boote' (863). Aaron refers deferentially to Tamora, 'our Empress, with her sacred wit' (2.1.121), the Latinism 'sacred' meaning 'devoted': Vulcan says of Apollo (more appropriately) that 'We are beholding to his sacred wit' (1072). Marcus boasts that his dogs

> Will rouse the proudest panther in the chase
>
> (2.2.21)

Faunus is happy to have caught a runaway,

> The fattest fairest fawne in all the chace
>
> (36)

and Dover Wilson (p. 116) recorded that this non-Shakespearian usage, 'chase', recurred four more times in *The Araygnement of Paris* (151, 176, 218, 1092)—Shakespeare prefers the term 'park' (3.1.88). In this pastoral Peele used some of his favourite words: as in *Titus* (4.1.89) the rare word 'fe(e)re' or 'phere' (49, 1069, 1233), and the verb 'gratulate' (175). If Peele's fondness for the virtues of honour and service associated with medieval chivalry seemed out of place in *Titus Andronicus*, the repeated invocation here of 'the honour of chyvallrye' (469)[40] and its values sound equally anachronistic in an ancient Greek myth.

The most remote of Peele's plays to the Roman tragedy is his amiable comedy, *The Old Wives Tale*, but Peele remembered it when he wrote an out-doors scene for *Titus*, the hunt which begins so innocently:

> The hunt is up, the morn is bright and grey,
> The fields are fragrant, and the woods are green
>
> (2.2.1–2)

The conjurer Sacrapant begins a scene with exactly the same evocation of favourable weather and general happiness:

> The day is cleare, the Welkin bright and gray,
> The Larke is merrie, and records hir notes,
> Each thing rejoyseth underneath the Skie.
>
> (335–7)

Equally remote from *Titus* is Peele's *David and Bethsabe*, which derives its action and diction jointly from the Bible and Du Bartas.[41] None the less, it

---

[40] Cf. also 'Ladie of learning and of chivalrie' (159); 'With wealth, with beautie and with chivalrie' (931); 'Her shilde, her launce, ensignes of chivalrie' (1099).

[41] Cf. the edition by Elmer Blistein in Prouty 1952–70, iii. 133–295, at pp. 143–51.

shows two examples of the collocation we have met elsewhere, 'success' + 'battle' (228, 429–30), and includes four instances of the last line of a speech becoming the first line of the next:

> *Cusay.* Hath sent Urias from the Syrian wars.
> *David.* Welcome Urias from the Syrian wars
>
> (418–19)
>
> *Servus.* And Davids heart would not be comforted?
> *David.* Yea Davids heart will not be comforted
>
> (689–90, also 127–8, 215–16)

In *David and Bethsabe* Peele was unusually fond of this unimaginative form of repetition, for the play contains no fewer than eight instances of a half-line being so echoed from one speech to the next (e.g. 421–2, 458–9, 919–21, 1010–11, 1036–7, 1128–9, 1356–7, 1804–5). In this play we also find an instance of the symmetrical balancing of speeches so common in the first scene of *Titus Andronicus*. When David throws himself on the ground in remorse and self-abasement, Nathan delivers a ten-line speech, beginning 'David stand up. Thus saith the Lord by me: | David the King shall live . . .', and ending:

> The child shall surely die, that erst was borne,
> His mothers sin, his kingly fathers scorne.
>
> (660–9)

David answers in a matching ten-line speech, beginning 'How just is Jacobs God in all his workes!', and ending:

> The babe must die that was to David borne,
> His mothers sin his kingly fathers scorne.
>
> (670–9)

The repetition rounds off the exchange, the patterning giving it a ritual quality, rather like Titus' repetition of the line 'In peace and honour rest you here, my sons' to begin and end his farewell blessing after their interment (1.1.150, 156).

This selection from the parallels Dover Wilson cited between Peele's scenes in *Titus Andronicus* and his other poems and plays, to which I have added, indicates a remarkable overlap in attitudes—admiration for chivalric behaviour, the virtues of honour, duty, and self-sacrifice for the state—as well as in syntax, grammar, and diction. Although Wilson agreed that Peele was wholly responsible for Act 1, and largely responsible for 2.1, 2.2, and 4.1, he indicated in his notes (e.g. pp. 112–16, 135–8) passages in those scenes where he thought he could detect Shakespeare's hand, or Shakespeare's influence. Conversely, Wilson indicated other passages within scenes undoubtedly by

Shakespeare where he believed he could detect the style of Peele. In such cases, and we will meet several more in the other plays of joint authorship, three explanations are possible: the co-authors influenced each other; one of them inserted a passage of his own writing; or he modified his colleague's first draft. It is true that such 'over-writing' must have occurred, especially if the main author tidied up the text for the playbook scribe, and Cyrus Hoy, a scholar not prone to wild conjecture, indicated passages in Fletcher's co-authored plays where he felt that one collaborator had retouched the other's lines.[42] However, all the historical evidence reviewed in Chapter 1 indicates that co-authors normally contributed whole acts, or at least whole scenes, and the piecemeal over-writing that Dover Wilson claimed to discover seems improbable. Wilson suggested that other passages showed signs of Peele's hand,[43] but the evidence is not decisive. Wilson described what he felt to be a 'diffuseness and metrical monotony' in the sequence where Saturninus reads aloud the letter with which Aaron incriminates Titus' sons for Bassianus' murder:

> 'An if we miss to meet him handsomely,
> Sweet huntsman—Bassianus 'tis we mean—
> Do thou so much as dig the grave for him;
> Thou know'st our meaning; look for thy reward
> Among the nettles at the elder tree
> Which overshades the mouth of that same pit
> Where we decreed to bury Bassianus.
> Do this and purchase us thy lasting friends'.

(2.3.268–75)

The first Arden editor, H. C. Hart, had described the explanatory 'we mean' as ' "a weak poetical trick of Peele's" ', and Wilson added: 'note also the repetition in "meaning" (l. 271)' (p. 123). Twice over Saturninus begins a line 'Look sirs', and 'Sirs' (278, 283), for Wilson to comment: 'Shakespeare does not need such line-filling devices'. However, the ironic clarification identifying Bassianus as the 'sweet huntsman' whom Titus' sons are allegedly hunting is perfectly justified, given that a letter is being quoted, while it seems to me that the directness and simplicity of the language, syntax, and verse movement in this speech are quite beyond Peele. Similarly unconvincing are Wilson's comments on the speech where Titus appeals to the Emperor:

---

[42] C. Hoy, 'The Shares of Fletcher and his collaborators in the Beaumont and Fletcher Canon (II)', *SB* 9 (1957): 143–62, at pp. 144–55; IV, *SB* 12 (1959), 91–116, at pp. 108–9; V, *SB* 13 (1960), 77–108, at pp. 101–3.

[43] Other passages where Wilson saw traces of Peele include 2.3.91–115 (where he compared *Alcazar*, ll. 468–82); 2.3.116–33; 4.3.27–34; 5.3.19–25; 5.3.84–6 (cf. *Troy*, ll. 400–11); 5.3.120–40; 5.3.142–5.

> High Emperor, upon my feeble knee
> I beg this boon, with tears not lightly shed,
> That this fell fault of my accursèd sons—
> Accursèd if the fault be proved in them—
>
>   (2.3.288–91)

Wilson argued that this speech echoed Peele's opening scene, where Titus attributes 'feebleness' to himself (1.1.188), Tamora describes supplicants 'all humbled on your knees' (472), and there are several references to 'tears' (1.1.75–6, 159, 161–2). However, for these expressions several parallels can be found in roughly contemporary Shakespeare plays: 'I beg this boon' can be paralleled in *The Two Gentlemen of Verona*, 'A smaller boon than this I cannot beg' (5.4.24; also 5.4.150); in *Richard III*, 'I'll beg one boon' (4.1.302). The phrase 'feeble knee' can be matched several times: 'feeble steps' (*Two Gentlemen*, 2.7.10), 'feeble body' (2 *Henry VI*, 5.3.13); 'feeble hands' (*Richard III*, 2.2.58); 'feeble voice' (*King John*, 3.4.41); 'feeble wrong' (*Richard II*, 1.1.191); 'feeble key of untun'd cares' (*Comedy of Errors*, 5.1.311). Indeed, in a later scene in *Titus*, undubitably by Shakespeare, we find 'bow this feeble ruin to the earth' (3.1.207). As for the two highly rhetorical lines following, with their double repetitions:

> That this fell *fault* of my *accursèd* sons—
> *Accursèd* if the *fault* be proved in them—

such emphatic effects are common in early Shakespeare, as in Lady Anne's lines denouncing her husband's murderer:

> O, *cursèd* be the hand that made these holes!
> *Cursed* the *heart* that had the *heart* to do it!
> *Cursed* the *blood* that let this *blood* from hence!
> More direful hap betide that hated *wretch*
> That makes us *wretched* by the death of thee.
>   (*Richard III*, 1.2.14–18)

A glance at the concordance will show that Shakespeare regularly placed the word 'Accursèd' at the beginning of a line.

Peele's hand has been suspected in the sequence where Chiron stabs Bassianus:

> And this for me, *struck* home to show my *strength*
>
>   (2.3.117)

—as we shall see, double consonantal alliteration is a Peele speciality—and Lavinia braves Tamora's threat of violence:

> Ay, come, Semiramis, nay, barbarous Tamora,
> For no name fits thy nature but thy own!
>
>   (2.3.118–19)

echoing Aaron's celebration of Tamora, 'this Semiramis' (2.1.22). But, of
course, Shakespeare also used alliteration frequently in his early plays; he
may have taken the parallel with Semiramus from Peele; and, most impor-
tantly, the verse movement seems much more like Shakespeare. Although
Dover Wilson went on to hazard some wild theories about the play's theatrical genesis, and refused to take it seriously as a tragedy, he made on the whole
a strong case for the abundant presence of Peele's 'stereotyped phrases and
diction' (p. xliv).

With so much linguistic evidence of a diction common to *Titus* and to
Peele's other plays and poems we may expect that some favourite grammatical constructions will also appear. Dover Wilson attributed to Peele the
speech by Marcus ending 4.1, addressing himself and expressing compassion
for the sufferings of Titus:

> Marcus, attend him in his ecstasy,
> That hath more scars of sorrow in his heart
> Than foeman's marks upon his battered shield.
>
> (126–8)

Wilson noted 'the self-address (l. 126), and the passive antecedent (ll. 126–7),
a favourite construction of Peele's (cf. 1.1.5, 39, 41–2)' (p. 138). Apparently
independently of Wilson, J. C. Maxwell also identified a grammatical construction that, he claimed, was unusually frequent both in the first act of *Titus*
and in Peele, namely 'the use of a possessive (A) adjective or (B) pronoun as
antecedent of a relative clause'.[44] Maxwell cited, as an example of the first
type, these lines:

> I am his first-born son, that was the last
> That wore the imperial diadem of Rome
>
> (1.1.5–6)

—that is, 'the first-born son of him who . . .'. And as an example of the
second, Maxwell cited:

> Agree these deeds with that proud brag of thine,
> That saidst, I begged the empire at thy hands.
>
> (1.1.306–7)

This stylistic marker could be significant, Maxwell argued, since 'it is not
likely to be imitated by one author from another, consciously or even un-
consciously; and it is not likely to vary in frequency a great deal according to
subject-matter' (Maxwell 1950, p. 557).[45] Maxwell's main interest was in

---

[44] J. C. Maxwell, 'Peele and Shakespeare: A Stylometric Test', *JEGP* 49 (1950): 557–61, at
p. 557.

[45] Marco Mincoff agreed that this construction 'is unusually frequent with Peele', and that the
seven instances in Act I are 'certainly reminiscent of Peele rather than Shakespeare. The point is

TABLE 3.3. *Possessives as antecedents in* Titus Andronicus

	Total	Instances	Frequency
A scenes (Peele)	760 lines	7	108.6
B scenes (Shakespeare)	1,759 lines	3	586.3
Peele's poems	2,406 lines	20	120.3
Venus and Adonis	1,194 lines	2	597
Rape of Lucrece	1,855 lines	3	618.3

Source: Maxwell 1950, pp. 558–9.

distinguishing between Peele and Shakespeare, and his results endorsed Dover Wilson's argument that 'Act 1 of *Titus* is entirely by Peele and the remaining acts largely by Shakespeare' (p. 558). Again we see the bad effect of limited knowledge: had Maxwell used the metrical studies by Parrott and Timberlake he would have realized that 2.1 and 4.1 are probably also by Peele. Still, he did cite every instance of this construction (p. 560), which enables us to reprocess his data. If we divide the play into two parts, *A*, comprising 1.1, 2.1, 4.1, and *B*, the remainder, we can compare the two writers in terms of the frequency with which they used it (every *x* lines). Maxwell also provided data from their poems, which I treat in the same way in Table 3.3. As we instantly notice, Peele's rate for the poems closely approximates that for the three scenes in *Titus Andronicus* which Parrott and Timberlake identified as non-Shakespearian, while the authentically Shakespearian scenes from the play tally closely with Shakespeare's narrative poems written close in time. On average, Peele used this construction five times more frequently than Shakespeare did.

The scholarly debate over Shakespeare's co-authorship of *Titus Andronicus*, as with other plays, has spilled over into many areas of knowledge. The range and nature of his classical learning has often proved a key issue. H. T. Price, bent on proving that Shakespeare had written the whole play, faced the awkward fact that while 'Shakespeare's other plays are sparing of references to classical literature, *Titus* is full of them' (Price 1943, p. 66). The play 'contains frequent references to Roman beliefs and ritual', Price observed, yet 'Shakespeare is often mistaken about custom and ritual. Human sacrifices were not offered up at Rome (1.1.96); holy water was not used at Roman marriages (1.1.323–4); panthers were not hunted in Italy (1.1.493), etc.'. Perhaps 'the author of *Titus*' introduced reminiscences of

of importance, for while the patterns form a kind of jingle that imposes itself on the ear and lends itself very readily to imitation, voluntary or involuntary, the grammatical construction is comparatively unobtrusive, and less likely to be imitated' (Mincoff, *Shakespeare: The First Steps* (Sofia, 1976), p. 128).

Greek literature, for 'human sacrifices occur in the *Iliad*' (Books 21, 23), and panthers are also hunted in that poem (21.510–11—the correct reference is 21.573–81). Shakespeare, Price deduced, 'is trying to create atmosphere by bringing in what he remembers of classical customs', knowing that his audience won't 'ask where they came from. A University poet would have acted in a different way' (p. 67).

The line of argument here is that the play contains several erroneous references to Roman customs, but Shakespeare could not be expected to know better. Yet, at the same time, Price credited him with a knowledge of the *Iliad*, a strange discrepancy. But it is Price who ought to have known better. In Book 10 of the *Aeneid*, in the course of battle the Trojan warrior Pallas is killed. Aeneas joins the combat, vowing revenge:

> So now he captured
> Alive four warrior sons of Sulmo and four whom Ufens
> Had reared, designing to sacrifice them to the ghost of Pallas
> And sprinkle his funeral pyre with the blood of these captive youths.[46]

In Book 11, after Aeneas has defeated Mezentius, his first order is 'let us commit to earth our unburied comrades' (22), after which he intends to give Pallas an honourable burial, heaping on his pyre the 'spoil they had won in the battle':

> Horses and weapons, too, they had taken from the enemy.
> Manacled captives there were, consigned to be gifts to the dead—
> Victims whose blood would be sprinkled upon the altar flames.
>
> (79–84)

But then envoys from the defeated Latins arrive, asking to be able to bury their dead, and Aeneas relents—'Go now, and burn your unfortunate comrades on the pyre' (118). In due course both leaders, victor and defeated,

> Each, after his own traditional usage,
> Brought hither his dead. They applied to the pyres the funereal torches,
> And smoke rolled up, spreading out and palling the sky above.
>
> (185–7)

Virgil does not return to the fate of the captured prisoners awaiting sacrifice, but otherwise Peele has good Roman authority both for Lucius' appeal here to be allowed to 'hew' the 'proudest prisoner of the Goths', and for his subsequent report that they have correctly

---

[46] *Aeneid*, 10.517–20; trans. C. Day Lewis, *The Eclogues, Georgics and Aeneid of Virgil* (Oxford, 1966). This sequence clearly echoes the *Iliad*, where Achilles captures twelve young Trojans, duly slain by him on Patroclus' pyre (*Il.*, 21.26–33, 23.175–83). Although intended to show Aeneas' maddened loss of humanity, the language echoes Roman sacral rituals, which may have involved human sacrifice, cf. S. J. Harrison, *Virgil, Aeneid 10* (Oxford, 1991), pp. 202–3.

perform'd
Our Roman rites. Alarbus' limbs are lopp'd,
And entrails feed the sacrificing fire,
Whose smoke like incense doth perfume the sky.

(1.1.142–5)

As for panthers not being hunted in Italy, Price should have checked more carefully. Livy recorded the spectacular games given by M. Fulvius Nobilior in the second century BC, which included the hunting of panthers. In June 51 BC, when Cicero was governor of the province Cilicia, his young protégé Marcus Caelius Rufus requested him to send some panthers to Rome for a wild-beast hunt at the games Caelius would have to give on being appointed Aedile. In September, Caelius expressed his impatience: 'In almost every letter I have written to you I have mentioned the subject of panthers. It will be little to your credit that Patiscus [a Roman businessman in Cilicia] has sent panthers for Curio, and you not many times as many [for me]. Curio has given me those same animals and another ten from Africa.' Cicero finally replied on 4 April the following year, from Laodicea: 'About the panthers, the usual hunters are doing their best on my instructions. But the creatures are in remarkably short supply, and those we have are said to be complaining bitterly because they are the only beings in my province who have to fear designs against their safety . . . But the matter is receiving close attention, especially from Patiscus. Whatever comes to hand will be yours . . .' In his *Natural History* Pliny referred to the hunting of panthers, so that the topic must have been a familiar one in Roman culture.[47]

In place of H. T. Price's deduction, that erroneous classical references point to Shakespeare's authorship, we can see that they are perfectly Roman, and suggest the hand of Peele, who refers to panthers elsewhere, and was well versed in the *Aeneid*. His classical education, at Christ's Hospital and Christ Church, Oxford, extended from 1562 to 1581, enabling him to translate into English complex Latin texts, such as Erasmus's version of Euripides' *Iphigeneia*. Peele displayed his knowledge of Roman history somewhat ostentatiously on the title-page of *The Araygnement of Paris* (1584), adding an ornament which W. W. Greg described as 'a cut of a Roman coin or medal with the inscription "Imp Opilius Macrinus Aug" '[48]—so far as I know, the only such device in English Renaissance drama. Although the Yale edition reproduced the title-page, it made no comment on the medallion representing M. Opellius Severus Macrinus, Roman Emperor in AD 217–18. Macrinus, not exactly a well-known figure in Roman history, was only accessible to

---

[47] Cf. Livy, 39.22.2; Cicero, *Epistulae familiares*, 2.11, 8.2, 8.5, 8.9, trans. D. R. Shackleton Bailey, *Cicero's Letters to his Friends*, 2 vols. (Harmondsworth, 1978), i. 165, 170, 172, 190–1, and D. Stockton, *Cicero: A Political Biography* (Oxford, 1971), pp. 228–9; Pliny, *Natural History*, 8.100.

[48] Greg 1939–57, no. 83 (i. 162).

someone familiar with the minor historians, such as Cassius Dio (*c*.164–229), whose *Roman History*, originally in eighty books, is only partially extant, covering the period up to AD 46 (although an epitome of the later period survives); or Herodian (early third century), whose *History of the Empire after Marcus*, in eight books, covered the period from Marcus Aurelius to Gordian III (AD 180–238); or Sextus Aurelius Victor (active 360–80), whose *De Caesaribus*, based on Suetonius, gives moralized biographies of the emperors from Augustus to Constantius II (AD 360); or the authors of that collection of biographies of Roman emperors, Caesars, and usurpers from AD 117 to 284 known as the *Historia Augusta*, complied in the late fourth century.[49] This is not material with which Shakespeare is likely to have been familiar, though it was well within Peele's range. Indeed, it may be that Peele found Macrinus' medallion in an early edition of Aurelius Victor, since Richard Gordon has informed me that seventeenth-century editions of *De Caesaribus* (first printed at Antwerp in 1579, and often contained in a collection called *Historiae Romanae Breviarium*, together with *De viris illustribus* and *Origo gentis Romanae*, which are not by Aurelius) regularly add portrait medallions, including that of Macrinus, which bear a generic resemblance to the one used by Peele (although such portraits are quite stereotyped).[50] Alternatively, Peele may have taken it from one of the increasingly comprehensive collections of numismatic portraits of famous people which appeared in the sixteenth century.

Comparing Peele's medallion to those illustrated in the standard reference work on Roman imperial coinage brings out an interesting discrepancy. All the surviving coins abbreviate Macrinus' *nomen* as 'Opel.',[51] but Peele expanded and altered it to read 'Opilius'. Why he did so is a puzzle which Richard Gordon has brilliantly solved, to my mind, pointing out that the Latin word *opilio* (found in Cato, *De agricultura* and Virgil's tenth Eclogue, about the tensions in Arcadia) means a shepherd. 'So the coin is simply a sort of emblem, with a witty pun pointing up the notion of pastoral . . . through the Emperor's very name, a royal personage of antiquity who was a kind of model for Queen Elizabeth in her capacity as patroness/spectator of the *Araygnement* as a pastoral drama'. To be able to make such a learned pun, trusting that it would be understood, presupposes a high degree of Latinity in

[49] For basic information on these writers see *The Oxford Classical Dictionary*, 3rd edn., ed. Simon Hornblower and Antony Spawforth (Oxford, 1996), s.vv.

[50] Personal communications, 10 Oct.–13 Nov. 2001, 22–3 Mar. 2002.

[51] *The Roman Imperial Coinage*, iv. part II. *Macrinus to Pupienus*, by Harold Mattingly, Edward A. Sydenham, and C. H. V. Sutherland (London, 1938), pp. 1–22, and plate I. David Magie, in his translation of the *Scriptores Historiae Augustae*, 3 vols., Loeb Classical Library (Cambridge, Mass., and London, 1924), i. 48 n., recorded that, 'in the manuscripts of the *Historia Augusta*, Victor, and Eutropius, the gentile name of Macrinus is regularly spelled Opilius. On coins and in inscriptions, however, it is invariably given as Opellius, and this is evidently the correct form'. I thank Annette Baertschi for help in tracking down the historical material.

Peele's circle, demonstrated again in the Latin lyric Peele wrote for the Three Fates to sing in the concluding scene (1208–32). Indeed, the prominent Latin element in the *Araygnement* may even explain how *Titus Andronicus* came to be printed and/or issued by John Danter. John Jowett has shown that Danter 'played an active role in procuring manuscripts himself', and that many of the books he was involved in publishing were by the 'university wits'—Lodge, Greene, Nashe, and Peele, while Danter's partner in these activities was Henry Chettle, himself employed as a printing-house corrector of Latin (Jowett 1993, pp. 469–71, 486).

Peele's demonstration of his Latinity in the *Araygnement of Paris*, adding the image of the Emperor M. Opellius Severus Macrinus to the title-page, forms another link between his work and *Titus Andronicus*. Discussions of the play's sources have had difficulty in locating any clear models, and have commented on its heterogeneity. Terence Spencer argued that its sources 'probably belong to medieval legend', and pointed out that 'the political institutions in *Titus* are . . . certainly peculiar, and cannot be placed at any known period in Roman history'.[52] At times Rome seems to be a free commonwealth, with the emperor being elected on merit, but at other times a hereditary principle of succession is recognized. These 'elements of the political situation can be found in Roman history, but not combined in this way': indeed, the play 'includes *all* the political institutions that Rome ever had' (Spencer 1957, p. 32). In striking contrast to 'the care and authenticity' that Shakespeare showed in *Coriolanus* and *Julius Caesar*, *Titus Andronicus* 'seems to be a quintessence of impressions derived from an eager reading of Roman history rather than a real effort at verisimilitude' (ibid.). The discrepancy between individual merit and primogeniture as the valid principle of succession corresponds to another problem that scholars have located in the opening act of *Titus*, what Clifford Huffman described as 'the juxtaposition of the differing values inherent in the older brother Saturnine's decadent Empire and the younger brother Bassianus's older, true-Roman traditions'.[53] Add to this the presence of the Goths, and one can appreciate Spencer's complaint that 'the author seems anxious, not to get it all right, but to get it all in' (Spencer 1957, p. 32).

As for the actual historical sources lying behind the play, claims that the mid-eighteenth-century chapbook version may derive from a lost sixteenth-century source, accepted by Geoffrey Bullough, were definitively refuted by Marco Mincoff and G. K. Hunter.[54] C. C. Huffman showed that the life of the

---

[52] T. J. B. Spencer, 'Shakespeare and the Elizabethan Romans', *ShS* 10 (1957): 27–38, at p. 32.

[53] C. C. Huffman, 'Bassianus and the British History in *Titus Andronicus*', *English Language Notes* 11 (1974): 175–81, at p. 175.

[54] G. Bullough, *Narrative and Dramatic Sources of Shakespeare*, vi. *Other 'Classical' Plays* (London and New York, 1966), pp. 7–10; M. Mincoff, 'The Source of *Titus Andronicus*', *NQ* 216 (1971): 131–4; G. K. Hunter, 'The "Sources" of *Titus Andronicus*—Once Again', *NQ* 228 (1983): 114–16.

Emperor Bassianus, who killed his brother, Geta, was referred to twice in Holinshed's *Chronicles* (1587), drawing on Cassius Dio and Herodian, and that an English translation of Herodian (by N. Smyth) appeared in 1556 or thereabouts (Huffman 1974, pp. 178–9). In an exemplary study, G. K. Hunter commented on the two contrasting value systems in *Titus*, a 'compacting of primitive republican virtue and decadent imperial miscegenation'.[55] Hunter argued that the 'image of the severe virtue of the Andronici' derived from the opening book of Livy's history, while the 'picture of decadent imperial family disputes' derived from Herodian (Hunter 1984, p. 187). In addition to the general resemblances between the Andronici's republican austerity and the mores embodied in Livy, Hunter suggested Livy as a source for Lucius' appeal to be given

> the proudest prisoner of the Goths
> That we may hew his limbs and on a pile
> *Ad manes fratrum* sacrifice his flesh.
>
> (1.1.96–8)

In Livy's account of the battle between the three Horatii and three Curiatii brothers, the victorious Horatius, having avenged his brothers' death by killing two of the Curiatii in single combat, stands over the one survivor: '. . . exsultans "Duos", inquit, "*fratrum Manibus dedi*: tertium causae belli huiusce . . . dabo"' (Hunter 1984, p. 185). ('The Roman cried exultantly, "Two victims I have given to the shades of my brothers; the third I will offer up to the cause of this war . . ."').[56] Horatius' reference to human sacrifice here is clearly a rhetorical exaggeration, from the victor's viewpoint, of what had been a normal hand-to-hand combat, but it could be taken literally. Indeed, Richard Gordon has observed that 'the Romans certainly cut the heads off prisoners on a grand scale after battles, and Caesar famously chopped the right hands off 10,000 Gauls that he had captured. So there can be no doubt about the Romanness of "hew his limbs"'. And there is other evidence that the Romans performed human sacrifice in religious rituals.[57]

Herodian's *History of the Empire after Marcus*, the other classical source cited by Huffman, Hunter, and more recent commentators,[58] was available to

---

[55] G. K. Hunter, 'Sources and Meanings in *Titus Andronicus*', in J. C. Gray (ed.), *Mirror up to Shakespeare: Essays in Honour of G. R. Hibbard* (Toronto and London, 1984), pp. 171–88, at p. 183.

[56] Livy, *Ab urbe condita*, 1.25.12, trans. B. O. Foster, *Livy*, 14 vols., Loeb Classical Library (London and Cambridge, Mass., 1919), i. 89. Disappointingly, neither Alan Hughes in his new Cambridge edition (1994) nor Jonathan Bate in his New Arden (1995) record Hunter's suggestion.

[57] See the article 'Menschenopfer' in *Der Neue Pauly. Enzyklopädie der Antike*, 7 (Stuttgart, 1999) cols. 1254–8, referring to Plutarch, *Roman Questions*, 83, and *Marcellus*, 3.3; Livy, 22.57.2–6; Pliny, *Nat. Hist.*, 28.12; Suetonius, *Augustus*, 15; Cassius Dio, 48.14.4.

[58] Naomi Conn Liebler, 'Getting It All Right: *Titus Andronicus* and Roman History', *ShQ* 45 (1994): 263–78. This essay cites neither Huffman nor Hunter's work.

sixteenth-century readers in the Latin version of Angelo Politiano, and in numerous editions of the Greek text, notably those by Stephanus (Paris, 1581) and Sylburg (Frankfurt, 1590).[59] Several of these sixteenth-century editions had the Greek text and Politian's Latin on facing pages, and some included other early historians of the Roman Empire, such as Sextus Aurelius Victor and Eutropius. The passages relevant to *Titus Andronicus* concern the two sons of L. Septimius Severus (emperor AD 193–211), the elder—named M. Aurelius Antoninus when he became Caesar (better known to us as Caracalla), but whose real name was (L.) Septimius Bassianus (3.10.5)—and his younger brother P. Septimius Geta. Herodian describes the brothers as 'mutually antagonistic' since their childhood (3.10.3). Severus gave Bassianus a wife, the daughter of Plautianus, prefect of the praetorian guard (3.10.5–6), who became ambitious for greater power, even hoping to become emperor (3.11.1–3). Plautianus devised a plot, suborning a military tribune called Saturninus to use his 'right of entry to the sleeping chambers' and murder both Severus and Bassianus (3.11.4–7). Saturninus, however, persuaded Plautianus to give him written orders for the deed, which he then showed the Emperor, who laid a trap for Plautianus and had him executed (3.11.12–3.12.12).

Severus died in the middle of a military campaign against 'the barbarians' in Britain, and his two sons, sharing power, set off for home, bearing with them their father's ashes in 'an alabaster urn. This they now escorted to Rome to be placed in the sacred imperial mausoleum' (3.15.7). On their arrival the people and Senate greeted them with an address, the two brothers heading the procession, 'wearing the imperial purple, followed by the consuls who were then in office'. The urn was 'laid in the temple where the sacred memorials of Marcus and his imperial predecessors were displayed' (4.1.3–4). But the fraternal union was already cracking: each suspected the other of trying to poison him (4.1.1), and 'their rivalry and hatred and plots against each other broke out' openly, polarizing the courtiers (4.2.1–2). Their mother Julia tried to cure their 'bitter antagonism' (4.3.4–9), but Bassianus finally stabbed his brother, who 'died spilling his blood on his mother's breast' (4.4.3). Having slaughtered Geta's household and friends in a particularly brutal manner, Bassianus murdered men, women, and children indiscriminately (4.6.1–5). Herodian relates that, after many other murders, Bassianus became obsessively suspicious that 'everyone was plotting against him', and a consul in Rome falsely denounced one of his two military prefects, M. Opellius Macrinus (4.12.1–6). By chance, Macrinus intercepted the message, and in pre-emptive self-defence persuaded one of his centurions to murder Bassianus, becoming emperor. It can hardly be a coincidence that this is the

[59] See C. R. Whittaker (ed. and trans.), *Herodian*, 2 vols., Loeb Classical Library (London and Cambridge, Mass., 1969), i, pp. lxxxiii–lxxxvi. All quotations are from this edition, in the form '3.10.5'.

same Opellius whose image Peele prefixed to the quarto of *The Araygnement of Paris*.

From Herodian's *History*, then, Peele took the names of Bassianus—which becomes attached to the gentler of the two brothers—and Saturninus (Shakespeare never uses either name); the return of victorious soldiers to Rome; the idea of a pious ceremony placing the ashes of the dead in a family mausoleum; and the deadly rivalry between two brothers. These elements were mixed up with the stern ethos of early Rome, as depicted by Livy, and a rather vague invocation of the Goths (who only started attacking the Roman Empire in the mid-third century AD). But in the *Historia Augusta* the biographer of Bassianus, also known as Caracalla, records a 'gibe that was uttered at his expense . . . when he assumed the surnames Germanicus, Parthicus', and so on, commemorating his victories. Helvius Pertinax 'said to him in jest, . . . "Add to the others, please, that of Geticus Maximus also"; for he had slain his brother Geta, and Getae is the name for the Goths, whom he had conquered, while on his way to the East, in a series of skirmishes'.[60] This anachronistic joke (for no one had heard of the Goths around AD 200) may have given Peele the idea of an ongoing war between the Romans and the Goths. As for Aaron, a character introduced by Peele, it is worth noting that, in the epitome of Cassius Dio's *Roman History*, Macrinus is described as 'a Moor by birth'.[61] Peele's cross-section of a thousand years of Roman history is quite unlike the unified plots which Shakespeare constructed out of Plutarch for his three Roman plays, and justifies Terence Spencer's description of *Titus Andronicus* as 'a quintessence of impressions derived from an eager reading of Roman history'. Peele had good precedents in Livy and Virgil for the idea that the Romans practised human sacrifice, and for Romans hunting panthers. True, Peele erred in introducing holy water at Roman weddings, but the rest of his Latin background is authentic. If the result still seems to us a historical mish-mash, then we should remember that the *dramatis personae* of *The Araygnement of Paris* embrace seven pastoral characters, modelled on Spenser's *Shepherd's Calendar*, five 'Country gods', nine 'Olympian gods', Ate, who speaks a Senecan prologue, the Three Fates, and a series of masques, including 'The Nine Knights', 'Helen and the Four Cupids', and 'Eliza or Zabeta, Queen Elizabeth', to whom Diana presents the golden ball, much to the approval of the Three Graces. For *The Tale of Troy* (1589, but written earlier), 'Peele referred to all the accounts of the Troy story he could find, including the *Iliad*, Ovid's *Heroides* and *Metamorphoses*, the *Aeneid*,

---

[60] *Scriptores Historiae Augustae*, i. 26–8 ('Antoninus Caracalla', 10.6). The anecdote is repeated in the life of Antoninus Geta, 6.6. (i. 44–5). I thank Richard Gordon for this reference.

[61] Dio's *Roman History*, trans. E. Cary, 9 vols., Loeb Classical Library (London and Cambridge, Mass., 1927), ix. 361. According to this authority, it was Bassianus who persuaded the centurion Saturninus to allege that Plautianus had suborned him to murder the Emperor (ix. 343).

Chaucer's *Troilus and Criseyde*, and Caxton's *Recuyell of the Histories of Troye*', his 'chief debt [being] to Caxton for narrative material and Chaucer and Spenser for style' (Horne 1952, p. 149). Elizabethan writers did not have our highly developed sense of historical period, and Peele's eclecticism is not unusual. Yet he obviously tried to give his share of the play a classical patina, and it is significant that many of the Latinisms which H. T. Price singled out as showing Shakespeare's amateurish attempt to create a sense of verisimilitude ('A University poet would have acted in a different way') come from Peele's Act 1. Price argued that 'Shakespeare invents a special vocabulary' to 'strengthen the illusion that we are in Rome', using such words as *patron* (1.1.1, 65), *continence* (1.1.18), *receptacle* (1.1.92), *prodigies* (1.1.101), *piety* (1.1.115), *religiously* (1.1.124), *tributary* (1.1.159, 3.2.270), *ensigns* (1.1.252), and *trophies* (1.1.388). Price argued that

The desire to create a special Roman vocabulary for *Titus* accounts for such words as *palliament* (1.1.182), *successantly* (4.4.113), and especially the meaning given to *obsequious* (5.3.152) of 'having to do with obsequies or a funeral'. It is important that Shakespeare is the only person in the Elizabethan period to misuse the word in this way. We should not expect to find these blunders in the language of a poet trained in the Classics at the Universities. (Price 1943, p. 68)

Again we note that ten of the words singled out as specially 'Roman' occur in Act 1, and that there is a clear difference between the historical errors that Price identified in that act (the over-ambitious display of imperfectly remembered classical learning, as we might describe it), and the supposed misuse of 'obsequious' in the final scene.[62] Price stated that nobody 'has yet worked out a vocabulary-test that will bear looking at' (p. 59), but he was on the verge of discovering one, which could have differentiated Shakespeare's hand from Peele's.

Advances in knowledge move unevenly, as we well know, and so it is not surprising to find persisting in Price (as in later scholars) the eighteenth-century image of Shakespeare as a partly educated dramatist always liable to make blunders. But the confident identification of such 'blunders' presupposes a scholarly superiority which is not always justified. Price claimed, both in this and in another essay,[63] that in his *Honour of the Garter* poem Peele invented the word *palliament* to describe the robes of the Knights of the Garter as being purple, like 'the purple worn by the Roman Emperor', while later on referring to the white robe worn by the *candidatus*. But in fact Peele says nothing about the garment's colour. As we saw above, the poem describes

---

[62] The only two citations in *OED* for 'obsequious' in this sense are both from Shakespeare, this passage in *Titus*, and *Hamlet*, 1.2.92.

[63] 'The Language of *Titus Andronicus*', *Papers of the Michigan Academy of Sciences, Arts and Letters*, 21 (1935): 501–7.

> A goodly king in robes most richly dight.
> The upper, like a Romaine Palliament,
> In deede a Chapperon, for such it was.

> (91–3)

Later Peele apostrophized 'sacred loyalty', whose

> weedes of spotlesse white;
> Like those that stoode for Romes great offices,
> Makes thee renownd, glorious in innocencie.

> (314–16)

According to Price,

Shakespeare confused the two passages in his memory and used Peele's *palliament* for the white robe of the *candidatus*. In his mistake he has been followed by all scholars who have discussed the passage. They all say that Peele's *palliament* is a white garment. However, it is quite clear that they, like Shakespeare, have misread Peele. Since the author of *Titus* misunderstood Peele, it is a fair inference that he was not Peele. The passage is important, because it shows how Shakespeare snapped up unconsidered trifles of language. For his Roman play he needed a Roman-sounding word, and, as in the case of *obsequious*, he was not particular about its meaning. (Price 1943, p. 60)

Once again we see how plastic 'linguistic evidence' can be, bent either way to suit a critic's preconception of the writer. Unfortunately for Price, T. W. Baldwin applied his phenomenal knowledge of the classical tradition to this issue, with a rather different outcome.[64] Drawing on Cooper's *Thesaurus* (1566), Elias Ashmole's *History of the most Noble Order of the Garter* (1715), and many other sources, Baldwin showed that Peele coined the word *palliament* from the (purple) *paludamentum* of Roman chief captains, under the etymological influence of *pallium*, 'a mantle or cloak', but that he misunderstood a passage in his source, Holinshed, and 'confused the mantle or *pallium* with the hood or *chaperon*' (Baldwin 1959, p. 406). But while in error here, Peele was not at fault in describing 'This Palliament of white and spotless hue' in *Titus* (1.1.182): since this *palliament* 'is the robe of a *candidatus*, the *toga candida*, the color is now quite correctly specified as white' (p. 411). As Baldwin concluded, 'there is no evidence . . . that the author of this passage in *Titus* mistook the color of a *palliament* as Professor Price thought, or that he drew his alleged mistake from Peele, and hence could not have been Peele himself. On the contrary, Peele himself appears to have invented the word *palliament*', and did so (as we can tell from the poem's entry in the Stationers' Register) in June 1593. 'Further, Peele's use of the word *palliament* is a direct one, growing out of Peele's source, while that in *Titus Andronicus* is a derived one . . . Therefore, Peele as the inventor and

---

[64] T. W. Baldwin, 'The Work of Peele and Shakespeare on *Titus Andronicus*', in Baldwin, *On the Literary Genetics of Shakspere's Plays, 1592–1594* (Urbana, Ill., 1959), pp. 402–20.

only known purveyor of the word must remain grievously suspect' as the play's co-author (p. 412).

Baldwin's clarification of the 'palliament' issue, J. C. Maxwell judged in his 1961 revised Arden edition, 'strengthens the case for Peele's hand in *Titus*' (p. xliii). Yet Maxwell himself, despite his cogent demonstration of the presence in Act 1 of Peele's idiosyncratic syntactical construction, '*his . . . that*', was strangely reluctant to draw the obvious conclusion. Diffidently summarizing his earlier essay in a mere eight lines, giving neither statistics nor quotations from Peele (pp. xxvi–xxvii), he nevertheless agreed with Dover Wilson that the evidence for Peele's presence in Act 1 includes many 'striking resem-blances, and probably more suggestive . . . the tendency to mechanical repe-tition of words and phrases'. In a note on 1.1.294 he followed Wilson in pointing out four repetitions of the same construction within 130 lines of that act:

> Nor thou, nor he, are any sons of mine
>
> (294)
> Nor he, nor thee, nor any of thy stock
>
> (300)
> Nor thou, nor these, confederates in the deed
>
> (344)
> 'Tis thou, and those, that have dishonoured me
>
> (425)

Maxwell noted that this repetition carries with it a further repetition of 'dis-honour' (295, 303, 345, 425), and that lines 303 and 304 are linked by the word 'confederates', concluding: 'I share Wilson's reluctance to attribute these mechanical recurrences to Shakespeare at any point of his career' (p. 17). Yet somehow he balked at the admission that a second hand could have written this scene—while nevertheless adding that 'if there is a clean break between the two authors, I should be inclined to put it after 2.1.25' (p. xxix n.). Maxwell agreed with H. T. Price that it would be 'tempting to assert roundly that the whole play is by Shakespeare and no one else . . . My only defence is that I can never quite believe it *while* reading Act 1' (p. xxix). And with these unresolved doubts the Arden editor dropped the problem.

It is still frustrating, today, reconstructing the scholarly debate on the play's authenticity, to see the detailed case made in 1919 (Parrott) and 1931 (Timberlake) for the radically different verse style of 1.1, 2.1, 4.1 being simply ignored by its editors, who of all scholars ought to be the most dili-gent in searching through the secondary literature and addressing this fun-damental issue. Further evidence of stylistic incongruity within the play was provided in 1957 by R. F. Hill, studying the play's use of rhetoric.[65] Hill took 130 rhetorical figures, as expounded by Puttenham in his *Arte of English Poesie*, and studied their occurrence in eleven early plays, finding *Titus* anomalous in several respects (Hill 1957, p. 64). The play uses alliteration far more frequently than the other early plays (apart from 2 *Henry VI* and *Richard III*, the rest contain 'only half as much'), and it differs from them in kind as well as in degree. The 'general naiveté' of alliteration as used in *Titus*, Hill wrote, amounts to an 'excessive and tuneless playing on the letter' (p. 65), as in this instance:

> Clear up, fair queen, that cloudy countenance:
> Though chance of war hath wrought this change of cheer
>
> (1.1.263–4)

While exceeding the other early plays in its use of alliteration, Hill found that *Titus* was far below them in one of Shakespeare's most characteristic tropes, for it contains 'only half the number of continued metaphors usual in the early tragedies and histories'. Hill quoted these lines to illustrate the play's paucity in extended metaphors:

> the good Andronicus,
> . . . .
> With honour and with fortune is return'd
> From where he circumscribed with his sword,
> And brought to yoke, the enemies of Rome
>
> (1.1.64–9)

Compared to the 'richness of Shakespeare's diction' in the other early plays, these 'separate metaphors . . . typify the empty diction which prevails through much of *Titus*', partly accounting for its 'un-Shakespearian quality' (p. 65). It is significant that Hill should have singled out Act I as exemplifying both faults.

Hill was one of the first scholars to draw on Elizabethan rhetoric as a tool in attribution studies. This is a potentially important resource, for although every writer who received a grammar-school education was exposed to five or six years' intensive study, gaining first-hand knowledge of over a hundred rhetorical figures and tropes, and many types of composition process, how they applied their training was as varied as their choice of vocabulary, grammatical constructions, or verse form. Writers using rhetoric can be differentiated on qualitative and quantitative grounds—that is, both in their manner of handling such devices and the frequency with which they use them. Uniting

---

[65] R. F. Hill, 'The Composition of *Titus Andronicus*', *ShS* 10 (1957): 60–70. This essay drew on Hill's Oxford B.Litt. thesis (1954), 'Shakespeare's Use of Formal Rhetoric in his Early Plays up to 1596'.

both approaches, Hill judged *Titus* anomalous in several respects. He had expected to find in it 'an abundance of the figures of repetition', such as *antimetabole*, *symploke*, and *epanalepsis*, but the total for these figures was far lower in *Titus* than in the other early plays.[66] *Titus* had fewer instances of other rhetorical figures (*antithesis*, all types of pun, *asyndeton*, *brachyologia*), but it far exceeded the ten early plays that Hill studied in those figures classified by rhetoricians as exemplifying 'vices of language', topping the list in tautology (or *pleonasmus*), and in general the—alas, vaguely defined—category 'wordiness' (twelve and eighteen instances, respectively). Quoting examples, Hill argued that 'these faults alone should make one doubt the authenticity of *Titus*, especially when considered together with the abundance of empty, unmusical lines which are not susceptible of statistical treatment. *Love's Labour's Lost* is generally dated 1594–5, which makes one thing certain; to contend for sole Shakespearian authorship of *Titus* and composition in 1593–4 is nonsense' (p. 68). Reviewing the evidence for an early dating, Hill argued that if one were to accept the 'orthodoxy' of Shakespeare's sole authorship, 'it would be *just* possible to justify the presence of the excessive and mechanical alliteration, the tautology', and the use of clichés. 'Candour compels me to admit, however, that . . . certain elements in the style, characterization and moral position seem uncharacteristic and even unworthy of Shakespeare at any period in his writing. Collaboration might still be an explanation . . .' (pp. 69–70).

Hill had discussed the possibility of co-authorship earlier in his paper, stating that 'Peele's authorship of Act 1, often suspected on account of the flatness of the verse, its thin diction and Peelean tags, seems confirmed by the abundant alliteration, a device favoured by Peele. Unfortunately there is just as much alliteration in Act 2 . . .' (p. 60). But of course Parrott (whose essay Hill cites) had ascribed 2.1 also to Peele, and perhaps even 2.2, so that the presence of alliteration in those scenes could be significant, if only Hill had cited all his evidence. However, he did make a further observation which pointed towards Peele's co-authorship, observing that 'peculiarities of style' may 'possess great evidential value' in authorship studies, since 'they may constitute the special "tricks" of a writer'. Hill instanced the fact that *Titus* contains forty-five examples of *epizeuxis* (repeating a word with no other word intervening, as in 'come, come'), and that in sixteen cases a

---

[66] Hill's figures were: *Tit.*: 6; *2 H6*: 14; *3H6*: 22; *R3*: 47; *Err.*: 23; *Shr.*: 20; *TGV*: 23; *LLL*: 40; *Rom.*: 38; *R2*: 39; *MND*: 18. In this essay, unfortunately, Hill did not cite specific instances. The study by Stefan Keller (see p. 241 below) does not support Hill's diagnosis of a paucity of rhetoric in the play. For *Titus* his total for the three figures of repetition selected by Hill (*antimetabole*, *symploke*, *epanalepsis*) is 27 in the 1,733 lines ascribed to Shakespeare, a frequency of 15.6 per 1,000 lines; for *Richard III* it is 77, a frequency of 21.4. In his share of *Titus* Shakespeare used 135 puns, or 1 every 13 lines, while in *Richard III* he used 376, or 1 every 10 lines. The figure *antithesis*, similarly, occurs 147 times in *Titus* (once every 12 lines), 473 times in *Richard III* (once every 8 lines). In the earlier play Shakespeare was learning his art.

vocative was placed between the repeated words, as in 'Help, grandsire, help' (in effect, this would be an instance of *ploké*, repetition with other words intervening). Hill noted that 'all the other plays contain only two to six examples each, and in none does the iteration have the woodenness found in *Titus*. There it has the air of a cliché, a fault of which Shakespeare is seldom guilty. Oddly enough', he added, 'the trick is most apparent in the often suspected Act 1, where it occurs five times in one hundred and sixty-eight lines'. Hill pointed out another 'unusual feature' of the play's diction, 'the repetition of a clause with an inversion in the order of its grammatical parts', as in

> Hear me, grave fathers! noble tribunes, stay!
>
> (3.1.1)
>
> My lord, look here: look here, Lavinia.
>
> (4.1.68)

As Hill observed,

Although not classified by the English rhetoricians, it is a figure certainly used by Seneca in his tragedies. Doubtless it could add to the music of poetry, but the mechanism in *Titus* is palpable; it is only the stiffness which attracts attention. There are at least eleven examples in *Titus*; the trick was noticed no more than twice in any one of the remaining plays studied. One cannot avoid the question: could Shakespeare's love of honeyed speech ever have betrayed him into a succession of vain repetitions? The music of words was his birthright and his faults those of excess, never the poverty of invention witnessed by these jejune phrases. Prompted by this thought I glanced through [Peele's] *The Battle of Alcazar* and found five examples at random . . . (p. 68)

In this, as in other respects, Hill's essay was a tantalizing example of a promising line of research opened up, but not carried through. More than fifty years later, we are still waiting for a detailed comparison of Peele's use of rhetoric with Shakespeare's.

Hill was unusual among Shakespearians in his readiness to describe verbal structures with the appropriate rhetorical term (the few writers who comment on Shakespeare's language prefer not to be so specific). The Bulgarian scholar Marco Mincoff was also not afraid to use the correct names when studying the language of Elizabethan drama.[67] Commenting on and endorsing Hill's analysis, he pointed out that 'several minor patterns [of repetition] that run through the play . . . are in fact reminiscent of Peele' (Mincoff 1976, p. 127). One pattern that Mincoff found to be 'definitely reminiscent' of Peele 'is the appositional repetition with amplification, occurring here only in Act I' (p. 127), as in

---

[67] Cf. also his earlier study, 'Verbal Repetition in Elizabethan Tragedy', *Sofia University Annual* 41 (1944/5): 1–128.

> Victorious Titus, rue the tears I shed,
> A mother's tears in passion for her son.
>
>   (1.1.105–6)
>
> To re-salute the country with his tears,
> Tears of true joy for his return to Rome.
>
>   (75–6)
>
> But let us give him burial as becomes;
> Give Mutius burial with our brethren.
>
>   (347–8)

Mincoff noted another characteristic of Peele's style, occurring once only, 'the echoing of the last line of a speech by the following speaker' (p. 128), as in

> *Tit.* In peace and honour rest you here, my sons!
> *Lav.* In peace and honour live Lord Titus long;
>   My noble lord and father, live in fame.
>
>   (1.1.155–7)

Lavinia's welcome also takes the form of another Peelean stylistic mannerism, as Hill had pointed out, 'a kind of antimetabole, with the parts of a clause (but not necessarily the actual words) repeated in reverse order, as also in "Sit down, sweet niece; brother, sit down by me" ' (4.1.64).

Yet, despite acknowledging the presence in *Titus* of these and other distinct characteristics of Peele's style (such as the liking for a relative clause with a possessive for its antecedent, noted by J. C. Maxwell), Mincoff could not accept the possibility of Peele's co-authorship. He compared the opening speech by Saturninus with the beginning of *The Battle of Alcazar*, finding the *Titus* passage to have more symmetry (pp. 129–30). But of course *Alcazar* is an abridgement, the text having suffered serious damage, and if Mincoff had compared this passage in *Titus* with Peele's poems he might have reached a different conclusion. Two other stylistic features that he noticed in *Titus*, 'the extreme use of apostrophe and alliteration' (pp. 131–2), are highly characteristic of Peele, as we shall see. Mincoff had much evidence pointing to Peele's co-authorship, but could not think that stage further (p. 129). Like R. F. Hill, although he drew on Elizabethan rhetoric Mincoff made no use of the metrical studies by Parrott and Timberlake which point so clearly to Peele as the author of 1.1, 2.1, 2.2, and 4.1. Their failure to use this material highlights the importance in authorship studies of co-ordinating several different approaches, each testing the others. Instead of extending a scholarly tradition, as he later did so effectively in studying Fletcher's two collaborations with Shakespeare (see Chapter 6), discussing *Titus Andronicus*, Mincoff tantalizingly remained on its margin.

As the twentieth century grew older, it seemed that knowledge, far from advancing, was actually dwindling, for editors showed a decreasing inclin-

TABLE 3.4. *Compound adjectives and the* un-*prefix in* Titus Andronicus

	Part	Length	Instances	Frequency: every x lines
Compound adjectives	A	759 lines	9	84
	B	1,759 lines	49	36
un-prefix	A	759 lines	8	95
	B	1,759 lines	39	45

Source: Jackson 1979, p. 152.

ation to face the issue of authorship, and areas of research that had been opened up were left to wither. MacDonald Jackson has always been a healthy exception to this trend, indeed his awareness and generous recognition of earlier scholarship makes him an admirable role model. In his seminal *Studies in Attribution: Middleton and Shakespeare* (1979), Jackson reintroduced readers to the metrical tests of Parrott and Timberlake, citing Parrott's figures for the low proportion of feminine endings in 1.1, 2.1, and 4.1. (On my computation, the average for those three scenes is 2.8 per cent; for the remaining eleven scenes it is 9.9 per cent.) Grouping the two sets of scenes together as *A* and *B*, Jackson then applied two vocabulary tests suggested by Alfred Hart's argument, in 1934, that Shakespeare made much greater use than other contemporary writers of compound adjectives and words beginning with *un-*.[68] Checking their frequencies in *Titus Andronicus* Jackson produced the result presented in Table 3.4. The two tests correlate in clearly distinguishing *A* (Peele) scenes from *B* (Shakespeare). Jackson also documented another difference between the two parts, depending on whether or not 'the *-ed* ending to verbs such as *called, abandoned, discovered*, in which it would not normally be syllabic, [is] given full syllabic value to fit the metre'. The figures for Part *A* (Peele) were 11 instances, or once every 69 verse lines; for *B* (Shakespeare), full syllabic value was called for 58 times, or once in every 29 verse lines (p. 152). All three tests confirm the findings of Parrott and Timberlake that two different hands were at work on this play.

Jackson's most original test involved computing what he calls a 'vocabulary index', drawing on the work of Gregor Sarrazin in 1897–8 on Shakespeare's 'word-echoes'. As I recorded in Chapter 2, Sarrazin compiled lists for each Shakespeare play of the words which occurred elsewhere in Shakespeare only twice ('dislegomena') or three times ('trislegomena'),

---

[68] This claim is not entirely justified, for Hart offered no comparative evidence. Charles Barber did so for the *un*-prefix in his ground-breaking study, *Early Modern English* (rev. edn., Edinburgh, 1997), pp. 235–6 (in the first edition (London, 1976), p. 189). For the frequency of compounds formed with *un*- in Nashe, Chettle, and Ford see Vickers 2002, pp. 112–13, 519 nn. 19–20.

TABLE 3.5. *Rare words in Shakespeare*

Group	Time span	Number of plays	Number of rare words
I	*TA* to *MND*	10	1,926
II	*RJ* to *JC*	10	2,083
III	*AYLI* to *Tim.*	8	2,034
IV	*KL* to *H8*	9	1,975

Source: Jackson 1979, p. 149.

TABLE 3.6. *Vocabulary index for* Titus Andronicus

	Group 1 *TA* to *MND*	Group 2 *RJ* to *JC*	Group 3 *AYLI* to *Tim.*	Group 4 *KL* to *H8*	Index %
Titus (whole play)	70	35	27	31	35.6
A scenes	33	9	8	8	27.6
B scenes	37	26	19	23	40

Source: Jackson 1979, p. 212.

showing that the correspondences were greatest for plays of roughly the same date. Jackson reworked Sarrazin's data, arranging the plays in the chronological order proposed by Karl Wentersdorf (1951), and dividing them into four groups. I reproduce his findings in Table 3.5. Jackson then compiled two tables, one giving the links in rare words between each individual play and the four chronological groups (table XIX, p. 211), the other calculating the percentage of links with the third and fourth groups (table XX, p. 212). This second table produced a 'vocabulary index' that ties up with the suggested chronology, the lowest index being that for 2 *Henry VI*, 29.8 per cent, the highest for *Antony and Cleopatra*, 63.7 per cent. The significant information for *Titus Andronicus* is that when the vocabulary links are tabulated a clear difference can once again be traced between the two parts, as can be seen from Table 3.6. The figures there show that the Shakespearian segment of the play has many more vocabulary links with Shakespeare's plays yet to be written than does the Peele section, which correlates mostly with Shakespeare's early works—Peele died in 1596. In terms of chronology, the vocabulary index for the whole play (35.6 per cent) would put it in position 7 on the scale of thirty-seven plays, dating it to about 1591–2; that for the *A* (Peele) scenes, at 27.6 per cent, is lower than for any play in Shakespeare's canon, while that for the *B* scenes (40 per cent) is close to *The Taming of the Shrew*, in position 12, which would date the play to about 1594–5. 'Thus, while in part *B* of the play the vocabulary is definitely early, in Part *A* it is much more so—overwhelmingly so, in fact.' While 'this evidence supports the view that there are two strata in *Titus Andronicus*', Jackson conceded that the discrepancy could be explained in terms of Shakespeare revising his own earlier draft, but added: 'I am not prepared to reject outright the possibility that Part *A* is the work of Peele' (p. 153). As we shall see, Jackson soon returned to this issue, adding new confirmatory evidence.

Readers who have followed my narrative so far might well think that by 1979 the theory that *Titus Andronicus* is a co-authored play was firmly established. In 1984, however, Eugene Waith pronounced in his Oxford edition that 'the tide of disintegration was already ebbing' in 1959 (Waith 1984, p. 12), and showed that he wished it to dry up altogether. After a superficial review of the scholarly tradition he asserted: 'I believe that the evidence I have presented points to the conclusion that *Titus Andronicus* is entirely by Shakespeare' (p. 20). But his 'evidence' consisted largely in suppressing the evidence of other scholars. He cited Parrott's essay merely for its conclusion that 'Shakespeare revised the work of another playwright' (p. 16), without explaining Parrott's method, or quoting any of his statistics. Waith never mentioned (if he knew it) Timberlake's confirmation of there being two metrical strata in the play, and although he briefly alluded to Jackson's findings (pp. 10, 16) Waith did so without properly reporting or evaluating them. Waith referred equally briefly to J. C. Maxwell's 'stylometric test' of the unusual grammatical construction found in Peele's poems and plays and in *Titus*, but only to say that it 'kept Maxwell from believing in Shakespeare's authorship of that part of the play' (p. 16)—an unfortunate obstacle, as it were. Waith conceded that the rare word 'palliament' only occurs in Peele's *Garter* poem, but took refuge in H. T. Price's erroneous claim that 'the different sense in which the word was used in the play made borrowing by Shakespeare much more likely than repetition by Peele' (p. 14). This merely shows that although Waith cited T. W. Baldwin's 1959 essay (p. 12), he had not read it attentively. Unsurprisingly, Waith pooh-poohed 'the dangerous game of parallel passages' (p. 15) as far as it might prove Peele's hand in the play—these 'can readily be attributed to either influence or coincidence'—while being happy to accept that the 'close connections' between *Titus*, *Venus and Adonis*, and *Lucrece*, 'where verbal similarity is matched by similarity of thought and subject matter, present us with the overwhelming probability that Shakespeare wrote them all' (p. 16). Special pleading, we see again, is the common coin of the Shakespeare 'fundamentalists'—as W. W. Greg christened those who affirmed his sole authorship of *Titus*. Naturally, Waith never mentioned Dover Wilson's painstaking account of the hugely repetitive and mechanical language of Act 1, nor the doubts expressed by Maxwell that Shakespeare could ever have written in this manner. Faced with Waith's blanket refusal either to report the case for co-authorship fairly, or to engage in a

TABLE 3.7. *Stress profile for* Titus Andronicus

	Syllabic positions				Difference		
	2	4	6	8	10	4–6	8–6
A scenes	67.4	83.7	72.8	71.4	84.9	+10.9	−1.4
B scenes	68.7	85.6	69.9	75.2	88.0	+15.7	+5.3

Source: Tarlinskaja 1987, p. 122.

serious evaluation of its arguments—'No compelling evidence associates any other playwright with it' (p. 20)—open-minded readers can only conclude that, for defenders of Shakespeare's sole authorship, there must be two standards of proof.

Objective scholarship, based on empirical analysis and meticulous computation, was applied to *Titus Andronicus* three years later, in Marina Tarlinskaja's quantitative analysis of Shakespeare's metrics, with significant results. As I briefly noted in Chapter 2, her method computed in percentages the occurrence of stress in the syllabic positions within a decasyllabic line, given the normal iambic emphasis on every even-numbered 'ictus' or foot (positions 2, 4, 6, 8, 10). Tarlinskaja calculated the percentage difference between the sixth and fourth, and eighth and sixth feet, respectively, producing a 'stress profile' for each play studied. Showing a wider knowledge of the secondary literature than any editor of *Titus Andronicus*, Tarlinskaja endorsed the findings of both Parrott and Timberlake, adding to them her own earlier researches, which have shown that 'a low proportion of feminine endings is a sign of earlier Elizabethan verse'.[69] Accepting the arguments of Jackson and earlier scholars that the play's scenes can be divided into two groups according to the proportion of feminine endings, she made the calculation which I reproduce in Table 3.7 for what we have been calling the *A* (or Peele) scenes (1.1, 2.1, 4.1) and the *B* scenes, or remainder. As Tarlinskaja commented, the stress profile of the *B* scenes 'displays a stressing tendency typical of Shakespeare's first period: there is a "dip" in position 6', giving the figure of +15.7 in the penultimate column (the figure for position 4 minus that for position 6), while the difference between positions 6 and 8 (+5.3) is also typical of Shakespeare's early work. In the *A* scenes, by contrast, the dip from position 4 to 6 (+10.9) is less, while the relationship between positions 6 and 8 (−1.4) is reversed, pointing to a much more evenly stressed line. Once again we can see a clear difference: the *A* scenes have 'a more archaic rhythmical style' than the *B* scenes (p. 124). Judging purely on the metrical evidence, Tarlinskaja concluded that the difference could be due to Shakespeare having reworked his own, earlier play, but she was 'really tempted to attribute *Titus* to two different authors' (ibid.). In a later analysis of the incidence of feminine endings (pp. 192–5), Tarlinskaja corrected Parrott's figures slightly, and confirmed that 'Act 1 seems especially archaic in style'.

It begins to look as if the authenticity debate over *Titus Andronicus* runs along two parallel paths. On the one side are a group of researchers who build on previous scholarship, using newer methodologies which confirm, ever more clearly, the existence of two distinct styles in the play. On the other side are the conservative Shakespearians, several of them producing editions of the play, who insist that it is a work of single authorship. This divide ran right through the one-volume Oxford Shakespeare, on which a team of editors began work in 1978. One of the first fruits of the establishment of 'the Shakespeare department of Oxford University Press' was the lecture series given by Stanley Wells at the Folger Shakespeare Library on some basic issues involved in preparing a new edition.[70] Wells discussed 'Old and Modern Spelling', 'Emending Shakespeare', 'Editorial Treatment of Stage Directions', and finally 'The Editor and the Theatre: Act One of *Titus Andronicus*' (Wells 1984, pp. 79–113). This lecture, which 'represents the thinking behind my edition of *Titus Andronicus* in the forthcoming *Complete Oxford Shakespeare*' (p. 82 n.), included a sensible discussion of how an editor ought to infer stage-business from the printed text, adding and systematizing stage directions where necessary. But it is quite remarkable in refusing ever to mention the possibility that Peele may have been the author of at least three scenes in the play, although Wells has always been among the best-informed Shakespeare scholars, having edited numerous companions and reader's guides. We can see how Wells avoided the issue of joint authorship from his remark that 'the Folio is our only authority' for 'a whole additional scene' (the 'fly' scene, 3.2), which is 'generally agreed to be by Shakespeare, and for another line (1.1.398) usually regarded as authentic' (pp. 79–80)—that is, Titus' remark, 'Yes, and will nobly him remunerate'. Usually regarded as 'authentic', that is, by those who believe that Shakespeare wrote the whole play. However, as editors have pointed out, this line might have been written by Peele as part of the theatrical manuscript from which Q1 was printed, omitted by mistake, and restored by the Folio editors (Waith 1984, pp. 40–1). And the word 'remunerate' was a favourite with Peele, as Dover Wilson and H. Dugdale Sykes had observed.[71] Wells never mentioned the possibility of

---

[70] Stanley Wells, *Re-Editing Shakespeare for the Modern Reader* (Oxford, 1984).

[71] Wilson 1948, p. 110, cited Sykes 1919a, p. 130, who listed four instances, adding that the 'very rare word', *re-salute*, occurs in the *Garter* poem and 'in *Titus Andronicus* [1.1.75, 326], one of the many marks of Peele's hand to be found in that play'. For further comments associating Peele with *Titus* cf. Sykes 1919a, pp. 108, 125.

co-authorship, and simply assumed that, by analysing the text of Act 1, he could re-create 'Shakespeare's intentions' (Wells 1984, p. 83). As will be seen from my discussion in Chapter 7 of the problems of co-ordinating plot in co-authored plays, Wells was dissatisfied with the dramaturgy of this opening scene, and proposed a drastic editorial solution, omitting a hundred lines of the text. He could have reached an easier decision had he been prepared to consider that the 'poor stagecraft' he complained of was actually a sign of Peele's contribution. But one must first be able to *think* that Shakespeare had a co-author.

When the one-volume Oxford edition of the complete plays appeared in 1986, in his introduction to this play (p. 141) Wells still made no reference to the long-lived debate over the play's authorship. Yet at the same time, and in the same office, Gary Taylor, to whom Wells expressed his great indebtedness,[72] was preparing *A Textual Companion* (1987) to the Oxford Shakespeare, which accepted the whole scholarly tradition arguing for co-authorship, baldly stating that 'Shakespeare wrote only a part' of the play (*TxC*, p. 114). Taylor quoted with approval J. C. Maxwell's observation of 'a grammatical construction . . . rare in Shakespeare but common in Peele' (p. 114). Taylor not only knew but accepted the evidence drawn from feminine endings—'the most easily and reliably identified of all metrical criteria—criteria for which we possess comprehensive data for plays up to 1595' in Timberlake's work. He endorsed MacDonald Jackson's demonstration ('drawing on earlier work') of 'a remarkable discrepancy between the low frequency of feminine endings in three scenes of the play (1.1, 2.1, and 4.1) and the high, typically Shakespearian frequency elsewhere', and agreed with Jackson that this discrepancy 'corresponds to a significant disparity in rare vocabulary links with other plays'. Taylor also took the occasion to recant an earlier opinion of his own, quoted by Eugene Waith, that 'the three scenes comprising Jackson's Part A "are linked by no narrative or formal logic, and that dramatic collaboration almost always involved a division of the plot along some obvious lines" ',[73] now making the valuable point that

In fact the first two scenes [1.2, 2.1] are, in the 1594 edition . . . a single uninterrupted scene . . . the scene division was created by a change of staging associated with an act division. In the original division of labour between putative collaborators, the first 626 lines might well have been regarded as a single unit. In a collaborative play one writer might well be given responsibility for a single act, and for another scene elsewhere; in this instance, Act I initiates the play as a whole, and 4.1 initiates the counteraction. The division suggested by feminine endings is thus compatible with patterns of collaboration in the drama of the period . . . (p. 114)

---

[72] Taylor's 'rigorous sense of logic and extraordinary command of detail have been a constant stimulus and challenge', and while acknowledging 'specific suggestions' he had received from Taylor, Wells recognized 'a far more pervasive indebtedness' (Wells 1984, p. v).

[73] Waith 1984, p. 17, quoting a letter by Taylor dated 24 Nov. 1981.

Changes of mind are becoming increasingly rare in authorship studies, so that Taylor's reconsideration of this issue was all the more welcome for adding a new argument supporting the case for co-authorship.

It is impossible to know what Wells thought of his co-editor's confident identification of Peele as the author of at least three scenes, but, according to a recent compilation offering to identify the best editions of Shakespeare currently before the public, he showed signs of wavering. Ann Thompson recorded that Wells had not questioned Shakespeare's sole authorship in the *Complete Works* (1986),

> but in the introductory matter he contributes to the Royal Shakespeare Company text (1987), he devotes much of the space available to the question 'Did Shakespeare Really Write *Titus Andronicus*?' and cautions his readers to remember that this play belongs to the earliest, least documented part of Shakespeare's career, a time when he might have collaborated with other writers, as he was to do again at the end (in *Henry VIII* and *The Two Noble Kinsmen*). This ambiguous attitude is not untypical of modern editors: while generally accepting the play as canonical, they still linger sufficiently long over the authorship issue to sow serious doubts, usually focusing on whether someone else had a hand in Act 1, and whether the play as a whole shows signs of revision.[74]

To orthodox Shakespearians, we see once more, any 'ambiguous attitude' on authorship issues is foul play, while 'to sow serious doubts' in the reader's mind deserves a rebuke. Professor Thompson has written a valuable study of Shakespeare's use of Chaucer,[75] and has a respectable place among feminist critics. But her comments show that conservative attitudes to the authorship issue can coexist alongside much more 'advanced' critical affiliations.

The persistence of conservative attitudes among Shakespearians of the most diverse pedigree is a remarkable phenomenon, as if a common need to protect the text against interlopers unites scholars, whatever their background. Two major editions of *Titus Andronicus* appeared in the 1990s, one for the New Cambridge Shakespeare, edited by Alan Hughes, Professor of Theatre at the University of Victoria, the other for the third Arden series, by Jonathan Bate, well known for his books on the Romantics' Shakespeare criticism and for Shakespeare's use of Ovid. Diverse backgrounds, but identical attitudes: Peele's co-authorship must be denied. Alan Hughes, finding it 'odd that so many scholars' have questioned Shakespeare's sole authorship (Hughes 1994, p. 11), gave the usual brief and inaccurate summary of scholarship. He informed his readers that 'Dover Wilson mustered an impressive list of parallels which he believed show Shakespeare's hand in every act except the first', referring to that part of Wilson's introduction entitled '*Shakespeare*

---

[74] A. Thompson, with T. L. Berger, A. R. Braunmuller, P. Edwards, and L. Potter, *Which Shakespeare? A User's Guide to Editions* (Milton Keynes and Philadelphia, 1992), p. 168.

[75] *Shakespeare's Chaucer: A Study in Literary Origins* (Liverpool, 1978).

shows his hand' (1948 edn., pp. xix ff.). But Hughes failed to disclose that in the following section, called *'Peele also shows his hand'* (pp. xxv–xxxiv), Wilson made an equally 'impressive' case for Peele's authorship of Act 1, copiously documenting the presence there of Peele's monotonous verse, stilted diction, and constant self-repetition. Hughes mentioned the existence of 'several *attempts* to apply objective tests to the text' (my italics), but he cited only T. M. Parrott's 1919 essay, and out-trumped it (or so he thought) with G. Harold Metz's citation of A. Q. Morton's 'stylometric' findings in 1979. Although he published his edition of the play in 1994, Hughes did not know either Metz's 1985 essay, or—a more serious failing—M. W. A. Smith's multiple refutations of Morton's method, which I discussed in Chapter 2. Smith published several important essays on the deficiencies of stylometry between 1985 and 1992, all of which were listed in the admirable World Shakespeare Bibliography published by *Shakespeare Quarterly*, and an editor of a major edition should have taken note of them. The mere existence of Metz's note was sufficient for Hughes to proclaim that 'these apparently scientific studies [give] contradictory results', and to take comfort in doubts expressed by R. F. Hill as long ago as 1957, that the tests made up to that date were inadequate. Yet, in a move characteristic of the Shakespeare-text conservators, Hughes failed to quote the rest of Hill's argument, namely that the many anomalous elements in its language and rhetoric are enough to 'make one doubt the authenticity of *Titus*' (Hill 1957, p. 68).

Hughes's refusal either to cite the scholarly tradition fairly, or to think for himself about the large stylistic discrepancies within the play identified by Parrott, Dover Wilson, and Hill—setting aside the other scholars he would not deign to mention (Timberlake, Tarlinskaja, Jackson)—is all too typical of the 'it's all by Shakespeare' school. It takes a newer form with an argument common to several editors in the New Cambridge Shakespeare series, along the lines 'yes, it may be bad poetry, but it's good theatre'.[76] As Hughes expresses this strategy of allowing theatrical considerations to outweigh all others:

The search for internal evidence has concentrated upon language because that is the source of doubt about Shakespeare's authorship. While methods are questionable and

[76] Michael Hattaway, in his edition of *The First Part of King Henry VI* (Cambridge, 1990), dealt very briefly with 'Authorship' (pp. 41–3), rejecting the findings of all stylistic studies (including the essay of Gary Taylor, not published until 1998), and dismissing the issue with this statement: 'I do not believe that stylistic analysis is sufficient to prove or disprove authorship, as it is likely that at an early stage in his career Shakespeare was moving freely between the various registers that were being deployed in the plays in which he was probably acting'. Telling his readers that 'none of the other statistical analyses I have read makes an indisputable case for dual or multiple authorship', Hattaway collapsed the issue altogether: 'And even if it could be proved that the play was in whole or in part not by Shakespeare, should that affect the way in which we read or direct it?' (p. 43). The Cambridge editors of *Pericles* also claim that the theatrical effect displaces all considerations of authorship, as we shall see.

results inconclusive, many good scholars intuitively feel that much of the verse is too clichéd and monotonous to be Shakespeare's, particularly in Act 1. These doubts tend to evaporate, however, when we recall that he was a dramatist and theatrical crafts-man as well as a poet. Indeed, it is conceivable that his theatrical talents matured first. Perhaps when he first drafted *Titus Andronicus*, at the beginning of his career, Peele's literary influence stifled his embryonic style. Revising later, possibly in 1593, he may have left Act 1 substantially unchanged. That would explain why its poetry seems inferior to that of the remainder of the play. But if we turn from language to dramaturgy and stagecraft, his signature is everywhere. (p. 12)

Here Hughes displayed another stock reaction of the Shakespeare fundamen-talists, dismissing detailed linguistic studies, rigorously controlled and quan-titatively expressed, as mere 'intuition'.[77] Like them, again, he was forced into speculation about Shakespeare's 'embryonic style' having been 'stifled' by Peele's when he wrote the first draft, yet, revising it four years later, leaving Act 1 'unchanged'. This seems a desperate way of not recognizing that the three scenes identified as Peele's are substantially different from Shakespeare's early style in several respects. As for the 'stagecraft', heavily criticized by Stanley Wells, Hughes avoided this issue by indulging in bardolatry: 'In *Titus Andronicus* a master stage craftsman commands the resources of an Elizabethan playhouse and its company with an authority that neither Peele nor Kyd could match' (ibid.). Many readers and theatregoers might reply that *The Spanish Tragedy* is at least as successful theatrically as *Titus*, but in an appendix Hughes continued to downgrade other dramatists and heap superlatives on Shakespeare, particularly praising Act 1 (its 'stagecraft . . . is beyond the capacity of Peele or Marlowe. Its mastery of space, movement and grouping. . . . Shakespeare has little to learn': pp. 154–5). Such indiscrim-inate praise at the expense of his fellow dramatists actually damages our understanding of Shakespeare's place in Renaissance drama, and is in any case no substitute for a close analysis, which will inevitably bring out much clumsiness and repetition (see Chapter 7). It also coexists very oddly with Hughes's 'Textual analysis', where he cited with approval the theories of Dover Wilson and Wells that Shakespeare 'decided to stage the sacrifice' of Alarbus, even though 'the incident interrupts the funeral' and 'the revisions were careless'. Hughes followed Wilson again on Shakespeare's other 'second thoughts': 'the killing of Mutius is an addition: if the episode were omitted, there would be a smooth transition from 1.1.286 to 1.1.299', while 'the burial of Mutius might also be an afterthought' (p. 147). It is difficult to recon-cile acceptance of such theories of careless revision and added episodes

---

[77] In his 'Textual Analysis' (pp. 145–53) Hughes reported that 'Maxwell and Dover Wilson have noted apparent repetitions of phrasing between 1.1.294, 343, 300 and 344, suggesting careless revision; but these are only echoes' (p. 147). But of course neither editor said that these repetitions indicated revision, but rather that such 'mechanical recurrences' were not typical of 'Shakespeare at any point in his career' (Maxwell's note on 1.1.294).

which 'interrupt' the dramatic action, and destroy 'smooth transitions', with Hughes's blanket assertions that the stagecraft of Act 1 is superior to anything in Peele, Kyd, or Marlowe. Loyalty to the cause of text conservation can blind critics to their own self-contradictions.

Alan Hughes struck out in some new directions in his attempt to assign the whole play to Shakespeare. In his Arden edition Jonathan Bate gave the most perfunctory treatment of the authorship issue in any major edition so far, relying on old and tried methods of dismissing the 'disintegrators'. He referred to only a few of the earlier authorship studies, work by J. C. Maxwell and by MacDonald Jackson, adding the snide comment that Jackson's 'conclusions are enshrined in the Oxford *Textual Companion*' (Bate 1995, p. 81), but he cited their work so briefly that no reader could derive any reliable impression of the case for Peele's co-authorship. Bate cited one parallel only between Act 1 of *Titus* and Peele's work (from the *Garter* poem), although he must have read the pages of parallels quoted by Dover Wilson, and he dismissed the whole issue by claiming that 'there are equally striking parallels with anonymous plays', with Marlowe, Kyd, Lodge, 'and of course with Shakespeare's works'. If so, why not cite them? But, in the familiar manner of the 'sole authorship' advocates, Bate felt that the counter-evidence was too insignificant to be worth even mentioning, assuring his readers that, 'with all the arguments based on verbal parallels. . . . imitation is always as likely as authorship', and that 'all the parallels with other dramatists in *Titus* may, paradoxically, be evidence that Shakespeare was in fact the author. The one thing we know for sure about his early career was that he was notorious for making use of other writers' fine phrases' (p. 82). As can be seen from the work of Donald Foster, it is a recognized tactic among those wishing to ascribe mediocre work to Shakespeare—such as the repetitive and mechanical Act 1 of *Titus*, or the equally repetitive and stereotyped *Funerall Elegye* (1612)—to accuse him of plagiarism.[78] Unfortunately, the only evidence that Bate could cite was a well-known exchange between Nashe and Greene, where he repeated a common misinterpretation.

In his preface to Greene's *Menaphon* Nashe had provocatively set some contemporary dramatists against the actors ('taffety fools'), praising 'sundry other sweet Gentlemen I doe know, that have . . . tricked up a company of taffaty fooles with their feathers, whose beauty if our Poets had not peecte with the supply of their periwigs, they might have antickt it untill this time up and downe the Countrey with the King of Fairies . . .'.[79] In his putative deathbed pamphlet, *Greene's Groats-worth of witte, bought with a million of*

---

[78] Cf. Foster 1989, pp. 199–200, and B. Vickers, *'Counterfeiting' Shakespeare: Evidence, Authorship, and John Ford's* Funerall Elegye (Cambridge, 2002), pp. 86–90.

[79] *The Works of Thomas Nashe*, ed. R. B. McKerrow, 5 vols. (Oxford, 1904–10; rev. edn., 1958), iii. 323–4. See also McKerrow's commentary, iv. 444–7, 458.

Repentance, which, as we have seen, was written by Henry Chettle,[80] Greene (St John's and Clare Hall, Cambridge) is presented as warning these gentlemen playwrights, Marlowe (Corpus Christi, Cambridge), Nashe (St John's, Cambridge), and Peele (Christ Church, Oxford), to beware of the actors, 'those Anticks garnisht in our colours'—that is, who speak the lines of verse (or perhaps rhetorical 'colours') that they have written for them:

Yes trust them not: for there is an upstart Crow, beautified with our feathers, that with his *Tygers hart wrapt in a Players hyde*, supposes he is as well able to bombast out a blank verse as the best of you: and beeing an absolute *Iohannes fac totum*, is in his owne conceit the only Shake-scene in a countrey. (Chambers 1930, ii. 188)

The italicized English words parody a line in *3 Henry VI*, 'O tiger's heart wrapp'd in a woman's hide' (1.4.137), and make it clear that Shakespeare is being mocked. But rather than accusing him of plagiarism, the attack was really directed against the impudence of a 'common player', as actors were then called, setting himself up as able to write blank verse as competently as those three university graduates. 'Jack of all trades, master of none', as the old saying has it, smears those of many talents. The author, whether Greene or Chettle, seems to have seriously (if rather impracticably) advised these gentlemen playwrights to give up writing for the popular theatres altogether:

O that I might intreat your rare wits to be imploied in more profitable courses: & let those Apes imitate your past excellence, and never more acquaint them with your admired inventions . . . for it is pittie men of such rare wits, should be subject to the pleasure of such rude groomes.

The whole thrust of this passage is clearly directed against the actors, 'these buckram Gentlemen'—an ironic contradiction in terms—and has nothing to do with plagiarism. In any case, given that Shakespeare was the most inventive writer of his age, to write him down as a plagiarist on this feeble evidence seems perverse.

Having branded Shakespeare a plagiarist, Bate got rid of the whole troubling authorship issue by invoking 'computer analysis' of 'functional words' (*sic*), which 'suggests what literary judgment confirms: that the whole of *Titus* is by a single hand and that at this level its linguistic habits are very different from Peele's'. Bate ended by citing a comforting authority for the Shakespeare conservators: 'According to Andrew Q. Morton, who undertook the analysis, the statistical probability of Peele's involvement is less than one in ten thousand million' (Bate 1985, p. 83). All too many uninformed readers will have been impressed by those astronomically large, but quite fictitious numbers, all too typical of Morton's unreliable methods, discussed above. Bate's reliance on Morton's authority confirms T. H. Howard-Hill's diagnosis of 'the uneasy

---

[80] See Warren B. Austin, 'A Computer-Aided Technique for Stylistic Discrimination: The Authorship of *Greene's Groatsworth of Wit*' (Washington, 1969).

relationship' that exists between scholars using stylometry and literary critics, who often do not understand the methods used. Critics will accept faultily executed work, which they cannot evaluate, if it matches their own theories, but reject properly executed work if it does not. 'If different stylometric analyses differ or are inconclusive, the critic will use that to discredit the stylometric results and confirm his own judgements.'[81] Had Bate been aware of M. W. A. Smith's stylometric studies, which contradict Morton's and confirm the presence of a second author, it would be interesting to know whether he would have changed his mind about Shakespeare's sole authorship.

Some editors of Shakespeare feel no compunction about dismissing the issue of co-authorship, but in doing so they perform a disservice to scholarship. The common reader, and even the professional, relies on the editor appointed to produce a major edition to sift through all the scholarly and critical literature on a play and to pick out the most important discussions. These should be reviewed in the introduction, in honest detail, properly evaluated, and used in the commentary where relevant. Our collective understanding of Shakespeare, our need to distinguish his work from that of his co-authors, is not advanced by editors who treat the authorship question in such a partisan or perfunctory manner as Waith, Hughes, and Bate have done. The prestige that these major editions enjoy means that their pronouncements on the authorship issue can have a stultifying effect on other editors and critics. In the recent New Penguin edition the textual editor, Sonia Massai, simply capitulated before Jonathan Bate's authority, reporting that 'Bate distances himself from [J. C.] Maxwell's view that the first act was written by George Peele . . .':[82] as if no more needed to be said. There, more than eighty years of scholarship by a dozen reputable scholars was buried from view by citing one of the Shakespeare 'conservators', a deference which, on this issue, was unfortunately misplaced.

Fortunately, true scholarship continues its attempt to find new and better ways of identifying Shakespeare's share in the play. MacDonald Jackson returned to *Titus* in 1996, drawing on new evidence to make the case for Peele's co-authorship even stronger.[83] Jackson's argument was based partly

---

[81] See T. H. Howard-Hill (ed.), *Shakespeare and 'Sir Thomas More': Essays on the Play and its Shakespearian Interest* (Cambridge, 1989), p. 4, and 'Reinterpreting a Quotation', *ShN* 209 (1991), p. 30.

[82] *Titus Andronicus*, Introduction and Commentary by Jacques Berthoud, ed. by Sonia Massai (London, 2001). Professor Berthoud does not discuss the case for Peele's co-authorship in his Introduction, apart from the oblique comment on 1.1. that 'It has been argued that Shakespeare could not have written this scene (but Peele, we are told, could)', and rejecting this claim as 'surely mistaken' (p. 33). In his commentary on 1.1.185, the word 'palliament', he observes: 'This has been cited as evidence in favour of Peele's authorship of Act 1 of Shakespeare's play. See Introduction, p. 12'—but that page has no reference to Peele.

[83] Given that many Shakespeare critics take little notice of authorship studies, it is heartening to find that Emrys Jones recently read Jackson's essay, with its 'coolly measured and implacably rational presentation of different kinds of evidence', and pronounced himself 'wholly persuaded': see Jones, 'Reclaiming Early Shakespeare', *Essays in Criticism*, 51 (2001): 35–50, at pp. 38–9.

on bibliographical evidence linking the 1594 quarto of *Titus* with Peele—
stage directions and speech headings—and partly on a fresh linguistic analysis. One stage direction in *Titus* (see Plate 6), the instruction to '*Sound Drums
and Trumpets, and then enter two of Titus sonnes . . . and others as many as
can be*' (1.1.69) has long been understood as typifying an author's stage direction in its vagueness (since those involved in theatrical productions need to
specify just which actors/characters are involved), and W. W. Greg cited
another instance, '*& others as many as may be*', from Peele's *Edward I* (see
Plate 7). But, rather than typical of a widely shared practice, Jackson pointed
out that 'these are almost certainly the only two instances of the entry of "others as many as can/may be" in the whole of English Renaissance drama
1576–1642' (Jackson 1996, p. 136).[84] That is indeed a strong piece of evidence for Peele's authorship of Act 1, never before observed. Other, equally
striking links between Peele and *Titus Andronicus* concern not the content of
stage directions but their form, a curious hybrid combining both stage direction and speech heading. Thus the stage direction '*Marcus Andronicus with
the Crowne*' (1.1.17) is printed in the centre of the page and serves simultaneously as a speech heading, no other being given. Similarly with '*Enter a
Captaine*' (1.1.64), who speaks six lines without any speech heading, and
'*Enter Lavinia*' (1.1.156), a cue which is directly followed by her eight-line
speech. Other instances in Act 1 of stage directions doubling as speech headings are '*Titus two sonnes speakes*' (1.1.355), '*Titus sonne speakes*' (1.1.357),
and '*they all kneele and say*' (1.1.386).

As Jackson has established, 'nothing comparable to the mix of formulas
and oddities in the headings and directions of the opening pages of *Titus
Andronicus* can be found in any other Shakespeare play—in the First Folio
(1623) or in any of the twenty-two substantive quartos, "good" and "bad"'
(p. 137). But this hybrid form is frequently found in Peele's plays. In *Edward
I* (1593) a centred heading *The Queen Mother* (see Plate 7) introduces 'a ten-
line speech; after the lords have exited, "*Manet Queen Mother*" is centred
and she continues a very long speech' (p. 139). Jackson quoted twenty
instances from this play of stage directions preceding un-prefixed speeches,
such as '*The Friar and Guenthian sing; Lluellen speakes to them*'; '*Then
Lluellen spieth Elinor and Mortimer, and saieth this*'; '*Longshanks kisses
them both and speaks*'; '*Bishop speakes to her in her bed*'. These are exact
parallels to the three instances in Act 1 of *Titus* of the formulae '. . . *speakes*',
or '. . . *say*'. Most of the directions in *Edward 1* 'are centred; most fall within
a scene, not at its beginning'—where a different typographical treatment can
be expected, and the speeches introduced are up to ten lines long. Jackson

---

[84] Alan C. Dessen and Leslie Thomson, *A Dictionary of Stage Directions in English Drama
1580–1642* (Cambridge, 1999), *s.v.* 'permissive stage directions' (p. 162), list one additional
instance of the phrase 'as many as may be' from Fletcher and Massinger's *The Double Marriage*
(1620).

The moſt Lamen-

table Romaine Tragedie of

Titus Andronicus : As it was Plaide by
the Right Honourable the Earle
of *Darbie*, Earle of *Pembrooke*,
and Earle of *Suſſex* their
Seruants.

Enter the Tribunes and Senatours aloft : And then enter
Saturninus and his followers at one dore, and Baſſianus and
his followers, with Drums and Trumpets.

Saturninus.

Noble *Patricians*, Patrons of my Right,
Defend the iuſtice of my cauſe with armes.
And Countrimen my louing followers,
Plead my ſucceſſiue Title with your ſwords:

Sound Drums and Trumpets, and then enter two of Titus
ſonnes, and then two men bearing a Coffin couered with black,
then two other ſonnes, then Titus Andronicus, *and then* Ta-
mora the Queene of Gothes and her two ſonnes Chiron *and*

Demetrius, *with* Aron *the More, and others as many as can*
be, then ſet downe the Coffin, and Titus *ſpeakes.*

Titus. Haile Rome, victorious in thy mourning weeds,
Lo as the Barke that hath diſchargd his fraught,
Returnes with pretious lading to the bay,
From whence at firſt ſhee wayd her anchorage;
Commeth *Andronicus*, bound with Lawrell bowes,

PL. 6. Stage directions, *Titus Andronicus*, Quarto (1594), 1.1.1 (sig. A₃ʳ),
1.1.69 (sig. A₄ʳ⁻ᵛ). By permission of the Folger Shakespeare Library

THE
Famous Chronicle hiſtorie of King
Edwarde the firſt, ſirnamed Edwarde
Longſhankes : with the ſincking of Queene
Elinor at Charingeroſſe, and her riſing
againe at Potters hith, otherwiſe
called Queene hith.

Enter Gilbart de Clare *Earle of Gloceſter, with the Earle of* Suſſex, Mortimer *the Earle of March,* Dauid Lluel-lens *brother, waiting on* Helinor *the Queene mother.*

The Queene Mother.

Y L. lieutenant of Gloceſter, and L. Mortimer,
To do you honor in your Soueraignes eyes,
That as we heare is newly come aland,
From *Paleſtine*, with all his men of warret
The poore remainer of the royall Fleete,
Preſeru'd by miracle in *Sicill* Roade.

The Trumpets ſound, and enter the traine, viz. his maimed Souldiers with headpeeces and Garlands on them, euery man with his red Croſſe on his coate : the Ancient borne in a Chaire, his Garland and his plumes on his headpeete, his Enſigne in his hand. Enter after them Gloceſter and Mortimer bareheaded, & others as many as may be. Then Long-ſhanks and his wife Elinor, Edmund Couchback, and Ione and Signior Moumfort the Earle of Leiceſters priſoner, with Sailers and Souldiers, and Charles de Moumfort his brother.

Q. Mother. Gloceſter, Edward, O my ſweete ſonnes.
And then ſhe fals and ſounds.

PL. 7. Stage directions, *The Famous Chronicle historie of King Edwarde the first*, 1.1 (sig. A$_2$^{r}, A$_2$^{v}). By permission of the Bodleian Library, Oxford

TABLE 3.8. *Function words in* Titus Andronicus

	Mean rates	*and*	*with*
Shakespeare			
All plays		2.998	0.878
Titus	Whole play	3.844	1.136
	Act 1	4.809	1.282
	Acts 2–5	3.556	1.103
Peele			
Edward I		3.872	1.518
Battle of Alcazar		5.314	1.213
David and Bethsabe		4.329	1.644

Source: Jackson 1996, pp. 144–5.

quoted a further eleven instances of this formula—a centred stage direction doubling up as a speech heading—from Peele's *Araygnement of Paris* (1584), six instances in his *The Battle of Alcazar* (1594), and six from Peele's *David and Bethsabe* (1599).

MacDonald Jackson's identification of this 'combination of anomalies' in the stage directions and speech headings of *Titus Andronicus*, Act 1, will seem, to many readers, decisive proof of Peele's authorship. But Jackson, having recapitulated the evidence provided by linguistic and metrical studies linking Peele with the play, added new tests. Drawing on Marvin Spevack's *Shakespeare Concordance*, which gives the rates of occurrence for every word in every play, these being expressed as percentages of the total number of words (that is, of 'tokens', not 'types'), Jackson studied the occurrence in *Titus* of two function words, *and* and *with*, compared with the norm for Shakespeare and with the opening scenes of three plays by Peele, which provided samples of about 2,000 words. In Table 3.8 I summarize[85] his findings. It is immediately obvious that in both cases the mean rate for Act 1 of *Titus* is higher than elsewhere in Shakespeare, but remains well within Peele's range of usage. For *and*, Jackson stated, 'this disparity between Act 1 and Acts 2–5 is highly significant, statistically speaking. The odds are less than one in a thousand that it is a chance phenomenon . . .' (p. 144). Although the difference is not so great for *with*, all of Peele's rates are outside the normal Shakespeare range, and we may conclude that Peele 'shows the same partiality for *and* and *with* that distinguishes Act 1 of *Titus Andronicus* from the rest of the Shakespeare canon' (p. 145).

[85] I have not recorded all the statistical detail, which interested readers will want to consult for themselves.

TABLE 3.9. *Verbal formulae in* Titus Andronicus

Play	Frequency: every *x* lines
Titus, Act 1	12.7
Titus, Acts 2–5	24.7
Two Gentlemen	22.8
Shrew	37.3
2 Henry VI	20.6
3 Henry VI	19.3
1 Henry VI	21.9
Richard III	24.0
Comedy of Errors	17.6
Love's Labour's Lost	34.8
Peele, *David and Bethsabe*, Act 1	13.6
Peele, *David and Bethsabe*, Act 2	10.8
Peele, *David and Bethsabe*, Act 3	12.2
Peele, *David and Bethsabe*, Act 4	8.3

Source: Jackson 1996, p. 145.

Jackson linked Peele still further by studying 'a trick of style that recurs conspicuously in Act 1 of *Titus*', indeed in the very first line:

This is the ending of a blank verse line with a preposition or conjunction, followed by a possessive pronoun plus a monosyllabic noun, as in 'of my right', 'with your swords', 'to our foes', 'of his name', 'and his sons'. The formula, usually preceded by a two-syllable word stressed on its first syllable, produces a pyrrhic foot[86] followed by a foot that is some way between an iamb and a spondee; alternatively, one might say that each successive syllable carries marginally more stress than the one before it, but only the last of the four is strongly stressed. (p. 145)

Jackson counted this stylistic feature in *Titus Andronicus*, in the opening acts of Shakespeare's eight other earliest plays, and in all four acts of Peele's *David and Bethsabe*. I summarize his findings in Table 3.9. The overall rate for the Shakespeare plays is one in 22.8 lines, which matches that for Acts 2–5 of *Titus* (24.7), while the overall rate of 11.2 for Peele's *David and Bethsabe* matches that (12.7) for *Titus*, Act 1. Jackson computed that the odds for the disparity in the figures for the two parts of *Titus* being 'a matter of chance . . . is less than one in a thousand' (p. 145). I imagine that most reasonable readers will now accept that, in terms of verse style, vocabulary, syntax, and other linguistic habits, two distinct strata exist in this play. In some of the later scenes, Jackson recorded, the two hands do not divide up so clearly, but he judged it hardly surprising 'if collaboration between Peele and Shakespeare,

[86] That is, one having two light stresses: 'sea/sŏn ŏf / mists'.

or the revision of one dramatist's script by the other, were to create such a stylistic mix. When two authors combine in the composition of a play, it is not uncommon for some mutual adjustment to take place . . .' (pp. 146–7).

Peele's participation in *Titus Andronicus*, already firmly established, was given more body by Brian Boyd, a colleague of Jackson's at the University of Auckland, in a detailed study of the play's language.[87] Having absorbed the work of Timberlake, Hill, Tarlinskaja, and Jackson, Boyd chose to extend the work of John Dover Wilson on the astonishing repetitiveness of the play's 'suspect parts', which show 'the lazy repetition of a few common words the author has retrieved from his wordbox and keeps on reshuffling. At times he may let them sink below the top of the pile, but he soon gropes again for his favourites. Nothing, it need hardly be said, could be less like Shakespeare' (Boyd 1995, p. 301). Boyd endorsed Wilson's description of Peele's fondness for self-repetition, but tried to express it in quantitative terms, beginning with the references to *Rome* (also *Rome's, Roman, Romans*). As we have seen, Hereward T. Price thought that the frequent allusions to Roman customs was part of Shakespeare's earnest (if amateur) attempts to lend a classical patina to the play. But Boyd showed a striking difference between Act 1, where 68 such terms recur in 495 lines, a frequency of 1 in 7, and the remaining acts, with 54 instances in 1,944 lines, a frequency of 1 in 36. This lower degree of reference closely matches the figures for Shakespeare's other Roman plays: *Julius Caesar* (1 in 38 lines), *Coriolanus* (1 in 34), *Antony and Cleopatra* (1 in 39). In Boyd's pungent verdict, the preoccupation with *romanitas* in Act 1 'reflects not a Shakespearian capacity to focus a topic but a collaborator's inattention to his own repetitiveness' (p. 302).

An equally sharp distinction between Act 1 and the remainder of the play emerged when Boyd studied the incidence of abstract nouns, such as 'honour', 'noble', 'grace', and their compounds, throughout the play. His results, summarized in Table 3.10, reveal a huge discrepancy between these two sets of figures, confirming the existence of two hands in the play, and documenting again Peele's weakness for verbal self-repetition. Boyd demonstrated both points by quoting four speeches from Act 1 of *Titus*, italicizing the repeated phrases, which amount to 'fifty-seven repetitions in 38 lines, or one in just over two-thirds of a line', a 'formulaic repetition' which 'shows that verbal tics override appropriateness to the situation. Need it be said that of all writers in the world Shakespeare is the furthest from the automatism here?' (pp. 302–3). Boyd then showed this 'repetition compulsion' to be 'decidedly the hallmark of Peele', quoting a comparable sequence from *The Battle of Alcazar*, which recycles many of the abstract nouns found in the first act of *Titus*, achieving '42 repetitions in 29 lines, or again one in just over every two-

---

[87] B. Boyd, 'Common Words in *Titus Andronicus*: The Presence of Peele', *NQ* 240 (1995): 300–7. Professor Boyd is best known for his outstanding two-volume biographical and critical study of Vladimir Nabokov.

TABLE 3.10. *Abstract nouns in* Titus Andronicus

Word	Frequency (every *x* lines)	
	Act 1	Acts 2–5
honour	14	240
noble	22	175
grace	35	137
virtue	62	(none)
right	50	321
favour	99	1,923
cause	71	481
fame	99	(none)
worth	83	385
arms	83	240

Source: Boyd 1995, pp. 502–3.

thirds of a line', and displaying several of the Peele stylistic mannerisms found in *Titus* (pp. 304–5).

Boyd identified Peele as co-author in two other ways. One is the choice between the variant forms *brothers/brethren*, a peculiarly important choice in a play involving so many sets of brothers. In 1.1 the word *brethren* appears 4 times (1:124 lines), but in the Shakespearian Part *B* only once (1:1923). On the other hand, 1.1 uses *brothers* once (1:495), Part *B* has it 7 times (1:275). Peele elsewhere prefers *brethren* to *brothers*, unlike both Shakespeare and Kyd. Boyd's other linguistic detail linking Peele with *Titus Andronicus* took the form of challenging A. M. Sampley's 1933 essay, which attacked Robertson and Sykes for indiscriminately ascribing anonymous plays to Peele. As I noted earlier, Sampley was unusually coy in failing to disclose the words that he had identified as common to Peele and to *Titus Andronicus*, but Boyd shows that they amount to 17 words or phrases[88] which 'occur outside this play uniquely in Peele (11 instances) or with far greater frequency in his work than in that of any other writer (6 instances)'. Nearly all of them occur in the scenes already identified as Peele's, 8 of them in 1.1, 3 in 2.1, 2 in the very short scene 2.2, and 1 in 4.1. The word *panther*, which was used more frequently by Peele than by any other writer apart from Greene, occurs in the Shakespeare canon only in this play, in

---

[88] Namely: '*architect*; *bright and grey*; *chase* in the sense of "park"; *feere*; *gallop the zodiac*; *gratulate*; *laden with honour's spoils*; *palliament*; *Prometheus tied to Caucasus*; *remunerate*; *sacred wit*; *salute . . . with tears*; *séquestered*; *successful in*; *to virtue . . . consecrate*; *wreak* as a noun; *wise Laertes' son*' (Boyd 1995, p. 305 n.).

1.1, 2.2,[89] and 2.3, 'a continuation of the plot line started at the end of 1.1'. In Boyd's words,

The odds against these pronounced Peelisms occurring by chance in each of the scenes otherwise identified as being closer to Peele's norms than to Shakespeare's—and occurring so many times in the longer scenes—must be enormous. . . . Either Peele had at least a major hand in the scenes of Part A; or, like the creationists' God planting fossils to mislead scientists, Shakespeare assiduously copied, for four scenes only, the obvious and the obscure characteristics—the exceptional and the commonplace locutions, even the proportion of humdrum function words, the imagery, the alliteration, the metre, the syntax, the line and speech structures, even the stage directions—of a writer he already had nothing to learn from. (p. 306 n.)

It remains a hypothesis, of course, that Peele 'wrote at least 1.1 and 2.1 and perhaps a first version . . . of 2.2 and 4.1 of *Titus Andronicus*'. Yet, as Boyd concluded, 'it seems a hypothesis much more likely to be confirmed—and refined—than refuted' (p. 307).

MacDonald Jackson helped confirm this hypothesis with a note on the incidence of the alternative forms, *brothers* or *brethren*, drawing on the Chadwyck–Healey databases, which permit searches of the whole canon of Elizabethan poetry and drama. He showed that Boyd's figures were not quite accurate, but that his argument was even more telling than he had realized. 'In *Titus Andronicus* the plurals *brothers* and *brethren* each occur nine times', but with an almost clinical separation: 'eight of the examples of *brethren* are in the suspect Act 1, while eight of the examples of *brothers* are in the rest of the play.'[90] This is indeed 'a remarkable discrepancy: 8:1 in Peele's putative share as against 1:8 in Shakespeare's'. Checking the rest of the plays, Jackson found that *Titus* 'accounts for half the examples of *brethren* in the whole Shakespearian dramatic canon, and all but one of these are in the "Peelian" Act 1' (Jackson 1997*b*, p. 495). In Shakespeare's eleven earliest plays the count is 23 instances of *brothers*, 2 of *brethren*, exactly the opposite result to Peele's 9 instances of *brethren* (8 of them in *The Battle of Alcazar*) and only one of *brothers*. And the only example of either plural in both authors' poems is *brethren* in Peele's *Polyhymnia*. Given that Shakespeare's preferred plural is *brothers*, 'the repeated use of *brethren* . . . in Act 1 of *Titus Andronicus* thus differentiates this piece of writing from anything else of comparable size in the Shakespeare canon'. As Jackson concluded, 'this small but significant item of evidence' strength-

---

[89] Further evidence for ascribing 2.2 to Peele is that the line in which occurs the word *panther*, 'Will rouse the proudest panther in the chase', 'contains not only the Peelian "chase", but also his characteristic fondness for alliteration, his habit of recycling line-endings, and the superlative, all found in his line "The fattest fairest fawn in all the chase" (*The Araygnment of Paris*, 1.1.7)' (p. 306 n.).

[90] M. P. Jackson, 'Shakespeare's Brothers and Peele's Brethren: *Titus Andronicus* again', *NQ* 242 (1997): 494–5, at p. 494.

ens the case for thinking that Shakespeare's collaborator on *Titus* was George Peele.

NEW TESTS FOR PEELE'S CO-AUTHORSHIP

The case for Peele's co-authorship can be made even stronger by examining other aspects of the play's style: I have devised three new tests. First, I have compared *Titus Andronicus* with one play by Peele of comparable subject-matter, *The Battle of Alcazar*,[91] in terms of their use of polysyllabic words. As we recall, F. E. Pierce showed that words of three and more syllables were most likely to be derived from Latin roots, and that their computation could effectively distinguish the work of Webster, a more learned dramatist, from that of Dekker. I have shown elsewhere that the same test clearly distinguished John Ford's hand in collaborative plays from Dekker's, an allocation of authorship that was confirmed by other tests.[92] Applying this test to *Titus Andronicus* and to a play wholly by Peele gave the results set out in Tables 3.11 and 3.12. These figures show that Peele had a distinctly stronger preference for polysyllabic words than Shakespeare. Indeed, it is striking that the overall frequency for his scenes in *Titus Andronicus*—one polysyllabic word every 2.8 lines—closely matches the overall frequency for *The Battle of Alcazar*. In this test I have computed words of three or more syllables, excluding proper names, where again a distinct difference emerges between Peele and Shakespeare, as a later test will show.

The individual word lists also show up differences between the two writers. Peele tends to use more abstract nouns ending in a consonant plus *y* than Shakespeare does: in Peele's scenes in *Titus* (1.1, 2.1, 2.2, 4.1) we find 'extremity', 'impiety', 'indignity', 'integrity', 'liberality', 'nobility', 'opportunity'. In his scenes—which total twice as many lines as Peele's—Shakespeare uses the more generally available terms, 'obscurity', 'melancholy', 'flattery', 'possibilities', and 'testimony'. (Three other nouns ending in consonant plus *y* refer to concretes: 'ceremonies', 'auditory', and 'oratory'.) In *The Battle of Alcazar* Peele uses 'ability', 'extremitie', 'integrity', 'magnanimity' (twice), 'melancholy', 'necessitie', and 'unconstancie'. A more obvious difference between the two writers is in the number of times they reuse the same word. In *Alcazar* Peele uses 'honorable' 8 times, 'barbarous' 6 times, 'embassador' 4 times, 'expedition', 'resolution', 'conquering', 'dangerous', and 'enemies' 3 times each, while in his share of *Titus* 'nobility' occurs 3 times. On this level, too, as noted by John Dover Wilson and Brian Boyd, Peele's style is

[91] I have used John Yoklavich's edition of *The Battle of Alcazar*, in Prouty 1952–70, ii. 215–373. It is likely that *Alcazar* survives in an abridged version: cf. W. W. Greg, *Two Elizabethan Stage Abridgments* (London, 1922), and D. H. Horne, in Prouty 1952–70, i. 77–8.
[92] See Vickers 2002, Appendix III.

TABLE 3.11. *Polysyllabic words in* Titus Andronicus

Act/scene	3, 4, and 5-syllable words (tokens)	Total lines	Frequency
1.1 (P)	206	495	2.4
2.1 (P)	44	135	3.0
2.2 (P)	7	26	3.7
2.3	107	306	2.9
2.4	11	57	5.2
3.1	70	300	4.3
3.2	26	85	3.3
4.1 (P)	24	129	5.4
4.2	48	180	3.8
4.3	34	121	3.6
4.4	51	113	2.2
5.1	52	165	3.2
5.2	51	205	4.0
5.3	75	200	2.7
TOTAL	806	2,517	3.1

Peele scenes: 785 lines, 281 tokens, frequency: 2.8.
Shakespeare scenes: 1,732 lines, 525 tokens, frequency: 3.3.

characterized by the repetition of a somewhat limited vocabulary. In Shakespeare's share the maximum repetition of any word was three times, for the words 'charitable', 'honorable', 'barbarous', 'revered', and 'execution'. (These figures omit recurring uses of titles or ranks, such as 'emperor' and 'general'.)

A second test I have used to differentiate the two writers concerns their use of alliteration. Peele's fondness for alliteration has been known to some scholars since 1910, when the University of Breslau accepted a still serviceable dissertation by Erna Landsberg[93] (a pupil of Gregor Sarrazin), studying his style in both the authentic and the ascribed works. Landsberg showed a commendable knowledge of rhetoric, analysing both grammatical and rhetorical elements in Peele's style (inversion, ellipsis, address, exclamation; metonymy, synecdoche, metaphor, hyperbole, *epizeuxis*, *anaphora*, *epistrophe*, *anadiplosis*, *gradatio*, *polyptoton*, and several types of word-play). She discussed alliteration in the plays then accepted as Peele's (Landsberg 1910, pp. 51–4), counting 207 instances in *The Araygnment of Paris*, 100 instances in *David and Bethsabe*, and 110 instances in *Edward I*. Of the other plays she discussed which were then ascribed to Peele, only *The Battle of Alcazar* has

[93] E. Landsberg, 'Der Stil in George Peeles sicheren und zweifelhaften dramatischen Werken', Ph.D. Diss. (Breslau, 1910).

TABLE 3.12. *Polysyllabic words in Peele,* The Battle of Alcazar

Act/scene	3, 4, and 5-syllable words (tokens)	Total lines
1. Prologue	21	53
1.1	52	135
1.2	19	86
2. Prologue	22	53
2.1	17	55
2.2	46	84
2.3	38	102
2.4	66	167
3. Prologue	6	22
3.1	36	68
3.2	10	30
3.3	19	45
3.4	31	76
4. Prologue	4	13
4.1	34	73
4.2	43	97
5. Prologue	8	33
5.1	65	259
TOTAL	537	1,452

Frequency: 2.7.

been admitted to the Peele canon,[94] although it survives in an abridgment 'which has affected the style for the worst'.[95] Landsberg computed alliteration as occurring once in every eight lines of this play (pp. 94–6)—a distinct underestimate, I believe.

Landsberg showed that Peele (like other users of this device) mostly used alliteration for the initial consonants, with the basic doubling pattern (*aa*) amounting to half of the total occurrences in the three canonic plays—that is, about 200 instances, according to her count. But Peele also used triple alliteration (*aaa*) within a line 158 times in these three plays, quadruple (*aaaa*)

[94] Landsberg also discussed *Sir Clyomon and Sir Clamydes*, in which one verse in every eight displayed alliteration, a proportion similar to *The Araygnement of Paris* (1910, pp. 56–8, 73–5), and *Locrine*, where the ratio is lower, once in every fourteen lines (pp. 124–5).

[95] Wolfgang Clemen, *English Tragedy before Shakespeare: The Development of Dramatic Speech* (London, 1961); trans. T. S. Dorsch from *Die Tragödie vor Shakespeare: ihre Entwicklung im Spiegel der dramatischen Rede* (Heidelberg, 1955), p. 171 n. Clemen commented that in the many 'flights of passion' given to the Moor, Muly Mahamet, 'with the help of such devices as the repetition and sheer accumulation of words, thrown into glaring relief by means of alliteration, a blood-curdling effect is intended to be produced' (pp. 172–3).

some 29 times, and quintuple (*aaaaa*) 6 times. Landsberg also noted alliterative patterns involving two different consonants in one line, either in parallel (*aabb*: 16 times; *aabbb*: 4; *aaabb*: 4) or alternating (*abba*: 7; *aabba*: 1;
aabcbc: 1). In many cases, however, Peele's typical alliteration involved not
just the initial but the first two consonants of the key word, especially when
the second one was an *r* or *l*, as in these examples:

> Her *tr*ailing *tr*esses that hang *fl*aring round
> Of July *fl*owers so *gr*affed in the *gr*ound
>
> > (*Araygnement of Paris*, 112–13)
>
> *Dr*oop, *dr*own and *dr*ench in Hebron's fearful streams
>
> > (*David and Bethsabe*, 677)
>
> And never may the *gr*ass *gr*ow *gr*een again
>
> > (*Edward I*, 2203)

In *The Battle of Alcazar* (total length: 1,452 lines), the play I have chosen for
comparison with *Titus Andronicus*, Landsberg computed alliteration once in
every 8 lines, which would give about 181 instances in all. Two-thirds of these
(or 120 instances), she claimed, were of the basic double form (*aa*), 37 were
of the triple (*aaa*), and four of the quadruple (*aaaa*). Several lines contained
alliteration on two distinct consonants (*aabb*: 10; *aaabb*: 1; *abab*: 1; *aabbc*: 2;
abbba: 1). Landsberg also found many instances where Peele alliterated on
the first two consonants, as in:

> *Th*row up *th*y trembling hands to heaven's *th*rone
>
> > (57)
>
> To *wr*eak *th*e *wr*ongs and mur*th*ers *th*ou hast done
>
> > (306)
>
> *Th*e *tr*ophies and *th*e *tr*iumphs of *th*y men
>
> > (1379)

Computing alliteration, as with other details of style, turns out to be not as
easy as one might think. In my own count (see Table 3.13) I have taken alliteration to mean the repetition of consonants within one syntactical unit or
one line, together with the half-line preceding or following. One problem
concerns rhetorical repetition (the figures *anaphora*, *ploké*, *epizeuxis*), where
the repetition of a word inevitably carries with it the echoing of the initial consonant. In the following tables such rhetorical figures have been counted. To
begin with *The Battle of Alcazar*, my totals are higher than Landsberg's, perhaps because I have included rhetorical figures. (In my terminology, A2 corresponds to her *aa*, double alliteration; A3 to *aaa*; A4 to *aaaa*, and so on.) The
same approach applied to their co-authored play yielded the results set out in
Table 3.14. Although he used alliteration to a lesser extent in *Alcazar*, in *Titus
Andronicus* Peele used it almost twice as often as Shakespeare, with a pro-

TABLE 3.13. *Alliteration in* The Battle of Alcazar

Act/scene	A2	A3	A4	A5	A6	A7	A8	Totals	Total lines	Frequency
1. Prologue	9	6	3	0	0	0	0	18	53	3.0
1.1	37	9	5	2	0	1	0	54	135	2.5
1.2	23	6	4	1	1	0	0	35	86	2.5
2. Prologue	17	4	2	0	1	0	0	24	53	2.3
2.1	18	3	0	0	0	0	1	22	55	2.5
2.2	19	4	2	0	0	0	0	25	84	3.4
2.3	23	4	3	0	0	0	0	30	102	3.4
2.4	27	6	1	0	0	0	0	34	167	5.0
3. Prologue	4	1	0	1	0	0	0	6	22	3.7
3.1	14	4	1	0	0	0	0	19	68	3.6
3.2	10	1	0	0	0	0	0	11	30	2.8
3.3	13	0	1	0	0	0	0	14	45	3.3
3.4	14	3	1	0	0	1	0	19	76	4.0
4. Prologue	3	1	0	2	0	0	0	6	13	2.2
4.1	8	4	1	0	0	0	0	13	73	5.7
4.2	25	2	2	1	0	0	0	30	97	3.3
5. Prologue	13	0	4	0	1	0	0	18	33	1.9
5.1	79	11	8	0	1	0	0	99	259	2.7
TOTAL								507	1,452	3.9

portionally greater fondness for the more elaborate patterns. This point emerges more clearly in Table 3.15, where the figures for Peele have been adjusted to the difference in line-totals between the two writers (multiplying by 2.28).

In addition to this statistically significant difference, examination of the text will show a basic identity between Peele's alliterative style in *The Battle of Alcazar* and his share of *Titus*. Peele regularly used double consonant alliteration, which gives his verse an emphatic, powerful, but slow-moving quality, as in these examples from *The Battle of Alcazar*:

> Honor *the* spurre *that* prickes *the* princely minde
>
> (1)
>
> Blacke in *his* looke, and *bloudie* in *his* deeds
>
> (16)
>
> Whose pride doth *sw*ell to *sw*aye beyond his reach
>
> (160)
>
> Of *tr*agedies, and *tr*agic tyrannies
>
> (281)

TABLE 3.14. *Alliteration in* Titus Andronicus

Act/scene	A2	A3	A4	A5	A6	A7	A8	Totals	Total lines	Frequency
1.1 (P)	125	23	25	4	0	1	1	179	495	2.8
2.1 (P)	34	6	11	3	3	0	0	57	135	2.4
2.2 (P)	5	1	2	1	0	1	0	10	26	2.6
2.3	69	9	11	2	1	0	0	92	306	3.4
2.4	14	3	2	1	1	1	0	22	57	2.6
3.1	66	14	11	3	3	0	0	97	300	3.1
3.2	17	6	4	0	1	0	0	28	85	3.1
4.1 (P)	33	9	4	2	0	0	0	48	129	2.7
4.2	33	3	0	0	0	0	0	36	180	5.0
4.3	8	2	2	0	0	0	0	12	121	10.1
4.4	16	1	1	0	0	0	0	18	113	6.3
5.1	27	3	3	0	0	0	0	33	165	5.0
5.2	26	4	0	1	0	0	0	31	205	6.7
5.3	27	3	4	1	0	0	0	35	200	5.8
TOTAL									2,517	

Peele scenes: 785 lines, 294 instances, frequency: once every 2.7 lines.
Shakespeare scenes: 1,732 lines, 404 instances, frequency: once every 4.3 lines.

TABLE 3.15. *Forms of alliteration in* Titus Andronicus

	A2	A3	A4	A5	A6	A7	A8
Peele scenes	449	89	98	23	6.8	4.6	2.3
Shakespeare scenes	303	48	38	8	6	1	0

I will *pro*vide thee of a *pri*ncely osprie
(554)
And as *this f*lame doth fasten on *this f*lesh
(602)
*Pro*mise them *pri*ncely paie . . .
(641)
. . . *f*ranke and *f*ree relieve
(652)
*Spa*ine meanes to *spe*nd no pouder on the Moores
(820)
. . . hath the *ch*iefest *ch*arge
(1028)

It is in vaine to *stri*ve with such a *stream*e

(1098)

And let me *tr*iumph in the *tr*agedie

(1140)

. . . *in*famie of this *in*jurious warre

(1311)

There was I *gr*ac'd by *Gr*egory the *gr*eat

(1348)

The last example I have cited manages to run into one line no less than three 'gr' sounds, a challenge to any (non-Scottish) actor. In his scenes for *Titus Andronicus* Peele used the same double consonant alliteration, albeit not quite so emphatically:

Give us the *pr*oudest *pr*isoner of the Goths

(1.1.96)

To *tr*emble under *Ti*tus' *thr*eat'ning look

(1.1.134)

To *gr*atify the good Andronicus
And *gr*atulate his safe *r*eturn to Rome

(1.1.220–1)

*Cl*ear up, fair *q*ueen, that *cl*oudy *c*ountenance;
Though *ch*ance of *w*ar hath *wr*ought this *ch*ange of *ch*eer

(1.1.263–4)

This sandy *pl*ot is *pl*ain

(4.1.68)

Heaven guide thy *p*en to *pr*int thy sorrows *pl*ain,
That we may know the *tr*aitors and the *tr*uth!

(4.1.74–5)

But if you hunt *th*ese bear-*wh*elps, then bew*a*re

(4.1.95)

In his scenes for *Titus* Shakespeare used double-consonant alliteration far less often than Peele, and invested less plosive force in the operation:

Here, Tamora, though *gr*ieved with killing *gr*ief

(2.3.260)

That I may *sl*umber in eternal *sl*eep

(2.4.15)

In summer's *dr*ought I'll *dr*op upon thee still

(3.1.19)

Thy napkin cannot *dr*ink a tear of mine,
For thou, poor man, hast *dr*own'd it with thine own.

(3.1.140–1)

Sweet *bl*owse, you are a beauteous *bl*ossom, sure

(4.2.72)

Here *st*ands the spring whom you have *st*ained with mud

(5.2.170)

As reference to the dramatic context will confirm, Shakespeare's alliteration on double consonants achieves adequate emphasis, in a range of tones from irony to lament, but never matches Peele's heavy, at times clotted utterance.

Shakespeare used alliteration less frequently than Peele, I suggest, because he could draw on a wider linguistic range, a greater variety of style. Alliteration in Peele gives emphasis, but is used too often, distributed too widely, until it becomes monotonous and ultimately less effective.[96] Already in *Titus Andronicus* Shakespeare uses it with more discretion, obeying the principle of decorum by reserving it for situations calling for emotional intensification, such as the beginning of Marcus' anguished speech when he is confronted by the mutilated Lavinia (2.4.11–21). But when Marcus comes to realize that she cannot reply to him because her tongue has also been cut out, he describes the mutilation with an immediacy and sympathy that needs no help from alliteration (23–51). At the end of the speech, however, as he takes her back to her father, alliteration returns to give appropriate emphasis (52–7). Naturally, it is used freely in the great scene where Lavinia's family express their horror and compassion (3.1.66–149). Where the dramatic context calls for lighter emotions, such as Aaron's gleeful exulting in his Machiavellian tricks, alliteration is conspicuously absent, both in the scene where he murders the Nurse, only witness to his child's parentage (4.2.52–180), and his later capture (5.1.19–165). The fact that Aaron uses alliteration less often than any other major character shows Shakespeare's organic use of language, for his conception of a character affects every detail of style, from vocabulary to syntax, rhetoric, and other expressive devices. Peele makes no such adjustment of language to personality and role. For him alliteration is a source of verbal emphasis to be scattered indiscriminately across the play.

The third new test that I have applied to the authorship of *Titus Andronicus* takes up an observation made by John Dover Wilson in his New Cambridge edition (1948). As my quotation above records, Wilson pointed out that Act 1 scene 1 of the play included an unusual number of vocatives:

---

[96] Marco Mincoff commented that 'Alliteration does not necessarily make for stiltedness in itself, but it does, unless carefully managed, tend to make for artificiality and even clumsiness, when the words are too obviously chosen for their sound rather than their sense. Locutions like, "Alarbus' limbs are lopp'd" [1.1.143], or "Rome, be just and gracious unto me | As I am confident and kind to thee" [1.1.60–1], or "bound with laurel boughs" [1.1.74] do sound inept, and they draw the whole style with them' (Mincoff 1976, p. 131). It is significant that his three examples come from Peele's opening scene.

TABLE 3.16. *Vocatives in* Titus Andronicus

Act/scene	Total lines	Vocatives alone	Vocatives and imperatives	Total vocatives	Frequency every x lines
1.1 (P)	495	78	43	121	4.0
2.1 (P)	135	14	2	16	8.4
2.2 (P)	26	7	1	8	3.3
2.3	306	32	3	35	8.7
2.4	57	2	1	3	19
3.1	300	21	17	38	7.9
3.2	85	3	7	10	8.5
4.1 (P)	129	19	22	41	3.2
4.2	180	14	0	14	12.9
4.3	121	22	10	32	3.8
4.4	113	8	5	13	8.7
5.1	165	8	3	11	15
5.2	205	12	3	11	18.6
5.3	200	21	4	25	8
TOTALS					
Peele	785	118	68	186	4.2
Shakespeare	1,732	143	56	199	8.7

'Almost every speech . . . during the first half of the act, i. e. for some 240 lines, begins with a vocative and continues with a verb in the imperative mood. Saturninus opens the play with

Noble patricians, patrons of my right.

And when Bassianus follows on, seven lines later, like this:

Romans, friends, followers, favourers of my right,

he seems an auctioneer, outbidding his rival by one alliterative word' (p. xxvii). Dover Wilson's observation was perfectly just, and lends itself to further development. In Table 3.16 I have computed the number of vocatives, with or without an imperative, that occur in *Titus Andronicus*. In his scenes for *Titus Andronicus* Peele used vocatives overall more than twice as often as Shakespeare, at a rate of once every 4.2 lines. For comparison, I took Peele's *Edward I*, which gave the results set out in Table 3.17. (In both cases I have ignored terms of abuse used in the vocative, such as 'villain', 'rogue'.) Readers will notice at once the remarkable similarity between Peele's overall figure for *Edward I*, a vocative every 4.3 lines, and that for his share of *Titus*, one every

TABLE 3.17. *Vocatives in Peele's* Edward I

Scene	Total lines	Vocatives alone	Vocatives and imperatives	Total vocatives	Frequency every x lines
1	267	47	14	61	4.4
2	363	80	5	85	4.3
3	137	24	9	33	4.2
4	58	7	3	10	5.8
5	190	33	10	43	4.4
6	134	38	5	43	3.1
7	97	20	2	22	4.4
8	162	35	8	43	3.8
9	27	5	1	6	4.5
10	288	62	16	78	3.7
11	205	49	0	49	4.2
12	95	24	5	29	3.3
13	43	6	0	6	7.2
14	3	0	0	0	0
15	38	13	3	16	2.4
16	27	3	3	6	4.5
17	40	9	2	11	3.7
18	32	2	3	5	6.4
19	40	5	1	6	6.7
20	56	11	0	11	5.1
21	58	11	3	14	4.1
22	36	5	0	5	7.2
23	288	37	7	46	6.3
TOTALS	2,685	526	102	628	
Frequency			5.1	26.3	4.3

4.2 lines. One could hardly hope for a closer correlation, confirming the value of this test in authorship investigations. It may prove useful in examining claims made for Peele's authorship of anonymously published plays, a task needing fresh evaluation.

The fact that Peele uses vocatives in *Titus* about twice as frequently as Shakespeare is yet another indicator of his tendency to repetition, deploying the same verbal devices over and over. Properly speaking, vocatives are only needed in formal exchanges, such as a face-to-face confrontation of ambassadors or combatant generals before some crucial encounter, or as expressions of respect to a superior. But Peele uses them as an automatic reflex, two of his scenes in *Titus* (1.1 and 4.1) reaching the astonishing frequency of a vocative every four lines or less.[97] In Peele's dramas, characters who are not confronting each other for the first time nevertheless continue to use their interlocutor's—often polysyllabic—name with great emphasis, drawing their attention to the fact that they are being addressed, a completely superfluous gesture once a continuous conversation has got under way. (It is as if the actors don't know to whom they should address their lines.) Vocatives can have another basic function in drama, of course, that of identifying the characters on stage, but here again Peele's usage far exceeds necessity, and can only be described as dysfunctional. Even skimming through these scenes, the repeated names stand out—'Renowned Titus' (1.1.38), 'Marcus Andronicus' (47), 'Titus' (86: the vocative applied by the speaker to himself, a form of self-address, another Peele favourite throughout his plays), 'Victorious Titus' (105), 'Andronicus' (116), 'Thrice-noble Titus' (120), 'Lord Titus, my belovèd brother' (169), 'gentle Tribune, noble brother Marcus' (171), 'Titus Andronicus' (179), 'Titus' (201), 'Prince Saturninus' (203), 'Andronicus' (206), 'Proud Saturnine' (208), and so on. Even in the intimate family scene (4.1), where Lavinia's family discover the identity of her rapists, Peele makes his characters constantly address each other by their name or kinship term: 'Help, grandsire' (4.1.1), 'Good uncle Marcus' (3), 'sweet aunt' (4), 'Lucius' (5), 'Lucius' (9), 'Lucius' (10), 'My lord' (16), 'Lucius' (29), 'Lavinia' (30), 'Marcus' (30), 'Lucius' (41), 'Grandsire' (42), 'Lavinia' (46), 'sweet niece; brother' (64), 'Lavinia' (67), 'Lavinia' (87), 'Marcus' (100), 'Lucius' (113), 'Lavinia' (119), 'Marcus' (119), 'Marcus' (124)—another instance of self-address. They also repeat status markers, such as 'boy', or 'my lord', not only at the beginning of a speech but during it, sometimes using two vocatives in the same line (cf. 30, 32, 65, 87, 120). At other times Peele accumulates vocatives and imperatives in little sequences:

> Ascend, fair queen, Pantheon. Lords, accompany
> Your noble Emperor and his lovely bride
>
> (1.1.333–4)
> Come, come, sweet Emperor; come Andronicus
>
> (1.1.456)
> Sit down, sweet niece; brother, sit down by me.
>
> (4.1.64)
> My lord, look here; look here, Lavinia.
>
> (4.1.67)

[97] Mincoff also noted 'the extreme use of apostrophe' in *Titus*: 'In the opening act there are very nearly as many vocatives as there are speeches, which does not quite mean that every speech contains an apostrophe, for many of the longer ones contain several. And these apostrophes tend to assume very heavy, complex forms: "Romans, friends, followers, favourers of my rights" [1.1.9; also 1.1.18, 104, 142, 315] . . . And though in the more intimate scenes, like IV.i, the forms are simple, the vocatives still proliferate' (Mincoff 1976, p. 131). It is hardly a coincidence that Mincoff should have once again picked out two scenes by Peele to illustrate this linguistic preference.

My lord, kneel down with me; Lavinia, kneel;
And kneel, sweet boy, the Roman Hector's hope.

(4.1.86–7)

The formulaic nature of such utterances is a sure mark of Shakespeare's co-author.

The general characteristic of Peele's style, we may say, is of verbal expansiveness vitiated by two failings: an inadequate sense of economy, and an inability to vary utterance according to character or context. Renaissance rhetoric taught that language should be functional, adjusted to the speaker, person addressed, rank, emotional state, and so forth. The rhetoric-books contain many injunctions that the figures and tropes, in addition to their individual properties, should also be functional, conveying meaning and purpose. In the revised edition (1593) of *The Garden of Eloquence*, Henry Peacham instructed all budding poets and prose-writers learning to use *anaphora* (which repeats the same word at the beginning of a sequence of clauses, sentences, or verse lines) that 'the use hereof is chiefly to report a word of importance and effectual signification', adding the cautions that the figure must not be used too often, nor tautologically, and that 'heede ought to be taken that the word which is least worthie or most weake be not taken to make the repetition, for that were very absurd'.[98] The converse figure *epistrophe*, ending a sequence of utterances with the same word, must fulfil the same functional criteria: 'this figure . . . serveth to leave a word of importance in the end of a sentence, that it may the longer hold the sound in the mind of the hearer' (p. 326). With *ploké*, repeating a word within a speech-unit, the word chosen must be the most meaningful one, and the repetition should serve 'both to the pleasure of the eare and sense of the mind' (ibid.). For *antimetabole*, 'a forme of speech which inverteth a sentence by the contrary'—as in 'eat to live, not live to eat'—Peacham writes that it serves 'properlie to praise, dispraise, to distinguish, but most commonly to confute by the inversion of the sentence' (p. 327). Other rhetoricians emphasized the same need for functional utterance. In his *Directions for Speech and Style* (c.1599), John Hoskyns described *antimetabole* as 'a sharp and witty figure' which 'shows out of the same words a pithy distinction of meaning' (p. 329), and urged that the use of a figure 'should come from some choice and not from barrenness' (p. 330). Of the many other statements of that principle in Renaissance rhetoric I select one only, a scathing comment by George Puttenham in *The Arte of English Poesie* (1589) on dysfunctional repetitions in verse, such as

---

[98] Cit. B. Vickers, *In Defence of Rhetoric* (Oxford, 1988; 3rd edn., 1997), p. 325. Further page references are included in the text. Excerpts from two of these texts (Puttenham, Hoskyns) can also be found in B. Vickers (ed.), *English Renaissance Literary Criticism* (Oxford, 1999), pp. 190–296, 398–427.

'To love him and love him, as sinners should doo'. These repetitions be not figurative but phantastical, *for a figure is ever used to a purpose, either of beautie or of efficacie*: and these last recited be to no purpose, for neither can ye say that it urges affection [passion], nor that it beautifieth or enforceth the sence, nor hath any other subtilitie in it, and therefore is a very foolish impertinency of speech, and not a figure. (p. 332, my italics)

Judging by the standards of Renaissance rhetoric, it must be admitted that Peele's use of the figures is often dysfunctional, simply piling up words for emphasis, not doing anything with them.[99] In *The Battle of Alcazar*, for instance, the figure *antimetabole* has none of the functions that Peacham or Hoskyns ascribed to it, to praise, dispraise, confute by inverting the terms, or create 'a pithy distinction of meaning'. Rather, the words repeated in inverted order are simply shifted around, with no gain of insight or energy:

> Calcepius Bassa, Bassa Calcepius
>
> (65)
>
> Ride Bassa now, bold Bassa homeward ride
>
> (382)
>
> Meete of a princesse, for a princesse meet
>
> (539)
>
> Seest thou not Stukley, O Stukley seest thou not
>
> (1252)

Peele uses the figure *ploké*, repeating a key word for emphasis, with a comparable woodenness:

> But follow to the gates of death and hell,
> Pale death and hell to entertaine his soule
>
> (175–6)
>
> These three conspire, these three complaine & more
>
> (304)
>
> And lastly for revenge, for deep revenge
>
> (1187)

Peele's many other applications of *ploké* heap up words like bags of sand,[100] an effect also produced by his use of *anadiplosis* (where the last word of a clause or sentence becomes the first of the one following):

> And now draw neere, and heaven and earth give eare
> Give eare and record heaven and earth with me
>
> (339–40)

---

[99] I am glad to find that Wolfgang Clemen reached a similar verdict nearly fifty years ago: 'Peele was of course thoroughly familiar with all the . . . rhetorical figures . . . It cannot be said, however, that he uses them with discrimination, or with a conscious functional purpose' (Clemen 1961, p. 171).

[100] Cf. also e.g. 986, 1183–4, 1280–1, 1288, 1301, 1357.

And for this deede ye all shall be renowmd,
Renowmd and chronicled in bookes of fame,
In bookes of fame and caracters of brasse,
Of brasse, nay beaten golde, fight then for fame

(951–4)

Peele's other flights using *anadiplosis* thud heavily to earth,[101] as do his efforts
with *epanalepsis* (repeating the same word at the beginning and ending of a line):

Flie King of Fesse, King of Moroccus flie,
Flie with thy friends Emperor of Barbary

(252–3)
Tell me Lord Bishop, Captaines tell me all
(713)

Had Hoskyns or Puttenham been confronted with such dysfunctional use of
rhetoric, their verdict would have been pungent.

In his share of *Titus Andronicus* Peele's use of rhetoric was less flaccid, a
fact which may be put down to his greater maturity, but perhaps also to
Shakespeare's influence. Just as his co-author helped him to create a plot far
more coherent than anything in Peele's unaided works, so his presence may
have restrained Peele's normally verbose style. But Peele's habitual repeti-
tiousness can still be seen, especially if we juxtapose comparable utterances:

Welcome brave Queen of Moores, repose thee heere,
Thou and thy noble sonne, and souldiers all,
Repose you here in King Sebastians towne.

(*Battle of Alcazar*, 905–8)
In peace and honour rest you here, my sons,
Rome's readiest champions, repose you here in rest.

(*Tit.*, 1.1.150–1)

In both examples the repeated words acquire no extra charge of energy or
illumination.

Who take them to their weapons threatning revenge,
Bloudie revenge, bloudie revengefull warre.

(*Battle of Alcazar*, 233–4)
But yet so just that he will not revenge.
Revenge the heavens for old Andronicus.

(*Tit.*, 4.1.127–8)

In these two instances, again, the words are simply shuffled around, the
reader learning nothing new from the process, as in Peele's use of *antimetabole* and *ploké* here:

[101] Cf. also e.g. 765–6, 986, 1197–8, 1217–18, 1252, 1357.

May favour Tamora, the Queen of Goths
(When Goths were Goths, and Tamora was queen).

(Tit., 1.1.139–40)

Compare a similarly wooden instance from *Edward I*:

That Spaine reaping renowne by Elinor,
And Elinor adding renowne to Spaine.

(233–4)

Peele's rhetorical figures often have a superfluous quality, where we feel that
one word would have been better than two, or three:

No, Titus, no, the Emperor needs her not;
Nor her, nor thee, nor any of thy stock.

(Tit., 1.1.299–300)

No, foolish tribune, no; no son of mine,
Nor thou, nor these, confederates in the deed

(1.1.343–4)

But let us give him burial as becomes,
Give Mutius burial with our brethren.

(1.1.347–8)

Why, hark ye, hark ye, and are you such fools

(2.1.100)

Come, come, our Empress . . .

(2.1.121)

I think she means that there were more than one
Confederate in the fact; ay, more there was

(4.1.38–9)

My lord, kneel down with me; Lavinia, kneel;
And kneel, sweet boy . . .

(4.1.86–7)

In many of these examples the repetitions seem mere padding, as if the
writer were marking time while thinking of something else to say.
Throughout his scenes Peele especially misuses the figures *epizeuxis* and
ploké, repeating words without adding any urgency.[102] For him rhetorical
figures are merely another form of alliteration, adding emphasis but
blurring particularity.

Shakespeare's use of rhetoric in *Titus Andronicus*, by contrast, is precise,
economical, witty. In general, one has the impression of a young writer feeling his way, satisfied to achieve convincing local effects without attempting
anything more ambitious. He uses fewer rhetorical figures than in *Richard*

---

[102] Cf. also 1.1.261–2; 2.1.20–3; 2.2.25; 4.1.1, 50, 54, 78.

III, say, and nowhere sustains such long sequences as Queen Margaret's virtuoso speech in that play (4.4.82–113). Compared to Peele, he uses the figures of repetition more sparely, and brings into play a much wider range of figures, antithesis, oxymoron, *articulus*, *epanorthosis*, *epistrophe*, and *aposiopesis*. Above all, Shakespeare uses many more tropes, especially metaphor and simile, the difference in quantity corresponding to one in quality.

To bring out these differences more clearly I shall first quote some Shakespearian uses of figures already familiar from Peele, starting with *ploké*, repeating a word within a line or sentence:

> Thou canst not come to me; I come to thee
>
> (2.3.245)
> So now go tell, an if thy tongue can speak,
> Who 'twas that cut thy tongue and ravished thee.
>
> (2.4.1–2)

As we already see, Shakespeare's language is more simple, less literary, more closely approaching natural speech rhythms:

> Look, Marcus. Ah, son Lucius, look on her.
>
> (3.1.110)
> To weep with them that weep doth ease some deal
>
> (3.1.243)
> Thou art made of tears,
> And tears will quickly melt thy life away.
>
> (3.2.50–1)
> Ay, some mad message from his mad grandfather
>
> (4.2.3)
> She is delivered, lords, she is delivered
>
> (4.2.61)
> Tear for tear and loving kiss for kiss
> Thy brother Marcus tenders on thy lips.
>
> (5.3.155–6)

All the instances of *ploké* in Shakespeare's share of the play are brief, pointed, functional.[103] In his use of *epizeuxis*, a word repeated twice in succession, we again find emphasis properly intensified (needless to say, one needs to know the dramatic context to appreciate the figure's success):

> Ah, Marcus, Marcus!
>
> (3.1.139)
> O, O, O!
>
> (3.2.68)

---

[103] Cf. also 2.3.100–1, 3.1.41–2, 101–2; 4.2.107; 4.3.1, 11–12; 4.4.5; 5.1.82; 5.3.57, 65, 171.

What, what, ye sanguine, shallow-hearted boys

(4.2.97)

Die, die, Lavinia, and thy shame with thee.

(5.3.45)

In Peele *epizeuxis* seemed unnecessary; in Shakespeare it seems like a spontaneous utterance, in credible speech rhythms.[104]

The difference between Peele's lumbering way with rhetorical figures and Shakespeare's lithe, economical application can be seen equally well with *anadiplosis*, as when Lucius tells his father that his appeal to the Roman authorities for mercy on his sons falls on deaf ears, since 'no tribune hears you speak':

> Why, 'tis no matter, man; if they did hear,
> They would not mark me; if they did mark,
> They would not pity me, yet plead I must.

(3.1.33–5)

With this figure Shakespeare economically conveyed the Tribunes' resolute indifference to Titus' sufferings. That utterance also used *anaphora*, repeating a word at the beginning of successive clauses or verse lines. This is a figure which can result in shapeless lists; Shakespeare deploys it with economy and variety:[105]

> Shall we be thus afflicted in his wreaks,
> His fits, his frenzy, and his bitterness?

(4.4.11–12)

> I am not mad; I know thee well enough:
> Witness this wretched stump, witness these crimson lines,
> Witness the trenches made by grief and care,
> Witness the tiring day and heavy night,
> Witness all sorrow that I know thee well

(5.2.21–5)

Shakespeare uses even more effectively (and, I think, more often than usual) the converse figure *epistrophe*, where the same word ends a series of clauses or verse lines. Here his choice of 'the word of most importance', as Renaissance rhetoricians laid down, is exemplary (again, reference to the full context is necessary):

> *Marcus.* My hand shall go.
> *Lucius.*   By heaven it shall not go!

(3.1.176)

---

[104] Cf. also 3.2.1, 31; 4.3.18, 36; 5.2.166.
[105] Cf. also 4.2.156–8; 5.1.40–3; 5.2.186–90; 5.3.4, 97–8, 195–6.

Lucius. Then I'll go fetch an axe.
Marcus.   But I will use the axe.

                                         (3.1.184)

Fie, fie, how franticly I square my talk,
As if we should forget we had no hands
If Marcus did not name the word of hands!

                    (3.2.31–3)

Coal-black is better than another hue,
In that it scorns to bear another hue.

                    (4.2.99–100)

Publius. Till time beget some careful remedy.
Marcus. Kinsmen, his sorrows are past remedy.

                    (4.3.30–1)

In each of those examples Shakespeare places a key word at the end of the
line, to leave it echoing in the reader or spectator's mind.[106]

Shakespeare's ability to highlight a specific word or idea economically,
without pomp or circumstance, can be seen in his use of *polyptoton*, a figure
sometimes classified as a type of pun, which repeats the stem of a word while
adding the ending of a derivative:

Speak, Lavinia, what accursèd hand
Hath made thee handless in thy father's sight?

                    (3.1.66–7)

O, handle not the theme, to talk of hands

                    (3.2.29)

'To Saturn', Caius, not to Saturnine

                    (4.3.57)

All these instances of *polyptoton* are brief, to the point.[107] Another figure that
Shakespeare uses to point up meaning economically is antithesis, always one
of his favourite devices. This serves to differentiate characters and their goals,
as Aaron observes to Tamora:

Madam, though Venus govern your desires,
Saturn is dominator over mine

                    (2.3.30–1)

or to prefigure Tamora's revenge:

Your mother's hand shall right your mother's wrong

                    (2.3.121)

---

[106] Cf. also 5.2.67–8 (a less successful instance).
[107] Cf. also 2.3.51; 3.1.61–2, 102, 108, 185–7, 215–16; 4.2.131; 4.3.21; 5.1.140.

In all Shakespeare's uses of this figure we notice a basic clarity, creating a focus on, and distinction between, two states.[108] Clarity and economy of this order seem beyond Peele. So Martius reports the discovery of Bassianus' corpse:

> We know not where you left them all alive,
> But, out alas! here have we found him dead
>
> (2.3.257–8)

Titus reports his failure to secure a pardon for Martius and Quintus, wrongly suspected of killing Bassianus:

> A stone is soft as wax, tribunes more hard than stones;
> A stone is silent and offendeth not,
> And tribunes with their tongues doom men to death.
>
> (3.1.45–8)

In all these quotations we note the ease and directness of Shakespeare's language, truly that of common speech. But Shakespeare can also apply antithesis for witty dialogue, as in the divided reactions to the sight of the black baby that Tamora and Aaron have produced. Tamora's sons, Demetrius and Chiron, are outraged, Aaron unrepentant:

> *Dem.* Villain, what hast thou done?
> *Aar.* That which thou canst not undo.
> *Chi.* Thou hast undone our mother.
> *Aar.* Villain, I have done thy mother.
> *Dem.* And therein, hellish dog, thou hast undone her.
>
> (4.2.73–7)

Similarly in their reaction to the child:

> *Chi.* It shall not live.
> *Aar.* It shall not die.
>
> (4.2.80)

Aaron wins this exchange, saving the child but killing the Nurse. In addition to juxtaposing opposites, Shakespeare sometimes creates a more powerful verbal effect by collapsing the opposed poles into a single formula, the figure oxymoron or *synoeciosis* ('a composition of contraries'), as in Lavinia's appeal to Tamora to be killed outright, rather than endure her son's 'worse-than-killing lust':

> Do this, and be a charitable murderer
>
> (2.3.278)

[108] Cf. also 2.3.167; 3.1.2–3, 66–7, 148–9; 4.2.31, 48; 5.1.10.

So Titus recognizes that the mutilated Lavinia is unable to communicate with words or gestures:

> Speechless complainer, I will learn thy thought
>
> (3.2.39)

Another figure outside Peele's range, but well used by Shakespeare, is *articulus* (or *brachylogia*), the 'cut comma' in Puttenham's terminology,[109] by which words are run together without any conjunctions or prepositions intervening. Like all the figures, this can be used for varying effects of emphasis, such as Bassianus' contempt for Tamora's relation with Aaron:

> Believe me, Queen, your swarthy Cimmerian
> Doth make your honour of his body's hue,
> Spotted, detested, and abominable
>
> (2.3.72–4)

Saturninus uses this figure to bewail his lot, an emperor 'thus overborne, | Troubled, confronted thus' (4.3.2–3), and Aaron to boast of his vicious deeds:

> For I must talk of murders, rapes, and massacres,
> Acts of black night, abominable deeds,
> Complots of mischief, treason, villainies,
> Ruthful to hear, yet piteously performed
>
> (5.1.63–6)

—concluding with an ironic antithesis. It is used symmetrically by Titus, just before he kills Lavinia. She has been 'enforced, stained, and deflowered' (5.3.38), like the daughter of Virginius, whose father killed her, so that she 'should not survive her shame', thus giving Titus

> A reason mighty, strong, and effectual;
> A pattern, precedent, and lively warrant
> For me, most wretched, to perform the like
>
> (5.3.40–4)

But Shakespeare can deploy with equal economy and propriety the opposite figure, so to speak, *polysyndeton*, which deliberately heaps up conjunction, as in Titus' promise to Lavinia that he will 'interpret all her martyred signs':

> Thou shalt not sigh, nor hold thy stumps to heaven,
> Nor wink, nor nod, nor kneel, nor make a sign,
> But I of these will wrest an alphabet
>
> (3.2.42–4)

---

[109] *Arte*, in Vickers 1999, p. 263.

There the repetition is oddly comforting, promising as it does her father's total dedication. Elsewhere it can be grim, or even revolting, as in Aaron's disclosure to Lucius that Chiron and Demetrius mutilated Lavinia:

> They cut thy sister's tongue and ravished her,
> And cut her hands and trimmed her as thou sawest
>
> .   .   .   .
>
> Why, she was washed and cut and trimmed,
> And 'twas trim sport for them which had the doing of it.
>
> (5.1.92–6)

(Again, Aaron is given jocular wordplay, using *polyptoton*—'trimmed . . . trim'.) Appropriately, Shakespeare uses the same figure, and the same conjunction, when Titus explains to the two rapists what will become of them after their execution:

> Hark, villains, I will grind your bones to dust,
> And with your blood and it I'll make a paste,
> And of the paste a coffin [pie-crust] I will rear,
> And make two pasties of your shameful heads,
> And bid that strumpet, your unhallowed dam

—to eat her own flesh (5.2.186–91). Here the figure *polysyndeton* combines with *anadiplosis* to describe the inexorable sequence of events about to take place.

Whether using the same rhetorical figures as Peele had used, or deploying his own much wider thesaurus, Shakespeare distinguishes himself from his co-author by the economy, functionality, and expressive power with which he employs these traditional resources. He, truly, needed no reminder that 'a figure is ever used to a purpose, either of beautie or of efficacie'. But the biggest difference between the language of his scenes for *Titus Andronicus* and those by Peele lies in the category of tropes, especially metaphor and simile. The difference is one both of quantity and quality: Shakespeare creates many more tropes than Peele does, and most of them are memorable in a way that Peele's are not. The qualities that make Shakespeare's imagery outstanding among English Renaissance poets and dramatists—concreteness, vividness, the surprising collocation of associations, a great expressive range—can already be seen in this play. Chiron plans Lavinia's rape:

> Drag hence the husband to some secret hole,
> And make his dead trunk pillow to our lust.
>
> (2.3.129–30)

Demetrius urges Tamora to enjoy Lavinia's suffering:

> let it be your glory
> To see her tears, but be your heart to them
> As unrelenting flint to drops of rain
>
> (2.3.139–41)

Unwittingly stumbling on the scene of Bassianus' murder, Quintus finds 'rude-growing briers' covering the pit,

> Upon whose leaves are drops of new-shed blood
> As fresh as morning dew distilled on flowers
>
> (2.3.199–201)

An equally immediate and incongruous visual effect is provided by the ring on the corpse's finger,

> Which, like a taper in some monument,
> Doth shine upon the dead man's earthy cheeks
>
> (2.3.228–9)

These metaphors and similes are used with precision and economy, illuminating an event and the characters' differing emotional responses to it. Much of the play's most powerful imagery arises in response to the sufferings of Lavinia and Titus, and one could easily fill several pages with quotations. With strict self-discipline I select Marcus' shocked first view of the mutilated Lavinia (beginning with *polyptoton*):

> Speak, gentle niece, what stern ungentle hands
> Hath lopped and hewed and made thy body bare
> Of her two branches, those sweet ornaments,
> Whose circling shadows kings have sought to sleep in
>   .   .   .   .
> Alas, a crimson river of warm blood,
> Like to a bubbling fountain stirred with wind,
> Doth rise and fall between thy rosèd lips,
> Coming and going with thy honey breath
>
> (2.4.16–25)

Critics have long noted the Ovidian echoes, but the important point is that these sensuous, pictorial images are perfectly appropriate to Lavinia's beauty, now for ever destroyed. That is, they serve one of the constant functions of tragedy, to document the *metabolè* (as Aristotle named it), that tragic contrast between what people once were and what they have become. So Marcus evokes the fable of Tereus' rape of Philomela to observe how her ravishers have outdone that vicious exemplar, cutting off not only the tongue but the hands:

> O, had the monster seen those lily hands
> Tremble, like aspen leaves, upon a lute,
> And make the silken strings delight to kiss them,
> He would not then have touched them for his life
>
> (2.4.44–7)

For Titus the Ovidian mode would be inappropriate, and Shakespeare chooses a much barer, bleaker register, as in his bitterness once the tribunes have refused to spare his sons' lives:

> Why, foolish Lucius, dost thou not perceive
> That Rome is but a wilderness of tigers?
> Tigers must prey, and Rome affords no prey
> But me and mine.

(3.1.53–6)

(As so often, for expressive purposes Shakespeare blends tropes and figures, also using *anadiplosis* and *ploké* there.) But, as Titus immediately discovers, seeing his mutilated daughter, his position is worse than he had imagined. Marcus reports that he found Lavinia hiding, as a wounded deer withdraws to die alone, and Titus responds, translating the 'dear' to a human state:

> It was my dear, and he that wounded her
> Hath hurt me more than had he killed me dead;
> For now I stand as one upon a rock,
> Environed with a wilderness of sea,
> Who marks the waxing tide grow wave by wave,
> Expecting ever when some envious surge
> Will in his brinish bowels swallow him

(3.1.91–7)

It is above all through images of numbness, the correlative of great psychological shocks, that Shakespeare evokes the dreadful sequence of events in this scene. Shortly afterwards the Messenger returns with the hand that Titus had been persuaded to cut off by Aaron's 'villainy', and the heads of Titus' two sons. Lavinia (as Capell saw) kisses her brothers' heads, to the despairing comment by Marcus:

> Alas, poor heart, that kiss is comfortless
> As frozen water to a starvèd [numbed] snake

(3.1.249–50)

Marcus himself sums up the family's stunned response to these catastrophes:

> Thy other banished son with this dear sight
> Struck pale and bloodless, and thy brother, I,
> Even like a stony image, cold and numb.

(255–7)

Among Shakespeare's most imaginatively used rhetorical figures readers will have noticed *polyptoton*, the repetition of a word stem with variant endings. Stefan Keller, in a study of Shakespeare's use of rhetoric,[110] has identified

---

[110] Keller, 'Shakespeare the Rhetorician: A Statistical and Comparative Analysis of Rhetoric in Ten Plays', Ph.D. Diss., University of Zürich (in progress).

TABLE 3.18. Polyptoton *in Peele and Shakespeare*

Play	Lines	Instances of *polyptoton*	Frequency (every x lines)
Titus, Peele	790	10	79.0
Titus, Shakespeare	1,733	59	29.4
Richard III, Acts 1–3	2,296	86	26.6

TABLE 3.19. *Scholarly authorship tests on* Titus Andronicus

Date	Scholar	Test	Authorship of Act 1
1919	Parrott	Feminine endings	Peele
1931	Timberlake	Feminine endings	Peele or Greene
1948	Dover Wilson	Diction; vocatives	Peele
1950	Maxwell	Grammar	Peele
1957	Hill	Rhetoric	Peele
1979	Jackson	Vocabulary	Peele
1987	Tarlinskaja	Metrics	Not Shakespeare
1988	Taylor	Metrics; vocabulary	Peele
1996	Jackson	Stage directions; function words; verbal formulae	Peele
1995	Boyd	Common words; vocabulary	Peele
1997	Jackson	Vocabulary	Peele
2001	Vickers	Polysyllabic words; alliteration	Peele
	Vickers	Vocatives; rhetoric	Peele
2001	Keller	Rhetoric	Peele

thirty-nine of the most frequently used rhetorical figures, and counted their incidence in ten plays, early, middle, and late. His data allow us to compute the frequency of use for this figure in the scenes of *Titus Andronicus* ascribed to Peele and Shakespeare respectively. As a control text I have taken his data for the first three acts of *Richard III* (a sequence of approximately the same length), yielding the results set out in Table 3.18. As the figures show, Shakespeare's use of *polyptoton* in *Titus* is very similar to that in *Richard III*, at a rate three times higher than Peele's. Keller's study also confirms my suggestion that Shakespeare used *epistrophe* more frequently than Peele: he found only two instances in the group *A* scenes, or once every 395 lines, as against 18 instances in group *B*, once every 96.3 lines, a ratio of 4 to 1. Keller has also shown that in his scenes Shakespeare used oxymoron more than five times more frequently than Peele, hyperbole nearly three times more often, and *asteismus* nearly six times more often. These quantitative differences clearly distinguish two different hands at work.

Peele was no doubt a useful co-author for Shakespeare, with his longer theatrical experience and greater knowledge of the classical world, but his style was distinctively different. Over the last eighty years scholars have applied, by my count, twenty-one separate tests to the play, each of which has confirmed the presence of a co-author. This long scholarly tradition identifying at least Act 1 as Peele's work, often adding three other scenes (2.1, 2.2, 4.1) can be summed up in Table 3.19. Surely this quantity of independent tests, mutually confirming each other, will now be enough to gain Peele recognition as co-author of 'The Most Lamentable Romaine Tragedy of *Titus Andronicus*'.

4

Timon of Athens with Thomas Middleton

As we have seen, authorship studies of Elizabethan drama over the last century have passed through three stages. The first involved the identification of passages in anonymous or co-authored plays that closely echoed known work by one or more dramatists. This method considers longer verbal collocations, not single words or short phrases, and works best when it can show parallels of thought and attitude, in addition to verbal parallels. The second stage was the realization that different writers have different preferences within frequently recurring linguistic features: the use of contractions (*'em, 'ee, 'tis*), choice of alternative spellings (*while* or *whiles*), variant verb forms (*has* or *hath*, *does* or *doth*), or favourite exclamations (*pish, phew*). These usages could be located in a text, and systematically investigated, sometimes revealing clear differences. Variations in verse form could also be identified and tabulated. The third stage grew out of this, locating linguistic features—such as 'function words' (*to, of, the*), or the words beginning and/or ending sentences or speeches—and submitting them to detailed statistical analysis. All three approaches are independently valid, but the most satisfying results are obtained when their results support each other.

The history of *Timon of Athens* and its authorship has followed this pattern. Since the play's represented action was not as violent as *Titus Andronicus* it offended fewer critics. Throughout the period 1660 to 1800, *Timon* was praised as a 'Moral and Instructive' tragedy (James Drake, 1699), full of 'useful satire' (Charles Gildon, 1710), a 'warning against ostentatious liberality' (Dr Johnson, 1765), or the effects of 'inconsiderate profusion' (William Richardson, 1783).[1] The play could easily be absorbed into neoclassical theories of literature's moral function, despite the obvious defects of the text as printed in the First Folio. It was not until the 1840s that Charles Knight made a reasoned case for co-authorship, in the prefaces to his popularizing Shakespeare editions, collected as *Studies of Shakspere*.[2] Knight began his essay with a scathing account of the co-called 'regulation' of the play's verse made by George Steevens, anxious to reduce

---

[1] *CHS*, ii. 95, 255; v. 141; vi. 361–5.
[2] C. Knight, *Studies of Shakspere* (London, 1849).

lines 'to the exact dimensions of his ten-syllable measuring-tape' (1849, p. 48). The consequence of Steevens's textual alterations, Knight pointed out, was that 'some very important characteristics' of the play's language 'have been utterly destroyed in the modern copies—the record has been obliterated' (p. 68). One significant detail destroyed by editorial modernizing is the fact that the Folio 'presents to us in particular scenes a very considerable number of short lines, occurring in the most rapid succession. We have no parallel example in Shakspere of the frequency of their use. The hemistich is introduced with great effect in some of the finest passages in *Lear*. But in *Timon of Athens* its perpetual recurrence in some scenes is certainly not always a beauty' (p. 68). Knight was the first to notice this feature of the play's style, and he rightly deplored the effect of Steevens's regularizings of the metre, which

have given to the *Timon of Athens* something of the semblance of uniformity in the structure of the verse; although in reality the successive scenes, even in the modern text, present the most startling contrarieties to the ear which is accustomed to the versification of Shakspere. (p. 70)

Knight's highly sensitive ear, attuned to Shakespeare's authentic versification, allowed him to reject firmly both theories explaining the play's stylistic unevenness—the English, by which 'the ancient text is corrupt', and the German, which described *Timon* as a late, and probably unfinished play. Knight presented his own conclusions, 'which have been hitherto entirely overlooked', namely 'that the differences of style, as well as the more important differences in the cast of thought, which prevail in the successive scenes of this drama, are so remarkable as to justify the conclusion that it is not wholly the work of Shakspere' (ibid.). The play contains 'parts not only out of harmony with the drama as a whole, in action, in sentiment, in versification, but altogether different from anything he had himself produced in his early, his mature, or his later years' (p. 76).

Knight argued that Shakespeare had taken over some existing play, 'which probably retained possession of the stage for some time in its first form', and that *Timon* 'has come down to us not only re-written, but so far re-modelled that entire scenes of Shakspere have been substituted for entire scenes of the old play' (pp. 70–1). Whether or not we accept this theory, the importance of Knight's essay lay in the criteria he used in identifying two different hands. These criteria involved both questions of style, to be considered here, and of dramaturgy, postponed to Chapter 7 below. Knight began his detailed analysis with an observation repeated by many subsequent readers:

The contrast of style which is to be traced throughout this drama is sufficiently striking in the two opening scenes which now constitute the first act. Nothing can be more free and flowing than the dialogue between the Poet and the Painter [1.1.1–94]. It has all the equable graces of Shakspere's facility, with occasional examples of that condensation of poetical images which so distinguishes him from all other writers. For instance:

> All those which were his fellows but of late,
> (Some better than his value,) on the moment
> Follow his strides, his lobbies fill with tendance,
> Rain sacrificial whisperings in his ear,
> Make sacred even his stirrup, and through him
> Drink the free air.
>
> (1.1.78–83)

(p. 71)

Knight was sure that Timon, in this opening scene, was 'Shakspere's own conception', and although he found Apemantus' repartee not distinctly Shakespearian, 'no one can doubt to whom these lines belong':

> So, so; there!—
> Aches contract and starve your supple joints!—
> That there should be small love 'mongst these sweet knaves,
> And all this court'sy! The strain of man's bred out
> Into baboon and monkey.
>
> (1.1.247–51)

(ibid.)

When Knight reached the second scene of Act 1, however, he felt that Shakespeare's hand had suddenly vanished, for

we find ourselves at once amidst a different structure of verse from the foregoing. We encounter this difference remarkably in the first speech of Timon:

> I gave it freely ever; and there's none
> Can truly say he gives, if he receives:
> If our betters play at that game, we must not dare
> To imitate them; faults that are rich are fair.
>
> (1.2.10–13)

In the first scene we do not find a single rhyming couplet; in the second scene their recurrence is more frequent than in any of Shakspere's plays, even the earliest. This scene alone give us sixteen examples of this form of verse; which, in combination with prose or blank verse, had been almost entirely rejected by the mature Shakspere, except to render emphatic the close of a scene. (p. 72)

Knight was perfectly correct to point out the unusually high frequency of rhyme in this scene, running quite against Shakespeare's stylistic development. Even more perceptively, he observed both the awkward nature of the couplets and a striking difference in the imaginative element of poetry: 'In the instance before us, we find the couplet introduced in the most arbitrary and inartificial manner—in itself neither impressive nor harmonious. But the contrast between the second scene and the first is equally remarkable in the poverty of the thought, and the absence of poetical imagery' (ibid.).

One of the recurring experiences of studying co-authored plays is to discover that the same character seems to be quite different from one scene to the next. Charles Knight showed that in the parts of both Apemantus and Lucius (the Steward), quite different styles could be detected. In 1.2, a scene in which he could find no trace of Shakespeare, Apemantus makes this superficial moralizing commentary, complete with rhyming couplets and half-lines:

> Hey day,
> What a sweep of vanity comes this way!
> They dance! they are mad women:
> Like madness is the glory of this life,
> As this pomp shows to a little oil and root.
> We make ourselves fools to disport ourselves;
> And spend our flatteries, to drink those men,
> Upon whose age we void it up again,
> With poisonous spite and envy.
> Who lives that's not depraved, or depraves?
> Who dies, that bears not one spurn to their graves
> Of their friends' gift?
> I should fear, those that dance before me now,
> Would one day stamp upon me: It has been done:
> Men shut their doors against a setting sun.
>
> (1.2.131–45)

In 4.3, by contrast, the great scene where the cynic confronts Timon the misanthrope, Apemantus speaks with remarkable energy, fusing metaphors together to contrast Timon's previous and his present state:

> Thou hast cast away thyself, being like thyself;
> A madman so long, now a fool: What, think'st
> That the bleak air, thy boisterous chamberlain,
> Will put thy shirt on warm? Will these moist trees,
> That have outliv'd the eagle, page thy heels,
> And skip when thou point'st out? Will the cold brook,
> Candied with ice, caudle thy morning tast,
> To cure thy o'er-night's surfeit? call the creatures,—
> Whose naked natures live in all the spite
> Of wreakful heaven; whose bare unhoused trunks,
> To the conflicting elements expos'd,
> Answer mere nature,—bid them flatter thee;
> O! thou shalt find—
>
> (4.3.220–32)

Every reader, I imagine, will agree with Knight on 'the impossiblity of [this] character having been wholly minted from the same die' in the two contrasting scenes (p. 72). Knight performed the same test with the Steward, quoting his long aside in this scene (1.2), in which we note again the irregular length of the verse lines and the unexpected use of couplets.

> *Flav.*   What will this come to?
>   He commands us to provide, and give great gifts,
>   And all out of an empty coffer.—
>   Nor will he know his purse; or yield me this,
>   To show him what a beggar his heart is,
>   Being of no power to make his wishes good;
>   His promises fly so beyond his state,
>   That what he speaks is all in debt, he owes for every word;
>   He is so kind, that he now pays interest for't;
>   His lands put to their books. Well, 'would I were
>   Gently put out of office, before I were forc'd out!
>   Happier is he that hath no friend to feed,
>   Than such that do even enemies exceed.
>   I bleed inwardly for my lord.
>
>   (1.2.191–205)

Knight commented: 'We print the speech of the first act as we find it in the original. With the exception of the two rhyming couplets, it is difficult to say whether it is prose or verse. It has been "regulated" into verse, but no change can make it metrical;—the feebleness of the thought is the same under every disguise' (p. 72). Knight contrasted this speech with one in Act 2, where Timon accuses the Steward of not having warned him of his impending bankruptcy, and of having cheated the estate, to which Flavius offers this self-defence:

> *Flav.* If you suspect my husbandry, or falsehood,
>   Call me before the exactest auditors,
>   And set me on the proof. So the gods bless me,
>   When all our offices have been oppress'd
>   With riotous feeders; when our vaults have wept
>   With drunken spilth of wine; when every room
>   Hath blaz'd with lights, and bray'd with minstrelsy;
>   I have retir'd me to a wasteful cock,
>   And set mine eyes at flow.
> *Tim.*   Prithee, no more.
> *Flav.* Heaven, have I said, the bounty of this lord!
>   How many prodigal bits have slaves, and peasants,
>   This night englutted! Who is not Timon's?
>   What heart, head, sword, force, means, but is lord Timon's?
>   Great Timon; noble, worthy, royal Timon!
>   Ah! When the means are gone that buy this praise,
>   The breath is gone whereof this praise is made:
>   Feast-won, fast-lost; one cloud of winter showers,

These flies are couch'd.

> (2.2.155–72)

Knight judged that 'the harmony, the vigour, the poetical elevation of the second passage, like the greater part of the fourth and fifth acts, effectually prevent all substitution and transposition' by a regularizing editor (p. 73). As for the substance of this scene, Knight detected in it 'unquestionably . . . the master-hand of our poet. The character of Timon as his ruin is approaching him is beautifully developed. His reproach of his Steward, slightly unjust as it is, is in a tone perfectly in accordance with the kindness of his nature; and his rising anger is forgotten in a moment in his complete conviction of the integrity of that honest servant' (p. 73).

Charles Knight showed himself well able to distinguish Shakespeare's hand from that of his co-author—indeed, almost all of his judgements have been confirmed by many careful studies in the century and a half since he wrote. In Act 3, he judged,

very little . . . is Shakspere's. The ingratitude of Lucullus in the first scene, and of Lucius in the second, is amusingly displayed; but there is little power in the development of character—little discrimination. The passionate invective of Flaminius is forcible; but the force is not exactly that of Shakspere. The dialogue between the Strangers, at the end of the second scene, is unmetrical enough in the original; Steevens has made it hobble still worse. The third scene has the same incurable defects. It seems to us perfectly impossible that Shakspere could have produced thoughts so commonplace, and verse so unmusical, as we find in the speech of Sempronius. The fourth scene, again, has little peculiarity. It might be Shakspere's, or it might be the work of an inferior writer. (pp. 73–4)

In Knight's eyes this whole sequence, in which Timon's servants try without success to borrow money from the friends whom he had so lavishly enriched, formed a unit in which he could find no trace of Shakespeare. As for the scene (3.5) where Alcibiades petitions the Athenian Senate to pardon a friend of his who has been found guilty of murder, Knight objected to it both on grounds of its un-Shakespearian dramaturgy (see Chapter 7 below), and 'the internal evidence of thought and style'. As he was the first to observe,

The scene between Alcibiades and the Senate consists of about a hundred and twenty lines. Of these lines twenty-six form rhyming couplets. This of itself is enough to make us look suspiciously upon the scene, when presented as the work of Shakspere. Could the poet have proposed any object to himself, by this extraordinary departure from his usual principle of versification, presenting even in this play an especial contrast to the mighty rush and sustained grandeur of the blank verse in the speeches Timon in the fourth and fifth acts? (p. 74)

What Knight pungently described as 'the perpetual and offensive recurrence of the couplet' was only one of several un-Shakespearian elements he detected in this scene:

The whole of the senate scene in *Timon* is singularly unmetrical; but, wherever the verse becomes regular, it is certainly not the metre of Shakspere. Mark the pause, for example, that occurs at the end of every line of the first speech of Alcibiades. 'The linked sweetness long drawn out' is utterly wanting . . . From the first line of this scene to the last, the speeches, though cast into the form of verse, are in reality nothing but measured prose. (ibid.)

Knight's strictures applied not only to the *verba* but to the *res* of this scene, its thought, imagery, and feeling:

But in addition to the structure of the verse, the character of the thought is essentially different from that of the true Shakspearean drama. Where is our poet's imagery? . . . The action of this scene admitted either of passion or reflection; and we know how Shakspere puts forth either power whenever the occasion demands it. The passion of Alcibiades is of the most vapid character:

> Now the gods keep you old enough; that you may live
> Only in bone that none may look on you!

$$(3.5.103-4)$$

Let us contrast for a moment the Shakspearean Coriolanus, under somewhat similar circumstances:

> You common cry of curs, whose breath I hate,
> As reek o'th'rotten fens: whose loves I prize,
> As the dead carcasses of unburied men,
> That do corrupt my air: I banish you.

$$(3.3.120-3)$$

Some of the stylistic differences that Knight indicated—the unusual number of couplets in the scene, the sequence of irregular lines in Alcibiades' opening speech (3.5.7–23)—can be quantified, and show a distinct numerical discrepancy compared to Shakespeare's normal verse styles at this period. Other perceptible differences cannot be quantified, but a cogent analysis can elicit agreement. As Knight argued,

In this scene between Alcibiades and the senate, the usually profound reflection of Shakspere, which plunges us into the depths of our own hearts, and the most unfathomable mysteries of the world around us and beyond us, is exchanged for such slight axioms as the following:

> For pity is the virtue of the law,
> And none but tyrants use it cruelly.

$$(3.5.8-9)$$

> To revenge is no valour, but to bear.

$$(39)$$

> To be in anger is impiety,
> But who is man that is not angry?

$$(56-7)$$

The form of expression in these scenes with Alcibiades appears to us as remarkably unShaksperean as the character of the thought. By nothing is our poet more distinguished than by his conciseness, the quality that makes him so often apparently obscure. (pp. 73–4)

But such speeches are never obscure, only too obvious. This moralizing style, with its love of sententious couplets, became one of the stylistic markers which allowed later scholars to identify Shakespeare's co-author as Middleton.

Although Knight assigned most of Acts 4 and 5 to Shakespeare, he indicated some passages contributed by the collaborator: 'The second scene of the fourth act, between the Steward and his servants, has some touches undoubtedly of the master's hand; the Steward's speech, after the servants have left, again presents us the rhyming couplets, and the unmetrical blank verse' (p. 76). Knight referred to this un-Shakespearian speech, which clearly resembles the Steward's style in 1.2 and 2.2:

> O, the fierce wretchedness that glory brings us!
> Who would not wish to be from wealth exempt,
> Since riches point to misery and contempt?
> Who would be so mock'd with glory, or to live
> But in a dream of friendship . . . ?
>   .   .   .   .
>   Strange, unusual blood,
> When man's worst sin is, he does too much good!
>
> (4.2.30–9)

Knight's judgement lapsed only once, it seems to me, when discussing 'the scene between the Poet and the Painter at the commencement of the fifth act', which 'is so unmetrical, that it has been printed as prose by all modern editors'. Knight was tempted to describe 'this hobbling approach to metre' as un-Shakespearian; he believed that 'the Poet and the Painter of this scene are as unlike' those characters in the first act 'in the tone of their dialogues, as can be imagined'; and he thought that 'Timon, in the lines which he speaks aside, has caught this infection of unmetrical blank verse which reads like prose, and jingling couplets which want the spirit of poetry' (p. 76). Later scholars did not share these judgements. Although the Folio text is certainly uneven, they found the verse in this scene recognizably Shakespearian, and quite unlike the co-author; the two artists are just as verbose and insincere here as in the opening scene; and Timon's three asides only contain one couplet, which is quite unlike the co-author's flaccid moralizing:

> To thee be worship, and thy saints for aye
> Be crown'd with plagues, that thee alone obey!
>
> (5.1.52–3)

Knight was not alone, however, in having difficulty with this closing Act. But he fairly summed up his case for the presence of two different authors in the play by appealing to more general impressions:

It is not by looking apart at the scenes and passages which we have endeavoured to separate from the undoubted scenes and passages of Shakspere in this play, that we can rightly judge of their inferiority. They must be contrasted with the great scenes of the fourth act, and with Timon's portion of the fifth,—the essentially tragic portions of this extraordinary drama. In power those scenes are almost unequalled. They are not pleasing—they are sometimes positively repulsive in the images which they present to us: but in the tremendous strength of passionate invective we know not what can be compared to them. In _Lear_ the deep pity for the father is an ever-present feeling, mingling with the terror which he produces by his denunciations of his daughters. But in _Timon_ the poet has not once sought to move our pity: by throwing him into an attitude of undiscriminating hostility to the human race, he scarcely claims any human sympathy. Properly to understand the scenes of the fourth and fifth acts, we must endeavour to form a general estimate of the character which Shakspere has here created. (pp. 76–7)

We will return to questions of character and dramaturgy in a later chapter, in which Knight's qualities as a sensitive reader will again be apparent.

Charles Knight's essay on the two styles he could detect in _Timon of Athens_ is a remarkable performance, which has never received the recognition it deserves. English Shakespearians ignored this problem for a generation, and the next scholar to take it up was Nikolaus Delius,[3] who had produced the first critical edition of Shakespeare's works in Germany (7 vols., 1854–61). Delius prefaced his essay with an excerpt from an earlier work of his, a commentary[4] on Ludwig Tieck's Shakespeare criticism (1846), in which he had drawn attention to the 'striking contrast in style, versification, and characterization that occurs throughout the whole drama, not only between separate scenes but even within the same scene' (Delius 1867, p. 335). Delius rejected both of the standard explanations of this contrast, textual corruption or the play's unfinished state, dismissing the latter by observing that 'the weaker passages', or 'those which stand in glaring contradiction to the supposedly complete parts', are not limited to one part of the play but alternate throughout, making it incomprehensible that Shakespeare could have put down on paper the finished and the unfinished parts not just next to each other but intertwined (p. 336). (This comment should be remembered when the 'unfinished play' theory crops up again in the 1930s.) In this 1846 essay Delius cited

³ N. Delius, 'Ueber Shakespeare's Timon of Athens', _ShJb_ 2 (1867): 335–61. All translations mine.

⁴ N. Delius, _Die Tieck'sche Shakespearekritik beleuchtet. Ein Supplement zu Shakespeare's dramatischen Werken_ (Bonn, 1846; Hildesheim, 1981). For information on German Shakespeare criticism see the admirable annotated bibliography by Hansjürgen Blinn, _Der deutsche Shakespeare_ (Berlin, 1993).

with respect Charles Knight's attempt (originally published in his 'Pictorial Shakespeare') to solve this embarrassment by postulating that Shakespeare had extensively rewritten an earlier play.

Although he praised 'the astuteness and fine aesthetic feeling' with which Knight had pointed out the variations in style running through the whole play, at this point Delius had rejected his theory on two grounds. First, he argued, there is no example of Shakespeare ever having treated an earlier play in this manner, 'leaving one half of the original untouched in all its metrical and stylistic deficiencies, while transforming the other half to a Shakespearian property'. When he transformed the source-plays for *King John* and *The Taming of the Shrew* Shakespeare did so completely, not leaving them half-complete, half-incomplete (pp. 336–7). Secondly, Delius judged in 1846, those parts of the play which Knight had allocated to the co-author, 'with all their faults, still bore the stamp of Shakespeare's individuality', so he concluded that the play was a reworking by the dramatist of some youthful work of his own (p. 337).

But Delius soon came to reject his own theory, recognizing that in Shakespeare's early period a play's whole design may be simpler, but it is still 'logically clear and coherent', and 'nowhere suffers from the internal contradictions, the unmotivated transitions and insertions that confront us in *Timon*' (p. 338). Characterization in the early plays may be neither deep nor precise, but it is always consistent, and gives us the impression of 'dealing with figures of real flesh and blood, not merely with the silhouettes or pure genre figures which appear here and there in some scenes of *Timon*'. The style or diction of Shakespeare's early plays, also, in contrast to 'the partially compressed and intellectual difficulty' of his later work, shows a clarity and ease of understanding quite unlike the 'deliberate obscurity and unpleasing strangeness' of the non-Shakespearian parts of *Timon*. These inauthentic scenes also differ totally in versification from the early plays, in which Shakespeare took over the regular, monotonous blank verse of his predecessors, gradually transforming it to 'the most lively and varied medium, perfectly adapted to dramatic purposes'. Compared to these strictly observed metrical conventions, Delius judged that, in the un-Shakespearian scenes of *Timon*,

complete metrical anarchy reigns, defeating all editorial attempts to regularize the verse. And in a completely unShakespearian manner, rhymed couplets are plentifully inserted into the limping and stumbling iambs, which look like prose, as well as into prose passages, rhyming verse whose otiose tinkle is doubly objectionable in such a context. . . . (p. 338)

In Shakespeare's early and late work, by contrast, rhyme is never introduced without some inner justification and motivation, usually at the end of either a scene or a long speech (p. 339).

For all these reasons, then, Delius had rejected his own theory of *Timon* being Shakespeare's revision of an earlier play, and in his edition of the text (1855) had signalled his complete acceptance of Charles Knight's identification of two different hands at work throughout (ibid.). Now, in 1867, Delius produced a new analysis, independent of Knight's, based on four general assumptions. First, that Shakespeare's revision dates from a late period in his career (pp. 339–40); secondly, that the play to which he contributed new additions must have existed complete, and may have already been a favourite with the public, so that Shakespeare could insert whole scenes without having to alter the plan of the whole (p. 340)—a point taken from Knight; thirdly, that the play which he worked over was not that old, since its verse style suggested that the co-author was one of Shakespeare's younger contemporary dramatists (p. 341); and fourthly, that since the extant play had already digested the classical sources, Shakespeare had no need to exert himself in that respect (pp. 341–2). I summarize these arguments merely to show the difficulties which meet even someone as knowledgeable as Delius, once scholars begin to speculate about the putative old plays which Shakespeare may have known, attempting to re-create them *ex nihilo* in order to legitimize their own indeterminable theories. Here Delius made 'den Vorgänger' responsible for the overall design of the play and for its handling of the sources, so exonerating Shakespeare from any blame for whatever structural deficiencies it might have. But at least Delius is to be praised for recognizing that the co-author was younger than Shakespeare, writing a newer form of verse.

Although Delius's theories of revision need not concern us, his commentary on the co-author's language and style remain highly perceptive. Having assigned Act 1 scene 1 mostly to Shakespeare, Delius observed of 1.2 that nowhere in his work can we find 'such verse and such prose, such sudden transitions from one to the other and back again'. A strikingly un-Shakespearian detail is that Apemantus 'decks out his lame iambics with rhymes completely lacking the epigrammatic balance and antithetical point that Shakespeare gives to his couplets' (p. 345). As an example of this stylistic feature I cite Apemantus' speeches at the first banquet, which move unpredictably from prose to blank verse, and to rhymed verse having eight, ten, or even twelve syllables:

> *Apem.* I scorn thy meat, 'twould choke me, for I should ne'er flatter thee. O you
> gods! what a number of men eats Timon, and he sees 'em not! It grieves me to see
> so many dip their meat in one man's blood, and all the madness is, he cheers them
> up too.
> I wonder men dare trust themselves with men.
> Methinks they should invite them without knives:
> Good for their meat, and safer for their lives.
> There's much example for't: the fellow that sits next him, now parts bread with
> him, pledges the breath of him in a divided draught, is the readiest man to kill

him; 't 'as been prov'd. If I were a huge man, I should fear to drink at meals,
Lest they should spy my windpipe's dangerous notes:
Great men should drink with harness on their throats.

Tim. My lord, in heart; and let the health go round.

2. Lord. Let it flow this way, my good lord.

Apem. Flow this way? A brave fellow! he keeps his tides well. Those healths will
make thee and thy state look ill, Timon.
Here's that which is too weak to be a sinner,
Honest water, which ne'er left man i' th' mire.
This and my food are equals, there's no odds;
Feasts are too proud to give thanks to the gods.

Apemantus' grace.

Immortal gods, I crave no pelf,
I pray for no man but myself.
Grant I may never prove so fond,
To trust man on his oath or bond

(1.2.38–65)

In 3.3 Delius again pointed to the 'wildness and waywardness' of the verse, and the 'trivial and tasteless rhyming couplets' which the other dramatist constantly introduced into his blank verse, ending this scene, like its predecessor, with banal moralizing couplets:

And this is all a liberal course allows;
Who cannot keep his wealth must keep his house.

(3.3.40–1)

and

Men must learn now with pity to dispense:
For policy sits above conscience.

(3.2.87–8)

'How can anyone have ever taken these inept attempts at rhyme for Shakespeare's?', Delius asked (p. 349). In 3.5, Alcibiades' scene before the Senate, he judged, the blank verse only appears to be such, mixed with incomplete lines and sententious couplets, the couplets often being elliptical and obscure (pp. 350–1). The soliloquy of Flavius, ending 4.2, also bears all the marks of Shakespeare's co-author, 'the moralizing commonplaces whose triviality is made more obvious by the rhymes strewn among the unrhymed, jerky and incomplete verses', the 'oblique and obscure' language, the inconsequential reasoning, and the curious alternation of an 'otiose jumble of *sententiae* with factual utterances' relating to the plot and its development (p. 353). In sharp contrast to this clumsy and incoherent use of poetic forms is Shakespeare's verse, which in 2.2 'shows all the living dramatic variety, the strength, zest and fullness characteristic of his middle period' (p. 347). Delius believed that Shakespeare's interest in the play reached its liveliest and most energetic point in the scenes of Timon's misanthropy (4.1 onwards), for which he reserved his most powerful verse (p. 352).

Delius gave both a general account of the differences between the two dramatists and a detailed division of their authorship (pp. 344–61), which can be summarized as follows:

Shakespeare: 1.1; 2.2.123–233; 3.4.79–117; 3.6.86–105; 4.1; 4.2.1–29; 4.3.1–299, 381–457; 5.1.47–228; 5.2; 5.4.1–64

Co-author: 1.2; 2.1; 2.2.1–122; 3.1; 3.2; 3.3; 3.4.1–78; 3.5; 3.6.1–85, 106–120; 4.2.30–50; 4.3.300–80, 458–536; 5.1.1–46; 5.3; 5.4.65–85

Modern scholarship, which has developed a much wider range of approaches, would endorse about three-quarters of Delius's assignations, giving Shakespeare all of 2.1, and only the first forty-five lines of 2.2. In the second banquet scene, where Timon feasts his guests on stones and warm water, scholars today attribute to Shakespeare not only the verse diatribe (85–105) but the bitterly ironic prose prayer which precedes it (65–84). Modern authorities would agree with Delius's division of 4.2, but would assign to Shakespeare the whole of 4.3—the scene where various groups visit Timon as he digs up roots and gold—up to the concluding sequence between Flavius and Timon. Here Delius judged the Steward's soliloquy on Timon's misery (458–71) to be identical in content and attitude to his soliloquy closing 4.2, both un-Shakespearian (again echoing Knight). In the dialogue following Delius pointed to the unmistakable signs of the co-author's hand in the blank verse, with its 'faulty construction and scansion', and attempt at rhyme:

> and believe it,
> My most honour'd lord,
> For any benefit that points to me,
> Either in hope or present, I'd exchange
> For this one wish, that you had power and wealth,
> To requite me by making rich yourself.
>
> (517–22)

Delius was certainly right to give this closing sequence to the co-author. But where he assigned several passages in Act 5 to 'the predecessor', mostly on the grounds of awkward dramaturgy, modern scholars tend to think it all Shakespeare's, explaining the inconsistencies and loose ends in terms of the rough and untidy 'foul papers' (pre-theatrical manuscript) from which it derived. These exceptions apart, Delius made a judicious division of responsibilities between Shakespeare and the other dramatist, which agreed on many details with that made by Charles Knight.

F. G. Fleay, that pioneer of scientific verse tests, discussed *Timon* in two essays produced (or so he claimed) in 1869 and 1874.[5] Fleay disagreed with Delius's theory of Shakespeare having revised a predecessor's work, arguing that 'the un-Shakespearian parts were certainly the latest written' (Fleay 1874c, p. 139). Using a number of different criteria, Fleay presented his results in tabular form, asserting that his table had been 'grounded on an examination of every line of the play, one by one, as regards the metre; on a specific analysis of the plot with regard to the bearing of each scene or portion of a scene on every other; and on a minute examination of the Folio of 1623, with regard to the printing and spelling of proper names, stage directions, etc., which have been altered by modern editors . . .' (p. 140). Fleay is to be commended for the range of approaches he applied and indeed, for his conclusions, which agree surprisingly well with more recent scholarship—I see no grounds for denying Fleay the title 'modern'. Fleay divided the play as follows:

Shakespeare: 1.1; 2.1; 2.2.1–193, 205–42; 3.6; 4.1; 4.2.1–29; 4.3.1–291, 363–97, 414–52; 5.1.50–231; 5.2; 5.4

Unknown: 1.2; 3.1; 3.2; 3.3; 3.4; 3.5; 4.2.30–50; 4.3.292–362, 398–413, 453–543; 5.1.1–50; 5.3

More recent scholars would reject Fleay's division of Act 4 scene 3 into so many small parts, on the grounds that co-authors normally took responsibility for whole scenes; but they would agree that the final part of that scene (lines 458–536 in the Riverside edition) is not by Shakespeare.

This unnecessarily fragmented treatment of 4.3 shows Fleay's weak spot, his treatment of Shakespeare's prose. Whereas his ear for authentic verse was often unerring, he found Apemantus' prose, in scenes which are undisputedly Shakespearian, to be 'bald, cut up' (p. 130) or 'chopt-up' (p. 135), and he impatiently ascribed these passages to the other hand. When it came to Shakespeare's verse, Fleay believed that he could detect 'the true ring' of Shakespeare in 2.1, and in 2.2 he judged the verse to be 'pure Shakespeare. No one else could have written it. The "drunken spilth of wine", the "one cloud of Winter showres, | These flyes are coucht", the "halfe-caps and cold moving nods, | They froze me into silence", bear the lawful stamp of his mintage' (p. 133). But Fleay's judgements, based on long and wide reading, were not merely impressionistic. He supplied a metrical table with precise computations, which I reproduce in Table 4.1. Rearranging Fleay's data gives the information supplied in Table 4.2. Those figures clearly show that Shakespeare used far less rhyme than his co-author, and much less prose. More important than the statistics, however, was Fleay's penetrating analysis

---

[5] F. G. Fleay, 'On the Authorship of *Timon of Athens*', *TNSS* 1 (1874): 130–51; repr. in Fleay, *Shakespeare Manual* (London, 1876), pp. 187–208.

TABLE 4.1. *Metrical table for* Timon of Athens

	Shakespeare					Unknown			
	A Prose	B Blank	C Irregular	D Rhymes		A Prose	B Blank	C Irregular	D Rhymes
1.1	58	208	25	2	1.2	64	126	21	36
2.1		31	2	2	2.2	11			
2.2	85	133	8	6	3.1	49	11	3	2
3.6	111	12	2	6	3.2	58	30	2	4
4.1		33	2	6	3.3	8	19	9	6
4.3		339	28	2	3.4	18	78	12	8
5.1		162	14	6	3.5		73	14	30
5.2		14	1	2	4.2		36	4	10
5.4		77	4	4	4.3	85	53	9	18
					5.1	46			4
					5.3		5	1	4
Totals	254	1,009	86	36	Totals	339	441	75	122

Source: Fleay 1874c, p. 141.

TABLE 4.2. *Rhyme and blank verse in* Timon of Athens

Division	Length	Percentage of rhyme to blank verse (cols. B + C)	Percentage of prose to all verse (cols. B + C + D)
Shakespeare's scenes	1,385 lines	3.28	18.3
Unknown's scenes	977 lines	23.64	34.7

of the stylistic confusion in the non-Shakespearian part of the play, which echoed those made by Knight and Delius. The 'style of these [scenes], and especially the metre, is utterly unlike anything in the other plays of Shakspere. It is marked by great irregularity, many passages refusing to be orthodox, even under torture; it abounds in rhymes, in emphatic and unemphatic passages alike; the rhymes are often preceded by incomplete lines; one of the rhyming lines is frequently imperfect or Alexandrine' (p. 144). More particularly,

The rhythm of the two portions of the play differs in every respect. The Shakspere parts are in his third style (like *Lear*), with great freedom in the rhythm, some 4 and 6 syllable lines, some Alexandrines with proper caesuras, and rhymes where the emphasis is great, at the end of scenes, and occasionally of speeches in other places. The other parts have irregularities, both in defect and excess, of every possible kind. There are lines of 8 and 9 syllables, Alexandrines without caesura, imperfect lines in rhyming couplets, broken lines preceding rhymes, and other peculiarities, not one of all which is admitted in Shakspere's rhythmical system. [1.2.257–9] is one of many instances of intolerably bad rhythm:

> I'll lock thy heaven from thee.
> O that men's ears should be
> To counsel deaf, but not to flattery!

Fleay added that 'one point in the metre may appear clearer if expressed statistically', namely that 'there are proportionally 8 times as many rhymes' in the portion by 'Unknown' as in Shakespeare's part (p. 148). He also noted that in the scenes where the creditors dun Timon (3.1–3.4) 'there is not a spark of Shakspere's poetry, not a vestige of his style', nor of his ability to differentiate characters through their language. The 'creditors' servants, who can rhyme much more easily than the best-educated personages in the Shakspere part of the play', he complained (echoing both Knight and Delius), are not individualized: 'they speak the same dialect, and use the same rhetoric, as all the characters of the second author; any speech of any one might be spoken by any other, so far as the language and form of expression are concerned' (p. 133).

Fleay used other, non-stylistic arguments to differentiate the two hands involved. He observed that one character 'is called Ventidius in the Shakspere part of the play', such as 1.1, but 'Ventigius' in the scenes by 'Unknown', such as 1.2 and 3.3 (pp. 131, 146). Fleay pointed out (p. 147) that the name 'Apemantus' is also spelled 'Apermantus' in some scenes, and he showed that in the non-Shakespearian 1.2, 'and here only', the steward is called Flavius, while in 2.2 'Flavius is given by Shakspere as the name of one of Timon's servants who is not the steward' (pp. 131, 146–7). Fleay also observed that the value of the Greek 'talent' varies considerably throughout the play, a loan of 5 talents being a considerable sum in 1.1, and 3 talents forming an acceptable dowry in 2.1. In 2.2, 3.1, and 3.4, however, sums of 50 talents are mentioned, while at 2.2.205 Timon even asks for 'A thousand talents'. In 3.2 we find both the completely vague 'so many talents' (12, 24, 37) and 'fifty-five hundred talents' (39). Fleay tried without success to correlate these striking discrepancies with his authorship division (pp. 144–5), and was forced to start emending the text (for 'thousand talents . . . I would read 1000 pieces'), a dangerous step in authorship studies.

Fleay had devoted a lot of thought to *Timon*, and made several intelligent observations. He deduced from the Folio pagination that *Troilus and Cressida* had originally been designed to fill this space, and that when that play was moved to its place between the Histories and Tragedies (for copyright reasons, as we now think), 'this space, then, of pp. 80–108 . . . being left unfilled, it became necessary to fill it' (p. 137). Credit for this discovery is

TABLE 4.3. *Verse table for* The Revenger's Tragedy

Total number of lines	over 2,400
Number of rhyming lines	exactly 460
Double endings	exactly 443
Alexandrines	exactly 2
Deficient and short lines	about 125

Source: Fleay 1874c, p. 138.

usually given to J. Q. Adams in 1908,[6] but Fleay must be awarded some share, even though he used it to support his completely improbable theory of a second playwright being engaged by Heminge and Condell in 1622–3 to pad out the play in order to fill the vacant space—which he signally failed to do, since the Folio pagination still has a gap between pp. 98 and 109.

I have left till last Fleay's one suggestion as to the identity of the second hand:

Having then, laid down as certain the division of the play, and the assignment of the nucleus to Shakspere, . . . we come to the more difficult question still—who was the second author? The ratio of rhyme to blank verse, the irregularities of length (lines with four accents and initial monosyllabic feet), number of double endings &c., agree with only one play of all that I have analyzed (over 200), viz., *The Revenger's Tragedy*. But I am doubtful as to pressing this argument very strongly, unless we give up (as I am quite ready to do) the notion of the play being finished in 1623, as *The Revenger's Tragedy* was written in 1607. The evidence of general style, however, appears to me strongly to confirm the conjecture that Cyril Tourneur was the second author. (pp. 137–8)

Now that we know that Middleton, not Tourneur, wrote *The Revenger's Tragedy*, Fleay's suggestion seems uncommonly prescient. He supported it (see Table 4.3) with 'numerical data . . . as near as I can count them in such a badly printed edition, as we yet have'. Although Fleay did not provide exactly the same range of statistics for *Timon*, if we accept his figures here, the percentage of rhymed verse (19.1) is close to that of the 'unknown' dramatist in *Timon* (23.6), and far above Shakespeare's rate in that play (3.3). My own calculation for *The Revenger's Tragedy*, based on Foakes's edition, with a total of 2,192 lines of verse, 243 lines of prose, and 380 rhymes, would be 17.3 per cent rhyme, which is not dissimilar to the figure for the non-Shakespearian scenes in *Timon*. Fleay then quoted (from a corrupt text) several passages of verse from *The Revenger's Tragedy* which seemed to

---

[6] J. C. Maxwell (ed.), *The Life of Timon of Athens* (Cambridge, 1957), p. 87 n.; J. Q. Adams, 'Timon of Athens and the Irregularities in the First Folio', *JEGP* 7 (1908): 53–63.

him to have 'exactly . . . the metre' of the co-author in *Timon*, including part of Vindice's concluding speech. I print the whole speech from a modern scholarly edition:[7]

> May not we set as well the duke's son?
> Thou hast no conscience; are we not reveng'd?
> Is there one enemy left alive amongst those?
> 'Tis time to die, when we are ourselves our foes.
> When murd'rers shut deeds close, this curse does seal 'em:
> If none disclose 'em, they themselves reveal 'em.
> This murder might have slept in tongueless brass,
> But for ourselves, and the world died an ass.
> Now I remember, too, here was Piato brought forth a knavish sentence once: no doubt, said he, but time will make the murderer bring forth himself. 'Tis well he died, he was a witch.
> And now, my lord, since we are in for ever,
> This work was ours, which else might have been slipp'd,
> And, if we list, we could have nobles clipp'd,
> And go for less than beggars; but we hate
> To bleed so cowardly. We have enough, i'faith;
> We're well, our mother turn'd, our sister true;
> We die after a nest of dukes. Adieu.

(5.3.117–25)

As we saw in Chapter 1, this jumbling of blank verse, rhyme, and prose is typical of Middleton, and if the reader will compare this speech with the same stylistic mélange in Apemantus' speeches in *Timon*, 1.2 (quoted above), the affinity will be instantly visible. It was not until 1928 that E. H. C. Oliphant suggested Middleton's authorship of *The Revenger's Tragedy*, an identification subsequently confirmed by the work of R. H. Barker, David Lake, and MacDonald Jackson, so it is hardly surprising that Fleay's identification has been either ignored or ridiculed.

In 1910 an American scholar, E. H. Wright, published his dissertation on the play's authorship,[8] following a by now firmly established tradition in identifying two authors on the grounds of wide variations in style, characterization, and dramaturgy. The co-author, to whom Wright attributed about one-third of the play, strove hard to be a poet by seeking 'rhetorical effect', but Wright found his work 'too thin in substance, too halting in expression, too tame and trite in imagery, too clumsy in characterization, too lacking in dramatic fitness, in a word too uninspired, to pass unsuspected' (Wright 1910, p. 27). Wright selected three passages from the play as illustrating the co-author's style, first that sequence in the opening banquet scene (1.2.38–65), previously singled out by Delius and quoted above, drawing

---

[7] *The Revenger's Tragedy*, ed. R. A. Foakes (London, 1966).
[8] E. H. Wright, *The Authorship of Timon of Athens* (New York, 1910).

attention to the 'quick and aimless shifts from prose to verse' and back—found in Apemantus' speech and elsewhere—'usually not even due, as in that excerpt, to a desire to rhyme' (p. 31). In this banquet scene, Wright pointed out, the language 'staggers aimlessly from prose to verse, from verse back to prose, sixteen times in 257 lines' (p. 36). Following Knight, Delius, and Fleay, Wright noted that the co-author is also very fond of rhyme, indeed 'twenty per cent of his verses rhyme. The ratio is practically constant with him; and the rhymes are scattered indiscriminately throughout his scenes. Shakespeare has only four per cent of rhymes and almost all of these at ends of scenes.' If one omits such final couplets, the difference is even more striking, the proportion of rhymes being less than 1 per cent for Shakespeare, 18 per cent for his co-author (p. 30). Another characteristic of the co-author is his fondness for irregular verse lines, which Wright computed to amount to 18 per cent of his verse, while for Shakespeare he counted only 4 per cent (p. 31). Taking the three characteristics together, Wright judged the co-author's technique to be 'irreconcilable with Shakespeare's . . . Frequent and useless shifts from prose to verse were never part of Shakespeare's practice; irregular verse was always scarce with him; and by the period of *Timon* he had all but discarded rhyme' (p. 30).

Although coming to similar conclusions as Knight, Delius, and Fleay had done about the two different verse styles in the play, Wright (correctly) criticized Fleay's treatment of prose. 'Bent on giving all the prose to the inferior author' (p. 35), Fleay had to evolve complicated theories to account for prose passages in scenes that otherwise seem Shakespearian. Thus in Act 1 scene 1, undoubtedly by Shakespeare, Fleay wanted to ascribe the 'bald' and 'cut-up' style of Apemantus' prose speeches to the other hand. But, Wright objected, 'the change [at 1.1.180] from verse to prose—definitive, and by no means like the uncertain vacillations of the inferior author into and out of meter—may . . . prove nothing but that prose is the natural, almost the only suitable, medium for Apemantus' brand of sarcasm. The balder this is, the better it suits Apemantus; its "cut-up" nature is its merit' (p. 34). Wright also showed the pernicious effect of Fleay's blind spot concerning prose in two later scenes, 4.3. and 5.1. In the first of these Timon the misanthrope is visited in his cave by various groups of people, including some bandits, a passage which Fleay had assigned to the co-author, his 'sole reason for thinking . . . the bandits' dialogue . . . spurious [being] that it is prose. When we find that Mr. Fleay has given the inferior writer every word of prose, without exception, in the play, we begin to doubt his judgment where it has no further basis . . .', especially when we see 'that Shakespeare meant the bandits to hold some dialogue before addressing Timon' (p. 50). Here, as in the scene following, where the Poet and the Painter approach Timon's cave, 'the prose is Shakespearean enough' (p. 52) to leave no case for assigning it to the other hand.

Having well characterized the style of the co-author (who would 'habitually hash his prose and verse': p. 49), Wright described Shakespeare's style in terms that we can still accept. In 1.1, for instance, he noted 'the rare quality of the copious and involved imagery', but at the same time 'the orderly technic of the verse' (p. 33). In 2.1, 'the solidity and dignity, yet delicacy, of the thought and verse alike, unmarred by metrical deformity, the unerring stroke of every sentence, driven home with telling phrases and with striking images, leaves no doubt' as to Shakespeare's authorship (p. 36). 'He alone was capable' of Timon's blistering address to the 'knot of mouth-friends' gulled and assaulted at the mock banquet (3.6.98), and in Timon's curse on Athens (4.1.1 ff.) 'the majesty of the style' declares his hand (p. 46). Wright judged the parting of the servants (4.2.1–30) to be 'the tenderest scene in *Timon*; in it is concentrated more pure poetry, perhaps, than is found in any scene of equal length in the play. All the critics note the break between it and the twenty-line soliloquy the Steward stays to speak after the servants go; which is little more than prose run mad', completely in the co-author's manner (p. 46). The most recent scholarship would support all these ascriptions.

Wright's cogent analyses of discrepancies in the plotting, and his description of the two different styles in the play, show the strengths of traditional aesthetic criticism. But its weaknesses are also apparent. Convinced as he was that Shakespeare would never have left a play in such a mess, and that the other dramatist made 'interpolations' with little concern for unity (pp. 39 ff., 47 ff., 58 ff.), Wright evolved a complex theory which involved postulating insertions into the text which the modern scholar is able to identify without difficulty, and which, once removed, restore the coherence of Shakespeare's pure invention before the interpolator tampered with it. Thus in 2.2, where the loyal Steward tells Timon how parlous his finances are, Timon dispatches three of his servants to his friends to request a loan, in a prose passage (2.2.186–94 in the Riverside text). Wright argued that 'this bit of prose, intrinsically trivial, [forms] a kind of keystone in the entire structure of the first three acts' (p. 61), for it was originally written by Shakespeare in verse, but had to be set as prose once the interpolator had inserted the words '—I hunted with his honour to-day; you to Sempronius': as Wright put it, 'one line out, the passage settles into blank verse. Even the pieces of the broken lines fit. So, we may be sure, Shakspere wrote it. Such a reconstruction is not possible by accident' (p. 66).

The self-serving nature of such speculations, all too common in authorship studies, needs no comment. But they drove Wright on to deny Fleay's argument that the three dunning scenes that open Act 3 were written by the co-author, claiming instead that 'a purely esthetic judgment as to the first two of the three scenes . . . indicates that Shakespeare wrote them; but an esthetic and technical judgment as to the third scene, which is mainly in bad verse, points to the other author' (pp. 39–40). But aesthetic reasons are not enough: authorship studies must pursue differing approaches independently. If the

methods are valid they will converge, giving the same result, mutually supporting each other. What was needed at this point was a close examination of
the language of these scenes, and this was soon provided. The studies by
William Wells in 1920 and H. D. Sykes in 1921 showed the linguistic unity of
3.1, 3.2, 3.3, and 3.4, giving them all to the co-author. Wright's stylistic analyses, and his apportionment of responsibility to the two dramatists, displayed
critical acumen but were vitiated by his theory that Shakespeare wrote the
original draft, which the co-author revised. All the inconsistent and uncoor-
dinated plot elements that he pointed to can be explained by a much simpler
hypothesis, namely that Shakespeare and his co-author drafted the play
together, each writing their allotted scenes, but failed to complete the final
stage, which might—or should—have involved checking the joint work for
internal coherence and rewriting where necessary. Of course, we will never
be able to reconstruct the compositional process of this, or any other
Elizabethan collaborative play, but experience of the severe distortion and
special pleading produced in the work of Delius and Wright by either of the
two arguments involving a temporal dislocation between the two writers'
contributions—Shakespeare wrote first; Shakespeare wrote last—suggests
that we should keep open the third possibility, which does at least correspond
to what we know about co-authorship in this period, that both writers
worked on the play simultaneously.

The first four serious students of the authorship problem in *Timon of
Athens*, Knight, Delius, Fleay, and Wright, had all given abundant evidence of
the existence of two discrepant verse styles in the play, and of a whole series
of differences in characterization and dramaturgy. The only attempt to identify the co-author had been Fleay's indication that several stylistic features
were shared by *The Revenger's Tragedy*, now known to be by Middleton. The
next two scholars to study the play's authorship each made an explicit case
for Middleton as co-author of *Timon*. William Wells cited a whole series of
verbal parallels between *Timon* and Middleton,[9] particularly convincing for
the sequence from 2.2 to 3.3, 'the abortive attempts of Timon to borrow
money', which forms a frequently recurring situation in Middleton's plays.
The idiosyncrasy of Middleton's language in these situations consists in
his frequent use of 'the verbs "to supply", "to furnish", and "to pleasure", in
situations where other terms could be employed just as correctly' (Wells
1920, p. 267). I select a few of the many parallels cited by Wells. Particularly
striking are those from *Michaelmas Term*,[10] the scene where Shortyard
tries in vain to raise money:

---

[9] William Wells, 'Timon of Athens', *NQ* 12th ser. 6 (1920): 266–9.
[10] Quotations have been checked against G. R. Price (ed.), '*Michaelmas Term*' and '*A Trick to
Catch the Old One*' (The Hague, 1976). Cf. also Shortyard's assurance that Easye will 'not want
money' since he feels bound 'to see you *furnish*' (2.1.15–17).

(a) '. . . commend me to their loves; and I am proud, say, that my *occasions* have found time to use 'em towards a *supply* of money' (*Tim.*, 2.2.197 ff.). 'Let them both rest till another *occasion*; you shall not need to run so farre at this time, take one near hand to Master Quasimodo the Draper, and will him to *furnish* me instantly' (*Michaelmas Term*, 2.1.93–6).

(b) '. . . I come to entreat your honour to *supply*; who having great and instant *occasion* to use fifty talents, hath sent to our lordship to *furnish* them' (*Tim.*, 3.1.17 ff.). '. . . Run presently to Master Goome the Mercer, and will him to tell out two or three hundred pound for mee, or more according as he is *furnished*' (*M.T.*, 2.1.81–3).

(c) 'My lord . . . has only sent his *present occasion* now . . . requesting your lordship to *supply* his instant use with so many talents' (*Tim.*, 3.2.35 ff.). 'Run to Master Goome, or Master Profite, and carrie my *present occasion* of money to 'em' (*M.T.*, 2.3.156–7).

(d) 'I count it one of *my greatest afflictions*, say, that I cannot *pleasure* such an honourable gentleman' (*Tim.*, 3.2.56 ff.). 'It is *my greatest affliction* at this instant, I am not able to *furnish* you' (*M.T.*, 2.3. 117–18).

(e) '*What a wicked beast was I* to *disfurnish* myself against such a good time . . .' (*Tim.*, 3.2.45 ff.). '*What a beast was I* to put out my money t'other day' (*A Mad World, My Masters*, 2.4.26–7).

These, and other parallels cited by Wells, formed conclusive evidence for Middleton's authorship of the satirical dunning scenes in Act 3.

The whole justification for authorship study is that it helps us understand the nature of a collaborative play, and the differences it displays between the writers involved. When I worked on Shakespeare's prose I was struck by several oddities in the scene (1.2) where Timon feasts his friends. There was the great stylistic variation in Apemantus' speeches, which I could describe —with 'their curious mixture of prose and couplets of ten, twelve, and eight feet'—but could not account for, and there was the strange oscillation between verse and prose in Timon's part, culminating in his prose speech in what seemed to me 'an artificial style, with its inflated language . . . and its expanded images'.[11]

> O you gods, think I, what need we have any friends, if we should ne'er have need of 'em? They were the most needless creatures living, should we ne'er have use for 'em; and would *most resemble sweet instruments hung up in cases, that keeps their sounds to themselves.* (1.2.95–9; my italics)

[11] B. Vickers, *The Artistry of Shakespeare's Prose* (London, 1968; repr. 1979), pp. 373–4.

This concluding image still seems affected, and is no doubt a deliberate effect, but it was not until I (belatedly) read William Wells's essay that I could identify its real author:[12]

> I commend
> The virtues highly, as I do *an instrument*
> *When the case hangs by the wall.*
>
> (Middleton, *More Dissemblers*
> *besides Women*, 1.3.22–4)

Wells also identified words and phrases characteristic of Middleton, such as 'apperie' (1.2.32) and 'rioter' (3.5.68), neither of which is found in Shakespeare. In 3.6 we find the phrase 'draw near', which occurs four times in *Timon* and often in Middleton, together with Middleton's favourite expletive 'push'. Wells also pointed to a characteristic grammatical usage in Middleton, who 'habitually dropped the personal pronoun in the nominative case'. Among the instances Wells cited are 'Has only sent his present occasion now' (3.2.34); 'Must I take the cure on me? | Has much disgraced me in't' (3.3.13); 'How fairly this lord strives to appear fine! Takes virtuous copies to be wicked' (3.3.30–1)—all Middleton scenes. The point is valid, but unfortunately Wells worked from a modernized edition. It was left to H. D. Sykes to consult the Folio text and to provide a more precise account.

Of many other significant parallels cited by Wells, I quote one from the subplot, the scene where Alcibiades pleads with the Senators to issue a pardon for his friend, who has committed murder:

> *Alcib.* Must it be so? it must not be. My lords.
>   I do beseech you know me.
> *Sec. Sen.* How?
> *Alcib. Call me to your remembrances.*
> *Third Sen.* What?
> *Alcib.* I cannot think but your age has forgot me;
>   It could not else be I should prove so base
>   To sue and be denied such common grace:
>   *My wounds ache at you.*
>
>   (3.5.90–7)

Both italicized phrases recur within a short passage in *A Chaste Maid in Cheapside*:

---

[12] The phrase recurs in a Dekker–Middleton play, *The Roaring Girl* (1608), this time with a bawdy meaning. Moll Cutpurse, dressed as a man, having drawn her sword against Sebastian, is handed a viol instead, with the words 'Hold, there shall need no weapon at this meeting', and replies: 'it shall ne'er by said I came into a gentleman's chamber and let his instrument hang by the walls!' (4.1.76–87). See the Revels edition by P. A. Mulholland (Manchester, 1987), pp. 10–11, for the ascription of this scene to Middleton.

Sir Wal. Touch me not, villain! *my wound aches at thee*,
   Thou poison to my heart!
Allwit.   He raves already:
   His senses are quite gone, he knows me not.
   Look up, an't like your worship; heave those eyes,
   Call me to mind! is your remembrance left?
   Look in my face.

(5.1.15–20)

As Wells showed, 'the same association of an aching wound with anger is seen in *Your Five Gallants*: 'Forgive me, dear boy; *my wound ached* and I grew angry' (3.3).

This pioneer essay by William Wells, identifying Middleton as the co-author of *Timon*, inspired H. Dugdale Sykes to a more detailed analysis. Citing Fleay's theory that Shakespeare was the original author, into whose work an interpolator placed his own 'inferior' additions—a theory which had apparently convinced K. Deighton, editor of the first Arden edition (1905)—Sykes set out to argue the opposite case, already urged by Wright and Delius, that 'Shakespeare worked over an existing play, or draft of a play'.[13] I shall not summarize Sykes's thesis, nor his attempt to prove the additional presence of John Day's hand (Sykes 1924, pp. 12–20), since neither argument carried conviction. The valuable parts of Sykes's essay were his general observations on the characteristics of Middleton's style found in *Timon*, and his detailed commentary on the individual scenes. Developing the observation made by Knight, Fleay, and E. H. Wright, that the play contains much more rhyme than any of Shakespeare's other plays of this date, a proportion rising to 20 per cent in some scenes (pp. 2–3), Sykes also echoed earlier scholars by observing that *Timon* had many 'irregular unscannable verse lines', and 'frequent and aimless shifts from verse to prose', all features 'characteristic of Middleton at the time this play was written'. Sykes instanced *The Phoenix* (1604) and *Michaelmas Term* (1606) as being 'most closely akin to *Timon* . . . In these plays we find the same high proportion of rhyme, the same irregularities of metre, the same habit of jumbling together verse and prose, rhymed verse and unrhymed' (p. 22). The passages that Sykes quoted for comparison are well worth a modern reader's attention:

> (*a*)   Poor honest lord, brought low by his own heart,
>   Undone by goodness! Strange unusual blood
>   When man's worst sin is, he does too much good!
>   Who then dares to be half so kind agen?
>   For bounty, that makes gods, does still mar men.
>   My dearest lord, blest to be most accurst,

---

[13] H. D. Sykes, 'The Problem of *Timon of Athens*', in *Sidelights on Elizabethan Drama* (Oxford, 1924), pp. 1–48 (originally as essays in *NQ*, 1921), at p. 1.

Rich only to be wretched, thy great fortunes
Are made thy chief afflictions. Alas, kind lord,
He's flung in rage from this ungrateful seat
Of monstrous friends;
Nor has he with him to supply his life,
Or that which can command it.
I'll follow and inquire him out:
I'll ever serve his mind with my best will;
Whilst I have gold, I'll be his steward still,

(*Tim.*, 4.2.37–50)

(*b*)   None can except against him; the man's mad,
And privileged by the moon, if he say true:
Less madness 'tis to speak sin than to do.
This wretch that lov'd before his food his strife,
This punishment falls even with his life.
His pleasure was vexation, all his bliss
The torment of another;
Their hurt his health, their starved hopes his store;
Who so loves law dies either mad or poor;

(*The Phoenix*, 4.1.138–47)

(*c*)   The happiest good that ever Shortyard felt!
I want to be express'd, my mirth is such.
To be struck now e'en when his joys were high!
Men only kiss their knaveries, and so die;
I've often mark'd it.
He was a famous cozener while he liv'd
And now his son shall reap't; I'll ha' the lands,
Let him study law after; 'tis no labour
To undo him for ever; but, for Easy,
Only good confidence did make him foolish
And not the lack of sense; that was not it:
'Tis worldly craft beats down a scholar's wit.

(*Michaelmas Term*, 4.2.10–19)

Looking at these three excerpts, with their incomplete verse lines and unpredictable use of couplets, we may well agree that 'it would be difficult to find passages more alike in style' (p. 23). Sykes pointed out that Apemantus' speeches at the first banquet (1.2.38–72) exhibit 'the same features (irregular metre, and jumbling together of rhymed and unrhymed lines and prose) as are found in Middleton's plays at this time' (pp. 32–3). This confusing mixture of styles is also found in the Steward's soliloquy (4.3.458–71), which has several echoes of earlier scenes (3.5, 4.2), proving that it, too, was written by Middleton. Sykes identified another characteristic of Middleton's style, his liking for 'antithetical couplets', shown three times in the first banquet scene of *Timon*,[14] and he noted that *The Phoenix* 'contains above a score' of such couplets (p. 34).

Sykes praised Wells for pointing to the dunning scenes in Act 3 as providing 'the clearest evidence of Middleton's authorship' (p. 23), and cited even more parallels between them and the acknowledged work of Middleton, who '. . . dwells much upon duns and debtors' (pp. 24–9, 37). He also showed that these scenes contain several Middletonian expressions which are either never or seldom used by Shakespeare. The word 'free-hearted' (3.1.10) 'occurs nowhere else in the Shakespeare Folio'; the expression 'give thee thy due' (35), occurs only once in the rest of Shakespeare (*1 Henry IV*, 1.2.59), but frequently in Middleton; and the word 'endeared' (3.2.31) regularly has in Middleton, but nowhere in Shakespeare, 'the sense of "obliged" or "bound" to a person'. Correcting a point made by Wells, Sykes pointed to other linguistic details indicating Middleton's hand, such as 'the contraction of "he has" to "h'as" ', which occurs six times in the folio text of *Timon*, always in Middleton's scenes.[15] Another characteristic Middleton contraction, according to Sykes, is ' 'tas' for 'it has', which occurs twice in another scene identified as Middleton's (1.2.49, 144). Both contractions 'are so frequent in Middleton as to attract the attention of the least observant reader', the two together occurring six times in *Michaelmas Term* and eight times in *Your Five Gallants* (p. 20). Returning to an observation of Fleay's, Sykes added a 'purely bibliographical' argument for the presence of two authors, namely the occurrence of the spelling 'Apemantus' in Shakespeare's 1.1 (10 times in full, 33 times abbreviated as 'Ape.'), as against 'Apermantus' in Middleton's 1.2 (4 times in full, 14 times abbreviated as 'Aper.'). In 2.2 and 4.3, both by Shakespeare, the spellings are 'Apemantus' (9 times) and 'Ape.' (38 times, once as 'Apem.'). Sykes recognized some exceptions—in 1.1 the stage direction is 'Enter Apermantus', and Timon once addresses him in that form; 'Apermantus' occurs once in 2.2.76—but argued that here 'for once the compositor failed to follow his copy' (pp. 21–2).

Between them, developing earlier demonstrations by Knight, Delius, Fleay, and Wright that two clearly distinguishable authors had collaborated on *Timon*, William Wells and H. Dugdale Sykes provided challenging evidence that the second hand was Middleton's. But despite these six independent studies, which reinforced each other's findings, the Shakespeare world once again closed ranks against the entry of an outsider. The most common all-purpose validation of the case for Shakespeare's sole authorship was to revive the favourite theory of early nineteenth-century German critics, and pronounce *Timon* an unfinished play. E. K. Chambers, a considerable scholar,

---

[14] Namely: '. . . invite them without Knives: | Good for their meat, and safer for their lives' (1.2.44–5); 'Methinks false hearts should never have sound legs' (233–4); 'O that men's ears should be | To counsel deaf, but not to flattery!' (249–50)

[15] 'Including one case of *had* (= he had)'. Cf. 3.2.34; 3.3.13, 23; 3.5.62; 4.3.450, 469.

but seldom willing to conceive of Shakespeare having collaborated with anyone, recognized that the play contains several scenes 'in which the verse at least cannot be the complete and jointed work of Shakespeare'. It is significant that most of the scenes in which Chambers pronounced the verse to be untypical of Shakespeare are those already identified as being by the second author, probably Middleton: 1.2; 3.1; 3.2; 3.3; 3.4.1–79; 3.5; 4.2.30–50; 4.3.1–47, 464–543; 5.1.1–118. Indeed, the account Chambers gave of the un-Shakespearian quality of this verse closely echoed the description of Middleton's characteristic confusion of styles given by Wells and Sykes. These un-Shakespearian qualities are

> particularly noticeable in the longer speeches. These contain Shakespearean ideas, sometimes inchoate, and scattered Shakespearean phrases. But they are not constructed as articulated paragraphs at all. They consist of juxtaposed sentences, now in blank verse, now in rhyme, now in wording which can most easily be read as prose. There are many short lines, occasionally successive, for which no rhythmic or dramatic justification is apparent. There are unmetrical long lines. It must be added that the structure of *Timon* as a whole is incoherent. There are many small confusions and inconsistencies.[16]

Chambers reported that these features had given rise to theories which agree 'in the assumption of a second hand' at work—the hostile term 'assumption' being evidently chosen to deny such theories the status of rational argument. Making easy capital out of the disagreement between scholars as to who the second author was (the 'multiplicity [of theories] suggests that their exponents are on the wrong tack'), Chambers avoided discussing any of the voluminous evidence already assembled, and curtly dismissed the issue: 'I do not doubt that [*Timon*] was left unfinished by Shakespeare, and . . . that it is unfinished still. The passages of chaotic verse, in particular, look very much like rough notes, hastily jotted down to be worked up later' (Chambers 1930, i. 482). But Chambers hastened to deny that Shakespeare habitually worked in such a chaotic manner: 'I do not suggest that *Timon* throws much light upon Shakespeare's normal methods of working. It is, perhaps, a subjective view that he dealt with it under conditions of mental, and perhaps physical stress, which led to a breakdown'. So, after this life-crisis, Shakespeare 'seems to have abandoned [the play], and never to have taken it up again' (p. 483).

　　To anyone who has read the detailed case for a co-author's contribution already made by six careful scholars, it must seem that Chambers simply ignored all the evidence not suited to his biographical construction of a Shakespeare writing 'chaotic verse' on the verge of a nervous breakdown, and never returning to the residuum of that unhappy period. It is hardly good scholarship, needless to say, to take refuge in biographical speculations sim-

---

[16] E. K. Chambers, *William Shakespeare: A Study of Facts and Problems*, 2 vols. (Oxford, 1930), i. 481.

ply to avoid an awkward issue. It is particularly disappointing that Chambers himself should have described the chaos of styles in some scenes of *Timon* in terms that exactly echoed those made by two Middleton scholars identifying this characteristic feature of his early plays, yet refused to acknowledge the strength of this evidence of a second hand at work. It is also regrettable that Chambers did not refer to Delius's 1867 essay, which cogently refuted the theory of *Timon* being an unfinished play, the 'completed' and 'uncompleted' parts being so thoroughly intertwined. Predictably enough, many Shakespearians approved of Chambers reviving this older theory of an unfinished play, for it provided an easy answer to anyone tempted to propose a co-author. Una Ellis-Fermor developed the Chambers position in 1942, in an often-cited essay,[17] arguing that the large number of 'broken and irregular lines, the patchwork effect' of many speeches are the normal signs of a writer 'roughing out a scene' (Ellis-Fermor 1961, p. 163). In order to show 'the characteristics of these broken speeches', Ellis-Fermor quoted from Alcibiades' speech to the Athenian senators (3.5.38–58), a passage which includes several irregular lines and four rhymed couplets (45–6, 52–7), arguing that this 'preliminary rush of isolated fragments' was a common experience for anyone who 'has ever written blank verse' (p. 165). This claim left Ellis-Fermor open to the objection that arrived, with some delay, from David Lake, who declared her theory 'fantastic. In my own experience as a practitioner of verse (and I have written hundreds of lines of couplets and unrhymed verse), couplets are not a prelude to any tolerable kind of blank verse—indeed, they block the development of run-on blank verse of the kind used by Shakespeare about the presumed date of *Timon* (*c*.1607)', and which are found in *Timon* 'in the clearly Shakespearean sections such as 1.1.1–176'.[18]

As that riposte shows, the theory of *Timon* being an unfinished play forces critics to ignore the many visible differences between some parts of the play and others, differences which Knight, Delius, Fleay, Wright, Wells, and Sykes had defined by a number of scholarly approaches—metre, the proportion of rhyme, unmotivated oscillations between verse and prose, verbal parallels, linguistic preferences, orthography, even bibliographical variants—and which two of them had shown to typify, respectively, Middleton and Shakespeare. But upholders of 'Shakespeare the Non-collaborator' have never had any difficulty in ignoring unwelcome evidence, as the editors of the two major scholarly editions in modern times showed, J. C. Maxwell in his 'New Cambridge edition' (1957), and H. J. Oliver in his volume for the 'New Arden' Shakespeare (1959).[19] Maxwell devoted only three pages (pp. ix–xi)

---

[17] Una Ellis-Fermor, '*Timon of Athens*: An Unfinished Play', in Ellis-Fermor, *Shakespeare the Dramatist* (London, 1961), pp. 158–76; originally in *RES* 18 (1942): 270–83.

[18] D. J. Lake, *The Canon of Thomas Middleton's Plays* (Cambridge, 1975), pp. 279–80.

[19] H. J. Oliver (ed.), *Timon of Athens*, New Arden Shakespeare (London, 1959; rev. edn. 1963).

to the arguments for co-authorship—or, as he called it, 'disintegration'. He briefly alluded to the main lines of two opposed theories (Shakespeare rewriting an earlier play, or being in turn rewritten), but cited none of the detailed evidence that had accumulated from Knight in 1849, Delius in 1867, and on up to Sykes in 1924 concerning the strikingly discrepant treatment of prose and verse—clearly distinguished in Shakespeare's scenes, but in the scenes ascribed to Middleton mixed with each other, and with rhymes. In his dismissal of the authorship issue Maxwell never even mentioned the essays by Knight, Delius, Fleay, Wells, and Sykes, even though the last two scholars published in *Notes and Queries*, the journal of which Maxwell was co-editor from 1959 to 1976.[20] Nor did he draw the reader's attention to the play's high proportion of rhyme, which is completely unlike any authentic play by Shakespeare at this point in his career. Maxwell did mention E. H. Wright's 1910 monograph, even including it in his bibliography (1957, pp. x, 100), but he never cited it, and certainly did not mention that Wright, like the five other scholars who had investigated the co-authorship issue, had distinguished two different authors in terms of style, characterization, and dramaturgy. Maxwell dismissed Wright's book in the manner of E. K. Chambers, trying to make it seem self-defeating,[21] before observing that in the authorship debate 'the tide soon began to turn' against acknowledging any 'non-Shakespearian matter' in the play (p. xi)—a metaphor favoured by the 'fundamentalist' camp. Maxwell declared that the Chambers/Ellis-Fermor theory of the play being 'a Shakespearian rough draft that had never been completed' is now 'generally accepted'.

But although Maxwell totally rejected the case for co-authorship in the Introduction, his notes reveal some tensions. He several times cited specific Middleton parallels, as for the ellipsis in Timon's sententious observation that

'Tis not enough to help the feeble up,
But to support him after

(1.1.110–11)

—the 'But' implying 'but it is necessary to'—where he quoted a passage in Middleton (*More Dissemblers besides Women*, 1.3.38–9):

'Tis not enough for tapers to burn bright,
But to be seen.

Maxwell scrupulously recorded that this parallel was cited by H. D. Sykes in *Notes and Queries*, 1 (1923): 167, 'who attributes the *Tim.* passage to

---

[20] See the memoirs in *NQ* 221 (1976): 194–7 following his accidental death.

[21] 'But by the very thoroughness of his analysis, Wright demonstrated the weakness of his theory. A second writer had been called in to remove irregularities and inconsistencies in the play as Shakespeare left it, but all the irregularities and inconsistencies which Wright detected arose, according to him, precisely from the process of addition and revision' (p. x).

Middleton' (p. 107). On the one hand, since Maxwell gave his readers no information either as to the number of parallels cited by Sykes or to the full argument for Middleton's presence, this brief acknowledgement lessened Sykes's credibility. But on the other hand, the fact that Maxwell thought it worth recording, adding another Middleton instance, shows that it had aroused some agreement in him. Maxwell noted that Sykes attributed to the co-author 3.5, Alcibiades' fruitless appeal to the Senate (not observing that Knight, Delius, Fleay, and Wright had also done so), and he took over another Middleton parallel, between a Senator's complaint against Alcibiades,

> Your words have took such pains as if they laboured
> To bring manslaughter into form

$$(3.5.26–7)$$

—that is, an acceptable legal form or procedure—and a passage that Sykes had cited from Middleton's *Phoenix* (4.1.6–9): 'I'll strive to bring this act into such form | And credit among men ...'. Maxwell added several other Middleton parallels on his own account,[22] including a suggestive resemblance in one of the dunning scenes that we may confidently ascribe to Middleton, Sempronius' aggrieved remark:

> I was the first man
> That e'er received gift from him
> And does he think so backwardly of me now,
> That I'll requite it last?

$$(3.3.16–19)$$

which he compared to *The Phoenix*, 1.1.47: 'I did not think so unfashionably of you'. Finally, since Maxwell had at least read the work of Wright, who showed how the non-Shakespearian scenes jumble prose, verse, and rhyme indiscriminately, it is revealing that he should ignore that point and in his own edition strive to regularize the prose/verse distinction in scenes that we can attribute to Middleton, even following Alexander Pope's notorious attempts to regularize Shakespeare's verse.[23] Maxwell's silence on this issue is a disappointing exception to his otherwise open-minded scholarship.

The other major edition, two years later, by H. J. Oliver for the New Arden series, showed again how Shakespearians can be encouraged to close their mind on the question of co-authorship. Following the example of Chambers, Oliver lumped together all the candidates proposed as co-author, including an obviously dotty claim that the play was an allegory of Francis Bacon's treatment of Essex, and asserted that 'the various theories identifying the

---

[22] Cf. pp. 121 (on an ellipsis at 2.2.18 and in Middleton), 127 (on 2.2.224, a similar usage in *The Phoenix*).

[23] See e.g. p. 133, on 3.4.2–9, 13–17; and pp. 160–1, on 4.3.464, 471–4, 477, 512: twice here Maxwell adopts emendations from Pope, transposing prose into regular verse.

co-author also cancelled each other out, of course' (Oliver 1959, pp. xxii–xxiii)—of course. Like Chambers, Oliver did not deign to quote any of the many parallels already provided between the Middleton scenes and Middleton's known work, and he erroneously reported that proponents of co-authorship assigned 1.1 and 2.2 to Middleton.[24] In any case, Oliver decided, 'such theories defeated their own object', for they began by wanting 'to explain the presence in the play of "inferior" work and almost without exception ended up by assigning to Shakespeare's collaborator some of the best scenes in the play (e.g. the first three of Act 3) as well as parts that were crucial in the plot (such as 2.2)' (p. xxii). That remark was intended to make these eccentric theorists look ridiculous, but the fact that Oliver liked the dunning scenes in Act 3 does not mean that they must have been written by Shakespeare, and he breezily ignored the extraordinary number of parallels drawn by Wells and Sykes with Middleton's speciality, dunning scenes (after all, Middleton was a pioneer in Jacobean city comedy from whom Shakespeare could learn). Again, the fact that 2.2 is essential to the action only means that the co-authors had worked out their plot properly, and those scholars who claim part of it for Middleton (perhaps lines 1–45, 120–233) also detect Shakespeare's hand. Boosted by his own assertiveness, Oliver simply dismissed all the verbal parallels, claiming that 'the *Oxford English Dictionary* has . . . shown most of this alleged evidence in a new light and has made it impossible to believe any longer that most of the words quoted were in fact characteristic of one dramatist'. This was a particularly devious statement, for of course Wells and Sykes had access to the *OED*, and when discussing individual words they were careful to document their presence in Middleton and their (frequent) absence in Shakespeare. But in any case, they mostly quoted much longer verbal collocations, even whole sentences, syntactical or idiomatic constructions which went far beyond the scale of single words, and showed them to be indeed characteristic of Middleton. Sweeping away all unwelcome evidence for co-authorship, Oliver fell back on the Chambers case for the play being unfinished, only disagreeing with Sir Edmund's claim that this mode of composition was abnormal for Shakespeare, the product of a mind on the verge of a nervous breakdown. Rather, Oliver countered,

Timon would suggest that thoughts often came to him in a kind of incomplete verse form, sometimes in prose and sometimes (interestingly) in rhyme, and that only on revision did the text evolve into, predominantly, blank verse. (p. xxviii)

Once again we see that a 'Shakespeare sole author' case, while consciously denying the evidence that Middleton regularly wrote in a jumble of verse

---

[24] Oliver's lack of concern for authorship matters can be seen in his report that Charles Knight argued that *Timon* is 'a reworking by another dramatist of a tragedy originally by Shakespeare' (1959, p. xxii), when Knight argued the opposite case.

forms, is often forced to make other speculations, here biographical. Oliver somehow knew that Shakespeare's 'thoughts often came to him in a kind of incomplete verse form', and he even added a further deduction, that the dramatist 'wrote scenes as he felt in the mood for them, not bothering to complete one if at the minute he was more interested in another'. Theories of this generality, and generosity, can be used to account for any kind of anomaly in any text, and are fundamentally unscholarly.

Another editor who could not reconcile the oddities he noticed in *Timon of Athens* with Shakespeare's normal compositional practices was G. R. Hibbard, in his New Penguin edition.[25] Hibbard noted several respects in which the play differed from other Shakespeare tragedies: the hero is alive when we last see him, leaving the stage 'on his own two feet' (Hibbard 1970, p. 7); he is a socially isolated character, having neither 'close personal relationships' nor friends (pp. 8–9); we know nothing of Timon's past, indeed he is 'the most generalized of all the tragic heroes' (pp. 9–10); the play 'comes much closer to fable and parable than does any other of the tragedies' (p. 11). These are all justified observations on the peculiarities of the play's plot, which (I suggest) proved an inauspicious choice for dramatic treatment. Hibbard also noted deficiencies in the play's dramaturgy. The way in which Alcibiades 'is incorporated into the general design is far from satisfactory', he judged (p. 13). In his first appearance (1.1) he is a minor character, but in 3.5 'he suddenly and quite unexpectedly assumes a major role as he confronts the Senate and pleads passionately for the life of his friend. Viewed in isolation, the scene is highly dramatic, quite the most exciting thing in the play so far, but it loses some of the impact that it ought to make, because it has not been prepared for' (p. 13). The 'whole incident remains tantalizing and obscure when it ought to be explicit, for it is of considerable structural importance' in suggesting that the ingratitude shown to Timon by the rulers of Athens is a recurrent feature of that city (p. 14). Similar uncertainty, Hibbard complained, surrounded other key elements in Timon's relationship to Athens, the fact that he had performed the state some service (2.2.201–4, 4.3.93–6), giving it both financial and military help. 'Had we known' about these details from the beginning, Hibbard argued, we would have appreciated more clearly the city's ingratitude towards Timon, and the ironic reversal by which two of its Senators come to ask for his help (5.1.132–66), a scene as equally unprepared for as Alcibiades' petition to the Senate.

Something odd is happening when in a play by Shakespeare, who in the rest of his work is such a master in the art of plotting, it is possible to point to inadequacies in this respect that badly blunt the impact of what should have been two of the most significant scenes in the play. (pp. 15–16)

---

[25] G. R. Hibbard (ed.), *Timon of Athens* (Harmondsworth, 1970).

Hibbard listed other elements in the play's dramatic structure that he found 'otiose and irrelevant'.

Turning from the play's dramaturgy to its style, Hibbard complained that its 'writing . . . is uneven', in many places 'comparatively thin' (p. 16). Like so many scholars in the century or more since Knight and Delius wrote (although he cited none of them), Hibbard instanced several passages 'in which regular blank verse, what appears to be highly irregular blank verse, and what can most easily be read as prose, are found mixed with each other in an erratic and unpredictable manner' (p. 17). Hibbard pointed out that the scene between Alcibiades and the Senate,

though written in verse throughout, also has some unusual qualities. A high proportion of the lines are short lines, and the transitions from one idea to another are strangely abrupt. The firm yet flexible control of the complex verse paragraph which is one of the most impressive characteristics of Shakespeare's mature writing is absent from this scene. (pp. 17–18)

Hibbard was an experienced scholar, sensitive to Renaissance language, and he documented some striking anomalies in the play's dramaturgy and style (although, oddly, he did not notice the high proportion of rhyme in this scene). All these anomalies could have been accounted for on the supposition that Shakespeare had a co-author. Indeed, as we shall see in Chapter 7, it was precisely these uncharacteristic dramaturgical weaknesses that provoked nineteenth-century scholars to look for evidence of two authors at work. But Hibbard merely concluded that '*Timon of Athens* is not . . . a completely finished play', and that 'some scenes . . . still needed to be fitted in when Shakespeare laid the draft by' (p. 17). In his 'Account of the Text' Hibbard discussed the several striking discrepancies in spelling (Apemantus/ Apermantus; Ventidius/Ventigius; Flavius/Steward), 'which must go back to the manuscript' (p. 259), and briefly considered the 'possibility that Shakespeare had a collaborator', only to dismiss it: 'this seems unlikely in view of the consistency of the play's imagery' (p. 260). Instead, Hibbard fell back on the comforting idea that *Timon* 'was composed in an irregular manner', due to 'Shakespeare going off to Stratford, for example, and leaving the completed portions of the play behind him in London' (p. 261). Although he included a section on 'Further Reading' (pp. 45–9), which was even updated in April 1980, Hibbard at no point mentioned the studies identifying Middleton as the co-author. Hibbard's edition, excellent in many ways, is still in print, and one may well hope that Penguin, or its general editor (Stanley Wells) will soon add a note pointing out that, on the issue of the play's joint authorship, Hibbard, like so many of his predecessors, simply avoided the issue.

The orthodoxy of 'Shakespeare the Non-collaborator' undoubtedly proved influential on many generations of readers—indeed, I confess that the combined authority of the New Cambridge and Arden editions of *Timon* blocked me for many years from looking at the issue afresh. Yet, as we see time and again when anatomizing its defensive posture, it has shown itself to be not only conservative but evasive, ignoring genuine scholarship while clinging to a mantle of authority. Fortunately, the tradition of scholarly enquiry that has animated authorship studies proved its vitality once again in the 1970s, when David Lake and MacDonald Jackson, working independently on the Middleton canon, converged on *Timon of Athens* with a new set of methods. The effect of their work, as in several other instances we have been following, was not to overturn the authorship divisions made by earlier scholars, but to restate them with new force and precision.

David Lake found that the identifications of Middleton's share carried out by William Wells and H. D. Sykes made the case for Middleton's participation 'strong enough to warrant a careful check by means of fresh evidence', drawn from the Spevack concordances. Lake compared both writers' preferences in colloquialisms and contractions, showing that

through all his work Shakespeare prefers *them* to *'em* and *hath* to *has*; he makes very little use of *I'm* (only 5 authentic instances outside *Timon*) or of *'Has* for *he has* (14 authentic instances outside *Timon*). Middleton, of course, shows the opposite preferences and makes considerable use of *I'm* and *'Has*. (Lake 1975, p. 281)

The total figures for *Timon* show that the relative frequencies differ greatly from those of other late plays. 'The *'em*:*them* ratio of *Timon* is higher than that of any unassisted Shakespeare late play except *The Tempest*; the *has*: *hath* ratio is higher than any (*has* being uniquely more frequent than *hath*), and so are the relative frequencies of *I'm* and *'Has* (p. 282). Even more significant is the distribution of these features throughout the play. Accepting the Wells–Sykes ascription of Middleton scenes (1.2; 3.1; 3.2; 3.3; 3.4; 3.5; 3.6; 4.2.30–51; 4.3.458–536), Lake compared the distribution of these features in *Timon*, as presented in Table 4.4. Middleton's scenes have no instance of the Shakespearian forms *doth* and *moe* (for 'more'), indeed Middleton

TABLE 4.4. *Colloquialisms and contractions in* Timon of Athens

Ascription	Length	'em	them	has	hath	does	doth	I'm	I am	'Has	'tas	moe
Middleton scenes	897 lines	16	16	25	8	16	0	3	13	4	2	0
Shakespeare scenes	1,418 lines	4	50	6	21	8	9	0	27	1	0	4
Whole play	2,315 lines	20	66	31	29	24	9	3	40	5	2	4

Source: Lake 1975, p. 283.

never uses *moe*, and only uses *doth* once in each of his early comedies, and twice in *The Revenger's Tragedy*. Lake commented that 'the ratios of *'em* to *them* and *has* to *hath* are about normal' for Shakespeare's late plays (in *Lear* they are 9:45 and 13:49; in *Ant.* 3:52 and 22:43, respectively), and that in the Middleton scenes the ratios for these two features, and for *I'm*:*I am* are all within the dramatist's normal range (p. 284). Some of Middleton's linguistic characteristics, however, are underrepresented (the oath *faith*, the contractions *I'th'*, and *they're*), and one (*I've*) does not occur (p. 285). But of course collaboration does affect the styles of both writers, and 'accommodation theory' predicts that each will suppress some aspects of his normal usage while adapting to the other.

MacDonald Jackson, the most inventive scholar in attribution studies over the last thirty years, while also endorsing the authorship divisions proposed by Wells and Sykes, extended them in several new directions. He pointed out further parallels with Middleton's usage, for instance, the fact that '*shine* as a noun, a well-known favourite of Middleton's which Shakespeare uses in no other play . . . appears at 3.5.101'.[26] Like Knight, Delius, Fleay, and Wright, Jackson also diagnosed a 'stylistic unevenness' in the play which would be untypical of Shakespeare, for 'at times the diction degenerates into an uncharacteristic medley of prose, blank verse of varying degrees of regularity, and lurching rhyme' (p. 54), and he agreed with Wells and Sykes that this stylistic jumble was typical of Middleton's early comedies. Endorsing Sykes's observation about the presence of 'antithetical couplets' in the Middleton-ascribed scenes and in Middleton's known work, Jackson added (p. 61) that *Timon* also contains two instances of another Middleton trait, 'gnomic couplets of the kind in which one line begins with *who* (meaning "he who") plus verb', as in:

> And with their faint reply this answer join:
> Who bates mine honour shall not know my coin.
>
> (3.3.25–6)
>
> And this is all a liberal course allows:
> Who cannot keep his wealth must keep his house.
>
> (3.3.40–1)

with which he compared Middleton's acknowledged lines:

> O, they must ever strive to be so good!
> Who sells his vow is stamp'd the slave of blood.
>
> (*The Phoenix*, 2.2.23–4)

Like Sykes, Jackson cited a long passage of verse from Middleton (*Phoenix*, 1.4.197–227) to show that his style regularly produces what apologists for

---

[26] M. P. Jackson, *Studies in Attribution: Middleton and Shakespeare* (Salzburg, 1979), p. 59.

Shakespeare's sole authorship regard as 'Shakespearian jottings which remain to be worked up into fully coherent blank verse' (p. 61).

Jackson analysed the play's use of contractions and colloquialisms independently of Lake, but reached identical conclusions. He noted (pp. 56–7) that the ratios for *hath* and *has*, *doth* and *does* vary considerably between the Middleton and Shakespeare scenes, as Wells and Sykes had defined them, but in each case within the normal range for each writer.[27] Jackson then showed that the distinction between these two groups of scenes is further strengthened once we observe the occurrence of 'eight contractions, *h'as*, *h'ad*, *'tas*, *ha'*, *'em*, *I'm*, *e'en*, and *ne'er*, [which] occur uniquely or with unusual frequency for Shakespeare in *Timon*, and . . . mostly in those scenes in which the treatment of *hath*, *has*, *doth*, and *does* was found to be markedly un-Shakespearian' (pp. 57–8). When different approaches within authorship studies produce identical results, we can be sure that the methods being used are reliable. Jackson reported that all eight contractions are 'known Middleton favourites', but that even if one omits *h'as* and *h'ad*, the figures for the remaining six still support the division between the two authors. Proportionally measured, none of the 'one hundred non-Middleton plays' that Jackson studied had a higher total for these contractions than the Middleton part. Jackson argued that no one could 'satisfactorily explain this agreement between two different sorts of evidence except on the assumption that [several scenes in *Timon*] really are largely Middleton's work' (p. 63).

Jackson added several further tests, one involving the frequency of thirteen selected 'function words' in the play. Taking a thousand-word sample from each section of the play, Jackson (using a chi-square 'goodness of fit' test) compared it with three other plays by each dramatist. The Shakespeare sample turned out to correlate very closely with *Othello*, *Macbeth*, and *King Lear*, but not at all well with the Middleton samples. Conversely, the Middleton sample from *Timon* correlated very closely with *Women Beware Women*, *The Phoenix*, and *Michaelmas Term* (pp. 89–90). Moreover, 'the "Shakespearian" and "Middletonian" portions are extremely divergent from each other' (p. 90). Jackson achieved a similar result when applying his 'rare word' test, which showed that the Middletonian portion of *Timon* had 'proportionally fewer "rare" words than the rest of the play', and stood in a 'less plausible and clear-cut chronological relationship (as determined by an analysis of the vocabulary) to Shakespeare's other plays' (p. 155). In the 'Shakespearian' part of the play 'rare' words occurred once in every eight lines ('about right' for this period in his career) but in the Middletonian part once only in every thirty-eight lines, a much lower rate than for any Shakespeare play, and almost five times less frequently than in the Shakespearian scenes. Referring to the 'vocabulary index' that he had

---

[27] Jackson's figures (*hath* 29, *has* 33) differ slightly from Lake's (*has* 31), and also from those given by F. O. Waller: see Jackson 1979, p. 65 n. 15, and p. 66 n. 31.

constructed, Jackson found that the figures for the Shakespearian portion of
Timon would date the play to 1604–5, a date supported by other evidence,
whereas the Middletonian figures would place it in 1594–5, 'a ludicrously
inappropriate date. . . . I see no convincing way of reconciling this discrepancy between the "Shakespearian" and "Middletonian" portions of *Timon*
with the assumption that Shakespeare was sole author of the play' (p. 155).

Jackson's final piece of evidence unsettling that assumption was bibliographical, drawing on Charlton Hinman's work on the Folio, which showed
that *Timon* was printed by one craftsman, Compositor B, that the names
Apemantus and *Ventidius* were 'differently spelt and abbreviated in different
places', and that 'the variant spellings fall into more or less well-defined
groups'.[28] Since only one printer was involved, Hinman reasoned that this
variation must reflect peculiarities in the copy, for 'such patterned alternations inevitably suggest different hands', perhaps 'scribal or (as for various
reasons seems to me much more likely) authorial'. In other words, the compositor accurately reproduced the forms used in each author's manuscript.
Jackson showed that the variants *Apermantus* and *Aper.* occur consistently
in Middleton's 1.2, as do *Ventigius* and *Ventig.* (also in Middleton's 3.3),
whereas the Shakespeare scenes have *Apemantus* and *Ape.*, *Ventiddius* and
Ventid. (p. 213). Thus Fleay's observation a hundred years earlier was validated. Jackson (following J. C. Maxwell's 1957 edition) also showed that the
two conflicting valuations of the Greek talent corresponded to the authorship
division, 'the four unequivocal references to a "currently small" number'
occurring in Shakespeare's 1.2 and 2.2, while the four inappropriate or confused references occur in Middleton's 3.2. There are also four references in
the play to an inappropriately large number, two of which occur in the
Middletonian 3.1 and 3.4,

> the other two at the end of 2.2 within the dialogue between Timon and his Steward
> which prepares for Act 3. This short dialogue contains references to both small num-
> bers (2.2.230, 233) and large numbers (2.2.197, 203). The large numbers are only six
> lines apart, and each has the contraction *'em* in the line which precedes it; an example
> of the parenthetical 'say', which Wells pointed to as characteristic of Middleton,
> occurs in the same context. So there may be some of Middleton's writing in the latter
> part of 2.2, as both Sykes and Wells believed. (p. 214)

Where earlier scholars believed that Shakespeare, in the process of writing
Timon, came to learn the value of ancient Greek money,[29] we can now agree
with Jackson that 'Middleton was uncertain of the value of a talent, and that
he was responsible for the references to large and indefinite numbers' (ibid.),
while Shakespeare had a much more accurate sense of its worth.

---

[28] C. Hinman, *The Printing and Proof-Reading of the First Folio of Shakespeare*, 2 vols.
(Oxford, 1963), ii. 280–5. Lake (1975, p. 286 n.) had also cited Hinman.

[29] Cf. T. J. B. Spencer, 'Shakespeare Learns the Value of Money: The Dramatist at Work on
Timon of Athens', *ShS* 6 (1953): 75–8. Spencer accepted the Chambers/Ellis-Fermor theory of
the play being unfinished.

TABLE 4.5. *Exclamations in* Timon of Athens

	Oh spellings	*O* spellings
Shakespeare scenes	0	14
Middleton scenes	13	10

Source: Jackson 1979, pp. 214–15.

Jackson added to the varied and detailed arguments a previously unnoticed piece of bibliographical evidence which, as he put it, 'comes near to clinching the case for recognizing Middleton's presence in *Timon*'—many readers will think that case already clinched. This concerns the spelling distinction between *Oh* and *O*, which most sixteenth- and seventeenth-century compositors reproduced as they found it in their copy. Middleton, to judge from his holograph of *A Game at Chess*, 'strongly preferred the spelling *Oh*: in the Trinity College MS he uses *Oh* 36 times, *O* only once. Shakespeare, in contrast, seems to have preferred *O'*, as Jackson showed from an analysis of eight good Quartos, which have 'an overwhelming preponderance of *O* spellings', a total of 540 as against 31 of *Oh* (pp. 214–15). Since, as seems probable, the folio text of *Timon* was set from the authors' foul papers, it is likely to retain authorial spellings, as indeed Jackson's computation showed (see Table 4.5). Statistical tests show that the chances of this disparity being fortuitous are less than one in five hundred.

The combined studies of Knight, Delius, Fleay, Wright, Wells, Sykes, Lake, and Jackson, drawing as they did on an extensive knowledge of Elizabethan and Jacobean drama, using a varied set of approaches, and synthesizing impeccably scholarly work by other writers, have established Middleton's co-authorship of *Timon* beyond any doubt. In the Oxford Shakespeare, gratifyingly enough, Stanley Wells, who had been unwilling to recognize Peele's presence in *Titus Andronicus*, endorsed the case for Middleton's co-authorship, reporting that 'during the 1970s and 1980s strong linguistic and other evidence has been adduced' on its behalf (p. 997). Of course, the case is much older than that, for Wells in effect was endorsing the allocation made by his namesake William Wells and H. Dugdale Sykes in the 1920s. In the *Textual Companion* to the Oxford edition Gary Taylor described the work of Wells, Sykes, Lake, and Jackson, together with the still unpublished dissertation by R. V. Holdsworth,[30] as providing 'extensive, independent, and compelling evidence that approximately a third of the play' (38.7 per cent, if one

---

[30] R. V. Holdsworth, 'Middleton and Shakespeare: The Case for Middleton's Hand in *Timon of Athens*', Ph.D. Diss. (University of Manchester, 1982). In the *Textual Companion* (1987) Holdsworth was credited with a 'forthcoming' book, *Middleton and Shakespeare: The Case for Middleton's Hand in 'Timon of Athens'* (TxC, p. 128). I have twice attempted to obtain Dr Holdsworth's permission to read his thesis, but without success.

accepts David Lake's division), was written by Middleton. As Taylor summarized Holdsworth's case, based upon study of the whole Middleton canon,

Middleton's presence in *Timon* is indicated by the distribution of (*a*) linguistic forms, (*b*) characteristic oaths and exclamations, (*c*) function words, (*d*) rare vocabulary, (*e*) characteristic stage directions, (*f*) verbal parallels, (*g*) spellings, (*h*) inconsistencies of plotting, (*i*) rhyme. Holdsworth's investigation of verbal parallels for the first time comprehensively compares every phrase in an entire play with the complete corpus of both candidates for authorship; although, as might be expected, each author occasionally uses phrases which occur in the other's works, the great bulk of the verbal parallels, and all of the most striking ones, fall into distinct patterns, corresponding to the division of authorship already established on other grounds. The consistency of all these independent forms of evidence cannot be plausibly dismissed. (*TxC*, p. 128)

Two of the other Oxford editors, John Jowett and Stanley Wells, agreed that the case has been made 'conclusively', and gave some account of Holdsworth's authorship division (p. 501). Apparently, Holdsworth's researches endorsed the accepted attributions, giving Middleton 1.2, nearly all of Act 3—which the Oxford edition divides into seven scenes, making 3.4.103–117 (Riverside text) into 3.5—and 4.3.459–536. In addition, they report, Holdsworth assigned to Middleton 1.1.272–83, part of 2.2.118–233, and 3.7 (in other editions, 3.6), lines 1–36, 104–10. In fact, all of these passages had been singled out by earlier scholars as showing Middleton's hand. H. Dugdale Sykes pointed out that the brief dialogue at the end of 1.1 between two Lords who agree to go 'in | And taste Lord Timon's bounty' (1.1.273–4) links up with the scene following, by Middleton, where Cupid greets the host:

> Hail to thee, worthy Timon, and to all
> That of his bounties taste!

> (1.2.122–3)

And this in turn links up with the First Stranger's claim that 'I never tasted Timon in my life' (3.2.77–8), which may now be confidently ascribed to Middleton. Holdsworth's assignation to Shakespeare of 3.6.37–103 recognizes his hand in Timon's two speeches at the second banquet, first the mock prayer in prose, before the parasites are served dishes of warm water, followed by Timon's devastating denunciation in verse ('You knot of mouth-friends!'). The verse speech was ascribed to Shakespeare by Delius in 1867, Fleay in 1874, Wright in 1910, Wells in 1920, and Sykes in 1923. All five scholars assigned to Middleton the final sequence of 4.3, the dialogue between Timon and his Steward. Once again, more varied and detailed research at the end of the twentieth century has confirmed the findings of pioneers up to a hundred years earlier.

Although Holdsworth's main case for Middleton's co-authorship of *Timon* has not yet been published, he recently itemized some eighteen close verbal parallels between Middleton's scenes and *A Yorkshire Tragedy*, whose ascrip-

tion to Middleton now seems certain. The most striking of these is between
Alcibiades' sophistic attempt to exonerate his unnamed friend from a charge
of murder:

> in hot blood
>
> .   .   .   .   .   .
>
> Seeing his reputation touch'd to death,
> He did oppose his foe
>
>   (3.5.11, 19–20)

This situation, of a man 'goaded into fighting a duel to defend his honour',
actually occurs in *A Yorkshire Tragedy*, where the Gentleman prepares to
fight the Husband to defend his reputation:

> I am past my patient bloode: shall I stand idle
> And see my reputation toucht to death?
>
>   (ii. 166–7)

Apart from the resemblance between the two situations, Holdsworth could
'find no evidence that "touched to death" was a common idiom'.[31] Several of
the parallels Holdsworth cited (pp. 23–4) are indeed striking (*A Yorkshire
Tragedy* is quoted first):

> he that has no coyne | Is damnd
>
>   (ii. 28–9)
> moulten coine be thy damnation
>
>   (3.1.52)

> himselfe withered with debts
>
>   (iii. 11)
> Debts wither 'em
>
>   (4.3.531)

> pollitick . . . subtiller then nine Devils
>
>   (iii. 54–5)
> the divell . . . made man Politicke
>
>   (3.3.28)

> man . . . in the mire
>
>   (iv. 76–7)
> man i'th'mire
>
>   (1.2.59)
> [both are denunciations of drunkenness]

---

[31] R. V. Holdsworth, 'Middleton's Authorship of *A Yorkshire Tragedy*', *RES* 45 (1994): 1–25,
at p. 23.

I bleede for you

(ix. 14)

I bleed inwardly for my Lord

(1.2.205)

[in both *bleed* = grieve]

In addition to these verbal parallels, the general situation in the two plays is very similar, both protagonists being spendthrifts. The Steward in *Timon* laments that his master is 'so senseless of expense | That he will neither know how to maintain it, | Nor cease his flow of riot' (2.2.1–3), while the Wife in *A Yorkshire Tragedy* complains that 'My husband never ceases in expence', and warns that 'Ryotts child must needs be beggery' (ii. 2–5). And in due course, as Holdsworth puts it, 'having squandered their wealth, both are driven to vindictive misanthropy and despair by an obsessive consciousness of poverty and "desp'rate want" (*Timon*, 4.3.462)' (p. 24). Holdsworth made the case for Middleton's co-authorship of *Timon* so convincingly that we can look forward with some impatience to him publishing all his evidence.

At this point, chronologically speaking, one might be able to consult Marina Tarlinskaja's work on Shakespeare's metrics in the hope of finding an independent approach to the problem which would either corroborate or extend the work of these seven scholars. Unfortunately, Tarlinskaja did not study this play with her normal care, and she seems to have been confused by the rival claims of Winifred Nowottny (in a vague and impressionistic article)[32] that Act 5 was largely un-Shakespearian, and MacDonald Jackson's much more scholarly ascription to Middleton of 1.2, Act 3, and parts of Act 4 (Jackson 1979, p. 48). Regrettably, Tarlinskaja then conflated these heterogeneous analyses to conclude that 'the whole of acts III and V are suspected of not belonging to Shakespeare'.[33] She provided stress profiles for whole acts, but—unsurprisingly, given this confusion of methods—was unable to draw any firm conclusion (table 3.1, p. 101; pp. 195–6). Her hesitation here may also have been due to the fact that while she provided comparative figures for other Elizabethan dramatists, including Norton and Sackville, Marlowe, Jonson, Beaumont, and Fletcher, she seems not to have analysed Middleton's metrical practices. It is unfortunate that a book so helpful in other respects should have failed to treat *Timon of Athens* in the light of

---

[32] W. M. J. Nowottny, 'Acts IV and V of *Timon of Athens*', *ShQ* 10 (1959): 493–7. This is basically a discussion of moral and Christian 'themes', 'symbols', and 'world picture' in the play, towards the end of which Nowottny declared her belief that the play was 'the work of two hands'. She could find 'no compelling case for supposing Shakespeare to have written any more of Acts 1 to 3 than the dialogue of Timon and Flavius in Act 2, scene 2', and doubted whether Shakespeare contributed much after 4.3.464 (p. 497). These assertions showed no knowledge of authorship studies.

[33] M. Tarlinskaja, *Shakespeare's Verse: Iambic Pentameter and the Poet's Idiosyncrasies* (New York, 1987), p. 104.

modern scholarship, especially since the earlier study of pause patterns in Renaissance drama by Ants Oras also failed to follow up the evidence for Middleton's authorship, and only provided statistics for the play as a whole.[34] It would be a distinct service to Shakespeare studies if future researchers could apply these valuable techniques for analysing verse to the authorship division so clearly established by the seven scholars whose work we have examined.

However, some impression of the metrical differences between the two authors can be achieved if we return to the statistics provided by E. H. Wright, and rework his data according to the division of authorial responsibility which has achieved consensus in recent years. The information will not be perfectly comparable, since Wright assigned a much shorter part of 4.3 to Middleton than recent scholars would (Wright 1910, p. 56), and it is not possible to recalculate his data within a scene. That reservation apart, the metrical figures presented in Table 4.6 show a clear distinction, indicating that Shakespeare was more prone to use feminine endings than Middleton, and almost twice as likely to favour run-on lines. Conversely, Middleton used rhyme nearly six times more often than Shakespeare (this figure, 19.6 per cent, compares well with my calculation for *The Revenger's Tragedy*, 17.3 per cent), and produced irregular verse lines five times more often. All four tests clearly distinguish the two dramatists.

The division of authorship between Shakespeare and his co-author, solidly established by metrical and linguistic studies, was recently confirmed by Jonathan Hope's important analysis of Shakespeare's grammatical preferences from the viewpoint of socio-historical linguistics.[35] Hope first studied the use of the auxiliary *do* in *Timon of Athens*, that is, the degree to which Renaissance dramatists adopted the 'regulated' form, which is now standard ('I went home'; 'I did not go home', etc.). Hope had shown earlier that this grammatical feature, expressed as a relative percentage of regulated sentences, could distinguish authorial preferences: the regulation rate for Shakespeare 'never exceeds 84 per cent', while 'no other author shows a regulation rate below 85 per cent' (p. 17). From the statistical appendices, where Hope displayed all his data, we can see that the two Shakespeare samples (six early, ten late plays) showed an average regulation rate of 81 and 82 per cent respectively, while the Middleton sample (five plays) gave a figure of 90 per cent (pp. 156–7). Many scenes in *Timon* are short, and in statistical terms 'give too small a sample to be judged', but Hope found enough instances in 1.1 and 1.2 to perform a viable comparison. He showed that the figure for 1.1, 82 per cent, was typical for Shakespeare, while 1.2, with a figure of 90 per

[34] A. Oras, *Pause Patterns in Elizabethan and Jacobean Drama: An Experiment in Prosody* (Gainesville, Fla., 1960), pp. 68, 75, 88.
[35] J. Hope, *The Authorship of Shakespeare's Plays: A Socio-Linguistic Study* (Cambridge, 1994), pp. 100–4.

TABLE 4.6. *Verse tests for* Timon of Athens

Shakespeare scenes	Verse lines	Feminine endings	Run-on lines	Rhymes	Irregular
1.1	210	51	57	2	4
2.1	35	7	12	2	3
2.2a	46	11	10	2	3
2.2b	109	31	30	4	7
4.1	40	5	10	6	1
4.2a	29	8	4	2	1
4.3a	390	76	104	10	15
5.1	188	48	44	10	4
5.2	17	5	6	2	0
5.3	10	0	1	4	1
5.4	85	10	35	4	1
	1,159	252	313	48	40
Percentages		21.7	27.0	4.1	3.5

Middleton scenes	Verse lines	Feminine endings	Run-on lines	Rhymes	Irregular
1.2	156	24	19	32	24
3.1	16	4	4	2	2
3.2	32	7	6	4	4
3.3	34	7	5	6	9
3.4	72	7	7	8	12
3.5	117	20	18	30	20
3.6	18	2	4	4	1
4.2b	22	2	2	8	6
4.3b	13	0	1	0	2
	480	73	66	94	80
Percentages		15.2	13.8	19.6	16.7

cent, 'comes out as strongly unShakespearian and within the Middleton comparison sample range'. As Hope commented, the fact 'that two scenes of more or less equal length should vary by 8 per cent is strongly suggestive of there being two hands in the play' (p. 101). The figures for auxiliary *do* in the remaining scenes, Hope reported, 'provide broad support' for David Lake's division of authorship, with his claimed Middleton scenes having a regulation rate of 87 per cent, those by Shakespeare 83 per cent (pp. 101, 165). Hope commented that 'a 4 per cent difference is not clinching evidence', although of course the lower than usual figure for Middleton could reflect the well-known fact that authors collaborating on a text tend to be influenced by each other. Still, Hope added, the evidence from 1.2 'remains strongly suggestive of there being a non-Shakespearian presence in the play—and there is nothing in the auxiliary *do* evidence which would rule Middleton out from being that presence . . .' (p. 101).

Hope also studied the use of relative markers in the play, applying the categories he had described earlier (pp. 27–53). Present-day Standard English uses *who* or *whom* in connection with personal antecedents, *which* with non-personal antecedents; Early Modern English did not distinguish the two.[36] In the older usage, *that* could be used in non-restrictive relative clauses, and the zero relative could be used in the subject position, both usages that younger, upwardly mobile authors in Shakespeare's age would avoid (p. 28). Hope's detailed analysis clearly differentiated the normal usages of Shakespeare and Fletcher (pp. 34–40), but he recorded that 'Middleton's proportions of usage of relative markers do not provide a basis for distinguishing him from other early modern writers' (p. 49). However, when he came to study *Timon of Athens* Hope found that the relative marker evidence '*does* support the theory of collaboration', and that it endorsed Lake's division of authorship (pp. 102–3, with tables 5.10 and 5.11). The 'key feature' to emerge from these figures 'is the fact that the *who/which* distinction is almost fully observed in the Middleton scenes, but not in the Shakespearian—which is what the comparison samples would lead us to expect in a Shakespeare–Middleton collaboration'. The figures for Middleton were higher in one respect than those for his unaided plays, lower in another, both cases involving 'a shift towards Shakespearian usage, [which] either indicates that Middleton is accommodating' himself to his senior, or that some of the scenes that Lake (and others) have ascribed to Middleton are really by Shakespeare. Hope judged the 'collaborative nature of *Timon of Athens*' to be firmly established, but suggested the need for 'further work to improve the precise division of the play . . .' (p. 104).

It is highly satisfactory that Hope's approach, through socio-historical linguistics, should confirm the findings of nine earlier scholars, using a very different series of approaches, who showed the presence of two distinct hands in the play. Yet, however great the volume of research suggesting that Shakespeare shared composition with co-authors, the Shakespeare conservators still manage to avoid the issue. That witty and erudite scholar, A. D. Nuttall, in a 'New Critical Introduction' to the play,[37] followed H. J. Oliver in describing the variations in the spelling of Ventidius as forming the main basis for claims of 'multiple authorship' (Nuttall 1989, p. 31)—when of course this is a relatively minor sign of collaboration. Further, Nuttall conveniently

---

[36] Cf. B. Vickers, '*Counterfeiting*' *Shakespeare* (Cambridge, 2002), ch. 4.
[37] A. D. Nuttall, *Timon of Athens* (Hemel Hempstead, 1989).

ignored the parallel case of the spelling of Apemantus, not citing the demonstration by Jackson (whose work he knew, describing him in a back-handed compliment as 'the best of the disintegrators': p. 37) that the variants correlate with the authorship division. Nuttall then listed the names of some scholars in the authorship debate, siding with Chambers and Ellis-Fermor, whose 'unfinished play' theory 'is widely regarded as having finally routed the disintegrators' (pp. 32–3). Like every other defender of Shakespeare's sole authorship, Nuttall deigned neither to summarize the case made for Middleton nor to quote any of the parallel passages, merely stating his belief that 'the severest disintegrator cannot *confidently* banish Shakespeare from a single line or phrase' (p. 34). That is a challenging claim, but of course it is wrong, since Shakespeare can be *confidently* freed of responsibility for several hundred lines of this play. Nuttall concluded that 'The arguments for regarding *Timon of Athens* as a collaboration are too strong to be ignored' (p. 39), but his perfunctory treatment of them did just that.

The orthodox view continues to flourish, apparently immune to rational demonstration. Lois Potter, writing in 1992, could seriously cite J. C. Maxwell's 1957 edition as having 'succinctly disposed of' claims for co-authorship. Maxwell's view, we are told, 'which is also the consensus of the last thirty years, is that the play is an unfinished, but wholly Shakespearean, draft. However, the two-author theory recently resurfaced in the Oxford *Complete Works* (1968)' (*sic!*).[38] The question many readers will be asking, confronted with Nuttall's belief that Ellis-Fermor's 1942 essay is 'widely regarded as having finally routed the disintegrators', or Potter's belief that 'the consensus of the last thirty years' plumps for sole authorship, is, in what circles do these critics move? How is it possible to ignore so much scholarly work which challenges your belief in sole authorship?

The persistence of the Shakespeare conservators' denial of a scholarly tradition now dating back a century and a half is strikingly illustrated in the recent edition of *Timon of Athens* for the New Cambridge Shakespeare by the late Karl Klein.[39] This gives a brief and wholly inadequate survey (Klein 2001, pp. 62–3) of the scholarly tradition from the mid-nineteenth to the late twentieth century. Klein made no attempt to give a fair summary of the many linguistic features which have been repeatedly shown to be untypical for

---

[38] A. Thompson *et al.*, *Which Shakespeare? A User's Guide to Editions* (Milton Keynes and Philadelphia, 1992), pp. 164–5.

[39] *Timon of Athens*, ed. Karl Klein (Cambridge, 2001). Professor Klein died in 1997, and his edition was completed by colleagues at the Universität des Saarlandes. According to the publisher's note on the half-title, he 'establishes *Timon* as one of Shakespeare's late works, arguing, *contrary to recent academic views*, that evidence for other authors besides Shakespeare is inconclusive' (my italics): but these 'views' are 160 years old. Klein's all-too-brief discussion of the play's date (p. 1) ignored the many reliable studies of Shakespeare's chronology, verse style, and vocabulary, concluding that 'dating it will always remain a matter of conjecture'. He did, however, record the claim by F. Brownlow that it was 'written after 1614': no evidence would support this late date.

Shakespeare but characteristic of Middleton. He ignored the detailed work of William Wells and H. D. Sykes showing the presence of many Middleton usages in the sequence (2.2 to 3.3) dealing with Timon's abortive attempts to borrow money. He described Fleay (1874) and Wright (1910) as taking 'great pains to differentiate in detail between Shakespeare's authentic passages and those which they thought could not be his' (p. 62), without indicating the empirical evidence for their conclusion, other than that they judged some 'couplets as well as irregular and unscannable lines . . . *unworthy* of Shakespeare' (my italics). But their point, rather—following observations made by Charles Knight and Nikolaus Delius—was that such verbal features occurred far more frequently here than in any other Shakespeare texts of this period, and that they were in themselves distinctly different from Shakespeare's usage. Klein paid a little more attention to the work of Lake and Jackson, granting them 'more rational' and 'more methodical proce-dures', but he still swept aside the remarkable amount of detail they assem-bled, since after all, however 'cogent . . . these patterned resemblances may be in detail, they include . . . only a small percentage of the possible elements of the text' (p. 63). But no, the stylistic markers identified by these two schol-ars cover many aspects of both Shakespeare's and Middleton's style in verse and prose, a large percentage of the significant stylistic characteristics.

Klein reserved most of his scorn for the discussion by Gary Taylor in his essay on 'The Canon and Chronology of Shakespeare's Plays' in the Oxford *Textual Companion*, taking exception to his general remarks on authorship criteria (*TxC*, pp. 77–80). Oddly, Klein ignored two further discussions there (mentioned above), Taylor's specific discussion of the *Timon* authorship issue (pp. 127–8), and the remarks of Stanley Wells and John Jowett prefixed to the Textual Notes on the play (pp. 501–2), both of which add detail, and give more (albeit incomplete) information concerning the scholarly literature on the authorship question. Klein quoted Taylor's statement that ' "unusual mix-tures of rhyme, irregular verse, and prose in the suspect scenes of *Timon*" sub-stantiate a claim regarding authorship, since they "resist rationalization" ', but he complained that 'the Oxford editors give no clue as to why these met-rical anomalies, if such they be, should point towards Middleton . . .' (Klein 2001, p. 64). However, if Klein had actually read all the secondary literature he cited, he would have seen that critics have time and again observed that the 'aimless' shifting back and forward between prose and verse is highly unchar-acteristic of Shakespeare at any period, who regularly establishes clear-cut conventions for the two media, and sticks to them, but that it is found fre-quently in Middleton, together with the scattering of moralistic couplets *ad libitum* throughout the text. These observations were made, with an impres-sive agreement about the scenes where such a mélange occurs, by a whole series of critics: Delius (1867), Fleay (1874), Wright (1910), Sykes (1924), Chambers (1930), and Jackson (1979). As we have seen, later scholars have evolved many new tests, including verbal contractions, function words, exclamations, speech headings, and several grammatical features. It is particularly disappointing that Professor Klein did not cite Jonathan Hope's ground-breaking study, published by Cambridge University Press in 1994.

Having failed either to report or evaluate this scholarly tradition adequately, Klein endorsed the theory, which he believed was 'first proposed by Wilhelm Wendlandt' in 1888, and given 'its most powerful and persuasive presentation by Una Ellis-Fermor' in 1942, that *Timon* is an unfinished play (pp. 65–6). However, this theory had been discussed by Nikolaus Delius in 1846, by Charles Knight in 1849, and Delius again in 1867, both of whom rejected it. Knight observed that 'the differences of style . . . prevailing in the successive scenes of this drama' indicated the presence of two hands, easily distinguishable by regularly recurring linguistic features, and that *Timon* contains 'parts not only out of harmony with the drama as a whole . . . but altogether different from anything [Shakespeare] had himself produced in his early, his mature, or his later years' (Knight 1849, pp. 70, 76). In 1846 Delius had already dismissed the 'unfinished play' argument by pointing to the 'striking contrast in style, versification, and characterization that occurs throughout the whole drama', with 'the weaker passages'—or those standing 'in glaring contradiction' to the other style—being not limited to one part of the play but alternating throughout. Delius found it inconceivable that Shakespeare could have left the 'finished' and 'unfinished' parts so inextricably intertwined (Delius 1867, pp. 335–6). It is regrettable that Karl Klein, reviving the 'unfinished play' explanation, should have failed to address the cogent objections made by a German scholar one and a half centuries earlier. As MacDonald Jackson judged, this theory simply 'fails to account for the evidence' of two distinct styles in the play, one of which has all the characteristics of Middleton (1979, pp. 63, 89–90, 155–6).

With *Timon of Athens*, as with the other plays studied here, the impressive feature of authorship studies from the 1840s to the 1990s is that widely differing methodologies have converged, supporting sound attributions and discrediting others. The newer statistical methods build on, and should be taken in conjunction with, older approaches through verse styles, verbal collocations, and linguistic preferences.[40] All these methods agree in assigning to Middleton a substantial part of *Timon*, and Shakespearians who continue to deny this point risk forfeiting their scholarly credibility.

---

[40] M. W. A. Smith, in 'The Authorship of *Timon of Athens*', *Text*, 5 (1991): 195–240, applied purely statistical techniques to examining the case made by D. J. Lake and MacDonald Jackson for joint authorship. His methods (using a function word test, type-token ratios, and the first-word-of-speeches test) confirmed Shakespeare's part-authorship but left some doubts about Middleton's (pp. 202, 221–3). Since Smith limited his enquiry to statistical techniques, ignoring all the stylistic, linguistic, and lexical evidence for Middleton's authorship, we can conclude that stylometry on its own is not conclusive—as indeed Smith has frequently stated.

5

Pericles with George Wilkins

The first commentator to suggest that *Pericles* was not wholly Shakespeare's creation was Nicholas Rowe, who included it in his edition of the plays and poems (1709) with this observation: 'Mr. Dryden seems to think that *Pericles* is one of his first Plays;[1] but there is no judgment to be form'd on that, since there is good Reason to believe that the greatest part of that Play was not written by him; tho' it is own'd that some part of it certainly was, particularly the last Act' (*CHS*, ii. 192). In his edition of Shakespeare (1725) Alexander Pope brusquely rejected *Pericles* along with 'those wretched plays' of the Apocrypha, but in 1733 Lewis Theobald included it in his edition, albeit with a condescending note: 'This absurd Old Play . . . was not entirely of our Author's penning; but he has honour'd it with a Number of Master-Touches so peculiar to himself that a Knowing Reader may with Ease and Certainty distinguish the Traces of his Pencill' (*CHS*, ii. 413, 500). In the prologue to his *Marina* (1738), an adaptation of the last two acts of the play, George Lillo varied this image of Shakespeare's 'Master-Touches' revealing their author:

> We dare not charge the whole unequal play
> Of *Pericles* on him; yet let us say,
> As gold though mix'd with baser matter shines,
> So do his bright inimitable lines
> Throughout those rude wild scenes distinguish'd stand,
> And shew he touch'd them with no sparing hand.[2]

Yet not everyone shared this confidence. In 1748 Peter Whalley declared that the play 'abounds with many such palpable Absurdities' as to place it among 'those spurious Pieces which are attributed to Shakespeare' (*CHS*, iii. 277). In 1765 Richard Farmer thought it to be, like some plays ascribed to Plautus, one of those 'which he only retouched and polished' (*CHS*, v. 270).

The degree of Shakespeare's involvement in *Pericles* was the subject of a vigorous debate between George Steevens and Edmond Malone in 1780, in the two-volume *Supplement* to the 1778 Johnson and Steevens edition, which had not included the play. In that edition Malone had followed Dryden in assigning it an early date (1592) while doubting its authenticity (*CHS*, vi.

---

[1] For Dryden's utterance see *CHS*, i. 15.
[2] Cit. F. D. Hoeniger in his New Arden edition, *Pericles* (London, 1963), pp. lii–liii. I regret not having included Lillo's *Marina* in my *Critical Heritage* series.

190–1), but in 1780 he decided to admit the play since, having studied it more carefully, he found that 'the congenial sentiments, the numerous expressions bearing a striking similitude to passages in his undisputed plays, the incidents, the situations of the persons, the colour of the style, at least through the greater part of the play, all . . . conspire to set the seal of Shakespeare on this performance'. Malone quoted Farmer's more recent opinion that 'the hand of Shakespeare may sometimes be seen in the latter part of the play and there only', but disagreed: 'The scene in the last act, in which Pericles discovers his daughter, is indeed eminently beautiful; but the whole piece appears to me to furnish abundant proofs of the hand of Shakespeare. The inequalities in different parts of it are not greater than may be found in some of his other dramas' (ibid. 297).

Steevens countered that although Shakespeare's hand may be visible in several places, Shakespeare was not 'the original fabricator' of the play, but only its 'mender', having added some 'partial graces' to improve it.[3] Steevens cited the un-Shakespearian metre of the choruses, differences in vocabulary from the authentic plays, and the fact that Shakespeare seldom drew on Gower's works. In addition, he pointed out, the characters' names were 'almost unique' to *Pericles* (unlike the many others that recur in several different plays). What Malone 'called the *inequalities of the poetry*', Steevens would 'rather term *the patchwork of the style*, in which the general flow of Shakespeare is not often visible'. Steevens drew attention to 'one peculiarity' of the style which, he believed, called in question 'the complete genuineness of this play':

I shall not hesitate to affirm that through different parts of *Pericles* there are more frequent and more aukward ellipses than occur in all the other dramas attributed to the same author; and that these figures of speech appear only in such worthless portions of the dialogue as cannot with justice be imputed to him. Were the play the work of any single hand it is natural to suppose that this clipt jargon would have been scattered over it with equality. Had it been the composition of our greatest poet he would be found to have availed himself of the same licence in his other tragedies . . . (Steevens 1780, p. 300)

That perceptive observation, both of the frequency of ellipses in the play, and their uneven distribution, was repeated by other scholars many years later, unaware of their predecessor. Steevens also pointed out inconsistencies in the way names are pronounced, as adapted to the metre: no 'individual writer' would have

called the same characters and places alternately Perĭcles and Perīcles, Thaïsa and Thaïsa, Pentapŏlis and Pentapōlis. Shakespeare never varies the quantity of his proper names in the compass of one play. In *Cymbeline* we always meet with Posthūmus, not Posthŭmus; Arvirāgus, and not Arvirăgus. (pp. 300–1)

---

[3] G. Steevens, Notes on *Pericles*, in E. Malone (ed.), *Supplement* to the 1778 edn. of Shakespeare by Johnson and Steevens (London, 1780).

Steevens concluded that Shakespeare revised a play by 'some inglorious and forgotten playwright', improving 'his dialogue in many places, and knowing by experience that the strength of a dramatic piece should be augmented towards its catastrophe, was most liberal of his aid in the last act' (p. 301). Steevens's arguments evidently influenced Malone, who in his 1790 edition revised his judgement, arguing that it was common in Shakespeare's day 'to alter, new-model, and improve the unsuccessful dramas of preceding writers'. Malone now claimed to have some (undivulged) 'internal and irresistible proofs that a considerable portion of this piece' was written by Shakespeare. 'The greater part of the last three acts may, I think, . . . be safely ascribed to him; and his hand may be traced occasionally in the other two divisions' (p. 536).

Modern study of the authorship of *Pericles* began in 1868, with an essay by the leading German Shakespearian, Nikolaus Delius.[4] Delius detected an 'evident disparity' of styles in the play (Delius 1868, p. 175), which divides into 'two fairly sharply defined halves', the first part being that of some preceding dramatist whose work Shakespeare revised (p. 182). Delius noted the uneven tone of the first two acts, unpredictably changing from the serious to the trivial and back, 'an oscillation of tone which inserts into the often jerky ['holpricht'] blank verse sequences of rhymed *sententiae* containing misplaced and inappropriate moralizing' (p. 185). The author of these first two acts had indulged his rhetorical skills by lumping together antitheses and hyperboles, not noticing that he was making one character tell another what they already knew (pp. 185–6). When Shakespeare picks up the pen in Act 3, however, all the rhymed *sententiae* disappear, together with the awkward and obscure diction, and a new economy and sensitivity of style is felt, as in the resuscitation of Thaisa: 'not one word too many, but each word hitting its target' (pp. 187–8). Delius noted some Shakespearian parallels to the last three acts, the Chorus opening Act 3 echoing the final scene of *A Midsummer Night's Dream*[5] (p. 187), while the brothel scenes match those in *Measure for Measure* in vigour and richness (p. 189).

Delius then proposed George Wilkins as the author of Acts 1 and 2, describing his novel, *The Painful Adventures of Pericles, Prince of Tyre* (1608) as a fusion of the existing play, *Pericles*, with material plagiarized from Lawrence Twine's novel on the Apollonius of Tyre legend, *The Patterne*

---

[4] N. Delius, 'Ueber Shakespeare's Pericles, Prince of Tyre', *ShJb* 3 (1868): 175–204. The translations are mine.

[5] Cf. *Pericles*, 3 Chorus 1–11: 'Now sleep y-slacked hath the rout; | No din but snores the house about | . . . The cat . . . | Now couches from the mouse's hole . . . | Hymen hath brought the bride to bed, | Where, by the loss of maidenhead, | A babe is moulded . . .', and *Midsummer Night's Dream*, 5.1.360 ff., *Puck*. 'Now the hungry lion roars, | . . . While the heavy ploughman snores . . . | . . . Not a mouse | Shall disturb this hallowed house', and *Oberon*. 'To the best bride-bed will we, | Which by us shall blessed be; | And the issue, there create, | Ever shall be fortunate'. F. D. Hoeniger cited this 'cluster of images' as proving Shakespeare's authorship of the *Pericles* chorus (1963, pp. lv–lvi, 75), but believed that the parallel had been first pointed out in 1939.

of *Paineful Adventures* (1576, 1607). Delius pointed out that Wilkins, while copying out large sections of Twine's novel, fitted them into a framework which retained the form of the play, and also preserved the names of the characters as in the play (p. 193), two points which a plagiarist unconnected with the theatre would not have observed. He suggested that Wilkins had written a complete play on this subject, and that Shakespeare rewrote the second half, his interest having been caught by the story of Marina (pp. 187, 193). The complete play then became the property of the King's Men, who allowed Edward Blount to publish it under Shakespeare's name. Publication of the play made it impossible for Wilkins to claim co-authorship, but he could at least compose a novel based on the play, eked out with material from Twine, 'as a surrogate for the play not yet published' (p. 194). This was a coherent and plausible scenario addressing the problem of priority between the play and Wilkins's novel.

Finally, Delius argued for Wilkins's authorship of *Pericles* 1 and 2 on the basis of the 'continuous stylistic, metrical, and dramatic relationship' between those two acts and Wilkins's *Miseries of Enforced Marriage*, published in 1607 (pp. 195–6). He summarized the play, quoting several long speeches in which the alert reader soon notices the same arbitrary switching from blank verse to rhyme and back as in *Pericles*. One blank verse speech of 24 lines in Wilkins's *Miseries* contains 4 inserted pairs of rhymed lines (pp. 196–7); another of 16 lines contains 4 couplets (p. 198), and so on. As a specimen of this unpredictable mixture of verse forms in Wilkins to which Delius drew attention, I select Scarborough's speech deploring his dissolute existence:

> What is prodigality? Faith, like a Brush
> That weares himself to florish others cloathes,
> And having worne his heart even to the stump,
> Hees throwne away like a deformed lump.
> Oh such am I, I ha spent all the wealth
> My ancestors did purchase, made others brave
> In shape and riches, and my selfe a knave.
> For tho my wealth raisd some to paint their doore,
> Tis shut against me, saying I am but poore:
> Nay, even the greatest arme, whose hand hath grac'd,
> My presence to the eye of Maiesty, shrinkes back,
> His fingers clutch, and like to lead,
> They are heavy to raise up my state, being dead.
> By which I find, spendthriftes, and such am I,
> Like strumpets florish, but are foule within
> And they like Snakes, know when to cast their skin.
>
> (2234–50)[6]

---

[6] Quotations are from *The Miseries of Enforced Marriage*, ed. G. H. Blayney (Oxford, 1964) for the Malone Society.

Delius observed that Wilkins's *Miseries*, like *Pericles* and the non-Shakespearian parts of *Timon of Athens*,[7] contains 'a mixture of prose, blank verse and rhymed verse without any detectable reason for the mixture' (pp. 200–1). The passages quoted from *The Miseries*, he wrote, show Wilkins's weakness for introducing 'trivial and tasteless rhymed *sententiae*' into a passage of blank verse, *sententiae* chosen primarily for their rhyme but adding obscurity to the utterance rather than point (p. 201). Delius then quoted a number of these awkwardly introduced rhyming antitheses from *Pericles*, such as Pericles' words concluding a scene:

> That time of both this truce shall ne'er convince,
> Thou show'dst a subject's shine, I a true prince.
>
> (1.2.123–4)

Delius drew particular attention to the fact that Wilkins often repeats his own rhymes within a few scenes: 'bred'/ 'head' (1.1.107–8), 'dead'/ 'head' (1.2.168–9); 'will'/ 'ill' (2.1.133–4, again 2.1.165–6); 'fall'/ 'burial' (1.4.48–9 and 2.4.11–12). One rhyme-pair links the two works, for Act 2 of *Pericles* ends with these words:

> It pleaseth me so well, I'll see you wed;
> Then with what haste you can get you to bed.
>
> (2.5.92–3)

while the final scene of *Miseries* ends with the same rhyme:

> And in your eies so lovingly being wed,
> We hope your hands will bring us to our bed.
>
> (2867–8)

Commenting on a reference in *Pericles* to 'all those eyes ador'd them', Delius glossed 'that is, "which adored them"', adding: 'this incorrect omission of the relative pronoun in the nominative case is, in its constant repetition, characteristic' of Wilkins (p. 202 n.). This perceptive observation, like the other stylistic markers that Delius identified in Wilkins, was not systematically developed until the 1970s, by scholars unaware of their pioneering German predecessor.

English Shakespearians soon followed the path that Delius had opened up. In 1876 F. G. Fleay could simply 'take it at once for granted, that the first two acts are not by Shakespeare', a conclusion, he believed, that 'the metrical evidence' alone would prove, for it shows 'so marked a difference between the first two, and last three acts as to render it astonishing that they could ever have been supposed to be the work of one

---

[7] It was perceptive of Delius to link these two plays, for as we saw in Chapter 4, Middleton had a similar habit of mixing up verse, prose, and rhyme.

TABLE 5.1. *Verse tests for* Pericles

	Pericles, Acts 1, 2	Acts 3–5
Total number of lines	835	827
Number of rhyme lines	195 (23.3)	14 (1.7)
Number of double endings	72 (8.6)	106 (12.8)
Number of Alexandrines	5 (0.6)	13 (1.6)
Number of short lines	71 (8.5)	98 (11.9)
Number of rhymes not dialogue	8 (1.0)	16 (1.9)

Source: Fleay 1876a, p. 195.

author'.[8] Fleay set out his data as presented in Table 5.1 (the bracketed figures are percentages). Fleay found the general difference striking, but in particular 'the difference of the numbers of rhymes, the proportion being 14 in the one part to 1 in the other, is such as the most careless critic ought to have long since noticed' (Fleay 1876, p. 195). As I observed earlier, Fleay's good ear for Shakespeare's verse did not extend to the prose ('it is scarcely possible to test the prose in the same way as we can the verse': p. 198), and he indignantly rejected all the brothel scenes in Act 4 as un-Shakespearian,[9] assigning them to Rowley. But he perceptively noted that the choruses given to Gower in Acts 4 and 5 'are in lines of five measures, and not of four, as those in the earlier acts' (ibid.), and he took seriously Delius's suggestion that George Wilkins was probably the original author of *Pericles*. Accordingly, Fleay appended

> an analysis of the metre of the only play of G. Wilkins which we possess—*The Miseries of Enforced Marriage*,—which will be found to coincide very closely with that of Acts 1–2 of *Pericles* given above, and which is more like it than that of any other play among the hundreds I have tabulated. There are in that play 526 rhyming lines, 155 double endings, 15 Alexandrines, 102 short lines, 14 rhyming lines of less than five measures, and a good deal of prose, which, seeing that the play is about three times the length of the first two acts of *Pericles*, gives a marvellously close agreement in percentage. (p. 201)

---

[8] F. G. Fleay, 'On the Play of *Pericles*', *TNSS* 3 (1876): 195–209; this study repr. in Fleay, *Shakespeare Manual* (London, 1876), pp. 209–23.

[9] 'These scenes are totally unlike Shakspere's in feeling on such matters. He would not have indulged in the morbid anatomy of such loathsome characters; he would have covered the ulcerous sores with a film of humour, if it were a necessary part of his moral surgery to treat them at all—and, above all, he would not have married Marina to a man whose acquaintance she had first made in a public brothel, to which *his* motives of resort were not recommendatory, however involuntary *her* sojourn there may have been' (p. 196). This last point still exercises critics and editors of the play.

Fleay did not disclose his figures, but if we take the play's length to be 2,868 lines, as in the Malone Society text, the percentage of rhymes in *Miseries* is 18.3, compared to 23.3 in *Pericles* Acts 1–2 and 1.7 in *Pericles* Acts 3–5. Whether that is 'a marvellously close agreement' I leave for others to judge; the figure is certainly far greater than anything in Shakespeare's output at this period. A pioneer in so many respects, Fleay was the first to point out, from a reading of Wilkins's novel, *The Painful Adventures of Pericles, Prince of Tyre* (1608), that Wilkins 'has many blank-verse lines in the midst of his prose', whole passages of verse occurring throughout the novel, and he cited several of them to show that 'very often his prose is in better iambic rhythm than his verse' (pp. 204–6). Fleay concluded that Shakespeare's 'work was not founded on Wilkins' play, but done previously and independently' (p. 208).

For many years there was general agreement that the last three acts of *Pericles* were by Shakespeare, although it was recognized that the printing of the 1609 Quarto was unusually defective, both verse and prose being mangled, and the text confused in many places. Some issues in the debate over authorship continued to divide critical opinion, such as the exact relationship of Wilkins's novel to the play, and whether Shakespeare revised an earlier play or took part in a straightforward collaboration, with a clear-cut division of responsibilities. Robert Boyle strengthened the case for Wilkins as co-author by showing that Acts 1 and 2 contained a large number of close verbal parallels both with Wilkins's *Miseries of Enforced Marriage* and with the scenes that Wilkins contributed to the play that he had jointly written with William Rowley and John Day, *The Travels of the Three English Brothers* (1607). Boyle identified several characteristics of Wilkins's style:[10] constant repetitions; a fondness for placing a negative before the verb ('I not love her sex'); 'the omission of the relative in the nominative', as in 'those men [who] | Blush not in actions blacker than the night' (*Per.*, 1.1.134 ff.)—a point that both Steevens and Delius had noted; and a tendency to use verbs 'followed by an infinitive without "to"' (as in 'Entreats you pity him', 2.1.65). Boyle also noted that Wilkins frequently echoed his own rhymes, as in 'relieve them/grieve for them' (1.2.99–100), which echoes 'greevous/releeve us' (*Miseries*, 1443–4), or even to repeat rhymes within a short space, as in 'grave/crave', which occurs at *Pericles* 2.1.10–11 and at 2.3.46–7. These are all suggestive observations, but with Boyle, as with so many earlier scholars, we lament the absence of system or method.

Such criticisms inevitably apply to the work of H. Dugdale Sykes, a sensitive and widely read critic whose work blended perceptive insights with an uncritical methodology. Sykes's sixty-page essay on *Pericles*[11] was a notable achieve-

---

[10] R. Boyle, 'On Wilkins's Share in the Play Called Shakspere's *Pericles*', *TNSS* 8 (1880–2): 323–40, at pp. 327–31.

[11] H. D. Sykes, 'Wilkins and Shakespeare's *Pericles, Prince of Tyre*', in Sykes, *Sidelights on Shakespeare* (Stratford-upon-Avon, 1919), pp. 143–203.

ment for its day, and is still worth reading, since much of the material he pre-
sented has been ignored by later scholars, especially those determined to uphold
Shakespeare's sole authorship. Sykes had studied the whole of Wilkins's oeuvre,
as then defined, using not only *The Miseries of Enforced Marriage* (1607) and
The Painful Adventures of Pericles (1608), but also the collaborative play (with
Day and Rowley), *The Travels of the Three English Brothers* (1607). In addi-
tion, Sykes drew on a short prose pamphlet, *The Three Miseries of Barbary:
Plague. Famine. Civil War. With a relation of the death of Mahamet the late
emperour* [1607],[12] and a collection of jests that Wilkins composed with
Dekker, including an appendix describing prison life, called *Jests to Make You
Merrie . . . [Also] the miserie of a prison, and a prisoner* (1607).

Sykes noted many parallels between these works and *Pericles*, including a
strikingly similar account of the famine given by Cleon in the play and by
Wilkins describing Barbary:

> But see what heaven can do! By this our change,
> These *mouths*, who but of late, earth, sea, and air,
> Were all too little to content and please,
>
> .   .   .   .
>
> They are now starv'd for want of exercise;
>
> .   .   .   .
>
> Those mothers who, to nousle up their babes,
> Thought nought too curious, *are ready now*
> *To eat those little darlings whom they lov'd.*
> So sharp are hunger's teeth, that man and wife
> Draw lots who first shall die to lengthen life.
> *Here stands a lord, and there a lady weeping*;
> Here many sink, yet those which see them fall
> *Have scarce strength left* to give them burial.
>
> (*Per.*, 1.4.33–49)

> God . . . sent famine to breathe upon them . . . so that they, that before durst not
> come near one another for fear of . . . the pestilence, *are now ready* to lay hold of
> each other, and to *turn their own bodies into nourishment. . . . They had once
> more meat than mouths, now they had many mouths and no meat.* O Hunger!
> how pitiless art thou! Thou hast heard children crying for bread to their parents,
> yet wouldest not relieve them, whilst *the parents went mourning and pining up
> and down* that they wanted food themselves. Men that were strong of body didst
> thou . . . *bring so low*, that *they could scarce stand on their legs.* (*The Three
> Miseries of Barbary*, Sig. D₂ʳ)

As Sykes observed, the two pictures overlap, both of them using the words
'mouths' and 'are now ready', both referring to cannibalism, 'while the parents *mourning and pining up and down* of *The Three Miseries of Barbary* are

---

[12] I accept the dating of this item in the revised *Short-Title Catalogue*, no. 25639. For the other
Wilkins works see STC 25635–8, 6417 (*Three Brothers*), and 6541 (*Jests*).

represented by "here . . . a lord and there a lady weeping" in the play' (Sykes 1919c, p. 167). The inhabitants of Barbary 'could scarce stand on their legs', being so feeble with hunger, those at Tarsus 'Have scarce strength left' to bury the dead, a detail found twice in Wilkins's prose narrative: 'the living were not able to inter the dead', and 'the living . . . were scarce able to bury the dead' (Sig. C$_3$^{r}, D$_4$^{r}). These parallel passages were cited neither in the New Arden edition (1963), nor the New Cambridge (1998), further proof that modern Shakespeare scholars have short memories. Sykes added another significant verbal detail, that the expression 'nousle up' in *Pericles*, meaning 'rear up, nourish', nowhere used by Shakespeare, recurs in the Wilkins–Dekker collection, *Jests to Make You Merry*, describing the human body, cosseted and preserved, 'yet thus *nusled up* . . . but for worms' (p. 168).

One other of the Wilkins–*Pericles* parallels cited by Sykes is worth quoting, since it shows Wilkins's fatal tendency to repeat himself from one work to another. In Act 2 of the play Pericles overhears a conversation between fishermen:

> *3rd Fisherman.* Master, I marvel how the fishes live in the sea.
> *1st Fisherman.* Why, as men do a-land; the great ones eat up the little ones. I can compare our rich misers to nothing so fitly as to a whale; a' plays and tumbles, driving the poor fry before him, and at last devours them all at a mouthful.

> (2.1.29–34)

Sykes (following A. H. Bullen and Robert Boyle) pointed out that part of this dialogue reappears in the Wilkins–Day collaboration, *Law Tricks*:

> *Joculo.* But, madam, do you remember what a multitude of fishes we saw at sea? And *I do wonder how they can all live by one another.*
> *Emilia.* Why, fool, *as men do on the land; the great ones eat up the little ones.*

> (Act 1 sc. ii. p. 25)

And, as Sykes pointed out, the same idea occurs in *The Miseries of Enforced Marriage*:

> These men like Fish, do swim within one streame,
> Yet theyd eat one another. . . .

> (1841–2)

Also, he observed, the comparison of rich misers to a whale which '*plays* and tumbles, driving the poor fry before him, and *at last devours them*' recalls another passage in *The Miseries*:

> young heires left in this towne where sins so ranke,
> And prodigals *gape* to grow fat by them,
> Are like young whelps throwne in the Lyons den,
> Who *play with them awhile, at length devoure them.*

> (1271–4)

In *Pericles* the fishermen develop the jest to a rather laboured conclusion, imagining that the whales might 'never leave gaping till they've swallowed the whole parish, church, steeple, bells and all', so that a man caught 'in his belly' might draw attention to his plight by making 'a jangling of bells' (32–43). As Sykes observed (pp. 169–70), in the same scene (1.2) of *Law Tricks* Wilkins recycled the joke:

> *Adam.* I know of one of that faculty (the law) in one term eat up a whole town, church, steeple, and all.
> *Julia.* I wonder the bells rang not all in his belly.

Sykes drew many other parallels between Wilkins's works and *Pericles*, claiming that he could 'demonstrate [Wilkins's] authorship of the whole of the first two Acts (including the Gower choruses) to the satisfaction of any person not obstinately determined to shut his eyes and ears to the evidence' (p. 143). He also believed that 'the rest of the play, though freely revised by Shakespeare, nevertheless contains a substantial substratum of Wilkins material' (p. 144). Although the second claim seems to me unproven, Sykes certainly established his first point, adding to the evidence from parallels in thought and language a detailed analysis of the 'outstanding peculiarities' of Wilkins's style, starting with his 'frequent omission of the relative pronoun in the nominative case' (p. 150). He acknowledged that Boyle had noticed this trait (as indeed had Steevens and Delius, earlier), but that no one had appreciated the frequency with which Wilkins used it. This 'ellipsis of the relative pronoun in the nominative', represented as [o]—or the 'zero relative', in modern terminology—he stated, is found 'in most writers of the Elizabethan period, Shakespeare himself included', but nowhere else to the same extent. Sykes had earlier listed some instances of the omission of the relative pronoun in the subject position in Wilkins's *The Miseries of Enforced Marriage*:

> . . . would I had a son [o]
> Might merit commendations even with him.
>
> (334–5)
> Divert the good [o] is lookt from them to Ill
>
> (351)
> . . . to see this girle, [o] shal be your sister.
>
> (680)
> Be iudge you Mayds
> [o] Have trusted the false promises of men.
>
> (852–3)
> The murther of a creature, [o] equald heaven
> In her Creation
>
> (953–4)
> Shame on them [o] were the cause of it.
>
> (981)

> . . . nor that you keepe
> The companie of a most Leprous route
> [o] Consumes your bodies wealth

> (1281–3)
> . . . that would not suffer him
> To kill our elder brother, [o] had undone us

> (2622–3)

And he cited another from *The Travels of the Three English Brothers*:

> But prove like those [o] resist to their own ill.

> (II. 15) (p. 81)

Sykes found 'over twenty instances of this ellipsis' in *The Miseries*, and identified fourteen instances of the zero relative in the subject position in Acts 1 and 2 of *Pericles*, quoting five of them:[13]

> Bad child, worse father! to entice his own
> To evil [o] should be done by none.

> (1 Chorus 28)
> . . . her thoughts the king
> Of every virtue [o] gives renown to men.

> (1.1.14)
> Of all [o] say'd yet, may'st thou prove prosperous!

> (1.1.59)
> . . . the sore eyes see clear
> To stop the air [o] would hurt them.

> (1.1.99)
> . . . those men
> Blush not in actions worser than the night,
> [o] Will shun no course to keep them from the light.

> (1.1.135)

In the third passage quoted he found 'a double ellipsis—of relative and auxiliary verb' (p. 151). Sykes found some of these ellipses 'uncouth', as for instance

> For flattery is the bellows [o] blows up sin

> (*Per.*, 1.2.39)

but conceded that 'Wilkins would not have found it offensive', since he created others just as awkward:

> Heeres fellows [o] swarme like flies to speake with you.

> (*Miseries*, 2397)

---

[13] Sykes (p. 151 n.) identified others at 1.2.39, 1.2.73, 1.4.74, 1.4.93, 2 Ch. 7, 2 Ch. 32, 2.3.55, 2.4.11, 2.5.53.

But prove like those [o] resist to their own ill

(*Travels*, 1.15)

Although the modern study of Shakespeare's grammatical preferences by Jonathan Hope (1994) will provide much more systematic evidence, it is fair to say that Sykes 'arrived at the right conclusions, though with slightly shaky counting, and fuzzy argumentation'.[14]

The second stylistic characteristic that Sykes pointed to, Wilkins's 'immoderate use of verbal antithesis, especially in riming couplets' (p. 150), was less distinctive, since the pairing of such antithetical concepts as soul and body, life and death, eyes and hands, is extremely common in Renaissance literature. Still, the argument of unusual frequency is valid, as is that of Wilkins's self-repetition, while some of the parallels Sykes quoted are suggestive:

> we are gentlemen
> Have neither in our *hearts* nor outward *eyes*
> Envied the great nor do the low despise

(*Per.*, 2.3.24–5)

> And tho I must be absent from thine *eye*,
> Be sure my *hart* doth in thy bosome lie

(*Miseries*, 316–17)

> How durst thy *tongue* move anger to our *face*?

(*Per.*, 1.2.54)

> . . . they have felt thy *cheek* Clare, let them hear thy *tung*

(*Miseries*, 672)

> Which welcome we'll accept; feast here awhile,
> Until our stars that *frown* lend us a *smile*.

(*Per.*, 1.4.108)

> If [men] prove true,
> Heaven *smiles* for ioy, if not it *weepes* for you

(*Miseries*, 286–7)

> That all those *eyes* ador'd them ere their fall
> Scorn now their *hand* should give them burial.

(*Per.*, 2.4.11–12)

> And in your *eies* so lovingly being wed,
> We hope your *hands* will bring us to our bed.

(*Miseries*, 2867–8)

As Sykes tartly commented, 'the range of Wilkins's ideas was so limited that it is no surprise to find' such frequent self-repetitions (p. 164).

The third stylistic characteristic that Sykes pointed out, 'the trick of repeating a word within the line' (pp. 155–6) may well link *Pericles* with *The*

---

[14] J. Hope, personal communication (29 Nov. 1999).

Miseries of Enforced Marriage, but of course this is a common rhetorical figure (*ploké*), not in itself distinctive. Sykes was on stronger ground when he discussed Wilkins's use of rhyme, echoing Delius's observation that in *The Miseries* Wilkins 'not only mingles blank verse and prose but introduces riming lines into his blank verse' (p. 156). Later scholars would systematize that insight into a valid stylistic discriminator.[15]

Sykes followed Fleay by pointing to the high proportion of rhyme in Acts 1 and 2 (24 per cent, not counting the Gower parts), far higher than in any purely Shakespearian work of this period, and he developed further Delius's demonstration that Wilkins constantly repeated the same rhymes (p. 156). In the first two acts of *Pericles* at least three rhymes recur within a very short distance of each other: 'fall'/ 'burial' (1.4.48–9, 2.4.11–12); 'seas'/ 'ease' (2 Chorus 27–8; 2.4.43–4); and 'grave'/'crave' (2.1.10–11, 2.3.45–6). Other rhymes recur across Wilkins's oeuvre: 'wife'/ 'life' occurs five times in *The Miseries* (112–13; 431–2; 652–3; 2044–5; 2464–5) and twice in *Pericles* (1 Chorus 37–8; 1.4.45–6); 'will'/ 'ill' occurs five times in *The Miseries* (350–1; 725; 827–8; 2736–7; 2774–5), twice in *The Travels*, and three times in *Pericles* (1.1.103–4; 2.1.136–7; 2.1.168–9); 'this'/ 'kiss' occurs four times in *The Miseries* (169–70; 396–7; 934–5; 2000–1) and once in *Pericles* (1.2.77–8); 'breath'/ 'death' occurs once in *The Miseries* (1859–60), four times in *The Travels*, and once in *Pericles* (2.1.6–7). Some of these rhymes are quite distinctive, and deserve quoting:

dead/ burièd:

> Your daughter,
> That begs of you to see her burièd,
> Prayes Scarborow to forgive her: she is dead.
>
> (*Miseries*, 880–2)
> Which of you shall refuse, when I am dead,
> For that I am a man, pray see me burièd.
>
> (*Per.*, 2.1.76–7)

consist/ resist:

> So that my griefe doth of that waight consist,
> It helpes me not to yeeld, nor to resist:
>
> (*Miseries*, 836–7)
> Welcome is peace if he on peace consist;
> If wars, we are unable to resist.
>
> (*Per.*, 1.4.83–4)

---

[15] Sykes noticed the same mingling of verse, prose, and rhyme in *A Yorkshire Tragedy* (pp. 80, 156), and can now be forgiven for attributing that play to Wilkins, just as Delius had ascribed the non-Shakespearian portion of *Timon* to him. As we have seen, Middleton indulged in the same jumbling of verse forms, and scholars now attribute both plays to him.

And Sykes (following Boyle) quoted a double rhyme shared by the two works, 'greevous'/ 'releeve us' (*Miseries*, 1443–4), and 'relieve them'/ 'grieve for them' (*Per.*, 1.2.99–100).

In pointing to Wilkins's fondness for recycling rhymes, Sykes hit on most valuable evidence, as scholars realized a half-century later. Some of these rhymes, he noticed, were 'false' (p. 187), the vowels rhyming, so to speak, but not the consonants. Twice in *The Miseries* 'we find "him" doing duty as a rime for "sin" ' (p. 158):

> . . . with one sinne,
> Done by this hand, ende many done by him.
>
> (866–7)
>
> My child, my childe, was't periury in him
> Made thee so fayre, act now so foul a sinne
>
> (910–11)

This false rhyme recurs twice in *The Travels*, and twice in *Pericles*:

> They do abuse the king that flatter him;
> For flattery is the bellows blows up sin.
>
> (1.2.38–9)
>
> How Thaliard came full bent with sin
> And had intent to murder him.
>
> (2 Chorus 23–4)

Sykes pointed to other false (or assonantal) rhymes in Wilkins, such as 'done'/'Rome' in *The Travels* (p. 187), 'men' and 'them' four times in *The Miseries* (717–18; 800–1; 2596–7; 2785–6) and argued that 'Wilkins is as likely to have been guilty, as Shakespeare innocent, of the false rhymes' in *Pericles*, 5.2, a short choric scene: 'run'/ 'dumb' (1–2) and 'soon'/ 'doom' (19–20), since the second of those rhymes resembles the earlier coupling of 'moons' and 'dooms' (3 Chorus 31–2).

All this detailed linguistic inquiry, it seems to me, provided strong evidence for Wilkins's authorship of Acts 1 and 2. But Sykes was less successful in his other main argument, that Wilkins's novel, *The Painful Adventures*, was in fact the source of the play (pp. 176–84). Sykes had earlier cited nine parallel passages from Acts 1 and 2 of *Pericles* and the novel, virtually identical in content and phrasing (pp. 147–9), but this in itself does not prove that the novel came first. Sykes interpreted correctly Wilkins's claim on the title-page of *The Painful Adventures*, that it contained 'the true history of the play of *Pericles*', namely that the novel 'is the true and original version of the story of Pericles used in the play' (p. 178). But it is highly unlikely that 'the allusions to Gower in the novel [and other] references to the play were added afterwards to help the sale of the novel' (p. 179), and Sykes never considered the simpler hypothesis, that the novel was based on the play. This explanation would have been within his grasp, since he rightly pointed out that in the play a banquet takes place at which Pericles supposedly performed 'sweet music', for which his host thanks him next morning (2.5.24 ff.), but that in the play-text as we have it no such incident occurs, although it is referred to in the novel (pp. 181–3). But instead of taking this to indicate an omission in the play-text, Sykes puzzlingly made the opposite deduction, that 'this incident cannot have found its way into the novel from the play' (p. 183). Sykes even quoted Collier's suggestion[16] that in several places 'the novel preserves bits of Shakespearian phrasing omitted from the text of the drama as printed in the quarto', before dismissing it (pp. 194–5). It was perhaps due to his theory of the novel's priority that Sykes claimed to find signs of Wilkins's hand in the last three acts, for, he argued, when the novel's text agreed with the play's it must mean that Wilkins had created the original, which Shakespeare had only partly effaced (pp. 193–7).

Despite his admirably detailed demonstration of Wilkins's hand in the first two acts, Sykes's essay lost its way once he decided that the novel was the source of the play. But his work deserved far more recognition than it ever received at the hands of the Shakespeare establishment. It was typical of E. K. Chambers's deep-seated conservatism, and insensitivity to literary criteria, that in his two authoritative-seeming volumes, *William Shakespeare: A Study of Facts and Problems*, he should dismiss Sykes's case, made 'on the basis of a stylistic comparison with other work of Wilkins', with the words 'there is . . . little to go upon'. But Sykes drew on four works by Wilkins, with a plethora of detailed parallels, and it is hard to know how much evidence the defenders of Shakespeare's sole authorship would need—if indeed they are at all willing to examine this issue with an open mind. Chambers announced that he did not 'feel any very strong conviction for or against a common style between *Pericles* 1.2 on the one hand, and the *Miseries* and *Travels* on the other',[17] a statement nicely calculated to place the issue in the realm of the undecidable and unrewarding. But he did concede that the play 'cannot all be by one writer', since he found 'an unmistakable difference of style' between the first two and the last three acts, the latter being 'clearly Shakespeare's in the temper and manner of his late romances', the former's verse not reading 'like Shakespeare at any stage of development . . . Many rhymed couplets are awkwardly interspersed, and there are only two-thirds as many feminine endings as in' Shakespeare's part (Chambers 1930, i. 521). Chambers discussed the many parallels between Wilkins's *Painful Adventures* and the play, concluding (with Delius) that 'the novel rests on the play, and on the play with Shakespeare's contribution in it' (i. 525). And he finally admitted: 'I do not think it is inconceivable that Wilkins was Shakespeare's collaborator'

---

[16] In his introduction to T. Mommsen's edition of *The Painful Adventures* (Oldenburg, 1857).
[17] E. K. Chambers, *William Shakespeare: A Study of Facts and Problems*, 2 vols. (Oxford, 1930), i. 522–3.

(i. 526), even though he had just cast doubt on Sykes's detailed demonstration of precisely that point.

The most valuable part of Chambers's remarks on *Pericles* was his application of A. W. Pollard's categorization of the 'Bad Quartos' as corrupted reconstructions of play-texts from the actors' memory. He described the 'extremely corrupt' text as 'a report, possibly with the aid of shorthand.[18] There may have been some omissions' (i. 520–1), Chambers added, emphasizing that 'we do not know what the reporter of the play may have omitted' (i. 523), and warning scholars to 'keep the reporter and his perversions in mind' (i. 526). The relation between the play and the novel was much clarified in 1933 by Sina Spiker,[19] who was convinced that 'Wilkins wrote his [novel] with a model in mind that corresponded closely with our known Shakespearean play—even the uncorrupted original of this play' (Spiker 1933, p. 552). Spiker valuably showed that Wilkins's novel 'makes clear a number of passages unintelligible, or at best cryptic, in the corrupt play that we read' (p. 553). In the play the counsellor Helicanus refers defensively to the 'reproof, obedient, and in order' that a counsellor ought to give his ruler (1.2.42), even though he has not done so: but this incident is fully reported in the novel (ibid.). Spiker listed other corrupt passages in the play which were clarified by Wilkins's full treatment in the novel (pp. 553–4), and showed that the play-text contained verbal errors (mishearings or misreadings) which could be corrected from the novel. In the play Pericles vows to keep his hair 'unsistered', while the novel has 'uncisserd'; in the play Dionyza accuses her husband of playing 'the impious Innocent', where the novel correctly reads 'pious'; in the play Cleon describes the plague in Tarsus as affecting 'Those pallats who not yet too sauers younger', where the novel reads 'two summers younger'.

Yet Spiker could also show that 'Wilkins' familiarity with the play was not thoroughly intimate'. He followed 'the general direction of the story, capturing many of its details, and was reminiscently familiar with its phrasing. Verbal resemblances there are a-plenty, but they are fragmentary and incomplete, quite unlike the parallels to the Twine version, where Wilkins, with the translation obviously before him plagiarizes from it sentence after sentence' (p. 555). Spiker identified forty-five parallels between the novel and the play, quoting a dozen of them, but pointing out that they were 'such scraps of speeches and such short passages as an attentive person might easily retain and record' from a memory of theatrical performances (p. 558). Several passages in the novel suggest the action of the play, the parallels having the 'characteristics of explanatory stage direction', or 'recalling bits of stage business

---

[18] Cf. also W. W. Greg's summary: '*Pericles*: Bad or Doubtful Quarto: 1609: From a Report of Some Kind, Perhaps Stenographic', in *The Editorial Problem in Shakespeare: A Survey of the Foundations of the Text*, 3rd edn. (Oxford, 1954), p. 187.

[19] S. Spiker, 'George Wilkins and the Authorship of *Pericles*', *SP* 30 (1933): 551–70.

as cues for action' (pp. 559–60). All this evidence suggests that Wilkins was 'describing a performance' of the play, 'very likely from memory instead of from a manuscript copy' (p. 560), for there remain several 'unintelligible corruptions in the play' that Wilkins's novel fails to clarify. Spiker took Wilkins's dependence on a staged version to prove that he could not have been the author of the original play (p. 570), and it was not until 1987 that the Oxford editors produced a plausible explanation of why Wilkins relied on memory in compiling these parts of his *Painful Adventures*. As Gary Taylor reasoned, 'the part-author of a Jacobean collaborative play need never have possessed a personal copy of the whole manuscript', and might not even have possessed his own 'foul papers' (rough drafts), if they had been used by the playhouse scribe to prepare the prompt copy and actors' parts. 'Moreover, once the play was purchased by a theatrical company they became sole owners', and would hardly allow loose copies to circulate (*TxC*, p. 557).

A somewhat unexpected insight into the double authorship of *Pericles* was provided by Charles A. Langworthy in two enterprising essays,[20] studying verse–sentence patterns in English poetry, and specifically in Shakespeare. Langworthy analysed the relations between the verse line as a metrical unit and the sentence as a syntactical unit, studying the varying degrees of parallelism and divergence between the two. In the simplest state, a verse line consists of a single sentence or independent clause. In the most complex, a sentence stretches over several lines of verse and can include an 'initially-incomplete-dependent clause line', a 'compound free-overflow line', and many other varieties of syntactical dependence (Langworthy 1928, pp. 284–93). Taking samples of 500 lines of verse, Langworthy was able to show considerable developments within Shakespeare's style between one early and one late play, *The Two Gentlemen of Verona* and *The Winter's Tale* (pp. 295–6). In a later study he applied his method to the whole canon, showing that 'the evolution of Shakespeare's style consists in both the diminishing proportion of parallel types and the increasing proportion of divergent types' (Langworthy 1931, pp. 738–47). He then established for each play a quotient, 'obtained by dividing the number of parallel types by the number of divergent types', and found that when the results were arranged in descending order of magnitude they correlated surprisingly well with the plays' chronology, as this had been established by quite different criteria, internal and external (pp. 747–8). The scale ran from *1 Henry VI*, with a quotient of 61.03—well outside Shakespeare's range—through *Two Gentlemen* (41.14), *Taming of the Shrew* (40.00), and so on, down to *The Tempest* (0.76), *Cymbeline* (0.61), and *The Winter's Tale* (0.47). Langworthy provided two significant results for *Pericles*, first a breakdown of his data, act by act, here

TABLE 5.2. *Syntactical quotients for* Pericles

Acts 1, 2		Acts 3–5	
Chorus	25.00	Chorus	3.71
Act 1	27.09	Act 3	1.83
Chorus	11.50	Chorus	1.00
Act 2	18.67	Act 4	2.22
		Chorus	1.17
		Act 5	2.66

Source: Langworthy 1931, p. 748.

set out in Table 5.2. As Langworthy observed, 'the quotient of 23.04 for Acts 1 and 2 differs so widely from the quotient of 2.33 for Acts 3, 4, and 5, that the hands of two authors are unmistakable. Indeed, about one-fourth of the difference would be sufficient to establish the contention' (p. 750). Secondly, Langworthy placed the figures for each part of the play within Shakespeare's overall chronology. The quotient for Acts 1 and 2 would place the play 'back in Shakespeare's earliest period', between *Love's Labour's Lost* and *A Midsummer Night's Dream*. That for Acts 3–5 would place it near *Timon of Athens* (3.08), *King Lear* (2.93), and *All's Well* (2.11), 'in the general period favored by the external evidence' for its composition. Langworthy's figures also indicated 'a strong probability that Shakespeare was the author of those parts of the Chorus associated with Acts 3, 4, and 5, with the exception of the brief Chorus at the conclusion of the play', although he acknowledged that parts of the Chorus 'are too brief for the best workings' of his analysis. Still, the difference in pattern they showed was 'closely analogous to the difference in pattern of the acts with which they are associated . . .'. Langworthy's test is hard to replicate, but it gives all the appearance of having been applied systematically, and demonstrates numerically what anyone can recognize in a close reading, that Wilkins's syntax was much simpler than Shakespeare's.

Between the 1930s and the 1960s a number of studies cast further light on the two authors involved in the play. Ants Oras, studying the internal pauses within the blank verse line in Elizabethan and Jacobean drama, discovered an enormous difference in verse style between the non-Shakespearian and Shakespearian parts. This can be seen from the statistics he compiled of the point in the verse line where pauses occur, reproduced here as Table 5.3. As the figures indicate, Wilkins made many more pauses after the fourth foot—typical for writers of an earlier generation—while Shakespeare made his greatest number of rests after the sixth foot. If we look at the 'first half figure' ('a percentage figure indicating the ratio of such pauses before the fifth pos-

TABLE 5.3. Pericles: *pauses within the blank verse line*

Title	Basic figures											
	1	2	3	4	5	6	7	8	9	Total	First half	Even
Pericles (non-S)	13	23	13	141	55	130	35	16	4	430	50.7	72.1
Pericles (S)		5	26	17	97	60	168	79	47	23	522	31.4	64.6

Source: Oras 1960, p. 68.

ition, i.e. in the first half of the line, to pauses after that position'[21]), we note that the result for Wilkins is much higher than that for Shakespeare. In order to relate this result to Shakespeare's chronology, reference to the comprehensive tables that Oras provided (pp. 67–9) shows that the figure for Wilkins's part of the play (50.7) correlates with that for four plays that Shakespeare wrote between 1596 and 1602: *Merchant of Venice* (51.7), *Henry V* (49.4), *Julius Caesar* (51.8), *Othello* (49.2)—in other words, this verse style would be quite anomalous for Shakespeare in 1607–8. The 'first half figure' for Shakespeare's Acts 3–5, however, at 31.4, correlates well with the figures for *Cymbeline* (30.0), *The Winter's Tale* (31.2), and *The Tempest* (33.6). The difference can be seen even more clearly in the graphic analysis that Oras provided for each part (see Appendix I). This meticulous study demonstrated afresh the wide variation between the two parts of the play.

A generation after Ants Oras, Marina Tarlinskaja confirmed his diagnosis that *Pericles* contains two distinctly different verse styles. Where Oras had studied pause patterns, Tarlinskaja concentrated on the variation in emphasis within the blank verse line, and several related phenomena. Her computation of the emphases on each syllable neatly differentiated between Acts 1–2 (720 lines) and 3–5 (598 lines), as can be seen in Table 5.4. Positions 2, 4, 6, 8, and 10 in a normal iambic pentameter are those of a strong stress (or 'ictic', as Tarlinskaja calls them), while the weak syllabic (or 'non-ictic') positions are 1, 3, 5, 7, and 9. The mean values are shown as S and W, respectively. As can be seen, of the ictic positions, the fourth, ending the first hemistich, is much more strongly stressed in Acts 1–2, indeed, 'stronger than in Shakespeare's other plays of the last period. Such a strong stress in position 4 ... was last observed in *Othello*' (1602). Non-ictic stresses are much the same for the first part of the line, but they 'display a maximum on position 7 in Acts 3–5, similarly with all other Shakespearean dramas beginning in at

---

[21] A. Oras, *Pause Patterns in Elizabethan and Jacobean Drama: An Experiment in Prosody* (Gainsville, Fla., 1960), p. 4.

TABLE 5.4. *Stress profile for* Pericles

Acts	Syllabic Positions									
	1	2	3	4	5	6	7	8	9	10
1–2	22.1	66.8	9.3	85.0	9.2	73.2	7.6	70.2	3.8	89.0
3–5	22.0	64.9	8.5	80.1	9.2	73.8	12.9	68.6	8.5	86.5

Acts	S (2–8)	W (3–9)	Iambic Index (S–W)
1–2	73.8	7.4	66.4
3–5	71.8	9.8	62.0

Source: Tarlinskaja 1987, p. 125.

least 1599–1600 (*Twelfth Night*)'. Thirdly, 'the iambic index of Acts 3–5 is close to those of all other plays' by Shakespeare written between 1603 and 1613, 'while in Acts 1–2 it is untypically high; such a high iambic index is found only in' Shakespeare's first period, in *Romeo and Juliet* and *Richard II*. Indeed, 'an iambic index exceeding 65 per cent has not occurred in Shakespeare's canon for 13 years, since 1594–95'.[22] Such anomalous results within the otherwise well-established chronology of Shakespeare's output clearly indicate a different author at work.

Other tests by Tarlinskaja revealed comparable anomalies. Study of the cases where a verse line is split between two or more characters, taking into account the place of the split in the pentameter line—that is, 'the final syllabic position of the preceding utterance' (p. 136)—showed that 'the proportion of split lines in Acts 1–2 is only 1.8 per cent, as low as in *Henry V*, eight years earlier', which was itself an exception (p. 143). In Acts 3–5, by contrast, the proportion (12 per cent) 'increases almost seven times', placing *Pericles* close to its 'chronological neighbours' (p. 143). This affinity is seen more clearly from her tabulation (here abridged in Table 5.5) of the place in the verse line where such junctures occur (in a percentage of all split lines). When Tarlinskaja computed the structure of line endings in the whole of Shakespeare's plays, Acts 1–2 of *Pericles* again emerged as anomalous, as Table 5.6 (abridged) shows. As its figures indicate, 'the incidence of unstressed and weakly stressed monosyllables in the final ictic position in Acts 3–5 [5.2 per cent] is three times higher than in Acts 1–2', but is close to that of other plays from the period 1606–9 (which range between 5.2 and 6.3 per cent). The low figure for the first two acts (1.7 per cent) reflects the 'more frequent occurrence of end-stopped lines', and would place that stratum of

[22] M. Tarlinskaja, *Shakespeare's Verse: Iambic Pentameter and the Poet's Idiosyncrasies* (New York, 1987), p. 125.

TABLE 5.5. *Places of utterance junctures in late-period Shakespeare*

Date	Drama	Positions of splits									Mean position	Number of split lines	% of split lines
		1	2	3	4	5	6	7	8	9			
1606–7	Antony and Cleopatra	0.2	0.4	0.9	13.5	16.0	41.8	24.8	4.2	3.7	6.3	450	18.2
1607–8	Pericles	—	—	—	17.6	12.9	35.3	23.5	8.2	2.3	6.0	85	6.4
	Acts 1–2	—	—	—	30.8	7.7	38.5	7.7	15.4	—	5.7	13	1.8
	Acts 3–5	—	—	—	15.2	13.9	34.7	26.4	7.0	2.7	6.0	72	12.0
	Coriolanus	—	0.2	0.5	10.5	12.1	30.5	32.1	5.5	3.9	6.4	380	17.0
1608–9	Cymbeline	0.2	0.2	0.5	13.4	18.5	37.1	23.4	6.1	2.5	6.0	393	15.4

Source: Tarlinskaja 1987, pp. 137–8.

TABLE 5.6. *Structure of line endings in late-period Shakespeare*

Date	Drama	Accentual Loss of stress caused by		Syllabic						Dactylic
				Masculine Total	Feminine					
		monosyllables	polysyllables		Total	Simple	Compound			
							light	heavy		
1606–7	Antony and Cleopatra	5.2	6.1	73.1	26.3	21.9	4.3	0.2		0.6
1607–8	Pericles									
	Acts 1–2	1.7	8.9	84.0	16.0	11.1	3.2	0.8		0.9
	Acts 3–5	5.2	8.4	72.7	27.3	20.7	5.3	0.5		0.7
	Coriolanus	5.9	5.1	69.8	29.6	22.6	6.4	0.6		0.6
1608–9	Cymbeline	6.3	4.2	69.7	29.4	23.7	5.0	0.7		0.3

Note: All figures given are a percentage of total lines.
Source: Tarlinskaja 1987, pp. 183–4.

the play—if it had been by Shakespeare—close to *Julius Caesar* (also 1.7 per cent), that is, in about 1599. Finally, the percentage of feminine endings in Acts 3–5 (27.3 per cent) is normal for the period 1606–9 (values from 26.3 to 29.4 per cent), while 'the percentage for Acts 1–2 (16.0 per cent) suggests either an impossibly early date, somewhere close to *Henry V* and *Julius Caesar* (1598–1600), or the presence in *Pericles* of another hand' (p. 197). In order to settle this point Tarlinskaja considered the possibility that the

TABLE 5.7. *Structure of line endings in* Cymbeline

Acts	Loss of stress caused by			
	Monosyllables	Polysyllables	Masculine endings %	Non-masculine endings %
1–3	7.7	4.6	69.1	30.9
4–5	5.2	3.7	70.5	29.5

Source: Tarlinskaja 1987, p. 198.

differences in verse styles within *Pericles* might be the sign of 'an evolution of rhythm within a play', only to reject that theory:

However, the more generalized rhythmical characteristics of a play definitely written by one author within a short period of time always indicate a more homogeneous rhythm or a smoother evolution than is observed in plays written in collaboration or reworked at a later date.

To prove this point Tarlinskaja divided *Cymbeline* into two quantitatively comparable parts, Acts 1–3 and 4–5, which yielded the data set out in Table 5.7. As we instantly note, the two parts are much more homogeneous than the two parts of *Pericles*, the last piece of evidence justifying her conclusion that 'the first two acts of *Pericles* were indeed written by another, probably earlier author' (pp. 198, 349).

Although Oras and Tarlinskaja jointly established beyond any question the presence of two different verse styles in *Pericles*, neither of them, unfortunately, applied their tests to the verse of George Wilkins (which should not deter some future scholar from doing so). But the study of Wilkins was carried on by other hands. In 1960 Kenneth Muir reiterated the stylistic difference between Wilkins and Shakespeare in more traditional terms, finding no definite trace of Shakespeare in the first two acts, but registering the marked change of style in Act 3: 'It is a thrilling moment in the theatre when at the beginning of Act III the voice of Shakespeare is heard, indubitable and potent, with a tempest at sea to match the storm in *King Lear*':[23]

> Thou god of this great vast, rebuke these surges,
> Which wash both heaven and hell; and thou that hast
> Upon the winds command, bind them in brass,
> Having call'd them from the deep! O, still
> Thy deaf'ning dreadful thunders; gently quench
> Thy nimble sulphurous flashes!

(3.1.1–6)

[23] K. Muir, *Shakespeare as Collaborator* (London, 1960), pp. 88–9.

As Muir says, such verse 'could have been written only in Shakespeare's final period' (p. 72), with its 'colloquial ease and magical phrasing' (p. 89), as again in Pericles' speech over the newborn Marina:

> A terrible childbed hast thou had, my dear;
> No light, no fire. Th'unfriendly elements
> Forgot thee utterly: nor have I time
> To give thee hallow'd to thy grave, but straight
> Must cast thee, scarcely coffin'd, in the ooze;
> Where, for a monument upon thy bones,
> And aye-remaining lamps the belching whale
> And humming water must o'erwhelm thy corpse,
> Lying with simple shells.

(3.1.56–64)

Muir wrote eloquently about the many affinities between *Pericles* and the other late plays, dealing with 'the restoration of the lost and the conquest of death by love' (pp. 93–7).

As for Wilkins, Muir (unwittingly echoing Fleay) showed that many passages in Wilkins's prose novel, *The Painful Adventures of Pericles*, are in fact 'concealed blank verse', using this fact to argue that they represent reminiscences of the original play-text, of which the 1609 Quarto is a garbled report (pp. 60–70). The possibility that Wilkins's verse passages might preserve parts of the original *Pericles* was also suggested by Geoffrey Bullough in his study of the play's sources, and he attempted to reconstruct long passages of 'latent verse'.[24] This line of enquiry culminated in the 1987 Oxford edition of the 'Complete Works', in which Gary Taylor and MacDonald P. Jackson published '*Pericles* by William Shakespeare and George Wilkins. A Reconstructed Text', which draws more heavily than is usual on Wilkins's novel (p. 1167), using it to provide phrases, lines, and indeed a whole scene not in the 1609 Quarto. It is unfortunate that (presumably) the Oxford edition's typographical fastidiousness prevented these two new co-authors indicating their insertions by the use of italics or square brackets, especially as readers had to wait until the companion volume appeared to discover what exactly they had done.[25] Still, at least the presence of Wilkins was freely acknowledged.

Other valuable work on *Pericles* came from scholars knowledgeable in bibliography. E. A. J. Honigmann, in his influential querying of the notion of a

---

[24] G. Bullough (ed.), *Narrative and Dramatic Sources of Shakespeare*, vi (London, 1966), pp. 358–9, and Appendix (pp. 549–64). Bullough found Acts 1 and 2 to be 'jejune, rigid, and apart from one or two passages, unlike anything in Shakespeare' (p. 350). Conversely, 'Wilkins's quasi-verse passages are un-Shakespearean, but they often resemble in style Acts I and II as reported, e.g. in the occasional use of an abstraction qualified by an epithet at the end of a sentence' (p. 359).
[25] Cf. *TxC* 1987, pp. 556–92, and my comments in *RES* 40 (1989): 402–11, at pp. 408–9.

'final text' of Shakespeare,[26] suggested that Wilkins 'threw together the prose *Pericles* (which on the title-page and in the Argument he entreats the reader to accept as the equivalent of a play, a most extraordinary proceeding) against the wishes of the [King's Men], perhaps because he felt he had a right in the play (as part-author?) and yet was forbidden to publish' (Honigmann 1965, p. 180). Honigmann presented new evidence of Wilkins's co-authorship, drawing attention to another work by him so far ignored in discussions of *Pericles* i.e., *The Historie of Justine*, 'newly translated into English by G. W. ... 1606'. Although purporting to be a translation from the Latin, in fact Wilkins had blatantly plagiarized from Arthur Golding's translation, *Thabridgment of the histories of Trogus Pompeius, collected by Justine*, published in 1564, 1570, and 1578. Honigmann endorsed the ascription of *Justine* to Wilkins, made in the *Short-Title Catalogue*, by pointing to some striking parallels between it and his other writings. In his *Painful Adventures* Wilkins ('an essentially parasitic writer', as Honigmann described him) borrowed a conceit from Sidney's *Arcadia*, in which Pyrocles describes Zelmane to Philoclea as someone who 'did resemble you: though as farre short of your perfection, as her selfe dying, was of her flourishing'.[27] Wilkins reproduced this conceit verbatim both in the *Painful Adventures* and in *Justine*, and recycled his dedication to the Latin history in his novel, in exactly the same words. Studying the links between these works led Honigmann to notice some stylistic habits of Wilkins not recorded by Sykes:

In the *Pericles* novel he repeatedly begins sentences, and clauses after a colon or semi-colon, with 'which' or 'by which', 'to which', 'of which' etc.; and he uses participial constructions far more than is normal in the same positions. Less significant, but still indicative, he has a partiality for starting sentences with 'this' or 'by this', 'to this' etc.; with 'thus'; with 'in brief', and other similar locutions. Examples of the two principal features ('which' and 'participial' openings) crop up on almost every page, as on p. 50:[28] 'Which name of Traytor being againe redoubled, *Pericles* then ... boldely replyed ...'; 'Which noblenesse of his, the king inwardly commending ... he answered ...'; 'Which wordes were no sooner vttered, but *Thaysa* ...'. (pp. 193–4)

Honigmann found 'the same striking mannerisms' in *Justine*, and, more important, in *Pericles*, 'where "which" openings occur in considerable numbers' (p. 195). Honigmann quoted two speeches showing this 'partiality', Pericles' account of how he had solved the riddle of Antiochus' incest:

---

[26] E. A. J. Honigmann, *The Stability of Shakespeare's Text* (London, 1965), pp. 178–80, and Appendix B: 'George Wilkins and *Pericles*', pp. 193–9.

[27] *Arcadia* (1590 version), Book 2, ch. 23; pointed out by Sykes 1919c, pp. 175–6. Sykes had recorded (pp. 174–5) that Steevens already identified three borrowings from *Arcadia* in Acts 1 and 2 of *Pericles*.

[28] Quotations are from K. Muir (ed.), *The Painfull Adventures of Pericles Prince of Tyre* (Liverpool, 1953).

Which by my knowledge found, the sinful father
Seem'd not to strike, but smooth. But thou know'st this,
'Tis time to fear when tyrants seem to kiss.
Which fear so grew in me I hither fled

  .   .   .   .

When all, for mine, if I may call offence,
Must feel war's blow, who spares not innocence;
Which love to all, of which thyself art one,
Who now reprov'dst me for't—

(1.2.77–95)

and this exchange:

  Cleon. The which when any shall not gratify,
    Or pay you with unthankfulness in thought,
    Be it our wives, our children, or ourselves,
    The curse of heaven and men succeed their evils!
    Till when,—the which I hope shall ne'er be seen—
    Your grace is welcome to our town and us.
  Pericles. Which welcome we'll accept; feast here awhile,
    Until our stars that frown lend us a smile.

(1.4.101–8)

In a footnote Honigmann drily recorded that 'the "which" test confirms the usual division of the play into two parts, Acts 1–2 by another, Acts 3–5 by Shakespeare', while adding: 'this "test" should not, of course, be taken too seriously' (p. 196 n.). However, a later scholar showed that it could indeed be used seriously.

The Arden edition of *Pericles* by F. D. Hoeniger, published in 1963,[29] was happy to accept the traditional authorship division:

About one matter there can at any rate be no doubt: Shakespeare wrote most or all of Acts 3–5. His hand is most obvious in 3.1, the scene of the storm and the casting overboard of Thaisa's body, and in 5.1, the first recognition scene. The two brothel scenes are also clearly by him, even if the Victorians disliked them. . . . They resemble parts of *Measure for Measure* and *All's Well* much more than any scene with similar low characters elsewhere in Jacobean drama. Leaving the Gower choruses aside for the moment, Shakespeare's late style is likewise evident in most other scenes of Acts 3–5, though much of it has been obscured by the reporter's inadequate transmission. These observations will be shared by every sensitive reader. They require no defence. (Hoeniger 1963, p. liv)

Hoeniger, like Fleay, recorded that the choruses from Act 3 onwards differ from the 'stiffer, more regular' style of the first two acts, with their 'predominantly end-stopped tetrameter lines'. With the exception of the chorus

---

[29] F. D. Hoeniger (ed.), *Pericles*, New Arden Shakespeare (London, 1963).

between the two recognition scenes (5.2), which reverts to the earlier manner, he described the verse of the later choruses as being handled more freely, with more lines of ten, nine, or eleven syllables, 'and with significantly more syncopation and variation in the use of the caesura' (p. lv). This change of style in the choruses, Hoeniger acutely observed, goes along with 'a difference in attitude towards the audience', the later choric passages resembling those in *Henry V*: 'Gower no longer merely presents the scenes to our eyes and judgment: he asks us to co-operate imaginatively with the action'. So in the Chorus to Act 4 scene 4 Gower comments on the artistic freedom with which the acting company works ('we . . . make short' distances, 'to take our imagination, | From bourn to bourn'), and counts on the audience's understanding—'By you being pardon'd'—for all the characters speaking the same language. He urges the audience to 'bear in mind' what is happening, while their 'thoughts' shall accompany the characters' movements. All these details recur in *Henry V*, including the direct appeals to the audience's imagination:

> In your supposing once more put your sight
>
> (Chorus 5.21)

(a detail which suggests to me that Shakespeare learned from *The Mirror for Magistrates*).[30] Hoeniger also echoed Delius (unknowingly) in pointing out that the third chorus resembles Puck's speech (*MND*, 5.1.360 ff.), both passages sharing 'a complex cluster of images, a feature which in recent years has come to be thought of as one of the most reliable literary criteria for authorship' (pp. lvi, 75). In addition, he observed, of twenty-three verbal parallels between *Pericles* and *Cymbeline*, *The Winter's Tale*, and *The Tempest*, 'some of them very remarkable, only three occur in Acts 1 and 2' (p. lvi).

As for the authorship of the first two acts, Hoeniger quickly disposed of Rowley and Heywood as candidates (pp. lvii–lix), and endorsed the case made for Wilkins, despite the opposition to it from those whom W. W. Greg dubbed 'fundamentalists', to whom 'the very idea that Shakespeare could have collaborated with such a minor dramatist near the end of his career was repugnant' (p. lix). But all of Wilkins's works appeared in 1606–8, exactly contemporary with *Pericles*, and Hoeniger found the many parallels in phrasing and use of rhyme presented by H. D. Sykes completely convincing. 'Cumulatively, this evidence is just about as considerable as any internal evidence can be. It would seem an incredible coincidence if all these similarities in style and close textual echoes between *Pericles* and Wilkins's work should have arisen accidentally' (p. lxii). While conceding that Wilkins shared in the play's composition, Hoeniger argued that John Day was also involved

---

[30] See Brian Vickers, 'Suppose You See: The Chorus in *Henry V* and *The Mirror for Magistrates*', in J. Batchelor, T. Cain, and C. Lamont (eds.), *Shakespearean Continuities: Essays in Honour of E. A. J. Honigmann* (London, 1997), pp. 74–90.

(pp. lxii, 171–80). However, the parallel passages he cited are not all convincing, nor did Hoeniger give adequate weight to the facts that Wilkins was a notorious plagiarist, and collaborated with Day (and Rowley) on one play, *The Travels of the Three English Brothers* (1607), and may have done so with Day on another, *Law Tricks* (1604), neither of which can be used as independent evidence for co-authorship.

In his 1963 edition F. D. Hoeniger happily accepted the co-authorship of *Pericles*. However, he subsequently published an essay recanting that opinion, now casting doubt on 'the notion that late in his career Shakespeare collaborated with such a hackwriter as George Wilkins . . .'.[31] Hoeniger admitted that 'the humdrum verse of the play's opening scene, and indeed of most of the first two acts, does indeed smack of a hackwriter: *as drama* the scene is singularly weak. And yet the early scenes work much better *in the theatre* than critical-minded readers of the text have assumed' (Hoeniger 1982, p. 468; my italics). If 'weak drama' can succeed 'in the theatre', a strange suggestion, that is surely due to the efforts of the director, designer, actors, and musicians, and it is in any case irrelevant to the issue of co-authorship. Hoeniger tried to extract himself from that contradiction by arguing that if these scenes 'had been conveyed in Shakespeare's characteristic blank verse and splendid dramatic manner, the effect . . . would have been jarring', so that Shakespeare deliberately wrote in an archaic style closer to the 'pseudo-Middle English and sing-song rhythm' of the Gower choruses (p. 468). Hoeniger then offered a commentary on the first two acts (pp. 468–74), which itemized a number of stylistic and dramaturgical features long associated with George Wilkins—'the great liberty taken with the rhyme', as in 'sin'/'shame', 'sin'/'him', the mixture of blank verse and rhyming couplets, the repetition of the same rhymes and half-rhymes, the excessive use of asides. But instead of pointing to the presence of Wilkins, Hoeniger argued that Shakespeare had fallen into all these oddities by having allowed 'a spillover from Gower into the enacted episodes', his archaic style somehow affecting all the other verse. Hoeniger added to this unconvincing suggestion a series of deductions concerning the crude dramaturgy of the first two acts as being a deliberate burlesque (see below), which hardly helped his case.

Responding to Hoeniger, Sidney Thomas objected that Shakespeare would hardly, 'especially in his opening acts, [choose] an inferior and ineffective style in deference to an arcane theory of what a Medieval mode of narration requires'.[32] The style of the first two acts, Thomas countered, 'is not archaic or formalized; it is simply incompetent, flat in diction, lifeless in rhythm, and unconvincing in content'. Quoting the speech in which Helicanus narrates the terrible punishment visited on the incestuous Antiochus (2.4.1–12), Thomas

---

[31] F. D. Hoeniger, 'Gower and Shakespeare in *Pericles*', *ShQ* 33 (1982): 461–79, at p. 463.
[32] Sidney Thomas, 'The Problem of *Pericles*', *ShQ* 34 (1983): 448–50, at p. 449.

described the style as 'bad in its very ordinariness, its lack of any quality that might suggest the legendary, remote world supposedly conjured up by Gower ...'. If, on Hoeniger's implausible theory, Shakespeare had deliberately adjusted his style to that of the 'archaic narrator', the question remains why he should have suddenly changed it at the beginning of Act 3, a change which Hoeniger explained in terms of an artistic 'compromise'. Thomas understandably dismissed the 'lameness and inadequacy' of Hoeniger's explanation, but it shows in vivid detail the consequence of ignoring scholarly evidence in order to preserve a belief in Shakespeare's 'sole authorship'.[33] Detailed work over the last thirty years by three scholars—David J. Lake, M. W. A. Smith, and MacDonald P. Jackson—has made it impossible for anyone to maintain that belief.

Lake's first study concerned the play's rhymes, in particular the peculiar number of false rhymes in Acts 1 and 2, 'assonances consisting of an identical vowel but different nasal consonants', such as *home–Drone* (2 Chorus 17–18), *sinne–him* (2 Chorus 23–4), *moones–doomes* (3 Chorus 31–2), *run–dum* (5.2.1–2), *soone–doome* (5.2.19–20). Lake scotched any notion that these false rhymes were introduced to create 'an archaic effect' by showing that 'the audience of *Pericles* were accustomed to hearing similar assonances in contemporary plays on contemporary themes',[34] namely the Wilkins–Rowley–Day collaboration, *The Travels of the Three English Brothers*, and Wilkins's own *The Miseries of Enforced Marriage*, both published in 1607. *The Travels* uses a Chorus or presenter who has a very similar role to Gower in *Pericles* as 'spokesman of the players', and who 'indulges in the same nasal assonances', such as *dumbe–tongue, done–Rome, him–sinne.* No archaicism was intended, for 'assonance, especially with nasals, is evidently the author's normal practice' and very different from Shakespeare's, a statement that Lake could make with some authority, having examined 2,000 rhyming lines in Shakespeare and found only five assonances (Lake 1969, p. 140). It is unlikely, Lake argued, that Shakespeare wrote 'all of the Act 3 Chorus (*moones–doomes* occurs at lines 31–2); or any part of the 5.2 Chorus, which begins and ends with nasal assonances'.

Designating the non-Shakespearian part of the play 'Pericles X', comprising Acts 1, 2, the Chorus to Act 3, lines 15–60 (since lines 1–14, as we have seen, echo *MND*), and 5.2, Lake eliminated Day and Rowley as possible authors, since the proportion of assonance in their unaided plays is far smaller than that in Wilkins's share of *The Travels*, or in *Pericles*. Acknowledging the work of H. Dugdale Sykes, who showed that the proportion of rhyme in Wilkins's *Miseries* (37 per cent) is comparable to that in *Pericles*, Acts 1 and 2 (25 per cent), and who also discovered identical rhymes

---

[33] Cf. e.g. Karen Csengeri, 'William Shakespeare, Sole Author of *Pericles*', *ES* 71 (1990): 230–43.

[34] D. J. Lake, 'Rhymes in *Pericles*', *NQ* 214 (1969): 139–43, at p. 139.

TABLE 5.8. *Assonance in* Pericles *and Wilkins*

	Total nasals	Total non-nasals	Total assonances
Pericles X	7	4	11
Travels W	15	6	21
Miseries	12	6	18

Source: Lake 1969a, p. 141; table simplified.

TABLE 5.9. *Rhyme and assonance in* Pericles *and Wilkins*

	Rhyming lines	Assonances	Frequencies
Pericles X	344	11	32
Travels W	515	21	41
Miseries	564	18	32

Source: Lake 1969a, p. 142.

in all three works, Lake made a more systematic study, finding 'in the *Miseries* the whole range of assonances that occur in *The Travels* and in *Pericles*, and in much the same proportions'. Lake proved the first point by detailed quotation, and the second by tabulating the figures for assonances in the three works, having established Wilkins's share in *The Travels*[35]—called '*Travels W*' in Table 5.8 (a simplified version of Lake's data). Lake computed the number of rhyming lines in the three plays, and the total assonances, to arrive at the frequencies per 1,000 rhyming lines, as set out in Table 5.9. If the figures for *Travels W* and *Miseries* are pooled, 'we get a frequency of assonance for Wilkins of 36 per 1,000. The agreement with *Pericles X* is startling; and it is now reasonable to conclude that he is the author of all three works' (p. 142).

Lake added another valuable stylistic criterion for identifying Wilkins's hand, his tendency to mingle blank verse and couplets indiscriminately. Delius had noticed this point in 1868, and Sykes had echoed him in 1919, but Lake was the first to treat it systematically. He showed that Wilkins often interrupted a single speech in couplets by inserting an unrhymed line (what Lake calls a 'rift'), and also wrote 'rhymed sections preceded and followed by blank verse in the same speech' (what Lake calls 'rafts'). Lake then computed the distribution set out in Table 5.10. Such mingling of blank verse and rhyme 'on a large scale co-occurs with assonance in *The Travels* only in the scenes attributable to Wilkins; and both are super-abundant in *The Miseries* and

[35] Cf. Lake's list of the scenes involved, p. 142 n. 19.

TABLE 5.10. *Rhymed and unrhymed lines in*
Pericles *and Wilkins*

	'Rifts'	'Rafts'
Pericles, 1–2	8	28
Travels W	13	25
Miseries	20	41

Source: Lake 1969a, p. 142.

Pericles 1–2'. Professor Lake was careful not to claim that Wilkins's co-
authorship of *Pericles* was 'now proved beyond all reasonable doubt', but he
certainly brought that conclusion much nearer.

   In two other essays Lake added further supporting detail. He showed that
yon and related words (*yond, yonder*) occur with surprising frequency in
the non-Shakespearian scenes of *Pericles* (eleven times, as against none in
Shakespeare's part), especially as deictics used in 'celestial' contexts.[36] This
habit, much rarer in Shakespeare, who only uses *yon* in this connection about
twice per play, is also visible in Wilkins's *The Miseries of Enforced Marriage*
(four instances), and *Travels* (seven instances in Wilkins's part). In these
plays, as in *Pericles*, the uses of *yon* occur in brief clusters, and in very similar
verbal forms: 'yon file of stars' (*Travels*), 'yon field of starres' (*Per.*, 1.1.37);
'yon heavenly frame' (*Travels*), 'yon celestiall tree' (*Per.*, 1.1.21). Lake also
showed that while the word *sin* occurs not at all in *Pericles*, Acts 3–5, it is
found frequently both in Acts 1 and 2 (eleven times in 1,033 lines), and in *The
Miseries* (twenty-nine times in 2,795 lines)—that is, one instance in about
every 100 lines of both works, and thirty-two times in Wilkins's share of
Travels. This insistent usage makes sin an agent in human activities, one sin
leading to another: 'as near as . . . sin to sin' (*Travels*), 'One sinne . . . another
doth provoke' (*Per.*, 1.1.137–9). In *Pericles* the rhyme *sin–him* occurs
(1.2.38–9, 2. Cho. 23–4), as it frequently does in Wilkins (Lake 1969c, pp.
290–1). In a further study Lake used his rhymed assonance test and the
linguistic preferences ('*em/them; has/hath; does/doth*) to eliminate Rowley
and Heywood as possible co-authors of *Pericles*, strengthening the case for
Wilkins.[37]

   That claim was made even more firmly by M. W. A. Smith in a series of stylometric studies, discussed in Chapter 2. As we saw there, Smith performed
four separate sets of tests, in each of which pairs of authors were compared in

[36] D. J. Lake, 'Wilkins and *Pericles*—Vocabulary (1)', *NQ* 214 (1969): 288–91, at p. 289.
[37] D. J. Lake, 'The *Pericles* Candidates: Heywood, Rowley, Wilkins', *NQ* 215 (1970):
135–41.

terms of their verbal preferences. In every test Smith's method correctly identified the authors of *The Alchemist* and *The Duchess of Malfi*, while endorsing the attribution to Shakespeare of *Pericles*, Acts 3–5, and indicating Wilkins as the most probable author of the play's opening acts.

Smith's expertise has proved especially valuable in dealing with some recent claims of Shakespeare's sole authorship that invoke stylometric studies, claims made by critics who are (as MacDonald Jackson puts it) 'oblivious to the difference between the stilted verse of *Pericles* 1–2 and the vigorous poetry of *Pericles* 3–5'.[38] Despite Smith's care in setting up a coherent methodology, established in advance of the computation, including a meticulous analysis of the evidence, his endorsement of the traditional attribution of Acts 1 and 2 to Wilkins was disputed by critics who believed that Shakespeare had written them earlier in his career, or who just denied Wilkins's co-authorship. Smith answered the first challenge by applying a new statistical method, 'Principal Component Analysis',[39] which again differentiated two authors, placing *Pericles* 1–2 closer to Wilkins, and *Pericles* 3–5 closer to Shakespeare's romances. This test produced 'no evidence', indeed 'no hint that these two Acts represent early Shakespeare' (Smith 1992*b*, p. 347), a conclusion that squares with other findings using purely linguistic evidence.

As for the second objection, by Thomas Merriam, which claimed that Wilkins's *Miseries of Enforced Marriage* could not be distinguished from either part of the play, and that since '*Pericles* 3–5 are generally acknowledged to be Shakespeare's work, a reasonable inference is that the first two acts are Shakespeare's as well',[40] Smith objected that Merriam had misinterpreted his findings,[41] in which 'dissimilarity is still discernable' (Smith 1994, p. 57). He also pointed out that Merriam, in his papers on *More* and *Pericles*, began by calculating Euclidian distances for 22 Shakespeare plays but continued 'by taking the 36 plays of the First Folio. Such an unexplained change invites suspicion and violates scientific practice'. Further, he showed that Merriam's experiment was 'based on a *selected* subset of tests', namely only 9 of the 46 he had described, without any explanation why these 9 had been chosen, when some of the other 37 were 'based on more frequently occurring features' in the texts concerned, and therefore likely to be more reliable. As Smith put it, 'if the tests were selected to provide a desired result, in the manner of quoting particular examples to sustain an argument, then one of

---

[38] M. P. Jackson, 'Rhyming in *Pericles*: More Evidence of Dual Authorship', *SB* 46 (1993): 239–49, at p. 240.

[39] M. W. A. Smith, 'The Problem of Acts I–II of *Pericles*', *NQ* 237 (1992): 346–55. Smith protested that T. Merriam 'distorts my argument to precisely its opposite' (p. 346).

[40] T. Merriam, '*Pericles* I–II Revisited and Considerations Concerning Literary Medium [*sic*] as a Systematic Factor in Stylometry', *NQ* 237 (1992): 341–5, at p. 344.

[41] M. W. A. Smith, '*Sir Thomas More*, *Pericles*, and Stylometry', *NQ* 239 (1994): 55–8. Here again Smith protested that 'Regrettably my words are reinterpreted in isolation to present the opposite meaning' to that stated in the article concerned (p. 57).

the most fundamental principles of statistical experimental design has been violated: the experimentalist should not be able to influence the outcome'. If indeed a small subset of tests had been 'selected in order to provide a certain result, then . . . the entire experiment is rendered null and void' (p. 58). I quote those words in order to counter the naïvety about statistics that still exists in literary circles. Figures do not always prove what their authors claim.

In an essay on Acts 1 and 2 MacDonald Jackson cited new evidence for George Wilkins. As we have seen, Ernst Honigmann observed that in the *Pericles* novel Wilkins repeatedly begins sentences and clauses with 'which' in various forms. Jackson noted that 'while the use of a Latinate "resumptive which" is common enough among seventeenth-century English prose writers, it is rare in drama'. In order to make an 'objective statistical comparison' Jackson limited his attention to

three clearly definable types of unusual 'which' in *Pericles*: (*a*) 'which' meaning 'and this' and qualifying a noun that immediately follows; (*b*) 'which' preceded by the definite article ('the which'); and (*c*) 'which' (or 'the which' or 'which' preceded by a preposition) beginning a speech that is not a question. (Jackson 1990, p. 193)

We can find examples of all three forms in the brief exchange concluding Act 1:

> Cleon. *The which* when any shall not gratify,
>   Or pay you with unthankfulness in thought,
>   Be it our wives, our children, or ourselves,
>   The curse of heaven and men succeed their evils!
>   Till when,—*the which* I hope shall ne'er be seen—
>   Your grace is welcome to our town and us.
> Pericles. *Which welcome* we'll accept; feast here awhile,
>   Until our stars that frown lend us a smile.

$$(1.4.101-8)$$

As Jackson indicated, in l. 101 Cleon's 'The which' is types *b* and *c*, while in l. 107 Pericles' 'Which welcome' is types *a* and *c* (p. 193).

Jackson counted 20 peculiar instances of 'which' in Acts 1 and 2 of *Pericles* (8 of type *a*, 8 of *b*, and 4 of *c*), none at all in Shakespeare's Acts 3–5. The figures for all 37 plays of Shakespeare show that he made relatively little use of this resumptive 'which', for Jackson counted 74 examples of type *a*, 99 of type *b*, and only 25 of type *c*. Examination of these usages in context disclosed another distinction, according to whether the word 'which', following a noun, 'is also preceded by a preposition, as in such standard expressions as "at which time" or "to which place"'. Distinguishing types *a* and *b* into the categories of (i) instances preceded by a preposition, and (ii) instances not so preceded, Jackson computed occurrences in the whole canon of Shakespeare's plays, in 21 plays by early seventeenth-century dramatists, and in 10 plays by the other candidates suggested as co-author (Rowley, Day, and

TABLE 5.11. *Occurrences of* which *in* Pericles, *late-period Shakespeare, and Wilkins*

Play	Resumptive *which*					Totals	
	Type *a*		Type *b*		Type *c*	All types	*a*(ii) + *b*(ii) + *c*
	a(i)	a(ii)	b(i)	b(ii)	c		
WT	2	1	1	1	0	5	2
Cym.	1	1	2	1	2	7	4
Tem.	4	0	1	0	0	5	0
H8	1	1	0	3	1	6	5
TNK	1	0	1	3	0	5	3
Per. 1–2	3	5	0	8	4	20	17
Per. 3–5	0	0	0	0	0	0	0
Miseries	0	4	1	5	9	19	18
Travels W	1	6	0	0	2	9	8
Travels non-W	0	0	0	0	1	1	1

Source: Jackson 1990, pp. 194–5.

Heywood). His tables show quite unmistakably that Wilkins's peculiar uses of 'which' occur far more frequently than in any of the other 23 dramatists that Jackson studied. I have abridged his tables in Table 5.11, reproducing only the data for Shakespeare's late plays, *Pericles*, Wilkins's *Miseries*, and his share of *The Travels of the Three English Brothers*.[42] The figures for *Pericles* 1–2 (only two-fifths of a play) are far outside Shakespeare's range, but correlate exactly with Wilkins's. As Jackson says, rejecting complicated theories of Wilkins having been the reporter of the first two acts, 'it is much easier to believe that he was their author in the first place' (p. 196).

MacDonald Jackson added still more weight to this belief in three further studies, beginning with the use of function words.[43] Jackson praised M. W. A. Smith's work for 'its objectivity', each step in his investigations having been made 'according to clearly defined rules that have already been laid down' before research began (rather than being selected in order to give favourable results). However, he pointed out that in investigating Wilkins's authorship Smith's work was 'limited by the small range of dramatists examined' and the

[42] For bibliographic details of Wilkins's share see M. P. Jackson, '*Pericles*, Acts I and II: New Evidence for George Wilkins', *NQ* 215 (1990): 192–6, p. 196 n. 12, which agrees with the allocation made by Boyle, Sykes, and Lake.

[43] M. P. Jackson, 'George Wilkins and the First Two Acts of *Pericles*: New Evidence from Function Words', *LLC* 6 (1991): 155–63. See also M. W. A. Smith, 'Function Words and the Authorship of *Pericles*', *NQ* 234 (1989): 333–6.

small number of plays involved—only two by Shakespeare (Jackson 1991, p. 156). Accordingly, Jackson studied the use of 13 'high-frequency' or 'function words' in 86 samples from plays by 20 known Jacobean dramatists, and from 18 disputed plays associated with Middleton. The words counted were *a, and, but, by, for, from, in, it, of, that, the, to,* and *with,* and each sample 'consisted of 1,000 instances of the selected function words, drawn from consecutive lines of text; this means that counts were of rates of function words in relation to one another, not in relation to the total number of all words within a particular block of text' (p. 156). Jackson also added samples from Wilkins's *The Miseries of Enforced Marriage,* his share of *The Travels of the Three English Brothers,* and of the play *A Woman Never Vexed* (Acts 3–4). Using chi-square values to establish the closeness of fit to the two sections of *Pericles,* Jackson discovered that for Acts 3–5 the closest fit was afforded by *Cymbeline,* the third closest by *The Tempest,* Shakespeare providing three of the six top-ranked plays. For Acts 1 and 2 the results were 'strikingly different', the closest fit being afforded by one sample from Wilkins's *Miseries* (the one containing most verse), with other Wilkins samples occupying the 3rd, 5th, and 8th positions (p. 157). These findings confirm Wilkins as the most likely author, and give no support to the theory 'that the first two acts of *Pericles* are a survival from an early Shakespeare play'. They also confirm Gary Taylor's earlier analysis using function words, which showed the last three acts to be perfectly Shakespearian, the first two highly anomalous, especially in their exceptionally high rate for *to.*[44] Jackson showed that 'unusually high tallies for *to* are characteristic of the Wilkins samples among the 112' he had studied (p. 159). 'The studies of Smith, Taylor, and myself', Jackson observed, 'have different strengths and weaknesses, yet all three converge on the same conclusion' (p. 161).

Jackson approached this issue from two different angles a few years later,[45] studying the play's use of infinitives and its idiosyncratic rhymes. Counting 'the number of occurrences of "to + infinitive" per thousand words', Jackson found 'a remarkable degree of separation between the eleven scenes in Acts 1–2 and the sixteen in Acts 3–5' (Jackson 1993a, p. 198). In the Shakespearian acts infinitives occur at a rate of 12.1 per thousand words, 'close to the average for Shakespeare's plays', as opposed to the 'anomalously high' rate of 20.1 per thousand for Acts 1–2. At no point in his career did Shakespeare use the infinitive with that frequency, although Wilkins did elsewhere, Jackson quoting rates of 16.2 and 17.5 for *The Miseries* and Wilkins's share of *The Travels* respectively (p. 198). Jackson went on to show that the evidence from rhymes, previously used by H. D. Sykes and David Lake, could be reworked from a new perspective, adding further likelihood to Wilkins's

[44] *TxC,* pp. 80–9. See also ibid. 130–1, 556–60.
[45] M. P. Jackson, 'The Authorship of *Pericles*: The Evidence of Infinitives', *NQ* 238 (1993): 197–200.

co-authorship. He compiled an alphabetical list of all the individual rhymes in *Pericles* and in *The Miseries of Enforced Marriage*, tallying the number of occurrences. As we might expect by now, the great majority of rhyme links, fifty-eight, occurred in the first two acts, as against thirteen in the last three (Jackson 1993*b*, pp. 242, 249). Further, 'three of the rhyme pairs common to *Miseries* and *Pericles* occur nowhere else in the Shakespeare canon', namely *consist/resist*, *him/sin*, and *impudence/offence*, while four others occur only once elsewhere in Shakespeare. Jackson then undertook the laborious task of counting all the rhymes in Shakespeare's poems and plays (some 8,170), computing for each work the number of rhyme links with *Miseries* as a percentage of the total number of rhymes, and ranking them in order. The result was that *Pericles* 1–2 headed the list 'with a percentage of rhyme links with *Miseries* that is almost double that of the highest authentic work by Shakespeare', with Wilkins's share of *Travels* taking second place (Jackson 1993*b*, p. 245). *Pericles* 3–5 falls about midway on Jackson's list, its percentage of rhyme links (10.2) corresponding to those of *The Winter's Tale* (11.3) and *Cymbeline* (8.8). Once again Jackson emphasized that his evidence provided no support for theories of Acts 1 and 2 being an early composition, and none for the suggestion that Shakespeare wrote those acts in a deliberately archaic style, for the vast majority of rhyme links with *Miseries* occur in the dialogue, not in the Gower choruses (46 against 12). 'At present', he concluded, 'the evidence favours the identification of . . . George Wilkins' as co-author (p. 248).

The recent sociolinguistic study by Jonathan Hope shed further light on this issue, while acknowledging that the evidence is not entirely clear-cut. Hope compared both parts of *Pericles* with Wilkins's *Miseries of Enforced Marriage*, applying two tests, the use of auxiliary *do* and the use of relative markers. Hope divided instances of the auxiliary *do* into 'regulated sentences' (conforming to what is now standard usage), and 'unregulated' (now non-standard), such as 'I did go home', 'I went not home'. By counting the number of regulated sentences in a text we can estimate the degree to which a writer follows older or newer usages. Where none of the sixteen plays in Hope's Shakespeare comparison samples has a rate greater than 84 per cent overall regulation, *Pericles* has a regulation rate of 85 per cent, which turns out to be the same in both sections, and closely matches the rate of 86 per cent found in Wilkins's *Miseries*.[46] This shows that the auxiliary *do* test 'can only distinguish between writers if their usages are sufficiently distinct', which is not the case here; but equally, 'if Wilkins is Shakespeare's collaborator here, then this is precisely the result we should expect'. Obeying his own injunction, that authorship studies should be 'cumulative, . . . cases to be built on a

---

[46] J. Hope, *The Authorship of Shakespeare's Plays: A Socio-Linguistic Study* (Cambridge, 1994), pp. 16–18.

variety of independent tests, rather than just one type of evidence', Hope
then applied his 'relative marker' test, whether writers use such non-standard
usages as *which* with a human antecedent, *whom* with a non-human
antecedent, *that* in non-restrictive relative clauses, and zero in the subject
position—as in 'I have a minde (o) presages' (*MV*, 1.1.175–6). Taking all
four tests together, he found the figures for *Pericles* to be anomalous in
several respects, matching simultaneously the highest and lowest rates in
Shakespeare, further evidence that the surviving text of the play has been dis-
rupted in some way, by 'collaboration, scribal interference, or oral or memorial corruption' (p. 110). Comparison with *The Miseries* showed that 'the
pattern of relatives is closer to that of Wilkins's play' than to the Shakespeare
sample, so supporting the evidence for collaboration, and in two respects
Wilkins's hand could be clearly distinguished. In three scenes of Act 1 there
are six instances of the non-personal *who*, a much higher rate than normal for
Shakespeare: 'only eight non-personal *who* forms appear in the five plays of
sample one; and twenty in sample two. Here there are six in three scenes'.
In the Shakespearian Acts 3–5 there are no instances of non-personal *who*
forms, but in Wilkins's *Miseries* there are seven instances. Secondly—and
here Hope followed in the path of Steevens, Delius, and Sykes, while providing far more accurate figures—Wilkins's fondness for zero forms emerges
very clearly. Where Sykes found 'over twenty' instances of subject zero forms
in *Miseries*, Hope found 39, with a further 44 in the object position. The figures for *Pericles*, Acts 1–2, are 18 in the subject, 9 in the object position (p.
111). In the early scenes of *Pericles* Hope found 'up to five non-restrictive zero
forms', that is, where a relative pronoun has been omitted, such as

> Bad child, worse father, to intice his owne
> To evill, (o) should be done by none.

(1 Chorus 27–8)

As Hope pointed out, 'this is a highly marked form—and it is completely
absent from either Shakespeare comparison sample (indeed, it is a very rare
form—only occurring in the Massinger and Fletcher comparison samples)'
(pp. 112–13). It is highly significant that there are so many of these forms in
Acts 1–2, none at all in Acts 3–5, and eight instances in Wilkins's *Miseries* (p.
113). Furthermore, within the zero form usage Shakespeare showed 'a consistent preference for the object position: in each sample, only 17 per cent of
zero forms appear in the subject position', while the rate for *The Miseries* is
47 per cent (ibid.). Hope rejected theories attempting to explain these differences in terms of *Pericles* being an early Shakespeare play, for the use in Acts
1–2 of zero relative markers in non-restrictive clauses is 'a highly unusual feature absent from Shakespeare's work (in both the early and late periods) but
present in Wilkins's play', and thus supporting the case for his authorship of
the first two acts (p. 152).

Reading and rereading all this literature on the authorship of *Pericles*, in order to summarize its arguments as briefly and clearly as possible while giving enough detail to make those arguments comprehensible, I have been impressed more than ever by the cumulative weight of scholarship in author-ship studies over more than one hundred years. From the suggestive, widely read but methodologically primitive work of Delius, Fleay, Boyle, and H. Dugdale Sykes to the rigorous studies by Lake, Smith, Jackson, and Hope the case for Wilkins's co-authorship has been made from a dozen different approaches, all of them yielding the same result. The other candidates—Day, Heywood, Rowley—have been eliminated, and a unanimous consensus points to Wilkins. While I certainly do not believe in the automatic progress of scholarship, it seems to me that the case of *Pericles* supports two conclu-sions, first that 'knowledge does advance', but secondly 'that it also stands still, or reverts to earlier states, unless it keeps a grasp on basic principles and can justify its deductions by reference to a valid methodology' (*CHS*, vi. 47). I wrote those words in commenting on a regressive phase in the late eight-eenth century, where Steevens and Ritson ignored the scholarly advances made by Edward Capell in validating the authenticity of the First Folio plays, harking back to the whimsical methods of Pope, who simply rejected words, lines, scenes, or plays which did not please his taste. Yet they turn out to be equally applicable in the late twentieth century, for the recent edition of *Pericles* in the New Cambridge Shakespeare[47] wilfully ignores the whole weight of scholarship proving that Shakespeare was one of the play's two co-authors.

Doreen Del Vecchio and Anthony Hammond, both Professors of Drama, dismissed the authorship issue as if a hundred years of scholarship had never existed. Their coverage of the secondary literature was highly selective: there is no sign that they knew the relevant essays and books by the older scholars—Delius, Boyle, Fleay, Sykes—nor the more recent work by Oras, Honigmann, or Tarlinskaja. They listed only one of D. J. Lake's essays, giving the barest references to 'his other articles on related topics' (Del Vecchio and Hammond 1998, p. 212), and subjected M. W. A. Smith to the same

---

[47] D. Del Vecchio and A. Hammond (eds.), *Pericles, Prince of Tyre* (Cambridge, 1998). On the many deficiencies of this edition see the review article by Roger Warren (who is editing *Pericles* for the one-volume Oxford series), 'Theatrical Use And Editorial Abuse: More Painful Adventures for Pericles', *RES* 49 (1998): 478–86. Warren showed that Hammond and Del Vecchio stubbornly clung to the 1609 Quarto text, not only ignoring the many helpful emend-ations which (following Spiker's lead) editors had derived from Wilkins's novel, based on the play, but not even recording them in their collations. This doctrinaire approach meant that they retained many 'corrupt or nonsensical passages' from the Quarto (p. 479), a misplaced fidelity to the text which denied their readers the fruits of two centuries' editorial labours. Regrettably, Laurie E. Maguire, in her review (*ShQ* 51 (2000): 362–4), praising the editors for 'vigorously defend[ing] Q readings . . . in eloquent miniature essays', and approving their rejection of the 'prejudicial' distinction between Good and Bad Quartos, hailed the New Cambridge as a 'bold and exciting edition'.

treatment: neither scholar's work was deemed worthy of discussion. They did record 'the widespread perception that there is a change in the style of the play after Act 2', but generously described the 'characteristic style of the first two acts' as 'a leisurely and formal use of verse' (p. 9). Other readers have used such terms as '*holpricht*', 'stilted', 'flat', 'lifeless'. Like E. M. Waith on *Titus*, or J. C. Maxwell on *Timon*, Del Vecchio and Hammond pretended that authorship studies died out long ago—'When disintegration was fashionable', they wrote, 'it seemed to many a reasonable inference' that the play had two authors (p. 9). Ignoring several generations of attribution scholars, they made the Oxford editors guilty of a 'revival of the practice of disintegration' in the 1987 *Textual Companion* (p. 12). They described F. D. Hoeniger's survey of the authorship debate in his Arden edition as 'full, though misguided' (p. 9 n.), evidently because it accepted Wilkins as a co-author. They themselves, denying more than a century of scholarship, expressed 'the gravest doubts that Wilkins had anything to do with *Pericles*'.

It is sad to realize that Del Vecchio and Hammond's discussion of the authorship issue followed the worst traditions of the 'it's all by Shakespeare' conservators, being misleading and evasive. The Oxford editors' claim that Wilkins wrote the first nine scenes, they judged, in so far as it 'is based on statistical evidence, . . . is fresh, interesting, and open to challenge by better evidence'—of which they had none. 'Insofar as it still rests on subjective impression', they went on, 'it adds nothing to the case' (p. 11). In boxing, this would be described as a blow below the belt, for Del Vecchio and Hammond completely failed to identify anything 'subjective' about that discussion. Huffing and puffing, they felt it 'necessary to say outright that we do not regard the stylistic differences in the play (which have often been exaggerated) as in any way conclusive evidence of collaboration' (ibid.). Who exaggerated these differences, and in what way? We are not told, but we are informed that in *Pericles*, as in other plays by Shakespeare, 'different styles [are used] for different dramatic purposes'. The examples cited are vague ('the multiple languages of some of the comedies'), or unconvincing (*Measure for Measure* has 'a folk-tale conclusion'), the argument driven on to a desperate extreme: 'indeed, any play which contains complex stylistics invites disintegration to those so minded' (p. 11). This is to give a wholly false description of the differences of style in *Pericles* between Acts 1–2 and 3–5, which are far greater in every respect than any variation within a play wholly written by Shakespeare. Repressing the very notion of two authors evidently made the editors blind to the changes within the play: so they documented in detail the ways in which Gower's chorus makes a 'direct appeal for the audience's assistance' (pp. 31–2), not observing that all the instances they quote come from Acts 3–5.

If we recall for a moment the catalogue of linguistic habits which careful scholars have shown to characterize George Wilkins—the omission of relative pronouns; various peculiar ways of using 'which'; the high incidence of verbs in the infinitive, and the related high frequency in using the word 'to'; the idiosyncratic mixture of rhyme interrupting blank verse, or blank verse interrupting rhyme; the large number of rhymes shared between *Pericles* and authenticated work by Wilkins, including several rhymes not otherwise found in Shakespeare—recalling all these points, laboriously established by painstaking scholarship, we can see that Del Vecchio and Hammond simply closed their eyes to every scholarly issue. They claimed to find it 'anomalous that there are so few verbal links between *Pericles* and *The Miseries of Inforst Marriage*', blandly ignoring the large number of such links that had already been shown. In a footnote they grudgingly conceded that 'there are a few lines in *Miseries* which make one think of *Pericles*', but made only three quotations before adding that 'more than one explanation is possible for these parallels' (pp. 13–14 n. 4)—such as? The only modern essay they cited was MacDonald Jackson's 'Rhyming in *Pericles*' (1993*b*), with its exhaustive demonstration that *Pericles* 1–2 has nearly twice as many rhyme links with Wilkins's *Miseries* than any play by Shakespeare, followed by Wilkins's share of *The Travels of the Three English Brothers*.[48] Del Vecchio and Hammond dismissed Jackson's essay by claiming that 'the anomaly, involving as it does a relatively small number of items (in statistical terms), is not beyond the bounds of coincidence' (p. 13). This was an extremely unwise remark, for anyone familiar with statistics will recognize that Jackson's analysis is in no way reliant on coincidence. Another unfortunate attempt to brush away unwelcome evidence was their report that Jonathan Hope's sociolinguistic study 'does little to strengthen the Wilkinsites' (p. 13 n.): the opposite is true.

It is sad to have to record such a wilful rejection of a solidly established scholarly tradition, since after all readers of a major edition legitimately expect its editors to have sifted through all the relevant secondary literature and to evaluate the case for co-authorship in a fair and open-minded manner. It is symptomatic of Del Vecchio and Hammond's evasion of these issues that they should argue that 'the early scenes of *Pericles* have been proved to harmonise with the later scenes and to work well on stage, the only real court of appeal' (p. 11). But the stage is not in any sense a court of appeal in authorship studies, for quite different concerns are involved. The Bad Quarto of *Hamlet* can 'work well' in a good production, after a fashion, but that does not mean we should accept any theatrical text, however corrupt, as Shakespeare's. Their further claim, that 'a play, any play, is *ipso facto* a work of collaboration' (p. 14), was equally evasive, and irrelevant. All of the performing arts depend on collaboration, but that takes place on a quite different plane from a jointly written primary text. As for their explanation of the

---

[48] In a note Del Vecchio and Hammond claimed that Wilkins's 'share in *The Three English Brothers* has never been established by any reliable method', which is also untrue: cf. n. 35 above.

text's many anomalies as being 'based upon incompletely revised draft papers, written by the author or copied from authorial papers by a scribe or scribes', and thus being comparable with the 1608 quarto of *King Lear* (pp. 79, 197–210), that, too, was a throwback to a now discredited stage of scholarship. They began their edition 'with a mandatory Government Health Warning: THIS EDITION OF *PERICLES* MAY BE HARMFUL TO YOUR PREJUDICES' (p. vii). But in fact it only documented their own prejudices,[49] resistant to the many rational demonstrations by painstaking scholars that the play is the product of two different, and easily distinguishable authors. Readers of *Pericles* deserve better than this.

By now, I hope, readers will be in a position to judge for themselves whether the Cambridge editors fairly reflected the weight of scholarship documenting Wilkins's involvement in this play. Happily, the vitality of that tradition is unabated, for MacDonald Jackson is about to publish a critical monograph which will definitely settle the case for Shakespeare and Wilkins as co-authors.[50] In a recent essay[51] Jackson returned to the question of Wilkins's verse, demonstrating by 'illustration and analysis along traditional literary critical lines' the affinities between the verse of *Pericles* 1–2 and that of *The Miseries of Enforced Marriage*. Whereas 'Shakespeare's poetic style is marked by its concentration, energy, particularity, and concreteness', he wrote (Jackson 1999, p. 2), in *Pericles* 1–2 Wilkins displayed 'a wordiness that seems half way between the pointless and the cryptic'. The imagery in these acts hints at 'interesting ideas, but there is a curious arbitrariness about it', as if it were dragged in for decoration, a 'hit-or-miss quality' quite unlike Shakespeare's focus and condensation. Jackson judges Pericles' apostrophe to the tempest at the opening of Act 3 (quoted above) both 'vivid in its parts and beautifully shaped' in its progress from the cosmic upheaval to the entry of Lychorida with the baby. 'Rhythmically, it is strong and varied, with its high proportion of run-on lines, heavy stops within the line, and sprinkling of

---

[49] One sign of prejudice is the abusive tone with which they referred to anyone (especially the Oxford editors) who suggests that the play was written by Shakespeare and Wilkins. They rejected 'hostile and disintegrative views of [the play's] text' (p. vii), an indignant metaphor which begs the question, for if a play was indeed written by two collaborators to recognize that fact is not to 'disintegrate' it but to render both authors their due. They accused theatrical directors of having 'rearranged . . . and Wilkinsised' the play (p. 20); Roger Warren has compared three stagings of the play, 'but his missionary view of the Oxford adaptation colours and distorts many of his statements and all of his opinions' (p. 20 n.); the 1986 Stratford, Ontario, production was good, 'despite the intrusion of some of the Oxford adaptation's fantasies' (pp. 22–3); to condemn the verse of Acts 1 and 2, they protested, is 'perverse, old-fashioned and unproductive', showing an 'implied hieratic elitism' (p. 37); and they repeated their disapproval of 'the Wilkinsisers' (p. 72 n.). This sustained abuse ends up by being counter-productive.

[50] The monograph is entitled *Defining Shakespeare*: Pericles *as Test Case*, and will be published by Oxford University Press.

[51] 'Medium and Message: Authors and Poetic Styles in *Pericles*', delivered to the Shakespeare Association of America's conference, 1–3 Apr. 1999: I am grateful to Professor Jackson for letting me read it.

feminine endings . . . Much of the poetic energy is generated by the verbs: "rebuke", "wash", "bind", "still", "quench", "stormest", "split", "cry", "convey", "make". The active diction provokes continual activity in the reader's or playgoer's mind' (p. 3). By sharp contrast, in both *Pericles* 1–2 and *Miseries*, Wilkins's 'stilted, predominantly end-stopped verse', with its 'rhythmic gawkiness', is sententious but vague and 'approximate', often relying on 'a set of associations' rather than observation freshly derived from the immediate dramatic context. His *sententiae* are generally conveyed in rhyme, and Jackson summarized the scholarly tradition identifying Wilkins's idiosyncratic rhymes, regularly repeated and recycled, adding some new detail. Sykes showed in 1919 that the unusual rhyme 'consist'/'resist' occurs in *Pericles* (1.4.83–4) and in *Miseries* (836–7): Jackson is now able to report that apart from these two instances, 'if the Chadwyck–Healey search functions are to be trusted', it occurs nowhere else in their 'English Drama' or 'English Poetry' databases (pp. 6–7). Such a unique parallel must strengthen even further the case for Wilkins as co-author.

The distinction that Jackson draws between the verse of Wilkins and that of Shakespeare is a distinction in kind or quality, which can be expressed quantitatively, as shown by his own earlier studies, along with those of Lake, Smith, and Hope. In this essay he abjured statistics, confident that the differences between the two dramatists 'can be discerned by an attentive reader' in 'a sensitive reading'. Jackson drew together all the linguistic habits long known to characterize Wilkins—the constant use of antithesis, often to add emphasis to a sententious couplet, which is given even more emphasis by alliteration; the idiosyncratic use of 'which' to open a speech; the frequent use of 'this' or 'thus' to point towards some moral or maxim; the elision of the relative pronoun; the unpredictable insertion of rhyme into blank verse speeches—and showed how they all come together in long sequences of *Pericles* and *Miseries*.

I cannot reproduce here his detailed analyses, but one especially convincing parallel involves that speech from *The Miseries of Enforced Marriage* which Delius singled out in 1868 (above, p. 294). Jackson compares it with Pericles' speech after he has solved Antiochus' riddle encoding his incestuous relationship with his daugther.

> How courtesy would seem to cover sin,
> When what is done is like an hypocrite,
> The which is good in nothing but in sight!
> If it be true that I interpret false,
> Then were it certain you were not so bad
> As with foul incest to abuse your soul;
> Where now you're both a father and a son,
> By your uncomely claspings with your child,—
> Which pleasure fits a husband, not a father;

And she an eater of her mother's flesh,
By the defiling of her parent's bed;
And both like serpents are, who though they feed
On sweetest flowers, yet they poison breed.
Antioch, farewell! For wisdom sees, those men
Blush not in actions blacker than the night,
Will 'schew no course to keep them from the light.
One sin, I know, another doth provoke;
Murder's as near to lust as flame to smoke.
Poison and treason are the hands of sin,
Ay, and the targets, to put off the shame;
Then, lest my life be cropp'd to keep you clear,
By flight I'll shun the danger which I fear.

(1.1.122–43)

Both speeches are soliloquies, and both display Wilkins's characteristic stylistic habits. In the first, 'the intermingling of rhyme and blank verse creates two "rifts"'—in Lake's terminology, one four-line 'raft' and two couplet 'rafts'. In the second, 'blank verse over the first half gives way to rhymes over the second', but Wilkins still inserts a couplet 'raft' in the blank verse section (123–4) and a blank verse 'rift' in the rhymed section (135), as if unable to decide on either medium. In the *Miseries* soliloquy 'the end-of-line full stops all follow rhymes'; in that from *Pericles* 'the heavy stops occur at line-endings, grouping lines in twos and threes'. Jackson's commentary on Pericles' speech captures well the basic linguistic qualities which define Wilkins's verse, and by the same token differentiate it from Shakespeare's:

The units of meaning are small, following each other by a simple process of accretion. Conjunctions, prepositions, and relatives make the joins. The result is rhythmic monotony and somewhat jerky progress. While lines end with strong content words, too many of the initial iambs consist entirely of colourless function-words, as in the sequence 'When what', 'The which', 'If it', 'Then were', 'As with', 'Where now', 'By your'. (p. 12)

I submit that if this speech is compared with any extended speech of Pericles in the last three acts then, as Lewis Theobald pronounced in 1733, 'a Knowing Reader may with Ease and Certainty distinguish' two different authors.

6

Henry VIII and *The Two Noble Kinsmen* with John Fletcher

Scholarly discussion of the two plays that Shakespeare wrote together with John Fletcher has followed a by now familiar pattern: (i) in the mid-nineteenth century pioneering work identifies the scenes written by each dramatist; (ii) these findings are consolidated by other scholars, using different methods; (iii) Shakespeare 'conservators' deny the findings, asserting his sole authorship; (iv) a recent generation of scholars, using more powerful analytical tools, validates the originally proposed divisions. The pattern being familiar, in discussing these two co-authored plays there is little need to follow out every move for and against. But I want to discuss the respective methodologies in enough detail to enable readers to understand and evaluate them.

HENRY VIII

In the history of canonical studies *Henry VIII* has a particular importance, since it inspired the first serious discussion of Shakespeare's verse style. As early as 1758, Richard Roderick's 'Remarks' on the verse of *King Henry VIII*[1] drew attention to three peculiarities in 'the measure [metre] throughout this whole Play':

There are in this Play many more verses than in any other which end with a redundant syllable—such as these:

> Healthful | and e | ver since | a fresh | admi | rer.
> Of what | I saw | there an | untime | ly a | gue.
> I was | then pre | sent saw'em | salute | on horse | back.
> In their | embrace | ment as | they grew | toge | ther—&c.

(I.I.3 ff.)

---

[1] Roderick was a poet and a Cambridge don, whose Shakespearian notes were inserted by Thomas Edwards in the sixth edition of his spirited attack on Warburton's edition of Shakespeare, *The Canons of Criticism . . . with Additions* (1758), pp. 225–8. Quotations are from the selections in *CHS*, iv. 338–40.

The measure here ends in the syllables '—mi—a—horse—ge', and a good reader will, by a gentle lowering of the voice and quickening of the pronunciation, so contract the pairs of syllables '—mirer—ague—horse-back—gether—' as to make them have only the force of one syllable each to a judicious hearer.

This Fact (whatever Shakespeare's design was in it) is undoubtedly true, and may be demonstrated to Reason and proved to Sense. The first, by comparing any Number of Lines in this Play with an equal number in any other Play, by which it will appear that this Play has very near *two* redundant verses to *one* in any other Play. And to prove it to Sense, Let any one only read aloud an hundred lines in any other Play, and an hundred in This, and if he perceives not the tone and cadence of his own voice to be involuntarily altered in the latter case from what it was in the former, I would never advise him to give much credit to the information of his ears. (*CHS*, iv. 338–9)

Citing Cranmer's last prophetic speech about Queen Elizabeth (5.5.17 ff.), Roderick became the first scholar to produce statistics for Shakespeare's style. He computed that 'in the 49 lines which it consists of, 32 are redundant and only 17 regular. It would, I believe, be difficult to find any 50 lines together (out of this Play) where there are even so many as 17 redundant'.

Roderick's second observation was equally important, sketching in some of the norms for Shakespeare's metrical practice. The later course of authorship studies will show how often critics have erred, not appreciating the increasing flexibility with which Shakespeare used the iambic pentameter.

Nor is this the only peculiarity of measure in this play. The *Cæsuræ*, or Pauses of the verse, are full as remarkable. The common Pauses in English verses are upon the 5th or the 6th syllable (the 6th I think most frequently). In this Play a great number of verses have the Pause on the 7th syllable, such as (in the aforesaid speech of Cranmer) are these:

> Which time shall bring to ripeness—she shall be.
> A pattern to all princes—living with | her.
> More covetous of wisdom—and fair vir | tue.
> Shall still be doubled on her—truth shall nurse | her.
> And hang their heads with sorrow—good goes with | her.
> And claim by those their greatness—not by blood.
> Nor shall this peace sleep with her—but as when.
> As great in admiration—as herself.
> Who from the sacred ashes—of her ho | nour.
> Shall be and make new nations—he shall flou | rish.
> To all the plains about him—children's children.

(5.5.20 ff.)

(*CHS*, iv. 339–40)

The third type of metrical irregularity that Roderick noted in *Henry VIII* derived from an intelligent observation of the interplay between metre and meaning:

Lastly, it is very observable in the measure of this Play, that the emphasis arising from the sense of the verse very often clashes with the cadence that would naturally result from the metre; i.e., syllables that have an emphasis in the sentence upon the account of the *sense* or *meaning* of it are put in the uneven place of the verse, and are in the scansion made the first syllables of the foot, and consequently short, for the English foot is Iambic.

Take a few instances from the aforesaid speech:

> And all that shall succede. Shĕbā was ne | ver. (23)
> Than this blĕst sōul shall be: all princely gra | ces. (25)
> Her foes shăke, līke a field of beaten corn.
> And hang their heads with sorrow; gŏod grōws with | her.
> In hēr dăys, every man shall eat in safe | ty,
> Under his ōwn vĭne what he plants, and sing. (31 ff.)
> Nor shall this pēace sleĕp with her; but as when. (39)
> Wherever the brĭght sūn of heav'n shall shine. (50)
> Shall be, and māke nĕw nations. He shall flou | rish (53)
> Shall sēe thĭs, añd blĕss heav'n— (55)

What Shakespeare intended by all this, I fairly own myself ignorant; but that all these peculiarities were done by him advertently, and not by chance is, I think, as plain to all sense as that Virgil intended to write Metre, and not Prose, in his *Æneid*. (*CHS*, iv. 340)

Having demonstrated these recurring deviations from the iambic norm, Roderick's immediate deduction was that textual editors such as Pope and Warburton ought not to have amassed such a 'heap of emendations founded upon the presumption of his being either unknowing or unsollicitous about [metrical norms]. Alterations of this sort ought surely to be made more sparingly than has been done, and never without great harshness indeed seems to require it, or great improvement in the sentiment is obtained by it' (ibid.).

Roderick's perceptive remarks were not altogether ignored by his successors, but they were not applied to considerations of the play's authorship. Nor were the observations made by Charles Knight some fifty years later, concerning another unusual feature in the style of *Henry VIII*:

It is remarkable for the elliptical construction of many of the sentences and for an occasional peculiarity in the versification, which is not found in any other of Shakspere's works. The Roman plays, decidedly amongst the latest of his productions, possess a colloquial freedom of versification which in some cases approaches almost to ruggedness. But in the *Henry VIII* this freedom is carried much farther. We have repeated instances in which the lines are so constructed that it is impossible to read them with the slightest pause at the end of each line: the sentence must be run together, so as to produce more the effect of measured prose than of blank-verse. As an example of what we mean, we will write a sentence of fourteen lines as if it had been printed as prose:

Hence I took a thought this was a judgment on me; that my kingdom, well worthy the best heir of the world, should not be gladded in't by me: Then follows, that I weigh'd the danger which my realms stood in by this my issue's fail: and that gave to me many a groaning throe. Thus hulling in the wild sea of my conscience, I did steer towards this remedy, whereupon we are now present here together; that's to say, I meant to rectify my conscience,—which I then did feel full sick, and yet not well,—by all the reverend fathers of the land, and doctors learn'd.

If the reader will turn to the passage [2.4.194–207] he will see that many of the lines end with particles, and that scarcely one of the lines is marked by a pause at the termination. Many other passages could be pointed out with this peculiarity.[2]

Knight's observation was correct: in this fourteen-line passage only two of the lines are end-stopped. Knight concluded that this stylistic feature ran through the whole play, and that Shakespeare used it with a distinct artistic purpose: 'The elliptical construction, and the licence of versification, brought the dialogue, whenever the speaker was not necessarily rhetorical, closer to the language of common life' (p. 404).

These observations by Roderick and Knight on the play's peculiarities of style were capable of being applied to the authorship question, as James Spedding, the distinguished editor and biographer of Francis Bacon, realized. In 1850 Spedding submitted to the *Gentleman's Magazine* an essay setting out a reasoned argument for Shakespeare and Fletcher as co-authors. Spedding summarized critical opinion that 'there was something singular and exceptional' about the play, that it contained 'certain singularities . . . which require to be accounted for', among them two features of the verse style. Spedding echoed Roderick on the first point, 'the unusual number of lines with a redundant syllable at the end, of which it is said that there are twice as many in this as in any other play of Shakespeare's'. His second point, deriving from Charles Knight, concerned 'the number of passages in which the lines are so run into each other that it is impossible to separate them in reading by the slightest pause at the end of each'.[3] Spedding recorded that 'I had often amused myself with attempting to trace the gradual change of [Shakespeare's] versification from the simple monotonous cadence of *The Two Gentlemen of Verona*, to the careless felicities of *The Winter's Tale* and *Cymbeline*, of which it seemed as impossible to analyse the law as not to feel the melody', but of some speeches in *Henry VIII* he could only ask himself, 'was it possible to believe that these lines were written by Shakespeare?' (Spedding 1850*a*, p. 117). Accordingly, he 'determined to read the play through with an eye to this special point', well aware that the issue could not be settled 'by detached extracts':

the only satisfactory evidence upon which it can be determined whether a given scene was or was not by Shakespeare, is to be found in the general effect produced on the mind, the ear, and the feelings by a free and broad perusal.

---

[2] C. Knight, *Studies of Shakspere* (London, 1849), pp. 403–4.
[3] J. Spedding, 'Who Wrote Shakspere's *Henry VIII*?', GM 178, NS 34 (1850): 115–23, at p. 115; repr. as 'On the Several Shares of Shakespeare and Fletcher in the Play of *Henry VIII*', TNSS 1 (1874): 1*–18*.

There Spedding formulated what should be a fundamental principle of authorship studies, that we must pay attention to every element in our experience of a text. The result of his 'examination was a clear conviction that at least two different hands had been employed in the composition of *Henry VIII*; . . . and that they had worked, not together, but alternately upon distinct portions of it' (p. 118).

Spedding supported his argument at first by a general characterization of the two different styles that he could distinguish. The opening scene, the conversation between Buckingham, Norfolk, and Abergavenny, Spedding recorded,

seemed to have the full stamp of Shakespere, in his latest manner: the same close-packed expression; the same life, and reality, and freshness; the same rapid and abrupt turnings of thought, so quick that language can hardly follow fast enough; the same impatient activity of intellect and fancy, which having once disclosed an idea cannot wait to work it orderly out; the same daring confidence in the resources of language, which plunges headlong into a sentence without knowing how it is to come forth; the same careless metre which disdains to produce its harmonious effects by the ordinary devices, yet is evidently subject to a master of harmony; the same entire freedom from book-language and commonplace; all the qualities, in short, which distinguish the magical hand which has never yet been successfully imitated. (p. 118)

That remarkably sensitive impressionistic description of Shakespeare's late style, partly indebted to Charles Lamb (see below), could be illustrated by at least twenty different speeches in the opening scene, such as this, where Buckingham utters his *ressentiment* against Wolsey:

> To th'king I'll say't, and make my vouch as strong
> As shore of rock: attend. This holy fox,
> Or wolf, or both—for he is equal rav'nous
> As he is subtle, and as prone to mischief,
> As able to perform't, his mind and place
> Infecting one another, yea reciprocally—
> Only to show his pomp as well in France
> As here at home, suggests the king our master
> To this last costly treaty; th'interview
> That swallowed so much treasure, and like a glass
> Did break i'th'wrenching.

> (1.1.157–67)

Spedding found the same stylistic characteristics equally strong in the council chamber scene following (1.2), where Katherine utters her hostility to Wolsey.

But the instant I entered upon the third scene, in which the Lord Chamberlain, Lord Sands, and Lord Lovel converse, I was conscious of a total change. I felt as if I had passed suddenly out of the language of nature into the language of the stage, or of some conventional mode of conversation. The structure of the verse was quite different and full of mannerism. The expression became suddenly diffuse and languid. The wit wanted mirth and character. And all this was equally true of the supper scene which closes the first Act. (p. 118)

Spedding's remarks well apply to passages such as these, where two courtiers mock the English fondness for French fashions:

> *Chamberlain.* As far as I see, all the good our English
>   Have got by the late voyage is but merely
>   A fit or two o'th'face—but they are shrewd ones,
>   For when they hold 'em, you would swear directly
>   Their very noses had been counsellors
>   To Pepin or Clotharius, they keep state so.
> *Sands.* They all have new legs, and lame ones; one would take it,
>   That never see 'em pace before, the spavin,
>   A springhald reigned among 'em.
> *Chamberlain.*   Death, my lord,
>   Their clothes are after such a pagan cut to't,
>   That sure th'have worn out Christendom.
>
>   (1.3.6–14)

It is precisely from the observation of such stylistic differences in the course of a normal reading that authorship studies arise.

Spedding then looked for an objective test that might confirm his subjective impression, drawing on Richard Roderick's point about the profusion of 'redundant syllables'. Spedding, however, argued that his observation 'does not apply to all parts of the play alike, but only to those which I have noticed as, in their general character, un-Shaksperian. In those parts which have the stamp of Shakspere on them in other respects, the proportion of lines with the redundant syllable is not greater than in other of his later plays . . .' (p. 121). Spedding set out his computation in numerical form, computing the relation between lines containing 'a redundant syllable' and regular verse lines in proportional terms. In Table 6.1 I have recalculated these figures as percentages, and rearranged the scenes into two groups. Spedding offered some comparative figures from Shakespeare's other, sole-authored late plays (again as proportions: I recalculate as percentages). In the opening scene of *Cymbeline*, he computed, 'an unimpassioned conversation, chiefly narrative, we find twenty-five such lines in sixty-seven' or 37.3 per cent. In 3.3, 'which is in a higher strain of poetry but still calm', he found 23 such lines in 107, or 21.5 per cent, while in 3.4, 'which is full of sudden turns of passion', his figures were 53 in 182, or 29.1 per cent; taken together, the three scenes gave a 'proportion of about two to seven', or 29 per cent. In Act 3 scenes 2 and 3 of *The Winter's Tale*, 'selected at random', the figures were 71 in 248, or 28.6 per cent. As can be seen, these rates are comparable to those for

TABLE 6.1. Henry VIII: *redundant syllables*
(*a*) Shakespeare scenes

Scene	Total lines	Redundant syllables	
		Total	%
1.1	225	63	28.0
1.2	215	74	34.4
2.3	107	41	38.3
2.4	230	72	31.3
3.2a	193	62	32.1
5.1	176	68	38.6
Shakespeare average: 33.8			

(*b*) Fletcher scenes

Scene	Total lines	Redundant syllables	
		Total	%
1.3 & 1.4	172	100	58.1
2.1	164	97	59.1
2.2	129	77	59.7
3.1	166	119	71.7
3.2b	257	152	59.1
4.1	116	57	49.1
4.2	173	102	59.0
5.2	217	115	53.0
5.4[a]	—	—	—
5.5	73	44	60.3
Fletcher average: 58.9			

Note: [a] Spedding did not compute the redundant syllables in this scene, since it is 'almost all prose'.

Source: Spedding 1850a, p. 121.

Shakespeare's scenes in *Henry VIII*, and substantially lower than those for Fletcher's scenes.

Spedding noted that the rates for each dramatist moved within relatively stable bounds: in my computation, from 28.0 to 38.6 per cent for Shakespeare, with an average of 33.8, and for Fletcher from 49.1 to 71.7 per cent, with an average of 58.9. (Most significant to a modern statistician is the fact that there is a clear gap of 10 percentage points between the two authors, with no overlap.) Furthermore, Spedding indicated, the difference in styles was not affected by the 'subject or character of the several scenes'. In Fletcher's scenes, 'the light and loose conversation at the end of the first Act, the plaintive and laboured oration in the second, the querulous and passionate altercation in the third, the pathetic sorrows of Wolsey, the tragic death of Katherine, the high poetic prophecy of Cranmer, are equally distinguished by this peculiarity' of a redundant syllable at the end of the verse line (p. 122). Spedding's deduction, made 150 years ago, seems entirely justified:

A distinction so broad and so uniform, running through so large a portion of the same piece, cannot have been accidental; and the more closely it is examined the more clearly will it appear that the metre in these scenes is managed upon entirely different principles, and bears evidence of different workmen. (p. 122)

While happily accepting that conclusion, the reader would naturally like to see it confirmed by a comparable analysis of Fletcher's style in other plays. Spedding recognized this need, but was unwilling to tackle the work involved: 'to explain all the particular difference would be to analyze the structure first of Shakespeare's metre then of Fletcher's; a dry and tedious task', he judged (ibid.). Spedding was sure that clear differences would appear once 'any undoubted specimen of Shakespeare's later workmanship' were placed next to a similar specimen from Fletcher's middle period, but he pointed out the very real difficulty (in 1850) of finding 'a serious play known to be the unassisted composition of Fletcher, and to have been written about the year 1612'. It was many years before scholars such as E. H. C. Oliphant and Cyrus Hoy could develop any reliable methods of distinguishing Fletcher's authorship from that of his collaborators, so we may excuse Spedding for not attempting that task. He did suggest three Fletcher plays which might be studied, and offered data for one of them, in which 154 out of 232 lines ended with a redundant syllable, or 66.4 per cent, which certainly matches the rate for the Fletcherian scenes in *Henry VIII*.

By one of those occasional scholarly coincidences, no sooner had Spedding published his essay than Samuel Hickson wrote a letter to the *Gentleman's Magazine*, announcing that he had reached 'exactly the same conclusion' some years earlier. His division of the play corresponded entirely to Spedding's, including ascribing the Prologue and Epilogue to Fletcher, and marking the change of authorship in 3.2 at line 203, following the King's exit.[4] In response, Spedding commented 'that two independent inquiries should thus have arrived at the same conclusions upon so many particulars' showed that 'the conclusions are according to reason'. Spedding also

---

[4] S. Hickson, Letter to the Editor, *GM* 178 (NS 34) (1850): 198; repr. as 'A Confirmation of Mr. Spedding's Paper on the Authorship of *Henry VIII*', in *TNSS* 1 (1874): 18*–20*.

acknowledged that 'the resemblance of the style, in some parts of the play, to Fletcher's, was pointed out to me several years ago by Alfred Tennyson', and that he had learned of 'the general distinctions between Shakespeare's manner and Fletcher's' from remarks on *The Two Noble Kinsmen* by Charles Lamb, William Spalding, and Hickson himself (see below). 'But, having been thus put upon the scent and furnished with principles, I followed the inquiry out myself, without help or communication'.[5]

Spedding's pioneering essay, one of the first classics of Shakespeare authorship studies, was reprinted in the New Shakspere Society's *Transactions* in 1874, with a new title,[6] and given deserved recognition. J. K. Ingram described it as 'the first example . . . of the application to Shaksperian metre of the strict numerical analysis', while the Society's president, F. J. Furnivall, paid a warm tribute to Spedding for having 'led the way, in which we, thus late, are following him'.[7] Furnivall then gave a 'fresh confirmation' of Spedding's division of authorship by computing the number of 'unstopped' (or run-on) lines in the play. I give his results in Table 6.2, again converting proportions to percentages. (Furnivall's totals for scene lengths differ slightly from Spedding's.) These figures again show a relatively narrow range for each dramatist, from 43.8 to 54.4 per cent for Shakespeare, with an average of 48.5 per cent, and a slightly greater range (bearing in mind the unrepresentative figures generally supplied by short scenes, such as the two concluding ones) for Fletcher, from 15.6 to 33.7 per cent, with an average of 24.8. Once again the two ranges are clearly separated, the highest value for Fletcher being some 10 per cent lower than the lowest value for Shakespeare.

Spedding's essay also stimulated the Irish scholar, John Ingram, to introduce a new verse test, measuring 'light' and 'weak' endings.[8] Acknowledging that Spedding's essay, together with Hickson's on *The Two Noble Kinsmen*, were 'the earliest examples of the systematic use of verse-tests to discriminate the work of different authors in the same play' (Ingram 1874, p. 444), Ingram developed a classification already made by George Craik[9] distinguishing two kinds of weak endings, previously treated as a single group. Craik and Ingram pointed out that in one of these groups 'the voice can to a certain small extent dwell [on the words] whilst the others are so essentially *proclitic*[10] . . . that we

---

[5] J. Spedding, 'Who Wrote Shakspere's *Henry VIII*?', Letter to the Editor, *GM* 178, NS 34 (1850): 381–2, at p. 382.

[6] 'On the Several Shares of Shakespeare and Fletcher in the Play of *Henry VIII*', *TNSS* 1 (1874): 1*–18*.

[7] F. J. Furnivall, 'Another Fresh Confirmation of Mr. Spedding's Division and Date of the Play of *Henry VIII*', *TNSS* 1 (1874): 24*.

[8] J. K. Ingram, 'On the "Weak Endings" of Shakspere, With Some Account of the History of the Verse-tests in General', *TNSS* 1 (1874): 442–64.

[9] G. Craik, *English of Shakespeare, illustrated in a philological commentary on his 'Julius Caesar'* (London, 1857); rev. edns., 1859, 1864, etc.

[10] Ingram took this term from the German scholar Hertzberg, who had used it in his preface to *Cymbeline*, in Ulrici's edition of the Schlegel–Tieck translation (1871), describing the many

TABLE 6.2. Henry VIII: *unstopped (run-on) lines*
(*a*) Shakespeare scenes

Scene	Total lines	Unstopped lines	
		Total	%
1.1	226	123	54.4
1.2	214	115	53.7
2.3	107	45	42.1
2.4	241	113	46.9
3.2a	203	101	49.8
5.1	178	78	43.8
		Shakespeare average: 48.5	

(*b*) Fletcher scenes

Scene	Total lines	Unstopped lines	
		Total	%
1.3 & 1.4	174	45	25.9
2.1	169	57	33.7
2.2	134	39	29.1
3.1	172[a]	36	20.9
3.2b	257	75	29.2
4.1	117	39	33.3
4.2	173	38	22.0
5.2	213	47	22.1
5.3	41	8	19.5
5.4	77	12	15.6
		Fletcher average: 24.8	

Note: [a] Not including the song 'Orpheus with his lute . . .'.
Source: Furnivall 1874*a*, p. 24*.

are forced to run them, in pronunciation no less than in sense, into the closest connection with the words of the succeeding line' (p. 447). They called the first of these groups 'light endings', the second 'weak endings'. Ingram itemized fifty-four monosyllabic words that could be used for light endings, such as the pronouns *I, thou, you, he*, and so forth, *do*, and *have* in various

weak endings in that play as 'proklitische Formwörter'. The word 'proclitic', which *OED* traces from 1864, is used in Greek grammar to describe 'a monosyllabic word that is so closely attached in pronunciation to the following word as to have no accent of its own', and is applied generally to a similar word in any language.

forms, when used as an auxiliary. As an example of a 'strong' ending, we could cite

> If I say sooth, I must report they were
> As cannons overcharged with double cracks
>
> (*Mac.*, 1.2.36)

Other monosyllabic words used to create light endings include the relatives *who, which, that*, the prepositions *upon, through, into*, and *yet* (in the sense of Latin *tamen*). The monosyllables yielding weak endings are fewer (twenty in all), such as the prepositions *at, by, for, from, in, of, on, to, with*, the conjunctions *and, as, but, of, for, nor, than, that*. As an example of a 'weak' ending we could cite Banquo's report of Duncan in Dunsinane:

> He hath been in unusual pleasures, and
> Sent forth great largess to your offices.
>
> (*Mac.*, 2.1.13–14)

Ingram counted the instances of light and weak endings in the whole of Shakespeare, showing a remarkable increase in the final ten plays (p. 450). *Twelfth Night* has 3 light endings and 1 weak ending; *Antony and Cleopatra* has 71 and 28 respectively; *Winter's Tale* 57 and 43. For *Henry VIII* Ingram computed in Shakespeare's scenes '45 light endings against 7 in Fletcher's part, and 37 weak endings against 1 in Fletcher's part' (p. 453). Every Shakespearian scene in the play contains weak endings, only one of Fletcher's (4.1), such scarcity being apparently normal for Fletcher. Ingram checked Fletcher's *The Custom of the Country*, and found just three (*and, from, with*). He could find no indication that a third dramatist was involved in *Henry VIII*.

In this way, the three independent verse tests carried out by Spedding, Furnivall, and Ingram agreed on the division of authorship in *Henry VIII*, their assignation of scenes coinciding exactly with that already made by Hickson. However, the division of the play between Shakespeare and Fletcher did not suit every student. Robert Boyle[11] and H. Dugdale Sykes[12] each claimed a share for Massinger, but neither of them convinced other scholars. Boyle worked by intuition, and could seemingly detect the exact point in a scene where Massinger took over from Fletcher, or even where Fletcher inserted a single verse line, while Sykes based his claims on parallel passages alone. I shall not summarize their cases, since they were well refuted by Marjorie Hope Nicolson and Baldwin Maxwell, respectively.[13] Further

---

[11] R. Boyle, '*Henry VIII*: An Investigation into the Origin and Authorship of the Play', *TNSS* 11 (1885): 443–87.

[12] H. D. Sykes, '*King Henry VIII*', in Sykes, *Sidelights on Shakespeare* (Stratford-upon-Avon, 1919*b*), pp. 18–47.

[13] M. H. Nicolson, 'The Authorship of *Henry the Eighth*', *PMLA* 37 (1922): 484–502, at pp. 485–7; B. Maxwell, *Studies in Beaumont, Fletcher, and Massinger* (Chapel Hill, NC, 1939; repr. New York 1966), pp. 63–73 (originally a review essay in *MP* 23 (1925–6): 365–72).

TABLE 6.3. *Contraction preferences:* 'em / them *in Fletcher and Shakespeare*

	'em	*them*	Proportion
Fletcher			
The Woman's Prize	60	4	15:1
Bonduca	83	6	13.8:1
Shakespeare			
Cymbeline	3	64	1:21.3
The Winter's Tale	8	37	1:4.6
The Tempest	13	38	1:2.9

Source: Thorndike 1901, pp. 25–6.

TABLE 6.4. *Contraction preferences in* Henry VIII

	Total lines	*'em*	*them*	Proportion
Shakespeare's part	1,168	5	17	1:3.4
Fletcher's part	1,604	57	4	14.3:1

Source: Thorndike 1901, pp. 40–1.

lingustic evidence supporting the division, quite independent of the verse tests, was produced by Ashley Thorndike in 1901, and by Willard Farnham in 1916.

Thorndike had noticed the great frequency with which Fletcher uses *'em* instead of *them*, and argued that the preference for either of these forms could be a fair indication of authorship. The preliminary figures he offered applied to plays of sole authorship,[14] and are set out in Table 6.3 (with the figures for proportions added). Although the Shakespeare figures vary, they all show his distinct preference for the full form, 'them'. Thorndike agreed that Spedding's 1850 essay 'conclusively proved that there were two authors of the play and that the second was Fletcher', and added: 'Fletcher's share is doubted by no one who has systematically studied his versification' (p. 39). He then gave his figures for *Henry VIII*, calculated according to Spedding's division, which I show in Table 6.4. As Thorndike commented, this test 'very strongly confirms the accepted division of the play between the two authors', and 'strongly

[14] A. H. Thorndike, *The Influence of Beaumont and Fletcher on Shakspere* (Worcester, Mass., 1901; repr. New York, 1966), pp. 24–6.

confirms the assignment of these parts to Shakspere and Fletcher' (pp. 40–1), since the figures for Shakespeare's part correspond closely with his practice in *The Winter's Tale* (1611), while those for Fletcher closely match his preferences in *Bonduca* (1616). For Thorndike the evidence showed the Fletcher and Shakespeare parts to be 'distinct, free from interpretations and revisions. There is only one scene (2.3) which contains neither *'em*s nor *them*s', and in each of the other scenes *them* predominates in Shakespeare, *'em* in Fletcher's part. Taken in conjunction with the clear division made by the three independent verse tests, Thorndike reasoned, this detail makes it probable 'that we have Shakspere's and Fletcher's work intact' (p. 42).

Thorndike initially claimed that his figures demonstrated 'the worthlessness' of Boyle's division of the play between Massinger and Fletcher, since Massinger rarely used *'em* (pp. 26–7, 41–2), a claim he subsequently withdrew in an errata slip, having discovered that modern editors had converted all Massinger's *'em*s to *them*s. That issue, however, was definitively settled by Willard Farnham, who tested plays by Beaumont, Fletcher, Davenport, Shakespeare, and Massinger in terms of their use of colloquial contractions, his results successfully distinguishing between them.[15] As we saw above, Farnham distinguished three groups of contractions, those clipping the *i* from the word *it*, and replacing it with a ' (*in't* for *in it*, similarly *to't*, *on't*, *offer't*); those contracting both *the* and the preceding preposition (*i'th* or *i'th'* for *in the*, similarly *o'th'*, *to'th'*, *by'th'*); and those contracting *us* or *his*, joining them to the preceding word (*on's* for *on us* or *on his*, similarly *in's*, *make's*). The third of these groups, the *s* contraction, being 'the most uncommon of all', proved particularly important (pp. 328–9). Farnham documented (pp. 342–4) an enormous rise in Shakespeare's use of contractions between *The Merchant of Venice*, with a total of 6, and *The Winter's Tale*, with a total of 164 (96 of these being *t* contractions, 42 being *the* contractions, and 16 *s* contractions). Farnham showed that Fletcher could be differentiated from Beaumont in each of the three categories (pp. 336–7), while Massinger was unusual in that none of his examined plays used *s* contractions (p. 338).

Farnham then analysed the use of contractions in *Henry VIII*, according to the accepted division (see Table 6.5). In purely statistical terms, Shakespeare used a consistently large number of contractions, almost three times as frequently as Fletcher. The total for Fletcher, thirty-nine for over half the play, agrees well with the average total that Farnham had computed for a Fletcherian play, about seventy (pp. 337, 350). An equally clear distinction emerges when the character of the contractions is studied, for Shakespeare's scenes use seven *s* contractions, as against Fletcher's two; they use more *the* contractions; and they use 'not only more *t* constructions . . . , but these

[15] W. E. Farnham, 'Colloquial Contractions in Beaumont, Fletcher, Massinger, and Shakespeare as a Test of Authorship', *PMLA* 31 (1916): 326–58, at pp. 326–8.

TABLE 6.5. *Colloquial contractions in* Henry VIII

Author	Line total	Total contractions	Average per line	Frequency: every *x* lines
Fletcher	1,597	39	0.24	40.9
Shakespeare	1,166	77	0.66	15.1

Source: Farnham 1916, pp. 348–50.

are more varied', including several with verbs (p. 350). Finally, Farnham juxtaposed Shakespeare's usage with Massinger's, as computed for the early plays, discovering that *t* contractions were 'many and varied' in Shakespeare, but 'rather few' in Massinger. Shakespeare had 'many' instances of *the* contractions, Massinger 'very few', and whereas Shakespeare made 'occasional use' of *s* contractions, Massinger used 'none' at all. Shakespeare emerges as 'a decidedly colloquial writer', Massinger a 'decidedly uncolloquial' one, who 'could not possibly have written *all* of the non-Fletcherian parts of *Henry VIII*'. Farnham checked on specific scenes claimed for Massinger, only to find them 'as un-Massingerian as the rest of the non-Fletcherian scenes' (p. 351).

Throughout the scholarly discussion of *Henry VIII* and its authorship, two main types of evidence have been used, metrical and linguistic. Rather than keep to a strict chronological order, I propose to deal with the verse tests first, picking up the story again in 1927, when E. H. C. Oliphant published his comprehensive analysis of the Beaumont and Fletcher canon. As we saw in Chapter 1, Oliphant characterized Fletcher's verse as having 'the most distinct and individual style' of all the dramatists involved, marked by an 'excessive use of double endings', regularly amounting to 70 per cent, coupled with many trisyllabic endings.[16] Oliphant perceptively noted that Fletcher often obtained this effect 'by means of some conventional and wholly unnecessary end word . . . thrown in for no other purpose', such as 'still', 'else', 'too', 'sir', or 'lady' (p. 33). Another distinctive feature of Fletcher's style is his avoidance of 'run-on verse', for Oliphant computed that about 90 per cent of his lines are end-stopped (pp. 34–5). Despite this potentially monotonous feature, Fletcher achieved an effect of 'careless ease' and conversational freedom in his verse, scarcely ever using rhyme (p. 36). Oliphant also computed that about 45 per cent of Fletcher's speeches 'end where the verses end', in sharp contrast with Massinger's 15 per cent (p. 60). Yet, despite this pioneering attempt to

[16] E. H. C. Oliphant, *The Plays of Beaumont and Fletcher: An Attempt to Determine their Respective Shares and the Shares of Others* (New Haven, 1927; repr. New York, 1970), p. 32.

identify and quantify the characteristics of Fletcher's verse style, when he came to discuss *Henry VIII* (pp. 302–16) Oliphant made no use of his statistics, falling back on generalities ('the style of the verse is decidedly Fletcher's', p. 316; some lines are 'reminiscent of the manner of Fletcher', p. 312). Oliphant had expressed diffidence about the value of verse tests (p. 5), but it is disappointing that he did not realize the value of these tools. In the light of the important demonstration that Marco Mincoff was to make in 1961 comparing the distinct changes that Fletcher's style underwent according to the collaborator with whom he worked (see below), it was prescient of Oliphant to point out that in *Henry VIII* 'the Fletcherian characteristics [appear] in greatly modified form . . . Fletcher seems more in earnest (because, I suppose, he was more on his mettle) here than elsewhere; and in consequence we have here his best work. Beaumont apparently exercised a certain amount of good influence over him; but Shakspere seems to have exercised more.' Still, Oliphant added, although occurring 'less frequently than ordinarily in Fletcher's work . . . the characteristics are there', and 'are of the peculiar Fletcher quality' (pp. 315–16).

After Oliphant's disinclination to use verse statistics, it comes as a pleasure, and a surprise, to find E. K. Chambers doing so in his two-volume *William Shakespeare*. Having been so sceptical about the evidence for Shakespeare's co-authorship in *Titus Andronicus* and *Timon of Athens*, Chambers accepted Spedding's division of *Henry VIII* without demur, finding that 'a general impression of stylistic differences is confirmed by the tests of double endings, overflows, and speech-endings. . . .'[17] Chambers believed that the process of collaboration might explain why both writers do not seem their normal selves: 'I should agree that *Henry VIII* is not very characteristic Fletcher, and should add that it is not very characteristic Shakespeare either. Shakespeare must have been writing in a tired vein and with some loss of concentration' (i. 497). Chambers found the strongest evidence of Fletcher's hand 'in the light scenes', 1.3 and 5.4, which have a 'superabundance of double endings, often with stressed final syllables', and also in 'the comparatively colourless state scenes' (2.2; 4.1; 5.2, 5.3), and the pathetic scenes (2.1; 3.1; 3.2.203–end; 4.2). 'There is some very good writing for him in the pathetic scenes and the play as a whole is a little out of his ordinary line. He may well have been working under the influence of Shakespeare.' Chambers argued that 'some kind of collaboration . . . is more plausible than revision' (ibid.), and in 'Appendix H: Metrical Tables' he produced three tables for what he dubbed the 'Abnormal Plays' which clearly differentiate the two dramatists (see Table 6.6, an abbreviated version of these).

Chambers provided firm quantitative evidence for the two dramatists' joint labours, clearly distinct—but Shakespeare scholars have always claimed it

---

[17] E. K. Chambers, *William Shakespeare: A Study of Facts and Problems*, 2 vols. (Oxford, 1930), i. 496.

TABLE 6.6. *Verse forms in* Henry VIII

	Feminine endings	%	Extra mid-line syllables	Overflow %	Light endings	Weak endings
Shakespeare	374	32	34	39	45	37
Fletcher	892	59	3	24	7	1

Source: Chambers 1930, ii. 403–5.

their 'old prerogative' to ignore unwelcome statistics, and to call in question the tests which have produced them. Two who did so at this time were Baldwin Maxwell and Peter Alexander. Neither scholar gave a fair indication of what their predecessors had achieved. Maxwell made the severe accusation that 'in a strict sense, Spedding cannot be said to have made any tests whatsoever', and alleged that he 'did no counting at all', writing 'under the influence of previous articles by Spalding and Hickson', only mentioning Fletcher because he considered him co-author of *The Two Noble Kinsmen*: 'but this collaboration is still doubted' (Maxwell 1939, p. 56). Alexander was equally unfair, suggesting that 'Spedding applied a test borrowed from Hickson', and pooh-poohing any idea that their independent agreement could be significant: 'Much is made of Hickson's reaching the same results in *Henry VIII* as Spedding, but once the test proposed by Hickson was accepted it was merely a matter of counting double endings. It would have been strange had they not succeeded in counting alike.'[18] But anyone who has read Spedding's work, as summarized above, will see how false these accounts are. Spedding made it very clear that his enquiry into the double authorship of *Henry VIII* began from the general impression he had gained from reading the play, and he certainly did all the counting himself. He did not take over a test proposed by Hickson, for Hickson's essay on *The Two Noble Kinsmen* includes no tables or verse tests of any kind. Spedding's affirmation that 'I followed the inquiry out myself' cannot be doubted, and it is regrettable that scholars who do not like other scholars' results should misrepresent their achievements.

Maxwell agreed that 'the strongest argument for Fletcher's participation in *Henry VIII* is certainly the great number of lines ending in a stressed extra syllable', this being 'the most pronounced characteristic of [his] style, and is most marked in certain scenes . . .' (p. 58). Maxwell had compared this play with four others by Fletcher, finding the proportion of stressed extra syllables in the Fletcherian scenes of *Henry VIII* to be much the same in *Bonduca* and *Valentinian*, plays written by Fletcher alone, but 'almost twice as great as . . .

[18] Peter Alexander, 'Conjectural History, or Shakespeare's *Henry VIII*', *Essays and Studies* 16 (1931): 85–119, at p. 103.

in the Fletcherian scenes of *Philaster* and *The Maid's Tragedy*' (p. 58), plays written with Beaumont. Although his findings here partly endorsed Spedding's, Maxwell did not attempt to estimate what degree of variation might be normal within a dramatist's work, nor what effect collaboration might have on his style. For three other tests, Baldwin argued, the figures for *Henry VIII* were uncharacteristic of Fletcher. Fletcher's rate for unstopped lines in that play, 26 per cent, according to Furnivall's figures, was higher than in the four other plays Maxwell had tested, their range being from 20.4 to 16.6 per cent (p. 61; I have recalculated proportions as percentages). But, we must respond, five Fletcher scenes in *Henry VIII* show values below 22 per cent, as can be seen from Table 6.2, and in any case the crucial point is the clear distance between Fletcher's highest score (33.7) and Shakespeare's lowest (42.1). Maxwell performed three other tests, finding that Fletcher used more 'general truths' (maxims, proverbs) in this play than in others, more parenthetical interruptions, and far less repetition than elsewhere (pp. 60–3). Maxwell concluded that, if Fletcher did write part of this play, 'either he was revising another's work, or the peculiarities of his style and method were modified by a collaborator' (pp. 58, 63). The second of those options is surely the one to endorse. Maxwell failed to discredit Spedding's findings, and he signally ignored Ingram's most revealing weak and light endings test, but he did show that a Renaissance dramatist's style can vary considerably.

The problem that Baldwin Maxwell raised, in effect, was the extent to which particular features of a writer's style would vary under normal conditions, when he was working alone, as opposed to when he was working together with one or more other dramatists. It was not until 1961 that any scholar addressed this issue, but Marco Mincoff did so then with enormous energy and authority. Mincoff, demonstrating a wide knowledge of Fletcher, took issue with Maxwell's claim that Fletcher's scenes for *Henry VIII* differed from his other work by pointing out that Fletcher's style varied greatly according to whom he worked with. With some collaborators, such as Field or Massinger, 'Fletcher did not trouble to adapt his style to theirs in any way, but he certainly subordinated himself very strongly to Beaumont', and did so equally strongly when working with Shakespeare.[19] Objecting that Maxwell's metrical statistics were taken from various sources, and revealed great differences (the counting of run-on lines being notoriously subjective), Mincoff offered his own figures for Fletcher's single and collaborative work between 1609 and 1614, figures which were derived from counting 'separate acts or scenes, and have been chosen to illustrate the limits of fluctuation within a play' (Mincoff 1961, p. 240). Mincoff analysed ten plays, and I abbreviate his findings in Table 6.7 to show the range of values in each of his three groups. (The figures in the latter category of this table refer to Fletcher's

---

[19] M. Mincoff, '*Henry VIII* and Fletcher', *ShQ* 12 (1961): 239–60, at p. 239.

TABLE 6.7. *Metrical figures for Fletcher plays*

Author(s)	Double endings (%)	Run-on lines (%)
Fletcher alone	66–80	8–17
Fletcher and Beaumont	38–50	11–24
Fletcher and Shakespeare	59–61	19–23

Source: Mincoff 1961, p. 241.

Act 2 of *The Two Noble Kinsmen,* and to all of Fletcher's scenes for *Henry VIII.*) Table 6.7 shows very clearly the considerable stylistic changes that are brought about by collaborative writing. In the Beaumont collaborations 'Fletcher's peculiar and very marked style appears only in short passages here and there', and 'the test figures fluctuate very much more erratically in these plays than when Fletcher was writing alone . . .' (ibid.). In the Shakespeare collaborations Mincoff noted a similar phenomenon, 'a certain veiling of Fletcher's stylistic peculiarities and a rather more marked dislocation of his metrical characteristics, though in neither case so great as in his work with Beaumont'. In both plays 'the double endings are considerably reduced and the run-on lines increased in comparison with . . . Fletcher's independent work . . .'. But the variations do show the need for caution when comparing statistics derived from sole and from co-authored works, a consideration that Baldwin Maxwell did not observe.

Furthermore, Mincoff argued, comparisons such as Maxwell made between the amount of repetition in one play and another, or the number of 'general truths' they may contain (a phenomenon affected by genre),[20] can be expressed statistically but are not necessarily illuminating. Statistical evidence of this type, Mincoff objected, 'comparatively seldom touches directly on the really characteristic features of a writer's style', which are 'more often qualitative than quantitative. Sometimes metrical counts do seem to reflect something that one consciously feels in the style, but equally often they do not.' Only a slight increase in the figures from one play to another can create a marked difference in stylistic texture. More important,

the statistically measurable features need to be evaluated with regard to the part they play in the styles as a whole, for their importance lies as a rule not so much in their effect individually but as the reflection of a more elaborate system that cannot be reduced to percentages.

[20] Mincoff found it 'scarcely very surprising' that Fletcher's portion of *Henry VIII* contained more 'general truths' than his other plays, for it is, after all, 'a chronicle play, heavy with political implications, in which the fall from greatness is a recurrent and heavily underlined theme . . .' (Mincoff 1961, p. 240).

Maxwell had found in Fletcher's share of *Henry VIII* only six examples of accretive repetition of the characteristic Fletcherian type, 'Oh, very mad, exceeding mad, in love too' (1.4.27), at a rate some four times less than his norm elsewhere (Maxwell 1939, p. 62). But, Mincoff replied, accretive repetitions, more generally defined, play a huge role in the system of speech patterns that determine Fletcher's style. 'For his sentence structure is based largely on accretive appositional phrases forming a series of variations on a theme', of which the example that Maxwell quoted 'is only a variant of many other patterns'. Mincoff cited several examples from *Bonduca*, such repetitions as 'Are these the men . . .? These the Julians', 'Twice we have beat 'em . . . scatter'd 'em', 'as short . . . as high . . . as subtle'. These and similar patterns, Mincoff suggested,

make up at least 50 per cent of a normal Fletcher play, and it is they that determine his rhythm, the constantly recurring cadences, and to a large extent the end-stopping too. For the short appositional phrases by which the thought expands itself in little rushes and eddies greatly increase the number of pauses in general and, naturally, of end pauses too.

Challenged by those who denied the metrical evidence, Marco Mincoff here produced a truly fruitful insight into Fletcher's style, and the interconnection between its components. Fletcher's great fondness for double endings, he suggested, derives from the same principle, 'for they break the finality of the end pause on a stressed syllable and secure a certain measure of flow in spite of the pause'. In Fletcher's work, uniquely in this period, 'end-stopping and double endings go hand in hand, nearly always rising or falling together', and 'the ratio of run-on lines is from two to five times as high among the comparatively rare masculine endings as among the feminine ones'.[21]

Mincoff's essay raised many important issues for attribution studies, of which I can only discuss a few. His demonstration that Fletcher's style changed according to his co-author enables us to revalue retrospectively studies that were affected by this factor without realizing it. For example, in a pioneering essay,[22] Karl Ege performed a 'systematic stylistic comparison' of *Henry VIII* with other, accredited plays by Shakespeare and Fletcher, studying four elements of style: '1. Imagery, 2. Rhetorical repetition[23] (all the rhetorical figures of repetition and accord), 3. Alliteration, 4. Antithesis (and related figures)' (Ege 1922, p. 99). Ege showed a good grasp of methodology, choosing plays of a comparable date: for Shakespeare, *Cymbeline*, *The Winter's Tale*, and *The Tempest*, for Fletcher, *The Mad Lover*, *Valentinian*,

---

[21] Mincoff gave these figures: 'In *The Woman's Prize*, e.g., 25 per cent of the masculine endings run on, but only 12 per cent of the feminine ones; in *Monsieur Thomas* the ratio is 21 to 10, *Wit without Money* 21 to 6, *The Mad Lover* 31 to 7' (Mincoff 1961, p. 242).

[22] K. Ege, 'Shakespeares Anteil an *Henry VIII*', *ShJb* 58 (1922): 99–119; translations mine.

[23] This is my translation of a term which has different connotations in English, 'die Wort-Parallelen (sämtliche Figuren der Wiederholung mit Gleichklang' [assonance]).

TABLE 6.8. *Stylistic elements in Shakespeare and Fletcher*

Dramatist	Images	Rhetorical repetition	Alliteration	Antithesis
Shakespeare				
Cymbeline	10	9	10	9
Winter's Tale	10.5	9	10	8
Tempest	10	9	11	8
Fletcher				
Mad Lover	6	17	21	3
Valentinian	6	13	19	2
Monsieur Thomas	6.5	14	18	2.5

Source: Ege 1922, p. 101.

and *Monsieur Thomas*. He also realized the importance of standardizing computation, choosing to express his results in terms of 'the relative density of the individual figures per 100 lines of verse' (p. 100). His computation for the control plays already displayed a clear difference between the two dramatists, set out in Table 6.8. As the table shows, Fletcher used fewer images than Shakespeare, and more irregularly, with a considerable fluctuation (from three to ten images per 100 lines) as opposed to Shakespeare's fairly constant usage. Ege found a difference in quality, too, for although capable of striking comparisons Fletcher often uses conventional images, stock classical allusions, and superficial and traditional personifications, quite unlike Shakespeare's metaphors, which are 'bold, like lightning flashes'. Fletcher is more prone to use simile, 'a weakened form of metaphor', the proportion of metaphor to simile in his control texts being 10:15, as against Shakespeare's 10:30. The dramatists differed also in their use of rhetoric. In the last phase of his career, Ege observed, Shakespeare used the resources of rhetoric economically, while Fletcher employed figures frequently but often excessively, indulging in whole sequences of repetition not having a truly organic function (p. 102)—a judgement echoed again in our time.[24] Fletcher also used alliteration to excess, 'extending alliteration on the same letter across several lines, which would be inconceivable with Shakespeare'. His use of alliteration in the last three Romances is more controlled, reserving it for passages of emotional intensity, often in love scenes (Ege 1922, p. 109).

    Ege also showed a clear difference between the two dramatists, quantitative and qualitative, in their use of antithesis, which Shakespeare employed nearly three times more frequently (8.5 instances per 100 lines as against

---

[24] C. Hoy, 'The Language of Fletcherian Tragicomedy', in J. C. Gray (ed.), *Mirror up to Shakespeare* (Toronto and London, 1984), pp. 99–113.

Fletcher's 3.5). 'In Fletcher we mostly find a purely stereotyped confrontation between two opposed concepts, frequently repeated.' No fewer than twelve of the sixty-three antitheses in *Valentinian* consist of 'live–die', other conventional pairings including 'peace–war', 'win–lose', 'joy–misery', 'love–hate'. Shakespeare treated antithesis as an important element in both thought and language, 'deliberately avoiding the set phrase' (p. 103).

> In Shakespeare antithesis frequently helps to clarify a thought by referring to its opposite; the confrontation is usually very effective. He avoids too abrupt oppositions, preferring to choose some related expression from a series of antithetically opposed concepts, as a result of which his antitheses sometimes seem concealed, felt rather than heard, but appearing none the less vivid.

Ege remains one of the few critics to have recognized this important feature of Shakespeare's style and thought.

Having described and exemplified his rationale for choosing these four stylistic resources, Ege then computed their occurrence in *Henry VIII*, discovering that although his results for Shakespeare corresponded to those for the three late Romances, some of those for Fletcher differed from the control texts. In this collaboration Fletcher used 6.5 images per 100 lines (as against 6 elsewhere), 4 instances of rhetorical repetition (15), 11 of alliteration (19), and 3 of antithesis (2.5). Faced with this discrepancy, Ege bluntly concluded that Fletcher could not have been co-author of *Henry VIII* (p. 106). Since Mincoff's demonstration that many features of Fletcher's style were affected by co-authorship, we can understand why Ege's figures for two of the four stylistic markers in Fletcher's scenes here should deviate from the other three plays tested. Despite the numerical discrepancy, Ege's analysis showed several continuities with qualities he had earlier identified as typifying Fletcher, such as the 'completely conventional' imagery in the non-Shakespearian scenes of *Henry VIII* (pp. 106, 114) as in Fletcher's sole-authored plays (pp. 101, 104). Ege admitted that the unknown co-author was 'close to Fletcher' in several respects (pp. 106, 114), and his results for the first three acts were actually very close to those yielded by the control texts.[25] But, like some other commentators on *Henry VIII*, Ege simply could not accept the idea that Shakespeare could have allowed Fletcher to write the 'great speeches' of Buckingham's and Wolsey's farewells, or Cranmer's prophetic speech over the newborn Elizabeth (pp. 109–14). This preconceived idea seems to have even influenced his counting of the four stylistic features from 3.2 onwards. Ege's failure to trust the evidence of his own computations shows, retrospectively, the value of Mincoff's demonstration that Fletcher's normal idiolect was affected by the collaborative process.

[25] Ege's figures for antithesis per 100 lines in Shakespeare's 1.1, 1.2, 2.3, and 2.4 (8, 8, 10, 8), show the same contrast with those for Fletcher's 1.3, 1.4, 2.1, and 2.2 (3.3, 3.5, 2.5). The highest figures for alliteration come in Fletcher's 1.3 (27), 1.4 (13), and 3.1 (14)—and so on.

Mincoff's essay also drew attention to the crucial process by which we define the stylistic markers to be computed. Baldwin Maxwell had claimed that there is suspiciously more use of parenthesis in the scenes ascribed to Fletcher in *Henry VIII* than in his other work, namely once in every 89.2 lines, as opposed to four other plays, where it only occurs once every 141–254 lines (Maxwell 1939, pp. 60–1). But Maxwell defined parenthesis very strictly, as a syntactically separate unit occurring in the middle of a clause. By taking a slightly more flexible definition, allowing the comment to be attached to the main clause by a conjunction, Mincoff produced figures of one parenthesis in 75.7 lines for *Henry VIII*, and one in 62.2 'for a piece of pure Fletcher of similar length', Acts 3 and 4 of *Valentinian* (Mincoff 1961, p. 243). In stylometry the definition of a stylistic marker plays a crucial role in influencing all subsequent computations and arguments, and should be chosen—and evaluated—with great care.

As I mentioned before, Baldwin Maxwell was one of the two sceptics in the inter-war years who challenged the case for Fletcher having written part of *Henry VIII*. The other was Peter Alexander, who attacked several proponents of Fletcher's co-authorship, while not always reporting them accurately.[26] Alexander challenged the accuracy of Richard Roderick's two-century-old estimate of the number of double endings in Shakespeare's late plays (Alexander 1931, p. 104), not a difficult task, we might think, and he dismissed with equal ease the theories of Boyle (pp. 105–6), and J. M. Robertson (pp. 109–10). As for E. A. Abbott's claim that *Henry VIII* was unique, and therefore inauthentic in its treatment of feminine endings, breaking Abbott's supposed 'rule (that the extra syllable is rarely a monosyllable)', Alexander readily disproved it with instances from *The Tempest* and *The Winter's Tale* (pp. 106–7). These were valid corrections of unscholarly claims. However, Alexander also called in question Ingram's statistics for light and weak endings because they appeared to show great variations within a play (pp. 108–9), hinting that the stylistic variations within *Henry VIII* might be due to as sudden a change in Shakespeare's style as that found with *Antony and Cleopatra*. Alexander did not argue this point in any detail, preferring to attack Spedding's speculations about Shakespeare's original conception of the play, another easy target. But he unsettled the received picture—as he had represented it, at least—sufficiently for some orthodox Shakespearians to feel reassured that Fletcher's contribution had been called in question. For others, prepared to do the detailed and often tedious work involved in authorship studies, computing minute qualities of style, these objections were merely a

---

[26] It is not true that 'Spedding also pointed to a difference in the proportion of run-on lines in the two parts, these varying inversely with the double endings' (Alexander 1931, p. 104). Spedding merely observed that 'this play is remarkable for the prevalence of *two* [metrical] peculiarities of different kinds, which are in some degree irreconcilable with each other' (1850a, p. 115).

challenge to find more conclusive stylistic markers with which to define each writer's work.

Alexander's denial of Fletcher's co-authorship was in turn contested by three scholars, Ants Oras, Robert Adger Law, and Marco Mincoff. Oras agreed that Alexander had exposed some of the exaggerations of the Fletcherian school concerning 'the use of "extra monosyllables", that is, monosyllables forming the last metrically unstressed part of feminine endings'[27]—as David Lake later remarked, 'extra monosyllables are . . . merely a sub-class of feminine endings (those in which the final trochee is formed by separate words)'.[28] But Oras observed that Alexander had not addressed the undeniable fact of their high frequency in Fletcher's verse, in particular 'the frequency of extra monosyllables in relation to the total number of feminine endings' (Oras 1953, p. 199). Oras then analysed this phenomenon in both Fletcherian collaborations, *Henry VIII* and *The Two Noble Kinsmen*, three other plays by Shakespeare (*Cymbeline, Winter's Tale, Tempest*), and three by Fletcher alone (*Valentinian, Bonduca, Monsieur Thomas*). In his analysis Oras considered 'only blank verse, and only "full lines", i. e., lines with at least five metrical beats. Triple endings are counted as feminine endings', scenes in prose or rhyme are omitted (p. 200). Oras supplied remarkably full data, which I have rearranged in tabular form in Table 6.9. For the remaining plays Oras gave the totals given in Table 6.10. As Oras observed, 'even a cursory glance at the figures' for *Henry VIII* 'shows unmistakable differences between the Shakespeare and the Fletcher parts of these plays. The division between the two groups, while not absolutely consistent, is about as sharp as can be expected of prosodical statistics, and the divergences are, on the whole, very definitely in the "orthodox" directions: high percentages for Fletcher, low percentages for Shakespeare' (p. 201). The average for Fletcher's part is close to that for *Bonduca*, that for Shakespeare's 'falls short of the other Shakespearean averages for complete plays but is very like that of the third act of *Cymbeline* (= 14.9 per cent)' (p. 201). Oras described the fluctuations within Shakespeare's scenes for *Henry VIII* as being 'even less pronounced than in the unquestionably Shakespearean sequences', and drew attention to the similarity between the percentages for 3.2, the scene of Wolsey's fall, where Fletcher 'takes up Shakespeare's thread at a half-line [203], which he completes . . . This might, though it need not, suggest closer collaboration than elsewhere in the play' (p. 202).

Having disproved Alexander's suggestion that the stylistic variations within the play might simply be those of Shakespeare's late style, Oras responded to the other implication of that thesis, namely that there are no

---

[27] A. Oras, ' "Extra Monosyllables" in *Henry VIII* and the Problem of Authorship', *JEGP* 52 (1953): 198–213, at p. 198.

[28] D. J. Lake, 'Stylistic Variation in *Henry VIII* and *The Two Noble Kinsmen*' (unpublished typescript), p. 5.

TABLE 6.9. Henry VIII: *extra monosyllables and feminine endings*

(*a*) Shakespeare scenes

Scene	Total lines	A Extra monosyllables	B Feminine endings	C Percentage of A to B
1.1	226	8	66	12.1
1.2	214	7	73	9.6
2.3	107	5	38	13.2
2.4	241	9	74	12.2
3.2a	203	15	63	23.8
5.1	178	10	66	15.2
Total	1,169	54	380	

Average for Shakespeare: 14.2

(*b*) Fletcher scenes

Scene	Total lines	A Extra Monosyllables	B Feminine endings	C Percentage of A to B
1.3	67	9	45	20.0
1.4	107	17	59	28.8
2.1	169	30	94	31.9
2.2	134	24	77	31.2
3.1	172[a]	36	113	31.9
3.2b	257	44	152	28.9
4.1	117	7	59	11.9
4.2	173	29	99	29.3
5.2	35	6	17	35.3
5.3	181	31	99	31.3
5.4	85	5	20	25.0
5.5	76	16	44	36.4
Total	1,573	254	878	

Average for Fletcher: 29.0

Note: [a] Without the song.

Source: Oras 1953, p. 200.

'important qualitative differences' between the line-endings in Fletcher's part and in Shakespeare's (p. 203). Oras studied this issue in relation to the plays already analysed, with some additional Fletcher material. In Shakespeare's three late Romances, he found, 'the extra monosyllable is in

TABLE 6.10. *Verse statistics for Shakespeare and Fletcher plays*

Play	A Extra monosyllables	B Feminine endings	C Percentage of A to B
Cymbeline	142	792	18.1
Winter's Tale	136	672	20.2
Tempest	112	483	23.2
Valentinian	608	1,881	32.4
Bonduca	460	1,511	30.4
Monsieur Thomas	766	1,808	42.4

Source: Oras 1953, p. 201.

most cases a light one. Care appears to have been taken not to impede the flow of the verse, and when heavy monosyllables occur, they are nearly always made to fall naturally and easily into their metrical positions' (ibid.). His examples included:

> But being so allow'd: to apprehènd thus
>
> (*Cym.*, 3.3.7)
> I learnt it out of women's faces. Prày now,
> What colour are your eyebrows?
>
> (*WT*, 2.1.12–13)
> The washing of ten tides! *Gon.* He'll be hàng'd yet.
>
> (*Temp.*, 1.1.61)
> The very thought of my revenges thàt way
> Recoil upon me.
>
> (*WT*, 2.3.19–20)

The same concern 'to keep the monosyllables from obstructing the free progression of his blank verse' can be seen in Shakespeare's part of *Henry VIII*:

> How he determines further. *Aber.* As the Dùke said,
> The will of heaven be done.
>
> (1.1.214–15)
> Now all my joy
> Trace the conjunction! *Suf.* My amen to't! *Nor.* Àll men's!
>
> (3.2.44–5)

Oras described the latter instance as 'an especially deft method of emphasizing the penultimate [syllable] in the second line' through the echoing of 'all', a 'clearly felt connection' which 'makes us place an especially strong

emphasis on the word at its second appearance' (pp. 204–5), while still preserving natural speech stresses.

Oras contrasted Shakespeare's 'fluent ease' in *Henry VIII* with Fletcher's
high use of 'heavily weighted extra monosyllables', due to which—as Roderick
had seen—'the normal sentence stress and the metrical stress tend to clash'. As
examples of this 'distinct tension between speech stress and meter' he cited:

> Go, give 'em welcome; you can speak the Frènch tongue
>
> $\qquad\qquad\qquad\qquad\qquad\qquad$ (1.5.57)
>
> $\qquad\qquad\qquad$ I know it;
> But 'tis so lately alter'd that the òld name
> Is fresh about me
>
> $\qquad\qquad$ (4.1.97–9)
> Nor build their evils on the graves of grèat men.
>
> $\qquad\qquad\qquad\qquad$ (2.1.67)

In none of these instances is there 'adequate logical motivation for the strong
emphasis on the adjective', and in the third 'the purely phonetic trick of
increasing this emphasis by making the adjective alliterate with a stressed
word earlier in the line (*graves—great*) is characteristic of Fletcher' (pp.
205–6; four examples quoted). Fletcher achieved his heavily weighted extra
monosyllables in various ways: by a 'heavy stress on the genitive',

> These articles, my lord, are in the Kìng's hand
>
> $\qquad\qquad\qquad$ (3.2.299)

by a 'stressing of the numeral in phrases defining time',

> $\qquad\qquad\qquad\qquad\qquad$ Or I'll find
> A Marshalsea shall hold ye play these twò months
>
> $\qquad\qquad\qquad$ (5.4.89–90)

or by using heavier vocative nouns: 'Can you thìnk, lords' (3.1.83); 'not wèll,
lords' (3.1.133); 'Lead the wày, lords' (5.5.73). I have quoted only the
Fletcherian examples in *Henry VIII*, but Oras cited many from other Fletcher
plays to show that in Fletcher's verse the penultimate syllable 'has to be somewhat over-emphasized to counterbalance the accented extra monosyllable:
the rhythm is dictated by the meter rather than the meaning in a manner not
found in the Shakespearean evidence, except perhaps in the combination of a
numeral with noun' (p. 207).

Oras supported his convincing contrast between Shakespeare's light touch
and Fletcher's heavier one with further detail. Fletcher uses a 'noticeably
weighted group of extra monosyllables' consisting of a group of six adverbs,[29]

---

[29] Oliphant had drawn attention to this preference, picking out the words *still*, *else*, and *too*
(Oliphant 1927, p. 33).

of which 'too and *else* are conspicuous, and often tedious, favorites of his. Shakespeare, on the contrary, seems to dislike the dragging effect of appending them to a stressed word: even *inside* his pentameter lines it is very scarce ... The normal position for these expressions in Shakespeare is metrically stressed' (p. 208). Fletcher, in *Henry VIII* as everywhere else, 'decidedly prefers them in unstressed positions, whether medially or terminally'. Among the Fletcherian instances that Oras cited of *too* in the terminal position I pick out

> O, very mad, exceeding mad, in lòve too.
>
> (1.4.28)
> Earl Surrey was sent thither, and in hàste too
>
> (2.1.43)

and in the medial:

> Your lordship is a gùest too. *Cham.* O, 'tis true
>
> (1.3.51)
> And at the dòor too, like a post with packets.
>
> (5.2.32)

Similarly for *else*:

> Pray God he do! He'll never know himsèlf else.
>
> (2.2.23)
> Get up o'th' rail. I'll pack you o'er the pàles else!
>
> (5.4.94)
> We shall be làte else; which I would not be.
>
> (1.3.65)

We can also gauge Fletcher's fondness for the combination of feminine endings with extra monosyllables in his scenes for *Henry VIII* from 'the way the same sounds are crowded in them, even to the point of becoming impediments to enunciation: "Prepàre there" (2.1.97); "How can màn then" (3.2.441); "himsèlf else" (2.2.23); "what's thàt, Butts?" (5.2.20)'. (To a reader of modern poetry these occasionally sound like the heavily emphatic verse of Gerard Manley Hopkins.) Oras could find 'nothing of the kind anywhere in Shakespeare's easily flowing endings', whereas their insistent use by Fletcher here and elsewhere may 'be a deliberate trick' of style to emphasize the feminine endings, 'on which he seems to be lingering with relish' (p. 209).

The impression given by this analysis is of Shakespeare's metrical flexibility as against Fletcher's monotony. Fletcher, Oras found, was 'less versatile than Shakespeare in his methods', often repeating identical sentence patterns in his emphasis on personal pronouns, such as lines ending 'Ì do' (3.1.32;

5.3.41), or 'yòu are' (5.3.140), or 'thìs is' (5.5.27) and 'shè was' (5.5.46–7)—to cite only the *Henry VIII* examples (p. 210). Fletcher was also 'too obviously fond of repeating the same final monosyllables in close succession, often in lengthy series', revealing 'his passion for parallelism' as against Shakespeare's choice of variety. In Shakespeare's scenes for *Henry VIII* Oras found only three such repetitions of paired monosyllables at the line ending (1.1.102–3; 2.3.103, 107; 3.2.161, 165), whereas in Fletcher's scenes 'there are fifteen groups of two, seven of three, one of four', and one of eight, namely Cranmer's speech in the final scene, which has lines ending '*about her* [5.4.18], *with her* (23); *nurse her* (29), *bless her* (31), *with her* (33), *about her* (37); *see her* (58), *mourn her* (63). The refrain-like effect is unmistakable' (p. 211). This was the last link that Oras had freshly forged in 'that long chain of arguments, metrical and non-metrical', which differentiated the two dramatists. His completely new test showed another clear difference:

Shakespeare's extra monosyllables are varied, usually light, and, when heavier, then at least easy to fit naturally and smoothly into their metrical context; their retarding effect is slight. Fletcher's monosyllables often create an effect of top-heaviness; the endings appear artificially weighted, as though conceived according to a monotonous tune in the author's ear which imposes itself on the verse and not infrequently distorts the normal speech rhythm: the writer seems to be lingering on them, and they tend considerably to slow up the verse. (p. 212)

Oras concluded that here, as in other respects, Fletcher displayed 'some toning down of his habitual style' in this play, and agreed with E. K. Chambers that Shakespeare's influence may have caused him 'somewhat to restrain his extreme tendencies while at work on *Henry VIII*' (p. 213). That is, of course, a well-observed phenomenon in co-authorship.

Throughout the authorship debates we can observe a series of pendulum swings by which a case made by one scholar is rejected by another, rejection in turn provoking a new attempt to strengthen the original thesis. Just as Ants Oras was stimulated by Peter Alexander's scepticism to define Fletcher's idiosyncratic verse style more closely than ever before, so R. A. Law responded to the scepticism expressed by R. A. Foakes in his New Arden edition (discussed below).[30] Law argued that Spedding's authorship division was correct, and had been confirmed by both metrical and linguistic tests. He pointed out that the 'most convincing' of the verse tests, Ingram's figures for weak and light endings, had been 'overlooked by recent controversialists'—a familiar tactic of those wanting to preserve their belief in Shakespeare the sole author—and he went on to document another 'fairly regular habit . . . or trick of style' in Fletcher, namely 'the ending of a feminine line with a verb followed by an unstressed pronoun. For example, "I knew him, and I know him; so I *leave*

---

[30] R. A. Foakes (ed.), Shakespeare, *Henry VIII* (London, 1957; rev. edn., 1962).

TABLE 6.11. Henry VIII: *lines ending with a verb followed by an unstressed pronoun*

(*a*) Shakespeare scenes

Scene	Blank verse lines	Verb/Pronoun	Percentage
1.1	226	2	0.9
1.2	212	3	1.3
2.3	107	4	3.7
2.4	231	4	1.7
3.2a	202	9	4.4
5.1	176	2	1.0
Total	1,154	24	
			Shakespeare average: 2.1

(*b*) Fletcher scenes

Scene	Blank verse lines	Verb/Pronoun	Percentage
1.3	67	4	6.0
1.4	108	8	7.4
2.1	169	14	8.5
2.2	134	9	6.1
3.1	170	17	10.0
3.2b	253	27	11.0
4.1	117	3	2.6
4.2	172	13	7.5
5.2	34	3	8.6
5.3	178	17	9.5
5.4	39	2	4.5
5.5	71	8	11.3
Total	1,512	125	
			Fletcher average: 8.3

Source: Law 1959, p. 474.

him" '.[31] Surprisingly, Law did not know the recent essay by Oras, and the data he provided do not altogether square with his predecessor's. (In Cranmer's final speech he has missed two lines ending 'with her' and 'about her': Law 1959, p. 473.) But he collected enough material to be able to make a useful series of comparisons, as we can see from Table 6.11. Law provided

[31] R. A. Law, 'The Double Authorship of *Henry VIII*', *ShQ* 56 (1959): 471–88, at p. 472.

TABLE 6.12. *Verse statistics for Shakespeare and Fletcher*

	Blank verse lines	Verb/Pronoun	Percentage
Cymbeline (1609–10)	2,607	82	3.1
A Winter's Tale (1610–11)	2,107	52	3.1
The Tempest (1611–12)	1,445	60	3.6
Bonduca (1614)	2,427	218	9
Valentinian (1611–12)	2,763	276	10
The Wild-Goose Chase (1621)	2,293	252	11.2

Source: Law 1959, p. 477.

parallel figures, set out in Table 6.12, for the three Shakespeare plays nearest in date to *Henry VIII*, and for three Fletcher plays, both close to that date and later. As the two tables reveal, 'Shakespeare's three plays of this period show a consistent proportion of three per cent of such feminine endings while Fletcher's show a gradual rising of nine to eleven per cent'. The figures for their shares of *Henry VIII*—2.1 and 8.3 per cent—reflect this basic stylistic difference, while being slightly below each dramatist's norm elsewhere, a by now familiar result of co-authorship.

Like Oras, R. A. Law felt the need to support his quantitative analysis with traditional literary criticism, in order to define some characteristics of the two dramatists' individual verse styles. He did so by taking up a well-known contrast made by Charles Lamb in *Specimens of English Dramatic Poets* (1808):

> [Fletcher] lays line upon line, making up one after another, adding image to image so deliberately that we see where they join. Shakespeare mingles everything, embarrasses sentences and metaphors; before one has burst its shell, another is hatched and clamours for this disclosure. (p. 478)

Law illustrated this observation by juxtaposing two passages from *Henry VIII* on the same topic, Henry's wish to divorce Queen Katherine. First, from a scene ascribed to Fletcher, Norfolk's account of Wolsey's influence on the King:

> He counsels a divorce, a loss of her
> That like a jewel has hung twenty years
> About his neck, yet never lost her lustre;
> Of her that loves him with that excellence
> That angels love good men with; even of her
> That when the greatest stroke of fortune falls,
> Will bless the King.

(2.2.31–7)

As Law commented, 'here we have in simple direct language the thought expressed with three images separately developed' (p. 478). In the scene following, ascribed to Shakespeare, 'exactly the same thought is put into the mouth of unsophisticated Anne Boleyn':

> Not for that neither! Here's the pang that pinches;
> His Highness having liv'd so long with her, and she
> So good a lady that no tongue could ever
> Pronounce dishonour of her—by my life
> She never knew harm-doing!—O, now, after
> So many courses of the sun enthroned,
> Still growing in a majesty and pomp, the which
> To leave a thousandfold more bitter than
> 'Tis sweet at first t'acquire—after this process
> To give her the avaunt, it is a pity
> Would move a monster.

$$(2.3.1\text{--}11)$$

Here, by contrast, 'at least five images are mingled in complex sentences by the maid of honor sympathizing with her mistress' (p. 479). A similar difference can be seen in the two dramatists' use of animal imagery, Fletcher's (5.3.126–9) tidy and sequential, Shakespeare's (1.1.158–67: quoted above) involved, the thought forcing out of one idea into the next, the syntax keeping up as best it can. Fletcher gives us a 'clear succession of images', separately conceived, without Shakespeare's energetic but untidy fusion of metaphors.

The interplay between a quantitative approach, subjecting particular stylistic features to statistical computation, and a literary–critical one, working by verbal analysis, was fruitfully demonstrated by Marco Mincoff, defending the traditional ascription against the sceptics (Baldwin Maxwell, Peter Alexander, and R. A. Foakes). In the course of a devastating refutation of Alexander's essay (Mincoff 1961, pp. 244–52), Mincoff showed that stylistic evidence needs to be interpreted in context, not as a separable statistic having an autonomous significance. Alexander may have easily refuted Abbott's claim that Shakespeare never used redundant endings on a monosyllable, but he failed to observe how differently Fletcher uses such forms. In his work

these forms stand out so clearly not only because of their frequency and because the monosyllable is so often a superfluous addition, very often a vocative like *sir*, but above all because they so often form part of a short comment at the end of a series of variations, clinching it and underlining the coincidence of sentence and verse-ending. (p. 247)

Mincoff quoted several examples of Fletcher using the redundant monosyllable to bring the thought to a conclusion, of which I select three from one scene (1.3) of *Henry VIII*:

> To Pepin or Clotharius, they keep state so.
> The lag end of their lewdness, and be laughed at.
> The beauty of this kingdom, I'll assure you.

Mincoff computed that 'in the first three Fletcher scenes of *Henry VIII* (1.3, 1.4, 2.1), 19 per cent, nearly every fifth line, is of the heavy type; in the two preceding Shakespeare scenes only 3 per cent, every thirty-third line. And of the 64 Fletcher examples 9 are superfluous while of the 14 of Shakespeare's not one is' (ibid.).

As we read Mincoff's discussion we will be compelled to agree that 'every single test applied' to the play, whether metrical or linguistic, 'leads to the same clear division into two separate styles, and one of these styles always points to Fletcher' (p. 252). Indeed, it is surprising that proponents of 'Shakespeare the Non-collaborator' should continue to dispute this issue, since Fletcher's style is so clearly distinguishable from Shakespeare's in so many respects. All the accounts of Fletcher's verse that I have summarized itemize a whole series of metrical mannerisms, found across his whole writing career. Ralph Waldo Emerson, in *Representative Men* (1850), had found in *Henry VIII* two distinct verse styles, and identified the un-Shakespearian 'cadence' in

> Wolsey's soliloquy [3.2.350–72], and the following scene with Cromwell, where, instead of the metre of Shakespeare, whose secret is that the thought constructs the tune, so that reading for the sense will best bring out the rhythm; here the lines are constructed on a given tune . . .[32]

Mincoff agreed that, in the prime act of reading, 'the cadence of the two styles strikes my ears at once and I feel no need of tests to prove what is so clearly to be heard' (Mincoff 1961, p. 248). This 'fixity of melody' in Fletcher can be partly defined by the statistics for end-stopped lines, but it also depends on verse movement and syntactical patterns, which are not so amenable to computation. To illustrate this point Mincoff cited Katherine's speech of self-defence, in Fletcher's hand:

> Have I liv'd thus long—let me speak myself,
> Since virtue finds no friends—a wife, a true one?
> A woman, I dare say, without vain glory,
> Never yet branded with suspicion?
> Have I with all my full affections
> Still met the king? Lov'd him next heaven? obey'd him?
> Been, out of fondness, superstitious to him?
> Almost forgot my prayers to content him?
> And am I thus rewarded? 'tis not well, lords.
> Bring me a constant woman to her husband,
> One that ne'er dream'd a joy beyond his pleasure,

---

[32] Quoted in *NQ* 2/307 (Oct. 1850), and in *TNSS* 1 (1874), p. 21*n.

And to that woman, when she has done most,
Yet will I add an honour, a great patience.

(3.1.125–36)

Mincoff observed 'how the sentences fall either into couplets or single lines, and how frequently they are rounded off with a short cadence separated from the rest':

> a wife, a true one?
> obey'd him
> 'tis not well, lords.
> a great patience.

In addition, 'most of these concluding cadences re-echo the tunes cited above', while 'the frequent medial pauses tend to break up the lines into smaller, constantly recurring units'. We also see how the speech 'is built up of variations of a phrase', each having a simple grammatical structure, the whole speech being carried and given 'unity [by] the rapid rush of these variations—all points eminently characteristic of Fletcher' (p. 249). Emerson rightly described such lines as being 'constructed on a given tune'.

For comparison, Mincoff cited the self-defence that Shakespeare wrote for Katherine in an earlier scene, which derives closely from the source, Holinshed. For this reason, perhaps, it lacks the syntactical complexities of other Shakespearian speeches of free composition in this play: but it is still markedly different from Fletcher.

> Heaven witness,
> I have been to you a true and humble wife,
> At all times to your will conformable,
> Ever in fear to kindle your dislike,
> Yea, subject to your countenance, glad or sorry
> As I saw it inclin'd: when was the hour
> I ever contradicted your desire,
> Or made it not mine too? Or which of your friends
> Have I not strove to love, although I knew
> He were mine enemy? What friend of mine
> That had to him deriv'd your anger, did I
> Continue in my liking? nay, gave notice
> He was from thence discharg'd? Sir, call to mind
> That I have been your wife, in this obedience,
> Upward of twenty years, and have been blest
> With many children by you: if in the course
> And process of this time you can report,
> And prove it too, against mine honour aught,
> My bond to wedlock or my love and duty
> Against your sacred person, in God's name,
> Turn me away, and let the foul'st contempt

Shut door upon me, and so give me up
To the sharp'st kind of justice.

(2.4.20–42)

As every reader will have noticed, here 'is no rhythmical monotony, no forcing everything into the Procrustean bed of a few, fixed, short melodies. The
sentences form lengthy, sweeping, and very varied units, and every sentence
pause comes in the middle of the line. There is no question here of fixed
cadences in fixed positions. Variation there is, but it is not verbal variation
merely, as so much of the first passage, but variation of thought, and it does
not harp on one string, varying a single point in a series of graduations. The
whole texture of the passage is incomparably more complex and weighty'
(p. 250). I can only salute Mincoff for that perceptive analysis, which fully
justifies Emerson's description of Shakespeare's 'secret . . . that the thought
constructs the tune', and 'the sense [creates] the rhythm'. Mincoff also
brought out—to my mind, unanswerably—the implications of recognizing
this difference for the issue of co-authorship:

To suppose that Shakespeare could have given these two speeches to the same person
shows an astonishing lack of appreciation of what is perhaps his greatest gift of all as
a dramatic poet, his power to give his characters an individual verse melody of their
own, so that Othello and Iago or Macbeth and Banquo speak with different voices
throughout. Contrasts of melody such as this are inevitable in a work of collaboration,
but to suppose that either Shakespeare or any other dramatist worth his salt would
make all his characters chop and change between two distinct rhythms and two distinct styles for no reason at all, as they do in *Henry VIII*, is to suppose him incapable
of entering into the personality of his characters or of conceiving them as individuals.
(p. 250)

As I observed earlier, it is inevitable, even normal, that a character who
appears in scenes written by different dramatists will show visible differences
of style. How could it be otherwise?

Mincoff's essay was a major contribution to the discussion of *Henry VIII*,
and to authorship studies in general. He rejected with some authority
attempts to undermine the case for Fletcher as co-author by citing apparently
significant differences between his style here and elsewhere. These 'slight
divergences from his unadulterated style . . . vanish into utter insignificance
before the number and variety of the similarities through which the quality of
his style is preserved for long stretches at a time. Even if it were possible to
throw far graver doubts on each of these tests taken separately, the cumulative effect of this variety of unrelated and independent testimony is not to be
shaken. It is not a question of slight, or even of marked, fluctuations with
regard to one or two indicators alone, but of two fundamentally different
styles, poles apart in every respect' (p. 252).

Mincoff also valuably defined the range of fluctuations within Fletcher's

TABLE 6.13. *Fletcher's scenes in* Henry VIII: *double endings and run-on lines*

Scene	Subject-matter	Double endings	Run-on lines
1.3	Satire on foreign fashions	69	24
3.1	Katherine and the cardinals	66	18
5.5	Cranmer's prophecy	66	16
2.1b	Buckingham's farewell	63	15
3.2b	Wolsey's farewell	63	24
4.2	Katherine's death	60	20
2.2	Discussions of divorce	58	22
5.3	Trial of Cranmer	57	27
2.1c	Conversation—rumours of divorce	57	42
1.4	Wolsey's banquet	55	26
5.2	Cranmer before the council chamber	54	21
4.1	Conversation—the coronation	53	28
2.1a	Conversation—Buckingham's trial	50	36
5.4	Crowd scene	48	23

Source: Mincoff 1961, p. 257.

style, far greater than earlier discussions had led us to expect. Collaborating with Shakespeare created several 'modifications [in] Fletcher's style', but these are not evenly distributed, as some critics had thought. 'There are scenes that ring like the purest Fletcher', such as that between Katherine and the cardinals (3.1), or Buckingham's farewell (2.1.100–35), others of 'a dry, pedestrian verse', as in the conversations before Buckingham's farewell (p. 256). Mincoff demonstrated these fluctuations within Fletcher's style very clearly, as can be seen from Table 6.13, by arranging his scenes in descending order, according to the number of double endings (the second—less revealing—figures being for run-on lines). As Mincoff observed, the fluctuations of metre are greater here than in Fletcher's independent plays or in his collaborations with Massinger, but are comparable to those found in *The Two Noble Kinsmen* and in his collaborations with Beaumont, both cases where working with a co-author caused him to vary his style more than usual. Particularly interesting here is that

there seems to be a distinct connection between the double endings and the subject matter. The lower part of the scale is taken up with static, undramatic scenes, largely of fairly rapid conversation and mostly between minor characters describing events on or off the stage. The upper part, on the contrary, consists mainly of scenes of strong pathos, of the long, oratorical tirades that Fletcher loved, while in the middle come two scenes of dramatic dispute or discussion, the preparations for the divorce and Cranmer's trial. (pp. 257–8)

TABLE 6.14. *Pause patterns in* Henry VIII

	1	2	3	4	5	6	7	8	9	Half	Even
Shakespeare	2.1	2.8	2.2	14.8	13.1	27.4	20.6	11.0	5.9	25.2	56.1
Fletcher	1.6	6.3	3.9	16.0	14.7	18.9	23.9	12.3	2.4	32.6	53.5

Source: Oras 1960, p. 68.

The only exception to this allocation is the first scene on the list, satirizing the English vogue for foreign fashions, partly drawn from Holinshed, but which 'gives in easy, humorous talk a satirical comment on the times' (p. 258). Mincoff's preferred explanation for the 'dislocations of metre' is that Fletcher 'was deliberately attempting to tone down his style to his partner's, and that he succeeded best when he was least involved emotionally. In the scenes of pathos and comic satire, where he warmed to his task, he let himself be carried away, and dropped inevitably into his more usual style. And that in its turn would suggest that the dominant partner was Shakespeare' (p. 259).

Mincoff's essay endorsed the validity of those 'objectively measurable and essentially independent indicators' (pp. 259–60) that clearly divided responsibility for *Henry VIII* between Fletcher and Shakespeare, and he showed that the quantitative verse tests could be supplemented by qualitative stylistic analyses which—if performed with sensitivity—could strengthen their findings. The metrical evidence produced between 1850 and 1959 was reassessed by two modern scholars using more rigorous statistical approaches, Ants Oras and Marina Tarlinskaja, both of whom strengthened still further the evidence for co-authorship. As noted in Chapter 2, Oras analysed more than 700 Elizabethan and Jacobean plays, computing 'the incidence of internal pauses in each of the nine positions possible within an iambic pentameter line in relation to the totals of such pauses'.[33] He then converted the basic figures into percentages, and calculated 'the ratio of such phrases before the fifth position, i. e. in the first half of the line, to pauses after that position', the result being labelled 'First Half'. He also provided figures 'showing the percentage of pauses in even positions, that is, pauses after an even-numbered syllable', or 'Even' (p. 4). His results for *Henry VIII* are set out in Table 6.14. In Shakespeare's verse line the first three feet are evenly stressed, the next two reach a higher plateau, rising to a peak stress on the sixth foot, and subsiding by regular degrees over the last three feet. In Fletcher's line the second foot is more strongly stressed, but the progress from the fourth to the seventh foot

[33] A. Oras, *Pause Patterns in Elizabethan and Jacobean Drama: An Experiment in Prosody* (Gainesville, Fla., 1960), p. 2.

rises at a more even rate than Shakespeare's, while the rate of emphasis on the two last feet drops off much more sharply. These differences are clearly visible in the frequency polygons that Oras provided for the two dramatists' shares (see Appendix I). Having studied Fletcher's whole prosodic development, Oras observed that his collaboration on *Henry VIII* fell in 'an early phase of Fletcher's career, when his full personal manner was only beginning to show itself', becoming 'the junior partner who had his peculiarities subdued'. However, although other features of Fletcher's style were affected, his pause patterns are already characteristically his own. Confirming the earlier observations of Spedding, Furnivall, Fleay, and others, Oras observed that 'one of the most immediately noticeable features among many striking peculiarities' of Fletcher's verse

is the unusual scarcity of run-on lines. . . . His line-endings tend to be heavily, often top-heavily, marked and underscored by extremely strong stresses to make readers linger over them. (p. 25)

Using various devices ('accumulating closely cognate sounds', and alliteration) Fletcher emphasizes the strong final effect, and carefully fences off 'the brief verse segments coming after a late pause'—usually at the seventh foot—'both by punctuation and by the use of double and triple endings, which prevent the iambic or anapaestic lilt from being continued without interruption into the next verse. This is the very opposite of a technique intent on run-on effects', such as Shakespeare's. Oras defined 'the special "tune" of Fletcher's verse' as being 'an extremely powerful, almost incantatory rhythm, usually in three waves, with three very prominent stress peaks, placed on the second or fourth, the sixth or eighth, and the tenth syllables. These sharply marked peaks make the typical verse of Fletcher predominantly dipodic . . .'—that is, with two metrical feet making up the measure (pp. 25–6). The unusual strength of these main stresses 'permits Fletcher to weight some of the metrically unstressed syllables to an extent seldom risked by other writers . . .' (p. 26), and helps give individuality to his style. Oras concluded with an observation that Shakespeare fundamentalists should note: 'the peculiar nature of Fletcher's verse distinguishes it sharply from everybody else's, but this nature appears with particular clarity if compared with that of his collaborator, Massinger'—or, we can add, Shakespeare.

The even more elaborate statistical study of Shakespeare's metrics by Marina Tarlinskaja put this issue beyond question. Her method, we recall, analysed the placing of emphasis by syntax and meaning on the normally strong or 'ictic' positions in an iambic decasyllabic verse line (the even syllables: 2, 4, 6, 8, 10), and on the theoretically weak or 'non-ictic' positions (the odd syllables: 1, 3, 5, 7, 9). She demonstrated the gradual evolution of Shakespeare's style, in both ictic and non-ictic positions, towards

TABLE 6.15. *Stress profiles for* Henry VIII *and* Bonduca

| | Syllabic Positions | | | | | | | | | | | |
	1	2	3	4	5	6	7	8	9	10	S (2–10)	W (1–9)
Shakespeare scenes	20.7	64.9	11.0	79.2	8.0	75.6	19.5	67.4	13.0	86.9	74.8	12.6
Fletcher scenes	24.5	63.7	16.6	83.6	12.3	75.7	13.3	71.9	13.2	92.0	77.4	16.0
Bonduca	32.0	65.3	14.9	88.2	12.8	79.9	20.1	74.4	18.6	95.7	80.7	19.7

Source: Tarlinskaja 1987, p. 127.

emphasizing the later part of the line,[34] a movement which his scenes for *Henry VIII* continued to follow. Accepting Spedding's division of the play, Tarlinskaja calculated stress profiles for each dramatist's part, taking a large sample (eight scenes, totalling 757 lines) from Fletcher's *Bonduca* (1614) for comparison, with the results set out in Table 6.15 (the last two columns give the mean figures for strong and weak syllables respectively). Although both portions of *Henry VIII* reflect the general pattern of 'a later Elizabethan–Jacobean rhythmical style', the figures bring out several differences between the two writers. The high incidence of stress on positions 4 and 10 of both Fletcher plays 'are signs of a rhythmical-syntactical break after position 4 (5) and of "end-stopped", syntactically complete lines. A "dip" in position 8 and a relatively strong non-ictic stress on 7 and/or 9 indicate another rhythmical-syntactic break after positions 6, 7, or 8. Such a three-part line segmentation into relatively simple sometimes structurally recurrent, grammatical phrases is characteristic of Fletcher' (pp. 127–8)—a point made independently by both Mincoff and Oras. Fletcher's verse also 'abounds in extra-metrical stresses', the syntactical and rhythmical structure making it 'sound much "heavier" than Shakespeare's (p. 128).

All of Tarlinskaja's subsequent tests confirmed the distinctions which, she recorded—in an unusually complete survey of scholarship—had been made by critics for over a hundred years (pp. 125–7, 198–9). An equally clear difference emerged when she analysed the 'places of utterance junctures' in Shakespeare, that is, where verse lines are split between personages. The juncture is recorded for each syllabic position, and is expressed in Table 6.16 as a percentage of all split lines. As she commented, the proportion of split lines in Shakespeare's scenes is identical to that of his three preceding plays, while that for Fletcher comes quite outside Shakespeare's

[34] M. Tarlinskaja, *Shakespeare's Verse: Iambic Pentameter and the Poet's Idiosyncrasies* (New York, 1987), pp. 53–79.

TABLE 6.16. *Places of utterance junctures in late-period Shakespeare*

Drama	Position of splits								
	1	2	3	4	5	6	7	8	9
Cymbeline	0.2	0.2	0.5	13.4	18.5	<u>37.1</u>	23.4	6.1	2.5
Winter's Tale	—	0.3	0.6	14.8	15.2	<u>39.5</u>	23.3	6.5	1.8
Tempest	—	0.9	0.4	11.9	14.2	<u>40.7</u>	28.4	4.1	3.2
Henry VIII									
Shakespeare scenes	0.6	—	0.6	9.1	13.6	<u>34.6</u>	<u>35.2</u>	6.2	6.1
Fletcher scenes	—	1.9	0.9	10.9	14.7	19.0	<u>35.7</u>	19.1	2.4

Source: Tarlinskaja 1987, p. 138; table 4.1.

TABLE 6.17. *Line endings in* Henry VIII

	Accentual			Syllabic				
	Loss of stress caused by			Non-masculine	Feminine		Compound	
	Monosyllabic	Polysyllabic	Masculine	Total	Total	Simple	Light	Heavy
Shakespeare	8.2	4.7	67.2	33.8	32.8	27.5	4.6	0.8
Fletcher	1.0	7.2	40.6	59.4	58.7	40.6	13.2	4.9

Source: Tarlinskaja 1987, p. 200.

chronology, and would correspond to his verse style in *Macbeth*, seven years earlier (p. 143). The 'split maximum' for both writers occurs after position 7, but Shakespeare has a second highest score after position 6, which—I suggest—shows his tendency to let the second half of the verse line run over into the line following. Conversely, Tarlinskaja pointed out, position 8 differentiates the two even 'more strikingly: utterance junctures occur after position 8 three times more frequently in Fletcher's than in Shakespeare's portions of the play' (p. 147). A split coming so late in the line, as Fletcher scholars have shown, leaves room for a short additional phrase before the line-ending. Quantitative and qualitative analyses confirm each other.

Praising that 1953 article in which Ants Oras, 'with his typical deep inquiry into the subtleties of the text structure', analysed Fletcher's use of heavy feminine endings (p. 199), Tarlinskaja gave her own figures for line-endings as a percentage of total lines, which I reproduce in Table 6.17. There we can see that 'the incidence of unstressed monosyllables, a sign of acute run-on lines, is almost nine times more frequent in Shakespeare's than in Fletcher's scenes'. The figure of 8.2 per cent correlates with those for *The Winter's Tale* (6.7) and *The Tempest* (6.6), and is far removed from Fletcher's. Equally revealing is the percentage of non-masculine endings, where the Shakespeare index of 33.8 is close to that of *Winter's Tale* and *Tempest* (34 and 35 per cent, respectively). Fletcher's figure of 59.4 per cent, nearly twice as high, compares with about 48 for the four Fletcherian scenes in *The Maid's Tragedy* and roughly 70 per cent for *Bonduca*. 'The higher figure in *Bonduca* can be explained by the fact that the tragedy, written by Fletcher alone, was not influenced by the style of a co-author' (p. 200). (Tarlinskaja added further statistics to show that the fluctuation of verse styles in co-authored plays is much greater.) The differences between the Shakespearian and Fletcherian scenes 'in terms of compound feminine endings is even more revealing: the index for compound light endings is three times heavier' in Fletcher's scenes (13.2 against 4.6 per cent), and that for compound heavy endings (4.9 against 0.8 per cent) is more than six times higher (pp. 200–1).

As if this were not already enough proof, Tarlinskaja reported two further tests that distinguish Shakespeare's contribution to *Henry VIII* from Fletcher's. The first test moved from analysing line-endings to considering the structure of phrase-endings within the verse line, looking at 'two-element phrasal combinations of words found in verse (micro-phrases)'. In some cases the stressed syllable of these combinations 'falls on an ictic, or strong (S) syllabic position of the verse line, while the other element falls on a non-ictic, weak (W) syllabic position, either preceding or following S. In the former case the word on W becomes, as it were, a proclitic, in the latter case an enclitic to the stressed word on S' (p. 203). Tarlinskaja's example is a line from Shakespeare's Sonnet 65:

$$\text{Ɜ} \qquad\qquad\qquad\qquad \text{Ɛ}$$

$$\text{⊥} \qquad\quad \text{⊥} \qquad\qquad\qquad \text{⊤}$$

Or what <u>strong</u> hand (proclitic) *can hold his swift* <u>foot</u> (enclitic) *back*

As Tarlinskaja showed, English verse is marked by a prevalence of proclitic structures, due to 'the prevailing tendency of English speech to stress the last notional word of a phrase (sentence) particularly strongly' (p. 214). However, poets vary greatly in their allegiance to enclitics or proclitics, as my excerpt from one of her tables in Table 6.18 shows. As the reader can see, in *Henry VIII* 'enclitic phrases are over *three* times more frequent in Fletcher's than in Shakespeare's scenes' (p. 215). This test also clearly differentiates the collaborators on *The Maid's Tragedy*, for Fletcher 'used enclitic phrases 2.5 times more frequently' than Beaumont. Typically for an author being freed from

TABLE 6.18. *Proclitic and enclitic phrases*

Author and title	Proportion of proclitic and enclitic phrases (%)		Number of enclitic phrases per 1,000 lines
	Proclitic	Enclitic	
The Winter's Tale	82	18	73
Henry VIII			
Shakespeare scenes	85	15	58
Fletcher scenes	63	37	201
Fletcher, *Bonduca*	59	41	295
Beaumont and Fletcher, *The Maid's Tragedy*			
Beaumont scenes	75	25	92
Fletcher scenes	64	36	220

Source: Tarlinskaja 1987, p. 215; table 4.1.

TABLE 6.19. *Proclitics and enclitics in Fletcher and Shakespeare*

Drama	A	B
Fletcher, *Bonduca*	66; 34	55; 45
The Maid's Tragedy	63; 37	68; 32
Henry VIII	60; 40	44; 56
Shakespeare, *Henry VIII*	79; 21	79; 21
The Winter's Tale	86; 14	70; 30

Source: Tarlinskaja 1987, pp. 219–20.

the constraints of co-authorship,[35] Fletcher's highest rate for enclitic phrases comes in *Bonduca*, all his own work (p. 217). Tarlinskaja subsequently computed two further statistics, the 'proportion of proclitic versus enclitic *attributive* phrases', and the 'proportion of proclitic versus enclitic phrases of the type *verb + adverb* (adjective)'. In Table 6.19 I select the data of interest to us, 'arranged in order of decreasing percentage of enclitic', labelling

[35] Tarlinskaja suggested earlier (pp. 198–9) that Shakespeare and Fletcher influenced each other reciprocally and offered to illustrate it from *Henry VIII*, 'the first scene of Act 3, written, as everybody seems to agree, by Shakespeare' (p. 217). But she had herself already recorded the traditional authorship division, on which her computations throughout are based, in which 3.1 is clearly ascribed to Fletcher (p. 208).

TABLE 6.20. Henry VIII: *disyllabic rhythmical figures*

	Positions				Total number
	3–4	5–6	7–8	10–11	
Shakespeare scenes	43.8	6.2	43.8	6.2	16
Fletcher scenes	41.0	33.3	25.7	—	39

Source: Tarlinskaja 1987, p. 261.

them A and B respectively. Once again we notice the fluctuations in Fletcher's style as measured from his norm, *Bonduca*, according to whether he collaborated with either Shakespeare or Beaumont. And once again we can identify the figures for Shakespeare's part of *Henry VIII* with those for *The Winter's Tale*.

Finally, Tarlinskaja studied disyllabic 'rhythmical figures' and their syntactical combinations. One such figure combines 'a loss of stress on a strong syllabic position (S) coupled with an extrametrical strong stress on either of the adjacent weak positions (W), to the left or to the right of S'. The variation on this, a figure she christens 'WS-1', is formed by two monosyllables, with an extrametrical stress on the preceding weak position. I select from a later stage in her highly technical discussion just one table (reproduced in Table 6.20), in which she gave the percentage distribution for 'the figures WS-1 coupled with a monosyllabic noun on W preceded by an attribute and followed by an unstressed monosyllable on S', according to four positions within the verse line, as found in this play. In Shakespeare's scenes the emphasis falls on positions 3–4 and 7–8, mirroring 'the looser iambic form . . . of Shakespeare's later verse'. Fletcher, by contrast, has a greater stress in position 5–6, which 'reflects a more frequent 4 + 6 or 5 + 5 bipartite line variant' in Fletcher (p. 262), a conclusion echoing Oras's earlier description of Fletcher's 'dipodic' verse line. Oras and Tarlinskaja raised the study of Shakespeare's metrics to an altogether higher level of complexity, but their findings for *Henry VIII* restate in other terms those made by Spedding, Furnivall, Ingram, Law, and Mincoff. Scholarly agreement of this order, stretching across one and a half centuries, is surely remarkable.

As I mentioned earlier, the two main approaches to the authorship question in *Henry VIII* have been metrical and linguistic. It is now time to take up the second of these threads, beginning with a scholarly work on Shakespearian syntax which supports Tarlinskaja's highly technical results from a quite different direction. As we saw above (p. 307), Charles Langworthy studied the relation between the verse line as a metrical unit and the sentence as a syntactical unit, computing the degrees of parallelism and divergence between the

TABLE 6.21. *Verse–sentence analysis of*
Henry VIII
(*a*) Shakespeare scenes

1.1	0.21
1.2	0.30
2.3	0.31
2.4	0.42
3.2	0.80
5.1	0.61
Average	0.44

(*b*) Fletcher scenes

1.3	1.91
1.4	0.42
2.1	1.02
2.2	1.90
3.1	2.52
4.1	1.50
4.2	3.31
5.2	2.00
5.3	1.50
5.4	1.71
5.5	2.56
Average	1.85

Source: Langworthy 1931, p. 748.

two. He established a quotient for each of Shakespeare's plays 'by dividing the number of parallel types by the number of divergent types', and showed that the results, when arranged in descending order of magnitude, correlated well with the plays' chronology.[36] Langworthy also applied this test to both parts of *Henry VIII*, discovering that the quotient for Fletcher's part was 1.85, which would place it chronologically alongside *Macbeth*, in 1606— precisely the same chronological discordance that Tarlinskaja was to discover fifty years later—while that for Shakespeare's part was 0.36, which would place it exactly among the later Romances. As presented in Table 6.21, Langworthy's figures for the individual scenes of *Henry VIII*, as he observed, led to a 'division of the play . . . substantially the same as that made by James

[36] C. A. Langworthy, 'A Verse–sentence Analysis of Shakespeare's Plays', *PMLA* 46 (1931), at pp. 738–74.

Spedding' a century earlier (p. 750 n.). Langworthy's figures 'show clearly that one author wrote' 1.1, 1.2, 2.3, 2.4, 3.2 'as far as the exit of the King',[37] and 5.1, and that the other 'wrote the remainder of the play, with the exception of 1.4, where the evidence is inconclusive' (p. 751). That such a completely different linguistic or syntactical approach should confirm the findings of the verse tests is highly significant.

Indeed, it seems as if any systematic and open-minded study of the play, whatever its approach, will yield the same result. Alfred Hart, in his pioneering investigation of Shakespeare's vocabulary,[38] computed for each play the number of words in its vocabulary, and the proportion of these that were peculiar to each work (Hart 1943a, pp. 131–3). Grouping the plays by genre, he detected in *Henry VIII* 'a falling-off; though longer than each of three of the earlier histories, it has a considerably smaller vocabulary'. The play was also anomalous when checked against the Romances, as Hart's figures show: *Cymbeline* has 219 'peculiar' words, *Winter's Tale* 219, *The Tempest* 202, *Henry VIII* 127. Hart checked his findings against the accepted authorship division, and concluded that 'this deficiency is a result of composite authorship. Shakespeare contributes a little more than two-fifths, Fletcher nearly three-fifths of the play, but the respective vocabularies are almost equal. Had Shakespeare written the whole play, the vocabulary would have had at least three thousand words' (instead of 2,659), and a correspondingly greater number of peculiar words (p. 134). From Hart's table we note that two other plays of part authorship also have a lower proportion of peculiar words than those by Shakespeare alone: *Timon* has 138, *Pericles* only 105. A similar anomaly emerged from Molly Mahood's study of Shakespeare's word-play.[39] Having immersed herself in Shakespeare's intense and varied playing on the word, she found that this approach could 'strengthen the case for or against the inclusion of a play in the Shakespeare canon, for once we have grown accustomed to Shakespeare's verbal habits the absence of any one of them from a play casts doubts upon his authorship. The part of *Henry VIII* held to be non-Shakespearean contains remarkably few puns, except for some *double-entendres* which do not recur among the Folio plays' (Mahood 1957, pp. 26–7).

These three scholars—Langworthy on syntax, Hart on vocabulary, and Mahood on word-play—broke new ground in Shakespeare studies, each confirming the long-established division of authorship between Fletcher and Shakespeare. A. C. Partridge strengthened that case still further in a detailed linguistic study combining several approaches. When two authors worked on a play, Partridge argued, 'it seems fair to assume that small mannerisms of grammatical usage, easily passed over in the weightier aesthetic consider-

---

[37] Unfortunately, Langworthy failed to provide a statistic for Fletcher's part of 3.2.
[38] A. Hart, 'The Vocabularies of Shakespeare's Plays', *RES* 19 (1943): 128–40.
[39] M. M. Mahood, *Shakespeare's Wordplay* (London, 1957).

ations, are most likely to betray their several hands'.[40] A writer will normally be 'quite unconscious of his ingrained grammatical habits', and will be unable to vary them, however much he adjusts in other ways to his co-author. Reading the play, Partridge—like Spedding a century earlier—'was struck by the fairly sharp transitions from one grammatical idiom to another. These divisions seemed to correspond to differences in the method of developing the thought through the style; in the one case involved, though poetically pregnant; in the other, fluent and lucid in syntactical pattern, almost anticipating Dryden' (Partridge 1964*a*, pp. 146–7). Quoting with approval Emerson's contrast between Shakespeare's style, in which 'the thought constructs the tune', and Fletcher's, in which 'the lines are constructed on a given tune', Partridge characterized Shakespeare's syntax vividly:

Shakespeare cannot serve as a stylistic model for anyone, because his rhythms are individual and accommodated to the needs of the moment; his ideas outstrip his syntax. On the track of the telling and indelible image, he may leave behind anacoluthons and hanging relative clauses in the most inconsequent fashion; he compresses his meaning and tortures his syntax, so that while the effect of the passage may be poetically grand, the meaning is wrung from it with extreme difficulty. (p. 147)

Partridge, continuing a stylistic analysis going back to Lamb and Spedding, contrasted Shakespeare's 'difficult syntactical progression . . . with the clarity of Fletcher', suggesting a comparison between Shakespeare's presentation of the King angrily questioning a courtier about Buckingham's treachery (1.2.177–199) and Fletcher's last speech for Buckingham (2.1.100–36). As Partridge put it, 'the power of Shakespeare's imagination, especially where the emotional tension of a scene is heightened, called for rapid transitions of feeling, thought and figure, and for these the syntax of the time, of any time, was too halting' (p. 157). This innate energy accounts for the many passages of involved syntax in his share of the play, such as Wolsey's anguished self-defence:

> I do profess
> That for your highness' good I ever laboured
> More than mine own; that am, have, and will be—
> Though all the world should crack their duty to you
> And throw it from their soul, though perils did
> Abound as thick as thought could make 'em, and
> Appear in forms more horrid—yet my duty,
> As doth a rock against the chiding flood,
> Should the approach of this wild river break
> And stand unshaken yours.

> (3.2.190–9)

---

[40] A. C. Partridge, '*Henry VIII*: Linguistic Criteria for the Two Styles Apparent in the Play', in Partridge, *Orthography in Shakespeare and Elizabethan Drama: A Study of Colloquial Contractions, Elision, Prosody and Punctuation* (London, 1964), pp. 141–63, at p. 144.

Partridge cited several other passages 'equally involved in their syntactical building' (including 1.1.158–90, 1.2.151–99, 5.1.95–108), and declared that 'few dramatists, except Shakespeare, could have drafted such structurally entangled accounts of events' (p. 158). Fletcher nowhere produced syntactical complexity of this order.

In grammar, as in syntax, Partridge found that he could easily distinguish the two writers. 'At the beginning of the play grammatical idiosyncrasy shows variations between one scene and another', as between 1.2 and 1.3, and may at first suggest that Shakespeare simply varied his style. 'But, as the play develops, it becomes clear that . . . the different grammatical forms and constructions occur in the speeches of the same character under similar dramatic conditions in different parts of the play' (p. 147). In Act 3 scene 2, where all the metrical tests point to Shakespeare having written the first part of the scene, up to the King's exit (l. 203), with Fletcher taking over at that point, Partridge found 'no less than twelve uses . . . of the periphrastic auxiliary verb *do*, as a mere expletive in affirmative statements', as with the three instances in this passage:

> the cardinal *did* entreat his holiness
> To stay the judgement o'th'divorce; for if
> It *did* take place, 'I *do*' quoth he, 'perceive . . .'

> (3.2.32–5)

Fletcher's remaining 256 lines contain only one instance of the expletive *do*, in the final couplet, doubtless for the sake of the rhyme ('Farewell | . . . my hopes in heaven do dwell'). Shakespeare's scenes have fifty uses of the expletive *do* in 1,165 lines, Fletcher's only five in 1,584 lines, and some of these have special causes (p. 148). Partridge recorded that elsewhere Fletcher rarely uses the expletive *do*, and showed that he was equally more likely to use the newer verb forms *has* and *does*, while Shakespeare preferred the older *hath* and *doth* (pp. 149–50). Partridge then applied the *'em/them* test, as developed by A. H. Thorndike, and the contraction tests worked out by W. E. Farnham, tabulating his findings (pp. 150–4) as set out in Table 6.22, giving the frequency of occurrence for each co-author's scenes. I have omitted from Partridge's counts instances where the grammatical form occurs in stage directions (five uses of 'them' in Shakespeare's 2.4, one in Fletcher's 4.2), since there is no way of telling who wrote these directions; also data for Fletcher's Prologue (one instance of *them*, two of *'em*, and two of *ye*).

Although Partridge concluded that these 'grammatical peculiarities . . . substantiate broadly the divisions of the play, made upon other grounds, by Spedding and Hickson' (p. 153), he conceded that his evidence included some anomalies, 'for instance the occasional appearance of *'em* and *ye* in the parts assigned to Shakespeare, and *hath* and the expletive *do* in those assigned to Fletcher' (p. 152). Anomalies also troubled Cyrus Hoy, whose account of

TABLE 6.22. *Grammatical preferences in*
Henry VIII

	Shakespeare	Fletcher
Expletive 'do'	45	5
Hath	22	2
Has	14	33
Doth	2	0
Does	10	6
Them	18	5
'em	5	57
Ye	1	70
y'	4	9

Source: Partridge 1964*b*, p. 152.

Henry VIII and *The Two Noble Kinsmen* completed his seven-part study of Fletcher's authorship in both single and collaborative plays. Hoy acknowledged A. C. Partridge's pioneering work and accepted his conclusions,[41] but was bothered by another anomaly, the fact that in some scenes traditionally ascribed to Fletcher the proportion of *ye* to *you* forms was lower than one would expect. He reviewed the bibliographical evidence of the Folio text having been set by two compositors, the experienced Compositor B and his less experienced partner (previously labelled A but now known as I),[42] according to which Compositor B set 208 *you*'s to 25 *ye*'s, a ratio of eight to one, while Compositor I set 191 *you*'s to 48 *ye*'s, a ratio of four to one (Hoy 1962, p. 78). Still, even accepting the compositors' influence, Hoy was disturbed by the seemingly low proportion of *ye* to *you* forms in some Fletcherian scenes (1.4, 3.2b), which otherwise faithfully reproduced the Fletcherian *'em*. Observing that the *ye*'s tended to 'fall into little clusters', Hoy became convinced that there Fletcher was merely 'the interpolator and not . . . the original author' (pp. 80–1). Accordingly, he argued that five of the scenes hitherto attributed to Fletcher—2.1, 2.2, 3.2b, 4.1, 4.2—should be assigned to both dramatists.

It is regrettable that Hoy did not review the many additional types of evidence then available demonstrating a complete continuity between these five and the six other scenes attributed to Fletcher, both in terms of verse style, measured in several different respects, and of grammatical and syntactical

[41] C. Hoy, 'The Shares of Fletcher and his Collaborators in the Beaumont and Fletcher Canon (I)', *SB* 8 (1956), at pp. 129–30; 'The Shares of Fletcher and his Collaborators in the Beaumont and Fletcher Canon (VIII)', *SB* 15 (1962), at p. 77.

[42] Following Gary Taylor, 'The Shrinking Compositor A of the Shakespeare First Folio', *SB* 34 (1981): 96–117.

habits. However, he did admit that none of the five scenes for which he was claiming joint authorship contained 'convincing traces of Fletcher's syntactic or rhetorical practices', some of which he usefully analysed (pp. 82–4). These include such typical Fletcherian line structures as 'This night he makes a supper, and a great one';[43] 'O, very mad, exceeding mad, in love too', such 'repetition with different modifiers' being a frequent Fletcher mannerism; and some peculiarly Fletcherian syntactical constructions, as in Wolsey's lines to Katherine:

> Noble lady,
> I am sorry my integrity should breed,
> And service to his Majesty and you,
> So deep suspicion, where all faith was meant.

> (3.1.50–3)

Hoy declared that this construction, 'wherein the elements of a compound subject ("integrity", "And service") are separated by an intervening verb phrase ("should breed")—is distinctly Fletcherian', and he argued that 'there is no stronger evidence for Fletcher's presence in *Henry VIII* than the occurrence in the play of this particular syntactic arrangement. In the passage in question, it makes for an extreme parenthetical inversion, but so it often does in Fletcher's unaided plays', as six quotations proved (Hoy 1962, pp. 82–3). Hoy also analysed four longer sequences (3.1.115–20; 3.1.125–33; 5.3.137–40; 5.5.25–35) which show 'Fletcher's rhetorical cascades', built up out of 'a number of separate devices', including a 'towering spiral of appositives, each dilating in its small way on the subject at hand', together with 'parenthetical insertions', and successive lines ending with a pronoun, 'him' (3.1.130–2) or 'her' (5.5.28 ff.—Cranmer's speech over the babe Elizabeth). These are, by now, familiar features of Fletcher's style.

Hoy's position as the leading modern authority on the Fletcher canon meant that his article, forcibly arguing for Fletcher's presence in the play, while apparently increasing Shakespeare's share by these newly ascribed five scenes of 'joint authorship', attracted wide attention. In recent years scholars have drawn attention to several faults in Hoy's reasoning, and suggested different explanations for what he thought to be Fletcherian anomalies. But it is interesting to see how his arguments were weighed up, in relation to the century-long discussion of the play's authorship, by editors of the three major modern editions so far published: R. A. Foakes's New Arden edition (1957; revised 1962); J. C. Maxwell's Cambridge New Shakespeare (1962; revised 1969);[44] and John Margeson's successor in this series[45]—it cannot be

---

[43] See also C. Hoy, 'The Shares of Fletcher and his Collaborators in the Beaumont and Fletcher Canon (V)', *SB* 13 (1960), at p. 96.

[44] J. C. Maxwell (ed.), *Henry VIII* (Cambridge, 1962; rev. edn., 1969).

[45] J. Margeson (ed.), Shakespeare, *Henry VIII* (Cambridge, 1990).

described as 'replacing' Maxwell's, which was far more scholarly and judicious.

Of the three, only J. C. Maxwell had read the scholarly literature thoroughly and with an open mind. He devoted more than half of his introduction to the authorship issue (Maxwell 1969, pp. xii–xxviii), and provided fair-minded accounts of the work of previous commentators. He summarized the metrical evidence, emphasizing that Spedding's sense of two styles in the play derived, as Spedding had claimed, from 'the general effect produced on the mind, the ear, and the feelings by a free and broad perusal' (1850a, p. 118), and judged that the evidence computed from feminine endings was 'quite remarkably consistent with that derived from Spedding's sense of style'. Still, Maxwell added, it was no longer 'necessary to remain content with the unanalysed category of "feminine endings"' after the meticulous computations of the ratio of final monosyllables to feminine endings made by Ants Oras (1953). He hailed this essay for providing 'a completely new test applied to the division of the play originally arrived at on other lines, and giving a wide divergence, in the right direction, between the figures for the putative authors', an 'analysis . . . also valuable on the qualitative side' for identifying scenes having the 'idiosyncratically Fletcherian' style. Although he accepted and endorsed the metrical evidence for co-authorship, J. C. Maxwell felt that 'trivial habits of syntax and accidence which a writer is not likely to be aware of' provided a more satisfactory linguistic approach, in which 'twentieth century investigation has confirmed Spedding's findings in several mutually independent ways; I find it quite impossible to regard the convergence of these results as fortuitous'. Maxwell cited the relative frequency of the pronominal forms *them* and *'em* (Thorndike 1901), and of *hath* and *has* (Partridge 1949),[46] commenting: 'cumulatively, these and some other less striking examples seem to me to establish the case for Fletcher beyond any reasonable doubt; especially in conjunction with the greater frequency of such contractions as *'t* and *'th* in Shakespeare'.

Maxwell also took note of his namesake Baldwin Maxwell's arguments concerning some 'unFletcherian' aspects of the style in Fletcher's scenes, but observed that 'almost all critics have recognized that Fletcher seems to have toned down some of his mannerisms in this play', perhaps due to Shakespeare's influence: 'indeed, the notion that collaboration with Shakespeare might be expected to have no effect on him would be a curious kind of tribute to either dramatist'. Taking all the evidence together, J. C. Maxwell felt that 'the case for joint authorship is as fully established as such a case ever can be on purely internal evidence' (p. xvi), a balanced and fair appraisal of the scholarly tradition.

---

[46] A. C. Partridge, *The Problem of Henry VIII Re-opened* (Cambridge, 1949); revised as Partridge 1964b.

In his New Arden edition R. A. Foakes showed no such openness to the possibility of co-authorship. He devoted much less space to the matter (Foakes 1957, pp. xvii–xxvi), and minimized the significance of both the metrical and linguistic evidence. Spedding is said to have 'claimed' that his computations distinguished the two dramatists' styles, but Foakes did not deign to quote any statistics from Spedding—nor from Furnivall, Ingram, or E. K. Chambers. Foakes referred to W. E. Farnham's analysis (1916) of colloquial contractions, but dismissed it as 'of doubtful importance, for the range of evidence presented is so narrow as to establish little more than that both authors were inconsistent in their usage'—a patently unfair account. Foakes recorded that Ants Oras had pointed to 'a high proportion of . . . extra weighted monosyllables' in 'the scenes said to be Fletcher's', but added: 'they occur occasionally in Shakespeare's other work'. Foakes seemed to relent in this negative attitude to the co-authorship claims when he reached A. C. Partridge's 1949 essay, 'the fullest and most compelling argument yet put forward' for Fletcher's co-authorship, and he even devoted a page to citing Partridge's 'formidable evidence' concerning the two authors' clearly distinguishable preferences in the use of the expletive *do*, *hath/has*, *them/'em*, and *ye* (some of which evidence, of course, derived from Farnham and Thorndike). 'These statistics', Foakes informed his readers, 'reinforce the arguments from style, phraseology, rhythm, and the frequency of double-endings and end-stopped lines.' Moreover, he added, 'there is nothing suspicious about claiming collaboration between Fletcher and Shakespeare', as we know from *The Two Noble Kinsmen* and, perhaps, *Cardenio*.

Just at the point when Foakes seemed to be conceding the case for Fletcher's participation, the reader turns the page and is rudely awakened:

> Most of the evidence for Fletcher is, however, suspect on one ground or another, as a few scholars writing in defence of Shakespeare's authorship have sought to demonstrate. *The statistics relating to tricks of style have been shown to mean little.* Double-endings become increasingly common in Shakespeare's later plays, and vary in frequency from scene to scene. (p. xx; my italics)

And so on, reiterating the views of Alexander (1931), and Baldwin Maxwell (1939). It is hard to know what to make of the sentence I have italicized. It seems to assure readers that the scholarly literature has been carefully studied, and the appropriate conclusion reached. But Foakes nowhere discussed this material, and showed no signs of having understood its significance. He was clearly able to understand the complicated bibliographical evidence concerning the two compositors' stints in the play, so we can only wonder why he refused to make a rational evaluation of the many stylistic arguments for Fletcher's participation.

Foakes went on to cast further doubt on all the linguistic evidence (*you/ye*, contractions), since 'the occurrence of all of these forms may . . . have been affected by scribal or compositorial interference'. Foakes reminded his readers yet again that 'stylistic evidence is notoriously unreliable', but that did not prevent him from essaying the same approach, arguing that the play's 'structure of imagery . . . cuts across the proposed authorship division and suggests a single mind at work'. Foakes cited imagery of bodily movement, sickness, sun and light, storms and shipwrecks, as occurring in both parts of the play, and as being typically Shakespearian. However, as Marco Mincoff countered, although one could imagine co-authors having worked out 'a scheme for the imagery' together, in *Henry VIII* 'there is nothing that one can really seriously claim as a running image'. The fact that the many images in the play can be classified into three or four spheres does not constitute a deliberately thematic use of imagery, especially when the associations described are so universal as that between light and royalty, or between storms and passion or destruction (Mincoff 1961, p. 254). Taking each group of images defined by Foakes, Mincoff quoted abundant examples in Fletcher's plays of metaphors that Foakes claimed to be specifically Shakespearian. In *Valentinian* alone he found ten images of disease connected with wrongdoing or mental suffering, seventeen images of the sea and shipwrecks, and at least thirty images of bodily movement (pp. 254–6). Some of the metaphors that Mincoff quoted are very similar to Fletcher's imagery in *Henry VIII*, but he was not arguing for parallel passages, rather making the general point that 'all four "running" images are as characteristic of Fletcher as they are of Shakespeare' (p. 256).

Once again, it seems, when a scholar takes on the role of editing a Shakespeare play his instincts to legitimize his own activity lead him to defend it from any claims of part authorship, as if that would somehow reduce the play's value, or diminish his own profession. When Foakes issued a second, revised edition in 1962, he had had the chance of reading Marco Mincoff's wide-ranging and cogently argued essay, which a noted attribution scholar described in that year as presenting 'the case for co-authorship in virtually irresistible form'.[47] Foakes, however, passed over Mincoff's new and important material showing the varying effect on Fletcher's style of writing alone, collaborating with Massinger, or with Shakespeare, and misleadingly reported that Mincoff had 'set out again, with some new emphases . . . the statistics concerning what he calls "objective differences of style and metre"', only to dismiss the whole enterprise: 'Mincoff's vehement partisanship is evident throughout this essay, and he does not observe that the interpretation of internal evidence is subjective, depending on a personal reaction to style and rhythm . . .' (Foakes 1962, p. xxvii). To be both partisan and subjective is obviously a damning condition; but again we see the Shakespeare conservators' blanket refusal to recognize that concrete statistical evidence, brought

[47] M. P. Jackson, 'Affirmative Particles in *Henry VIII*', *NQ* 206 (1962): 372–4, p. 372n.

together over a hundred-year period by many different metrical and linguistic tests, is anything but 'subjective'. Not surprisingly, Foakes felt comforted by Cyrus Hoy's suggested reassignments, which 'would thus reduce Fletcher's share in the play considerably from the usual ascription of ten and a half scenes to six, or, in terms of lines, by rather more than half'. Still, Foakes avoided explicitly commenting on the other side of the case, that Hoy 'finds consistent strong evidence of Fletcher's linguistic habits' in those six scenes, which would have seriously qualified his belief that the whole play is Shakespeare's work.

Thirty years on, John Margeson was still falling back with relief on Hoy's essay as 'the most carefully worked out evidence to date as to the actual fact of Fletcher's participation and also to its extent'—which, he happily added, was not great: 'the narrative plot, characters, the major confrontations, the interplay of ideas and the over-all pattern of the play . . . are Shakespeare's' (Margeson 1990, pp. 13–14). But, we would have to reply, all collaborations jointly agree on plot, characters, and related thematic issues, and in fact several of the most celebrated speeches in this play—Wolsey's two soliloquies, Cranmer's prophecy over the future Queen—are unmistakably Fletcher's. The Shakespeare fundamentalist may find himself compelled to take notice of some arguments for co-authorship, but he will do his best to minimize them. One popular strategy recently has been to suggest that Victorian and modern 'disintegrators' did not like the play, and therefore sought to ascribe it to a divided authorship, while our larger-souled generation scorns such a judgemental approach. As Margeson put it, 'recent criticism' displays 'an awareness . . . of the dramatic integrity of *Henry VIII* rather than *a desire to emphasise its dramatic faults and moral incoherence and then to explain them by a theory of dual authorship*. The varied interpretations of a number of recent staged representations have demonstrated the potentialities that lie within its text . . .' (pp. 11–13; my italics). Indeed, Margeson himself defended at great length 'the unity of the play' (pp. 11, 32–46), and interpreted the stage history as showing that the play 'now appears able to stand on its own merits' (pp. 48–59).

This whole apologetic vein contributes to what we might call the 'wellness' or 'feel good' factor so important in recent Shakespeare criticism. Our ancestors did not like the play, so they evolved these unpleasant theories—but we are more broad-minded, we reject the whole notion of a play having 'faults'. However, this is another instance of special pleading that quite falsifies the motives of the dozen or more scholars, from Spedding to Partridge and Mincoff, who recorded the fact that, while reading the play, they had noticed clear differences in verse, grammar, and other linguistic forms when moving from 1.2 to 1.3, from Shakespeare to Fletcher, or in reverse, from 2.2 to 2.3, or between the first and the second half of 3.2. Their motives for recording these impressions were purely scholarly, not designed to justify a pre-existing theory of the play's 'dramatic faults and moral incoherence'. It is entirely typical of Margeson's defensive fundamentalist attitude that, publishing in 1990, he did not cite the recent work on the play's verse style by Oras (1953 and 1960), Law (1959), Mincoff (1961), and Tarlinskaja (1987), a selective take that no doubt lightened his editorial task. Like Foakes in 1957, Margeson in 1990 was still content to summarize the case against Fletcher's co-authorship made by Alexander (1931) and Maxwell (1939), unaware that it had been disproved by the scholars he had ignored. Like Foakes, again, Margeson gave the briefest possible survey of the case before dismissing it:

Non-linguistic tests for authorship based on style, structure, characterisation and the use of imagery have tended to cancel one another out because of their widely differing conclusions and their apparently subjective nature. (p. 8)

But no, the uncomfortable fact is that all these varied scholarly approaches have confirmed each other to a quite striking degree. Oblivious to several generations of scholarship, Margeson argued that any variations in the verse style are 'functional and dramatically appropriate to the scenes where they are used' (pp. 10, 46–8), essentially Alexander's claim, but one discredited many times over. Given his unwillingness to rethink this issue, it is understandable that Margeson should have fallen back so gratefully on Cyrus Hoy's 'firmly based' reassignment, 'reducing Fletcher's share of the play from over two-thirds in the traditional division to less than one-third' (p. 8). That is a comforting calculation:

> Thy fifty yet doth double five and twenty,
> And thou art twice her love.

> *(Lear, 2.4.259–60)*

Yet Cyrus Hoy's inferences have not satisfied other scholars. In 1969 J. C. Maxwell added a brief note to his introduction recording Hoy's suggestion that 2.1, 2.2, 3.2b, 4.1, and 4.2 are 'basically touched up and added to by Fletcher . . . because the Fletcherian *ye* tends to occur in little clusters'. Maxwell commented: 'I find this unconvincing: *you* speeches such as 2.1.55–8 are just as Fletcherian in style as the supposed *ye* insertions. Except for 4.1, the scene for which Hoy's theory seems to me most plausible, the "extra monosyllables" in these scenes are on a Fletcherian scale' (p. xxxvii). By citing the work of Ants Oras, and by pointing to the consistency of style within Fletcher's scenes, despite the supposedly anomalous *you* instances, Maxwell showed how Hoy had failed to take into account all the other evidence for Fletcher's presence. In 1989 Fredson Bowers,[48] one of the leading textual scholars of our time, while welcoming Hoy's demonstration 'by

---

[48] F. Bowers, *Henry VIII*: 'Textual Introduction', in Bowers (ed.), *The Dramatic Works in the Beaumont and Fletcher Canon*, vii (Cambridge, 1989), pp. 3–20. Note a slight misprint, p. 5, 14 lines up: read 'I i–ii', not 'II'.

refined linguistic evidence that Fletcher was the second author in *Henry VIII*', regretted that no scholar had 'made a closer study of the evidence' in the quarter of a century that had elapsed since the essay was published (Bowers 1989*b*, pp. 5, 17 n. 10). Pointing out that Hoy's 'suspicion that Fletcher was not the main author rests exclusively on one range of linguistic evidence, the irregularity of his characteristic use of *ye*' (ibid.), Bowers proposed another explanation for 'the disproportionate number of *you*'s to *ye*'s in the admitted Fletcherian scenes' than just 'compositorial neglect'. A similar phenomenon occurs in the Fletcherian scenes of *The Two Noble Kinsmen*, which has a 'relative paucity of the *ye* form', and where several scenes mix *you* and *ye* indiscriminately, details which can be plausibly explained by 'the intervention of a copyist between Fletcher's autograph and the compositor'. In other words, the fluctuations in grammatical usage are not signs of a different author at work but derive from the nature of 'the printer's copy, which on the evidence seems to have been a scribal transcript' (p. 6). Bowers also pointed out that 'the Fletcherian *'em*—not unknown to Shakespeare but still not common—is sprinkled in these scenes in the midst of the *you*'s that were taken to represent Shakespeare' (p. 7), a sign that the copyist was inconsistent in reproducing his author's preferences. He also showed that on Hoy's theory 'the distinct stylistic and linguistic breaks between 3.2*a* and 3.2*b* remain unaccounted for if both were basically Shakespearian'. Bowers concluded with an observation important for authorship studies:

In sum, in the scenes Dr Hoy believes to have been initially Shakespeare's no positive evidence against Fletcher's sole authorship is advanced but only the negative evidence that in these scenes *ye* is likely to cluster instead of appearing sporadically spaced as in Fletcher's acknowledged scenes. The force of this observation, unaccompanied by other evidence for Shakespearian involvement, is blunted by the lack of any obvious signs of rewriting and by the periodic presence in these scenes of such Fletcherian signs as *'em* versus *them*, no different from what is found in his undisputed scenes. At best, a Scottish verdict of 'not proven' must be suggested at the moment, and the traditional assignment to Fletcher reaffirmed of 2.1, 2.2, 3.2*b*, and 4.1, 4.2. (p. 7)

More evidence disproving Hoy's thesis came from Jonathan Hope, in his sociolinguistic study of the Shakespeare collaborations.[49] Like Bowers, Hope objected to Hoy's treatment of the scenes where, because of the low number of *ye*'s, Fletcher was reduced to a sporadic interpolator: 'a positive ascription (to Shakespeare) is being made on the basis of negative evidence: the lack of Fletcherian features, rather than presence of Shakespearean ones' (Hope 1994, p. 69). Hope supported Bowers's indication of the potential scribal influence by citing the well-known 'tendency of Knight, the bookkeeper of the King's Men, to change *ye* to *you* when copying texts' (p. 69; Hoy 1956, pp.

[49] J. Hope, *The Authorship of Shakespeare's Plays: A Socio-linguistic Study* (Cambridge, 1994), pp. 67–83.

139–41). Other linguistic differences that Hoy cited, 'such as *th* and *s* endings are similarly unstable', liable to be affected by printing-house practice, as has been shown for three Shakespeare plays (pp. 69–70). Hope claimed that the sociolinguistic evidence he had used is unaffected either by scribes or compositors,[50] not being based on 'semantically equivalent variants (that is, *ye* and *you*, or *them* and *'em*) . . .'. The use of such a grammatical form as the auxiliary *do*, by contrast, 'involves a substantial difference in word order', which in turn has further significance for the verse line. There is no evidence that the older—or, as Hope calls them, 'unregulated'—habit, the use of *do* in positive declarative usages, such as 'did almost sweat to bear' (1.1.24), or 'they did perform' (1.1.35), was ever interfered with by scribes or compositors, since the more modern—or 'regulated' forms (here, 'sweated' and 'performed'), would ruin the metrical structure and necessitate further alterations, a messy and uneconomical task (pp. 73–6).

Hope studied three grammatical forms in *Henry VIII*, the auxiliary *do*, the relative marker *who*, and the personal pronoun option *thou* or *you*. Taking Hoy's tripartite scene division (A = Shakespeare, B = Fletcher, C = Fletcher touching up Shakespeare), Hope's computations for the regulation rate for *do* gave a score to the A scenes of 80 per cent, comfortably within the normal range for Shakespeare (79–84 per cent); for the B scenes the figure was 93 per cent, well within the normal Fletcher range (90–4 per cent); for the C scenes the figure was 95 per cent (pp. 70–1, 163). The huge gap of thirteen percentage points between A and B shows, once again, that 'the evidence for the presence of two hands in the play is overwhelming'. As for the C scenes, if Fletcher had merely sporadically interpolated lines or words into a Shakespeare scene, we could expect a value somewhere between those for A and B, so that the result Hope achieved, a figure 'slightly higher than the upper limit of the Fletcherian sample' is 'the least likely outcome' according to Hoy's thesis, which now seems untenable. Hope's figures for auxiliary *do* were 'calculated by adding the usages of several different types of sentence', but in a further test he considered 'the most frequent type, positive declaratives'. Having analysed ten plays by each dramatist he found that Shakespeare regularly used the older, unregulated form, his usage rate never falling below 8 per cent (or once every thirty-seven lines), while the more up-to-date Fletcher's rate never rose above 4 per cent (or once every ninety lines). The average usage for

---

[50] While this may be true in general, Ernst Honigmann has recently pointed out that both compositors and scribes did change some details. The 1619 Pavier reprint of *Sir John Oldcastle* introduced colloquial contractions (*d'ye* for *do ye*, *I'me* for *I am*), some of which produced 'metrically irregular lines' (E. A. J. Honigmann, *The Texts of 'Othello' and Shakespearian Revision* (London, 1996), pp. 52–3). This practice justified the complaints of Thomas Heywood (in 1612) that 'the negligence of the Printer' included 'misplacing of syllables', and Ralph Brooke (in 1621) that printers fathered 'syllabical faults' on their authors (pp. 51, 57). The scribe Ralph Crane, 'in one of his transcripts of *A Game at Chess*, . . . wrote "hath" some three dozen times where Middleton wrote "has" or "ha's"' (p. 68), and regularly changed *it* to *'t* (p. 69).

the ten plays examined was: Shakespeare 11.5 per cent, Fletcher 2.2 per cent (pp. 72–3).

Hope's second test, the use of relative markers (*who* with personal and impersonal antecedents; the 'zero' relative; *that*) again showed a marked affinity between the A scenes and Shakespeare's normal usage, and between the B scenes and Fletcher's. As for the C scenes, they were 'clearly closer to the Fletcherian comparison sample', once more scotching Hoy's attempt to father these scenes on Shakespeare (pp. 78–9, 163). However, within the Fletcherian range, the figures for these grammatical features were closer to Shakespeare's than were those for the auxiliary *do*, which led Hope to suggest that Fletcher may have been 'influenced by Shakespeare's style' (pp. 79–81). Hope carried out his third test, that for *thou/you*, even though he had shown its deficiencies as socio-historical linguistic evidence for authorship (pp. 54–64), because of the extraordinary figures for *Henry VIII*. These show 618 *you* forms (330 in Shakespeare's scenes, 288 in Fletcher's) and only 74 *thou* forms (22 in Shakespeare's scenes, 52 in Fletcher's), the percentage of *you* forms being Shakespeare 93.8 per cent, Fletcher 84.7 per cent. In other recent plays Shakespeare had a much lower percentage of *you* forms: *Antony and Cleopatra*: 59 per cent; *Coriolanus*: 62 per cent; *Cymbeline*: 60 per cent; *Winter's Tale*: 70 per cent; *Tempest*: 38 per cent, while figures for five Fletcher plays ranged from 55 to 78 per cent (p. 59). This comparative evidence suggests that in *Henry VIII* both Shakespeare and Fletcher altered their normal pronoun usage to achieve a stylistic effect, and Hope made the interesting suggestion that they may have adopted 'a specific linguistic tactic' as 'an attempt to write what was perceived as a new form of historical drama . . . a sort of documentary history', as suggested by the play's variant title, *All Is True*, in which the language would be 'deliberately modern, aping contemporary court usage' (pp. 82–3). Whatever we might do with that suggestion (in part anticipated by Charles Knight's description of the play's dialogue being deliberately 'closer to the language of common life'), we must give considerable weight to Hope's revalidation of the Spedding–Hickson ascription, and to his belief that 'the collaboration of Shakespeare and Fletcher in this play was interactive—that the two men wrote and planned together', rather than Fletcher finishing off a play that Shakespeare had abandoned (p. 82). At all events, editors who had taken refuge in Hoy's thesis are shown to have been deluded.

In authorship studies, as elsewhere, knowledge undergoes a cyclic structure of affirmation, denial, and reaffirmation. A case made on inadequate grounds can be refuted, sometimes conclusively. Another case made on an eminently rational interpretation of the evidence can be denied by those unwilling either to entertain the hypothesis or to examine the evidence with an open mind. But such denials can, in turn, stimulate other scholars into making new tests, finding more and even stronger evidence. The denial of Fletcher's authorship made by R. A. Foakes in 1957 sparked off the essays by R. A. Law (1959) and Marco Mincoff (1961), as we have seen, each of whom brought new evidence to bear and restated the traditional authorship division with greater force. It also provoked responses by MacDonald Jackson (1962) and David Lake (1969, 1970) which added still more evidence.

Jackson studied the distribution of the affirmative particles 'Yes', 'Yea', and 'Ay' in *Henry VIII* and in other plays by both dramatists.[51] According to *OED*, ' "Yes" was formerly more emphatic than "Yea" or "Ay" and was used in particular in answer to a question involving a negative . . .'. However, not long after 1600 'Yes' became the normal form, and already by 1610 dramatic texts showed 'a general tendency for "Yes" to replace "Ay" as the particle occurring most frequently' (Jackson 1962, p. 372). The new style is visible in Jonson, for 'while "Ay" appears nearly a hundred times' in the early *Every Man out of his Humour* (1599?), in *The Alchemist* (1610?) ' "Yes" takes over all [the] functions' of 'Ay', and 'occurs twice as often'. Fletcher, like Jonson, followed the newer mode, using 'Yes' almost exclusively, but 'Shakespeare throughout his career seems to have restricted his use of "Yes" to the special circumstances indicated by O. E. D.', that is, 'for special emphasis and in order to contradict a negative'. Jackson provided figures for both writers, here presented in Table 6.23. As the figures show, Fletcher clearly preferred 'Yes' to 'Ay', while Shakespeare made the opposite choice. Jackson's demonstration that *Henry VIII* precisely reflects the preferences of Fletcher and Shakespeare elsewhere strengthens the accepted authorship division still further.

David Lake documented another difference, if less decisive, showing that Fletcher always used the plural form *more* 'as an adjective with a substantive in the plural', never the older form *mo* (also spelled *moe*). In the five plays of sole authorship that he checked Fletcher had forty-three instances of *more*, none of *mo*. It is entirely consistent with Fletcher's preferences that in the *Henry VIII* scenes ascribed to him, *more* occurs six times with plural substantives, *mo* not once.[52] However, Shakespeare used both *more* and *mo* throughout his work, *The Winter's Tale* having 5 instances of *more* and 3 of *mo*, his scenes for *Henry VIII* showing 2 instances of *more* and 4 of *mo*. Lake's statistical calculations established 'a nine-to-one probability *on this piece of evidence alone*' that Shakespeare did not write the Fletcher scenes, a

---

[51] E. H. C. Oliphant, a pioneering scholar in many respects, was the first to notice, in Shakespeare's scenes for *The Two Noble Kinsmen*, 'the great use of "yea" in the sense of "more than that" '. He cited 6 instances of it in this play, 9 in *Henry VIII*, 5 in *Cymbeline*, and 3 in *The Tempest*. As he cogently commented, 'This is then a characteristically Shakespearean expression, used mainly in his later period; and its occurrence here is therefore not without significance. Its importance as testimony rests upon its literary unimportance. Except the hardened imitator that some investigators are so fond of imagining, no one was likely to copy so insignificant a trick' (Oliphant 1927, p. 338).

[52] D. J. Lake, ' "More" and "Mo(e)" in *Henry VIII*', NQ 214 (1969): 143–4, at p. 143.

TABLE 6.23. *Affirmative particles in* Henry VIII

Author	Play	'Ay'	'Yes'	'Yea'
Fletcher	*Bonduca*	3	16	1
	Valentinian	2	28	0
	Monsieur Thomas	6	15	1
	Henry VIII scenes	3	15	0
Shakespeare	*Henry VIII* scenes	3	3	9
	Cymbeline	16	6	7
	Winter's Tale	16	2	7
	Tempest	14	3	3
	Average for all plays	18	4	—

Source: Jackson 1962, pp. 372–3.

detail that favours the traditional division but 'does not prove it' (Lake 1969*b*, p. 144).

Lake also took a wider view in an as yet unpublished essay on 'Stylistic Variation in *Henry VIII* and *The Two Noble Kinsmen*'.[53] Observing that several of the linguistic features used to discriminate authorship do not occur in a tidy distribution within texts, Lake adopted the method used by Alvar Ellegård to overcome this problem, 'grouping together several features and plotting their combined frequency' (Lake unpublished, p. 4). Lake took as 'Fletcherian' features 'occurrences of (i) *'em*; (ii) *ye*; (iii) "extra monosyllables"', and as 'Shakespearian' features (i) 'the use of the auxiliary DO as a mere metrical expletive'; (ii) third-person singular verbs in *-th*'; and (iii) run-on lines, or 'rough endings', as he called them, which 'correspond approximatively to the categories of "light" and "weak" endings of traditional description'. Lake then divided the texts into blocks of approximately 100 lines each, counting the number of distinctive features and then processing the result: 'for each section of text, a subtraction of the number of "Shakespearisms" (S) from "Fletcherisms" (F) will give us a general "stylistic coefficient", given as a score per 100 lines: high coefficients will indicate "Fletcherisms" and low coefficients "Shakespearisms"' (pp. 4–7). For his control sample Lake analysed three Shakespeare and three Fletcher plays, as chosen by Ants Oras (1953), and presented his statistical data for each play in the form of a histogram, a diagram used in statistics for recording frequency distribution.[54] Single-authored plays, Lake reasoned, 'will show random variations in the stylistic coefficient, i. e. . . . . their histograms will approximate to normal curves, with scores clustering about a single mean in each case' (p. 7).

[53] I am most grateful to Professor Lake for letting me use this paper, written *c*.1970.
[54] See e.g. C. S. Butler, *Statistics in Linguistics* (Oxford, 1985), pp. 18–20.

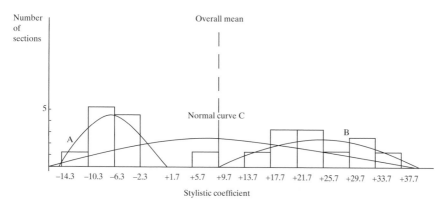

FIG. 6.1. Stylistic variation in *Henry VIII*
Source: Lake unpubl., p. 15.

As a layman might put it, in a typical histogram the vertical blocks reach their highest point in the middle, falling away symmetrically on either side.

Lake's analyses of stylistic variation in *Cymbeline*, *The Winter's Tale*, and *The Tempest* produced histograms of this form, largely symmetrical around a central block. Those for the three Fletcher plays (*Bonduca*, *Valentinian*, *Monsieur Thomas*) were visibly different, having many more blocks of a lower height, spread evenly over the whole horizontal scale, but still approximating to 'a normal curve, humping about the overall mean and tailing off on either side' (p. 14). The six tests showed that 'the styles of late Shakespeare and Fletcher are clearly distinguished numerically, with mean scores of about 0 to −5 for Shakespeare, and +35 to +50 for Fletcher. Nor is there any overlap; no Fletcherian section has a score of less than +19, and no Shakespearian section has a score of more than +6', apart from three short scenes in *The Tempest*, where Caliban's speeches have extra monosyllables, a form of characterization through style that Ants Oras had commented on (1953, p. 20). The results for *Henry VIII*, however, were startlingly different, as Fig. 6.1 shows. The pattern of variation in *Henry VIII* is quite unlike any of the other six plays. 'The mean stylistic coefficient for the whole play is about +9.7, and the standard deviation about 16; "Normal Curve C" on the diagram shows the random distribution one would expect with these parameters'. But the specific data do not fit the normal curve at all, producing what Lake terms a 'bimodal' curve (Lake 1970, pp. 3–4): the histogram 'humps twice, approximating to the two separate normal curves A and B, which have means about −6 and +24 respectively. In other words, there are two clearly distinct styles in the play' (p. 16). The first curve corresponds to the results Lake obtained for the three Shakespeare late plays, the second 'shows all the characteristics of Fletcher, but, on the whole, to a less extreme degree, its mean coefficient being at least 10 units lower than those of *Bonduca* and *Valentinian*'. This result confirms everything that we have learned about Fletcher's collaboration with Shakespeare, that the usual characteristics of his style were 'veiled' or toned down. Lake calculated that the probability was 'slightly more than 0.001 . . . against a single random distribution falling by chance into two such maxima'. Thus, 'it is 1000 to 1 probable that there are really two distinct styles in *Henry VIII*', and furthermore, Lake observed, the odds may actually be much higher, 'for other tests which we have not used—counts of vocabulary, repetitions and contractions—point in the same direction'. Lake's allocation of the individual scenes turned out to be 'almost exactly the "orthodox" division of Spedding', confirming that apart from 3.2, which Spedding split at line 203, the King's exit, 'no other long scenes need to be divided between the two styles' (p. 18).

David Lake ingeniously combined several stylometric analyses to create a new evaluative tool. In his most recent essay on the play's authorship,[55] MacDonald Jackson has shed still more light on this issue. Always innovative, Jackson devised a completely new test for *Henry VIII*, measuring the 'lengths of phrase' throughout—that is, 'the number of words intervening between any of the [eight standard] marks of punctuation' (Jackson 1997a, p. 76). Jackson counted phrases consisting of one word, two words, and so on, up to thirteen or more, in the scenes traditionally ascribed to each dramatist, expressing the result both as numbers and as percentages. Next, he performed 'a chi-square test comparing the overall distribution of phrase lengths' for the Fletcherian and Shakespearian scenes, which showed a 'highly significant difference', statistically speaking, and confirmed that the portions of the play assigned by Spedding and Hickson to each dramatist 'constitute two distinct populations'. Jackson then divided the Fletcherian material into the two groups which, Hoy claimed, were either pure Fletcher or basically Shakespeare with some minor revision by Fletcher, and tested them again. As Jonathan Hope had also found, performing the same exercise, the two 'Fletcherian' groups were 'indistinguishable' from each other, and 'statistically different from the uncontested "Shakespearian" matter' (p. 76).

Having disproved Hoy's thesis, Jackson went on to rearrange his material according to the individual scenes, so as to be able to measure each writer's phrase-length preferences. It transpired that Fletcher 'uses a higher proportion of phrases of two, three, four, five, six, and twelve words', a fact that Jackson illuminatingly linked with 'Fletcher's tendency to build up a passage of verse through a succession of simple grammatical units—by the accretion of "short appositional phrases by which the thought expands itself in little rushes and eddies"' (p. 78)—to quote Mincoff (1961, p. 242). In the

---

[55] M. P. Jackson, 'Phrase Length in *Henry VIII*: Shakespeare and Fletcher', NQ 242 (1997): 75–80.

TABLE 6.24. *Phrase lengths in* Henry VIII

Scene	Phrases of 2–6 or 12 words (%)	Spedding ascription
5.3	76.0	Fletcher
1.4	72.5	Fletcher
1.3	69.1	Fletcher
*4.1	67.2	Fletcher
*2.2	65.7	Fletcher
5.2	65.3	Fletcher
*4.2	63.9	Fletcher
3.1	63.6	Fletcher
*3.2b	63.3	Fletcher
5.4	61.0	Fletcher
*2.1	59.1	Fletcher
5.1	58.9	Shakespeare
3.2a	58.2	Shakespeare
1.2	57.9	Shakespeare
2.3	56.6	Shakespeare
2.4	55.0	Shakespeare
1.1	52.4	Shakespeare

Source: Jackson 1997a, p. 79; table 3.

Shakespearian scenes, by contrast (how often I have used that phrase!), there is a higher proportion of phrases of 7, 8, 9, 10, 11, and 13 or more words, Shakespeare being 'more apt than Fletcher to use longer, more complex phrasing, as sentences straddle line endings in energetic imitation of the tortuous movements of the mind' (p. 78). Jackson presented these findings in a particularly revealing table, which I reproduce as Table 6.24. This ranks the play's scenes 'according to their percentage of phrases of 2, 3, 4, 5, 6, or 12 words', marking with asterisks those scenes which Hoy considered to be basically Shakespeare's, with sporadic interpolations by Fletcher. As we can see, 'all eleven of the "Fletcherian" scenes are ranked higher than any of the "Shakespearian" scenes'. The percentage for the lowest Fletcher scene, 2.1, 'is the merest fraction above' that for the highest Shakespeare scene, 'but the separation is nevertheless perfect' (p. 78). Interestingly, other studies have put 2.1 nearer to Shakespeare, so that the two writers may have overlapped in this scene. Otherwise, Jackson's results 'indicate that there really are two authorial styles present in the play and that Spedding's allocations are fairly accurate'.

At much the same time that Lake and Jackson were scrutinizing linguistic differences in the two strata of *Henry VIII* using the naked eye, W. M. Baillie was using a 'sophisticated [computer] program for stylistic analysis'.[56] Baillie took as control texts Shakespeare's *Cymbeline* (1609) and *The Winter's Tale* (1611), Fletcher's *The Woman's Prize* (1611) and *Valentinian* (1614). He took ten 500-word samples from each play 'in three categories: standard-size units, whole scenes, and individual characters' (Baillie 1974, p. 74). Concentrating on syntactic features, Baillie found that several tests successfully discriminated the two writers, including 'their percentage of descriptive adjectives' (p. 75) and 'the proportion of words in complement structures' (pp. 75–6). Studying word-class and function categories, Baillie found that 'noun modifiers' provided an excellent discriminator between Shakespeare and Fletcher, a difference which emerged even more clearly when he combined two or more variables, achieving '95 per cent accuracy' (pp. 76–7). Confirming most statisticians' experience that smaller samples are less reliable, the statistical methods used (including 'multivariant discriminant analysis') could none the less distinguish the two dramatists at the level of whole scenes, and in the language of individual characters (p. 78). Much of Baillie's paper was concerned with methodological issues, but he certainly established that electronic means could 'consistently discriminate Fletcher from Shakespeare at a high level of significance' (p. 81). He also showed that 'the overall variance among samples is much less for Fletcher than for Shakespeare' (p. 80), confirming an evaluation of the two dramatists' respective inventive powers made by more traditional studies.

Throughout my studies of these five plays I have emphasized the importance of modern editions and their power either to advance or retard the current of knowledge concerning Shakespeare's activities as a co-author. After a number of regressive editions in the 1980s and 1990s, it was a pleasure to welcome Jay Halio's recent edition of *Henry VIII*.[57] Halio gives a judicious account of the authorship issue, commendably up to date, showing that the work of Marco Mincoff, Marina Tarlinskaja, and Jonathan Hope, using quite different approaches, confirmed the traditional assignment of scenes. Halio contributes two new stylistic markers from his study of the Folio text,

---

[56] W. M. Baillie, 'Authorship Attribution in Jacobean Dramatic Texts', in J. L. Mitchell (ed.), *Computers in the Humanities* (Edinburgh, 1974), pp. 73–81. The program is known as EYEBALL. Thomas B. Horton, in another computer-based study, 'Frequent Words, Authorship, and Characterization in Jacobean Drama', in I. Lancashire (ed.), *Research in Humanities Computing* 1 (Oxford, 1991), pp. 47–69, reported on his doctoral dissertation (University of Edinburgh, 1987), 'The Effectiveness of the Stylometry of Function Words in Discriminating between Shakespeare and Fletcher' (not seen). Unfortunately, Horton devoted most of this essay to applying J. F. Burrows's use of 'word-rate variations in Jane Austen's novels to determine relationships between characters' (p. 47). The only findings of interest to us are that 'most of the Shakespeare and Fletcher characters fall into two separate regions' of the statistical diagram, and that 'Fletcher has not succeeded in creating differing idiolects for the major characters in his tragedy' *Valentinian* (p. 66), a linguistic stereotyping that will be discussed in Chapter 7.

[57] *King Henry VIII, or All is True*, ed. Jay L. Halio (Oxford, 1999): see my evaluation in *RES* 53 (2002): 119–21.

first 'the frequency throughout the play of *y'are* (= *you're*) and similar contractions (for example, *y'have, th'have, th'ave*) . . . A tabulation of incidences shows that of the dozen *y'* contractions, 10 are in scenes assigned to Fletcher, and only 2 in Shakespeare's . . .' (Halio 1999, p. 20). Secondly, the frequency of parentheses may be tabulated according to the two dramatists' shares, 'and here again the proportions are revealing. In the Shakespearian scenes, parentheses appear 37 times among a total of 1,167 lines, giving a ratio of once every 31.5 lines; in Fletcher's scenes, they appear 255 times among 1,599 lines, giving a ratio of once every 6.27 lines' (pp. 20–1). Halio's computations, based on the original text, are more reliable than those provided by Marco Mincoff from a modernized text, but confirm his diagnosis of Fletcher's 'parenthetical mode of construction', that is, 'the way in which the flow is frequently broken by sharp, clear-cut parenthetical comments' (Mincoff 1961, p. 243). The interaction between these scholars, two generations apart, typifies the scholarly tradition in Shakespeare authorship studies, as later workers devise more accurate and more reliable tests.

To sum up 'this tale of length' in numerical terms, the scholars whose work I have been discussing have established that, in their respective portions of the play, Shakespeare's rate of using feminine endings was 34 per cent, Fletcher's 59 per cent, with a clear difference of ten percentage points between Shakespeare's highest and Fletcher's lowest scores. For run-on lines the relation is reversed, Shakespeare's average being 48.5 per cent, Fletcher's 25 per cent, again with ten percentage points between Fletcher's highest and Shakespeare's lowest score. In their use of the auxiliary 'do' the gap is even wider, thirteen percentage points (Shakespeare 80 per cent, Fletcher 93 per cent). Shakespeare's use of light endings far outnumbers Fletcher's (45 to 7), and the weak endings even more so (37 to 1). The ratio of Shakespeare's use of *'em* to *them* is 1 to 3.4, Fletcher's 14.3 to 1; their use of 'Ay' and 'Yes' shows the same different preference. Shakespeare uses a colloquial contraction once every fifteen lines, Fletcher once every forty. The percentage of extra monosyllables to feminine endings in Fletcher's scenes is 29 per cent, as against 14.2 per cent in Shakespeare's. Fletcher ends lines with a verb followed by an unstressed pronoun four times more frequently than Shakespeare (8.3 to 2.1 per cent), but Shakespeare's use of unstressed monosyllables at line endings is more than eight times as great as Fletcher's (8.2 to 1 per cent). Fletcher used enclitic phrases in his scenes nearly four times more often than Shakespeare did (201 against 58), and his verse–sentence quotient is more than four times greater than Shakespeare's (1.85 against 0.44). The 'stylistic coefficient' clearly differentiates the two writers, as does the phrase-length test. Finally, Fletcher uses both *y'* contractions and parentheses five times more frequently than Shakespeare. All of the scholars who have performed objective tests on the play agree with the authorship division proposed by James Spedding and Samuel Hickson in 1850.

It might seem that we have travelled an awfully long way, only to reaffirm the authorship division made so long ago. The evidence for the traditional ascription is now overwhelming, not to be dismissed by any suggestion that scholars who argued it were 'subjective' or 'partisan'. There is, in effect, no coherent evidence against the co-authorship of Shakespeare and Fletcher, but some Shakespeare conservators will no doubt continue to dispute it. Another type of challenge to authorship studies has emerged in recent years following some supposed revolutions in Literary Theory, one effect of which would be to outlaw such studies altogether. In a recent consumer's guide to Shakespeare editions, commissioned by the Open University, and appropriately called *Which Shakespeare?*, A. R. Braunmuller informed those needing to choose an edition of *Henry VIII* that

Since the 1960s, criticism has increasingly suspected authorship study and has denied, on theoretical grounds, the relevance of the single historically definable author.[58]

Braunmuller singled out for special odium the New Penguin edition (1971) by A. R. Humphreys, who is sternly criticized for discussing 'authorship and collaboration', an issue which 'does not prove a very attractive introduction to the play', and for having even worse vices:

Humphreys's assumptions about authoritative organic form (or collaborative disunity), sequential versus dynamic episodes, 'symbolical or conceptual unity', and so forth form a short list of all that post-structuralist criticism finds wrong with authorship study. While it seems certain that few spectators or readers will come to *Henry VIII* without already having a fair knowledge of Shakespeare's plays, they can hardly be assumed to know, or care, about Fletcher's. (p. 80)

From that lordly pedestal Braunmuller also berated J. C. Maxwell's New Cambridge edition for spending more than half of his introduction 'reviewing the history of the authorship debate and awarding merits or demerits to the contributors' (p. 79). Curiously like the old-fashioned Shakespeare fundamentalists, Braunmuller had no criticism to make of David Bevington's Bantam edition (1988), which 'begins with the question of collaborative authorship and concludes that the play is entirely Shakespeare's', nor of John Margeson's New Cambridge text, in which 'arguments over authorship and shares are extensively considered and then dropped as critically nugatory' (p. 81). And he naturally approved of R. A. Foakes's 'hopes of dismissing the matter from critical debate', while recklessly claiming that 'Foakes's view now prevails among most literary and theatrical critics', always excepting the villains of the piece, 'the Oxford Complete Works'.

Braunmuller seems to be invoking two standards, demonizing editors who give too much space to discussing co-authorship while lauding those who

---

[58] A. Thompson *et al.*, *Which Shakespeare? A User's Guide to Editions* (Milton Keynes and Philadelphia, 1992), p. 78.

ascribe *Henry VIII* to Shakespeare alone. Similarly, despite his notionally dismissing 'the single historically definable author' as a myth put about by the bourgeoisie in the late eighteenth century, Braunmuller still talks of 'Shakespeare', is happy to accept him as the sole author, and vastly prefers him to another 'single historically definable author', the evidently far inferior 'Fletcher', whose work no student can be expected 'to know, or care about'. Notwithstanding Braunmuller's dismissive remarks, Fletcher was an inventive dramatist, whose many gifts are worth our attention, and the desire to differentiate his share of the play from Shakespeare's remains a fundamental and legitimate approach.

Gordon McMullan's recent Arden edition seems to have accepted that goal, since it announces the play on its title-page as being by William Shakespeare and John Fletcher.[59] However, in order to discover why he gives Fletcher equal billing, one has to turn to the very end of an enormously long introduction (200 pages) to find a section on collaboration, which is unsatisfactory in several respects. McMullan distorts this issue (and many others)[60] by linking authorship studies to 'the prejudiced, bardolatrous environment out of which the study of authorship attribution grew' (McMullan 2000, p. 186). But although some of the early practitioners expressed a belief in Shakespeare's superiority, their primary concern was the empirical study of the plays' language. The original essay on *Henry VIII* by James Spedding was not based on 'intuition'—a 'wholly subjective and thus unsatisfactory analytical approach', as McMullan weightily pronounces (pp. 186–7)—but on repeated experience of the whole play, resulting in an objective attempt to distinguish by linguistic means the presence of two styles which he, like many other readers, had noticed there. There is no truth in the allegation that critics who do not like the play 'have found it useful to be able to lay the blame on Fletcher' (p. 180). Such allegations are becoming habitual for Shakespeare fundamentalists wishing to deny the presence of a co-author. As we have seen, John Margeson alleged that 'disintegrators' of *Henry VIII* shared 'a desire to emphasize its dramatic faults and moral incoherence and then to explain them by a theory of dual authorship' (Margeson 1990, pp. 11–13). In the same vein, Jonathan Bate claimed that scholars studying *Titus Andronicus* 'have been prejudiced by their distaste for the play . . . [and] have been anxious to find grounds for . . . dismissing it from the canon of his works' as 'a patched-together collaborative effort'.[61] The popularity of such allegations shows that they have become a stock in trade of the Shakespeare conservators, but by ascribing to scholars some prior and concealed aesthetic distaste they evade confronting the historical phenomenon of co-authorship.

---

[59] Gordon McMullan (ed.), William Shakespeare and John Fletcher, *King Henry VIII* (London, 2000).

[60] See my comments in *RES* 53 (2002): 121–7.

[61] J. Bate (ed.), Shakespeare, *Titus Andronicus* (London, 1995), p. 3.

McMullan muddles this issue further by claiming that 'the New Biblio-
graphers in the mid-twentieth century began to revisit and revise the long-
dismissed "disintegrative" practices of the mid- to late nineteenth century,
by which plays could be attributed scene by scene to the collaborating
writers' (p. 185). But all the historical evidence indicates that co-authors did
indeed usually write whole scenes (the switching of responsibility that takes
place in *Henry VIII* in the middle of 3.1 is unusual), and to identify their
respective shares is not to 'disintegrate' a play but to give its creators their
due. McMullan's sole exemplar of this supposed 'disintegrative' revival is
Cyrus Hoy, who produced a series of essays on the authorship of the plays in
the Fletcher canon (Hoy 1956–62). But Hoy had nothing to do with the New
Bibliography of the generation from McKerrow to Greg and beyond, his
interests being solely in devising a series of linguistic tests which would effectively distinguish Fletcher's work from that of his many collaborators—
Beaumont, Middleton, Ford, and Shakespeare, among others. In so doing,
Hoy was in a direct line of descent from earlier attribution scholars, such as
F. G. Fleay (1874), A. H. Thorndike (1901), W. Farnham (1916), and above
all E. H. C. Oliphant (1927). The tradition of authorship studies has nothing
to do with either bardolatry or with the New Bibliography.

    Collaboration was a frequent practice in the drama between 1580 and
1642, and cannot be dismissed as an irrelevant issue by claiming that theatre
by its very nature is 'collaborative' (McMullan 2000, p. 196). All the performing arts are collaborative in the sense that they rely on a number of
people bringing them to fulfilment in a particular space at a particular time,
but that is very different from the kind of collaboration in which Elizabethan
dramatists took part. McMullan surveys some of the scholarship which
has clearly distinguished Fletcher and Shakespeare's work, but in a disap-
proving manner, as in his reference to the 'best-known Victorian disintegrators, Fleay and Furnivall of the New Shakespere [*sic*] Society'—a pedantic
parenthesis which ruins its point by not reproducing that Society's true
spelling, 'Shakspere'—without actually disclosing what methods they used.
McMullan does cite some of the scholars concerned in a footnote (p. 187),
but gives no sign that he has actually absorbed their arguments or noticed the
wide range of linguistic evidence that they brought to bear on the issue. He
also leaves out many relevant studies that I have discussed here, by F. J.
Furnivall (1874), John Ingram (1874), Marjorie Nicolson (1922), Karl Ege
(1922), Charles Langworthy (1931), Alfred Hart (1943), Ants Oras (1960),
Marco Mincoff (1961), MacDonald Jackson (1962, 1997), David Lake
(1969, 1970), Marina Tarlinskaja (1987), and Fredson Bowers (1989). Taken
together, these studies provide compelling evidence of a consensus now 150
years old confirming the original attributions made by Spedding and
Hickson. McMullan gives the main authorship division in a chart on pages
448–9, listing only five authorities, one of whom is the not always reliable

Fleay, who was convinced that Massinger had contributed three scenes to the play. However, the next authority cited, Willard Farnham, decisively disproved Fleay's thesis, as did Nicolson, Baldwin Maxwell, and Hoy.[62] To cite Fleay here is to show that the basic scholarship on this issue has not been digested. McMullan mentions Jonathan Hope's recent and valuable discussion (1994) for its critique of Hoy's attempt to reassign several Fletcher scenes to Shakespeare on the basis of one verbal marker only, but does not realize that Hope totally demolished Hoy's case. It is misleading, then, to refer in the Notes to every scene which Hoy attempted to reclaim for Shakespeare.

One further source of dissatisfaction for readers of McMullan's edition is the degree to which it has adopted sceptical attitudes to authorship put about by Current Literary Theory. He prefaces his discussion of collaboration with an epigraph from Michel Foucault's essay 'What is an Author?' (1969):

> The author does not precede the works, he is a certain functional principle by which, in our culture, one limits, excludes, and chooses. (p. 180)

Readers may wonder what to do with this oracular pronouncement, since every shred of evidence that we have from the Renaissance, or indeed from classical antiquity, plainly shows that the author does precede the works, and is in no sense a source of limitation or exclusion. McMullan pays homage to what he calls the 'ground-breaking work on the historical construction of the concept of authorship' by Michel Foucault, as processed by such recent critics as Stallybrass and Masten, who have uncritically accepted Foucault's claims that the individual writer's 'proprietorship' of his work was a phenomenon of the eighteenth century and after (pp. 196–7). I have given separate consideration (see Appendix II: 'Abolishing the Author? Theory *versus* History') to Foucault, and to the book by Masten, who gets himself into great difficulty trying to apply Foucault's ahistorical theory to the conditions of authorship in the seventeenth century, adding a further level of anachronism by interpreting utterances from that period in a heavily sexualized way, so as to claim that collaboration in Renaissance drama was a 'homoerotic' activity.[63] All I need to say here is that Foucault's theory of the author not 'emerging' until the eighteenth century, and of authors having no sense that they owned their work before the introduction of the copyright laws, lacks any

---

[62] McMullan regularly cites Fleay's Massinger ascriptions in his notes (e.g. pp. 212, 329, 388), unaware that they have been discredited.

[63] McMullan emulates Masten in giving anachronistic sexualizing interpretations of the play's language, this time for a heterosexual agenda. He claims that the word '*conscience*' in the play is always given a sexual meaning, and 'becomes curiously synonymous' with *vagina* (pp. 280, 289, 310); he believes that the word '*nothing*' [also] has its early modern significance of *vagina* (p. 295); he takes a reference to Anne Boleyn's receiving of gifts from Henry to imply 'oral sex' (pp. 296–7); and does wonders with the innocent words *bosom* and *prick* (p. 311). While Shakespeare, like Fletcher, often indulged in bawdy, reference to these dramatic contexts will show that the innuendo exists in the editor's brain.

historical validity. We may understand this anachronistic conception as deriving from Foucault's constant obsession with the issues of power and powerlessness, which led to his idiosyncratic linking of writing with 'penal transgression' and the institution of prisons, but as a version of history it has nothing to recommend it. As a model for scholarly research into authorship problems in Renaissance drama, it is hard to think of anything more irrelevant, or more destructive.

Given this allegiance to Current Literary Theory, it is not surprising that McMullan's discussion should be burdened by its heavy weight of interpretative expectations, claiming that 'the issue of collaboration' raises 'larger debates . . . about authorship, the construction of the subject and the possibility of human agency' (p. 182). These expectations lead him to make utterances in a theoretical vacuum, far removed from the practical conditions of the theatres. 'Collaboration, by definition, disperses the authority of the author', he asserts (p. 182): but no, the two or more authors share a joint authority, and a joint reward. There is no evidence to support the claims that co-authors 'work simultaneously on a scene', or even 'work together in a single room' (pp. 192, 197). Robert Daborne, according to his own testimony, was busily writing in his own lodgings when Philip Henslowe's assistant called to collect the next instalment of the play. A further sign that McMullan's scholarly competence has been damaged by his allegiance to theory is his ignoring of the standard authorities on co-authorship, giving only the most superficial attention (pp. 183–4) to G. E. Bentley's discussion, and (like Masten) never using Henslowe's Diary. He remains unaware of the considerable evidence that co-authors delivered their share in the form of whole acts or scenes, often distributed across the play, presumably as an aid to continuity.

McMullan approvingly summarizes Hope's work, but then appropriates it to Foucauldian theory, praising him for 'projecting authors who are the products of their linguistic environment rather than autonomous agents freely choosing a particular, and unique, mode of expression' (p. 195). But the exclusive dichotomy is his own, for Hope shows that authors are *both* products of their linguistic environment *and* autonomous agents. His book demonstrates that, because authors come from different sociolinguistic environments, we can differentiate their contributions to a play on the objective evidence of verbal preferences. This does not mean that they did not, also, have a 'particular, and unique, mode of expression', indeed Hope builds on earlier studies of the authorship division made for *Henry VIII* derived from the differences between Shakespeare's and Fletcher's versification, and nowhere denies the validity of these studies. McMullan, following Masten, believes that 'the professional nature of the playwright's task undermines the notion of fixed style', since, by creating dramatic personae he ' "refracts the supposed singularity of the individual in language' " (p. 195). This is what we might call an utterance of pure theory, unsullied by any actual knowledge of nineteenth- and twentieth-century scholarship. But although playwrights, since the time of Greek tragedy and comedy up to and beyond the Renaissance, have expended remarkable labour on individualizing the characters represented on stage, according to gender, age, political status, personal preoccupations, it is a demonstrable fact that their own linguistic and stylistic habits can be traced in the speeches of many characters who are individualized in other ways. In John Ford's plays characters both of low and high rank use the abbreviated forms *'dee* and *'tee*; in Middleton's, a wide range of characters prefer some verbal contractions to others, choose from the same group of oaths and ignore others; and so on. All the dramatists we know of have an individual practice both in the placing of pauses within the verse line and in the use of extra-metrical lines; in an extensive oeuvre, such as Shakespeare's, we can trace a strikingly regular progression over time.

The individualizing of characters through their speech is a striking feature of *Henry VIII*, where we can juxtapose the variety and individuality of Shakespeare's inventions against Fletcher's use of verbal and situational stereotypes (see Chapter 7). McMullan observes in his notes that 'Katherine expresses herself much more vehemently' in a Shakespeare scene than in Holinshed (p. 302), but does not ask himself whether Katherine has the same vehemency in the scenes that Fletcher provided; reference to the text will show distinct differences. In his introduction McMullan juxtaposes two speeches by Katherine, one written by Shakespeare (2.4.72–82), the other by Fletcher (3.1.102–11), observing that 'the second is . . . heavily end-stopped, whereas in the first longer units of meaning extend across several lines of verse' (p. 190). This is an accurate observation, although at a far lower level than the analyses of Oliphant, Oras, Mincoff, and others. But McMullan uses the speeches as examples of differing linguistic habits (the contraction *'em* for *them*; a preference for *ye* over *you*), to illustrate Hoy's methodology for differentiating Fletcher and Shakespeare—a method he here endorses, although he later sides with Masten's ill-informed critique of Hoy (p. 191). McMullan describes Victorian critics' 'sense of a writer's characteristic way with verse form' as an 'intuitive' approach (p. 185), but it is only his resolute refusal to take note of the many valuable quantitative, statistical approaches to the prosody of *Henry VIII* that leaves the issue of verse form at this pre-scholarly level.

For all his editorial labours, McMullan seems to have become fatally divided between accepting and rejecting the rationale of attribution scholarship, leaving himself sitting painfully on the fence between theory and history. In his notes he gives many helpful citations from Holinshed and other sources, and occasional comments prove the point made by R. A. Law and others, that Fletcher generally followed his sources carefully (e.g. pp. 269,

285, 356, 402), while Shakespeare deviated at will (e.g. pp. 298, 339). It is obvious on any analysis that the two authors must have planned their selection of a limited number of usable episodes from this vast body of historical material, and that their planning also included agreement on thematic issues, such as the importance given to Henry's conscience. It is disconcerting, then, to find McMullan recording that one passage in the play (3.2.213 ff.) shows that 'Fletcher has read Holinshed on *Henry VII* too', only to draw this conclusion:

That a 'Fletcher' section and a 'Shakespeare' section demonstrate knowledge of the same page in Holinshed's 'Henrie the seventh' underlines the closeness of the collaboration (or the irrelevance of authorial attribution). (p. 344)

Once again he rushes to an exclusive position: despite the shared planning, with the sources as with so many other issues we can still tell Fletcher and Shakespeare apart. McMullan's Foucault-generated scepticism would destroy the possibility of historical scholarship in all literary study. Although paralysed by theory, McMullan still defends *Henry VIII* against detractors— 'I like the play, I think it is a fine play, and I think it a collaboration' (p. 180). At least we can agree with that.

THE TWO NOBLE KINSMEN

The co-authorship of this play was affirmed by the very first document mentioning it, the entry in the Stationers' Register for 8 April 1634:

Master John Waterson Entred for his Copy under the hands of Sir Henry Herbert and master Apsley warden a Tragi Comedy called the two noble kinsmen by John ffletcher and William Shakespeare, vjd.

The quarto edition, which Waterson published later that year, added some new information:

> The Two Noble Kinsmen: Presented at the Blackfriars by the Kings Maiesties servants, with great applause: written by the memorable Worthies of their time:
>
> M[r]. *John Fletcher*, and
> M[r]. *William Shakespeare.*   Gent.
> Printed at *London* by *Tho. Cotes*, for *Iohn Waterson* . . .
>
> (Chambers 1930, i. 528)

Waterson's statement that Shakespeare's company performed the play at their regular winter playhouse, the indoor theatre at Blackfriars—a declaration unlikely to be false—is already sufficient indication that his authorship ascription may be trusted. As Eugene Waith noted in his edition, Waterson 'published several other plays of the King's Men, none of them falsely attributed', including Webster's *The Duchess of Malfi*, and Fletcher's *The Elder Brother* and *Monsieur Thomas*.[64] Cotes, interestingly enough, was associated with publishing Shakespeare's Second Folio in 1632, and in 1635 brought out a (sixth) quarto of *Pericles*.

Much of the best commentary on the play's co-authorship appeared in the early nineteenth century, a period when interest in Elizabethan and Jacobean drama, previously focused on Shakespeare, was being extended to the other dramatists. A convenient starting-point is the edition of Beaumont and Fletcher by Henry Weber (1783–1818). In some 'Observations on the Participation of Shakespeare in *The Two Noble Kinsmen*',[65] Weber summed up earlier critics, starting with the editions of Fletcher by Thomas Seward (1750) and George Colman (1778). Seward had argued that 'either Shakespeare had a very great hand in all the acts of this play, . . . or else that Fletcher more closely imitated him in this than in any other part of his works' (cit. Weber 1812, xiii. 151). Seward had pointed out parallels with both dramatists: the prison scene between Palamon and Arcite (2.2) resembles a scene (4.3) in Fletcher's *Love's Progress*; the pedantic schoolmaster's Latinisms (3.5) seemed the work of Fletcher; but Emilia's description of female friendship (1.3) closely resembled that in *Midsummer Night's Dream* (3.8), while the madness of the Jailer's Daughter (4.3) has 'such strong features of both Ophelia and Lear in their phrensies, that one cannot but believe that the same pencil drew them all' (xiii. 153). In his edition Colman defended Fletcher from Seward's jest, that 'Shakespeare's second-best manner' was 'not easily distinguishable [from] Fletcher's best' (cit. Weber 1812, xiii. 152), objecting that Fletcher has 'so much poetical merit, that to attribute his most exquisite beauties to Shakspeare is doing him an injury' (xiii. 155). As for the Jailer's Daughter, her madness contains 'much poetical fancy' but does not equal 'the *natural* madness painted by Shakspeare. Like the assumed distraction of Hamlet and Edgar, "Though this be madness, yet there's method in't"; more *apparent* method than in the drawing of Ophelia and Lear' (xiii. 155–6). Colman pointed out several other parallels with Fletcher's work, but denied any contribution from Shakespeare.

The question of distinguishing Shakespeare's style from Shakespearian imitation, a particularly tricky issue in *The Two Noble Kinsmen*, also exercised George Steevens in a long note which Weber reprinted from Malone's edition of *Pericles* (1780).[66] Steevens observed that 'the language and images of this piece coincide perpetually with those in the dramas of Shakespeare. The same frequency of coincidence occurs in no other individual of Fletcher's works;

---

[64] E. M. Waith (ed.), *The Two Noble Kinsmen* (Oxford, 1989), p. 50.
[65] H. Weber (ed.), *The Works of Beaumont and Fletcher*, 14 vols. (Edinburgh, 1812), xiii. 151–69.
[66] See Malone, *Supplement* to the 1778 edition of Shakespeare by Johnson and Steevens (London, 1780), ii. 168–76.

and how is so material a distinction to be accounted for?' Steevens answered his question by categorically denying that Shakespeare would have stolen so many scraps from his own work had he been engaged in a collaboration. In that case he would 'studiously have abstained from the use of marked expressions', and he 'cannot be suspected of so pitiful an ambition as that of setting his seal on the portions he wrote, to distinguish them from those of his colleague. It was his business to coalesce with Fletcher, and not to withdraw from him' (xiii. 158). With that a priori pronouncement about the 'business' of co-authors to write in the same style, not enquiring whether such a thing were possible, Steevens then compiled a list of more than forty parallels between *The Two Noble Kinsmen* and Shakespeare's plays, concluding that 'this tragedy [was] written by Fletcher in silent imitation of our author's manner. No other circumstance could well have occasioned such a frequent occurrence of corresponding phrases . . .' (xiii. 163). In any case, Steevens claimed, the 'sagacity' of earlier critics 'was insufficient to observe that the general current of the style was even throughout the whole, and bore no marks of a divided hand'. Steevens did not deign to enlighten them further, concluding with a casual remark on the play's style, that 'there are fewer hemistichs in it than in any other of Shakespeare's acknowledged productions. If one speech concludes with an imperfect verse, the next in general completes it. This is some indication of a writer more studious of neatness in composition than the pretended associate of Fletcher' (xiii. 165).

But, despite Steevens's dismissal, other readers recognized the hands of both dramatists. Weber instanced (xiii. 165–6) the play's inclusion by Charles Lamb in his *Specimens of English Dramatic Poets who lived about the Time of Shakespeare* (1808). Lamb anthologized three scenes from the play, and commented that although the dialogue of Palamon and Arcite in prison (2.2) 'bears indubitable marks of Fletcher', the two preceding scenes—that is, 1.1, where the three Queens appeal to Theseus, and 1.3, the dialogue on female friendship between Hippolyta and Emilia,

give strong countenance to the tradition that Shakspeare had a hand in this play. The same judgment may be formed of the death of Arcite [5.4.48–84], and some other passages not here given. They have a luxuriance in them which strongly resembles Shakspeare's manner in those plays where, the progress of the interest being subordinate, the poet was at leisure for description. I might fetch instances from *Troilus* and *Timon*. That Fletcher should have copied Shakspeare's manner in so many entire scenes (which is the theory of Steevens) is not very probable; that he could have done it with such facility is to me not certain. His ideas moved slow; his versification, though sweet, is tedious, it stops every moment; he lays line upon line, making up one after the other; adding image to image so deliberately that we see where they join: Shakspeare mingles every thing, he runs line into line, embarrasses sentences and metaphors; before one idea has burst its shell, another is hatched and clamorous for disclosure. If Fletcher wrote some scenes in imitation, why did he stop? Or shall we say that Shakspeare wrote the other scenes in imitation of Fletcher? that he gave Shakspeare a curb and a bridle, and that Shakspeare gave him a pair of spurs: as Blackmore and Lucan are brought in exchanging gifts, in *The Battle of the Books!*[67]

After nearly two centuries, that is still a remarkably perceptive comment on both writers, one echoed by many modern scholars. Lamb enlarged here on an earlier passage in which he had contrasted the two dramatists' styles, having praised a scene from Fletcher's *Thierry and Theodoret*:

Yet, noble as the whole scene is, it must be confessed that the manner of it, compared with Shakspeare's finest scenes, is slow and languid. Its motion is circular, not progressive. Each line revolves on itself in a sort of separate orbit. They do not join into one another like a running hand. Every step that we go we are stopped to admire some single object, like walking in beautiful scenery with a guide. This slowness I shall elsewhere have occasion to remark as characteristic of Fletcher. (Lucas 1904, iv. 329)

Lamb's account of Fletcher's style, the verse moving a line at a time, deliberate but static, was impressionistic but remarkably accurate, as later studies confirmed.

None of the critics cited by Weber had practised what he called 'the minute criticism which is required for a subject like the present', but he went on to do so himself, rejecting Steevens's description of the play's style as 'even throughout', showing 'no marks of a divided hand'. Weber affirmed that 'the strongest argument to prove the co-operation of Shakspeare in *The Two Noble Kinsmen*, is, certainly, the entire difference between some scenes and others, in point of language, metaphor, and versification; which is so strong, that it is very wonderful how Steevens could fail to be struck with it' (Weber 1812, xiii. 166). Going into detail, Weber argued that

Nothing can be more distinct than the style, for instance, of the first and second act. In the first, the language is far more metaphorical and involved, so that the body of notes requisite to illustrate the text, is about three times the volume of those necessary in the latter. Another and a still more decisive variation appears in the versification. In the first act, the lines, as Mr Lamb observes, are run one into the other; in the second, the peculiarities of Fletcher's versification, which the same critic notices, are extremely apparent. Most of the lines finish a division of a sentence; a full point very rarely occurs in the midst of a verse; and, what Mr Lamb has not noticed, the number of double terminations of the verses is greater here, as well as in all the plays of Fletcher, than in the metre of any contemporary dramatist. (xiii. 166)

All of these observations—the correspondence between line length and sentence patterns; the absence of mid-line pauses; Fletcher's fondness for double endings—were accurate, as the scholarly tradition analysing

---

[67] E. V. Lucas (ed.), *The Works of Charles and Mary Lamb, iv. Dramatic Specimens and the Garrick Plays* (London, 1904), pp. 341–2. For that episode in *The Battle of the Books* see Jonathan Swift, *The Prose Writings*, ed. H. Davis, 14 vols. (Oxford, 1939–68), i. 158.

Fletcher's style in *Henry VIII* has shown. Weber then emulated Richard Roderick, who in 1758 had been the first scholar to attempt a statistical analysis of verse styles:

Taking an equal number of lines in the different parts which are attributed to Shakspeare and to Fletcher, the number of female, or double terminations in the former, is less than one to four; on the contrary, in the scenes attributed to Fletcher the number of double and triple terminations is nearly three times that of the single ones. (xiii. 166 n.)

Weber added linguistic to his metrical analyses, pointing to 'the number of uncommon words in the particular scenes which [Shakespeare] may be supposed to have written', words which 'Fletcher's language is, in general, peculiarly free from'. Weber cited as examples '*counter-reflect* (a noun); *meditance*; *couch*, and *corslet* (used as verbs); *operance*; *appointment*, for military accoutrements; *masoned*; *globy eyes*; *scurril*; *disroot*; *dis-seat*, &c' (xiii. 166 n.). It was not until 1934 that Alfred Hart's systematic study of the play's vocabulary confirmed the specifically Shakespearian nature of these words.

Ahead of his time in so many respects, Henry Weber also challenged the evidence of the parallel passages selected by Steevens

from the present play and the dramas of Shakspeare, which, instead of rendering the co-operation of the latter improbable, strongly support the likelihood of it. About two-thirds of them, and those in general the most striking, occur in those portions which exhibit so strongly the style and language of Shakspeare. Mr Steevens observes, that they are more numerous than the coincidences in any other plays of that poet, in the ratio of ten to one; but his assertion is made at random, and might be easily disproved. (xiii. 168)

Equally decisive was his rejoinder to the single piece of stylistic evidence that Steevens cited, the presence of 'hemistichs', incomplete or half-lines:

Finally, the number of hemistichs may not be equal to that in some others of Shakspeare's plays, but they are far more numerous than in the acknowledged productions of Fletcher; and almost all which do occur are in those parts which are written in Shakspeare's style. That poet is peculiarly fond of finishing a scene with a hemistich, as in the first, second, and fourth scenes of the first act, and in the very conclusion of the drama. In the same manner the addresses of Palamon, Arcite, and Emilia, to Mars, Venus, and Diana, contain a great number of hemistichs, and are generally finished with one. (xiii. 169)

All these observations are accurate, as can be seen by examining the text. Having given so many pioneering examples of the 'minute criticism' needed for authorship studies, Weber was convinced that

an attentive reader will easily perceive that some of the scenes so strongly resemble the style of Shakspeare, and that of none of his contemporaries, and others bear the equally well-marked stamp of Fletcher, that no adventitious circumstances can over-weigh this evidence, when combined with the authority of the title-page, and the play-house tradition . . . (xiii. 167)

Weber concluded by giving a detailed authorship ascription:

Act 1: Shakespeare
Act 2: Fletcher[68]
Act 3, scenes 1 and 2:[69] Shakespeare
————scenes 3–6: Fletcher
Act 4, scenes 1–2: Fletcher
————scene 3: Shakespeare
Act 5, scenes 1, 3–4: Shakespeare
————scene 2: Fletcher (xiii. 169)

The soundness of Weber's judgement, in 1812, can be gauged from the fact that Eugene Waith, in his excellent Oxford edition, summarizing nearly two centuries of scholarship, gave the same division of labour, only ascribing 2.1 to Shakespeare (Waith 1989, p. 22). It is heartening to find 'an attentive reader' so long ago coming to a conclusion that much subsequent scholarship would confirm.

The growing interest in Shakespeare during this period easily declined into bardolatry, a conviction of his superiority to other dramatists, and even a belief that he could do no wrong. These attitudes mar the essay by a promising young scholar, William Spalding (1809–59), *A Letter on Shakspere's Authorship of 'The Two Noble Kinsmen'; a Drama commonly ascribed to John Fletcher* (Edinburgh, 1833). Spalding's essay was reprinted in 1876 for the New Shakspere Society by F. J. Furnivall, who hailed it as 'one of the ablest (if not the ablest) and most stimulating pieces of Shakspere criticism I ever read' (Spalding 1876, p. v), and added a new subtitle describing its general drift: *On the Characteristics of Shakspere's Style and the Secret of his Supremacy*. After Furnivall's praise the essay proves to be rather disappointing, diffuse, generalized, and over-long. Most of the ideas in it, especially those differentiating Shakespeare's style from Fletcher's, derive from Lamb and Weber, as Spalding acknowledged:

Shakspere's versification is broken and full of pauses, he is sparing of double terminations to his verses, and has a marked fondness for ending speeches or scenes with hemistitches. Fletcher's rhythm is of a newer and smoother cast, often keeping the lines distinct and without breaks through whole speeches, abounding in double endings, and very seldom leaving a line incomplete at the end of a sentence or verse. (Spalding 1876, p. 11; similarly, pp. 32, 36–8, 47)

---

[68] Weber treated the prison scene as a single unit; later editors made the opening prose dialogue into 2.1, the verse scene following into 2.2.
[69] Weber treated 3.1 and 3.2 as one scene.

Spalding elaborated on this basic idea, describing Shakespeare's style as having an energy which could relapse into obscurity (pp. 13–14, 28, 32, 34, 46, 54), an 'oracular brevity' (pp. 13, 15, 28), a rapidity of mental conception and imagination (pp. 14, 16), a 'prevailing tendency to reflection' (p. 20), a liking for personifications (p. 25), and a 'clearness' in its use of imagery (pp. 27, 33, 40). Fletcher's style, he judged, suffers from 'the want of distinctness in grasping images, and the inability to see fully either their picturesque or their poetical relations' (p. 16), 'a slowness of association' in developing ideas (p. 37), proving that he had 'a less fertile fancy and a more tardy understanding than Shakespeare's' (p. 38), and so on. Such predetermined judgements simply elevate Shakespeare and depress all other dramatists by comparison (pp. 23, 57–8, etc.): 'in the fifth act we again feel the presence of the Master of the spell' (p. 45). Spalding added only two points to the received picture, one describing Fletcher's tendency towards sudden switches of mood (p. 38), abrupt alternations of feeling (p. 44), effects of hurry and surprise (p. 73); the other observing Shakespeare's fondness for 'verbal names expressing the agent' (p. 29), as in 'Thou *purger* of the earth' (1.1.48).

That Spalding's essay was so admired shows that it performed a useful function in familiarizing nineteenth-century readers with the fact that two dramatists collaborating on a play could be clearly distinguished in terms of verse style, language, characterization, and morality. Spalding believed that Shakespeare had designed the whole play (pp. 59, 62–5, 77), but he rejected the subplot as having been planned and executed by Fletcher (pp. 35, 60). This self-contradiction was pointed out by Samuel Hickson in 1847, in a journal essay reviewing recent work on the play, which was also reprinted by the New Shakspere Society in its *Transactions* for 1874.[70] Hickson urged that 'some such invention as these characters'—the Jailer and his daughter—'was necessary to the escape of Palamon' from prison, and he defended their first introduction (2.1) as Shakespearian, the scene being written in prose, a common medium for him but rare in Fletcher, and lacking the 'grossness' that Fletcher showed elsewhere (Hickson 1847, pp. 62, 69). Hickson also argued that the verse soliloquy for the Jailer's Daughter (3.2) was designed and written by Shakespeare, giving an instance of that dramatist's 'fine judgment' in two respects: supplying 'the due gradation between a mind diseased and madness', necessary to the development of her character, and displaying 'a depth of insight into the psychological character of this state only excelled by Shakespeare himself in *King Lear*' (p. 73). Hickson attributed to Fletcher the next subplot scene, the soliloquy and song displaying the Daughter's madness (3.4), with its 'mere incoherent nonsense' (p. 74). But he ascribed the prose scene (4.3), where the Doctor, the Jailer, and her Wooer observe and comment

---

[70] S. Hickson, review essay on *The Two Noble Kinsmen*, *Westminster and Foreign Quarterly Review*, 92 (1847): 59–88; repr. as 'The Shares of Shakspere and Fletcher in *The Two Noble Kinsmen*', *TNSS* 1 (1874): 25*–61*.

on her madness, to Shakespeare, describing it as 'the most important scene of the whole play' (p. 76).

Hickson justified this surprising judgement by reverting to a topic that Steevens had mentioned, only to dismiss, the nature of literary imitation. He began by proposing a general principle concerning the *plagiarius* (Latin for 'kidnapper'), namely

that a wholesale plagiarist or imitator will infallibly betray himself by the bad use he makes of his stolen property. By such, a sentiment or illustration is more easily kidnapped than the grace of doing it. Aptness of illustration, truth of sentiment, justness of thought, fitness to the character using it, all considered in the original, may all be missing in the theft of such a writer. If all these indications of the imitator be wanting, we may fairly conclude the passage in question to be original, notwithstanding any resemblance in thoughts or sentiments to other works. (p. 77)

As an example of imitation, Hickson cited Arcite's question, in a Fletcher scene:

Am not I liable to those affections
Those joys, griefs, angers, fears, my friend shall suffer?

(2.2.189–90)

juxtaposing it with Shylock's

Hath not a Jew eyes? Hath not a Jew hands, organs, dimensions, sense, affections, passions? (*MV*, 3.1.59–60)

Fletcher, he argued, imitated Shakespeare when writing Arcite's speech, but whereas 'we all know the use made by Shylock of the latter question, . . . Arcite merely opens what is, in his case, an untenable argument. It leads to nothing: it is a mere flash in the pan' (p. 77). Similarly, when the Jailer's Daughter says, 'I know you, you are a tinker' (3.5.79), this is an opportunistic imitation of Hamlet's reply to Polonius: 'Do you know me, my lord?'—'Excellent well, you are a fishmonger' (2.2.173–4), another borrowing that leads nowhere. In the prose scene of the Daughter's madness, by contrast, the several echoes of other passages in Shakespeare are resemblances 'in style or structure, which go to prove identity of writer, [rather] than in either sentiment or imagery', the mark of an imitator (p. 79). When the Jailer's Daughter describes the pains of hell—'such burning, frying, boiling, hissing, howling, chatt'ring, cursing'—she peoples it with those who deserve to be punished:

Lords and courtiers that have got maids with child, they are in this place; they shall stand in the fire up to the navel and in ice up to th'heart, and there th'offending part burns and the deceiving part freezes—in truth a very grievous punishment . . . (4.3.29–30, 37–41)

Hickson compared this speech with mad Lear's diatribe against women:

> Down from the waist they are Centaurs,
> Though women all above;
> But to the girdle do the gods inherit,
> Beneath is all the fiend's: there's hell, there's darkness,
> There is the sulphurous pit, burning, scalding,
> Stench, consumption.

$$(4.6.124–9)$$

As he put it, 'comparing the women, who "down from the waist are centaurs", with the lords and courtiers who stand "in ice up to the heart", we may perceive that there is not one circumstance that is common to both images, and that the resemblance is entirely that of manner' (p. 79). Similar though this scene is to passages in Shakespeare—I should want to add Claudio's imagined picture of hell in *Measure for Measure* (3.1.117–22)—Hickson argued that the resemblances were 'not so much copies as variations of phrase, equally in place', and appropriate both to the character and her condition (p. 80). In this way we can distinguish between Shakespeare echoing himself, and Fletcher imitating him.

Hickson's treatment of imitation can still help to solve the difficulties many readers have had with the Shakespearian reminiscences in *The Two Noble Kinsmen*. His discussion of the play's authorship corrected Spalding's blanket rejection of the subplot as non-Shakespearian, while not modifying the authorship division set out by Henry Weber. But Hickson's juxtaposition of the two dramatists' verse styles varied the accepted image, with some freshness:

Of all writers of blank verse, Shakespeare is the most musical. His verses flow into each other with the most perfect harmony; never monotonous, but seldom rugged. His words seem rather to fall naturally into verse, than to be measured out into lines; and his varied pauses break without disjoining the longest passages, so that none can be said to be long-winded, nor to add to their untiring effect. (p. 66)

Unfortunately, like many admirers, Hickson exaggerated Shakespeare's uniqueness, claiming that 'he uses redundant syllables very sparely', and 'double endings . . . but occasionally'. His account of Fletcher was more accurate:

the measure of Fletcher's verse is extremely peculiar: double and triple endings, and redundant syllables, may be said to form the character of his system; so much so that the line is frequently eked out with an expletive, after the verse is complete. The result of this is, what was introduced for the sake of variety, and which has that effect when Shakespeare uses it, in Fletcher becomes excessively monotonous, giving something of a sing-song effect. (p. 66)

That description of the main features of Fletcher's verse style, well illustrated by a comparison of Arcite's pathetic speech (2.2.37–45) with one from

Fletcher's *Elder Brother* (pp. 66–7), was confirmed in the following century by the detailed studies of E. H. C. Oliphant, Ants Oras, R. A. Law, Marco Mincoff, and Marina Tarlinskaja. Hickson made one specific observation worth recording, Fletcher's liking 'to use in the plural certain nouns of quality or circumstance commonly used in the singular', such as 'our honours' (1.2.37), and 'our banishments' (2.2.37), both instances where 'Shakespeare would have used the singular number' (p. 68).

The studies by Lamb, Weber, Spalding, and Hickson had established by 1847 the broad general differences between the styles of Shakespeare and Fletcher. If research were to be carried further, more detailed indicators were needed, involving some degree of quantification. Two such indicators were forthcoming in what Harold Littledale described as 'the wave of metrical tests which inundated criticism in 1874'.[71] Following the reprinting of Hickson's article in the New Shakspere Society *Transactions* for that year, F. G. Fleay added a note confirming Hickson's authorship division.[72] Fleay accepted that the play had been 'conclusively shown to be a joint production of Shakespeare and Fletcher, and the portion written by each author . . . accurately assigned', and he agreed with Hickson that Shakespeare had written two of the prose scenes in the subplot (2.1, 4.3). Fleay described the various verse tests he had applied, conceding that he had found 'no aid as to discriminating these authors' by computing the number of rhymes, Alexandrines, and very short lines. The one decisive test, he believed, was that for the number of double endings, and his findings are set out in Table 6.25. Fleay pointed out that 'the metrical evidence confirms the results of the higher criticism in the strongest manner', for the Shakespearian average agreed exactly with that for *The Winter's Tale*, while that for Fletcher corresponded to the figure Fleay had computed for 'his undoubted works'.

Fleay was followed by F. J. Furnivall,[73] who added further confirmation to Hickson's division[74] by computing their percentage of 'unstopt' or run-on

---

[71] H. Littledale (ed.), *The Two Noble Kinsmen. By William Shakspere and John Fletcher. Edited from the Quarto of 1634. Part II. General Introduction and List of words* (London: The New Shakspere Society, 1885), p. 79*. Part I of this edition was *The Two Noble Kinsmen. Reprint of the Quarto, 1634* (London: The New Shakspere Society, 1876). I shall mostly refer to Part II, in which the page numbers are followed by an asterisk.

[72] F. G. Fleay, 'Mr. Hickson's division of *The Two Noble Kinsmen*, Confirmed by Metrical Tests', *TNSS* 1 (1874): 61*–64*; repr. in Fleay, *Shakespeare Manual* (London, 1876), pp. 172–4.

[73] F. J. Furnivall, 'Mr. Hickson's Division of *The Two Noble Kinsmen*, Confirmed by the Stopt-line Test', *TNSS* 1 (1874): 64*–65*.

[74] I have adjusted Furnivall's tables by moving 2.2 to the Fletcher table: as J. K. Ingram pointed out, Furnivall originally concluded that his test 'fails in part because it gives Shakespeare's 2.1 to Fletcher. Now the fact is, that Mr. Hickson assigns this scene to Fletcher, and thus the test in question really confirms, in this instance, the orthodox view as to authorship. Mr. Furnivall was led into mistake by the different numeration of the scene in different editions. What he calls 2.1 contains the prison-scene, which Mr. Hickson, separating it from the prose which precedes it, calls 2.2. Here, then, is an interesting unconscious testimony to the value of the verse-tests' (Ingram 1874, p. 455).

TABLE 6.25. *Double endings in* The Two Noble Kinsmen

Author	Total lines	Double endings	Percentage
Shakespeare	1,124	321	28.6
Fletcher	1,398	771	55.2

Source: Fleay 1874*d*, pp. 62*–63*.

TABLE 6.26. *Run-on lines in* The Two Noble Kinsmen

Author	Total lines	Run-on lines	Percentage
Shakespeare	1,095	517	47.2
Fletcher	1,439	257	18.0

Sources: Furnivall 1874*b*, p. 65*.

TABLE 6.27. *Light and weak endings in* The Two Noble Kinsmen

	Light	Weak
Shakespeare scenes	50	34
Fletcher scenes	3	1

Source: Ingram 1874, p. 454.

lines, as shown in Table 6.26. Furnivall noted the affinity between the Shakespearian average, 47.2 per cent, and those for *Cymbeline* (39.6 per cent) and *The Winter's Tale* (47.1 per cent). But he warned that the test could be unreliable 'in single scenes . . . Counting can never be a better judge than real criticism' (p. 65*).

J. K. Ingram applied his 'light' and 'weak' ending test to this play, also, as can be seen from Table 6.27, confirming that 'here again there are two different systems of verse', and producing results very similar to those for *Henry VIII*. Ingram offered a full tabulation of his results (Ingram 1874, p. 462), pointing out that 'the weak endings are found in every non-Fletcherian scene but two'. One is the very short 1.5 (the three Queens' funeral song), the other 3.3, a scene which Weber gave to Fletcher, as did Furnivall. Ingram was convinced of Fletcher's authorship, but recorded his feeling that the

Shakespearian scenes were below his best. None the less, he concluded, 'the manner, in general, is more that of Shakespeare than of any other contemporary dramatist', and 'the system of verse is one which we do not find in any other', being, 'in all essentials, that of Shakspere's last period' (p. 454).

In addition to pioneering verse tests, the New Shakspere Society performed another great service to the study of this play by publishing Harold Littledale's excellent edition of it in two parts, the first containing a reprint of the 1634 Quarto, the second a modernized text of the play with notes. Littledale provided new and more correct statistics, praising Ingram's light and weak endings test as 'a most trustworthy witness of lateness of composition, and an index of truly Shaksperian peculiarity', worked out by Ingram 'with great precision' (Littledale 1885, p. 19*). Then he gave his own count, based on a better text, which slightly increased the figures for Shakespeare: 'light' endings, from 50 to 52; 'weak' endings, from 34 to 35; while those for Fletcher remained unchanged (p. 20*). Littledale perceptively dismissed the rhyme test as useful for 'determining the relative lateness or earliness of plays in the whole series of Shakspere's works, [but] not one which throws any light upon the question of authorship' (p. 19*). But he described the 'stopt-line' and 'double-ending' test as most important, and he drew

particular attention to the fact that, the division of the scenes between the two authors having been made originally before any systematic application of tests had taken place, these tests are now found to confirm that apportionment made primarily upon aesthetic grounds. (p. 21*)

Littledale gave fresh data, tabulating both tests together (in Table 6.28 I have substituted percentages for his proportions). As Littledale commented, the figures clearly differentiate the two dramatists. Proportionally speaking, 'while Shakspere has only 1 double ending in every 3.49 lines', Fletcher has '1 in every 1.89 lines, or nearly twice as many; and . . . while Shakspere has 1 unstopt line in every 1.78 lines Fletcher has only 1 in every 4.06 lines. Such divergences, consistently preserved throughout, cannot be lightly scorned as the frenzied fancies of maniacal metremongers'—to quote A. C. Swinburne's animadversions (p. 23*).

Littledale then offered a scene-by-scene commentary justifying his authorship attributions by citing extensive parallel passages from Shakespeare and Fletcher, aware that no such systematic comparison had ever been made. This is a remarkable sequence (pp. 29*–68*), and must still be read by every serious student of this play—especially since modern editors increasingly ignore such material. Littledale realized 'the danger of too readily relying upon apparently parallel passages', pointing out that a seeming 'self-repetition from *Macbeth*' in one piece derives from Shakespeare having closely followed Chaucer (p. 43*). He abjured any 'survey of the "finger-post" kind'—alluding to one of Francis Bacon's aphorisms in the *Novum Organum*, proposing

TABLE 6.28. *Double endings and run-on lines in* The Two Noble Kinsmen
(*a*) Shakespeare scenes

Scene	Number of lines	Double endings	Percentage	Run-on lines	Percentage
1.1	210	49	23.3	106	50.5
1.2	116	35	30.2	75	64.7
1.3	97	39	40.2	60	61.9
1.4	49	13	26.5	26	53.1
2.1 (prose)	—	—	—	—	—
3.1	123	33	26.8	74	60.2
3.2	38	10	26.3	11	28.9
4.3 (prose)	—	—	—	—	—
5.1	173	49	28.3	105	60.7
5.3	146	39	26.7	79	54.1
5.4	137	45	32.8	74	54.0
Totals	1,089	312		610	
Averages			28.6		56.0

(*b*) Fletcher scenes

Scene	Number of lines	Double endings	Percentage	Run-on lines	Percentage
1.5	6	0	0	1	16.7
2.2	281	159	56.6	72	25.6
2.3	83	39	47.0	21	25.3
2.4	33	19	57.6	10	30.3
2.5	64	47	73.4	13	20.3
2.6	39	22	56.4	15	38.5
3.3	53	29	54.7	9	17.0
3.4	20	11	55.0	4	20.0
3.5	150	59	39.3	24	16.0
3.6	310	184	59.4	79	25.5
4.1	151	58	38.4	49	32.5
4.2	156	79	50.6	48	30.8
5.2	112	63	56.3	14	12.5
Totals	1,458	769		359	
Averages			52.7		24.6

Source: Littledale 1885, p. 22*.

a new scientific methodology[75]—'in order to ascertain the actual number and intensity of the flashes of genius which are to be found in the Shakespearian scenes', holding it enough to show 'by comparisons that the thoughts in general are Shakespeare's thoughts, and the phrases peculiarly his phrases . . .' (p. 28*). Taking up Hickson's discussion, Littledale found it 'easy to distinguish

[75] Bacon, *Novum Organum*, Book II, aphorism 36; in *The Works of Francis Bacon*, ed. J. Spedding *et al.*, 7 vols. (London, 1857–9), i. 294–304, iv. 180–90.

between plagiarisms and self-reproductions. A plagiarism is betrayed by its environment, 't will out, be the plagiarist never so skilful . . .'. But 'with a self reproduction the case is different. The resembling passage occurs naturally, incidentally; some familiar word associates an old train of ideas', or some familiar phrase structure will carry a fresh idea. Littledale showed the difference between imitation and self-reminiscence by citing the scene where Emilia recalls her childhood friendship with Flavina. This is said to be an imitation of Helena's reproach that Hermia had forgotten their 'school-days friendship' (*MND*, 3.2.195–216), but the similarities are 'coincidences, and not conscious imitations.—Each passage has a fitness of its own' (p. 42*), and Shakespeare wrote both. However, 'the description of the mad girl floating on the lake, making the flower-posies, and singing her snatches of song' (4.1.52–93), is 'an imitation obviously of the flower-scene and death of Ophelia' (p. 55*). It is understandable that 'Shakspere repeats himself regularly and frequently; he is like the ocean, *ce vaste prodige de la monotonie inépuisablement variée*, never quite the same, yet never wholly different'— quoting from Victor Hugo's 'magnificent rhapsody', *William Shakespeare* (1864).

Littledale's forty pages of detailed parallels certainly establish beyond question Shakespeare's authorship of part of the play. As he pointed out, few of his Shakespeare parallels were 'drawn from the early or even second period plays: all the closer self-reproductions are traced from the last two groups, and especially from the plays of the fourth period' (p. 68*), many from *Coriolanus*, *Cymbeline*, and *The Tempest*. In the course of his scene-by-scene analysis Littledale brought several kinds of criteria to bear, both linguistic—commenting on Fletcher's liking for 'plural nouns, especially abstracts', finding no less than 44 in the first 50 lines of 2.2 (p. 48*)[76]—and metrical, suggesting that the first 17 lines of 5.1 may be by Fletcher: '17 verse-lines, 13 double-endings' (p. 62*). Littledale was also sensitive to the effect of dramatic context on style. In the night-time soliloquy where the Jailer's Daughter looks for Palamon in order to give him a file with which to escape from prison (3.2.1–38), Littledale noted that the proportion of double endings (26.3 per cent) is well in line with Shakespeare's average for the play as a whole (28.6 per cent), whereas that for run-on lines (28.9 per cent) is far below his average (56.0 per cent). Notwithstanding, Littledale argued, 'all the metrical evidence except the "stopt-line" points to Shakspere as the author, and the "stopt-line" can be given no weight here, the spasmodic versification, full of jerky pauses, being an artistic reflection of the mental whirl

---

[76] Littledale's list of Fletcher's plural nouns in 2.2.1–50 is: 'prisoners, friends, kindreds, comforts, youths, games, favours, ladies, ships, clouds, praises, garlands, twins, arms, horses, seas, swords, sides, temples, gods, hands, armies, hopes, prisoners, graces, youths, embraces, kisses, cupids, necks, figures, selves, eagles, arms, fathers, maids, banishments, songs, woes, delights, hounds, echoes, javelins, rages' (p. 48*).

and bewilderment of the speaker' (p. 53*). That comment illustrates a fundamental principle of authorship studies, that variations in statistical data should send a scholar back to the play, in order to see what effect the dramatist might have been intending in a specific context, before drawing any far-reaching conclusions.

Littledale confirmed most of the authorship ascriptions made by his predecessors, but queried some. The short scene (1.5) where the three Queens enter with attendants bearing the hearses of their knights, and sing a mourning song, the only scene of whose authorship Hickson was uncertain (1847, p. 69), Littledale assigned to Fletcher: 'First, the song is very poor stuff, and contains several Fletcherian phrases, as "quick-eyed pleasure" '—which he paralleled with comparable Fletcher compounds, here 'fair-eyed maids' (2.2.37), 'fair-eyed honour' (2.5.29), and 'fair-eyed Emily' (4.1.8)—also 'sad and solemn', the latter phrase occurring 'in a *Fletcherian* stage-direction in *Henry VIII*, 5.2: "sad and solemn music" '. Secondly, the song concludes with the line, twice repeated:

> We convent naught else but woes
>
> (9–10)

and Littledale noted that 'the word *convent* [was] evidently imitated from the preceding scene'—by Shakespeare—'where it is correctly used: "all our surgeons convent in their behoof" [1.4.30]; here it is meaningless. It is not likely that the writer of scene 4 would have repeated such an unusual word' (p. 45*). The modern reader, having profited from the many analyses of Fletcher's style produced since 1885, is tempted to cite, in addition, the unnatural emphasis that the metre gives to the word 'darken', which must either be read as an iambic foot, stressing the second syllable, or as a trochaic, with a heavy initial emphasis, reinforcing the alliteration:

> Vapours, sighs, *darken* the *day*
> Our *dole* more *deadly* looks than *dying*.
>
> (1.5.2–3)

Both effects are typically Fletcherian. Littledale also gave detailed indications of where Fletcher may have added touches of his own to Shakespeare's scenes, such as 1.1.1–37 (p. 31*), 5.1.1–17 (p. 62*), 5.3.105–14, 136–46 (p. 66*), and 5.4.23–38 (p. 67*), suggestions still worth consideration. Harold Littledale's edition of *The Two Noble Kinsmen* is one of the best that any co-authored Shakespeare play has ever received, and deserved to become better known. Its publication by the New Shakspere Society was 'for members only', unfortunately, and many libraries never acquired it.

Several scholars who have studied this play did so alongside *Henry VIII*, the other joint Shakespeare–Fletcher creation, and recorded very similar results. In 1916 W. E. Farnham considered 'the use of colloquial contractions as a test of authorship', his figures for *Henry VIII* being 39 contractions in Fletcher's scenes, or an average of 0.024 per line, as against 77 contractions in Shakespeare's scenes, or an average of 0.066 per line (1916, p. 350). For *The Two Noble Kinsmen*, unfortunately, Farnham did not know Littledale's authorship division, relying on other less well-informed accounts, which ascribed '2.1', 411 lines long (that is, the prose scene now known as 2.1, together with the verse scene, now 2.2), to Shakespeare, also '2.2', now 2.3. Since Hickson, Littledale, and other scholars have reliably ascribed 2.2 and 2.3 to Fletcher, I have taken the liberty of recalculating Farnham's figures, as follows:

> Shakespeare scenes (1,089 lines): 13, 11, 6, 5, 2, 2, 6, 6, 6, 10, 7
> = Total 74. Average per line: 0.067.
> Fletcher scenes (1,458 lines): 0, 9, 7, 1, 1, 1, 13, 2, 6, 8, 8, 2, 9
> = Total 67. Average per line: 0.046.

(Farnham's figures were 0.062 and 0.046 respectively: pp. 353–5.) His conclusion, that the evidence concerning the author of the non-Fletcherian scenes in both plays is 'on the side of their being identical', is even stronger now with my revised figure for the Shakespeare scenes here (0.067), which is indistinguishable from that for *Henry VIII* (0.066). The average for the Fletcher scenes here is considerably higher than those in the history play, 0.046 as against 0.024, further evidence of the fluctuations in Fletcher's style caused by collaboration. Farnham reviewed other authorship claims for the non-Fletcherian scenes, his evidence clearly ruling out either Beaumont or Massinger (his average being only 0.01), and he concluded that the contractions in these scenes are 'later Shakespearean in number and character' (p. 356).

Massinger's co-authorship was also excluded by A. C. Bradley, who studied the degree to which the 330 scenes in Shakespeare concluding in blank verse (according to the Globe edition) ended with four possible types of line: a '*complete* line spoken by one person' (A), 'a *complete* line, spoken by more than one person' (B), 'a *part*-line closing a speech' (C), and 'a *part*-line consisting of a whole speech' (D). Bradley computed figures for the whole of Shakespeare as against selected plays by eight other contemporary dramatists, whose average *CD* endings, as a percentage of the whole, turned out to be less than 10, as against Shakespeare's average of 36.9.[77] Bradley then divided Shakespeare's output at the year 1600, showing that the 21 plays written before that date yielded only 21 *CD* endings, the 16 after it, 102. For the last six plays Shakespeare wrote (omitting *Timon* and *Pericles*), the percentage of scenes ending with part-lines was 59.6; for the five scenes ascribed to him in *Henry VIII* the percentage was 60.0; for the twelve Shakespearian scenes in *The Two Noble Kinsmen* it was 66.0, all strikingly similar rates. By

---

[77] A. C. Bradley, 'Scene-endings in Shakespeare and in *The Two Noble Kinsmen*', in Bradley, *A Miscellany* (London, 1929), pp. 218–24, at pp. 218–20.

contrast, only one (perhaps) of Fletcher's scenes ends with a part-line, giving a rate of 8.3 per cent: Massinger scored even lower (Bradley 1929, pp. 221–2). These findings, from a scholar not otherwise associated with authorship studies, showed that the clear difference between Shakespeare and Fletcher was constant in both of their joint-authored plays.

Karl Ege, applying to *The Two Noble Kinsmen* the same stylistic tests that he had used for *Henry VIII*, again showed that Shakespeare consistently used more imagery and more antithesis than Fletcher, but less alliteration and less rhetorical repetition.[78] However, once again Ege's method proved not wholly reliable, since he felt that the style of 2.2 (the prison scene where Palamon and Arcite indulge their self-pity, see Emilia, fall in love, and quarrel over her) was not even throughout, and so he ascribed the first part, up to Emilia's entrance, to Shakespeare, the second part to Fletcher (Ege 1923, pp. 70–1). To every other commentator this scene has seemed a unity, and Ege evidently attached too much weight to fluctuations in the incidence of stylistic elements without regarding the dramatic context. However, his results did support the ascription of 5.1.1–18 to Fletcher (p. 76).

The growing acceptance of Shakespeare's co-authorship derived from the recognition in it of his authentic modes of utterance, in syntax and in verse movement. E. H. C. Oliphant instanced 'numerous examples of his characteristic constructions' (citing 1.2.58–60, 71, 95–8, 100–1), and quoting the suppliant First Queen's appeal to Theseus:

> Remember that your fame
> Knolls in the ear o'th'world; what you do quickly
> Is not done rashly; your first thought is more
> Than others' laboured meditance; your premeditating
> More than their actions. But, O Jove, your actions,
> Soon as they move, as ospreys do the fish,
> Subdue before they touch.
>
> (1.1.133–8)

Also instancing Emilia's prayer to Diana, 'O sacred, shadowy, cold, and constant queen' (5.1.137–73), Oliphant commented: 'It is not only the run of the verse, the compressed and elliptical methods of utterance that stamp the work as his; but also the sovereign way in which words are bent to his purpose, the boldness of the imagery, the grandeur of the thought' (Oliphant 1927, pp. 340–1). Such appreciative remarks are not susceptible to quantification, but they valuably recognize authentic Shakespearian qualities in the play's verse.

---

[78] K. Ege, 'Der Anteil Shakespeare's an *The Two Noble Kinsmen*', *ShJb*, NS 1 (1923): 62–85, at p. 67. Ege's figures (Shakespeare first, Fletcher second), given in percentages, are: (1) Metaphors, 11/6.5; (2) Alliteration, 10/18; Antithesis, 10/2. For comments see Oliphant 1927, pp. 347–8.

TABLE 6.29. *Extra monosyllables and feminine endings in* The Two Noble Kinsmen

Author	Play	Totals	Percentage
Shakespeare	*Henry VIII*	54/380	14.2
—	*The Two Noble Kinsmen*	60/310	19.4
Fletcher	*Henry VIII*	254/878	29.0
—	*The Two Noble Kinsmen*	276/766	36.0

Source: Oras 1953, p. 200.

Quantification has never been lacking in discussions of *The Two Noble Kinsmen*. Ants Oras, comparing it with *Henry VIII*, studied both plays' verse in terms of 'the frequency of extra monosyllables as compared with the total number of feminine endings' (Oras 1953, p. 199), his results confirming the stylistic identity between them. Displayed in abbreviated form, his computations were as set out in Table 6.29 (the percentage figure indicating 'the proportion of extra monosyllables in the total of feminine endings'). The far greater number of both extra monosyllables and feminine endings in the Fletcher scenes, and the far higher proportion of the former, together differentiate the two writers 'about as [sharply] as can be expected of prosodical statistics' (p. 201). As we saw above, Oras then analysed the function of these extra monosyllables in the verse, in terms that—consciously or otherwise—closely echo the descriptions made by Lamb, Weber, and Hickson, contrasting Shakespeare's 'fluent ease', his 'light, varied, and smooth' endings with Fletcher's 'heavier', 'artificially weighted', over-emphatic ones, which considerably slow up his verse (pp. 203–13). In *The Two Noble Kinsmen*, Oras judged, Shakespeare's 'skilful handling of sentence stress precludes any metrical awkwardness' (p. 204), for example:

> Excess and overflow of power, an't mìght be
>
> (1.3.4)
> Your ire is more than mortal; so your hèlp be!
>
> (5.1.14)
> What canon ìs there
> That does command my rapier from my hip
>
> (1.2.55–6)

Fletcher's stresses are much heavier, sometimes running against the metre:

> And let them all alone. Is't not a wìse course?
>
> (4.1.127)

> This only, and no more: thou art mine àunt's son
>
> (3.6.94)

Fletcher's emphatic extra monosyllable sometimes has an extremely disruptive effect on the metre:

> Heigh-ho! *Pal.* For Emily, upon my lìfe. Fool,
> Away with this strain'd mirth!
>
> (3.3.42–3)
> Your teeth will bleed extremely. Shall we dànce, ho?
>
> (3.5.81)

A whole group of 'weighted' extra monosyllables that Shakespeare avoided, but Fletcher indulged in, consists of adverbs, which produce a 'dragging effect [by] appending them to a stressed word':

> And she must see the Duke and she must dànce too
>
> (2.3.45)
> I am very cold; and all the stars are òut too
>
> (3.4.1)
> Fit for the honour you have won; 'twere wròng else
>
> (2.5.61)
> To put my breast against! I shall sleep like a tòp else.
>
> (3.4.26)

One Fletcherian speciality that Oras illustrated from *Henry VIII* but not from this play, concerned the repetition of identical monosyllables, such as the repeated word 'her' ending the lines in Cranmer's speech over the babe Elizabeth (p. 211). I can cite a similar example here, in the soliloquy of the Jailer's Daughter, in love with Palamon, where the word 'him' is repeated 12 times in 31 lines (2.4.7–31), 8 times ending a clause, 6 of which are also line-endings:

> Then I loved him,
> Extremely loved him, infinitely loved him.

Cyrus Hoy has also noted this feature of Fletcher's style.[79]

In his later work on pause patterns Ants Oras documented from another perspective the clear difference between Shakespeare and Fletcher. His analysis of the distribution of emphases in *The Two Noble Kinsmen* (Hoy 1960, p. 68) gave the result shown in Table 6.30. Comparison with the results for *Henry VIII* will show that while the overall patterns continue to differ, the

---

[79] C. Hoy, 'The Language of Fletcherian Tragicomedy', in J. C. Gray (ed.), *Mirror up to Shakespeare* (Toronto and London, 1984), pp. 99–113.

TABLE 6.30. *Pause patterns in* The Two Noble Kinsmen

	1	2	3	4	5	6	7	8	9	First Half	Even
Shakespeare	1.2	4.1	1.6	15.2	14.6	27.7	19.5	11.6	4.5	25.8	58.6
Fletcher	2.1	3.7	4.3	17.1	15.3	21.8	21.4	11.3	3.0	32.0	53.9

Source: Oras 1960, p. 68.

TABLE 6.31. *Line endings in* Henry VIII *and* The Two Noble Kinsmen

Henry VIII	Blank Verse	Verb–Pronoun	Percentage	*Two Noble Kinsmen*	Verb–Pronoun	Percentage
Fletcher	1,512 lines	125	8.3	1,423	134	9.4
Shakespeare	1,154 lines	24	2.8	982	25	2.5

Source: Law 1959, pp. 474–7.

difference is less marked in some respects, such as the second foot, now stressed more often by Shakespeare, less often by Fletcher. Shakespeare still places his main pause most often after the sixth foot, the distribution of pauses thereafter declining by regular degrees. Fletcher once again stresses the sixth and seventh positions almost equally, and still has a steeper falling-off at the line-ending, albeit less marked than in *Henry VIII*, a year or so earlier. Fletcher may have adjusted his verse style more towards Shakespeare, but it still differs markedly from his co-author's.

Other studies of the play's verse styles confirmed the authorship division. R. A. Law analysed a 'habit or trick of style' common to Fletcher, 'the ending of a feminine line with a verb followed by an unstressed pronoun' (Law 1959, p. 472). As we saw above, his computations for *Henry VIII* revealed that Fletcher used this verbal pattern considerably more often than Shakespeare, a finding repeated for this play, as a summary tabulation shows (see Table 6.31). The remarkable closeness of *The Two Noble Kinsmen* to *Henry VIII*, shown by every type of metrical analysis, is strong confirmation that Shakespeare and Fletcher were involved in both plays. As Marco Mincoff wrote, the separate independent evidence for attributing each of these plays to them is great, while 'the combination of the evidence constitutes an almost impregnable position. For it is in the nature of evidence that the probability rises with each independent corroboration not arithmetically but geometrically'.[80] Describing Shakespeare (b. 1564) as representing the style of an older

---

[80] M. Mincoff, 'The Authorship of *The Two Noble Kinsmen*', ES 33 (1952): 97–115, at p. 99.

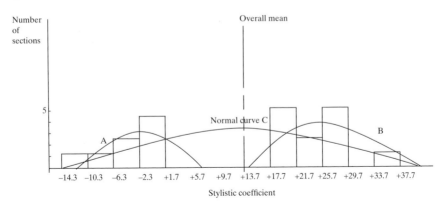

FIG. 6.2. Stylistic variation in *The Two Noble Kinsmen*
Source: Lake unpubl., p. 17.

generation, which produced 'a poetry of power flashes' with moments of 'obscurity and involvedness', Fletcher (b. 1579) that of a younger one, which followed 'a classical ideal of lucidity and correctness, a style that scarcely ever startles or reveals by flashes', Mincoff could

> think of no other play, except *Henry VIII*, in which the contrast between these two stylistic tendencies is so marked, more marked even than the metrical peculiarities which separate the two parts so clearly. One might say that not only are two distinct authors represented in this play, but two generations even. (Mincoff 1952, p. 104)

That perceptive suggestion was confirmed by Jonathan Hope in his sociolinguistic study of the Shakespeare authorship problem (1994).

A further, extremely vivid representation of the differences between the two authors' styles was devised by David J. Lake. As we saw with *Henry VIII*, Lake took three characteristic features of Shakespeare's style (the auxiliary *do*, verbs ending in *-th*, and run-on lines), and three of Fletcher's (the use of *ye*, *'em*, and feminine endings), computing their occurrence in 100-line blocks of text. For each text-section he subtracted the number of 'Shakespearisms' from the number of 'Fletcherisms', to yield a stylistic coefficient, the results being set out in tabular form. In three plays of single authorship by each dramatist Lake's results approximated to the standard curve, peaking around the mean, and dropping away symmetrically on either side (Lake unpublished, pp. 1–14). For *Henry VIII*, however, the results produced two quite distinct curves, separated by many points on the scale, a 'bimodal' result suggesting the presence of two distinct styles (pp. 15–16). *The Two Noble Kinsmen* yielded exactly the same bimodal curve, as illustrated in Fig. 6.2. As Lake commented, 'we see again two styles, one with Shakespearean characteristics, and a mean about −3, the other with Fletcherian features and a mean about +25. No section has a score between +1 and +18, which is precisely the region where we would expect to find scores, if a single author were under investigation' (p. 18). The two styles are identical with those of *Henry VIII*, and we can 'see once more that when [Fletcher] collaborates, his normal style is toned down or "veiled" to some extent'. Lake also showed that this method, bundling together several stylistic features, could be meaningfully used on smaller sections of text. Following up Cyrus Hoy's suggestion that 5.1.1–33 should be ascribed to Fletcher, Lake tested that section and found that it had a 'Fletcherian stylistic coefficient +33', while the scene's remaining 139 lines yielded a 'Shakespearean stylistic coefficient –7'. As he suggested, smaller sections of text can be investigated in this way, 'once the general distribution of stylistic scores suggests double authorship', but he urged that 'in all such cases, the postulated change of author should coincide with some natural articulation of the scene, such as an entrance or an exit' (p. 19). This is certainly the case here, given the stage direction 'Exeunt Palamon and his knights'.[81]

With *The Two Noble Kinsmen*, as with *Henry VIII*, the firm authorship division established on literary–critical and metrical grounds was strengthened still further by linguistic approaches. Alfred Hart, in a pioneering essay on the play's vocabulary,[82] recorded his impression, reading 'certain scenes' of the play, that 'I was listening to the voice and music of the master, to the language and verse of the man who wrote *Coriolanus, Antony and Cleopatra, The Winter's Tale*, and *The Tempest*'. In the hope of showing that 'Shakespeare had a hand in writing this play', he analysed the vocabulary, sorting his material into two groups, following the division suggested by some 'competent critics' (Hart 1934*b*, p. 242). Unfortunately, Hart did not know Littledale's edition, and the division he accepted was less than accurate, ascribing to Shakespeare (Part A) Act 1, Act 3 scene 1, and Act 5 except the second scene, a total of 1,091 lines, and giving the remainder (Part B) to Fletcher, totalling 1,681 lines. Littledale (and most other critics) ascribe 2.1, 3.2, and 4.3 to Shakespeare, giving 1.5 and some additional passages to Fletcher. This misallocation had some effects on Hart's discussion, none of them serious.

Hart, who had studied the vocabulary of 'nearly 80' Elizabethan plays, selected 'the "rarer" words' of the play and checked them against Alexander Schmidt's *Shakespeare Lexicon* (rev. edn., 1902). He found 188 words not in

---

[81] Fredson Bowers, however, disagreed with Hoy, suggesting that Fletcher's authorship extended only to l. 17, where Theseus leaves the stage (Bowers, 'Textual Introduction' to *The Two Noble Kinsmen*, in Bowers 1989*a*, pp. 157–8). Lake's detailed analysis seems more convincing.

[82] A. Hart, 'Shakespeare and the Vocabulary of *The Two Noble Kinsmen*', in Hart, *Shakespeare and the Homilies: And Other Pieces of Research into the Elizabethan Drama* (Melbourne and London 1934; repr. New York, 1970, 1977), pp. 242–56; from *RES* 10 (1934): 278–87.

TABLE 6.32. *Previously unused words in* The Two Noble Kinsmen

Play	Line total	Total first used words	Frequency: every x lines	Number of first used main words	Number of first used compound words	Percentage of compounds
Antony and Cleopatra	3,016	273	11	218	53	19.4
Coriolanus	3,279	267	12.3	228	39	14.6
Cymbeline	3,264	231	14	164	67	29.0
The Winter's Tale	2,925	225	13	161	64	28.4
The Tempest	2,015	192	10.5	118	74	38.5
The Two Noble Kinsmen	2,772	188	14.7	113	75	40.0
Part A	1,091	111	10	76	35	31.5
Part B	1,681	77	22	37	40	52.0

Source: Hart 1934*b*, p. 245.

the *Lexicon*, of which 111 occurred in Part A (1,091 lines), 77 in Part B. His comparison with five other Shakespeare plays near in time gave the result presented in Table 6.32. While the figures given for Part A (a new word being introduced every 10 lines), 'due allowance being made for its length, agree very closely with those for *The Tempest*' (one every 10.5 lines), 'the number of words in Part B is little more than a half of the number in Part A', one new word occurring only every 22 lines. Checking the number of these words which were repeated in one, two, and three other plays by Shakespeare, Hart found that the results for Part B (Fletcher) were consistently lower, and concluded that 'the want of agreement between Parts A and B is too well maintained throughout the table to be accidental' (p. 244). Hart's evidence from vocabulary confirmed those differences other critics had already noticed in 'characterization, moral tone, treatment of subject matter, style and metre', namely that two different authors worked on the play, 'one of whom has a less copious and more commonplace vocabulary than the other'. The table also 'illustrates the rate at which Shakespeare revivified his vocabulary even during the last years of his dramatic career by a continuous inpouring of previously unused words into each play', thus providing 'a measure of his imaginative and creative activity'.

Hart's next two columns give data for first-used main words, the more important category, and compound words (showing that 'compounds increase as main-words decrease'). Here the ratio for Part A (one new main word every 14.3 lines of text), compares well with that for *The Tempest* (one every 17 lines), while 'the ratio for Part B—one fresh main-word to each 45 lines of text—is . . . lower than for any play of Shakespeare, and indicates the poverty of the author's vocabulary' (p. 246). Fletcher may have come from a more privileged social background, but his linguistic inventiveness never

TABLE 6.33. *Words new to English literature in* The Two Noble Kinsmen

Play	Number of words peculiar to play	Number of new main words	Number of new compounds	Total new words	Number of new words repeated from earlier plays	Total new words	Frequency: new words every x lines
Antony and Cleopatra	231	51	47	98	21	119	25.4
Coriolanus	242	58	31	89	22	111	29.5
Cymbeline	219	40	48	88	40	128	25.5
The Winter's Tale	214	34	49	83	22	105	27.9
The Tempest	190	25	59	84	27	111	18
The Two Noble Kinsmen	188	34	47	81	25	106	26
Part A	111	27	27	54	12	66	16.5
Part B	77	7	20	27	13	40	42

Source: Hart 1934*b*, p. 247.

matched Shakespeare's. As for the percentage of compounds, the score for B 'is exceeded only in *Richard II*; perhaps it would be more accurate to say that the high percentage of compounds in Part B conceals the poverty in the matter of fresh main-words. Tested by the totals of first-used words Part A and Part B are by different authors' (ibid.). The difference between the two parts emerged again when Hart computed the 'new' words in the play, it being 'an important and unvarying characteristic of Shakespeare's vocabulary at any period of his career' that it contains 'a large number of words previously unused not merely by himself but by any other known author . . .'. Table 6.33 describes this phenomenon most clearly. As for new words, Part A is again comparable to *The Tempest* (one every 16.5 and one every 18 lines, respectively), while Part B, containing 'the insignificant number (7) of "new" main-words', one every 42 lines, scores well below Shakespeare's rate, although it is 'almost identical with the number (6) of "new" main-words in the non-Shakespearean portions of *Henry VIII* . . .' (p. 248).

In the second part of his essay Hart complemented his quantitative approach with a commentary on individual word-groups, beginning with 'parasynthetic formulations such as *black-haired, hard-hearted*'. Shakespeare made such coinages freely, some 350 altogether, averaging about ten a play. *The Two Noble Kinsmen* contains more of these compounds than other plays (10 in Part A, 13 in Part B), but Hart pointed to a great difference in quality. Part A contains such original creations as *high-speeded* (1.3.83), *scythe-tuskt* (1.1.79), *best-tempered* (1.3.10), and *leaden-footed* (1.2.84) (p. 248), while Part B has four ending in -*eyed* (*fair-eyed, great-, grey-, red-*),[83]

[83] Had Hart known Littledale's edition he might not have ascribed 'quick-eyed' (1.5.8) to Shakespeare: it clearly belongs to Fletcher.

three in -*haired* (*black-, white-, hard-*), three in -*hearted* (*honest-, soft-, stout-*), and two in -*faced*. As Hart observed,

Those in Part B connote simple attributes of person or of disposition, they are obvious epithets used in every-day speech, not unsuitable to drama but merely descriptive and without any poetic quality. How much more varied in form, compact and expressive are the similar compounds in Part A! Emilia, describing herself as 'bride-habited / But mayden-harted' [5.1.150], epitomizes in five words her part in the play. (p. 249)

The group of parasynthetic compounds in Part A recall such formations as 'soft-conscienced' and 'tiger-footed' in *Coriolanus*, 'loose-wived' and 'three-nooked' in *Antony*, 'full-acorned' in *Cymbeline*, 'wide-chopped' and 'short-grassed' in *The Tempest*, all bearing 'the hall-mark of the mature Shakespeare; every one of those in B could find a place in the most common-place prose' (p. 249).

Another notable feature of the diction in Part A, Hart showed, 'is the number of substantives which are used as verbs; they add vigour, vividness and imagination to the verse'. Several critics had commented on such striking usages as the three Queens' appeal to be allowed to burn their husbands' 'bones, | To *urn* their ashes' (1.1.43–4), or to receive their bones 'that we may *chapel* them' (50). Other nouns used as verbs, equally remarkable, include

> Fortune at you
> *Dimpled* her cheek with smiles
>
> (1.2.69–70)

a word that Hart found 'used participially only in Shakespeare'; 'they have *skiffed* | Torrents' (1.3.37–8); and 'the wolves would *jaw* me' (3.2.7)—accepting this as a Shakespearian scene. Hart found twelve such substantives used as verbs in Part A, none in Part B. Wanting to use some other recalcitrant nouns as verbs, Shakespeare 'transmuted them into participles used adjectively by adding -*ed* to them', the word so formed being sometimes an adjective, sometimes the past participle of a verb used in the passive voice. From this play Hart found six examples, all in Part A, including 'the *helmeted* Bellona' (1.1.75); 'his action's *dregged*' (1.2.97)—that is, as E. M. Waith glosses it, 'rendered turbid as with dregs'; '*scissored*' hair (1.2.54); and 'the *masoned* turrets' (5.1.55).

One particularly important group of words here is that 'beginning with the prefix *un-*', which, Hart estimated, 'amounts to nearly 4 per cent of Shakespeare's vocabulary; about a quarter are "new" to literature' (p. 253).[84] Hart tabulated this usage, too (see Table 6.34). The totals for Part A, nineteen in fewer than 1,000 lines, correspond well to those for *Hamlet*, *King Lear*,

---

[84] Not having performed comparative analyses, Hart did not realize that words beginning with *un-* were widely coined in Elizabethan and Jacobean English: see B. Vickers, *Counterfeiting Shakespeare* (Cambridge, 2002), pp. 111–13, 303–5.

TABLE 6.34. *Words in Shakespeare beginning with* un-

Play	Total number of words	Number used for first time	'New' words
2 *Henry VI*	34	28	7
Romeo and Juliet	44	16	4
Richard II	52	22	8
1 *Henry IV*	39	9	4
Twelfth Night	33	17	7
Hamlet	71	35	17
Lear	55	21	12
Coriolanus	48	23	8
The Tempest	20	6	3
The Two Noble Kinsmen			
Part A	19	10	7
Part B	8	0	0

Source: Hart 1934*b*, p. 253.

and *Coriolanus*, while 'the seven "new" words, three being repeated from earlier plays, exhibit the author's power of invention. Part B seems to have been written by a man whose vocabulary is almost entirely derivative' (p. 253). Hart also noted the 'remarkable' fact that in *Pericles*, *Timon*, *Henry VIII*, and *The Two Noble Kinsmen*, 'all the "new" words beginning with *un-* are in the portions usually assigned to Shakespeare' (p. 254).

Whichever category Hart investigated, he found the vocabulary in Shakespeare's scenes to be larger and more creative than in Fletcher's. Shakespeare regularly made 'a very free use of compound words consisting of a noun or its equivalent followed by a participle', such as 'brow-bound', 'grief-shot' (*Cor.*), 'lust-wearied', 'war-exercised' (*Ant.*), and 'cloud-capped', 'sight-outrunning' (*Temp.*). Part A has five such formations ('blood-sized', 'heart-pierced', 'wind-fanned', 'all-feared', 'bride-habited'), Part B only one ('beast-eating'). Part A contains three words in another of Shakespeare's special forms, ending in -like ('dove-like', 'Phoenix-like', 'pig-like', the two latter being 'new' words), Part B has none of this type. Two other 'new' words in Part A, 'smel-lesse' and 'tasteful', show Shakespeare's fondness for adjectives ending in these suffixes; Part B has no 'new' adjectives of this type. Echoing observations made by Steevens and Littledale, Hart drew attention to the fact that 'in the last scene of the play two strikingly expressive "new" words, viz., *disroot* and *disseat* occur in the space of four lines. Shakespeare coins 32 such words in all: in his last group of plays he gives us *disproperty*, *disbench* (*Coriolanus*), *discandy*, *dislimn* and *dispunge* (*Antony and Cleopatra*) . . .' (p. 256)—and we can add Macbeth's awareness

TABLE 6.35. *Contraction preferences in* The Two Noble Kinsmen

	Total lines	*'em*	*them*	Proportion
Shakespeare scenes	1,034	5	15	1 : 3
Fletcher scenes	1,579	45	5	9 : 1

Source: Thorndike 1901, p. 49.

that the impending battle 'Will cheer me ever, or *disseat* me now' (5.3.21), validating Charles Jennens's emendation of the Folio's *dis-eate*.

Hart concluded this impressive analysis with an important methodological observation, pointing out that, unlike previous vocabulary tests in authorship studies, his

method of investigation rests not on sameness but on differences in vocabulary, and requires rather the absence than the presence of identical phrases and parallel passages. My arguments are based upon words not common to Part A and Shakespeare's latest plays, on 'new' words of Part A not in the concordance, on words that Shakespeare had not used before. The diction of Part A I take to be his because nearly every line bears the stamp of the essential qualities of his vocabulary, simplicity, directness, originality and copiousness, the whole shot through with imagination and alive with metaphor. (p. 256)

It would be a peculiarly stubborn reader to resist the conclusion that Hart's study of the vocabulary 'strongly supports the claim made by many critics that *The Two Noble Kinsmen* should be included in the Shakespeare canon', with Fletcher as the co-author.

The evidence drawn from parts of words—colloquial contractions—also supports this claim, if not quite so neatly, due to the intermittent intervention of scribes and compositors. Ashley Thorndike's pioneering work computing the occurrence of *them* and *'em* (1901, pp. 44–55) was one of the few studies to draw on Littledale's penetrating evaluation of the play's authorship. In addition to the accepted ascription, Littledale and Thorndike treated several passages as Fletcherian interpolations into otherwise Shakespearian scenes (1.1.1–37; 1.4.28–37; 5.1.1–17; 5.3.104–46). Adding these to Fletcher's part, Thorndike produced the result given in Table 6.35 (prose scenes omitted). Thorndike reminded readers that the comparable figures for *Henry VIII* were: for Shakespeare, 17 *thems* and 5 *'ems*, for Fletcher, 4 *thems* and 57 *'ems*. 'The *'em–them* test thus confirms the assignment of the play to Shakespere and Fletcher and the approximate accuracy of its division between the two.' However, the division by scenes is not as exact as in *Henry VIII*, suggesting that in this collaboration Fletcher was more active

TABLE 6.36. *Colloquial contractions in* The Two Noble Kinsmen

	ye	y'	you	hath	doth	'em	them	i'th'	o'th'	's	t'
Shakespeare scenes	o	2	118	13	1	16	23	10	21	1	1
Fletcher scenes	37	8	262	3	o	39	8	12	8	4	1

Source: Hoy 1962, p. 89.

in retouching Shakespeare's lines and adding to them. The test certainly disproved 'the theory that Massinger wrote the non-Fletcherian part, and there is no evidence for any other author except Shakespeare' (p. 50).

When Cyrus Hoy applied his contraction test to the play, some sixty years later (Hoy 1962, pp. 71–6, 89), he recognized (as Thorndike had not) the possible influence of the compositors who set the 1634 Quarto edition. Hoy ascribed to Shakespeare the whole of Acts 1, 2.1, 3.1, 3.2, 5.1.34–173, 5.3, and 5.4, unfortunately not recognizing the strong case that Littledale had made for regarding 1.5 as Fletcher's, 4.3 as Shakespeare's. (This slightly affects his totals for *you*.) Otherwise, Hoy's basic computations, by whole scenes, now including those in prose, produced the following results (I have recomputed them in Table 6.36 for the play's two parts). Hoy also provided linguistic tables showing these contractions in eight unaided plays by Shakespeare (p. 88), which established that the significant stylistic markers are 'Shakespeare's use of the third person singular verb forms *hath* and *doth*, and his general avoidance of pronominal *ye*' (p. 74). *Doth* appears in all the Shakespeare plays Hoy had examined, ranging from 5 occurrences in *Antony and Cleopatra* to 36 in *Troilus and Cressida* (Q text), the figures for *hath* ranging from 26 occurrences in *The Tempest* to 80 in *Cymbeline*; neither form occurs frequently in Fletcher. On the other side, in *The Two Noble Kinsmen* 'all of the quarto's 37 *ye*'s are Fletcher's; none occur in scenes that do not otherwise bear the signs of his stylistic manner' (p. 88). The two authors are also clearly distinguished in Fletcher's marked preference for *'em*, Shakespeare's for *them*, and *o'th'*. Hoy found it worth noting 'that the use of *'em*, *i'th'*, and *o'th'* in the two shares of *The Two Noble Kinsmen . . .* is exactly comparable to the use of these forms demonstrated above in, respectively, the unaided work of Shakespeare and Fletcher'. The comparative data that Hoy had compiled enabled him to conclude with some authority that the two dramatists' 'contrasting practices . . . in the use of *hath* and *ye* complete the linguistic evidence for differentiating their shares in a play of their joint authorship' (p. 75).

The only anomaly in this division was the number of *ye*'s, far below that for other Fletcher plays. Responding to an account of the play's printing by F. O. Waller,[85] Hoy dismissed his suggestion that the play was printed from a

[85] 'Printer's Copy for *The Two Noble Kinsmen*', SB 11 (1958): 61–84.

prompt copy but accepted the alternative hypothesis, that it was set from 'an annotated intermediate scribal transcript', perhaps by Edward Knight, book-keeper for the King's Men from *c*.1628 (p. 75). As Hoy had shown earlier, two scribal transcripts of Fletcher plays are extant, Knight's version of *Bonduca*, and an unidentified scribe's copy of *The Woman's Prize*, both of which sub-stantially alter the number of *ye* forms, as can be seen by reference to the 1647 Folio. In the former, they are reduced from 352 to 147 occurrences, in the latter they are increased from 84 to 133 occurrences (Hoy 1956, pp. 139–40). Fredson Bowers reviewed the evidence, concluding that a scribe might well have altered *ye* to *you* indiscriminately, but not the play's compositors (1989*b*, pp. 151–6).

In a careful bibliographical study Paul Werstine[86] strengthened the case for positing an intermediate scribal transcript on three grounds, stage directions, mislineation, and spelling. The 1638 Quarto contains some stage directions in the margins, suggesting the possibility that Knight may have inscribed these directions 'in the margins of the manuscript printer's copy' (Werstine 1989, p. 21). Furthermore, some of these directions contain 'syntactically dis-junct elements punctuated by colons', indicating theatrical additions, such as correcting the extant text's failure to provide attendants for the royal Theseus. Hence Werstine suggested that the printer's copy was a theatrical transcript (pp. 20–3). Secondly, although verse is mislineated as prose, the Quarto text preserves within the prose the capital letters normally reserved for making verse lines. This peculiarity is common to both compositors, and they jointly set 4.3, 'a verse scene set almost entirely in prose'. Thus, both errors can only derive 'from scribal copy itself'. Thirdly, Werstine drew on Richard Proudfoot's observation that the co-authors used two different forms of the name Pirithous. 'In Act 1 the name is trisyllabic, and is scanned "Pirithoús"; in Acts 2 and 4 it has four syllables and the correct classical accentuation "Piríthoús"'. Shakespeare may have learned the name from North's Plutarch, where the character is called Pirithous, Fletcher from Chaucer's *Knight's Tale*, where he appears as Perithous.[87] Proudfoot recorded some variations in the spellings, for which he subsequently held the com-positors responsible, but Werstine argued that 'the three anomalous [medial] –e- spellings in Shakespeare's portion and the four anomalous –i- spellings in Fletcher's', common to both compositors, prove the existence of 'a scribal transcript that intervened between authorial manuscript and printed text, and in which the pattern of authorial preferences was overlaid with a scribe's halfhearted attempts to regularize his copy' (p. 25). At all events, once again we see that Shakespeare's ideas about the scansion of proper names could

---

[86] 'On the Compositors of The *Two Noble Kinsmen*', in C. H. Frey (ed.), *Shakespeare, Fletcher and 'The Two Noble Kinsmen'* (Columbia, Mo., 1989), pp. 6–30.

[87] G. R. Proudfoot (ed.), Fletcher and Shakespeare, *The Two Noble Kinsmen* (London, 1970), p. xix.

differ from his co-author's, as Steevens and Fleay had pointed out in previous centuries.

A heartening feature of Shakespeare scholarship, old and new, is the readiness of some scholars to devote enormous care and energy to the most meticulous study of texts, whether Hart's scrutiny of Shakespeare's word-formation or Werstine's examination of the compositors' differing habits of inserting, or omitting, spaces after commas. Jonathan Hope's work on grammatical preferences is equally meticulous, and once again distinguished the co-authors beyond dispute (Hope 1994, pp. 83–9, 164). Unfortunately (like Hoy), Hope ascribed 1.5 (the three Queens' funeral song) to Shakespeare, and 4.3 (the prose scene where the Doctor monitors the insanity of the Jailer's Daughter) to Fletcher, instead of the other way round (p. 87), a decision that slightly affected his computations. Comparing the two dramatists' use of the auxiliary *do* in positive declarative sentences, Hope found that Shakespeare was appreciably below Fletcher in the degree to which he approached a 'regulated' usage (that is, one observing modern grammatical conventions). His figures were 86 per cent for the Shakespearian scenes, 95 per cent for the Fletcherian ones, both close to the results obtained for sole-authored plays by each dramatist, and confirming that two 'quite different' writers were involved (pp. 85–6). If we reassign the two scenes mentioned above, the newly computed figures would be 86.4 and 96.9 per cent, respectively, a higher figure than one might expect for either author, perhaps because several scenes gave values 'consistently near or below the minimum significant sample size'. Hope then studied the use of relative markers (*who, which, that,* and zero forms), his results showing that section A conforms closely to Shakespeare's usage elsewhere, as does section B to Fletcher's (pp. 87–9). Since it is 'much easier for one collaborator, producing a final fair copy of the whole play, to impose his own relative marker choices on the text, than it is for him to alter other linguistic features (such as auxiliary *do*)', the fact that 'the relativisation strategies' are so distinct in both *The Two Noble Kinsmen* and *Henry VIII*, Hope suggested, 'is evidence against any kind of final reworking of the plays by either of the collaborators' (p. 89). But of course, even within a straightforward joint authorship, one contributor may insert short segments of verse into the other's scenes, or even touch up passages, as several scholars have suggested for this play. It would be interesting to check all of Hope's evidence against the passages that Hickson, Littledale, Thorndike, and Hoy proposed as showing signs of Fletcher's intervention. Otherwise, Hope's careful study confirmed the findings of a dozen or more scholars who made independent analyses over a period of two centuries, that *The Two Noble Kinsmen* was the joint work of Shakespeare and Fletcher.

With other co-authored plays, as we have seen, modern editors in the three main series of individual play editions (the Oxford, Cambridge, and New

Arden) have rejected any possibility of Shakespeare having had a collaborator. For *The Two Noble Kinsmen*, I am glad to say, the two editions recently
published, by E. M. Waith in the Oxford series, and by Lois Potter for the
New Arden,[88] accept his co-authorship. Waith gave an unusually accurate
account of the authorship discussion from Weber to Hoy (1989, pp. 4–23),
and validated the use of verse tests—sometimes disputed, usually by proponents of Shakespeare's sole authorship. Waith confirmed the accuracy of
Littledale's figures for double endings (which were based on an edited text,
the Leopold Shakespeare), having checked them against the 1634 Quarto and
finding only slight differences. Taking two scenes which present Palamon and
Arcite in conversation, Shakespeare's 1.2 and Fletcher's 2.2, Waith found '32
instead of Littledale's 35 double endings in the 116 lines of 1.2, and 163
instead of 159 double endings in the 281 lines of 2.2—differences easily
accounted for by the inevitable slight variations between two readings of certain lines'. This single comparison shows 'the strikingly larger proportion of
double endings' in Fletcher's scene (p. 13), one of many stylistic markers differentiating the two authors. Lois Potter also endorsed the accepted division
(1997, pp. 16–34), although evidently unsure on several issues, and tending
to summarize every contribution without taking a position of her own.[89]
Neither editor took seriously the attempt of Paul Bertram to show that the
play is wholly Shakespeare's.[90]

The cumulative evidence of nearly two centuries of scholarly investigation,
from Charles Lamb (1808) and Henry Weber (1812) to Jonathan Hope
(1984) and Paul Werstine (1989), making possible a clear differentiation of
the respective shares in *The Two Noble Kinsmen* contributed by these two
'memorable Worthies of their time', may stand as one more validation of the
vitality and continuity within authorship studies. No one who cares for
Shakespeare can afford to ignore these findings.

---

[88] L. Potter (ed.), *The Two Noble Kinsmen*, New Arden Shakespeare (London, 1997).
[89] See my comments in *RES*, NS 50 (1999), pp. 82–4.
[90] Paul Bertram, *Shakespeare and the 'Two Noble Kinsmen'* (New Brunswick, NJ, 1965). See
the devastating review by Cyrus Hoy, *MP* 67 (1969): 83–8.

7

Plot and Character in Co-Authored Plays: Problems of Co-ordination

In considering Shakespeare's co-authorship of these five plays I have concentrated on their language, the many ways in which his style can be differentiated from that of his collaborators. Similar differences can be found on a larger scale, concerning the plays' plotting and characterization. As we saw in Chapter 1, writing a collaborative play necessitated some preliminary discussion by the dramatists involved as to the overall movement of the plot from first to last, and the main features of characterization. Some such detailed outline must have existed before an acting company would commit itself financially, and discussions between the author(s) and the company's sharers may have been prolonged. In 1614 Nathan Field, leader of the Lady Elizabeth's Men, 'a company which Henslowe continually oppressed by hard dealings in money matters and by a fixed policy of keeping it ever in debt to him',[1] wrote on behalf of the four sharers who had formed a committee to deal with the impresario, concerning a plot that had been offered them by Robert Daborne. Field, who was both a practical actor and an experienced dramatist, urged Henslowe to advance the necessary money (£10) to secure the play for the company, assuring him that 'Mr. Daborne and I, have spent a great deale of time in conference about this plott, which will make as beneficiall a play as hath come these seaven yeares'.[2]

If dramatists working on their own could provoke so much discussion of their projects, two or more working together would surely need to spend even more 'time in conference' to ensure a properly organized play. George Steevens, who added to his wide bibliographical knowledge an awareness of contemporary theatrical practice, recorded in 1780 the basic truth that

without frequent interviews between confederate writers, a consistent tragedy can hardly be produced. Yet such precautions will be sometimes inefficient in

---

[1] J. Q. Adams, 'The Author-Plot of an Early Seventeenth-Century Play', *Library*, 4th ser., 25 (1945): 17–27, at p. 19.
[2] W. W. Greg, *The Shakespeare First Folio: Its Bibliographic and Textual History* (Oxford, 1955), p. 164.

producing conformity of plan even when confederate authors are within reach of each other.

Steevens cited *Oedipus* (1678) by John Dryden and Nathaniel Lee, 'in the third act of [which] Dryden has made Tiresias say to the Theban monarch,

> . . . if e'er we meet again, 'twill be
> In mutual darkness; we shall feel before us
> To reach each other's hand.

'But, alas!', Steevens added, 'for want of adverting to this speech, Lee has counteracted it in the fourth act, where Tiresias has another interview with Oedipus before the extinction of his eyes, a circumstance that does not take place till the fifth act'.[3]

Steevens's term 'consistent' meant, at that time, 'holding together as a coherent material body' (*OED*), describing the notion of unity, the literary–critical concept according to which a literary work should have a beginning, a middle, and an end, coherently related. Renaissance literary theory lagged behind practice, of course, and readers who study contemporary treatises are more likely to find precepts urging the importance of variety.[4] But evidently dramatists were familiar with the notion of unity, and if they did not know Aristotle's *Poetics* they certainly knew Horace's *Ars Poetica*, that influential digest of a fully rhetoricized poetics, in which the opening lines describe the comical effects of a poem lacking unity:

Imagine a painter who wanted to combine a horse's neck with a human head, and then clothe a miscellaneous collection of limbs with various kinds of feathers, so that what started out at the top as a beautiful woman ended in a hideously ugly fish. If you were invited, as friends, to the private view, could you help laughing?

Such a painting would be ridiculous—but just so, 'a book whose different features are made up at random like a sick man's dreams, with no unified form to have a head or tail, is exactly like that picture' (1–8).[5] Horace warns poets not to unite extreme opposites, such as pairing 'snakes . . . with birds or lambs with tigers' (9–12), and although purple patches are allowed, they have to occur in the right place (13–16). The poet must always consider the unity of his design: 'let it be what you will, but let it be simple and unified' (20–1). The artfully oblique structure of Horace's *Art of Poetry* disguises its nature as a preceptive treatise, but it consistently reiterates certain key principles, above all careful choice, control, decorum. The main virtue of 'arrangement

---

[3] Cit. H. Weber, 'Observations on the Participation of Shakespeare in *The Two Noble Kinsmen*', in Weber (ed.), *The Works of Beaumont and Fletcher*, 14 vols. (Edinburgh, 1812), xiii. 164.

[4] See e.g. Bernard Weinberg, *A History of Literary Criticism in the Italian Renaissance*, 2 vols. (Chicago, 1961, 1974), ii, index, pp. 1182–3, s.v. 'Unity', 'Variety'.

[5] Trans. D. A. Russell, in D. A. Russell and M. Winterbottom (eds.), *Ancient Literary Criticism* (Oxford, 1972), p. 279.

[*ordo*] . . . consists in saying at this moment what needs to be said at this moment', postponing or omitting irrelevancies (42–4). 'Everything must keep the appropriate place to which it was allotted' (91–2), style being adjusted to subject-matter: 'sad words suit a mournful countenance, threatening words an angry one' (107–8). Concerning plots, Horace tells poets to 'invent a consistent story' (119), maintaining a character 'to the end as it began' (126–8). A character must be consistent, true to its own premises, having the appropriate 'manners of each time of life' (156–78). Horace illustrates this point with thumbnail sketches of the four ages of man, reiterating the injunction that 'your character should always remain faithful to what is associated with his age and suits it' (158–78). Horace's ideal author is 'that poet whose every endeavour is to the point! . . . He tells his fables and mixes truth with falsehood in such a way that the middle squares with the beginning and the end with the middle' (140–1, 148–51), achieving unity. It follows that dramatists should avoid choric songs which have 'no relevance to or cohesion with the plot' (196–7).

Any product of an English grammar school is likely to have known Horace's *Art of Poetry*. Horace's works were published many times in England, and the *Ars* was translated by Thomas Drant in 1567, and twice by Ben Jonson, in 1604 and again in 1610.[6] And although no English writer produced a comparable work in the preceptive tradition until much later in the seventeenth century, several critics emulated Horace's method of inculcating an important principle of composition by showing the bad effects of not observing it. In place of Horace's ludicrous woman–fish compound, in his Preface to *Promos and Cassandra* (1578) George Whetstone mocked the 'indiscreet'—that is, not observing decorum—English dramatist, who 'first grounds his work on impossibilities; then in three hours runs he through the world, marries, gets children, makes children men, men to conquer kingdoms, murder monsters'.[7] Writing his *Defence of Poetry* a few years later (*c*.1580–1; published 1595)—a work that Shakespeare may have known—Sir Philip Sidney poked fun at plays in which the action ranged from Asia to Africa, including a shipwreck, 'a hideous monster with fire and smoke', 'two armies . . . represented with four swords and bucklers' (Vickers 1999, p. 381). Although he did not refer to the Neo-Aristotelian categories by name, Sidney was concerned with the unities of action and place, and he deplored

---

[6] See *Horace his arte of poetrie, pistles, and satyrs Englished . . . by T. Drant* (London, 1567); *Q. Horatius Flaccus: his art of poetry. Englished by Ben: Jonson* (London, 1640). Jonson produced a first version of the *Ars* in about 1604, and a later one, following the rearrangement proposed in Heinsius' Latin text of 1610: see Jonson, *Works*, ed. C. H. Herford, P. and E. Simpson, xi (Oxford, 1952), pp. 110–14. On the *Ars Poetica* in English grammar schools, and for Shakespeare's specific knowledge of it, see T. W. Baldwin, *William Shakspere's 'Small Latine and Lesse Greeke'*, 2 vols. (Urbana, Ill., 1944), i. 328, 400, 669–72; ii. 402–6, 497–8, 500–1, 516, 518, 521–4, 547.
[7] B. Vickers (ed.), *English Renaissance Literary Criticism* (Oxford, 1999), p. 173.

the popular drama's freedom with time: 'for ordinary it is that two young princes fall in love; after many traverses, she is got with child, delivered of a fair boy; he is lost, groweth a man, falls in love, and is ready to get another child; and all this in two hours' space' (p. 382). Such drama is 'absurd . . . in sense', Sidney complained (that is, 'to the senses'), and he was echoed by Cervantes in *Don Quixote* (part 4, ch. 21), where the village Canon attacks modern (Spanish) comedies: 'what greater absurdity can be in such a subject than to see a child come out in the first scene of the first act in his swaddling clouts, and issue in the second already grown a man, yea, a bearded man?' (Vickers 1999, p. 526n.). As Gabriele Jackson pointed out,[8] in 1611–12 Thomas Shelton's translation of *Don Quixote* was being set in type by William Stansby, who at the same time was also printing Jonson's Folio, a coincidence which may account for Jonson's seemingly echoing it in the pro- logue to the revised version of *Every Man In His Humour*, published in the 1616 *Works*. There Jonson mocked 'th'ill customs' of the contemporary stage, such as

> To make a child, now swaddled, to proceed
> Man, and then shoot up, in one beard, and weed
> Past threesome years
>
> (Vickers 1999, pp. 526–7)

Jonson also mocked the Chorus who 'wafts you over the seas', as in Heywood's *The Four Prentises of London* (*c.*1594), or Shakespeare's *Henry V* (1599).

Such criticisms show at least that English poets and dramatists were well aware of the theorists' claim that dramas should have a unified action, even though they might choose to ignore one of the unities when it suited them. Shakespeare makes Time, his Chorus in *The Winter's Tale*, excuse the liberty he has taken with the normal course of events:

> Impute it not a crime
> To me, or my swift passage, that I slide
> O'er sixteen years, and leave the growth untried
> Of that wide gap, since it is in my power
> To o'erthrow law. . . .
>
> (4.1.4–8)

We willingly excuse him, since it is only by allowing Perdita—or Marina, in *Pericles*—time to reach a marriageable age that Shakespeare could achieve that distance between the generations which he needed in the late plays, in order to achieve those powerful actions of loss and reunion, harm and for- giveness. Both *Pericles* and *The Winter's Tale* seem to obey a more important

---

[8] G. B. Jackson, edition of *Every Man In His Humour* (New Haven and London, 1969).

law, the unity of action embracing a character or a family's whole life, that of Pericles, Thaisa, and Marina; Leontes, Hermione, and Perdita. Indeed, as Madeleine Doran pointed out in her sensitive discussion of the nature of unity in Elizabethan drama,[9] one way that dramatists achieved 'an organic structural form' was through 'the domination of a single striking figure', such as Tamburlaine, or Richard III. 'The danger here, of course, was that the unity would be only of the hero, and not of the action, that many of the events of the plot would stand together in the accidental relationship of biographical chronology rather than in the necessary relationship of cause and effect' (Doran 1954, p. 288). We may doubt whether Marlowe evaded that danger with Tamburlaine, but Shakespeare certainly did so with Richard III, joining a 'rise-and-fall pattern' (ibid.) to another common plot-form, involving the conflict between good and evil (pp. 303–6).

Other Elizabethan plays attempted to unify the plot by having several parallel actions run side by side, actions which, as Doran put it, were unfortunately 'more commonly allowed to run parallel courses than made to work together', as in *A Woman Killed with Kindness*, 'where the rivalry of Acton and Mountford, without essential connection to the Frankford story, follows even quite a different time scheme from the main plot' (pp. 289–90). At other times Elizabethan dramatists 'achieved a kind of unity which is one of feeling or tone rather than of structure', in Doran's terms 'a qualitative unity. They got it by throwing the different actions into some relation of reinforcing, complementary, or contrasting tones: for example, in repeating the same theme in different keys, as in the three love stories in *The Insatiate Countess*; in making the comic action parody the serious one', as in Lyly's *Endymion* (p. 290). Dramatists also unified their work by emphasizing its country or urban setting, to such a degree that 'setting becomes a means both of organizing action and of unifying emotional tone' (p. 293). Doran acknowledged the 'not infrequent failure [by Elizabethan dramatists] to bring their different actions together in a unified piece of plotting' (p. 290), and judged that, for them, 'unity . . . was hard to come by. For few were willing to sacrifice any variety to get it. In consequence, when it was achieved, it was a kind of multiple unity of many parts. It was bustling, lively, and generous' (p. 294).

We can happily endorse Doran's own generous attitude to the plotting in English Renaissance drama, and it would obviously be inappropriate to approach these plays with neoclassical expectations. None the less, given the widely shared concept of the need for plots to be unified, the question arises, to what extent the collaborative plays managed to meet it. With *Keep the Widow Waking*, for instance, when Dekker contributed the first act, 'and a speech in the last scene of the last Act of the boy who had killed his mother', how did the other writers—Webster, Rowley, and Ford—bridge the gap

---

[9] M. Doran, *Endeavors of Art: A Study of Form in Elizabethan Drama* (Madison, 1954).

between? Even if they kept to a detailed plot-outline, each writer must have enjoyed a great amount of freedom, and unless someone charged with continuity took that role seriously enough either to request rewriting, or to do so himself, divergences of motive, characterization, and plotting seem inevitable. John Jowett, trying to reconstruct the genesis of *Sir Thomas More*, suggested that Anthony Munday 'was in charge of the play, especially at the stages of its inception and its completion'. Since the evidence suggests that Henry Chettle was responsible for at least six of the original play's seventeen scenes, with Munday providing most of the remainder, Jowett imagined

Munday drawing together sources, plotting the play, and allocating work on it; after the text was assembled, he would scrutinise it with a view to consistency and coherence, then, perhaps still making minor alterations, transcribe the foul papers to create the extant text.[10]

That, no doubt, is how things ought to have been managed, in an ideal theatre; but the surviving text of *Sir Thomas More* shows that Shakespeare's addition, for one, was not properly integrated. As Scott McMillin observed, Shakespeare's contribution served no immediate theatrical purpose, and in several respects seems to stand apart from the other contributions. It is, to begin with, 'the largest scene in the play, involving thirteen speaking roles', and although the playhouse scribe (Hand C) made several alterations to it, carefully allotting the speeches to individual characters (Shakespeare merely specified 'other' or 'others'), he made no alterations to the casting.[11] This may suggest that the revisers wanted this scene to have its maximum impact, but it may also show that they had not yet registered the discrepancy.

Of course, with its chequered history of a twofold genesis, several writers being co-opted to rescue an unlucky project, *Sir Thomas More* is doubtless a special case, untypical of the several hundred normal collaborations that graced Elizabethan, Jacobean, and Caroline stages. It is tempting to assume that it differed in kind from other collaborations, but perhaps the differences are only of degree. At all events, Shakespeare's contribution was in some ways external to the others, for nobody seems to have informed him that the apprentices had been removed from the uprising scene, making his reference to them being 'undone' by the foreigners' success in business superfluous. Giorgio Melchiori, author of several acute studies of this text, pointed out that the presentation of the rioting citizens by Munday and Shakespeare is discordant: 'while Munday in the rest of the play presented the leaders of the rebellion as fairly substantial citizens, for D they seem to be thoughtless

---

[10] J. Jowett, 'Henry Chettle and the Original Text of *Sir Thomas More*', in T. H. Howard-Hill (ed.), *Shakespeare and 'Sir Thomas More': Essays on the Play and its Shakespearian Interest* (Cambridge, 1989), p. 132.

[11] S. McMillin, *The Elizabethen Theatre and 'The Book of Sir Thomas More'* (Ithaca, NY, 1987), p. 44.

apprentices one and all, an indiscriminate mass led by a trouble-maker'.[12] Shakespeare's addition to scene 6 'contradicts the way in which the citizens (whom he calls "prentices") had been presented up to that moment, and are to appear again in scene 7'. What Melchiori described as Shakespeare's 'careless treatment of Lincoln and company as a bunch of fools, in contrast with their painstaking individual characterization in the original draft' (p. 112), suggests that he had seen little of the original version, or of the other revisions perhaps being made at this time. Another sign of inadequate co-ordination is the fact that 'there was no Clown in Munday's original text: the role was introduced in the additions by Hand B', Thomas Heywood (p. 109). Shakespeare 'was unaware that in the meantime the reviser Hand B had created such a part and was to introduce it by adding speeches for him to scenes 4, the last part of 6, and 7 of the play'. Accordingly, Shakespeare wrote no speeches for the Clown, but the playhouse scribe (Hand C) reassigned to the Clown two speeches that Shakespeare 'had destined to an anonymous "other"' (p. 113). This discrepancy has led some critics to assume that Shakespeare's scene was part of the original composition (McMillin 1987, pp. 136–45), totally discordant though it is with Tilney's orders. But stylistic and other evidence puts his contribution much later, and perhaps we ought rather to conceive that Elizabethan theatrical companies accepted a certain amount of incoherence as inevitable, unlikely to be noticed in the excitement of performance. Perhaps the management of Elizabethan theatres made only sporadic attempts to achieve 'consistency and coherence'. Whatever they did, differences in style are only to be expected in co-authored plays, indeed precisely these differences allow us to identify the writers involved, even when no external evidence survives. Other, larger differences, involving coherence at the level of plot and character, may have been visible to those able to read the printed text, but it is a moot point whether or not structural incoherences affected the success of individual plays in performance.

Regrettably, scholars of Renaissance drama have not addressed these issues in any detail. Cyrus Hoy has made the most thoughtful contribution, discussing the critical and aesthetic problems involved,[13] and deploring that, although scholars had made great advances in establishing the canon of Middleton, Dekker, Beaumont, Fletcher, and Massinger, 'the criticism of collaborative drama has yet to catch up with—to make any real use of—the scholarly gains that have been made over the past quarter of a century' (Hoy 1976, p. 4). Another twenty-five years later, little has changed, and it seems as if an even wider gulf has opened up between attribution studies and the criticism of Elizabethan drama. As Hoy defined the issue,

[12] G. Melchiori, 'Hand D in *Sir Thomas More*: An Essay in Misinterpretation', *ShS* 38 (1985): 101–14, at p. 109.

[13] C. Hoy, 'Critical and Aesthetic Problems of Collaboration in Renaissance Drama', *RORD* 19 (1976): 3–6.

the aesthetic problem which collaborative plays pose will always involve in some measure at least questions of dramatic coherence. To what extent does the fact of multiple authorship impede the achievement of some degree of formal unity—some quality of thematic design—for the play as a whole? (Hoy 1976, pp. 5–6)

Hoy pointed to the tripartite structure of *The Witch of Edmonton* as one example of how 'multiple dramatic visions have fused into a single coherent one', for Dekker, Rowley, and Ford each handled a section of the play dramatizing 'a basic diabolism which gives coherence to the whole'. However, Hoy judged, 'coherence of this kind is rare in collaborative drama, and becomes even rarer in plays where the authorial shares are not neatly contained within specific areas of plotting, as they are in *The Witch of Edmonton*' (p. 6). Hoy defined a double process: once scholars have reliably identified the co-authors involved, critics must learn to relate a play 'to a plurality of *oeuvres*' (p. 6), comparing it with each dramatist's performance in his sole-authored plays. Middleton's collaborations with William Rowley, for instance, 'contain some of his finest work, including his masterpiece, *The Changeling*, which is also arguably the finest product of collaboration which the Jacobean theater produced' (p. 5). Indeed, this play challenges our ideas of how co-authors worked together. With its 'famous double plot', we might assume that the dramatists divided up their work on that basis, but this is not entirely true.

While Middleton was chiefly responsible for the tragic main plot involving Beatrice-Joanna and De Flores, and Rowley was entirely responsible for the comic sub-plot set in the mad house, Rowley also seems to have written the opening and closing scenes of the play, both of which are concerned with the tragic main plot: an ascription which may account for the fact that the denouement of *The Changeling* is so much better managed than the garish finale to Middleton's own earlier tragedy of a few years before, *Women beware Women.* (p. 5)

This play seems to be a (rare) instance of co-authorship diminishing each writer's faults, and allowing his virtues to emerge more clearly than elsewhere. Thus, discussions of *The Changeling*

must face the fact that the play's triumph is first and last a triumph of collaboration: that here, Rowley for once was lifted entirely beyond himself, to a strain quite above his usual bumptious garrulity, and that the satiric demon which throughout his career had turned Middleton's efforts at tragedy into so many exhibitions of the ironic grotesque (from *The Revenger's Tragedy* to *The Second Maiden's Tragedy*) is for once controlled by a humane sympathy. (ibid.)

The Changeling is an exception to 'the abiding weaknesses of collaborative drama', namely that 'when characters are subject to development by two or more dramatists, inconsistencies—of speech, of temperament, in a word, of character, are bound to appear' (p. 6). C. G. Petter made a similar comment in 1973 on the Jonson–Chapman–Marston collaboration, *Eastward Hoe!*, that 'masterpiece of city comedy': 'The unity and cohesiveness with which the three authors combined their mature skills are such that in some respects they surpass the major comedies written independently'. Petter quoted F. E. Schelling's apposite comment, made in 1903, praising the play's 'extraordinary success as a collaboration': ' "there is a geniality of spirit in *Eastward Hoe* foreign to Marston, a definition of character and a restraint in incident above Chapman, and a fluidity of movement and naturalness of manner not always to a similar degree Jonson's" ' (Petter 1973, p. xxvii).

Other collaborations were not so happy. Robert Kean Turner[14] has vividly shown the kinds of inconsistency that collaboration could produce in respect to two tragicomedies written by Massinger, Fletcher, and Field for the King's Men between 1616 and 1618, *The Queen of Corinth* and *The Knight of Malta*. As Eugene Waith showed,[15] one element in the former play's plot derives from Seneca, *Controversiae* 1.5, the celebrated rhetorical dilemma called 'The Man Who Raped Two Girls'. The law is that 'a girl who has been raped may choose either marriage to her ravisher without a dowry, or his death'; the case proposed is that 'on a single night a man raped two girls', one of whom 'demands his death, the other marriage'.[16] Massinger wrote the play's first act, introducing the Queen of Corinth and her son Theanor, who is in love with Merione, sister of Leonidas, general of Corinth. Leonidas has defeated Agenor, Prince of Argos, and 'they become friends, Agenor surrendering his territorial claims in exchange for the hand of Merione' (Turner 1987, p. 317). Ordered by his mother to abandon Merione, Theanor decides to possess her by force, the rape taking place at the end of Act 1. 'Act 2, Fletcher's work, opens just after Merione's rape', as she 'pleads with the masked Theanor to restore her honor by marrying her', but he refuses (p. 318). Field composed Acts 3 and 4, competently developing both plots (which are far more complicated than my summary can suggest), and continuing the action until the point where Theanor will rape Beliza, a friend of Merione, 'great in beauty, birth, and fortune' (p. 317). Massinger returned to the writing with the fifth act, in which the rape takes place, Theanor is caught and brought before the Queen (his mother) for judgment. She sentences him to marry Merione and then to be executed, but after the marriage takes place it is revealed that (*a*) Theanor's minion Crates had arranged the first rape, convinced that Merione was 'his wife before the face of heaven'; (*b*) but, rather than permit the second rape, Crates had 'persuaded Merione to allow herself, disguised as Beliza, to be a second time ravished, only she was

---

[14] R. K. Turner, 'Collaborators at Work: *The Queen of Corinth* and *The Knight of Malta*', in B. Fabian and K. Tetzeli von Rosador (eds.), *Shakespeare: Text, Language, Criticism. Essays in Honour of Marvin Spevack* (Zurich, 1987), pp. 315–33.

[15] E. M. Waith, *The Pattern of Tragicomedy in Beaumont and Fletcher* (New Haven, 1952; repr. Hamden, Conn., 1969), pp. 136–7, 204–5.

[16] See *The Elder Seneca, Controversiae*, trans. M. Winterbottom, 2 vols., Loeb Library (London, 1974), i. 120–34.

actually never ravished at all, having all along been Theanor's wife' (p. 321). Shakespeare's use of 'the bed-trick' in *All's Well* and *Measure for Measure* seems almost chaste by comparison.

Turner's detailed summary of this complicated plot reveals several 'lapses in motivation and logical continuity' (p. 321). Massinger set the serious parts going, but then Field invented a comic character, Onos, a ridiculous figure, recognizably Sir Abraham Ninny of Field's earlier play, *A Woman is a Weathercock* (1609), but now 'turned into a nitwit traveller in order to take advantage of a current interest in Thomas Coryate' (p. 322). Evidently Massinger had forgotten about Onos, for he introduced him awkwardly 'into the opening of 1.3, the failure of his part of the scene to connect at all with the rest marking it as an interpolation' (p. 322). Turner suggested that, 'after reading the first version of Act 1 and plotting the remainder of the play, Fletcher and Field set to work, probably independently because in several matters they go in different directions from Massinger and from each other' (p. 323). Fletcher was happy to deal with 'the high emotionalism of the rape's immediate aftermath', having handled a similar situation in *Valentinian* (1614), but he took only a perfunctory interest in the comic plot, renaming 'Onos' as 'Lamprias', and transferring the name Lamprias to the uncle (p. 324). (Something similar happened between Shakespeare and Middleton in *Timon of Athens*, with the name 'Flavius' and the Steward.) Field was 'sufficiently well informed to carry the main plot forward', but his 'handling of the fools indicates that he did not exactly know what Fletcher was doing with them' (ibid.). Evidently the co-authors had not seen each other's drafts, a feature of Shakespeare and Fletcher's collaboration on *The Two Noble Kinsmen*, as we shall see.

The biggest inconsistencies in the text of *The Queen of Corinth* derive from the co-authors' differing attitudes to the play's overall structure. 'Massinger's collaborators, Fletcher especially, had attempted striking local effects without much concern for their long-range consequences. In order to bring about the happy endings, therefore, Massinger needed to effect some powerful transformations of character' (p. 325). The ending required several 'egregious changes of character', for 'the Theanor and Crates whom Fletcher depicted as depraved, Field as cheaply vicious, and the Massinger of Act 1 as clumsily criminal are worlds away from the moral paragons of Act 5' (p. 326). A modern scholar notices the inconsistency: did the original audience? In *The Knight of Malta* Field took responsibility for the opening and closing acts, Fletcher writing Act 2, and two later scenes (3.4, 4.2), Massinger contributing one scene (3.2). Again Turner's analysis reveals each dramatist doing his own thing. Massinger contributes a 'workmanlike' section, Fletcher indulges in one of the 'double reversals' for which he was famous, the young Knight Miranda apparently attempting to seduce Lucinda, but then asserting that 'he was merely testing her integrity. Why he should do so is as much a mystery as the motives for most of the chastity trials in Fletcher's plays' (p. 328). Turner's summary shows the plot proliferating in several directions. As he drily observed, 'it is small wonder that Field, who composed Act 5, would not pick up all the threads of a story grown so complicated' (ibid.).

Already from this brief summary we can see that neither play would fulfil even a generously defined concept of unity. It is tempting to imagine that the texts as they have reached us represent some preliminary draft, for in both cases 'enough loose ends remain' to suggest that before they were staged 'further work on the text would have been done by the prompter if not by the authors'—one of whom, Field, acted in both plays (p. 326). However, Turner's scrutiny of the texts shows that *The Knight of Malta* was printed (in the Beaumont and Fletcher Folio, 1647) from the prompt-book, for the prompter's careful and systematic annotations survive (pp. 329–30). In other words, *The Knight of Malta* 'would have been performed as it stands', and although *The Queen of Corinth* was set from a scribal transcript, not the prompt-book, the similarity between it and the other play suggested to Turner that '[its] anomalies too may have been allowed to stand as being of no importance' (p. 330). That is in some ways a chastening conclusion for modern scholars, suggesting that the expectations of coherent characterization and plot design that we bring to a play may be misplaced.

However, the expectation of coherence or unity of action voiced by my representative critics—Whetstone, Sidney, Cervantes, and Jonson—encourages the counter-suggestion that they, too, would have recognized the inconsistencies, unexplained reversals, and inadequate motivation contained in these two plays. Perhaps the best argument for Renaissance dramatists having had a concept of unity is the continuing self-criticism by which some of them did achieve it. As Madeleine Doran wrote of the Elizabethan and Jacobean dramatists, 'their great problem was the achievement of unity out of diversity', and 'success in structural form was never very uniformly achieved'. Jonson and Shakespeare 'each solved the problem of achieving unity out of variety in a different way. Jonson did it by exclusion and repetition, Shakespeare by inclusion and complex harmony' (Doran 1954, pp. 19–20). Since Jonson edited out the contribution of his co-author in *Sejanus*, we shall never know whether his achievement of unity had been compromised by the collaborative process. In the five co-authored plays in which Shakespeare took a part, as we shall see, the presence of a co-author was a stimulus but in some cases a distinct obstacle. The problem remains, as Hoy defined it, that in dealing with a collaborative work we 'must be prepared to relate it to a plurality of *oeuvres*', a task that I shall now attempt.

Scholars have long noticed many inconsistencies in Shakespeare's co-authored plays. I shall draw on their discussions for the evidence it provides of collaboration, but in a rather different spirit from that shown by earlier commentators, in whose eyes the fellow dramatist was always 'the inferior author'.[17] The Revd F. G. Fleay poured scorn on

the monstrous theory . . . that 'the original composer of [*Pericles*] later on withdrew in favour of his co-worker Shakspere—so to say, allowing himself to be eclipsed'. Imagine Shakspere in his best period allowing this stuff to stand in a play over which he had the full control! It is impossible. Shakspere certainly never had any management or arrangement of the play: he only contributed the Marina story, which I have tried to separate and restore to him.[18]

According to Fleay, this section of the play formed 'a perfect artistic and organic whole', deserving to be printed on its own (p. 197), a resolution which he subsequently carried out in an edition for the New Shakspere Society. Acknowledging Wilkins as the author of Acts 1 and 2, Fleay criticized his 'poverty of invention' for not having made better use of the space available to him (p. 208), and rejected any notion that the two dramatists could have worked together on the play. Shakespeare's part was 'done previously and independently' (ibid.).

John Fletcher received an equally rough treatment as co-author from Shakespeare scholars. In his *Letter* on the authorship of *The Two Noble Kinsmen* William Spalding assured his readers that Fletcher's 'needless degradation of his principal characters is a fault of which Shakespeare is not guilty',[19] and he dismissed Fletcher's 5.2 (the scene with the Jailer's Daughter, her father, wooer, and the Doctor) as 'disgusting and imbecile in the extreme' (p. 49). In his otherwise excellent edition Harold Littledale also used Fletcher as a general whipping-boy, declaring that 'the Shaksperian two-fifths give us all the positive ideas we possess of Theseus, Hippolyta, Emilia, Palamon, Arcite, and Perithous; and the rest of the play is only a confusion and perversion and obscuration of the traits indicated by Shakspere'.[20] Littledale alleged that Fletcher's scenes had had a 'benumbing effect . . . upon the Shaksperian portion' (p. 27*), and although he accepted that 'Shakspere must have given some outline' of the subplot with the Jailer's Daughter, he complained that Fletcher submitted the characters outlined by Shakespeare to a process of 'degradation' (p. 46*). So we see the Jailer's Daughter 'moralizing on her love for Palamon [2.4] in Fletcher's peculiarly prurient way' (p. 49*), the co-author 'having made her passion extravagantly sensual, mere frenzy of lust'

---

[17] S. Hickson, review essay on *The Two Noble Kinsmen*, *Westminster and Foreign Quarterly Review*, 92 (1847): 59–88; repr. as 'The Shares of Shakspere and Fletcher in *The Two Noble Kinsmen*', *TNSS* 1 (1874): 25*–61*, at pp. 62, 86; E. H. Wright, *The Authorship of Timon of Athens* (New York, 1910), p. 51.

[18] F. G. Fleay, 'On the Play of *Pericles*, *TNSS* 3 (1876): 195–209, at p. 200.

[19] W. Spalding, *A Letter on Shakspere's Authorship of 'The Two Noble Kinsmen'* (Edinburgh, 1833; repr. London, 1876), p. 42.

[20] H. Littledale (ed.), *The Two Noble Kinsmen. By William Shakspere and John Fletcher. Edited from the Quarto of 1634. Part II. General Introduction and List of Words* (London: The New Shakspere Society, 1885), p. 25*.

(p. 50*) in her soliloquy (2.6), and later descending to 'filthy nymphomania' (p. 51*). Littledale quoted with approval Swinburne's attack on ' "the pestilent abuse and perversion" ' to which Fletcher put Shakespeare's ' "hints or sketches" . . .' for the underplot (p. 80*), but the Victorian critics' indignation seems out of place when we consider that Shakespeare collaborated voluntarily with Fletcher, three times in all.

PERICLES

Elevating Shakespeare so that one may downgrade his co-authors is an old vice that should have been stamped out long ago. Without indulging it, we can nevertheless register the problems of co-authorship in varying degrees in all five plays, depending on the initial division of labour. The simplest division is that found in *Pericles*, where each writer handled a self-contained section of the play, with some linking choric commentary. Evidently Wilkins and Shakespeare had sketched out the whole plot sequence, basing their version of the Apollonius of Tyre story on Gower's *Confessio Amantis* and Laurence Twine's *Pattern of Painful Adventures* (c.1594?; 1607). In Geoffrey Bullough's words, the play 'interweaves material from both of them in every scene, sometimes taking more from Gower, sometimes more from Twine',[21] a systematic treatment which suggests an approach agreed in advance. MacDonald Jackson judged that '*Pericles* derives its essential coherence from the ancient folk-tale, which has its own inner dynamic',[22] and he argued that the play's dual authorship did not produce a 'lack of cohesion':

Despite their stylistic awkwardness, the first two acts serve the play's action well enough and initiate its main concerns. *Pericles'* air of artlessness has been artfully created, and the play has imaginative unity—to a greater degree perhaps than Shakespeare's collaborations with John Fletcher, an infinitely more talented dramatist than Wilkins.[23]

Many readers would agree with that overall judgement, but it cannot be denied that the plot-structure and characterization in the first two acts differ considerably from those in the last three.

The opening acts conform to 'a species of play which had long been known on the Elizabethan stage', as Geoffrey Bullough observed, being 'mainly derived from medieval romances (many of which were still popular in sixteenth-century editions), but . . . also from the biographical Morality plays which represented a series of adventures or phases in a life-history'

---

[21] G. Bullough, *Narrative and Dramatic Sources of Shakespeare*, vi (London, 1966), p. 355.
[22] M. P. Jackson, 'Medium and Message: Authors and Poetic Styles in *Pericles*', unpublished paper delivered to the Shakespeare Association of America, 1–3 Apr. 1999.
[23] M. P. Jackson, '*Pericles*, Acts I and II: New Evidence for George Wilkins', *NQ* 215 (1990): 192–6, at p. 196.

(Bullough 1966, p. 369). Examples of this genre included the probably most popular Elizabethan play, *Mucedorus* (1598; printed fourteen times by 1639, and revived in 1609), *The Rare Triumphs of Love and Fortune* (1589), Heywood's *Four Apprentices of London* (1594?), Peele's *Old Wife's Tale* (*c.*1591–4), and Anthony Munday's Robin Hood plays (1598) (ibid.). The play's theatrical genealogy may explain its structure as 'a romantic biography' but it can also help account for its structural deficiencies. As F. D. Hoeniger put it, 'the play is unified by its central figure, Pericles, rather than by its plot . . . It presents us with Pericles' adventures over a period of many years, and to a lesser degree with those of Marina (Thaisa's are barely sketched). All other characters are strictly subordinate and most of them in fact episodic, drifting into Pericles' life on only one or two decisive occasions'.[24] If I may briefly summarize the action: Pericles, in his postings around the Mediterranean, has to undergo a series of unrelated tests: to solve Antiochus' riddle of his incestuous relationship with his daughter (1.1); to survive shipwreck (2.1); to win the joust for Thaisa, Simonides' daughter (2.2); and to brave the father's apparent displeasure in order to gain her hand in marriage (2.5). The incestuous ruler is rapidly introduced in the play's opening scene, but disappears just as rapidly, and his subsequent destruction by 'the most high gods' is narrated in a dozen lines (2.4.1 ff.), wrapping up a functionless piece of plotting. Meanwhile, Pericles is being pursued by the villain Thaliard, sent by Antiochus to poison him (1.1.154–71). Thaliard reaches Tyre, only to discover that Pericles has gone to Antioch, at which point he gladly returns home, like an undelivered letter (1.3.10–39).

In the first two acts both characterization and dramaturgy are often perfunctory, as critics have long observed. George Steevens complained in 1780 that the characters in *Pericles* were not individualized and that the plot was disorganized, for characters appear and disappear without any continuity or liaison between them (*CHS*, vi. 298–9). Nikolaus Delius could find no trace of dramatic design or character motivation in the first two acts.[25] In the scene (1.4) describing the famine at Tarsus, the ruler, Cleon, explains to his wife in laborious detail things that she knows as well as he does (p. 186), Dionyza being reduced to such comments as (to her husband's plea, to 'help me with tears')—'I'll do my best sir', and 'O 'tis too true'. Delius pointed out that Gower's chorus beginning Act 2 'recapitulates in a completely superfluous manner what was staged in Act 1, as if the spectator could have already forgotten it' (p. 186), and he described the Simonides–Thaisa scenes as putting the source-material's naïve narrative on to the stage without any dramatic reworking, a failure to develop either character or motive typical of the

---

[24] F. D. Hoeniger (ed.), Shakespeare, *Pericles*, New Arden Shakespeare (London, 1963), p. lxxix.
[25] N. Delius, 'Ueber Shakespeare's Pericles, Prince of Tyre', *ShJb* 3 (1868): 175–204, at pp. 185–6.

play's first half. Significantly, Delius discovered in Wilkins's *The Miseries of Enforced Marriage* the same 'lack of coherence and motivation in plot development and characterization' that he had diagnosed in *Pericles* (p. 196).

Indirect testimony to the oddities of plot and characterization in Acts 1 and 2 were provided a century later by F. D. Hoeniger's second thoughts on the play, in which he now ascribed these acts, also, to Shakespeare.[26] His new thesis forced Hoeniger to argue that Shakespeare deliberately used 'crude dramaturgical devices', superfluous asides, conspicuous repetition, including having to write 'a speech of a kind that dramatists normally do their best to avoid', namely Thaisa's report to her father (2.3.86–9), who is standing next to her, of the self-description that Pericles had just given (2.3.81–5). Why should Shakespeare make such uncharacteristic faults? Hoeniger's sole explanation was that 'the cumbersome-seeming repetition, with only slight variation, seems appropriate in *Pericles* . . .' (1982, p. 413). As for the equally 'crude and desperate characterization' in 2.5, with the constant interruption of the action 'by asides which the audience does not need, knowing, as it does from the start that the King is dissembling', Hoeniger could only suggest that 'the effect may well be intentionally burlesque' (p. 474), solemnly urging readers to accept it as an analogue of Chaucer's 'silly tale of Sir Thopas in jingling rhymes, which appears to go nowhere . . .' (pp. 476–7). So 'Shakespeare too may be winking at his audience in some of the play's most absurdly devised episodes' (p. 477), all the while creating a 'new form of drama' (p. 479). These desperate arguments are symptomatic of the strain produced by denying the overwhelming evidence that two authors were involved in the play, for to make Shakespeare sole author means that the visible discrepancies in dramaturgy and characterization have somehow to be laid at his door.

In claiming that *Pericles* is entirely Shakespeare's composition Dolores Del Vecchio and Antony Hammond found themselves obliged to follow Hoeniger's path. The 'misdirected . . . journeys of the plot', the editors argue, 'are emblematised by the language. What begins awkwardly and linguistically disappointing [*sic*] is made sharp, keen, vigorous, and intensely moving'.[27] Like Hoeniger, they could only suggest that Shakespeare deliberately wrote badly to start with. The perfunctory dramaturgy of the opening scene gets through about six major stages of plot 'in only 171 lines of dialogue', all of them being 'swiftly conveyed because of their stock conventionality: a quality facilitated and shared by the language, appropriately illustrating how the medium can be the message' (p. 38)—and so on. Rather than follow these attempts to claim Acts 1 and 2 for Shakespeare, we can happily agree with Nikolaus Delius's comment on reaching Act 3, that here, for the first time, Shakespeare's 'great skill in characterization turns characters

---

[26] F. D. Hoeniger, 'Gower and Shakespeare in *Pericles*', *ShQ* 33 (1982): 461–79.

[27] D. Del Vecchio and A. Hammond (eds.), Shakespeare, *Pericles, Prince of Tyre* (Cambridge, 1998), p. 37.

who have so far been mere puppets into figures truly capable of life, for whose happiness or sorrow we take a hitherto unexpected interest' (1868, p. 187). Every reader notices the intensity of feeling which Pericles suddenly displays, his sense of loss at his wife's apparent death, his acute awareness of the new-born child's vulnerability (3.1). In the final three acts Pericles remains the centre of interest, but for the first time he has a family, and Shakespeare devotes several scenes to the fortunes of his wife and child. In 3.2 Thaisa's coffin is rescued from the sea, the physician Cerimon miraculously restores her to life, and in order to remain faithful to her husband she takes on 'A vestal livery' in Ephesus (3.4). Meanwhile Pericles leaves Marina in the care of Cleon and Dionyza (3.3), a guardianship that turns vicious some sixteen years later as the Queen, jealous of Marina's superiority to her own daughter, orders Leonine to kill her (4.1). Marina is rescued from this fate by pirates, only to suffer a (threatening) fate worse than death, being sold to a brothel. It is typical of Shakespeare's interest in the richness of life that, in the brothel scenes (4.2, 4.5, 4.6) 'for the first time the play elaborates considerably on the story material' (Bullough 1966, p. 364). As with the brothel scenes in *Measure for Measure*, or the sheep-shearing scene in *The Winter's Tale*, Shakespeare provides us with a fullness of observed detail far in excess of what the dramatized events would need by any economic calculation. All of these events concerning his wife and child being known to the audience, but not to Pericles, our hopes that he will finally be reunited with them suffer a setback as he falls into a profound lethargy,

> A man who for this three months hath not spoken
> To anyone, nor taken sustenance,
> But to prorogue his grief
>   .   .   .   .
>   from the loss
> Of a belovèd daughter and a wife.
>
>   (5.1.22–8)

In choosing to contribute the play's final three acts, Shakespeare was able to involve us far more deeply in the pattern of loss and restoration associated with Pericles, Thaisa, and Marina, a pattern which anticipates the three Romances which he was soon to write, unaided. All four plays have a common plot-situation involving fathers and daughters, husbands and wives, separated by some alien force (storm, shipwreck, human evil or folly), who are reunited at the end, the daughter being either restored to her husband (Imogen to Posthumus) or given in marriage to a man matching her rare qualities (Marina, Perdita, Miranda). Although victims of fortune and human malice, the daughters are shown to be capable of acting for their own good, loyally defending the men they love, and entering a marriage which will bring happiness as much to their parents as to themselves. Perdita and Miranda have less room for independent action, but Imogen takes her fate into her own hands, and Marina's skills in music and language succeed in rescuing her father from a life-denying melancholy (5.1.71–254), in a sequence that sends shivers down my spine whenever I read it. The four Romances confront evil and misfortune, overcoming them with a beneficent dramaturgy—not to be confused with Christian providence[28]—and guarantee a fruitful and benevolent generation to follow. Their generally acknowledged power over readers and audiences springs in great part from their concern with legitimacy, authority, fertility, patrimony, and all the gifts that human beings can confer on each other, issues fundamental to human happiness, social or individual. Shakespeare's ability both to dramatize these sequences of loss and recovery, and to respond to them with poetry beyond expectations in its depth of feeling and richness of expression is already fully shown here, in the marvellously extended reunion between Pericles and Marina, and the briefer but no less moving restoration of Thaisa to her husband and daughter (5.3.1–84). In retrospect, it is easy to see what attracted Shakespeare to this story, and why he may have been happy to let Wilkins wrestle with a great deal of unpromising material.

TITUS ANDRONICUS

In *Titus Andronicus*, some twelve or fifteen years earlier, Shakespeare had agreed to a similarly clear division of labour, letting Peele set the play in motion by writing the whole of the first act and the first two scenes of the second, an opening stretch of some 656 lines. Thereafter Peele seems to have claimed for himself only one whole scene—but a plum one for a Latinist— where Lavinia identifies her rapists with the help of Ovid's *Metamorphoses* (4.1). In these scenes, as we have noted, Peele made use of a peculiarly formulaic diction, constantly recycling the same terms and attitudes, his characters addressing each other with frequent vocatives, granting their interlocutors rank and title but forfeiting intimacy, and making their utterances more emphatic by a heavy use of alliteration. Peele seems to invest so much energy in the act of utterance, and in the arranging of his characters into formal groupings, alliances, and oppositions that determine staging and speech-making (*opsis* and *lexis*, in Aristotle's terms), that he has little energy left for characterization. Many critics have commented that this opening sequence fails to individualize any of the characters, beyond their obvious roles—competing election candidates; the returning hero; the injured mother; the badly treated soldier. The very fact that we can describe them in terms of

---

[28] For examples of editors attributing a pseudo-Christian status to the Romances, see Hoeniger 1963, pp. lxxix–xci; Del Vecchio and Hammond 1998, pp. 51–78.

their roles shows that the characters are subordinated to plot in an un-Shakespearian way. Scholars who have compared Peele's dramaturgy with that of his contemporaries find it similarly lacking in the power that unifies the elements into a whole. Wolfgang Clemen, in his classic study of 'the development of dramatic speech' in Elizabethan drama, comparing Peele to Marlowe, judged his work to mark

a retrogression as far as the process of 'dramatizing' the set speech and making it an integral part of the dramatic composition is concerned. Peele had no talent for dramatic structure, for consistency in the handling of plot and the portrayal of character, for the harmonious interdependence of the various elements that make up the whole play; he had no sense of proportion, or order, of dramatic architecture. On the other hand, he possessed strongly marked powers of expression and a real gift for the effective presentation of individual episodes and situations.[29]

The language of *Edward I* is typical in that it has a 'variegated texture' but lacks both uniformity and any organic relation between speech and character: 'Peele does not use all this manifold variety in his language as a means of differentiating his *dramatis personae*. There are no signs yet of the association of a particular way of speaking with a particular character, such as we are later to find in Shakespeare' (p. 167). Every reader notices that the characters in the opening scenes of *Titus Andronicus* are not individualized through their language; indeed, it is not until Shakespeare takes over the character of Aaron in Act 2, and responds to Titus' increasing sufferings and mental breakdown in Act 3, that individual styles can be distinguished. As Clemen wrote, it is in the episode that Peele 'displays his sense of drama, and according to the requirements of the episode that he moulds his diction' (p. 168). Werner Senn, in his sustained comparison of Peele and Greene, reached a similar conclusion, warning readers of Peele not to expect 'character in anything like a Shakespearean sense'.[30] Like Greene, whenever Peele attempts 'to present an inward action, a debate in a person's mind . . . [he does] so in the form of a rhetorical exercise rather than of a psychological study, in an exterior, formal manner'. Peele's interest was 'not in a character as such but in story first and foremost', and it follows that major characters, not being individualized, display many inconsistencies (Senn 1973, pp. 127, 130); their utterances 'belong to a certain rhetorical style and are therefore useless as a means of character-drawing' (p. 131).

The dramaturgy of the opening act of *Titus Andronicus* shows Peele's liking for block-composition, presenting striking units of action, but often forgoing adequate preparation. Where Shakespeare might have given us some

---

[29] W. Clemen, *English Tragedy before Shakespeare: The Development of Dramatic Speech* (London, 1961), p. 163.
[30] W. Senn, *Studies in the Dramatic Construction of Robert Greene and George Peele* (Berne, 1973), p. 114.

preliminary hints—via two gentlemen encountering each other by chance, or officers strewing cushions—as to the significance of the scene that is to follow, Peele plunges us without warning into a crucial election campaign, with action on two stage-levels, and from both sides of the stage:

> *Enter the Tribunes and Senators aloft; and then enter below Saturninus and his followers at one door, and Bassianus and his followers at the other, with drums*

'*and trumpets*', according to the First Quarto, or '*Colours*', according to the Folio. Saturninus, eldest son of the late Emperor of Rome, first delivers his election speech (1.1.1–8), his brother Bassianus follows with his (9–17), exactly symmetrical utterances. But suddenly Marcus, the people's tribune and brother of Titus Andronicus, announces that the Roman people have summoned Titus home to be appointed emperor, and requests both brothers to suspend their campaigns (18–45). Saturninus and Bassianus withdraw their candidatures again in symmetrical speeches, like Tweedledum and Tweedledee, and '*go up into the Senate-house*' (46–63). That marks the end of the election process, for the moment.

In his speech Marcus had eulogized Titus' repeated sacrifices *pro bono Romano*:

> Ten years are spent since first he undertook
> This cause of Rome, and chastised with arms
> Our enemies' pride; five times he hath return'd
> Bleeding to Rome, bearing his valiant sons
> In coffins from the field,   35
> And now at last, laden with honour's spoils
> Returns the good Andronicus to Rome
>
>   (1.1.31–7)

After the 'short line' 35 (as the Riverside edition misleadingly describes it), the First Quarto (1594), the only authoritative text of the play, contains the following three-and-a-half lines:

>   and at this day,   35*a*
> To the Monument of that Andronicy   *b*
> Done sacrifice of expiation,   *c*
> And slaine the Noblest prisoner of the Gothes.   *d*

The Second and Third Quartos (1600, 1611) omitted these lines, as did the Folio (1623), while modern editors have mostly consigned them to the notes or textual appendix, as being supposedly superfluous given that the staged sacrifice of Alarbus follows (1.1.96–149). Two editors, as we shall see, have even recommended the drastic step of eliminating the whole Alarbus episode, as a later addition.

In 1929 J. S. G. Bolton made the first thorough examination of the text of *Titus Andronicus*, collating the recently discovered First Quarto of 1594 (it came to light in 1905) with its subsequent reprints, and vindicating its author-ity.[31] Bolton defended these three-and-a-half lines, suggesting two emend-ations, reading '*the* Andronicy' (not '*that*'), since the common abbreviation *y'* is easily misread; and altering '*at* this day' either to '*as* this day', or—more convincingly, I believe—to 'at this *door*', another easy misreading (especially if 'day' were spelt 'daie') (Bolton 1929, pp. 781–2). The emendation of 'day' to 'door', Bolton argued, 'would make clear, as early as line 36, the stage-setting for the scene—the entrance to the tomb of the Andronici—and would prepare for the opening of the tomb a page later and for the subsequent sacri-fice of Tamora's oldest son. Five times before would a noble prisoner of the Goths be known to have met death in expiatory sacrifice' (p. 781). That seems to me an elegant and plausible solution, and Bolton repeated it some forty years later.[32] Editors have ignored Bolton's arguments,[33] but MacDonald Jackson recently revived them, I think correctly—once one understands the characteristics of Peele's dramaturgy. Defending the emendation 'door', Jackson pointed out that it 'also vindicates the two pronouns in the Quarto text, "at" (where "on this day" would have been idiomatic), and "to" '. As he rightly observed, 'the whole movement of Marcus's speech requires that the sacrifice of propitiation to the *manes* of Titus's dead sons be described as habitual'.[34] Marco Mincoff, in his perceptive study of the play, had noted that the purpose of these lines is 'to prepare us for the repetition of a sacrifice that has already been enacted five times'.[35] Looking at Marcus' speech again, we can see its emphasis on a cyclic pattern:

expedition: war: Roman losses: victory: sacrifice.

'Ten years' have passed since Titus first 'undertook | This cause of Rome', we are told, and 'five times he hath return'd' with his 'valiant sons | In coffins'. On each occasion, then, he has performed a 'sacrifice of expiation' to the Andronici's family tomb, and on each occasion he has 'slaine the Noblest prisoner of the Gothes'. The 'door' is presumably an opening in the theatre's

---

[31] J. S. G. Bolton, 'The Authentic Text of *Titus Andronicus*', *PMLA* 44 (1929): 765–88.

[32] J. S. G. Bolton, 'A Plea for 3½ Rejected Shakespearian Lines', *ShQ* 23 (1972): 261–3.

[33] J. C. Maxwell, in his Arden edition 1953 (revd. 1961), included these lines in the text, but numbered them '35–35c'; Eugene Waith treated them as superseded by the staging of Alarbus' sacrifice (Waith (ed.), Shakespeare, *Titus Andronicus* (Oxford, 1984), pp. 39, 85), as did Alan Hughes (Hughes (ed.), Shakespeare, *Titus Andronicus* (Cambridge, 1994), pp. 54, 146–7). Jonathan Bate printed them in his text, but within wavy lines. In his introduction, however—to his credit—he declared them 'defensible', since they could be taken as 'an anticipation of the slay-ing of Alarbus, not an inconsistency with it. This interpretation could be strengthened by emend-ing "at this day" to . . . (Jackson, conj.) "at this door" ("here at the entrance to the tomb of the Andronici")' (Bate (ed.), Shakespeare, *Titus Andronicus*, New Arden Shakespeare (London, 1995), pp. 99–100, 129–30). Bolton's responsibility for the emendation seems to have been forgotten.

[34] See his review of Harold G. Metz, *Shakespeare's Earliest Tragedy: Studies in Titus Andronicus* (1996), in *PBSA* 92 (1998): 90–4, at pp. 92–3.

[35] M. Mincoff, *Shakespeare: The First Steps* (Sofia, 1976), p. 213.

rear wall, representing the door which—as in buildings to this day—gives access to a family tomb. The Andronici's tomb is going to be a main focus of the action for much of this opening scene, first in the sacrificial ceremony to appease the dead sons' spirits, whose coffins are finally placed in the tomb to the sound of trumpets (96–160), and then in the dispute as to whether the rebellious son Mutius, slain by Titus, should be accorded burial in the family tomb or not (341–90).

The reinterpretation of this passage made possible by the arguments of Bolton, Mincoff, and Jackson would make it an integral part of the scene, not a superfluous pre-echo of the action to be staged later. I would support their argument from other verbal links in the text. When Titus' procession arrives, graphically described in the stage direction—'*Sound drums and trumpets, and then enter two of Titus' sons; and then two men bearing a coffin covered with black . . . Then set down the coffin, and Titus speaks*'—he addresses Jupiter Capitolinus, asking him to 'Stand gracious to the rites that we intend!' (1.1.78), Peele thus emphasizing the religious element from the outset. One of these rites will be to give his sons 'burial amongst their ancestors', and once the family tomb has been opened Titus appeals for a respectful silence:

> There greet in silence, as the dead are wont,
> And sleep in peace, slain in your country's wars!

The other rite will involve that 'sacrifice of expiation' at which, as on previous occasions, they have 'slain the Noblest prisoner of the Gothes' (1.1.35*d*). Having prepared for this detail, Peele now returns to it in the speech which Lucius addresses to his father, the victorious general, appealing:

> Give us the proudest prisoner of the Goths
> That we may hew his limbs and on a pile
> *Ad manes fratrum* sacrifice his flesh
> Before the earthy prison of their bones
>
> (96–100)

Titus accedes to the request, formally repeating for the third time the condition that the chosen victim should be 'the noblest prisoner of the Goths' (35*d*), or 'the proudest prisoner of the Goths' (96):

> I give him you, the noblest that survives,
> The eldest son of this distressed queen.
>
> (102–3)

In another dramatist the repetition of an almost identical line twice within sixty lines might indeed arouse suspicion that one of those utterances is superfluous. But such verbal repetition is typical of Peele, as we know, and at the third occurrence we finally realize who the victim will be: Alarbus, Tamora's son. As I briefly indicated in Chapter 3, the choice forced on Titus by this habitual rite of appeasement to his dead sons' spirits becomes the first offence in the cycle of revenge which will ultimately destroy Titus and most of his family, Tamora and her sons, as well as Bassianus, Saturninus, and Aaron. Marco Mincoff well observed that this 'horrific blood-sacrifice', the fact that Tamora's son 'must be sacrificed to satisfy an inhuman but hallowed custom', constitutes Titus' *hamartia*, his fatal error (Mincoff 1976, pp. 115, 117). Rejecting the editorial deletion of that passage in the First Quarto, together with any notion that 'the episode of the sacrifice is a later insertion', Mincoff asked: 'what dramatist would have left the essential *hamartia* of his hero to be deduced from a single vague allusion like this, without making the reason for Tamora's rancour explicit?' (p. 213). Those three-and-a-half lines in the First Quarto, far from being a superfluous duplication, are part of Peele's carefully symmetrical handling of this sequence. Were they to be excluded, Lucius' request that Titus should 'give us the proudest prisoner of the Goths' to be slain would be quite unexpected, a sudden and unnecessarily vengeful request rather than part of a solemn rite. When Tamora has finished pleading for Alarbus' life, in vain, Titus justifies his sacrifice as an unquestionable right due to the deceased:

> Patient yourself, madam, and pardon me.
> These are their brethren, whom your Goths beheld
> Alive and dead, and for their brethren slain
> Religiously they ask a sacrifice:
> To this your son is mark'd, and die he must,
> T'appease their groaning shadows that are gone.

(121–6)

The whole episode is given pattern and symmetry through this sequence

request: request granted: objection denied: sacrifice executed.

When Titus ordered the tomb opened he had pronounced the *requiescat in pace* formula—'sleep in peace, slain in your country's wars'—and recalled how many of his sons the tomb already contained (91–5). Once his sons return, having 'perform'd | Our Roman rites', Titus can resume his formal exequy over the coffins:

> In peace and honour rest you here, my sons,
> Rome's readiest champions, repose you here in rest,
> Secure from worldly chances and mishaps!
>   . . . .
>   here are no storms,
> No noise, but silence and eternal sleep.
> In peace and honour rest you here, my sons!

(150–6)

The repetition of a whole line framing that utterance gives it the symmetry of ritual, an effect sustained with the greeting of Lavinia, as she comes to pay her respects, echoing the preceding line in a characteristic Peelean manner (as we saw in Chapter 3):

> In peace and honour live Lord Titus long!
>
> (157)

This is an impressive episode, with Tamora's passionate lament, the imagined offstage sacrifice, the sight of 'smoke, like incense' arising from 'the sacrificing fire' (144–5), and the 'loud 'larums' of the trumpets as the coffins are interred.

We readily grant Peele's skill in constructing an episode, but it is often at a cost. Throughout this sequence, for over a hundred lines (64–168), the election campaign has been suspended, and the candidates, Saturninus and Bassianus, together with Marcus Andronicus and the other Tribunes, have silently observed proceedings from the upper stage, imagined as the Senate House. Now Peele picks up this plot thread again, in a rather awkward piece of staging, for the next episode involves a heated interchange between Titus on the main stage and the others aloft (169–233). Marcus informs Titus that the people of Rome invite him to be emperor; he declines, on the ground of age; Saturninus threatens to seize power by force; Bassianus requests it gently; but Titus cedes the rule to Saturninus. That plot sequence concluded, the Folio text gives a stage direction, '*A long flourish till they come down*', trumpets covering the time it takes the actors to descend, and action proceeds on the main stage. Saturninus thanks Titus for his generosity, and as a reward announces that he will make Lavinia his Empress. The two men exchange compliments, and Titus formally gives his captive Tamora into the Emperor's care.

Peele had carefully prepared the sequence involving Titus' return, the sacrifice of Alarbus, and his sons' burial, even though it awkwardly interrupted the imperial election. At this point in the scene he has resolved both the burial ritual and the election, achieving a sense of closure. But now, suddenly, he pushes the action off into several unexpected directions. The Emperor Saturninus, having just ceremonially named Lavinia as his bride-to-be, receives the captive Tamora and instantly feels the pangs of desire:

> [*Aside.*] A goodly lady, trust me, of the hue
> That I would choose were I to choose anew.—
> Clear up, fair queen, that cloudy countenance
> .   .   .   .
>   Madam, he comforts you
> Can make you greater than the Queen of Goths.
>
> (211–19)

Peele had introduced Bassianus as worshipping Lavinia (51–2), and one might have expected him to protest earlier, when Saturninus announced his intention to marry her. But Peele postpones to this point his protest—'Lord Titus, by your leave, this maid is mine'—['*Seizing Lavinia*', editors add]—and within fifteen lines Marcus Andronicus has joined Bassianus in Lavinia's abduction, Titus has killed his son Mutius (who tried to help them), and the situation is plunged into chaos. Thereafter, Saturninus rewards Titus' great loyalty with great ingratitude, formally discarding Lavinia and choosing Tamora for his bride—'If thou be pleased with this my sudden choice' (321)— and insulting Titus into the bargain, who is left alone on stage, 'dishonoured' and accused of wrongs (277–340). This sensational reversal is completely unprepared for, and poorly motivated, both characteristics not usually found in Shakespeare's opening scenes.

We might expect Titus to draw the consequences of the Emperor's calculated insults, in some form of counter-action. However, Peele now offers another separately formed block of composition, also unprepared for, in which Marcus and Titus' three remaining sons plead with Titus to allow Mutius burial in the family tomb, finally persuading him with a series of symmetrically balanced speeches reminiscent of those from Saturninus and Bassianus at the outset:

> *Lucius.* But let us give him burial as becomes,
>   Give Mutius burial with our brethren.
>
>   (347–8)
> *Marcus.* My nephew Mutius' deeds do plead for him,
>   He must be buried with his brethren.
>
>   (356–7)
> *Marcus.* Brother, for in that name doth nature plead—
> *Martius.* Father, and in that name doth nature speak—
> *Titus.* Speak thou no more if all the rest will speed.
> *Marcus.* Renowned Titus, more than half my soul—
> *Lucius.* Dear father, soul and substance of us all—
> *Marcus.* Suffer thy brother Marcus to inter
>   His noble nephew here in virtue's nest . . .
>
>   (370–6)

The symmetrical patterning has an operatic quality, as if the characters were engaged in a trio or quartet. This self-contained sequence concludes with the four persuaders speaking in unison the formulaic farewell:

> No man shed tears for noble Mutius;
> He lives in fame, that died in virtue's cause.
>
>   (389–90)

Surprisingly, the personages we had just seen on the upper stage (298)—'*the Emperor, Tamora and her two sons, with the Moor*'—now enter '*at one door*' of the main stage, while simultaneously '*Enter at the other door Bassianus and Lavinia, with others*' (398), another symmetrical grouping demanding care from the actors and stage-manager. Symmetry of language is matched by the symmetry of actors' stage-positioning. The resentment that we might expect Titus to be feeling against Saturninus is now uttered by Bassianus (413–22), but Tamora unexpectedly emerges as peacemaker, in public at least (428–41, 456–85), apparently justifying Titus' naïve belief that, being indebted to him, she 'will nobly him remunerate' (376–8). In reality, though, as the audience learns from her speech aside to Saturninus (442–55), Tamora plans to 'massacre' all the Andronici, and we realize that the note of amity on which the scene ends, looking forward to the next day's hunting, is illusory.

In this opening scene Peele has put together about five large units of action, one following the other without preparation or internal logic. It might be possible to rearrange parts of the sequence without changing the overall effect. He has exploited theatrical resources vigorously, with a constant eye for symmetry, giving us action on two levels, above and below, groups of characters entering simultaneously right and left, with speeches self-consciously organized into symmetrical groups, echoing the patterned stage movements. We are conscious throughout of the scene's formal organization (it is what one imagines a Meyerbeer opera to be like), with characters living out their roles, speaking 'not what they feel, but what they ought to say'.

The dramaturgy of this scene resembles that of other Peele plays. More than a century ago Gregor Sarrazin pointed out the similarities with the opening of *Edward I*:

Return from the wars; coronation (choice of a ruler); triumph of the proud, cruel, adulterous queen [Elinor, Edward's Spanish wife], who—following legend, not historical reality—is characterized in such a way that she could have served as a model for Tamora.[36]

In that play Elinor, the Queen Mother, sends her attendant lords to greet her son Longshanks (the future Edward I) as the conquering hero returns from Jerusalem, imagining his triumphant progress.

> Veering before the winde, plowing the sea,
> His stretched sailes fild with the breath of men
> That through the world admires his manliness.
>
> (29–32)

As we saw above, MacDonald Jackson showed that the stage direction for the returning hero's entry in this play exactly parallels that for *Titus Andronicus*.[37] Jackson also pointed out significant parallels between the

---

[36] G. Sarrazin, *William Shakespeares Lehrjahre* (Weimar, 1897), p. 47; my translation.
[37] M. P. Jackson, 'Stage Directions and Speech Headings in Act 1 of *Titus Andronicus* Q (1594): Shakespeare or Peele?', *SB* 49 (1996): 134–48, at pp. 136–7.

dramaturgy of the first scene in this 'Romaine Tragedie' and other Peele plays:

> Even the stagecraft indicated by some of the directions seems characteristic of Peele. *Titus Andronicus* is the only play in the Shakespeare canon that begins with an entry 'aloft' followed immediately by entries (at separate doors) onto the main platform, and that proceeds with dialogue between characters on the two levels, and movement up and down. *David and Bethsabe* opens in a similar fashion, with David 'above' viewing Bethsabe below and calling on Cusay to enter at the upper level and then descend in order to fetch Bethsabe to him. In the next scene '*Ioab speakes aboue*', '*Enter Cusay beneath*', and Joab calls on Cusay to 'come vp' to join him, which he does. (Jackson 1996, p. 140)

My summary description of the opening scene of *Titus Andronicus* has emphasized its block composition—units following each other without preparation or interlinking, including several surprising reversals; its symmetrical construction; and its use of spectacle. These are characteristics that several critics have judged typical of Peele's plot structures. A. M. Sampley, in a rather unsympathetic essay,[38] found Peele's plays lacking in unity and coherence. He described *The Araygnement of Paris* as 'little more than a succession of pageants and songs bound together by slight threads of plot', violating unity by the plot's 'poor development' and lack of integration, a 'sudden shift of interest [occurring] in the middle of Act IV' (Sampley 1936, p. 690). But the play also shows a 'balancing or contrasting of one plot with another' (p. 691). *Edward I*, Sampley wrote, 'seems at first reading a maze of disconnected incidents' containing five separate main plots, and no less than seven 'scenes and incidents having little or no connection with these plots' (p. 692). But despite these structural faults the play abounds in 'stage effect', with a 'liberal use of pageantry . . . trumpets, horseplay and skirmishes', and 'the paralleling of one situation with another very similar' (p. 694). Sampley showed that two other plays, *The Old Wife's Tale* and *David and Bethsabe*, were similar, having 'a discursive, haphazard' structure enlivened by striking stage effects (p. 700). However, instead of recognizing here several characteristics of Acts 1 and 2 of *Titus Andronicus*, Sampley argued that that play was 'on the whole, well constructed', and so could not have been written by Peele (p. 701). Sampley was concerned to refute the claims made by J. M. Robertson and others for Peele's authorship of *Titus*, but he unwittingly strengthened them.

More recently, Wolfgang Clemen described a deficiency in Peele's dramaturgy by which 'a thread of plot . . . is so often interrupted', with 'many distracting episodes [being] grafted on to it', sometimes producing an 'incoherent succession of heterogeneous episodes' (Clemen 1961, pp. 164, 166). Peele, Clemen judged, is 'much more interested in the effect of the individual

---

[38] A. M. Sampley, 'Plot Structure in Peele's Plays as a Test of Authorship', *PMLA* 51 (1936): 689–701.

episode, and he pays no regard to anything that precedes or follows it' (p. 168). His plays contain a great variety of styles, 'but they are not in any sense assimilated, nor are the changes of tone prepared for' (p. 165). That is certainly true of the several surprising plot developments and reversals in the first act of *Titus Andronicus*. Werner Senn's searching study of Peele in the context of pre-Shakespearian drama brought out several other aspects of plot construction resembling the first act of *Titus*. Peele regularly juxtaposed parallel situations, so as to materialize 'the basic conflict in visual terms but in an utterly static manner' (Senn 1973, p. 92). Senn found that 'Peele's repetition of scenic situations and character-groupings remains somewhat mechanical and lifeless' in general (p. 208), and particularly in *Edward I* (pp. 98, 105), although in *David and Bethsabe* the antithetically opposed elements do converge (p. 156). I noted the same use of opposed character-groupings in *Titus Andronicus*, together with unprepared motivation and surprising reversals. Similarly, Senn diagnosed a 'blatant lack' of motivation in Peele's drama (p. 102), and noted the frequent presence of unconnected, unmotivated material (pp. 97, 101, 103, etc.). His plays abound in 'sudden reversals' (pp. 93, 205), and can use 'a stunning surprise' to work up dramatic tension, but at the cost of organic plot development (pp. 101, 205). If such local dramaturgical effects typify Peele's scenes in *Titus Andronicus*, the long-term effect of his plots is also very similar. In Senn's description,

Peele shows a predilection for a wealth of incidents which he is usually unable to arrange in a unified pattern. But the basic structure he uses in all three plays discussed here is the same: it consists of two antithetical strands of action of a varying degree of coherence . . . meeting in one or more points of contact and crisis, until one of the opponents is annihilated. (p. 160)

That is exactly the pattern found in the opening act of *Titus*, with the rise of Saturninus and Tamora and the successive defeats of Bassianus, Lavinia, and Titus. It is carried on in the following acts through the murder of Bassianus, the rape of Lavinia, the execution of Quintus and Martius, and Titus' final revenge. Peele, too, had paid his dues to the Senecan revenge tragedy, as Senn showed (pp. 57–9). Shakespeare ably worked out the consequences of the revenge plot, introducing a brilliant reversal by which Titus, with the new-found skills of a Machiavel, outwits Tamora and Saturninus, managing to 'o'erreach them in their own devices' (5.2.143).

Senn's analysis of Peele's characteristic dramaturgy was endorsed by A. R. Braunmuller, in particular his use of 'repetition for emphasis and structure'.[39] Braunmuller himself commented that in *The Battle of Alcazar*, as elsewhere in Peele, all too often 'stiff formality and heavily ritualized scenes substitute for conflict among the characters or for a single character's introspection. Most debates or hints of debate quickly become occasions for exhortation'

[39] A. R. Braunmuller, *George Peele* (Boston, 1983), p. 105.

(Braunmuller 1983, p. 82). Peele's plays abound in 'ceremonial and formal-ized effects', striking stage pictures echoing 'a patterned, ritualized stage action' (pp. 82–3). *Edward I* shows Peele trying to bring 'clarity and symme-try' out of the recalcitrant source-material (p. 94), yet allowing space for sen-sational reversals: Queen Elinor, 'at first loving and tender, becomes suddenly vicious' (p. 91). *David and Bethsabe*, Braunmuller showed, abounds in sudden transitions (p. 112), 'abrupt emotional changes' (p. 111), 'extraordi-nary swings of emotion and spirit', not found in the biblical source, creating a pattern 'deliberate and imposed' by Peele (p. 117). We recognize there several characteristics of Peele's dramaturgy in his four scenes for *Titus Andronicus*.

If we widen the term dramaturgy to embrace not just the organization of drama but its content, or recurring situations, we can bring out another important link between Peele's other plays and *Titus Andronicus*, the repre-sentation on stage of physical violence and sensational or shocking acts. Peele's choice and handling of subject-matter was often arranged to accom-modate extreme violence. The opening dumb show in *The Battle of Alcazar* shows Muly Mahamet ushering his two young brothers to their bed, then swiftly returning: '*Enter the Moore and two murdrers bringing in his Unkle Abdelmunen; then they draw the curtains and smoother the yong princes in the bed. . . . Which done in sight of the unkle, they strangle him in his chaire, and then goe forth*' (stage directions, 26 ff.). The Presenter promises that 'Nemesis high mistres of revenge' will soon arouse the Furies 'To range and rage, and vengeance to inflict | Vengeance on this accursed Moore for sinne' (39–40), and indeed a main thread of retribution in this gory play emerges from the initial act of violence presented in the opening scene (as in *Titus*). Soon Rubin Archis, Abdelmunen's widow, is pronouncing her dedication to avenging his murder:

> Of death, of bloud, of wreake, and deepe revenge,
> Shall Rubin Archis frame her tragicke songs,
> In bloud, in death, in murther and misdeede,
> This heavens mallice did begin and end.
>
> (162–5)

Abdelmelec describes her utterance—the text is heavily abridged, and some speeches were once clearly longer—in terms of a ritual:

> Rubin these rites to Abdelmunens ghost,
> Have pearst by this to Plutos grave below,
> The bels of Pluto ring revenge amaine . . .
>
> (166–9)

This sequence bears comparison with Titus' announcement of 'the rites that we intend' (*Tit.*, 1.1.78), 'our Roman rites' (142), performed to appease the

surviving sons, who 'for their brethren slain | Religiously . . . ask a sacrifice'
(123–4).

Retribution is never slow in Peele's drama. In Act 2 the Presenter tells us
that the 'barbarous Moore' Muly Mahamet has been already deposed by
Abdelmelec, and now lives 'forlorne among the mountaine shrubs', existing
on 'the flesh of savage beasts' (307–10). He soon enters *with raw flesh upon*
his sworde' (s.d., 536) intended for his wife Calypolis (537), repeatedly
urging her to 'Feede then and faint not faire Calypolis' (548, 561, 568)—an
utterance eagerly parodied by Shakespeare and others. In the scene following
Moorish ambassadors demonstrate their integrity by putting their hands into
'a blasing brand of fire' (590–606). The dumb show preceding Act 4 presents
a grisly feast given by Mahamet to the King of Portugal, which cannot help
remind us of the climactic revenge banquet in *Titus Andronicus*:

> *Enter a banket brought in by two moores. Enter to the bloudie banket Sebastian,*
> *Muly Mahamet, the Duke of Avero, and Stukley. To them enter Death and three*
> *Furies, one with Dead mens heads in dishes, another with Dead mens bones.*
> *Exeunt shew.* (s.d., 984 ff.)

In the surviving 'Plott' to this play the stage direction specifies that the actors
should include 'one with blood to Dy lights: one with dead mens heads
in dishes: another with Dead mens bones', so we may be sure that this is
exactly how the scene was staged. Throughout *Alcazar* Peele strives for violent, shocking effects, the final dumb show including '*Lightning and thun-*
der', '*Heere the blazing Starre*', and '*Fire workes*', predicting the fall of kings
(s.d., 1165 ff.). The rebel Tom Stukely is stabbed by his own Italian soldiers,
and '*dyeth*' after a long speech, his corpse remaining on stage (1321–72). The
corpse of Abdelmelec is put to better use in a 'pollitique' stratagem, being
dressed in his usual apparel and 'set . . . in his chayre with cunning props', so
that his soldiers will imagine that he's still alive (1242–7). As for the evil Muly
Mahamet, his corpse suffers a suitably deterrent transformation:

> His skin we will be parted from his flesh,
> And being stifned out and stuft with strawe,
> So to deterre and feare the lookers on,
> From anie such foule fact or bad attempt.

> (1443–6)

Throughout his plays Peele showed a keen appreciation of the pain and
humiliation that can be inflicted on the human body, nowhere more vividly
than in *Edward I*. The rebellious Lluellen, Prince of Wales, angry that King
Edward has stolen his fiancée, Elinor de Monfort, arranges with his brother,
David of Brecknock, that when the King lays siege to their castle he will pre-
tend to threaten David's life. They appear on the castle walls, '*Meredith hold-*
ing David by the collar, with a Dagger in his hande' (s.d., 830 ff.), and proceed

to carry out their threats: '*Meredith stabs him into the armes and shoulders*' (s.d., 894 f.), while Lluellen displays to Edward some other 'tooles': '*He showes him hote Pinsers*' (s.d., 897). But at the last moment Lluellen finds another mode of torture: '*He cuts his nose*' (s.d., 903), David pretending to cry out in pain. Meredith urges Lluellen to 'sacrifice this Tike in her sight, her friend, which beeing done, one of your soldiers may dip his foule shirt in his bloud . . .' (944–6), but Edward gives in, to prevent further suffering. These tortures may be a stratagem, but they are carried out realistically, like the other forms of violence in the play. In one of Peele's abrupt plot developments, Edward's Queen, Elinor of Castile, hitherto gentle and womanly, suddenly demands that all Englishmen shall cut off their beards, and their women cut off their right breasts (1633–50). Edward outwits her by offering himself as an example of the first punishment, inviting her to undergo the second.

Foiled in this attempt 'to give your English pride a Spanish brave', Elinor vents her anger on Maris, wife of the Lord Mayor of London, who had previously offended her. She orders her servant to 'binde her in the chaire' and 'draw forth her brest', on which they let an adder 'sucke his fil' (2090–2108). Gloating over Maris's agonies as the snake bites her—'Now she is a Nurse, sucke on sweet Babe'—Elinor leaves Maris tied in the chair, and '*Here she dies*', another vivid action which awkwardly leaves the body on stage. The next scene shows the end of the defeated Welsh: '*Enter Lluellen running out before, and David with a halter ready to hang himselfe*' (2108). David flees, but '*Lluellen is slain with a Pike staffe*' (2128), and his corpse is taken away to be decapitated. Queen Elinor, evil rampant, curses and blasphemes, and for her sins the ground suddenly swallows her up (2196–9), a spectacle advertised on the title-page of the 1593 Quarto, promising 'the sinking of Queen Elinor, who suncke at Charing Cross and rose again at Potters Hithe'. Having magically reappeared she reveals all her evil deeds, including fornication before marriage, and having begotten a bastard daughter with a Friar. Then '*Queen Elinor dies*' (s.d., 2506). When her daughter, Joan of Acon, is informed of her true parentage, '*Shee sodainly dies at the Queenes beds feete*' (s.d., 2607), leaving another corpse to be carried off stage. Other graphic stage directions include '*Enter David drawn on a hurdle*', being carried off to execution, '*with Lluellens head on a speare*' (2362), and '*Enter Mortimor with the head*' of Joan (2674), so that her husband can take his tearful farewell, at which point the play ends.

A. R. Braunmuller, having commented on Queen Elinor's 'sadistic demand' for mutilating English women, and the 'grotesque cruelty' with which she tortures the Lady Mayoress, fairly concluded that 'although Marlowe has a modern reputation for staging violence, *Edward I* exceeds in variety and number the scenes of cruelty shown in Marlowe's plays' (Braunmuller 1983, pp. 90, 91, 99). We know that *Edward I* was a popular play, Henslowe earning well from fourteen performances between August 1595 and July 1596

(p. 87), as audiences evidently enjoyed Peele's feast of horrors. When Peele treated a biblical subject, in *The Love of King David and Fair Bethsabe. With the Tragedie of Absalom*, he chose material from the Second Book of Samuel which presents an interlocking series of transgressions. David, King of Israel, spying Bethsabe bathing, sleeps with her (23–156), an adultery which has several disastrous consequences. David's son, Ammon, conceives an incestuous love for his half-sister Tamar, and with the help of Jonadab lures her to his bed and rapes her (in the biblical account, 'being stronger than she, [he] forced her, and lay with her': 2 Sam. 13: 14). Jonadab is left on stage while the rape takes place, and vividly imagines Tamar's unpreparedness for 'an action of such violence', carried out by 'Ammons lusty armes, | Sinnewd with vigor of his kindlesse love' (292–5). This dwelling on the violence of rape bears comparison with the treatment of Lavinia in *Titus Andronicus*. The play dramatizes with equal gusto Absalom's revenge murder of Ammon (307–64, 725–67, 853–69), Achitophel's suicide—the stage direction, '*Achitophel solus with a halter*' (1415) echoing one in *Edward I*, and Absalom's famous misfortune. His long hair having got caught in an oak tree—'*The battell, and Absalom hangs by the haire*', Peele specifies (s.d., 1469)—Joab, ignoring Absalom's pathetic appeals, is able to stab his defenceless body: 'Take that as part of thy deserved plague' (1527), he says, some '*five or six soldiours*' finishing him off (1550–61). The relish with which Peele represents these violent transgressions, from an adulterous love scene and a rape to a suicide and a stabbing to death, makes us wonder how much influence he exerted on the plot of *Titus Andronicus*. Co-authors are jointly responsible, of course, but Peele's fondness for scenes involving physical mutilation and violence performed on people unable to defend themselves may well have helped shape a plot which includes the sudden killing of Mutius (his corpse left lying on stage unattended), the rape and mutilation of Lavinia, Titus being fooled into chopping off his own hand, and the final banquet of horrors. Peele's special expertise with corporeal mutilation may have set the direction that the plot would take, leaving Shakespeare to flesh out the detail, so to speak.

This brief account of Peele's dramaturgy has described both the shape and substance of his preferred plots, which use bold effects—sharp contrasts, symmetrical structures, sudden reversals—and revel in human cruelty. Peele gave his audiences a swiftly moving spectacle, in which violence is a main ingredient, the victims' pleas being swept aside, their suffering represented without sympathy. By describing Peele's characteristic plot choices we can define his individuality, allowing us to recognize the identity between his scenes in *Titus Andronicus* and the rest of his oeuvre. But we can also see that Shakespeare's handling of both form and substance differed greatly. These characteristics of Peele's dramaturgy can be set in greater relief by comparing them with a typically Shakespearian plot sequence. In Peele's Act 2 scene 1, Aaron urges Demetrius and Chiron on to the 'rape and villainy' which they execute in 2.3 and following, written by Shakespeare. Having raped and mutilated Lavinia, gloating over her injuries, they abandon her in the forest (2.4.1–11), where Marcus finds her. While Peele rarely allowed any of his characters to express pity for, or give comfort to, the victims of mutilation, Shakespeare makes this a key element in all his scenes of suffering, from here to *King Lear* and beyond.[40] Marcus expresses at length his horror at whatever 'stern ungentle hands | Hath lopp'd and hew'd' Lavinia's arms, and cut out her tongue. Then he leads her to what will be a shattering confrontation:

> Come let us go, and make thy father blind,
> For such a sight will blind a father's eye
>
> .   .   .   .
>
> Do not draw back, for we will mourn with thee
> O, could our mourning ease thy misery!
>
> (2.4.52–7)

That comforting phrase, 'for we will mourn with thee', already marks a major difference between Shakespeare and Peele. Our knowledge of the shock that awaits Titus adds emotional intensity to the following scene, where we first find Titus pleading in vain with the Roman authorities to spare the life of his sons, unjustly accused of Bassianus' murder (3.1.1–57). The entry of Marcus with Lavinia—'Ay me this object kills me!' Lucius exclaims with anguished sympathy (64)—pushes Titus to new degrees of suffering:

> My grief was at the height before thou cam'st,
> And now like Nilus it disdaineth bounds.
>
> (70–1)

In a marvellously humane sequence, Titus and Marcus respond to Lavinia's mutilations with anguish and deep feeling, their tears matching hers (59–149). Then Aaron enters, with his fiendish pretence that Saturninus will spare the lives of Titus' two sons if someone from their family will chop off his hand, a contest which Titus wins by outwitting Marcus and Lucius, with the ready help of Aaron (150–205). This act provokes Titus to further outcries of anguish (206–33), but his sufferings become even more intense when a Messenger appears, *'with two heads and a hand'*, the sons having been executed all the same (234–40). Marcus and Lucius lament this tragic outcome (241–63), but Titus is silent, finally bursting out in laughter, a remarkable theatrical stroke (264). Having reached a point beyond suffering, with 'not another tear to shed', he devotes all his energies to revenge, while Lucius

---

[40] For an admirable account of compassion in *Titus Andronicus* see Brian Gibbons, 'A Speechless Dialect: Interpreting the Human Body in Shakespeare's Plays', in his *Shakespeare and Multiplicity* (Cambridge, 1993), pp. 48–59. Jacques Berthoud has given a sensitive commentary on this scene in J. Berthoud and S. Massai (eds.), *Titus Andronicus*, New Penguin Shakespeare (London, 2001), pp. 17–22.

goes off to 'raise a pow'r' among the Goths, | To be reveng'd on Rome and Saturnine' (266–300).

Emrys Jones, in a perceptive analysis of this scene,[41] has pointed out that it is 'carefully built in stages: a sequence of steps rising to a climax' (Jones 1985, p. 9). The brief episode following Titus' self-mutilation seems to reach 'a climax of pain and misery', but the real climax comes with Titus' fit of laughter, having 'no tears left, no more feeling or words. . . . This is the turning-point of the scene and of the entire play'. As Jones observes,

> The development of this scene could be described in various figurative ways, but what is essential to it is the idea of tension being increased to an almost intolerable point— the moment when Titus bursts into laughter. The tension is then quickly lost, and shortly after the scene closes. What is remarkable is the way tension is maintained through a long scene, and not only maintained but increased; the dramatist's control over his audience is never lost. (p. 9)

Jones rightly praises 'Shakespeare's feeling for audience response', being able 'to discriminate between degrees of misery, and . . . to distribute climaxes' across moments of relaxation. It seems to me that the dramatist displays another quality here, not found in Peele's scenes, the ability to sustain a focus on the events and feelings represented, making gesture, language, even the absence of language—Lavinia's mutilated silence, Titus' inability to speak— all cohere. As Jones notes, this long scene (300 lines) 'moves through five or six actions', but each addresses the same object, the four members of the Andronicus family and their incremental sufferings. If we took any sequence of 300 lines from Peele's opening scene, we would find a number of episodes, not always related, with many distractions, the whole written in unindividu-alized language, a formulaic style used by everyone present. By contrast, as Jones points out, 'Titus' grief . . . is expressed in several brief exchanges with Marcus and Lucius and in three long speeches, each of which develops an elaborate image-pattern. There is no wandering or inconsequentiality; each unit of action has its own form', and its own tempo. When the scene is acted, 'it seems to flow with an unpremeditated naturalness', but in reality 'the whole movement is deliberately planned so that everything occurs in the order best suited to the emotional effect' (p. 10). Digressions are eliminated, 'nothing is allowed to distract from the single-minded onward progression of the scene's movement (its continuousness is essential to the effect)' (p. 13). These qualities, the ability to concentrate on a single terrible action without distraction, to represent, and to share human suffering and human sympathy, orchestrating all the elements of drama into a coherent whole, mark Shakespeare's dramaturgy in these scenes as being quite distinct from Peele's, making this play a worthy precursor of *Othello* and *King Lear*.

The un-Shakespearian dramaturgy of Act 1 of *Titus* was attested to, rather

[41] E. Jones, *Scenic Form in Shakespeare* (Oxford, 1971; rev. edn., 1985), pp. 8–13.

obliquely, by Stanley Wells in 1984. At this time Wells was convinced of Shakespeare's sole authorship, and he simply assumed that he could discuss such matters as 'Shakespeare's carelessness in not providing' an entry for characters at the beginning of the first scene,[42] one of several points which showed that 'Shakespeare was thinking in terms of his fiction, not of his stage' (p. 87). Wells magnanimously suggested that 'Shakespeare himself may have' forgotten about the Tribunes and Senators being on stage (p. 88), as some editors have done, and he believed that he could tell just when 'Shakespeare changed his mind during the process of composition about who should take part in a particular scene' (p. 92). Wells's certainty that Shakespeare wrote the play, however, coexisted uneasily with a generally negative view of the dramatic structure of Act 1. He was quite critical about the sequence where Titus kills his son Mutius (1.1.290 ff.), after which the imperial party re-enters 'aloft', not having been given any direction to leave the stage: 'it is poor stage-craft', Wells commented (p. 99). Wells was willing to blame 'the uncertainties of this passage' on a messy 'foul-papers text', or even on Shakespeare revising 'in the course of composition', but he never entertained the possibility of collaboration. Rather surprisingly, Wells then endorsed John Dover Wilson's confident account of how this play was written:

> it is generally agreed that the sacrifice of Alarbus, earlier in the scene, is an addition; Dover Wilson plausibly argued that the later episode of the burial of Mutius is another; and if this is so, then it is not improbable that, as Wilson also suspected ([1948,] p. xxxvi), the slaying of Mutius, too, is an addition; he is, as Wilson says, 'a quite unnecessary complication'; moreover, and in spite of the fate in store for Aaron, people are usually dead before they are buried, and if Shakespeare, in his earlier draft, had killed Mutius he would probably also have arranged to dispose of him. (pp. 99–100)

It may be 'generally agreed'—although, as I have argued, erroneously—that the sacrifice of Alarbus was an addition, but Wilson's further suggestions, that the burial of Mutius (1.1.341–90) is another insertion, that these lines could be omitted, and that 'the text gains much and loses nothing by the omission',[43] have been ignored, evidently not seeming to many Shakespearians at all 'plausible'.[44] The really strange thing about Wells's subsequent argument,

---

[42] S. Wells, *Re-Editing Shakespeare for the Modern Reader* (Oxford, 1984), p. 86.

[43] J. D. Wilson (ed.), Shakespeare, *Titus Andronicus* (Cambridge, 1948), p. xxxvi.

[44] Marco Mincoff objected that it is only when the three-and-a-half lines that editors excise are 'read outside their context' that anyone could imagine 'that the sacrifice of Alarbus has already been completed, and therefore the episode of the sacrifice is a later insertion'. He added: 'It certainly is not true, as Dover Wilson maintained, that if we omit the sacrifice the pieces join on without a break. Titus makes his funeral speech, rounding it off with a peroration invoking peace on his sons' remains as he is about to consign them to the tomb, a peroration that concludes appropriately with a rhymed couplet. Then follows the supposed insertion, and Titus is once more called upon to conclude the ceremony of the entombment, which he does, repeating the substance of his first peroration, but in a more lyrical vein, with an intricate interweaving of word patterns. Standing by itself as it does, it is effective, but not as a second peroration to a speech that

however, will be invisible to the non-specialist reader unless he consults the 1948 Cambridge edition, namely that Wells was quoting from the sequence where Dover Wilson, *having established Peele's authorship of this act*, went on to discuss 'How it all happened', starting with 'yet another indication of the hand of Peele in Act 1' (p. xxxiv). In other words, Wells took over Wilson's rather tetchy objections to Peele's stagecraft—Mutius as 'a quite unnecessary complication'—but applied them to Shakespeare, silently suppressing any indication that the target of these criticisms was in fact Peele. As for Wilson's comment on Mutius, which Wells endorsed, it seems to me that Mutius, far from being 'unnecessary' to Peele and Shakespeare, is a crucial figure in the plot, for Titus' killing of his son shows how much he is prepared to sacrifice in his personal life in order to maintain his sense of duty, a moral principle against which the ingratitude of Saturninus stands out all the more glaringly. Equally, the sequence where Titus' brother and his three surviving sons finally succeed in persuading the general to allow Mutius to be buried, an action that is then solemnly performed, is an affecting (if somewhat long-drawn-out) scene on stage, arousing pathos and restoring some humanity to Titus.

Wells's discussion of this scene continued in a direction which is becoming familiar. The conservator of Shakespeare identifies clumsiness and repetition in a text which he is determined to take as Shakespeare's, and then postulates a complicated series of first drafts, revisions, additions, deletions that should have been made but were not, and so on. The simpler hypothesis, that we have here another instance of Peele's vigorous but chaotic dramaturgy, is ignored. Instead, Wells argued that in the immediately following 'episode, too, piecemeal composition might be suspected', for at this point 'Lucius accuses Titus of injustice in killing Mutius', and Titus responds:

> Nor thou, nor he, are any sons of mine;
> My sons would never so dishonour me
>
> (1.1.294–5)

As Wells noted,

Then follows the self-contained, upper-level episode, after which the substance of this interchange is repeated, this time between Marcus and Titus. Like Lucius, Marcus points out to Titus that he has killed his son:

has already had one, precisely similar in content. But we can hardly relegate it also to the insertion, for Lavinia, who now enters, takes up the burden of Titus' closing lines, and weaves it into her own words of welcome, in a manner reminiscent of Peele.' As for 'the other supposed addition', the burial of Mutius (1.1.341–91), Mincoff judged it 'not so essential to the action as this, though obviously something of the kind is needed to dispose of the corpse left prostrate on the stage. Mutius, with the family tomb lying so close to hand, could hardly be carried unceremoniously off, nor yet consigned to the grave without some sort of formality. And again the omission does not result in a smooth join, for it leaves Titus to spring without preparation from offence at being passed over by the new bride to a happy conviction that she must be grateful and nobly remunerate him. The mere detachability of an episode is not enough to stamp it as an insertion—for that a break in the texture of the style must be proved' (Mincoff 1976, p. 213).

> O *Titus* see: O see what thou hast done
> In a bad quarrell slaine a vertuous sonne. (341–2)

Titus again disowns those who, he believes, have dishonoured him:

> No foolish Tribune, no: No sonne of mine,
> Nor thou, nor these, confederates in the deede,
> That hath dishonoured all our Familie,
> Vnworthy brother, and vnworthy sonnes. (343–6)

Instead of recognizing that, as Dover Wilson had shown in great detail in the immediately preceding section of his introduction, such symmetrical patterning, echoing lines just spoken, is eminently characteristic of Peele, Wells weakly suggested that 'the repetitions of the rebukes to Titus and his self-defence may seem simply a way of recalling the situation to the audience's mind' (p. 103) . . . a mere fifty lines later. Finding another 'oddity of the stage-craft' in that Mutius' body, lacking any stage direction to the contrary, remains on stage 'throughout the upper-level episode'—an indifference to the presence of a corpse often shown by Peele—Wells complained that this

episode merely makes explicit what is already implicit—that Saturninus is taking Tamora to himself—and it would be easy to believe that Shakespeare originally intended to move straight from the killing of Mutius to his burial; but this conflicts with the notion, also plausible, that the killing and burial of Mutius are themselves interpolations. Shakespeare could not have interpolated a scene into one that was not written . . . (ibid.)

True enough. But whoever reads Peele will find many instances of scenes making dreadfully explicit things that seem obvious to an experienced modern theatregoer. Wells got 'Shakespeare' out of this difficulty by postulating that 'Mutius' body should not remain on stage, but should be dragged off by Lucius after the killing, and carried back again by Marcus' and others later on (surely a rather undignified way for a brother and uncle to treat a corpse), although he conceded that 'Shakespeare appears not to have written directions for these happenings' (ibid.).

I accept that many stage directions are lacking in early drama texts, but what disturbs me here is Wells's refusal ever to consider the presence of another hand in the play, and his ever-deeper plunge into speculations about passages having been added, revised, deleted, and so forth. Thus, one 'anomaly in the Quarto has been explained by the hypothesis that when the burial of Mutius was added the episodes were not brought fully into consonance with another . . .' (p. 104). Or again, 'It is possible that, as Shakespeare wrote the interpolated episode of Mutius' burial, he forgot that he needed to leave Titus' sons on stage . . .' (ibid.). As Wells's notes show, other eminent Shakespearians, such as W. W. Greg and R. B. McKerrow, were forced to indulge in similarly complex hypotheses to 'save the phenomenon' of

Shakespeare's sole authorship. It is rather incongruous, however, that Wells should have cited Dover Wilson's speculations when Wilson, all along, was arguing that 'we find Peele adding to his own play in Act 1, doing so in a manner which shows him compelled to *contrive* his additions, and not making a very neat job of it' (Wilson 1948, p. xxxvii). Shakespeare, Wilson believed, 'was called in to help Peele expand' the play partly because he was known to be writing *The Rape of Lucrece*, but mainly because 'The earl of Sussex's men were in a hurry' (ibid.). The play needed padding, Wilson thought, because he had just claimed 'that in the 1594 text two insertions . . . may be detected in Act 1, amounting to over a hundred lines when taken together', so that the act *was once shorter* than its present length by about a fifth'. The play's original length, then, must have been about 2,000 lines, 'and *for all we know, may have been a good deal shorter still*' (p. xxxvi; my italics). To all such speculations, 'for all we know', I can only answer with Wittgenstein, '*Wovon man nicht reden kann, sollte man schweigen*'.

At all events, it is clear that in 1984 Stanley Wells was faithfully following Dover Wilson's theories on how Peele's text was expanded by Shakespeare, while diligently suppressing any mention of Peele's name. His debt to Dover Wilson became even clearer in the Appendix to his book, which presented 'Shakespeare's First Draft of Act One of *Titus Andronicus*: A Conjectural Reconstruction' (pp. 114–25). This edition is the logical consequence of Wilson's theories, for as Wells explained, it 'omits the passages which there is reason to believe that Shakespeare added after his initial act of composition, that is, the episode of the sacrifice of Alarbus [1.1.96–149], Mutius' attempt to assist Bassianus in abducting Lavinia and Titus' killing of him (ll. 287–8, 289–98), the burial of Mutius (ll. 341–90), and Bassianus' subsequent allusion to the killing (l. 418)' (p. 114). The result is indeed, as Wilson surmised, an act which is one hundred lines shorter than in the Quarto or Folio texts. Wells made the three major cuts silently, the lines being renumbered to run consecutively, but for the fourth he simply suppressed the line 'With his own hand did slay his youngest son', leaving an empty line in the text, its absence marked by square brackets:

> This Noble Gentleman Lord *Titus* here,
> Is in opinion and in honour wrongd,
> That in the rescue of *Lavinia*,
> [   ]
> In zeale to you, and highly movde to wrath,
> To be controwld in that he frankelie gave,
> Receave him then to favour Saturnine . . .
>
> (p. 122)

Unfortunately, as every reader can see, the omission leaves the sense incomplete, and draws attention to an unnecessary and unsuccessful piece of surgery.

Wells believed that he had 'dealt empirically with a variety of features' concerning editing play-texts (p. 108)—the word 'empirically' suggesting pure logic, unaccompanied by theory, a naïve belief that one can act without having any theoretical assumptions—and he criticized J. C. Maxwell for being 'conservative' (p. 89). Yet Wells's own position on the co-authorship issue in this play was far more conservative than Maxwell's, and his unwillingness to consider the evidence for Peele's share in it made his theorizing anything but empirical. It seems as if Wells's drastic alterations to Act 1 were largely motivated by his aesthetic objections to its dramaturgy; if so, they could have been obviated had he recognized its many affinities with the stagecraft of George Peele. Fortunately, by the time the one-volume Oxford edition appeared in 1986, Wells had largely abandoned Wilson's theories, printing an almost complete Act 1, apart from two omitted passages.[45]

On the basis of this discussion we can conclude that Peele and Shakespeare neatly divided their writing assignments, the older dramatist setting the play in motion, writing Act 1 and the first two scenes of Act 2, while contributing the later scene (4.1) in which Lavinia identifies her harmers. In their discussions drafting the plot Peele and Shakespeare evidently agreed to emphasize certain features throughout, notably the motif of ingratitude. In Peele's opening scene, after the Emperor Saturninus has repaid Titus' generosity and self-sacrifice with injury and insult, Tamora warns him to

> Dissemble all your griefs and discontents
> .   .   .   .
> Lest then the people, and patricians too,
> Upon a just survey take Titus' part,
> And so supplant you for ingratitude,
> Which Rome reputes to be a heinous sin.
>
> (1.1.493–8)

In a later scene Peele made Marcus applaud young Lucius' resolve to destroy enemies:

> Ay, that's my boy! Thy father hath full oft
> For his ungrateful country done the like.
>
> (4.1.110–11)

---

[45] These passages are relegated to the end of the play, and printed under the Oxford soubriquet for all the parts of Shakespeare's text which the editors rejected for one reason or another, 'Additional passages' (they should really be called 'Subtracted passages'). They include those three-and-a-half lines found in the First Quarto but in no subsequent early edition and which 'presumably should have been deleted'; and another (1.1.284–6) which Wells (and presumably Taylor) find 'difficult to reconcile with the apparent need for Saturninus and his party to leave the stage at 275.1–2 before entering "above" at 294.2–4. It is omitted from our text in the belief that Shakespeare intended it to be deleted after adding the episode of Mutius' killing to his original draft, and that the printers of Q1 included it by accident' (p. 171). Speculation reigns; Peele is absent; *plus ça change* . . .

Similarly, in Shakespeare's scene, where Titus and his friends fire arrows to the gods outlining his grievances, Titus describes himself as 'old Andronicus, | Shaken with sorrows in ungrateful Rome' (4.3.16–17), and Marcus urges them to 'Take wreak on Rome for this ingratitude' (34). When Lucius marches on Rome to take his revenge, a Roman compares him to Coriolanus, who wanted to punish Rome's ingratitude (4.4.67–8), and a Goth describes Titus as one

> Whose high exploits and honourable deeds
> Ingrateful Rome requites with foul contempt.
>
> (5.1.11–12)

With this detail Peele and Shakespeare co-ordinated plot and motive.

Given the neat separation between their contributions, there are few places in the play which might show poor co-ordination. The only point where we may find it concerns the relative prominence of Tamora and Aaron. After Tamora has been proclaimed the future Empress of Rome she advises Saturninus to dissemble his 'discontents', and allow her to deal with the Andronici:

> I'll find a day to massacre them all,
> And raze their faction and their family.
>
> (1.1.449–51)

Yet, of course, the malignant queen does not bring about their sufferings: 'they have been devised and, for the most part, executed by a character scarcely noticeable at the beginning of the play . . .'.[46] J. S. G. Bolton observed that 'the black-faced scoundrel who for three acts displaces Tamora as protagonist of evil' appears in the stage directions for Act 1 (after lines 69, 291, 298), but does not speak until 'his racial superiors have withdrawn', when he tells us 'of his illicit love for his royal mistress' (Bolton 1933, p. 212). Aaron declares both his love and desire to 'mount aloft' with Tamora (2.1.1–25), and intervenes in the dispute between Chiron and Demetrius with 'policy and stratagem', urging them to abduct Lavinia and rape her (104–32).

As Peele handles him, Aaron is evil, but his speeches are predictable, lumbering in their argument, not witty. Every theatregoer and reader notices the difference when Shakespeare takes over his part two scenes later, as Aaron enters carrying a bag of gold and directly addresses us:

> He that had wit would think that I had none,
> To bury so much gold under a tree,
> And never after to inherit it.
> Let him that thinks of me so abjectly
> Know that this gold must coin a stratagem,

---

[46] J. S. G. Bolton, '*Titus Andronicus*: Shakespeare at Thirty', *SP* 30 (1933): 208–24, at p. 211.

Which, cunningly effected, will beget
A very excellent piece of villainy

(2.3.1–7)

Aaron's zest, his patent enjoyment of the sufferings he inflicts, his witty and
unfeeling commentary on them, all make him an attractive theatrical figure,
obviously indebted to Barabas in Marlowe's *Jew of Malta*, and looking forward to Richard III. Further, he lends a new sense of direction to the play. As
A. K. Gray wrote, 'outrage and horror abound' in the first two acts, 'but
whereas the rhetorician of Act 1 staggers clumsily from one horror to the
other, without stopping to wait, explain or analyze, the poet of Act 2 fore-
shadows his horrors by omens, dreams, and ironical asides . . .'.[47] The chief
agent of this foreshadowing is Aaron:

> Aaron looks an act ahead, and allows his audience to do likewise. He can be seen to
> plant the gold and the incriminating letter. He is heard to give instructions to the queen
> and her two sons. He is then observed as he works out the villainy step by step, impli-
> cating first Bassianus, then his bride, and, lastly, her two brothers, while at the same
> time so bewildering Titus and his remaining son with his sudden strokes that they are
> powerless to interfere. (Bolton 1933, p. 223)

His machinations may seem puerile to a sophisticated modern audience, yet
they were a great improvement on anything in Marlowe, Kyd, or Peele; and
Shakespeare continued to use 'similar structural devices' up to Edmund's
forged letter in *King Lear*, and Iago's manipulation of his conversation with
Cassio for Othello's benefit. 'Shakespeare took always much comfort in
dropped letters and overheard conversations' (ibid.).

Aaron, we might say, is the play's controlling intelligence for much of the
time. Yet, at the play's climax, when Titus takes a spectacular revenge on
Tamora for the crimes committed by her sons, Aaron's declaration of his
responsibility for suggesting the rape, and his revelation of all his subsequent
deeds, are made to Lucius (5.1.20–151), and Titus never learns who has been
the secret agent of his sufferings. Lucius, again, is entrusted with Aaron's final
punishment (5.1.1–16, 175–91). Aaron's fate is unrelated to that of the characters in the main plot, a failure in co-ordination that Shakespeare did not
make for Iago, or Edmund. In the First Quarto the play ends with six lines
execrating 'that ravenous tiger, Tamora', but (presumably) the editor of the
Second Quarto, who worked from a defective copy of the first edition, added
four lines marking the chief villain:

> See justice done on Aaron that damn'd Moor,
> By whom our heavy haps had their beginning:
> Then afterwards to order well the state,
> That like events may ne'er it ruinate.

---

[47] A. K. Gray, 'Shakespeare and *Titus Andronicus*', *SP* 25 (1928): 295–311, at p. 298.

Certainly Aaron had become one of the play's main characters, his role (353 lines) being second in length only to that of Titus (709), and ahead of both Marcus (313) and Tamora (256). It may be that Shakespeare developed the role far beyond what he and Peele had originally conceived, and this may have fulfilled a desire to give a leading role to a young male actor. (Tamora, an older woman, could have been an adult actor's role.) Tamora does not fade out of the action, but she never fulfils the vengeance she had threatened, and when she again occupies the centre of the stage (4.4, 5.2), as Dover Wilson observed, 'her scheming is foolish and ineffectual' (Wilson 1948, p. xi). Accepting Bolton's suggestion that co-authorship had resulted in uncoordination, Wilson judged that the liaison between Tamora and Aaron, 'stressed at the opening of Act 2, possesses no further dramatic significance . . . except in respect of its offspring, the black baby'. Many critics, however, have welcomed this plot invention as showing Shakespeare deliberately balancing Aaron's villainy with a father's humanity. 'Another anomaly', Wilson noted, 'is that though Tamora is Queen of the defeated Goths, it is to the Goths that Lucius son of Titus repairs to enlist help and raise an army against her and the emperor her husband' (ibid.).[48] These slight inconsistencies do not diminish the play's power, then or now (it continued in repertoire until 1606, at least), but they indicate some problems that Shakespeare and Peele had in unifying their joint labour.

TIMON OF ATHENS

Inconsistencies of several kinds confront us in *Timon of Athens*, as critics have long recognized. In the preface to his edition of the play in the early 1840s, Charles Knight identified Shakespearian and non-Shakespearian elements in style, characterization, and plotting. The opening scene, in which the Poet describes his allegory of Fortune's hill, where currently Timon's 'present grace' attracts flatterers and parasites who will abandon him 'When Fortune in her shift and change of mood | Spurns down her late beloved' (1.1.92–4), Knight recognized as typically Shakespearian: 'The foreshadowing of the fate of Timon in the conclusion of this dialogue is part of the almost invariable system by which Shakspere very early infuses into his audience a dim notion of the catastrophe, most frequently indeed in the shape of some presentiment'.[49] But in other parts of the play Knight observed a 'want of connexion' between scenes, as in the puzzling dialogue between Apemantus, the Fool, and the Page (2.2.46–118), where Knight conceded that 'it was of little consequence whether [the Fool's] speeches had any very strict connexion with the

---

[48] See 3.1.286; 4.2.173; 4.4.27–38; 5.1.16.
[49] C. Knight, *Studies of Shakspere* (London, 1849), p. 71.

more important scenes' (p. 73). Far more disturbing, however, was the scene (3.5) where Alcibiades pleaded to the Athenian Senate to pardon a friend of his, convicted of murder. Knight had shown that 'the internal evidence of thought and style' would ascribe this whole scene to the co-author, and he now pointed to its curiously unrelated existence in the plot:

this scene of the banishment of Alcibiades, and the concluding scene of his return to Athens, appear to belong to a drama of which the story of this brave and profligate Athenian formed a much more important feature than in the present play. That story stands here strictly as an episode. The banishment of Alcibiades is perfectly unconnected with the misanthropy of Timon; the return of Alcibiades takes place after Timon's death. We feel no interest in either event. Ulrici has noticed the uncertain connexion of this drama as a whole, particularly in the scene before us, 'where it remains quite unknown who is the unfortunate friend for whom Alcibiades petitions so earnestly that he is banished for it'.[50] In Shakspere's hand the banishment of Alcibiades is only used in connexion with the wonderful scene in the fourth act. (p. 74)

That is, his confrontation with Timon (4.3.49–175). Knight pointed to another dislocation in the plot, the extremely vague stage direction opening 3.6, 'Enter divers Friends at several doors', which hardly squares with 'the previous scenes in which these friends are introduced' and named, that is, 3.1 to 3.4. But since Knight had expressed doubts whether this sequence was by Shakespeare, this would explain the discrepancy.

　　Nikolaus Delius also argued that the play's dramaturgy, like its language, clearly showed the presence of two writers. As he pointed out, following Knight, Shakespeare 'regularly prepared his audience for an imminent peripeteia or catastrophe, never using the bombshell of surprise'.[51] While Shakespeare works by preparation, his co-author introduces without warning the scene (3.5) of Alcibiades pleading to the Senators of Athens for the life of some friend of his,

a nameless, unknown person who has never been mentioned before and never will be again . . . One can search the whole Shakespeare canon in vain for a scene thrust so suddenly between the ones surrounding it. This is quite unlike Shakespeare's art of allowing each scene to develop organically from the one preceding, never introducing a new thread into the fabric of a play which is not directly tied to one already existing. (p. 350)

The co-author's scenes also show inadequate motivation, Delius judged (p. 338), as in 3.2, where, 'in order to provide Lucius with an interlocutor, the co-author introduces three "strangers" in a clumsy and unmotivated way' (p. 348). In characterization, too, Delius pointed to some inconsistencies of motivation. The Senate scene was supposed to account for Alcibiades

　　[50] Hermann Ulrici, *Ueber Shakespeare's dramatische Kunst und sein Verhältnis zu Calderon und Göthe* (Halle, 1839), p. 254.
　　[51] N. Delius, 'Ueber Shakespeare's Timon of Athens', *ShJb* 2 (1867): 335–61, at p. 343; my tanslations.

reappearing as a Nemesis to Athens, but this motif is incoherently attached to the citizens' treatment of Timon, as if they—not his own prodigality—were responsible for his transformation from 'imperceptive philanthrope to imperceptive misanthrope' (p. 351). In their confrontation in Act 4, however, where Alcibiades recalls that he had earlier

> heard, and grieved,
> How cursed Athens, mindless of thy worth,
> Forgetting thy great deeds when neighbour states,
> But for thy sword and fortune, trod upon them

> (4.3.93–6)

at this point, 'Alcibiades suddenly emerges as no longer the avenger of his own disgrace, or that of his nameless friend, condemned to death, but as the avenger of the injustice that has befallen Timon', a plot development which Delius dismissed as 'forced and inconsistent' (p. 354). As we now know, Middleton was responsible for 3.5, Shakespeare for 4.3, and evidently their treatments were never co-ordinated. Similarly in the final sequence of this scene, written by Middleton (4.3.458–536), Delius commented: 'that Timon should affirm that he loves Flavius, taking him for a woman on account of his tears [482–6], totally contradicts the explicitly formulated character of a misanthrope who hates all mankind, men and women, without exception' (p. 356). As Delius observed, one need only compare Shakespeare's scene where Timon attacks Phrynia and Timandra, or his preceding soliloquies (4.1.1–41, 4.3.1–48), to put this point beyond doubt. Middleton's arousing of pathos, we might say, is totally consistent with his intensely emotional style throughout the play, a pathos which is well suited to Flavius but utterly inconsistent with Timon at this stage in his experience.

F. G. Fleay, having used several stylistic criteria to distinguish the co-authors, also pointed to differences in the dramaturgy. Fleay tended to worship Shakespeare, and to denigrate whichever unknown writer had been rash enough to alter any of his work, but he did make a fruitful analysis of the play's content in terms of main and subsidiary plot, diagnosing a weakness in the play, its 'wearisome want of action':

But this fault is due entirely to the passages which I assign to the second writer, not one of which adds anything to the development of the plot, for they are in every instance mere expansions of facts mentioned in the genuine parts of the play. Thus the germ of

	1.2	is in	1.1.270, &c.,
of	3.1–3.3	„	2.2.192,
of	3.4	„	2.2,
of	3.5	„	3.6.61,

and the added parts of Acts 4 and 5 are merely padding to fill out the deficiency in quantity. The Shakspere part is complete in itself, and never flags at all.[52]

---

[52] F. G. Fleay, 'On the Authorship of *Timon of Athens*', *TNSS* 1 (1874): 130–51, at pp. 147–8.

There is a touch of bardolatry in that estimate, but it does suggest that Shakespeare was the chief plotter, leaving Middleton a clearly marked section of the play in which to work out conflicts already prepared for. Fleay went on to indicate 'the main plot', or 'complete story . . . intended by Shakspere to be read as follows':

1 Act.	Timon's prosperity: 1.1 of present play.
2 "	Debts and Duns: 2.1, 2.2 of present play.
3 "	Farewell to Athens: 3.6, 4.1 of present play.
4 "	Cave life, 4.3 (part): 5.1 (1–118) of present play.
5 "	Death and indirect revenge through Alcibiades: 5.1
	(119–231), 5.2, 5.4 of present play. (p. 148)

While it is impossible to reconstruct the original genesis of *Timon*, nothing in Fleay's account would rule out the hypothesis of the play having been a collaboration between two writers working together at the same time. The division of roles left Middleton to dramatize the first banquet; the scenes where Timon's Steward tried to raise money from his friends; Alcibiades' appearance before the Athenian Senate; and the Steward's compassion for his ruined master.

The closer study of the play's structure made by E. H. Wright revealed inconsistencies in characterization and dramaturgy. Character continuity, Wright observed, was poor: 'Persons, and sometimes persons who would seem to be important, come into one scene unexpectedly, disappear hereafter, and remain enigmas' (Wright 1910, p. 2). Like Delius, he drew attention to the lack of preparation with which the scene of Alcibiades' banishment (3.5) is introduced, 'sundered from all else in the play' (p. 44). Further, echoing Knight and Delius, Wright showed that the two authors had treated the Alcibiades plot from two different perspectives. The co-author had dramatized the banishment, which gives Alcibiades a motive for avenging himself on Athens, yet Shakespeare's share of the plot would 'make Alcibiades the avenger of Timon's wrongs rather than of his own' (pp. 72–8). The two conflicting motivations were never reconciled. Wright pointed to another sign of uncoordination between the two dramatists in the treatment of Ventidius. In Shakespeare's 1.1 Timon ransoms Ventidius from a debtor's prison with five talents, a gift which leads us to expect a later scene in which Ventidius would deny Timon's request for help in his time of need. 'Such a refusal would have put the climax on the ingratitude of Timon's friends; and without it the part of Ventidius in the play is pointless' (p. 59). But when the co-author wrote the banquet scene that immediately follows (1.2), he 'could think of no better way to open it than by making Ventidius offer to repay Timon's loan' (1.2.1–7), a plot development by which Ventidius' future role as an ingrate 'is practically nullified'. Subsequently the co-author 'merely mentions the refusal casually in the scene where he displays that of his own Sempronius'

(p. 59)—that is, 3.3.3–8. It is untypical of Shakespeare, Wright noted, that three new characters should be introduced in the second, 'superfluous' dunning scene (3.4), and unlikely that he would show us 'three close friends of Timon pestering him for money' without either prior preparation or a subsequent reference (p. 43).

Between 1849 and 1910, then, these four scholars (two English, one German, one American) identified discrepancies in both characterization and dramaturgy which were uncharacteristic of Shakespeare at any point in his career. As we saw in Chapter 4, G. R. Hibbard repeated these observations in 1970, while avoiding any suggestion of co-authorship. Yet, while agreeing to their collective diagnosis of the play's lack of unity, the initial dramatic impetus was coherently planned. The dramatists had evidently agreed on the main lines of Timon's character, his nobility and reckless generosity, and the tragic effect that ingratitude would have on him.[53] Middleton's second scene shows him in a more critical light, self-admiring and sentimental, but this could be taken as more a development of his character than an alteration of it. Middleton handled the banquet scene well, and displayed many of his satiric gifts in the dunning scenes. Indeed, Middleton did everything that could be expected of him in the comic scenes, which are well adapted to the play's direction. It shows how successfully he adjusted to the evolving structure that a second author was not suspected until the 1840s, when scholars began to pay much closer attention to Shakespeare's language, also bringing to bear a wider knowledge of Elizabethan drama.

The only serious misjudgement that Middleton made (in the text as it has come down to us, at least), was Alcibiades' appeal to the Senate (3.5). This is not only unprepared for, but its intention is radically uncertain. Everyone can see that the Athenian Senators' banishment of him gives Alcibiades reason to complain of their ingratitude, and so makes his experience parallel Timon's. But Timon has just grounds for complaint, both against the private friends who turn out to be flatterers and against the state which, as we learn almost in passing (4.3.93–6; 5.1.145–6, 158–62), he had generously helped during a serious crisis, both with gifts and with military service. Alcibiades, however, appeals to the Senators to pardon a friend of his who is guilty of murder. The advocate admits the deed, but pleads extenuating circumstances, the friend's 'noble fury and fair spirit' having punished a slight to his honour by killing 'his foe' (3.5.10–23). One of the Senators fairly objects that Alcibiades is

---

[53] 'When Timon enters, we feel certain that he is the Timon of Shakspere's own conception. He is as graceful as he is generous; his prodigality is without the slightest particle of arrogance, he builds his munificence upon the necessity of gratifying without restraint the deep sympathies which he cherishes to all of the human family. He is the very model too of patrons, appearing to receive instead of to confer a favour in his reward of art,—a complete gentleman even in the act of purchasing a jewel of a tradesman' (Knight 1849, p. 71).

> striving to make an ugly deed look fair;
> Your words have took such pains as if they laboured
> To bring manslaughter into form

That is, legalize it (24–7). All the moral force is with the Senators—'To revenge is no valour, but to bear' (40)—and Alcibiades' further arguments can only seem specious: anger is a masculine virtue; it is natural; the accused served the state as a soldier, so did Alcibiades, therefore the state owes them a favour in return (41–98). The fact that Alcibiades accuses the Athenian Senate of endorsing usury (101–2, 109–11) is also irrelevant, and although their banishing him seems harsh, the scene shows him in a far worse light. If this confrontation were intended satirically, to expose the corruptions of office, as with Davy's appeal to Justice Shallow that 'a knave should have some countenance at his friend's request', and that if 'I cannot once or twice in a quarter bear out a knave against an honest man, I have little credit with your worship' (2 *Henry IV*, 5.1.38–52), then the scene could be thought to have a proper function. But as it stands, Alcibiades is clearly in the wrong, his wish to benefit from Athenian gratitude a perversion of that virtue. The whole scene is 'too strict a paradox', as the Senator describes Alcibiades' case, too uncompromising in challenging the distinction between right and wrong.

Alcibiades reappears in two later scenes, both by Shakespeare, now seeming morally unexceptionable, indeed sympathetic. First we see him marching 'with drum and fife, in warlike manner', yet attended by 'a brace of harlots', as Timon puts it (4.3.49–175). In this scene, as J. C. Maxwell noted,

Timon and Alcibiades meet for the last time. As the scene stands, the presence of Phrynia and Timandra provides an occasion for Timon's invective, but scarcely helps to elucidate the Alcibiades theme. I should be reluctant to regard it as intended to indicate that the claims of Alcibiades in the final scene to regenerate Athens are to be taken cynically.[54]

That comment indicates that neither author managed to integrate the subplot satisfactorily, since there is no way of coherently linking this scene with the play's ending. But certainly Shakespeare shows Alcibiades in a much more sympathetic light, asking solicitously

> How came the noble Timon to this change?

> (4.3.67)

He offers 'noble Timon' his friendship, excusing the misanthrope's bitter remarks, 'for his wits | Are drowned and lost in his calamities' (89–90), and although he has 'but little gold' Alcibiades generously offers it to Timon (91–101). When Timon gives him all the gold he can carry, provided he acts as 'a planetary plague' destroying every degree of Athenian society

---

[54] J. C. Maxwell (ed.), Shakespeare, *The Life of Timon of Athens* (Cambridge, 1957), p. xl.

(109–29)—so revealing his insane misanthropy—Alcibiades replies 'I'll take the gold . . . not all thy counsel' (130–1), and he leaves with the compassionate words 'We but offend him' (175). In the final scene Alcibiades is the embodiment of righteous indignation against Athens (5.4.1–13), but he yields to the two Senators' abject pleas that he should forgo revenge, expressing his 'more noble meaning' of justice to all (58–63), and displaying precisely the virtue of forbearance they had urged on him (in vain) in the Senate scene, 3.5. He has 'most nobly spoken', they say, and he reuses that word on the news that 'Dead | Is noble Timon' (79–80). The behaviour of Alcibiades here, as in his last encounter with Timon, corresponds in no way to that in Middleton's scene in the Senate: they seem like different characters.

As for Shakespeare's handling of plot and character, his overall conception of Timon's movement from philanthropy to misanthropy is clear, and consistently developed. But the great scenes of vituperation against all human vice, while marvellously demonstrating Shakespeare's imagination and linguistic inventiveness, are a dramatic dead end. There are some satisfying incidental ironies, such as Timon discovering gold when he no longer needs it, totally disillusioned by the human acquisitiveness that he had mistaken for friendship, and the remarkable transformation by which he descends to the level of Apemantus, yet with some crucial differences. Charles Knight described the contrast between the two as 'one of the most remarkable proofs of our poet's wonderful sagacity in depicting the nicer shades of character', and quoted with approval Burke's remark commending ' "the subtlety of discrimination with which Shakspere distinguishes the present character of Timon from that of Apemantus, whom to vulgar eyes he would now resemble" ' (Knight 1849, p. 77). Knight perceptively defined 'the beautiful distinction which Shakspere has drawn between the intellectual cynicism of Apemantus and the passionate misanthropy of Timon. The misanthropy of Timon is not practical—it wastes itself in generalizations; the misanthropy of Apemantus is not imaginative—it gratifies itself in petty insults and unkindnesses' (p. 81). But the situation, whereby a sequence of visitors come to Timon's cave and go away, richer in both abuse and gold, is inherently static, having no further possibility of development. As Knight saw,

The soldier, the courtezan, the thief, are equally included in Timon's fiery denunciations; but they are all equally gratified in essentials. The equanimity with which the fair companions of Alcibiades submit to his railings, when accompanied by his gifts, is profoundly satirical:

More counsel with more money, bounteous Timon. [4.3.167]

It tells, in a word, the impotence of his misanthropy. It is cherished for his own gratification alone. (p. 81)

Timon goes on cursing until Shakespeare has exhausted that vein, when he dies a solitary's death, survived by two epitaphs, one of which is superfluous.

The 'unity of design' that Hazlitt found in the play[55] is a conceptual unity only, issuing out in a drama of episodes, lacking direction or resolution. Looked at in comparison with Shakespeare's other tragedies, the great defect of *Timon of Athens* is the main character's solitariness, which is precisely the condition for his misanthropy. No other character in Shakespeare is as isolated as he is, lacking any blood relative or family.[56] *Vae soli*, as the preacher said, 'Woe to him that is alone when he falleth; for he hath not another to help him up' (Ecclesiastes 4: 10). That text was addressed to human beings in general, but it has a particular significance for the potential 'hero' of a potential tragedy. The basic plot-material, in the end, may just have been too recalcitrant for either Middleton or Shakespeare to have made a viable drama out of it. The fault lay not with the co-authors, but with the 'plott' from which they began.

HENRY VIII

A similar judgement could be made of *Henry VIII*, which covers about 'a quarter of a long reign, and begins and ends with firm landmarks: the Field of Cloth of Gold (1520) and the christening of Princess Elizabeth (1533)'. As J. C. Maxwell summarized the sources, the play's 'material consists mainly of three blocks from Holinshed: the fall of Buckingham (1521), the divorce, followed by the fall of Wolsey (1528–30), with which the coronation of Anne Boleyn (1533) is introduced, and the birth and christening of Elizabeth (1533) . . . The choice of a terminal point is eminently tactful; the bastardizing of Elizabeth and the execution of her mother (1536) lie safely in the future'.[57] Holinshed's *Chronicles* (second edition, 1587) was the source for the main events, and Foxe's *Acts and Monuments* (1563) for the Cranmer part of Act 5. In a detailed study R. A. Law showed how faithfully the dramatists followed their sources, the difference being that Shakespeare invented new and transformed existing material, while Fletcher was content to reproduce what he read.[58] This degree of loyalty to the sources means that the co-authors must have designed the play's overall shape, indeed, 'it is ludicrous to suppose that . . . any pair of collaborators' would not have fixed 'the general lines of the plot' before starting work.[59] Defenders of a 'sole authorship

---

[55] *Characters of Shakespeare's Plays* (London: Everyman edn. 1906), p. 47.

[56] Charles Knight commented on this aspect of the play, but favourably: Shakespeare 'completely remodelled the character of Timon. He left it standing apart in its naked power and majesty, without much regard to what surrounded it' (Knight 1849, p. 76).

[57] J. C. Maxwell (ed.), Shakespeare, *Henry VIII* (Cambridge, 1962; rev. edn., 1969), pp. xxx–xxxi.

[58] R. A. Law, 'Holinshed and *Henry the Eighth*', *Texas Studies in English*, 36 (1957): 3–11, at pp. 3–10.

[59] M. Mincoff, '*Henry VIII* and Fletcher', *ShQ* 12 (1961): 239–60, at p. 254.

theory' have pointed to the fact that the consensus authorship division assigns to Shakespeare two foreshadowings of Elizabeth's birth, in the Chamberlain's remark that from Anne Boleyn 'may proceed a gem | To lighten all this isle' (2.3.78–9), and Suffolk's conviction that 'from her | Will fall some blessing to this land' (3.2.50–2), while the scene itself (5.4) was written by Fletcher. But it is obvious that any competent dramatist, having agreed on a division of labour, will link events forwards and backwards through the play. As Mincoff argued, 'Shakespeare could not have written a line unless he had had from the first something more than merely a vague idea of how the play was to develop, and had not discussed it fairly thoroughly with his partner' (p. 256).

The structural deficiencies of *Henry VIII* lie not so much in the choice of material as in its handling. The incidents of the King's reign, James Spedding wrote, 'admitted of many different combinations, by which the effect of the play might have been modified to almost any extent either at the beginning or the end. By taking in a larger period and carrying the story on to the birth of Anne Boleyn's still-born son and her own execution, it would have yielded the argument of a great tragedy and tale of retributive justice'.[60] Or else the emphasis could have been shifted to the doctrinal struggles that produced the Reformation; indeed Spedding came to believe that this may have been Shakespeare's original idea (pp. 122–3). But it is clear that neither dramatist cared about 'the final separation of the English from the Romish Church'. What really caught their interest, as it has impressed so many who study the reign of Henry VIII, Marjorie Nicolson pointed out, were 'the tremendous reversals of fortune which characterized the individuals of that period'. As she asked, 'Buckingham, Wolsey, Katherine, Cranmer, Anne, Cromwell— where in one period would one find more characters who, through one man, the King, rose to greater heights or fell to more definite misery?'.[61]

The Prologue (by Fletcher) certainly promises to make us weep, not laugh, by presenting 'things . . . | Sad, high, and working, full of state and woe', and by showing the variable fortunes of people in high places, 'How soon this mightiness meets misery' (1–4, 30). The first four acts perform this promise, presenting the successive falls of Buckingham, Katherine, and Wolsey, but the final act imposes a happy ending, with the validation of Cranmer's loyalty and the birth of Elizabeth. For some critics this shift from tragic to comic— contradicting the Prologue—is a main reason to judge the play 'a poorly-connected series of episodes',[62] 'conspicuous [among Shakespeare's historical plays] for its disunity' (Waith 1952, p. 119). James Spedding spoke for many when recording his feeling that

---

[60] J. Spedding, 'Who Wrote Shakspere's *Henry VIII?*', GM 178 (NS 34) (1850): 115–23, at pp. 116–17.

[61] M. H. Nicolson, 'The Authorship of *Henry the Eighth*', PMLA 37 (1922): 484–502, at p. 491.

[62] Irving Ribner, *The English History Play in the Age of Shakespeare* (Princeton, 1957), p. 291.

the effect of this play *as a whole* is weak and disappointing. The truth is that the interest, instead of rising towards the end, falls away utterly, and leaves us in the last act among persons whom we scarcely know, and events for which we do not care. The strongest sympathies which have been awakened in us run opposite to the course of the action. Our sympathy is for the grief and goodness of Queen Katherine, while the course of the action requires us to entertain as a theme of joy and compensatory satisfaction the coronation of Anne Boleyn and the birth of her daughter; which are in fact a part of Katherine's injury, and amount to little less than the ultimate triumph of wrong. (Spedding 1850a, p. 116)

The King's cause, Spedding argued, is represented throughout as 'a bad one', and although we hear of 'conscientious scruples as to the legality of his first marriage' we are not made to believe them sincere, and his new liking for Anne Boleyn shows less 'the hand of Providence' than the workings of appetite.

The mere caprice of passion drives the king into the commission of what seems a great iniquity; our compassion for the victim of it is elaborately excited; no attempt is made to awaken any counter-sympathy for *him*: yet his passion has its way, and is crowned with all felicity, present and to come. The effect is much like that which would have been produced by *The Winter's Tale* if Hermione had died in the fourth act in consequence of the jealous tyranny of Leontes, and the play had ended with the coronation of a new queen and the christening of a new heir, no period of remorse intervening. (ibid.)

Spedding's comparison underlines the double-edged nature of dramatic sympathy: concern for the victim arouses resentment at the oppressor.

Structurally, the triangular relationship Katherine–Henry–Wolsey was divided between the two dramatists. Shakespeare wrote 1.2, where Katherine comes into conflict with Wolsey, altering the sources in two respects. As R. A. Law pointed out, Katherine 'is made responsible for the King's action in pardoning his rebellious overtaxed subjects [1.2.18–68], and then pleads for a second exercise of mercy towards the accused Duke of Buckingham [108–76]. These two changes place the Queen in opposition to the Cardinal and excite her suspicion of his motives before even gossip of a coming divorce' (Law 1957, p. 6). Like the two anticipations of Anne Boleyn's childbearing, this shows how Shakespeare introduced material in preparation for a significant development. He did so again at the opening of 2.3, for the grief expressed by Anne Boleyn at the imminent eclipse of Queen Katherine (1–49) is Shakespeare's own invention, as are the Old Lady's cynical remarks questioning Anne's sympathy should she become the next favourite (81–107). In the trial scene (2.4), as Law pointed out, by several additions to the sources Shakespeare 'once more emphasizes the Katherine–Wolsey conflict and prepares for the eventual downfall of the potent Cardinal' (p. 6).

Fletcher took up Katherine's story for the interview between her and the cardinals (3.1.15–183). Spedding observed that although the character of

Katherine was consistent in the council chamber scene (1.2), and in 'the famous trial-scene', evidently by 'the same hand to which we owe the trial of Hermione', in Fletcher's scene of her interview with Wolsey and Campeius 'I found her as much changed as Buckingham was after his sentence, though without any alteration of circumstances to account for an alteration of temper' (Spedding 1850*a*, p. 119). Fletcher based the scene on Holinshed, but J. C. Maxwell noted that

it adds a degree of petulance and unfair attack on the cardinals (3.1.102–24) that jars with her claim to 'a great patience' (1. 137). I do not think it helps much to see in this the attribution of a human (or feminine) inconsistency to Katherine. No unified impression, not even a complex one, emerges from the scene. It reads rather as if the cardinals were being used, not just by an understandably outraged Katherine, but also by the dramatist, to divert possible obloquy from Henry. (Maxwell 1962, p. xxxvi)

Fletcher also dramatized Katherine's sickness, dying vision, and final contact with the King, through his ambassador (4.1.1–179). In these scenes, too, she seems a different person. Marjorie Nicolson described the Katherine of the opening scenes as displaying 'those characteristics which we have learned to expect in the great women of Shakespeare: fearlessness, courage, steadfastness, keen judgment' (Nicolson 1922, p. 493). In this part of the play Katherine shares with Portia and Hermione 'the simplicity and courageousness of all of Shakespeare's women', but she suffers a drastic change in 'the long-drawn dream and death scene which delighted Fletcher' (p. 499). Katherine's character is so different in 4.2 that Fredson Bowers spoke of her 'unmotivated instantaneous capitulation', as abrupt as the transformation of Wolsey, 'both being characteristic of Fletcher's facile methods to the highest degree'.[63]

As with Middleton's unprepared introduction of the Alcibiades scene in *Timon of Athens*, we can again detect a clear difference between Shakespeare and his co-authors in the handling of dramatic preparation. But here not only Fletcher is at fault. J. C. Maxwell found 'the presentation of Henry himself' the 'most unsatisfactory' part of the play,[64] for

There is a curious half-heartedness and inconclusiveness about the way in which the divorce is handled. In the trial scene itself, keeping fairly close to the chronicle source,

---

[63] F. Bowers, *Henry VIII*, 'Textual Introduction' to Bowers (ed.), *The Dramatic Works in the Beaumont and Fletcher Canon*, vii (Cambridge, 1989), p. 7.

[64] Fredson Bowers agreed: 'Because of the collaboration, at least one character—the King—is inconsistently presented. How hypocritical he is supposed to be at the end of 2.2 in his regrets that his conscience forces him to leave Katherine and how much this suspicion may influence an audience in its view of the candour of his elaborate defence in 2.4 may be questioned. Since Fletcher wrote the first and Shakespeare the second, very likely Fletcher's superficial (and cynical?) treatment of character according to fashionable standards of morality affected the presentation of Henry, who is at his best in Shakespeare's 1.2, 2.4, and 5.1, although his decisiveness and force of character are not to be ignored in Fletcher's 5.2, different from the sentimental Henry in Fletcher's mystical 5.4' (Bowers 1989*b*, p. 19 n. 23).

Shakespeare gives us a moving presentation of Katherine and of a Henry who at least puts up a good show of a genuine unwillingness to repudiate her, and pays a tribute in which real warmth of affection seems to breathe at 2.4.133–43. But there are no convincing or even interesting links backwards or forwards. (Maxwell 1962, p. xxxiv)

The absence of such links is perhaps a sign of divided responsibilities. However, the good impression that Henry may have made here is soon forfeited. Having praised Katherine as a good wife—only after she has left the stage—the King proceeds to exonerate Wolsey of all charges of malice towards her, a reaction which, given the care Shakespeare took to add passages to the sources so as to highlight the enmity between Wolsey and Katherine, has the effect of suggesting that the King, despite his splendid appearance, is 'in reality weak and ineffectual, entirely under the domination' of Wolsey's intellect (Nicolson 1922, pp. 500–1). But this development, while it may strengthen the Wolsey–Henry relationship, dissipates sympathy for the Queen. Shakespeare then gives the King a long apologia in which he claims that doubts about the legitimacy of his 'marriage with the dowager, | Sometimes our brother's wife . . . shook | The bosom of my conscience' (2.4.167–228). In his scenes Fletcher also made several allusions to the King's conscience, some sceptical (2.2.16–17, 4.1.47), others apparently sincere (2.2.141–2), which suggests that the co-authors must have agreed to emphasize this point, as Holinshed had done. But, as Maxwell put it, 'these different allusions are simply laid side by side, without either a clear resolution of conflicting points of view or an interesting tension between them' (p. xxxv).

If the balance of dramatic sympathy weighs for Katherine and against the King, it does so even more powerfully against Wolsey. Shakespeare presents him as an unscrupulous manipulator, ambitious for power, hated and resented by the nobles, as we see from Buckingham's first reference to him— 'No man's pie is freed | From his ambitious finger' (1.2.52–3), a resentment shared by Norfolk and Abergavenny (55–99). But this opening scene also establishes Wolsey's power, for no sooner have his fellow noblemen warned Buckingham of the danger he is in than Wolsey has him arrested on a charge of conspiracy (100–226). Shakespeare displays Wolsey's power over the King and Queen in the following scene (1.2), and shows him dominating Katherine's trial (2.4). But in 3.2—as Marjorie Nicolson well observed, Shakespeare reserved for himself 'the pivotal scenes, the ones which are the crisis of each plot' (Nicolson 1922, pp. 501–2)—Wolsey's fall begins. The resentful nobles report that Wolsey's letter to the Pope (which asked him to block Henry's divorce from Katherine in order to prevent him marrying Anne Boleyn, 'a creature of the queen's'), has reached the King by mistake (1–75). Wolsey's dislike of Anne is a fatal error (since the King has already married her) which alienates Henry from him, a process completed by his discovery that Wolsey had illegally accumulated huge riches. R. A Law (1957, p. 5) showed that Shakespeare added to Holinshed a new sequence (105–203) in which the angry King hands Wolsey the schedule of all his wealth and leaves him to digest it: 'and then to breakfast with | What appetite you have'.

At this point in the scene Fletcher took over, writing a soliloquy for Wolsey in which he admits to both greed and carelessness (a speech based once again on Holinshed):

> This paper has undone me: 'tis the accompt
> Of all that world of wealth I have drawn together
> For mine own ends—indeed to gain the popedom
> And fee my friends in Rome. O negligence!
> Fit for a fool to fall by: what cross devil
> Made me put this main secret in the packet
> I sent the King? Is there no way to cure this?
> No new device to beat this from his brains?
>
> (3.2.210–17)

But at this make-or-break point all his wit disappears, and 'Wolsey as Shakespeare saw him, . . . the supreme character of the play; a later Iago, [with] . . . all the cunning and craft of Iago . . . far-sighted, shrewd, an intellectual incarnate' (Nicolson 1922, p. 500), Shakespeare's Wolsey becomes a quite different person. Suddenly quite unable to think of any 'device', four lines later he meekly accepts his fate:

> Nay then, farewell!
> I have touched the highest point of all my greatness
>
> (222–3)

This formula, redolent with pathos, appealed so much to Wolsey (or Fletcher) that he repeated it after the nobles have reported the King's judgment on him, and he is again left alone:

> Farewell, a long farewell to all my greatness!
> This is the state of man; today he puts forth
> The tender leaves of hopes, tomorrow blossoms,
> And bears his blushing honours thick upon him:
> The third day comes a frost, a killing frost . . .
>
> (351–5)

And so on, through the familiar patterns of Fletcher's style. In the brief encounter with Cromwell that follows (372–489), Wolsey professes himself 'a poor fall'n man, unworthy now | To be thy lord and master' (413–14), and he piously urges Cromwell to 'fling away ambition. | By that sin fell the angels; how can man then, | The image of his maker, hope to win by it?' (440–2).

Within just over 250 lines Wolsey has been transformed from an unscrupulous worldly prelate to a crushed, penitent Christian, who only has left 'My robe, | And my integrity to heaven' (452–3). Marco Mincoff described this process as 'a transition, such as Fletcher was especially fond of, but it is not so much an emotional transition . . . or a slick conversion. It is a complete change of the whole man, such as we find in *Lear*, but packed into a single scene. He changes from arrogance to humility, from the prime of life to broken old age, before our eyes, and the change rings true' (Mincoff 1961, p. 259). But the parallel with Lear surely points up a big difference: that transformation is a long-drawn-out process, stretching over nearly five acts, and lived through in the most intense sequence of emotional and physical shocks that any character in Shakespeare experiences. Wolsey's transition is remarkably quick, not the result of any extended suffering of disappointment, and seems by comparison a volte-face. Other critics have objected to 'Wolsey's complete change of character in his farewell to Cromwell, which in every sentence contradicts the character of Wolsey as Shakespeare planned it' (Nicolson 1922, p. 497), or have complained that the 'inconsistencies' make the play's portrait of Wolsey 'almost incomprehensible' (Ribner 1957, p. 290), or have described 'the almost unmotivated abrupt change, without transition, from pride to humility in Wolsey' as 'characteristic of Fletcher's facile methods' (Bowers 1989*b*, p. 7).

The drastic changes in the characterization of Katherine and Wolsey reflect the division of labour between the two writers. Anyone willing to accept the notion that Shakespeare could have shared the writing of this play with a rising young dramatist will notice that it was Shakespeare who sketched in the characters of Buckingham, Wolsey, the King, Katherine, Anne Boleyn (2.3), Gardiner (5.1), and Cranmer (5.1). He dealt with their beginnings, so to speak, leaving Fletcher to take care of their endings.[65] With Buckingham, also, we observe a distinct character change. The nobleman who had expressed his resentment of Wolsey with such energy in the opening scene makes a last appearance on his way to the executioner's block (2.1), transformed by Fletcher into a penitent forgiving all who have harmed him:

> The law I bear no malice for my death,
> 'T has done upon the premises but justice;
>
> (62–3)
> . . . Sir Thomas Lovell, I as free forgive you
> As I would be forgiven: I forgive all.
>
> (82–3)
> Commend me to his grace;
> And if he speak of Buckingham, pray tell him
> You met him half in heaven: my vows and prayers

---

[65] Marjorie Nicolson analysed Shakespeare's share of the plot, arguing that '[his] work was introductory', and that 'he brought no [plot-line] to its conclusion. Fletcher's was entirely formed upon the parts already written; he began no new story in the play' (Nicolson 1922, p. 497). Her comments echoed Fleay's similar suggestion that in *Timon of Athens* Middleton also took over plot-lines which Shakespeare had begun.

Yet are the King's, and till my soul forsake
Shall cry for blessings on him.

(86–90)

Fletcher wrote three such speeches for Buckingham, seventy lines of Christian humility, self-indulgent pathos, as this latest example of the fall from greatness ('When I came hither, I was Lord High Constable | And Duke of Buckingham: now, poor Edward Bohun', 102–3) quits the scene. Readers will notice a common pattern in these farewells. As Eugene Waith wrote,

> Though Buckingham and Wolsey are presented as totally different sorts of men, their farewells are surprisingly similar. The likeness is not explained by the source of the play, Holinshed's *Chronicle*, which contains suggestions for Buckingham's speech but not for Wolsey's. Nor is the likeness made probable by the circumstance that Wolsey has repented of his evil ways at the end. The truth is that these two dissimilar men conform to a stereotype in their final moments. Each one appears as the pitiable victim of forces largely exterior to him. (Waith 1952, p. 121)

As Waith pointed out, both men display 'lofty nobility' in their acceptance of fate, express undying loyalty to the King, and both 'approach death like model Christians'.

> The ultimate intention of these speeches, which have such a dying fall, is to persuade us of the pathetic discrepancy between the fate of the two men and their innate nobility and to elicit by a generalized presentation a general response to the waste of potential. The effect is well enough prepared in the case of Buckingham by early scenes in which Wolsey's plots against him are revealed. What is striking is the attempt to secure the same effect in the case of the man responsible for the misfortunes of Buckingham. The success of the venture rests entirely upon rhetoric. (p. 122)

Here again we see that Fletcher's intervention nullified the workings of dramatic sympathy. Our pity for Buckingham produces resentment at Wolsey, but shortly afterwards we are asked to pity Wolsey too. Waith's pioneering study showed for the first time how much Fletcher and his associates had taken from the *Suasoriae* and *Controversiae* of the elder Seneca, those strange collections of exercises used to train orators in the Roman declamation schools. These texts provided many (often fantastic) plots for Jacobean and Caroline plays, and also encouraged dramatists to emphasize the act of speaking, the construction of speeches in the opposed modes of accusation and defence. By agreeing to a division of labour in which Fletcher handled the endings of Buckingham, Wolsey, and Katherine, and the infinitely promising beginning of Queen Elizabeth, Shakespeare in effect granted Fletcher a licence to indulge his skills in writing set speeches. As Waith put it, 'since the narrative complications are relatively slight, the play seems, even more than other Fletcherian plays, a vehicle for declamation. Fluent rhetoric is its lifeblood' (p. 120).

The result of this division of labour is that Fletcher's characterization of Buckingham, Wolsey, and Katherine, although so different from Shakespeare's individualization of those characters, makes them resemble each other, as they take the centre of the stage and assume the centre of interest. For the two male characters their 'noble eloquence in the last dramatic moments of their lives' casts them in the role of suffering heroes—however incongruous that costume might be for the Cardinal. Waith brings out well this curious feature of *Henry VIII*, deriving from Fletcher's dramaturgy what might be described as 'three characters in search of a role': 'Wolsey in particular seems, like other Fletcherian characters, to be assuming a role, and an unexpected one. The part of the tragic hero, noble and pathetic victim, awaits Wolsey as it does Buckingham. It is fully prepared; they need only speak the lines' (ibid.). Yet, by the same token, the role is defined in terms of the speech spoken, the individual character being subordinated to the declamatory experience:

Not only are the great speeches of such a play as *Henry VIII* examples of oratorical art but they tend to become dissociated from the speaker, as ends in themselves. Wolsey's farewell speech is less an expression of his individual character than of what a hero might be expected to feel at the moment of his downfall. As such, the speech closely resembles a rhetorical exercise. Its value to the play consists in rendering an intense theatrical moment.

It is this levelling-out of individualization in the interests of effective oratory, I believe, that accounts for the disappointment many modern readers feel with *Henry VIII*. We do not share the interest that Fletcher and his colleagues had in speech-making as such, and we have also been spoiled—or rather, educated—by Shakespeare, who, apart from a few 'choric' passages, always made speeches express the personality of their speaker. Some critics might defend the similarities between the farewell speeches of Buckingham and Wolsey as deriving from their similar fates, but the really telling evidence for Waith's thesis of Fletcherian rhetoric as a generalized, not individualized mode, is the final scene for Katherine:

In her death scene (4.2) Fletcher emphasizes her noble forgiveness of her enemies and devises yet another farewell speech. Katherine assumes the discarded robes of Buckingham and Wolsey. If the division of labor between Fletcher and Shakespeare is that commonly accepted, with all the climactic scenes in Fletcher's portion, it is impossible to be entirely fair in comparing the treatment of any one character by the two men. The nature of the scenes necessarily influences the treatment. However, it is undeniably the scenes ascribed to Fletcher which present in the declamatory style the figure of the hero, larger than life, and clothed in a ready-made nobility. (pp. 123–4)

Although I entirely accept Waith's penetrating account of Fletcherian rhetoric, I think it is hardly a question of being 'fair' or unfair to Fletcher. The fact that both dramatists agreed on this sharing of composition means that both are responsible for the play's moments of success, and failure. All the linguistic evidence suggests that Shakespeare wrote the opening scene of Act 5, in which we learn that the new Queen is in labour (1–32), that Cromwell's star is rising, that Gardiner (Bishop of Winchester) regards Cranmer (Archbishop of Canterbury) as 'a most arch-heretic, a pestilence | That does infect the land' (32–55). At this point Shakespeare switched his sources, from Holinshed to Foxe, for the scene between the King and Cranmer (55–157), in which the Archbishop's 'truth and integrity' is tested and approved, returning to Holinshed for the news that Anne has given birth to a daughter (157–76). Fletcher then took over, using Foxe, to dramatize the conflict between the council and Cranmer, which the King resolves in Cranmer's favour (5.2, 5.3), and he drew from Holinshed the detail that a ceremony followed the christening (5.5.1–14). Fletcher invented both the crowd scene before the christening (5.4) and Cranmer's speech prophesying the future greatness of Elizabeth and her country (5.5.14–77).

This concluding section, planned by both dramatists, was obviously intended to reverse the play's three-times-repeated pattern of a fall from greatness with a birth into greatness. But for many readers it has proved to be a bridge too far. Maxwell noted 'the absence of any real incisiveness in the frankly episodic scenes devoted to Cranmer, well though they are handled in detail' (Maxwell 1962, pp. xxxvi–xxxvii). R. A. Law observed that the 'lack of unity in the composition of *Henry VIII*, as a whole, is quite evident and has called forth serious criticism. The portion attributed to Shakespeare might escape such censure were he not held responsible for 5.1, which opens the story of the Princess Elizabeth and that of the persecution of Cranmer, a double topic extraneous to the moving tragedy of Wolsey and Katherine' (Law 1957, p. 11). James Spedding expressed his dissatisfaction more forcefully:

The greater part of the fifth act, in which the interest ought to be gathering to a head, is occupied with matters in which we have not been prepared to take any interest by what went before, and on which no interest is reflected by what comes after. The scenes in the gallery and council-chamber, though full of life and vigour, and, in point of execution, not unworthy of Shakspere, are utterly irrelevant to the business of the play; for what have we to do with the quarrel between Gardiner and Cranmer? Nothing in the play is explained by it, nothing depends upon it. It is used only (so far as the argument is concerned) as a preface for introducing Cranmer as godfather to Queen Elizabeth, which might have been done as a matter of course without any preface at all. (Spedding 1850a, p. 116)

Although these scenes are picturesque, to judge 'poetically'—according to the norms of poetic drama—Spedding found them to 'have in this place no value, but the reverse', effecting an unwelcome change of mood, and genre:

The fate of Wolsey would have made a noble subject for a tragedy in itself, and might very well have been combined with the tragedy of Katherine; but, as an introduction to the festive solemnity with which the play concludes, the one seems to me as inappropriate as the other. . . . I know of no other play in Shakspere which is chargeable with a fault like this, none in which the moral sympathy of the spectator is not carried along with the main current of action to the end. (pp. 116–17)

The charge of disunity, which so many critics have applied to *Henry VIII* over the last 150 years, is not easily dismissed. In part it is due to the co-authors' very different approach to characterization and to language—the one, after all, presupposing the other, by all Renaissance criteria of the necessary homogeneity between *res* and *verba*. In Shakespeare's scenes, characters are individualized and differentiated through their diction, imagery, and verse movement. In Fletcher linguistic resources tend to be the expression of an authorial style, a combination of features common to all the characters, whatever their variations in personality and situation. Given this radical difference in dramatic methods, it was inevitable that characters taken over by Fletcher should differ from the Shakespearian premises as much as they resemble each other. Whether or not Shakespeare knew that this would happen, the play as a whole was planned by both dramatists, and it would be wrong to blame Fletcher alone for our dissatisfaction. The total change of direction effected by the fifth act might have been a deliberate gesture towards the new aesthetic of tragicomedy, which, as Fletcher explained in his epistle to *The Faithful Shepherdess* (1610),

is not so called in respect of mirth and killing, but in respect it wants deaths, which is enough to make it no tragedy, yet brings some near it, which is enough to make it no comedy. . . . (Vickers 1999, p. 503)

But of course *Henry VIII* includes three deaths, of Buckingham, Wolsey, and Katherine, and as a history play it evades both classical and Renaissance genre categories. The drastic change of direction in the final act occurs in another Fletcher play, *Valentinian* (*c*.1614), as Robert Wolseley complained in 1678, 'the chief business of it . . . ending with the Fourth Act, and a new Design, which has no kind of relation to the other, is introduc'd in the Fifth, contrary to a Fundamental Rule of the Stage'.[66] In *Henry VIII* the birth of Elizabeth is certainly prepared for, but all the subordinate business involving Gardiner, the council, and Cranmer is quite unexpected. The decision to include all this material was obviously a joint one, but it added the final distraction to a play that was already losing continuity and coherence at the level of character and motive. For Shakespeare this collaboration, working together with Fletcher throughout a whole play, unlike the neater separation of energies he had negotiated with Peele and Wilkins, may have cost him more than he had expected. The chief casualty seems to have been what Coleridge

---

[66] Wolseley, preface to Rochester's adaptation, *Lucina's Rape, or Valentinian*; cit. G. McMullan, *The Politics of Unease in the Plays of John Fletcher* (Amherst, Mass., 1994), p. 135.

called the 'esemplastic power' of the imagination, that 'shaping or modifying power' which 'struggles to idealize and to unify' poetic creation.[67] This is not a faculty which one author can delegate to another.

The pattern of collaboration in *The Two Noble Kinsmen* resembles that for *Henry VIII* in several respects. Again, Shakespeare takes over the exposition for the main plot, writing the first act and beginning the underplot (the Jailer's Daughter) in the first scene of the second act. He opens with an action framing the play, the marriage of Theseus, Duke of Athens, and Hippolyta, Queen of the Amazons. Their ceremony is interrupted by the unexpected arrival of three Queens pleading with Theseus to force Creon, the tyrannical ruler of Thebes, to allow them to bury their dead husbands' corpses. The Queens appeal in turn to Theseus (39–76), to Hippolyta (77–106), and to Emilia, Theseus' sister (107–29). Theseus at first rejects their appeals, but their renewed pleadings, coupled with those of Hippolyta and Emilia (186–205), finally persuade him to make war on Creon, and he leaves Pirithous to look after Hippolyta (206–33). This opening scene impressively combines generalized lament with direct personal appeal to the Athenians to recognize the values of love and dedication to the dead. Shakespeare's second scene also articulates moral values, the disgust that Arcite and Palamon feel for the 'city | Thebes, and the temptings in't' (1.2.3–4),

> where every evil
> Hath a good colour; where every seeming good's
> A certain evil

> (38–40)

Arcite takes the lead in denouncing this corrupt city, while his cousin Palamon utters a powerful condemnation of their uncle, Creon, 'A most unbounded tyrant' (60–74). Alerted to the imminent attack from the Athenian forces, they resolve to give their services 'for Thebes, not Creon' (99).

Shakespeare now takes up those left behind by the war, as Pirithous brings Hippolyta and Emilia to safety before going off to join Theseus' army (1.3.1–26). Once he has gone, the two women praise Pirithous' loyalty to Theseus (26–47)—they were, of course, a well-known classical *exemplum* of friendship—and Emilia recalls her own childhood friendship for Flavina (48–82), arguing that 'the true love 'tween maid and maid may be | More than in sex dividual'. Emilia announces her resolve to remain chaste, a vow that

---

[67] *Biographia Literaria* (1817), ed. G. G. Watson (London, 1956), pp. 91, 160, 167.

Hippolyta receives with scepticism. Shakespeare evidently articulates Emilia's rejection of marriage (a distaste expressed by several characters in his comedies, *before* they fall in love) with an eye on the play's denouement, in which Emilia will be asked to marry either Palamon or Arcite, whoever wins the joust for which she is the prize. The next two scenes resolve the opening action, Theseus defeating Creon and granting the Queens their burial rights, and also link it to the play's main business, for Palamon and Arcite have been taken prisoner and are brought back to Athens (1.4, 1.5). There we find their Jailer assuring his daughter's wooer that he will consider his proposal of marriage once the wedding of Theseus and Hippolyta has taken place. However, the Daughter has already fallen in love with these prisoners, who embody the classical ideal of triumphing over misfortune: 'they have patience to make any adversity ashamed'; they do their best to ignore captivity and to 'enforce a freedom out of bondage', for 'they eat well, look merrily, discourse of many things, but nothing of their own restraint and disasters' (2.1.24–6, 36–7, 39–41).

At this point Fletcher takes up the story with the imprisoned heroes, whose behaviour in his hands turns out to be anything but Stoic. Although Palamon claims to be 'strong enough to laugh at misery', he delivers nearly twenty lines of lamentation, beginning (quite unlike the Palamon of 1.2, who detested that corrupt city) by appealing

> Where is Thebes now? Where is our noble country?
> Where are our friends and kindreds? Never more
> Must we behold those comforts, never see
>   .   .   .   .
>   O never
> Shall we two exercise, like twins of honour
> Our arms again . . .
>
>   (2.2.7–9, 17–19)

Fletcher's emphasis on the phrase 'never more' is so intense that he even drapes it around the final item in this self-pitying list (the rhetorical figure *tmesis*, or *dissectio*):

> These hands shall *never* draw 'em out like lightning
> To blast whole armies *more*.
>
>   (24–5; my italics)

Arcite answers Palamon, but whereas we might have expected him to remonstrate with his cousin, urging him to recall his virtue or patience and scorn adversity, as the interlocutor does in many other Renaissance dialogues (think of Pyrocles and Musidorus in Sidney's *Arcadia*), Arcite chimes in with another twenty lines of self-centred pathos:

> here we are
> And here the graces of our youths must wither
> Like a too-timely spring; here age must find us,
> And—which is heaviest, Palamon—unmarried.
> The sweet embraces of a loving wife
> Shall never clasp our necks . . .

(26–32)

Never will they have children to emulate their successes, and so on. Palamon then takes up the threnos, with a twice-repeated 'no more' (48), ending with a tidy rhetorical *partitio* to mark the speaker's final point:

> we shall die—
> Which is the curse of honour—lastly,
> Children of grief and ignorance.

(53–5)

Fletcher, having written a duet full of pathos, entirely devoted to 'their own restraint and disasters', contrary to what Shakespeare had the Jailer's Daughter prepare us for, finally allows his two heroes (briefly) to come to terms with their captivity. Arcite delivers a paradox on the advantages of being in prison (69–75), and Palamon remembers the 'court of Creon, | Where sin is justice' (105–6). At this point they see Emilia from their prison window, and instantly fall in love with her:

> Palamon. I saw her first.
> Arcite.   That's nothing.
> Palamon.   But it shall be.
> Arcite. I saw her too.
> Palamon.   Yes, but you must not love her.

(161–2)

And so they begin their fateful quarrel (154–221).

As with *Timon*, *Pericles*, and *Henry VIII*, it is just at the transition point where the co-author takes up the story that we notice a second hand at work. While Shakespeare presented the cousins as fiercely moral, condemning a corrupt society and its tyrant in energetic verse, Fletcher allows his heroes to indulge their griefs for fifty-five plangent lines. No doubt Fletcher fulfilled the letter of the 'plott' in the second half of the scene, with their quarrel, but its beginning has troubled many readers for the evident discrepancy in values between it and Shakespeare's scene. As Theodore Spencer wittily described it,

the way Fletcher describes his two heroes is very different from the way Shakespeare had described them earlier, the first time we see them, in Act 1, scene 2. The words Shakespeare puts into their mouths are not the words of sentiment; Palamon and Arcite are not like two graceful saplings, swaying in unison in a sentimental moonlight. They are a pair of moralists, with a strong sense of evil and a strong sense of indignation at the corruption engendered in Thebes by their wicked uncle, Creon. What Fletcher tells us about them bears only on the immediate dramatic situation; they say no more than is necessary to put the particular scene across. But Shakespeare reveals their characters by their attitude to a general situation, and we are in a different, a wider world of perception.[68]

The opening scenes of Act 1, as we noticed, all illustrate the human value of loyalty, in the three Queens' dedication to their dead husbands, in Palamon and Arcite, 'dearer in love than blood' (1.2.1), in the friendship of Theseus and Pirithous, and in that of Emilia for Flavina. As Spencer observed,

> One of Shakespeare's favorite dramatic devices in his mature work is to establish a set of values and then to show how it is violated by the individual action which follows. He does this in *Troilus and Cressida* through the speeches of Ulysses; he does it more indirectly in *Hamlet*, *Othello*, and *King Lear*; he clearly had it in mind when planning *The Two Noble Kinsmen*. But Fletcher, tied by temperament to the immediate and the obviously practical, was not concerned with such matters, and, when he took charge of the situation after the first act, the wider implication, the fundamental and general contrast which the story, in Shakespeare's eyes, could be seen to illustrate, disappeared. It was not appropriate to Fletcher's romantic and myopic vision. (Spencer 1939, p. 270)

If 'myopic' seems unfair, we might agree that, as a dramatist, Fletcher was always concerned with immediate effect, here milking the cousins' pathetic situation for all that it was worth. Eugene Waith, in his important study of the pattern of tragicomedy in the Fletcher canon, included among its special features 'the discontinuity of plot which results from sacrificing a single action to a series of situations' (Waith 1952, p. 136). Fletcher was more interested in the events of the moment, surprising developments or reversals which would keep an audience constantly stimulated, even if it meant losing, or not attempting, longer perspectives. Shakespeare had a far deeper concern with long-term processes, dramatic coherence, and unity.

   Differences in dramaturgy and characterization between the two authors can also be seen in their treatment of Emilia. Shakespeare had emphasized her lack of interest in men, and her nostalgic memory of her girlhood friendship. When Fletcher brings her on stage for the cousins to see her, Emilia, attended by a waiting woman, reveals a quite different set of values. As they walk up and down Emilia examines the flowers in the garden outside the prison, commenting on the narcissus:

> That was a fair boy, certain, but a fool
> To love himself. Were there not maids enough?
> Or were they all hard-hearted?

(2.2.120–3)

[68] T. Spencer, '*The Two Noble Kinsmen*', MP 36 (1939): 255–76, at p. 267.

Emilia praises her 'good wench' for not being 'hard-hearted' towards men, both remarks completely at variance with Shakespeare's presentation of her. At the end of their brief conversation we have this exchange:

Emilia. I am wondrous merry-hearted, I could laugh now.
Woman. I could lie down, I am sure.
Emilia. And take one with you?

(151–2)

' "Laugh and lie down" was the name of a card game, but also a proverbial expression with sexual overtones', an editor tells us.[69] Perhaps the last thing we could have expected from Shakespeare's Emilia was a taste for innuendo.

Fletcher developed Emilia's role further in the long soliloquy (4.2.1–54), his own addition to Chaucer,[70] in which she examines the pictures of the rivals for her love. Here we find nothing of the virginality or indifference towards men that Shakespeare had created for her. Instead, she responds gushingly to each in turn: 'What a sweet face has Arcite! . . . What an eye . . . Just such another wanton Ganymede | Set Jove afire . . .'. But then she registers Palamon's attractions: 'What a bold gravity, and yet inviting, | Has this brown manly face!'. In this soliloquy Emilia conforms to the traditional stereotype of the changeable woman, *'varium et semper mutabile | femina'* (Virgil, *Aeneid*, 4.569): as she says herself,

O, who can find the bent of woman's fancy?
I am a fool, my reason is lost in me . . .

When Shakespeare takes up Emilia's part for the second time, we once again see the chaste maiden, praising Diana as a goddess with whose values she totally identifies:

O sacred, shadowy, cold, and constant queen,
Abandoner of revels, mute contemplative,
Sweet, solitary, white as chaste, and pure
As wind-fanned snow, who to thy female knights
Allow'st no more blood than will make a blush . . .

(5.1.137–62)

Emilia alludes to 'blood' as a symbol of sexual desire, only to reduce it to the blush which was traditionally the sign of virtue (*rubor est virtutis color*). The values of purity in thought and speech which Diana embodies—her ear 'nev'r heard scurril term . . . wanton sound'—are not the values of Fletcher's Emilia.

As these inconsistencies show, Fletcher and Shakespeare may have worked

---

[69] E. M. Waith (ed.), Shakespeare, *The Two Noble Kinsmen* (Oxford, 1989), p. 115.
[70] A. Thompson, *Shakespeare's Chaucer: A Study in Literary Origins* (Liverpool, 1978), p. 195.

out a coherent story line, but in dramatizing it the difference between their
values turn out to be as clearly marked as that between their verse styles. In
the remarkable scene with which Shakespeare opened Act 5, Palamon prays
to Venus, affirming his purity in speech and thought:

> I have never been foul-mouthed against thy law;
> Nev'r revealed secret
>
> .   .   .   .
>
>   I never practised
> Upon man's wife, nor would the libels read
> Of liberal wits. I never at great feasts
> Sought to betray a beauty, but have blushed
> At simp'ring sirs that did.
>
>   (5.1.98–104)

Shakespeare's Palamon denies having revealed anyone's love-life, and distances himself as much from licentious speakers as from men who boast of
their sexual conquests. Fletcher's Palamon, however, in the scene where
Arcite gives him food and drink to help him back to strength, invites Arcite to
drink a health 'to the wenches | We have known in our days', such as the 'Lord
Steward's daughter', who 'loved a black-haired man' called—Arcite:

> *Palamon.*   She met him in an arbour.
>   What did she there, coz? Play o'th'virginals?
> *Arcite.* Something she did, sir.
> *Palamon.*   Made her groan a month for't—
>   Or two, or three, or ten.

Now Arcite pulls his cousin's leg about the 'marshall's sister', who 'Had her
share, too' from Palamon, ending with a bawdy joke—'and thereby hangs a
tale'—matching his cousin's sexual word-play on 'virginals' (3.3.29–42). A
Victorian editor wrote: 'this is one of those scenes, by the introduction of
which Fletcher succeeded in spoiling a good play' (Littledale 1876, p. 141).
More recently, Ann Thompson judged that 'the flippancy of the discussion
of women reflects little credit on the heroes, is absent from the source,
and, especially in the case of Palamon, notoriously inconsistent with
Shakespeare's conception of their characters' (Thompson 1978, p. 191). We
are not surprised to discover that these two passages of innuendo were both
inventions by Fletcher, not found in the play's main source, Chaucer's
Knight's Tale.

Professor Thompson's study of the play's sources brought out several fundamental differences between the co-authors. Having started work without
any preconceptions as to the authorship division, she found that her detailed
analysis 'strongly . . . confirmed' the accepted assignation of scenes made by
nineteenth-century scholars on the basis of verse tests. Indeed, she discovered

that 'the contrast between the two dramatists' soon became 'the most important focus' of her discussion, as she realized that 'Shakespeare and Fletcher clearly saw completely different things in *The Knight's Tale* and dramatized it in quite independent ways' (p. 167). The difference can be seen both in their varying fidelity to the source, and in their attitudes to it. As he had done with Holinshed in *Henry VIII*, Fletcher tends to take over whole sequences from Chaucer with little change, although he 'exploits the more comic and superficial elements of the story such as absurdity and suspense', while Shakespeare 'seems to see something very serious, not to say gloomy, in *The Knight's Tale*' (p. 172). In Act 1, Thompson showed (pp. 172–9), Shakespeare boldly reshaped the source-material, making a 'free adaptation' for the first scene, and inventing the two following ones, showing first Palamon and Arcite (1.2), then Emilia (1.3). When Fletcher takes over, in 2.2, 'the action speeds up at the same time as it narrows in scope and declines in seriousness' (p. 181). The cousins' quarrel over Emilia may be based on Chaucer but, as Thompson pointed out, Fletcher 'trivializes the main issue by omitting Palamon's reminder that they both swore

> That never for to dyen in the payne
> Till that the deth departe us twayne
> Neither us in love to hindre other
> (*Knight's Tale*, 1135–7)

so that his "I saw her first" claim becomes ridiculous. Arcite's reply is likewise simplified' (p. 183). Although emptying Chaucer's poem of its seriousness, Fletcher adheres closely to his source in Act 2 (p. 187), and again in 4.6, where he copies many verbal details (pp. 196–8). Shakespeare follows Chaucer quite closely for the prayers in 5.1, but from 5.3 onwards 'the source is considerably altered, and treated with as much if not more freedom than in Act 1' (p. 203). The same contrast, we remember, between Shakespeare's free reshaping of the sources and Fletcher's more faithful adherence to them, has been found in *Henry VIII* (Law 1957).

The differences between the co-authors in their handling of source-material may derive from their different experiences as working dramatists. In his far longer career Shakespeare had learned how to abridge material, reshape it, and place it in a different context, as he did so effectively with the frame action involving Theseus and Hippolyta. His scenes are highly compressed in both thought and expression, Fletcher's more straightforward, easier to take in. Some commentators have pointed to the evidence of Fletcher's relative inexperience as a dramatist (Hickson 1847, pp. 85, 87), and these differences in experience and temperament make their work easily distinguishable, even though they must have 'agreed on such alterations [to Chaucer] as a dramatic compression of the time-scheme, a general tightening of the structure and a greater emphasis on characterization' (Thompson 1978,

p. 169). Due possibly to Shakespeare's influence, the plot of *The Two Noble
Kinsmen* is 'much more straightforward than those [Fletcher] usually chooses,
and the number of emotional climaxes and theatrical set-pieces is thereby limited' (p. 211)—especially compared to *Henry VIII*. The play's plotting did not
leave much opportunity for another (damaging) feature of Fletcherian tragicomedy, 'the poses which make many of the protagonists unconvincing or
inconsistent' (Waith 1952, p. 136). Instead, Fletcher could 'exploit a comparatively simple situation with great effect: 3.6 and 4.2 . . . are equal if not
superior to anything in the Fletcher canon' (Thompson 1978, p. 211).

But another shaping difference, Thompson showed, was the fact that
Fletcher adapted the basic Chaucer story to 'the successful tragicomic pattern', as he did again in *Women Pleased* (1620), which drew on *The Wife of
Bath's Tale* (pp. 51–7). Well aware how best to use his talents, Fletcher left out
the kind of material which would

be incongruous with his tragicomic conception . . . He omits Chaucer's ironic perspective because his kind of tragicomedy requires its pathos to be taken seriously.
Altogether he produces a well-constructed fast-moving tragicomedy that might have
seemed his best play if the presence of Shakespeare had not set up conflicting aims and
standards which act as a constant reminder to readers and audiences that, however
excellent Fletcher may be at his own craft, it is one which is bound to seem narrow and
limited in comparison. (p. 212)

I suggested above that the pattern of collaboration in *The Two Noble
Kinsmen* resembles that of *Henry VIII* in many respects, but one major difference is that Shakespeare reserved the ending of this play for himself. In 5.3,
set in the forest near the field of combat, Pirithous and Theseus urge Emilia to
witness the fight for which she is 'the prize and garland' (16), but she refuses
to 'taint mine eye | With dread sights it may shun' (9–10). Left alone, Emilia
examines the cousins' pictures, as Fletcher had made her do in 4.2, but now
in a quite different mood, not swooning over their beauty but objectively
recording their matching moral qualities, especially in view of the coming
contest:

> Arcite is gently visag'd; yet his eye
> Is like an engine bent, or a sharp weapon
> In a soft sheath; mercy and manly courage
> Are bedfellows in his visage. Palamon
> Has a most menacing aspect, his brow
> Is grav'd, and seems to bury what it frowns on,
> Yet sometimes 'tis not so
>   .   .   .   .
>   melancholy
> Becomes him nobly. So does Arcite's mirth,
> But Palamon's sadness is a kind of mirth . . .
>   (41–51)

As the combat begins, our point of view is limited to Emilia's, and like her we listen helplessly for the fluctuations of the battle, first Palamon seeming victorious (66–89), then Arcite (89–104). When all the other bystanders express joy at Arcite's triumph, which will win him Emilia's hand, she expresses her pity for Palamon, wishing 'to comfort this unfriended | This miserable prince' (141–2), who is sent to execution. In the next scene we see Palamon comforting his knights, also sentenced to death, in terms that echo Shakespeare's use of the *consolatio* tradition at similar points in other plays.[72] The beginning of his speech—'There's many a man alive that hath outlived | The love o'th'people' (5.4.1–2)—recalls Cordelia, 'We are not the first | Who with best meaning have incurr'd the worst' (*Lear*, 5.3.3–4). The later passage on the advantages of dying young—'we prevent | The loathsome misery of age, beguile | The gout and rheum . . .' (6–8)—recalls Posthumus' 'welcome, bondage! . . . yet am I better | Than one that's sick o'th'gout . . .' (*Cym.*, 5.4.3–5).

Shakespeare invented Palamon's consolatory speech, but he returned to Chaucer for the stunning final reversal, in which Arcite is crushed to death by his own horse, and Palamon wins Emilia after all (5.4.40–137). In *The Knight's Tale* the fatal fall is caused by Saturn, intervening on behalf of his daughter, Venus, but Shakespeare, as Ann Thompson put it, 'reduces Saturn to a simile'—'What envious flint, | Cold as old Saturn and like him possess'd | With fire malevolent, darted a spark' (61–3), and the event is made to seem more arbitrary (Thompson 1978, pp. 206–7). Shakespeare certainly took over Chaucer's expression of his characters' sense of the unpredictable reversals of life,

> Now with his love, now in his colde grave
> Alone, withouten any compaignye
>
> (KT, 2778–9)

and 'We witen nat what thing we preyen heere' (1260). As Thompson saw, Shakespeare's Theseus 'tries to rationalize the situation . . . but his final speech expresses bewilderment as well as resignation' (p. 208):

> O you heavenly charmers,
> What things you make of us! For what we lack
> We laugh, for what we have are sorry; still
> Are children in some kind. Let us be thankful
> For that which is, and with you leave dispute
> That are above our question. Let's go off,
> And bear us like the time.
>
> (131–8)

[71] H. Littledale (ed.), *The Two Noble Kinsmen. Reprint of the Quarto, 1634* (London: The New Shakspere Society, 1876), p. 141.

[72] See B. Vickers 'Shakespearian Consolations', *Proceedings of the British Academy*, 82 (1993): 219–84, at p. 253.

That conclusion says all that can be said about this amazing reversal, in which both Venus and Mars can be seen to have triumphed (105–21).

But the dominant impression the reader or playgoer takes away at the end is of the conflict between sexual love and friendship. Palamon reflects on the painful paradox:

> O cousin,
> That we should things desire which do cost us
> The loss of our desire! That naught could buy
> Dear love but loss of dear love.
>
> (109–12)

Throughout the play, Shakespeare followed Chaucer's emphasis on the destructive power of love and friendship (Thompson 1978, pp. 198, 204–5, 213–14). Fletcher's hand has been detected in this final scene (Littledale 1885, p. 67*), in the plangent but mercifully short leave-taking between Palamon and Arcite (86–98). I am glad that Shakespeare held the pen firmly in order to end the play on this black note, giving it a far more unified conclusion than had been achieved in *Henry VIII*. If their partnership there did not succeed, we should perhaps be grateful that Fletcher aided Shakespeare in realizing the serious implications of this Chaucerian story, far darker than the resolutions achieved in his last three Romances. Where critics have long regarded those plays as a fulfilment of Shakespeare's career, the way he adapted to a different challenge in *The Two Noble Kinsmen* suggests that he was still capable of something new. The experience of co-authorship could have its positive side.

Pause Patterns in
Elizabethan Drama

As described in Chapter 2, Ants Oras developed a methodology for establishing the position of pauses within a verse line, from which he produced a 'profile' for each of the 700 plays he studied.[1] He gave both raw figures and percentages for the internal pauses in each play (pp. 61–88), and converted the statistical data into a frequency polygon. These graphs show in visual form the percentage figures on the vertical axis, the horizontal axis representing the pause position within the five-stress, ten-syllable line. Decimal points below 5 are rounded down, those above are counted as a full unit; the figures at the top of each graph indicate the total number of internal pauses in each work (pp. 5–6). The following selection from these graphs, covering some of the plays I have discussed, is reprinted with the kind permission of the University of Florida Press.

1. A-GRAPHS

These record the 'pattern formed by all pauses indicated by internal punctuation' (p. 3). See Fig. A I.1.

2. B-GRAPHS

These record the 'pattern of "strong pauses", i.e. pauses shown by punctuation marks other than commas' (p. 3). See Fig. A I.2.

In both types of pause we witness the homogeneity of Shakespeare's verse style between *Macbeth* (1606) and *Pericles* (1607), against which the non-Shakespearian parts of that play are clearly differentiated. Unfortunately, Oras never studied the oeuvre of George Wilkins, so we lack any external point of comparison.[2]

In the two late collaborations with Fletcher, the methodology that Oras developed clearly distinguishes Shakespeare's pausation patterns from Fletcher's. Again we note a continuity between the patterns of *A Winter's Tale* (1609), *The Tempest* (1611), *Henry VIII* (1613), and *The Two Noble Kinsmen* (1613–14). The last two plays themselves represent a simplification of verse technique compared to the two preceding, but

[1] A. Oras, *Pause Patterns in Elizabethan and Jacobean Drama: An Experiment in Prosody* (Gainsville, Fla., 1960), p. 3.

[2] In his forthcoming monograph, *Defining Shakespeare*: Pericles as Test Case, MacDonald Jackson has performed this task. His results place *Pericles* 1–2 closest to Wilkins's *Miseries of Enforced Marriage* and to his share of *The Travels of the Three English Brothers*. The pattern for *Pericles* 3–5, on the other hand, is virtually identical with that for *Coriolanus*.

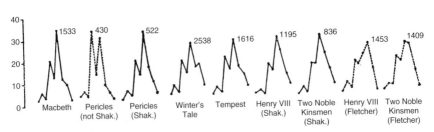

Fɪɢ. A I.1

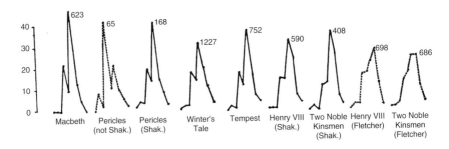

Fɪɢ. A I.2

their contours are still unmistakably clearer than those of Fletcher's scenes, which are altogether looser, more amorphous.

3. C-GRAPHS

These record the 'pattern of "splits" or "line splits", i. e. breaks within the pentameter line dividing speeches by different characters—by far the heaviest type of pause, rarely found before 1600' (p. 3). See Fig. A I.3.

As far as the Shakespeare collaborations go, the unity of style between *Macbeth* and *Pericles* is as clear in this test as in the two preceding, with Wilkins's scenes displaying a quite different distribution of breaks. For the last two collaborations, the stylistic homogeneity from *A Winter's Tale* to *The Two Noble Kinsmen* is once more instantly apparent. Fletcher's two contributions differ in these C-graphs to the same degree as in the A- and B-graphs, *The Two Noble Kinsmen* again having the more shapeless pattern.

Ants Oras was well aware that his method had a fruitful application to attribution studies. In the work of Dekker, for instance, Oras showed that his individual style is homogeneous between *1 Honest Whore* (1604) and its sequel (1605), against which Middleton's contribution to the first part forms a sharp contrast. At a much later stage of his career, Dekker collaborated with Massinger on *The Virgin Martyr* (1620), and

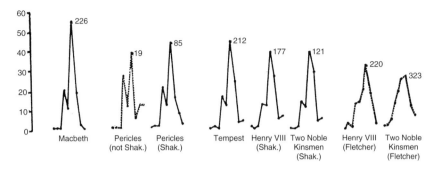

FIG. A I.3

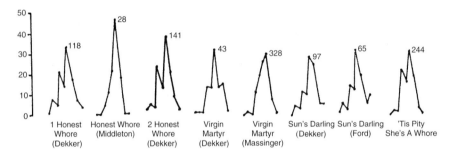

FIG. A I.4

with Ford on *The Sun's Darling* (1624). Ford's normal pausation practices in sole-authored plays can be gleaned from *'Tis Pity She's a Whore* (?1632) in Fig. A I.4; for Massinger's, see *The Duke of Milan* in Fig. A I.5.

We have seen something of Fletcher's characteristic use of pauses in his two collaborations with Shakespeare. His early verse style remained distinctively different from his co-author Beaumont, as can be seen from a comparison of Fletcher alone in *The Faithful Shepherdess* (1608) with their joint production *Cupid's Revenge* (1608). Beaumont's pause patterns in this collaboration correspond to those in his sole-authored play, *The Knight of the Burning Pestle* (1607). Later in his career Fletcher worked frequently with Massinger, whose style can be clearly differentiated in *The Little French Lawyer* (1619). Massinger's normal pause patterns can be seen from *The Duke of Milan* (1621), which in turn corresponds closely to that in his Dekker collaboration, *Virgin Martyr* (above).

Although his work remained unknown to many scholars, Ants Oras made a valuable contribution to Middleton's canon, both validating Middleton's claim to plays of disputed authorship and differentiating his style from that of his co-authors. Oras defined a common pattern in the Jacobean dramatists, having 'a gradual ascent up to the sixth or seventh position, sometimes showing distinctive curves and bulges on the

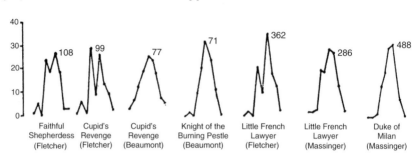

FIG. A I.5

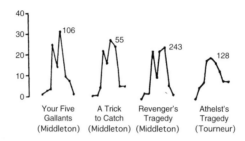

FIG. A I.6

way up, then dropping off suddenly', and lacking the 'late Shakespearean . . . sharp notch or depression in the middle' (p. 23). Middleton shares some features of this pattern, 'but his graphs have a special physiognomy of their own . . . They mostly culminate at the stressed sixth position, show a much steeper rise from the fifth position to the top, and drop even more suddenly from the seventh to the eighth. The upper part tends to be slimmer and more pointed, which makes them look strangely elegant' (pp. 23–4). As Oras pointed out, the iambic element is more prominent in Middleton's line splits than in most of his contemporaries, for although Middleton, in 'his fully formed style, avoided splits after the seventh position, the impression he creates is of more emphatic pausing, of more abrupt breaks—no doubt because of his more frequent use of the even position for his splits' (p. 27), so re-establishing an iambic pattern in a period showing a general trend towards the trochaic. This pattern can be seen in two of Middleton's early plays, *A Trick to Catch the Old One* (1605) and *Your Five Gallants* (1605), which demonstrate a clear homogeneity with *The Revenger's Tragedy* (1606). By the same token, Tourneur's *The Atheist's Tragedy* (1609) evidently comes from a completely different source, having a verse style that can be distinguished from Middleton's in several ways, but especially 'in the frequency of its almost foolhardy run-on procedures, more extreme even than Massinger's' (p. 28). See Fig. A I.6.

Applying his analytical method to Middleton's late works, Oras showed that the pause pattern of *Women Beware Women* (1621) corresponded both to Middleton's

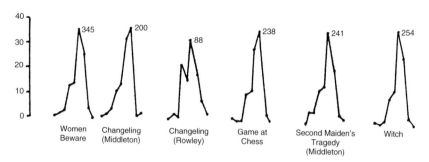

FIG. A I.7

share of *The Changeling* (1622) and to his sole-authored play, *A Game at Chess* (1624). As for *The Second Maiden's Tragedy* (1611), which a series of scholars using quite different methods have claimed for Middleton, alongside *The Revenger's Tragedy*, Oras concluded that 'the attribution of the play to Middleton, frequently made and as frequently attacked, would appear to receive considerable support from the extraordinary likeness of its line-split design to the mature patterns of Middleton, quite particularly in those plays closest to it in time, above all that of *The Witch*' (p. 32). *The Witch*, dated *c.*1609–*c.*1616 in the Harbage-Schoenbaum *Annals*, is indeed very similar. See Fig. A I.7.

Oras himself warned that this method alone could not settle authorship disputes, for 'a writer with a well-defined pattern of his own [may] deviate from it, if only once or twice in a long career', as can be seen with Massinger. Also, some surprisingly similar patterns emerge from plays that are otherwise different in every possible way, such as Chapman's *All Fools* and a play of unknown authorship, *The Trial of Chivalry*. It follows, then, that if the analysis of an anonymous work yields a pattern peculiar to a known writer, 'one had still better look for additional evidence before committing oneself to a definite opinion'. Oras modestly concluded that his analyses of over 700 plays 'may serve as corroboratory evidence or may supply clues for further study' (p. 31). I can only hope that future researchers will further develop this promising methodology.

Abolishing the Author? Theory *versus* History

I

The assumption governing my research, and that of all the scholars who have worked on attribution studies, is that writers have distinct and individual styles, both at the conscious level (the deliberate choice and handling of a verse form or stylistic resource, such as metaphor or verbal patterning) and at the unconscious (the use of abbreviations, a preference for one linguistic variant rather than another). These methodologies, and their practical applications, all rest on the further assumption that, when two or more writers collaborate on a play, we may be able to tell them apart, provided that we have access to other work by them, so that we can establish what their normal style(s) are when working alone. Both assumptions have been widely accepted, forming the basis of much scholarly work for over 200 years. Recently, however, we have been told that the methodology of authorship studies is 'problematic', since it rests on a concept of the author which must be dismissed as 'anachronistic'. As we saw in Chapter 6, in his edition of *Henry VIII* Gordon McMullan praised 'Michel Foucault's groundbreaking work on the historical construction of the concept of authorship', and endorsed two followers of Foucault who claimed that 'the proprietorship of individuals over "their own" work . . . in fact postdates the early modern period: Ben Jonson's highly conscious efforts to establish himself as an "author" mark only the beginning of a major shift in perceptions'.[1] I shall shortly discuss the claims made by one of these Foucauldians, Jeffrey Masten, in some detail, but I must first address their master's thesis that the whole concept of an author only emerged in the modern period.

Foucault made this pronouncement in a lecture given to an audience of philosophers in Paris, in February 1969, called 'What is an Author?'[2] To grasp its idiosyncratic emphases it helps to know the special sense in which Foucault used some key terms, especially 'discourse'. As Mark Bauerlein put it, 'Foucault gave to "discourse" an ominous and powerful new significance. Discourse was no longer a set of referentially similar statements. It was a historically developed and institutionally enacted mechanism of control geared to the production of putatively real and normal things like facts, rationality, and subjects'.[3] For Foucault, 'discourse' was intimately con-

---

[1] G. McMullan (ed.), William Shakespeare and John Fletcher, *King Henry VIII (All Is True)*, Arden Shakespeare, Third Series (London, 2000), pp. 196–7.

[2] M. Foucault, 'What is an Author?', trans. J. V. Harari, in Harari (ed.), *Textual Strategies: Perspectives in Post-Structuralist Criticism* (Ithaca, NY, 1979), pp. 141–60; here cited from David Lodge (ed.), *Modern Criticism and Theory* (London, 1988), pp. 197–210.

[3] M. Bauerlein, *Literary Criticism: An Autopsy* (Philadelphia, 1997), p. 52.

nected with power relations, social control, behavioural taboos, the police, and other forms of repression. This association of ideas accounts for the otherwise surprising opening claim in this lecture, that 'discourses are objects of appropriation', and that their 'ownership' involves an act of transgression. According to Foucault, 'the form of authorship from which [discourses] spring . . . has always been *subsequent* to what one might call penal appropriation. Texts, books, and discourses really *began* to have authors (other than mythical, "sacralized" and "sacralizing" figures) to the extent that authors became subject to punishment, that is, to the extent that discourses could be transgressive' (Foucault 1988, p. 202; my italics). In Foucault's peculiar version of history, it was only 'at the end of the eighteenth and the beginning of the nineteenth century', when 'a system of ownership came into being' and 'strict rules concerning author's rights, author–publisher relations, rights of reproduction, and related matters were enacted', that 'the possibility of transgression attached to the act of writing' allowed the emergence of the author, a process which began 'with the moment at which he was placed in the system of property that characterizes our society' (p. 202).

Foucault now started to erode the concept of an individual writer by referring to 'the author-function', another familiar move in French thought of the late 1960s, with its relentless attack on the notion of the subject.[4] His second claim was that this 'author-function' is a historical variable:

> There was a time when the texts that we today call 'literary' (narratives, stories, epics, tragedies, comedies) were accepted, put into circulation, and valorized without any question about the identity of their author. . . . On the other hand, those texts that we would now call scientific—those dealing with cosmology and the heavens, medicine and illnesses, natural sciences and geography—were accepted in the Middle Ages, and accepted as 'true', only when marked with the name of their author . . .
>
> A reversal occurred in the seventeenth or eighteenth century. Scientific discourses began to be received for themselves, in the anonymity of an established or always redemonstrable truth; their membership in a systematic ensemble, and not the reference to the individual who produced them, stood as their guarantee. The author-function faded away. . . . By the same token, literary discourses came to be accepted only when endowed with the author-function. We now ask of each poetic or fictional text: from where does it come, who wrote it, when, under what circumstances, or beginning with what design? (pp. 202–3)

Foucault's third claim, another familiar move in French thought at this period, was to demote the author from an actual human being to a social 'construct'. He declared that the 'author-function . . . does not develop spontaneously as the attribution of a discourse to an individual. It is, rather, the result of a complex operation which *constructs* a certain rational being that [*sic*] we call "author"'' (p. 203; my italics). Foucault's denial of the author as the originator of a text having its own meaning and value, whether trivial or profound, now reached its most extreme expression: 'these aspects of an individual which *we designate* as making him an author are only a projection, in more or less psychologizing terms, of the operations that *we force* texts to undergo, the connections that *we make*, the traits that *we*

---

[4] On the iconoclastic origins of Current Literary Theory in the Paris of the 1960s, see e.g. Brian Vickers, *Appropriating Shakespeare: Contemporary Critical Quarrels* (New Haven and London, 1993), pp. xii–xvi, 3–162, and the literature cited there.

establish as pertinent, the continuities that *we recognize*, or the exclusions that *we practice*' (p. 203; my italics).

Rather like Roland Barthes, whose essay of 1967 pronouncing the 'Death of the Author' had attracted notoriety,[5] Foucault took away power and identity from the author, transferring it to the reader. However, as Séan Burke showed in a classic study,[6] neither Barthes nor Foucault succeeded in constructing a coherent argument: both essays are riddled with ambiguities and inconsistencies, and despite their polemic both iconoclasts continued to rely on the concept of the author in their subsequent writings. Indeed, towards the end of this lecture Foucault actually reinstated the author, hailing Marx and Freud as writers who had not only authored memorable texts but had 'produced . . . the possibilities and the rules for the formation of other texts', so deserving to be acclaimed as ' "founders of discursivity" ' (pp. 206–8). As Burke observed, the phrase 'founders of discursivity' sounds particularly strange, 'for it is the concept of the subject as founder which has earned Foucault's most consistent and enduring disapprobation' (Burke 1998, p. 91). Despite beginning and ending his essay with a quotation from Beckett (' "What does it matter who is speaking?" '), Burke argued that

> Foucault here provides the most extreme example of why it does matter. The discovery of a text like Freud's 'Project for a Scientific Psychology' will modify psychoanalysis if and only if it is a text by Freud. Over and above the text's content, the fact of attribution—in and of itself—is the primary factor in establishing its significance for the psychoanalytical field. (p. 93)

That elucidation of Foucault's core assumption is a remarkably pertinent contribution to the argument of this book, even though it reveals the hopeless contradictions within his argument.

But Foucault's essay is not only incoherent, it bears no resemblance to historical argument. Despite the respect, even reverence with which Foucault's pronouncements have been accepted by some literary critics, his claim to be taken seriously as a historian seems increasingly slight. Vincent Descombes, a leading authority on modern French philosophy, judged that 'Foucault's historical works elude discussion, in that the gist of their argument remains indeterminate', belonging 'properly to the genre of fiction' (cit. Vickers 1993*b*, p. 105). J. G. Merquior's study of Foucault listed a large number of historians who had exposed the deficiencies of his historiography—although his admirers have either not read or refused to take note of these critiques.[7]

---

[5] See R. Barthes, 'The Death of the Author', in Barthes, *Image-Music-Text*, essays selected and translated by Stephen Heath (London, 1977), pp. 142–8.

[6] S. Burke, *The Death and Return of the Author: Criticism and Subjectivity in Barthes, Foucault and Derrida* (2nd enlarged edn., Edinburgh, 1998), especially ch. 1, 'The Birth of the Reader', pp. 20–61.

[7] See J. G. Merquior, *Foucault* (Berkeley and Los Angeles, 1985), especially the critiques reviewed there by Klaus Doerner, Jon Elster, Jan Miel, G. S. Rousseau, Peter Sedgwick, Peter Spierenberg, and Karen Williams. In addition, see Alan Megill, 'Foucault, Structuralism and the Ends of History', *Journal of Modern History*, 51 (1979): 451–503, and H. C. Erik Midelfort, 'Madness and Civilization in Early Modern Europe: A Reappraisal of Michel Foucault', in Barbara Malamont (ed.), *After the Reformation: Essays in Honor of J. H. Hexter* (Philadelphia and Manchester, 1980), pp. 247–65. On the unhistorical nature of Foucault's characterization of an early modern mentality see George Huppert, '*Divinatio et eruditio*: Thoughts on Foucault', *History and Theory*, 13 (1974): 191–207, and Ian Maclean, 'Foucault's Renaissance Episteme Reassessed: An Aristotelian Counterblast', *Journal of the History of Ideas*, 59 (1998): 149–66.

Every point in his history of the 'late emergence of the author' is dubious, if not obviously wrong. To begin at the end, scientific discourses in the seventeenth century ('or eighteenth' seems a disturbingly indecisive formulation), far from being 'received for themselves, in the anonymity of an established or always redemonstrable truth', were all explicitly identified with the author who had produced them. Anyone familiar with the publishing output and intellectual career of Kepler, Galileo, Descartes, Newton, and many others, will know that those philosophers were intensely conscious of their intellectual property, fiercely protective of their claims to originality and priority, and that this century saw an unparalleled emergence of distinctive systems identified with a specific author.[8] Nor did their work merely (re)affirm some established and demonstrable truth, for each of those philosophers issued profound challenges to extant theories, arousing intense controversy in their lifetime and beyond.

As for the time ('*a time there was* . . .') when 'epics, tragedies, comedies' were circulated and enjoyed without any consideration of their author, the vagueness of the formulation points to its unreality. It will never be possible to trace with any certainty the process by which the reciters of traditional epics gradually became separated from their composers, and the poems attributed to 'Homer' became canonic,[9] but the recognition of poets as professional writers, patronized by rulers, certainly took place in the late sixth century BC. Simonides, Pindar, and Bacchylides were 'fully professionalized itinerant craftsmen', accepting 'poetic commissions'. They can properly be called 'the first true authors', in whom 'individual poetic skill' was the defining factor.[10] When we reach Greek drama we know a great deal about named authors. In Athens, at the beginning of the fifth century, tragedies were performed as part of the Great Dionysia, the spring festival of Dionysus Eleuthereus, at which three poets competed, each presenting three tragedies and one satyric play. We know the names of several poets whose work has not survived (Phrynichus, Polyphradmon, Philocles, Meletus), but we can happily study the individual qualities and achievements of Aeschylus, Sophocles, and Euripides, whose successes and failures at the Dionysia are documented. For proof that the ancient Greeks recognized all three as the authors and in that sense 'owners' of their plays, each with an individual style, distinctive dramaturgy, and personal attitudes towards politics and society, we need look no further than Aristophanes' *Frogs*,[11] performed in January 405 BC. In the second half of this play Dionysus presides over a literary contest between Aeschylus and Euripides, in which each mocks the other's typical subject-matter and style. Euripides parodies Aeschylus' cumbersome diction (923–40), and describes his own drama as being the first that allowed women and slaves to talk freely on stage, one which taught the people of Athens to 'think evil and be always hypercritical' (948–58)—throughout,

---

[8] See Brian Vickers, review of *The Cambridge History of Seventeenth-Century Philosophy*, in *Renaissance Quarterly*, 54 (2001): 618–24.

[9] See e.g. Gregory Nagy, 'Early Greek Views of Poets and Poetry', in George A. Kennedy (ed.), *The Cambridge History of Literary Criticism*, i. *Classical Criticism* (Cambridge, 1989), pp. 1–77, especially §7, 'The Poet as Author' (pp. 35–8), and §10, 'The Singer as Author' (pp. 52–63).

[10] Leslie Kurke, 'The Strangeness of "Song Culture": Archaic Greek Poetry', in Oliver Taplin (ed.), *Literature in the Greek and Roman Worlds: A New Perspective* (Oxford, 2000), p. 63.

[11] Trans. T. F. Higham, in D. A. Russell and M. Winterbottom (eds.), *Ancient Literary Criticism: The Principal Texts in New Translation* (Oxford, 1972), pp. 8–38.

Aristophanes loads the scales unfairly against Euripides. Aeschylus, in turn, denounces Euripides for corrupting public morality, contrasting the wholesome lessons he himself had taught in *Seven Against Thebes* and *Persians*, and praising the poet's role as the teacher of virtue (1006–62). Aristophanes then makes Aeschylus attack Euripides for his distasteful realism, having represented on stage bawds and go-betweens, characters dressed in rags, and accouchements in shrines (1063–87). Both poets now mock each other's prologues, with increasingly vicious parodies and malicious quotations. Dionysus (like Aristophanes) sides with Aeschylus, who finally disposes of Euripides with a remarkable burlesque choric song ridiculing his boast of having democratized tragedy, and making fun of his metrical extravagances and lapses of decorum (1119–1483). The notion of authors being individual, having recognizably different styles and preoccupations, goes back to the early days of Western literature, long antedating 'post-Enlightenment' attitudes.

Authors, patrons, books, booksellers, libraries—all existed in antiquity.[12] In Greece, books (in the form of a papyrus roll) became available in the second half of the fifth century BC, and were soon in general circulation, with Athens having its own book trade by the fourth century. Individuals collected the best-known poets and philosophers: Plato records that a copy of Anaxagoras could be bought in the Agora, while the works of Lysias, a successful *logographos*, were much sought after. Authors sometimes distributed books to their friends after a public reading.[13] Many scholars built up their own collections: among the Greeks, Aristotle and his pupils assembled vast numbers of books, while Cicero accumulated several libraries. In the Hellenistic period public libraries were established, from Pergamon (with 200,000 papyrus rolls or volumes) and Alexandria (half a million) to Rome, where Augustus founded two, and the city eventually had twenty-eight. Contrary to Foucault's assertions, authors were indelibly associated with their works. The Hellenistic poet and scholar Callimachus compiled his *Pinakes*, 'Tables of Those who have distinguished themselves in Every Form of Culture and of What they Wrote', a work in 120 books which was both a bibliography of Greek literature and a catalogue of the Alexandrian Library, organized by subject and including biographical notes. That library kept their seventeen volumes of Pindar, for instance, in a vellum cover, of which the label has survived, identifying 'The Complete Pindar'.

If the Greeks established the author as originator and owner of his works, they also bore witness to the fact that wherever texts have authors, they will soon have plagiarists, real or imaginary. The Greeks had a word for it: *klopē*, theft, and numerous dissertations were written 'On Plagiarism' (*peri klopēs*). Accusations of, or fears of, plagiarism were common, from Aristophanes' attack on Eupolis (whose *Maricas* was his own *Knights*, he claimed, 'worn inside out'). In a collection dating from the sixth century BC, Theognis, in order to forestall plagiarism, put a 'seal' (*sphragis*) on his verses:

---

[12] In the following discussion I have partly relied on Simon Hornblower and Antony Spawforth (eds.), *The Oxford Classical Dictionary*, 3rd edn. (Oxford, 1996): see the entries on 'books, Greek and Roman'; 'books, poetic'; 'Callimachus (3)'; 'libraries'; 'ownership, Roman'; 'patronage, literary'; 'plagiarism'; 'sphragis'; and 'Theognis'. I thank Annette Baertschi for her assistance with some of the material involving Latin poetry.

[13] Russell and Winterbottom 1972, p. 25 n.

> When I make verses, Cyrnus, have them locked away—
>   though if they're stolen, it will always show;
> no one will choose the bad where better is to hand,
>   and all will say, 'This is Theognis' verse,
> from Megara': my name is famous everywhere.[14]

This motif, by which an author names or otherwise identifies himself, especially at the beginning or end of a poem or collection of poems, is found as early as Hesiod's *Theogony*, and may have originally functioned to identify a work with its author in a period of poetic fluidity. Subsequently it became a conventional way of ending a collection of poems, to identify them as an author's property, and to discourage theft.

All the connotations of authorship that I have documented for Greece existed in Rome, but in a more pronounced form. Roman authors were highly conscious of their individuality, especially so since they had been indebted to the Greeks for so much, from the major genres (except satire) to poetic conventions, prosody, and rhetorical figures. They acknowledged debts to specific Greek authors (Virgil to Theocritus and Hesiod; Propertius to Callimachus; Horace to Archilochus; Cicero to Demosthenes), while often claiming to have gone beyond them: *imitatio* led automatically to *aemulatio*.[15] Roman authors (apart from some working for the theatre) received no payment from booksellers, being dependent on friends and patrons for artistic and financial encouragement. Emperors promoted their favourite authors, while generous private patrons, such as Asinius Pollio (patron of Horace and Virgil), M. Valerius Messalla Corvinus (patron of Tibullus, Ovid, and others), and Maecenas (patron of Virgil, Horace, and Propertius) gave poets economic support and cultural stimulus. Poets became known through the organization of recitations and the private dispatch of copies of their works. Professional booksellers (*librarii*, which also means 'copyists') had staffs of scribes, while rich private patrons also employed copyists: Atticus published many of Cicero's works in this way. Martial (*Epigrams*, 1.117.11) describes Atrectus' bookshop in the Argiletum as having its *postes* covered with advertisements for books. All kinds of literature found their way into institutional libraries, indeed its acceptance into a great library marked a work as authentic, or at least politically acceptable.

Far from allowing them to circulate in anonymity, Roman authors made sure that their writings were identified as their property.[16] Poets, from the time of Callimachus onwards, formed their poems into collections, a self-conscious act which drew

[14] *Greek Lyric Poetry*, trans. M. L. West (Oxford, 1994), p. 64. This corpus (some 1,400 verses) is a composite from two or more ancient anthologies of elegiac excerpts. The authentic Theognis poems habitually address a friend Cyrnus, as throughout one whole section (ll. 19–254), in which the first and last excerpts serve as prologue and epilogue. On plagiarism in Greece see E. Stemplinger, *Das Plagiat in der griechischen Literatur* (Leipzig, 1912).

[15] See Doreen C. Innes, 'Augustan Critics', in Kennedy 1989, pp. 245–73, and Elaine Fantham, 'Latin Criticism of the Early Empire', ibid., pp. 274–96.

[16] Foucault connected the notion of property, intellectual and otherwise, with the modern period, but Roman society recognized and protected ownership. Goods and land changed hands in a contract of sale; one of the basic principles of Roman law was *suum cuique tribuere*, 'to render each man his due', and the transmission of property was a major preoccupation in wills. Questions of inheritance were dealt with by a special court, and formed a distinct specialization for lawyers—Pliny the Younger made his career in this branch of the law.

attention to their authorship and displayed the poems' unity and variety within a genre or theme. They called such collections their *liber*, or *libellus*, emphasizing its existence as a unit. Catullus' opening lyric discusses to whom he should 'present this | little book so carefully polished', settling on Cornelius and hoping that the Muse of poetry will 'turn as tolerant an eye upon these songs | in days to come'.[17] Ovid rounds off the first book of his *Tristia* with an epilogue (1.11) completing 'this whole book', and appealing 'for indulgence, generous reader'.[18] In such ways Roman poets made a direct link with their reading public, also making them aware that they were reading a composition that had been carefully put together.

Ovid was not alone in bringing the *auctor* and his *opus* to the reader's attention. In Latin poetry of the Augustan age poets regularly appear *in propria persona*, adding autobiographical information relevant to their vocation and poetic practice. Virgil concluded the *Eclogues* with a coda, formally bowing out of the poem (*Ecl.*, 10.70–2). But he completed the *Georgics* with a *sphragis*, a 'seal' or 'signature', in the manner of Callimachus (who had ended the four-book collection of his *Aetia* in this manner), recording that while Augustus Caesar was pursuing military victories,

> I, Virgil, nurtured in sweetest
> Parthenope, did follow unknown to fame the pursuits
> Of peace, who dallied with pastoral verse, and by youth emboldened,
> Tityrus, sang of you in the shade of a spreading beech.[19]

When Horace, who owed so much to Virgil, published his first book of verse *Epistles* in 20 BC, his concluding poem (1.20) addressed his book and revealed the poet who had created it, down to his physical appearance: 'of small stature, grey before my time, fond of the sun, quick in temper, yet so as to be easily appeased'.[20] There Horace left his 'seal' on the volume, as he did with the concluding poem (3.30) to his collection of *Odes* (23 BC), the famous assertion 'Exegi monumentum aere perennius . . .', which includes the prophetic lines:

> I shall not wholly die. A great part of me
> will escape Libitina. My fame will grow,
> ever-renewed in times to come . . .[21]

If any poet's work ever survived Libitina, the Roman goddess of funerals, it was Horace's. His prestige in Rome led to him receiving a commission from the Emperor Augustus to write a 'Secular Hymn' (*Carmen Saeculare*) for the Augustan Secular Festival, in June 17 BC, an invitation that gave this author an important position in the state (he was not the first to be so honoured). Horace's prophecy that his verse would outlive bronze and 'the procession of unnumbered years' was unexpectedly confirmed in September 1890, when a workman digging on the banks of the Tiber unearthed a large marble inscription which Augustus had set up, forming the Acts of the Games,

[17] *The Poems of Catullus*, trans. Peter Whigham (Harmondsworth, 1966), p. 49.

[18] Ovid, *The Poems of Exile*, trans. Peter Green (Harmondsworth, 1994), p. 23.

[19] *Georg.*, 4.559–66; trans. C. Day Lewis, ibid., 128. Cf. Richard F. Thomas (ed.), *Virgil, Georgics*, 2 vols. (Cambridge, 1988), i. 1–2, 7; ii. 239–41.

[20] Horace, *Satires, Epistles and Ars Poetica*, trans. H. R. Fairclough, Loeb Classical Library (London, 1929), p. 391.

[21] Horace, *The Complete Odes and Epodes*, trans. David West (Oxford, 1997), p. 108.

including an acknowledgement of the poet responsible for the ceremonial hymn: 'carmen composuit Quintus Horatius Flaccus'. In an ode composed for his fourth Book (*c.*13 BC) Horace referred to this commission (which he regarded as having crowned his life's work), claiming his descent from Phoebus Apollo, god of poetry, who 'has given me the art, the very breath I of song', and addressing a maiden who had taken part in the performance of his *Carmen Saeculare*:

> In time to come when you are a Roman wife, you will say,
>   'When the Secular festival brought back its lights,
> I performed the hymn which so pleased the gods,
>   and was taught the music of the poet Horace'.[22]

The public recognition of Horace as Poet Laureate would be alone sufficient to prove that the idea of the author was well established in antiquity.

In Latin poetry authors are regularly present in their poems, moving freely and apparently quite naturally within their own creations, to a degree that may surprise the modern reader. Beginning his sixth Eclogue, Virgil gave a quasi-autobiographical account of how he had been tempted to turn from pastoral to epic poetry, until Apollo intervened (*Ecl.* 6.1–13). In the first poem of his *Amores* Ovid turned his failure to write epic into a brilliant description of that genre to which he was best suited, the *elegia* or love-poem, with its characteristic metrical form:

> My epic was under construction—wars and armed violence
> in the grand manner, with metre matching theme.
> I had written the second hexameter when Cupid grinned
> and calmly removed one of its feet.[23]

The god of love then fired an arrow, setting the poet's blood 'on fire'. Now,

> Love has moved in as master of my heart.
> I choose the couplet—rising six feet, falling five.
> Farewell, hexameters and iron wars.
> Garland your golden hair with myrtle from the seaside,
> Hendecametric Muse, my Elegia.

> (27–30)

So a poem which began in the epic mode with the word 'Arma', ends by explaining how the elegiac couplet (the usual metre for love-poetry) came about, joining a pentameter to a hexameter.

Roman poets frequently addressed themselves by their own name in their poems, validating their authorship. In one lyric (49) Catullus greets Cicero—'gratias tibi maximas Catullus': 'Catullus, least of poets, [thanks] Marcus Tullius . . . prince of advocates'. Catullus cites his own name in nineteen other poems, often in conjunction with Lesbia's.[24] Catullus' example of the poet as not just an author but an actor in his

---

[22] *Odes*, 4.6, trans. West, pp. 119–21. The inscription is reproduced in Taplin 2000, p. 404.

[23] *Amores*, 1.1–4; trans. Guy Lee, *Ovid's Amores* (London, 1968), p. 3. Cf. also Propertius, 3.3, in which Apollo is brought in to dissuade him from writing epic.

[24] See *The Poems of Catullus*, nos. 2, 6, 7, 8, 11, 12, 13, 14, 15, 38, 44, 46, 56, 58, 68, 72, 76, 79, 82.

own poems was followed by Propertius and Tibullus, both of whom figure as lovers and poets in their own verses.[25]

The most brilliant presenter of the poetic self in Augustan poetry was Ovid. Having set his seal on the first Book of the *Amores* with the famous poem (1.15) dismissing envy and asserting that his work will survive his death, Ovid begins Book 2 with a jocular self-announcement, offering the reader

> A second batch of verses by that naughty provincial poet,
>   Naso, the chronicler of his own
> Wanton frivolities; another of Love's commissions (warning
>   To puritans: *This volume is not for you.*)[26]

Appropriately, Ovid ended his *Amores* by announcing the 'final lap' of his career as a love-poet, adding a postscript concerning the author:

> of Paelignian extraction . . .
>   Mantua boasts her Virgil,
> The Veronese their Catullus. *I* shall become the pride
> Of my fellow-Paelignians.
>
>   (3.15; trans. Green, pp. 164–5)

While bidding farewell to these 'unheroic elegiacs'—none the less 'Work born to live on when its maker's dead!'—Ovid lets us look forward to the next stage in his poetic career: as Virgil moved on to epic, he will to tragedy, producing a much-praised *Medea* (now lost).

If the poets of Augustan Rome regularly take part in their own poems, naming and describing themselves, explaining how they came to shift (or not) from one genre to another, and how the verse form they are using came into existence, they are also generous in their reference to other poets. In the *Eclogues* Virgil alludes to Gallus (10.2–73), Varius (9.35), and Asinius Pollio (3.84–8, 4.12), while Horace addresses an affectionate letter to Tibullus (*Epistles*, 1.4). Poets also constructed genealogies of descent within a genre. In one of his elegies Propertius lists the poets and their loves, moving from Homer and Virgil to Varro, Catullus, Calvus, and Gallus—all famous authors—concluding with himself (2.24):

> Last but not least Propertius, Cynthia's bard,
> If I be ranked with these by fame's award.
>
>   (trans. Watts, p. 121)

Augustan poets celebrated other poets, living or dead. In his *Amores* (3.9) Ovid included a marvellous tribute to Tibullus, who died in 19 BC. According to Aulus Gellius, three earlier Roman poets even wrote their own epitaphs. He included them (according to some modern scholars, doubtfully attributed) in his *Noctes Atticae*. The epitaph ascribed to Plautus is on the topos 'Comoedia luget':

---

[25] See e.g. Propertius, 1.14, 4.7, in *The Poems of Propertius*, trans. A. E. Watts (Harmondsworth, 1966), pp. 87–8, 185; Tibullus, 1.3, 1.9, in *The Poems of Tibullus*, trans. Philip Dunlop (Harmondsworth, 1972), pp. 69, 90.

[26] Ovid, *The Erotic Poems*, trans. Peter Green (Harmondsworth, 1982), p. 85.

> Since Plautus has met death, Comedy mourns,
> Deserted is the stage; then Laughter, Sport and Wit,
> And Music's countless numbers all together wept.[27]

Ben Jonson echoed that tribute in the closing lines of his poem 'To the memory of my beloved, the author Mr. William Shakespeare', in the 1623 Folio, invoking this 'star of Poets' to 'Shine forth' and 'cheer the drooping stage; | Which, since thy flight from hence, hath mourned like night, | And despairs day, but for thy volume's light'.[28]

Even on this brief survey it must be obvious that Roman poets were omnipresent in their poems, self-conscious authors alerting their reading public to the hand behind the *stilus*, recording how and why this poem had been written at that point in time, and in its genre or metrical form. The fact that Foucault could theorize about the late emergence of the author suggests that he had little knowledge of classical literature, or had forgotten what he knew. He claimed that the author's belated appearance was linked to the possibility of transgression and the establishment of a penal code in the eighteenth century. But Ovid fatally transgressed Roman public ethics in AD 8 with the publication of his *Ars Amatoria*, and Augustus banished him to Tomis (on the Black Sea) on two charges, his poem and a mistake of conduct ('duo crimina, carmen et error', *Tristia*, 2.207). In exile Ovid produced *Tristia*, a book comprising five books of epistles (AD 8–12) which matches Horace in its candid presentation of the poet in his work. The first poem of Book I (an *envoi*) imitates Horace's epistle by addressing his 'little book' on its way to the bookseller. A later poem gives the readers the blunt autobiographical facts:

> Listen, readers of the future, if you want to know who I was—the jesting author of light love poems whom you read. My birthplace is Sulmo, rich in cold streams, and ninety miles away from the City. Here I was raised: if you want to know the year, it was when both consulships met a like fate.[29]

That is, in 43 BC. Ovid then describes how his career diverged from that of his elder brother, preferring poetry to a public life. 'I cultivated the acquaintance of poets of the day', he goes on, listing the authors to whom he owes most: Macer, Propertius, Ponticus, Bassus, Horace. In another famous poem[30] (drawn on by Ben Jonson in his First Folio tribute to Shakespeare[31]), Ovid claims immortality for himself matching and indeed excelling the poets who preceded him—among the Greeks Homer, Hesiod, Callimachus ('his art is great'), Sophocles, Aratus, and Menander; among the Romans, Ennius ('for all his lack of art'), Accius, Varro, Lucretius, Virgil, Tibullus, Gallus. As a full reading could show, Ovid gives specific attributes to most of these poets, characterizing them by their preferred subject-matter or style.

Further proof that Roman poets already regarded their works as their own production and property is provided by their attitude to plagiarism. The term, derived from the Latin *plagiarius* or 'kidnapper', was applied to literary theft by Martial in Book I

---

[27] *The Attic Nights of Aulus Gellius*, trans. J. C. Rolfe, Loeb Classical Library, 3 vols. (London, 1961), i. 108–11.

[28] Cf. B. Vickers, *English Renaissance Literary Criticism* (Oxford, 1999), p. 540—where I had not spotted the allusion.

[29] *Tristia*, 4.10.1 ff., trans. M. Winterbottom, in Russell and Winterbottom 1972, pp. 292–3.

[30] *Amores*, 1.15; trans. M. Winterbottom, in Russell and Winterbottom 1972, pp. 297–8.

[31] Cf. Vickers 1999, pp. 530 and note, 539–40.

of his *Epigrams* (published in AD 80), where he appeals to a friend to preserve his poems from a poet who is going round reciting them as if they were his own: 'when that fellow calls himself their owner, say that they are mine, sent forth from my hand (*dicas esse meos manuque missos*). If thrice and four times you shout this, you will shame the plagiarist' (1.52).[32] In other poems the plagiarist is identified:

> There is one page of yours, Fidentinus, in a book of mine—a page, too, stamped by the distinct likeness of its master (*certa domini signata figura*)—which convicts your poems of palpable theft . . . My books need no title or judge to prove them; your page stares you in the face, and calls you 'thief'. (1.53)

By the claim that the plagiarized passage was 'stamped by the distinct likeness of its master' Martial shows his awareness of his own individual poetic style. In all these poems Martial protests that his own property is being stolen:

> Rumour asserts, Fidentinus, that you recite my works to the crowd, just as if they were your own. If you wish they should be called mine, I will send you the poems gratis; if you wish them to be called yours, buy my disclaimer of them. (1.29)

That disclaimer is contained in a later epigram, addressed to a 'greedy thief of my works', who thinks he can become a poet by buying 'a transcript and a cheap papyrus roll' for 'six or ten sesterces . . . Whoever recites another man's work, and so woos fame, ought not to buy a book, but—silence' (1.66). The plagiarist steals not only the poet's works but the fame due to him, a fame which Horace and Ovid equated with immortality. Horace had expressed a comparable dislike of plagiarism in a verse-letter some sixty years earlier, enquiring of his friend, Julius Florus,

> What, pray is Celsus doing? He was warned, and must often be warned to search for home treasures, and to shrink from touching the writings which Apollo on the Palatine has admitted: lest, if some day perchance the flock of birds come to reclaim their plumage, the poor crow, stripped of his stolen colours, awake laughter.[33]

(Florus had evidently been copying earlier writers, using the library in the temple of Apollo on the Palatine.) Horace's reference to the *cornicula*, or 'little crow' being stripped of his stolen plumage and becoming a source of ridicule, offered a description of the plagiarist which was to be quoted for centuries. He was probably alluding to the Aesopic fable of 'The vainglorious jackdaw and the peacock', which was retold in Latin verse by Phaedrus to point the following moral:

> Ne gloriari libeat alienis bonis,
> suoque potius habitu vitam degere.[34]

[32] Martial, *Epigrams*, trans. W. C. R. Ker, Loeb Classical Library, 2 vols. (London, rev. edn., 1968).

[33] *Epistles*, 1.3.14–20; trans. Fairclough 1929, pp. 271–3.

[34] Phaedrus, *Fables*, 1.3: 'to the end that none may borrow another's property with which to put on airs, but may rather pass his life in clothes that are his own, Aesop has set before us the following example.

A jackdaw, puffed up with empty pride, picked up some feathers that had fallen from a peacock and adorned himself with them. Next, scorning his own kinfolk, he pushed his way into a handsome flock of peacocks. But they stripped the brazen bird of those feathers and pecked him till he took to flight. Being thus roughly handled, the saddened jackdaw attempted to return to his own tribe; but, on being driven away by them also, he bore the burden of an ugly dis-

Despite the belief expressed by Foucault's followers that 'the proprietorship of individuals over "their own" work . . . in fact postdates the early modern period' (McMullan 2000, pp. 196–7), Phaedrus' lines reiterate the distinction, fully present in ancient Rome, between 'another's property' and 'his own'. Accusations of plagiarism were not limited to lyric poetry. In two of his prologues Terence defended himself against the charge, while Cicero apostrophized Ennius: 'you who from Naevius have taken much, if you confess the debt, or if you deny it, much have stolen.'[35] The Romans had no copyright law, but writers and readers were perfectly clear about the difference between imitation and plagiarism.

II

I have discussed the prominence given to the author in Greece and Rome partly because this material disproves Foucault's thesis that the author only emerged in modern times, and partly because many of these texts were well known to the classic-ally educated writers of Renaissance England. Virgil, Horace, Ovid, were all major authors in the grammar-school curriculum,[36] and were in fact the most important models for any English poet. Very few Englishmen could read Greek fluently—even George Chapman, in his famous versions of the *Iliad* and *Odyssey*, worked not from the original but from a Renaissance Latin translation, actually incorporating some of the editor's notes and glosses into his texts, as if they were Homer's words.[37] Elizabethan and Jacobean writers of love-poetry who had 'the tongues' might draw on the Petrarchists and anti-Petrarchists, or on the Pléïade school, but the major poets whom every beginner studied and emulated were Latin, and their prominent presence as authors in their own poems influenced many English poets. It is not necessary here to document the many allusions to, and imitations of, Latin poetry by writers of the English Renaissance. But we can remind ourselves that Horace's *Exegi monumentum*, together with the *sphragis* concluding Ovid's *Metamorphoses*, were echoed by Spenser in *The Shepheardes Calendar* and by Shakespeare in the *Sonnets*.[38] Spenser

grace. Then one of those jackdaws whom he had previously despised remarked: "if you had been content with our station in life and had been willing to take what nature gave you, you would nei-ther have experienced that first humiliation nor would your misfortune have felt the sting of our rebuff".' Trans. Ben Edwin Perry, in *Babrius and Phaedrus*, Loeb Classical Library (London, 1965), pp. 195–7. In his adaptation of the fable ('Le Geai paré des plumes du Paon', 4.9) La Fontaine made the connection with plagiarism explicit: 'Il est assez de geais à deux pieds comme lui, | Qui se parent souvent des dépouilles d'autrui, | Et que l'on nomme plagiaires.' Cf. Louis Havet (ed.), Phèdre, *Fables Ésopiques* (Paris, 1914), pp. 19–23.

[35] Terence, *Eunuchus*, 23, *Adelphi*, 13; Cicero, *Brutus*, xix. 76. Cf. J. F. D'Alton, *Roman Literary Theory and Criticism* (London, 1931; New York, 1962), pp. 18–19, 428–31.

[36] See T. W. Baldwin, *William Shakspere's 'Small Latine and Lesse Greeke'*, 2 vols. (Urbana, Ill., 1944), ii. 417–525, for analyses of 'Upper Grammar School: Shakspere's Latin Poets; Ovid, Virgil, Horace'.

[37] See F. L. Schoell, *Études sur l'Humanisme Continental en Angleterre à la fin de la Renaissance* (Paris, 1926).

[38] See 'December', in R. A. McCabe (ed.), *Edmund Spenser: The Shorter Poems* (Harmondsworth, 1999), pp. 155–6, 574; for Shakespeare's debt to Book 15 of the *Metamorphoses* see G. B. Evans's excellent edition of the *Sonnets* (Cambridge, 1996), pp. 127 (on Sonnet 15), 131–2 (on 19), 149 (on 39), 163 (on 55), 166 (on 59), 166–7 (on 60), 171 (on 64), 178–9 (on 73), 241–2 (on 126).

also knew the ancient tradition, still alive in Renaissance editions of Virgil, that the *Aeneid* originally began with four autobiographical lines recording the poet's switch from pastoral and georgic poetry to epic:

> Ille ego, qui quondam gracili modulatus avena
> carmen, et egressus silvis, vicina coegi
> ut quamvis avido parerent arva colono
> gratum opus agricolis: at nunc horrentia Martis
> arma virumque cano . . .[39]

So he began *The Faerie Queene* by imitating Virgil's autobiographical account of how he changed genres:

> Lo I the man, whose Muse whilome did maske,
> As time her taught, in lowly Shepheards weeds,
> Am now enforst a far unfitter taske,
> For trumpets sterne to chaunge mine Oaten reedes,
> And sing of Knights and Ladies gentle deeds;
> Whose prayses having slept in silence long,
> Me, all too meane, the sacred Muse areeds
> To blazon broad emongst her learned throng:
> Fierce warres and faithfull loves shall moralize my song.[40]

The English were perhaps less prone than Latin poets to include their own and other poets' names,[41] but they certainly imitated the Roman poetic elegy or epitaph, producing such notable examples as Surrey's Epitaph on Wyatt (Vickers 1999, pp. 70–2), Jonson's tribute to Shakespeare (pp. 537–40), John Ford's recently discovered 'Elegy on John Fletcher' (pp. 541–5), and Thomas Carew's 'Elegy upon the Death of Dr John Donne' (pp. 554–7).

   It would be an easy matter to show that English Renaissance poets are present in their poems, distinct biographical entities having all the properties that we associate with authors. Rather than labour that point, I would like to argue that the Roman poets' highly emphasized references to *auctor* and *opus* helped form English attitudes to authorship, especially the belief that a writer owned his own work. The best study of this topic is still H. O. White's path-breaking discussion, unsurpassed in its range of reference, of 'the attitude of English writers between 1500 and 1625 toward the ques-

---

[39] Cf. W. A. Camps, *An Introduction to Virgil's Aeneid* (Oxford, 1969), Appendix 2, pp. 121–3. Camps translates the lines, found in both *Lives* of Virgil by Donatus and Servius, but supposedly omitted by Varius, Virgil's first editor, as follows:

> I who once set my song to the music of a humble straw,
> and then forsook the woods and taught the neighbouring
> fields to obey the farmer's greediest demands—a boon
> for husbandmen—ah, now [of the horrors
> of war I sing, and of the man . . .]

> (p. 119, modified)

Camps gives cogent arguments for doubting that Virgil would have begun an epic in this way.

[40] Cf. William Nelson, *The Poetry of Edmund Spenser: A Study* (New York, 1963), p. 117.

[41] This may have something to do with the English language—it is hard to imagine anything matching 'Ronsard me célébrait du temps que j'étais belle'.

tion of literary property right'.[42] As is well known, the notion of copyright laws did not take shape until the eighteenth century.[43] In the sixteenth and seventeenth centuries the Stationers' Company protected the copyright of its members and adjudicated in many disputes. However, as in ancient Rome, writers vigorously asserted their moral rights to their own intellectual property, and despised plagiarism. In Renaissance England authors were recognized as such, whether amateurs (gentlefolk of both sexes) or professional writers who, from the 1580s onwards, eked out a living in London.[44] One excellent testimony to the universal recognition of the individual 'author' is the existence of so many book dedications.[45] In something like 90 per cent of all books published in England between 1475 and 1641 (which amount to over 30,000 publications), we find authors, writing as individuals, addressing individual patrons, thanking them for their support, hoping that the book will please, and often describing the circumstances which caused them to write it. Study of the patronage process will show even more clearly that, on both sides of the exchange, writer and patron existed as individuals, sharing interests and values.[46] The 'author-function', in Foucault's pseudo-scientific terminology, was performed by the authors themselves.

In discussing attitudes to plagiarism or surreptitious publication in the English Renaissance, as Leo Kirschbaum showed in a classic study, we must distinguish between the conflicting interests of the stationers (a term covering the activities of printers, publishers, and booksellers) and those of the writers themselves.[47] Although approximately one-third of the books published up to 1642 had not been entered in their Register, the Stationers' Company regarded all printed books as being the perpetual copyright of the stationer involved (Kirschbaum 1955, pp. 25–86). This convention was so absolute that when a stationer had printed the 'Bad' Quarto of a play he effectively established his right to print the 'Good' text issued to replace it (p. 89). Kirschbaum's detailed survey of 'surreptitious publication' (pp. 87–153) showed that publishers were not legally bound to secure an author's permission before publishing his work. Indeed, Kirschbaum quoted several instances where a publisher added a preface explicitly declaring that he had received the manuscript from a third party (usually 'a friend of the author's'), and was knowingly publishing it without the author's consent (pp. 92–118). However, Kirschbaum's collection of material may be reinterpreted to a different end, to suggest that such utterances were a kind of sales puff, whetting the reader's appetite to buy and read a text which

---

[42] H. O. White, *Plagiarism and Imitation during the English Renaissance: A Study in Critical Distinctions* (Cambridge, Mass., 1935; New York, 1965, 1973), p. vii.

[43] Cf. Mark Rose, *Authors and Owners: The Invention of Copyright* (Cambridge, Mass., 1993).

[44] See e.g. Edwin Haviland Miller, *The Professional Writer in Elizabethan England: A Study of Nondramatic Literature* (Cambridge, Mass., 1959); J. W. Saunders, *The Profession of English Letters* (London, 1964).

[45] Cf. Franklin B. Williams, Jr., *Index of Dedications and Commendatory Verses in English Books Before 1641* (London, 1962).

[46] See e.g. Eleanor Rosenberg, *Leicester: Patron of Letters* (New York, 1955); H. S. Bennett, *English Books & Readers 1558 to 1603: Being a Study in the History of the Book Trade in the Reign of Elizabeth 1* (Cambridge, 1965), pp. 30–55; Suzanne R. Westfall, *Patrons and Performance: Early Tudor Household Revels* (Oxford, 1990).

[47] *Shakespeare and the Stationers* (Columbus, Oh., 1955).

the author would otherwise have withheld (pp. 94–6, 99, 102–4). The piquancy of a publisher announcing that he was breaking the author's interdiction might make the text seem more desirable. Although they could ignore an author's wishes with impunity, publishers knew that he might be exceedingly displeased to be treated in this way. Richard Watkins issued a work by George Pettie in 1576, telling readers that in publishing it without the author's knowledge he knew that 'I am sure hereby to incur his displeasure', since he had 'willed me . . . to keep them secret: yet if it please you thankfully to accept my goodwill, I force the less of his ill will' (p. 95). The stationer hopes that the reader's gratitude will outweigh the author's indignation, an attitude often expressed.

The full treatment of this issue, both by Kirschbaum and by H. S. Bennett in his wide-ranging survey of 'demand and supply in the book trade',[48] shows very clearly that the category 'author' was well established in the sixteenth century, giving meaning to the term '*unauthorized* publication'. Authors objected to three dangers in books being published without their knowledge: that their work might be presented in a corrupt form, the text as they intended it having been mangled by repeated copying or incompetent printing; that their work might be mixed up with that written by others; or that credit for their own products might be stolen by someone else. Abraham Fraunce issued *The lamentations of Amyntas* in 1587 since he believed that his text was being 'pitifully disfigured by the barbarous handling of unskilfull pen men' producing copies (Bennett 1965, p. 21). Another stationer recorded in 1600 that 'the Author of these *Essayes*' (Sir William Cornwallis) was bringing them out reluctantly, to forestall their being 'by a mercenarie hand fowly corrupted and altered in sence', and then published 'unpolished & deformed without any correction' (cit. Kirschbaum 1955, p. 121).

Reading such utterances we must bear in mind that the Renaissance enjoyed a vigorous manuscript culture, as recent studies have shown,[49] in which scribes, both freelance and in the pay of rich collectors, made multiple copies of works in prose and verse on all manner of subjects. Many collectors of poetry compiled their own manuscript anthologies, verse miscellanies in which confusions over authorship were rife. We regularly find complaints at unauthorized 'imperfect and surreptitious' transcripts getting into print (Kirschbaum 1955, pp. 122, 127–9, 131, 144). Sir Thomas Browne complained that the 'imperfect and surreptitious copy of *Religio Medici*' published in 1642 was 'a broken and imperfect Copy, by frequent transcription . . . still run forward in corruption', with additions, omissions, and transpositions for which a copyist or printer was responsible, not the author himself (p. 145). The author most indignant at the way his writing had been treated may have been Sir Lewis Lewkenor, who in 1595 complained that 'the coppies of my letters' to private friends concerning the maltreatment of English fugitives in Spain had, 'contrarie to my intention', been given to a publisher, and not long since

---

[48] Bennett 1965; H. S. Bennett, *English Books & Readers 1603 to 1640: Being a Study of the Book Trade in the Reigns of James I and Charles I* (Cambridge, 1970).

[49] See e.g. Peter Beal, *Index of English Literary Manuscripts*, i. 1450–1625, 2 vols. (London, 1980); ii. 1625–1700, 2 vols. (London, 1987, 1993); id., *In Praise of Scribes. Manuscripts and their Makers in Seventeenth-Century England* (Oxford, 1998); Henry Woudhuysen, *Sir Philip Sidney and the Circulation of Manuscripts 1558–1640* (Oxford, 1996).

a discourse printed in Paules Church-yarde, conteining some parts of the substance thereof, but manye thinges that I had written left out, and manye thinges inserted that I never meant, and finally in the whole so falsified and chaunged, as well in matter as wordes, & ignorantly entermixed with fictions of the publisher,

that readers of any discrimination would reject it as 'grossly handled and full of absur-dities' (p. 142). These vigorous complaints show that although Current Literary Theory may deny that writers could ever have had a realizable intention, and hence a fixed and definite text, in the Renaissance these were fundamental concerns for authors at all levels.

In such unauthorized publications writers in the English sixteenth and seventeenth centuries were especially outraged when their work became indiscriminately mixed with that of other men. Given the wholesale practice of manuscript copying, such confusions were inevitable, but none the less disturbing. When Robert Tofte's poetry collection, *Laura*, appeared in 1597, it carried a public apology by the printer, Valentine Simmes, explaining that he had received the verses from a friend of the poet, one 'R.B.', and hence 'we are both to blame, that whereas he having promised to keepe private the originall, and I the copie, secret, we both have consented to send it abroad, as common'. 'R.B.' duly added a note at the end of the book, recording that the author had asked him to prevent it being printed:

> But I came at the last sheetes printing, and finde more than thirtie sonnets not his, intermixt with his. Helpt it cannot be, but by the wel judging Reader, who will with lesse paine distin-guish between them than I on this sodaine possibly can. (Bennett 1965, p. 23; Kirschbaum 1955, p. 105)

This little episode also shows that in the English Renaissance a poet's style was thought to be sufficiently individual for the presence of 'thirtie sonnets not his, inter-mixt with his' to offer readers no difficulty in distinguishing a poet's authentic intel-lectual property from an interloper's.[50] Nicholas Breton was another poet who suffered the indignity of having a book of his issued by the stationer 'in the Authors absence', and containing work not by him. In his next book, *The Pilgrimage to Paradise* (1592), Breton denounced the spurious work:

> Gentlemen, there has beene of late printed in London by one Richarde Joanes, a printer, a booke of English verses entituled *Bretons bower of delights*. I protest it was donne altogetheur without my concent or knowledge, and many thinges of other mens mingled with a few of mine, for except *Amoris Lachrimae*, an epitaphe upon Sir Phillip Sydney and one or two other toies, which I know not how he unhappily came by, I have no part with any of them, and so I beseech yee assuredly beleeve. (Bennett 1965, p. 24; Kirschbaum 1955, p. 115)

---

[50] George Wither's *Faire Virtue* (1622) was published without the author's consent, appearing in three issues, two with the poet's name on the title-page, the third with 'Written by himselfe'. In this issue the stationer, John Marriott, inserted an Epistle (which he had asked Wither to write for him) explaining that 'This being one of author's first poems was composed many years agone, and unknown to him gotten out of his custody by an acquaintance of his: and coming lately to my hands without a name, it was thought to have so much resemblance of the maker, that many upon the first sight undertook to guess who was the author of it, and persuaded that it was likely also to become profitable both to them and me' (cit. Kirschbaum 1955, p. 120).

The pain which Breton feels at having 'other mens [poems] mingled with a few of mine' expresses writers' widely felt concern to mark and respect the boundary between their own work and that of other authors.

If Elizabethan and Jacobean authors were indignant when their work appeared in print without their knowledge or permission, or in a garbled form, they were even more upset to discover that they had been plagiarized. English writers were familiar with Roman discussions distinguishing imitation from plagiarism. Among the many texts collected by H. O. White is John Hooper, *A Declaration of the Ten Holy Commandments* (1549), who, commenting on the commandment, 'Thou shalt not steal', included literary theft: 'Here is forbidden also the diminution of any man's fame; as when for vainglory any man attribute unto himself the wit or learning that another brain hath brought forth.' That sounds just like Martial's complaint about depriving a writer of his due fame, cited above, and indeed Hooper then quoted the protests of Virgil and Martial against plagiarism (White 1935, p. 41). George Puttenham gave a wider circulation to a famous anecdote concerning Virgil, recorded in Donatus' *Life* of the poet (many Renaissance writers would have found it in their edition of his works). Virgil had written a distich praising Augustus, which he fixed to the palace gate, without disclosing his authorship. The Emperor liked it, but could not discover the author, at which point 'a saucie courtier' named Bathyllus claimed it for his own, and was generously rewarded: 'whereupon Virgill, seing him self by his overmuch modestie defrauded of the reward, that an impudent had gotten by abuse of his merit, came the next night' and affixed four enigmatic, incomplete verse lines in the same place. The puzzle 'remained a great while because no man wist what it meant, till Virgill opened the whole fraud by this devise', completing the four lines and adding 'the whole verse hexameter:

Hos ego versiculos feci tulit alter honores'[51]

That is, 'I wrote these verses, but another stole the credit for them'. That text was quoted self-defensively by Greene in his dedication to *The Mirror of Modesty* (1584), and more aggressively by Heywood in *The Brazen Age* (1613), denouncing an impudent theft (White 1935, pp. 98–9, 188).

Many English writers regarded plagiarism as a shameful act.[52] A striking instance of this attitude came from Thomas Heywood in 1612, when William Jaggard reissued his spurious volume *The Passionate Pilgrim. By William Shakespeare* (1598–9). This is a small collection of twenty-one poems, of which only five are certainly by Shakespeare, including three sonnets from *Love's Labour's Lost* and two of the 'sugared sonnets' that were circulating among his private friends, as Francis Meres recorded in his compilation *Palladis Tamia: Wits Treasury* (1598). Jaggard, trying to cash in on Shakespeare's current popularity, repeated the offence in the third edition, which included additional poetry, this time lifted from Heywood's *Troia Britannica:*

---

[51] G. Puttenham, *The Arte of English Poesie*, ed. G. D. Willcock and A. Walker (Cambridge, 1936; 1970), p. 55.

[52] Sir John Harington was one of many Renaissance writers who regarded plagiarism as theft. In the preface to his translation of *Orlando Furioso* he described the task as time-consuming: he could have produced 'a just volume' of his own work in the time it has taken, especially 'if I wold have done as many spare not to do, flowne very high with stolen fethers. But I had rather men should see and know that I borrow all than that I steale any' (cit. White 1935, pp. 75–6).

or, Great Britaines Troy. A poem (1609), partly translated from Ovid. In the epistle to *An Apology for Actors* (1612) Heywood indignantly drew attention to the 'manifest injury done me in that worke' by Jaggard, having taken two of his verse epistles between Helen and Paris

> and printing them in a lesse volume [*The Passionate Pilgrim*], under the name of another [Shakespeare], which may put the world in opinion I might steale them from him; and hee to doe himself right hath since published them in his owne name [Shakespeare's *Sonnets*, 1609]: but as I must acknowledge my lines not worthy his patronage, under whom he [Jaggard] hath publisht them; so the Author I know much offended with M. *Jaggard* (that altogether unknowne to him) presumed to make so bold with his name.[53]

Shakespeare might well be angry with Jaggard, but the Stationers' Company existed to protect stationers, not authors. Greg noted that 'Jaggard at least had the decency to print a cancel title-leaf from which Shakespeare's name was removed' (1955, p. 9)—Malone's copy, now in the Bodleian.

Aesop's fable of the crow (or jackdaw) dressed in peacock's feathers recurred in many Renaissance anatomies of plagiarism. The most celebrated instance is the attack on Shakespeare delivered in a pamphlet, supposedly written by Robert Greene on his deathbed, *Greene's Groatsworth of witte, bought with a million of Repentance* (1592), which warned three fellow dramatists against trusting the common actors: 'Yes trust them not: for there is an upstart Crow, beautified with our feathers, that with his *Tygers heart wrapt in a Players hyde*, supposes he is as well able to bombast out a blanke verse as the best of you.' As White showed, with uncommon percipience, this 'is not an accusation of plagiarism' against Shakespeare but 'a diatribe against actors, if it is to be correctly understood' (1935, pp. 100–5). As we have seen, recent scholarship has proved that the writer of this attack was in fact Henry Chettle, himself the plagiarist.

H. O. White showed that English writers had 'deprecat[ed] certain types of incorrect imitation for nearly a century', while lacking the technical term (p. 120). In *Virgidemiarum* (1598), Joseph Hall introduced the word 'plagiary' when listing some unwelcome things that could happen to a person, including

> a Catch-pols fist unto a Bankrupts sleeve,
> Or an *Hos ego* from old Petrarchs spright
> Unto a Plagiarie sonnet-wright.[54]

To have Petrarch returning from the dead with Virgil's famous claim to authorship on his lips would indeed terrify the 'Plagiarie sonnet-wright', mocked in a later satire as one ready to

> filch whole Pages at a clap for need
> From honest Petrarch, clad in English weed.[55]

---

[53] Cit. W. W. Greg, *The Shakespeare First Folio: Its Bibliographic and Textual History* (Oxford, 1955), p. 9n.

[54] *Virgidemiarum*, IV. ii. 82–4, in A. Davenport (ed.), *The Collected Poems of Joseph Hall* (Liverpool, 1949), p. 57.

[55] Ibid., VI. i. 251–2, p. 94.

Other poets soon used the new word to attack an old vice. In his second *Satire* (*c.*1593–8) Donne surveyed various perversions of poetry, judging plagiarism the most serious:

> But he is worst, who (beggardly) doth chaw
> Others' wits' fruits, and in his ravenous maw
> Rankly digested, doth those things out spew,
> As his own things; and they are his own, 'tis true,
> For if one eat my meat, though it be known
> The meat was mine, th' excrement is his own.[56]

That repulsive metaphor shows how Renaissance writers regarded the theft of intellectual property. Several of Jonson's *Epigrams* (published 1616) denounce plagiarism, including one modelled on Martial (1.63), addressed 'To Prowl the Plagiary', a predator who claims for himself every line written by other poets, and lives off their work.[57] Another attacks 'Poor Poet-Ape', whose works are 'the frippery of wit' (rubbish, old clothes), and who has moved on from 'brocage' (dealing in cast-offs) to larger and bolder thefts:

> At first he made low shifts, would pick and glean,
> Buy the reversion of old plays; now grown
> To a little wealth, and credit in the scene,
> He takes up all, makes each man's with his own.

When 'Poet-Ape' is 'told of this, he slights it'. The poets from whom he steals—'we, the robbed', including Jonson—angry at first, 'leave rage, and pity it', for they realize that although an uninstructed audience may not notice the theft, good judges will spot a work made of shreds and patches:

> Tut, such crimes
> The sluggish gaping auditor devours;
> He marks not whose 'twas first: and after-times
> May judge it to be his, as well as ours.
> Fool, as if half-eyes will not know a fleece
> From locks of wool, or shreds from the whole piece![58]

There Jonson echoed Theognis (knowingly or not) in expressing his confidence that good judges will be able to detect authentic work from spurious. In his plays Jonson frequently attacked 'such crimes'. In the first version of *Every Man in His Humour* (1598) the scribbler Matteo 'is forced to admit that his verses are "translated . . . out of a booke, called Delia"' (White 1935, p. 128)—where the word 'translated' is a euphemism for piracy, and does not refer to working with a foreign language. In *Poetaster* one of Jonson's characters 'exclaims at a poem by Crispinus (Marston): "the ditti's all borrowed; 'tis Horace's: hang him plagiary"'—as White observed (p. 134), using 'the word "plagiary" just as Martial did for the outright literary pirate'. In

---

[56] *Satire* 2, 25–30; in A. J. Smith (ed.), *John Donne: The Complete English Poems* (Harmondsworth, 1971), p. 158.

[57] *Epigrams*, lxxxi, in George Parfitt (ed.), *Ben Jonson: The Complete Poems* (Harmondsworth, 1975), p. 60. Cf. also liii, 'To Old-End Gatherer' (p. 50).

[58] *Epigrams*, lvi, 'On Poet-Ape' (p. 51).

Epicoene 'two characters twit the significantly named Daw'—the vain jackdaw of the Aesopic fable—about one of his poems: "Admirable!—How it chimes . . . divinely!—Ay, 'tis Seneca.—No, I think 'tis Plutarch"' (p. 139).

The fact that writers could identify the plagiarists' victim reinforces the dominant impression produced by this enquiry, that in sixteenth- and seventeenth-century England an author was regarded as having a moral right in his or her works, whether published or still in manuscript. A vivid description of the plagiarist caught in the act is found in one of the three anonymously authored Parnassus plays, literary satires produced at St John's College, Cambridge, between 1598 and 1601, published in 1606.[59] In *The First Part of the Return from Parnassus* Gullio, 'the foolish courtier and admirer of Shakespeare', as J. B. Leishman described him, outlines to Ingenioso, 'a destitute scholar who has perforce taken service with him' (White 1935, p. 165), the 'enthusiasticall oration' he has just made to his 'new Mistress' ears', and offers to repeat it. At each stage Ingenioso comments scathingly to the audience on Gullio's plagiarisms from the current best-sellers by Shakespeare and Kyd:

> *Gullio.* Suppose also that thou wert my Mistress . . . thus I would looke amorously, thus I woulde pace, thus I woulde salute thee. . . .
> 'Pardon faire lady, thoughe sicke thoughted Gullio makes a maine unto thee, & like a bould faced sutore gins to woo thee.'
> *Ingenioso [aside].* We shall have nothinge but pure Shakespeare, and shreds of poetrie that he hath gathered at the theators.
> (a) *Gullio.* 'Pardon mee moy mittressa, as't am a gentleman the moone in comparison of thy bright hue a meere slutt, Anthonie's Cleopatra a blacke browde milkmaide, Hellen a dowdie.'
> *Ingenioso [aside].* Marke Romeo and Juliet: o monstrous theft, I thinke he will runn throughe a whole book of Samuel Daniells.
> (b) *Gullio.* 'Thrise fairer than my selfe,' thus I began,
> 'The gods faire riches, sweete above compare,
> Staine to all Nimphes, more lovely than a man,
> More white and red than doves and roses are:
> Nature that made thee, with herselfe at strife,
> Saith that the world hath ending with thy life.'
> *Ingenioso [aside].* Sweet Master Shakespeare.
> (c) *Gullio.* 'As I am a scholler, these arms of mine are long and strong withall:
> Thus elms by vines are compast ere they falle.'
> *Ingenioso.* Faith gentleman, youre reading is wonderfull in our English poets.
> *Gullio.* 'Sweet Mistress'—I vouchsafe to take some of their wordes and applie them to mine owne matters by a scholasticall imitation. Report thou upon my credit, is not my veyne in courtinge gallant & honorable?

> (Leishman 1949, pp. 183–4)

Like other plagiarists in this period, Gullio claims to be carrying out a 'scholasticall' *imitatio*, but he has in fact appropriated for his mistress, as if they were his own composition, excerpts from the following works: (a) 988 ff.: *Romeo and Juliet*, 2.4.38 ff.;

---

[59] All quotations are from the excellent edition by J. B. Leishman, *The Three Parnassus Plays* (London, 1949). See 3.1.968–1009.

(*b*) 995 ff.: *Venus and Adonis*, 7–12; and (*c*) 1002–3: Kyd, *The Spanish Tragedy*, 2.4.44–5.

Although this scene has been misunderstood as an accusation of plagiarism against Shakespeare,[60] it must be obvious that Ingenioso's 'Sweete Master Shakespeare' simply identifies the source of Gullio's preceding lines. Gullio is mocked as one of numerous uninventive lovers in Elizabethan drama who steal lines from other men's writings, in order to 'applie them to mine own matters'. True to type, Gullio subsequently commissions Ingenioso to write some New Year's verses for his mistress 'in two or three divers veyns, in Chaucers, Gowers and Spensers, and Mr Shakespeares', his preferred model:

> Marry I think I shall entertaine those verses which run like these:
>
> > 'Even as the sunn with purple coloured face
> > Had ta'en his laste leave on the weeping morne', etc.
>
> O sweet Master Shakespeare, Ile have his picture in my study at the courte.
>
> (3.1.1013–1033; Leishmann 1949, p. 185)

Ingenioso duly appears with verses 'in their severall [separate] veyns', reading out passages first in 'Chaucer's veine', then 'Spensers veine', quotations from *Troilus and Criseyde* and *The Faerie Queene* respectively, only for Gullio to reject them and demand to 'heare Mr Shakspears veyne'. Ingenioso obliges, no longer with a direct quotation from *Venus and Adonis* but with a pastiche stanza of his own invention, which sends Gullio (who is truly no judge of poetry, and whose praise may be intended satirically) off into more raptures: 'let this duncified worlde esteeme of Spenser and Chaucer, Ile worshipp sweet Master Shakespeare, and to honour him I will lay his *Venus and Adonis* under my pillowe . . .' (4.1.1137–1210; Leishmann 1949, pp. 190–3). The issues of authorship and authority crop up later in this play, when two Pages imitate their masters' behaviour, pretending to ask fiddlers to play:

> *Sir Roderick's page.* Have you never a song of maister Dowland's making?
> *Amoretto's page.* Or *Hos ego versiculos feci*, &c?
> —A pox on't, my maister *Amoretto* useth it very often. I have forgotten the verse.
>
> (5.2.1979–83; p. 353)

As H. O. White pointed out, the fact that 'Amoretto, who is satirized as a pretentious coxcomb without learning or poetic gifts, should have repeated the Virgilian accusation, "I made the verses, another has stolen the praise", so often that his page takes *Hos ego versiculus feci* to be the refrain of a song is ironic in the extreme', putting him in the category of authors 'who attempt to distract attention from their own dishonest borrowing by accusing others of the same practise' (p. 166). The metaphor repeatedly used in the *Parnassus* plays of an author's 'vein', his characteristic and recognizable style, existed in English since the 1560s, and was common throughout the English Renaissance.[61] One of Jonson's Epigrams (lxxiii), 'To Fine Grand', item-

---

[60] Cf. D. Foster, *Elegy by W. S.: A Study in Attribution* (Newark and London, 1989), p. 82, and B. Vickers, *'Counterfeiting' Shakespeare* (Cambridge, 2002), pp. 88–90.

[61] Cf. *OED*, 'vein', '12. A special or characteristic style of language or expression in writing or speech.' Bacon refers to 'the flowing and watery vein of Osorius' in 1605.

izes all the debts owed to the poet for the literary compositions he had supplied to this nobleman:

> *Item*, a fair Greek posy for a ring
>
> .   .   .   .   .   .
>
> *Item*, a gulling imprese for you, at tilt
>
> .   .   .   .   .   .
>
> *Item*, an epitaph on my lord's cock,
> In most vile verses, and cost me more pain,
> Than had I made them good, to fit your vein.[62]

The denunciations of plagiarists made by Renaissance authors address culprits who are partly real, partly imaginary. Such offences certainly took place, for in 1935 H. O. White could already list some striking instances: Brian Melbancke's *Philotimus* (1583) incorporates 'nearly two hundred borrowed passages' from Lyly's *Euphues* (p. 98); Dekker's *The Bellman of London* (1608) 'is, save for the introduction, a tissue of word-for-word copies or paraphrases from six similar works'—although Dekker himself denounced writers whose works are 'full of stolne patches', appealing: 'Banish these *Word-pirates*' (pp. 145–6). A pamphlet of Samuel Rowlands borrowed slavishly from one by Lodge, who in turn was indebted to Nashe (p. 156). Henry Pestowe's claim, in the dedication to *The Second Part of Hero and Leander* (1598), that he has made use of 'the true Italian discourse of those Lovers further Fortunes . . . to finish the Historie', is in fact 'dishonest camouflage to hide extensive paraphrasing and verbatim cribbing from *Tottel's Miscellany*' (p. 161). Scholarship in the seventy years since White wrote has accumulated many more instances of plagiarism in the Renaissance, each of which testifies to the existence of those key literary categories which, Foucault believed, must be dated much later.

III

Michel Foucault's claim that the concept of the author only emerged in the seventeenth or eighteenth century can now be seen as constituting myth, not history. The author emerged as a professional writer in the sixth century BC, and many of the attributes that we associate with authorship—a sense of individual identity, in style, attitude, literary structure; a hatred of plagiarism; a respected role in society—were already found in abundance in Greco-Roman antiquity. The status of the author undoubtedly fluctuated during the late classical period and the so-called Dark Ages, but a moment's reflection will recall that the patristic writers, Greek and Latin, enjoyed a great reputation during the Middle Ages, and that medieval *auctores* enjoyed a comparable prominence throughout the Renaissance. A glance at a catalogue of manuscripts, incunabula, or early printed books will reveal massive entries for Aquinas, Aristotle, Augustine, etc. As for the Renaissance, the rise of individuality was one of Jacob Burckhardt's markers for the new age (not without disapproval), while authors from Petrarch to Montaigne felt free to express their individual

---

[62] Parfitt 1975, p. 57.

attitudes and experience.[63] Anyone who had studied the Renaissance in even a per-functory manner would have to be suffering from amnesia to imagine that 'the author' had not then 'emerged'.

Yet, such is (or was) Foucault's cultural prestige that some impressionable students took his anachronistic myth to represent historical truth. Recently Jeffrey Masten, in a book ostensibly about authorship in Renaissance drama,[64] accepted Foucault's assault on the notion of the author as if it were a truly historical account, by reference to which all other conceptions could be dismissed as 'anachronistic'. Masten announced that,

> by demonstrating a thematics of collaboration in some 'Shakespearean' texts and by illustrat-ing the emergence of the author as *contemporaneous with (not prior to) those texts and their publication*, the present study will attempt to detach their significations from the domain of *the anachronistic author*. To do so, of course, is to argue im-plicitly the inappropriateness of an authorially based canon in this period. (Masten 1997, p. 10; my italics)

The phrase that I have italicized suggest that Masten silently revised Foucault's chronology, for instead of heralding 'the emergence of the author' in the late seven-teenth or eighteenth centuries, Masten saw it as 'contemporaneous' with 'some' Shakespearian texts, which would place it in the period 1590–1614. In other places, however, Masten's chronology was vague, or self-contradictory: Renaissance play-texts were created 'at a historical moment prior to the emergence of the author in its modern form' (p. 13). Since Masten invoked claims relating to history, we may pro-perly ask, at what 'historical moment' did the author emerge? No clear answer was provided. Masten asserted that the ascription of 'an authorial univocality' to Renaissance drama derives from 'later considerations' (p. 15), but did not disclose how much later. In Current Literary Theory it is always a safe option to attack the Enlightenment for having supposedly foisted on us such dubious conceptions as the autonomy and responsibility of the individual, so Masten proclaimed that these texts should no longer be 'read from the *post-Enlightenment* perspective of individual authorship, the now-hegemonic mode of textual production and the site of Foucault's critique' (p. 16; my italics). But a page later he asserted that the concept of a writer having an 'individuated style depends on a network of legal and social technologies specific to a *post-Renaissance capitalist culture* (e.g. intellectual property, copyright, individuated handwriting)' (p. 17; my italics). The more such statements, the more confusing the underlying chronology became: did Masten take 'post-Enlightenment' to be the same thing as 'a post-Renaissance capitalist culture'?

It is already evident that Masten copied Foucault's trick of making large historical generalizations without feeling the need to cite supporting evidence. Foucault man-aged to protect himself from the weaknesses of such a tactic with an evasiveness which Thomas Pavel has acutely described as ' "empirico-transcendental side-stepping",

---

[63] See J. Burckhardt, *Die Cultur der Renaissance in Italien. Ein Versuch* (1860), of which ch. 2 discusses the 'Development of Individualism'. See also Norman Nelson, 'Individualism as a Criterion of the Renaissance', *JEGP* 32 (1933): 316–34; Marvin B. Becker, 'Individualism in the Early Italian Renaissance: Burden and Blessing', *Studies in the Renaissance*, 19 (1972): 273–97.

[64] *Textual Intercourse: Collaboration, Authorship, and Sexualities in Renaissance Drama* (Cambridge, 1997).

which consists in conducting arguments on two levels at the same time without a system of transitions. If historical proof is missing in such a demonstration, the author will borrow from the language of metaphysics; when philosophical coherence is wanting, he will claim that the subject matter is only history'.[65] Masten did not pursue the transcendental, mercifully enough, but his claims about the emergence or non-emergence of authorship in the sixteenth and seventeenth centuries were equally lacking in any empirical grounding. Having simply asserted that a concept of the author did not exist in this period—assuming what he failed to prove—Masten shifted to a second level of theorizing, equally insistent, and equally unsupported with any historical evidence. In this second-level theory Masten constructed a new history of English drama according to which collaboration on plays *preceded* single authorship. He complained that 'scholars trained to organize material within post-Enlightenment paradigms of individuality, authorship, and textual production' have failed to realize that 'collaboration was a [*sic*] prevalent mode of textual production in the sixteenth and seventeenth centuries, *only eventually displaced by the mode of singular authorship* with which we are more familiar' (p. 4; my italics). Normally, we would expect such positivist-sounding utterances to be backed up with empirical evidence, such as a documentation of known collaborations (for which our major source of evidence is Henslowe's Diary), arranged in chronological order, and set in parallel with the evidence of sole-author composition, for which many other sources of information exist. But Masten did not offer such an analysis, indeed—amazingly enough—he never used any material from Henslowe, and appeared to be unaware of its significance. The reader of his book soon realizes that, although the author proclaimed an interest in 'a thematics of collaboration' (p. 10), it was only at an abstract or ideological level. He was not interested in the practice of co-authorship, discussing *Pericles* (pp. 75–93) without any consideration of how Shakespeare collaborated with George Wilkins, and *The Two Noble Kinsmen* (pp. 49–56) without taking stock of Shakespeare's very different collaboration with Fletcher. In fact, Masten urged scholars to 'no longer regard collaboration as an *aberrant* form of textual production in a period and genre in which it in fact *predominated*', and to 'forego *anachronistic* attempts to divine the singular author of each scene, phrase, and word' (p. 7; my italics). Further, he berated 'criticism' (whatever, or whoever, that refers to) for having

> viewed collaboration as a mere subset or aberrant kind of individual authorship, the collusion of two unique authors whom subsequent readers could discern and separate out by examining the traces of individuality and personality (including handwriting, spelling, word-choice, imagery, and syntactic formations) left in the collaborative text. (p. 16)

In claiming that collaboration 'predominated' in a given period Masten made another utterance apparently based on empirical evidence, without providing any; by introducing the word 'aberrant' he attacked a straw man, for no scholar in the field of Renaissance drama regards collaborations as anything other than normal; and by rejecting the identification of co-authors as 'anachronistic' Masten seemed to claim access to a more correct version of history. Unfortunately, his polemic did not affect

---

[65] Thomas Pavel, *The Feud of Language: A History of Structuralist Thought* (Oxford, 1989), p. 85.

the historical record, indeed, did not even impinge on it. He never attempted to justify his second-level theory, that collaboration preceded 'singular' authorship, by a review of the available evidence. Instead, he relied on a series of attempted connections between authorship and some other vaguely defined historical phenomena. But here again he did not work like a historian, who synthesizes a number of types of evidence, weighing their reliability and relative worth. Rather, he based historical-type pronouncements partly on a semantic reinterpretation of the English language (see below), partly on literary–critical readings of the preliminary matter of some seventeenth-century folio editions: the *Workes* (1616) of King James I (pp. 67–73), the *Comedies and Tragedies* (1647) of Beaumont and Fletcher (pp. 121–55), and the *Playes* (1662) of Margaret Cavendish, Duchess of Newcastle (pp. 156–64). In giving this preliminary material such importance, Masten dutifully followed Margreta de Grazia's treatment of the Shakespeare Folio,[66] but ran into several kinds of danger.

Masten's successive attempts to identify the point at which, or the process by which, collaborative authorship gradually 'gave way' to singular authorship, turn out to be opportunistic, attributing too much importance to a single text, and taking the attitudes expressed there as signifying some large cultural phenomenon. The fact that James Montagu, Bishop of Winton, dedicated James's *Workes* to his son, Prince Charles, allowed Masten to import the notion of 'patriarchal reproduction' and 'patriarchal control', resulting in the deduction that 'the idea of the author . . . *emerges* in conjunction with a language of patriarchal absolutism', or what is later dubbed 'the *emerging* patriarchal absolutist paradigm of singular authorship' (pp. 73, 131; my italics). Here Masten yoked uneasily together two clichés of recent politicized criticism, 'patriarchy', that baleful all-purpose source of evil first denounced by Lawrence Stone, and 'absolutism'—that is, 'the practice of absolute government; despotism', as the *OED* defines it, dating its first appearance to 1830. For the first, several social historians have shown that Stone both exaggerated and misdescribed the power of patriarchal attitudes in the English seventeenth century.[67] For the second, it is imperceptive to describe any English monarch in this period as 'absolutist' (*OED*: 1830; in the sense of 'despotic': 1837), when we recall all the troubles that James I and Charles I had with Parliament, resulting in civil war and regicide. Using two strikingly inappropriate categories, patriarchy and absolutism, Masten never explained how, and why, these two entities could be causally related to 'the emergence of the author'. His claim was nothing but an *ad hoc* deduction from a reading of the preliminary materials to James's *Workes*, attributing misplaced significance to what are quite conventional utterances. In another over-extended literary–critical discussion, concerning the introduction on stage of authors as presenters in *Pericles* and some other plays

---

[66] See *Shakespeare Verbatim: The Reproduction of Authority and the 1790 Apparatus* (Oxford, 1991). De Grazia was also much influenced by Foucault, claiming that Edmond Malone's edition was instrumental in 'individuating' Shakespeare for posterity. But a wider survey of Shakespeare's reception could show that that process had been at work since the late sixteenth century.

[67] See e.g. David Cressy, *Birth, Marriage, and Death: Ritual, Religion, and the Life-Cycle in Tudor and Stuart England* (Oxford, 1997), pp. 261, 538 n. 82, for critiques of Stone by E. P. Thompson, Alan MacFarlane, J. A. Sharpe, Martin Ingram, Eric Carlson, and Jeffrey Watt. See also Ralph A. Houlbrooke, *The English Family 1450–1700* (London, 1984), pp. 14–15, for a succinct account of Stone's deficiencies.

(pp. 74–102), only two pages after he had suggested that 'the idea of the author . . . emerges in conjunction with . . . patriarchal absolutism', Masten argued that 'the authorial presenters' in these plays 'establish a space for an identified author-figure on the stage'. This does not mean, he hastily added, 'that the author as we know it simply arises on the stage in the first decade of the seventeenth century' (p. 75), a possibility which always aroused his unease.

Having tried out patriarchal absolutism in connection with King James, and author-ial presenters in connection with *Pericles* (the two theories may also be combined, for *Pericles* contains two or three fathers . . .), Masten's third attempted explanation for the concept of authorship which was 'beginning to emerge' (p. 112)—it was always emergent, but never actually emerged—had to do with publishing history. Masten argued that printed play-texts functioned as 'marketable commodities' primarily advertising the theatre companies. This is unexceptionable, but he then claimed that 'a playwright's name [was] only occasionally present', and that even 'when play-wrights' names did begin to appear on quarto title pages . . . they remained only one of the many features recorded there', and were 'often typographically smaller' (pp. 114–16). What would one expect? But here Masten at last seemed to be working with empirical evidence, for he claimed to find an 'increasing frequency of title-page attri-butions to playwrights in the first three decades of the seventeenth century'. How could one explain this apparently unequivocal emergence of the author? First, Masten denied that 'authors took control of their texts' (obviously not, given the monopoly enforced by the Stationers' Company), or 'insisted upon attribution of properties rightfully theirs in a language of patriarchal-absolutism' (p. 116). But, as we have seen, a large number of authors did insist on their literary property rights, whatever language they used, and the failure to discuss the issues of plagiarism and piracy were major lacunae in Masten's work. And, despite his desperate attempts to play down the evidence of authors' names appearing on title-pages, this was not an occasional but a frequent phenomenon. As I showed in Chapter 1, declarations of authorship, single or joint, were common on quarto title-pages from the 1570s for both academic plays and the professional theatre, and continued to be given beyond the closing of the theatres (see Table 1.2). That survey allows us to draw two firm conclusions. First, although Masten attempted to limit attention to the three decades 1600–1629, it is obvious that the three preceding decades had already well established the practice of naming the writers responsible for a sole-authored or a collaborative play. Secondly, the whole record disproves Masten's case that naming authors at all was only an 'occasional' phenomenon.

Equal scepticism must greet his third explanation for the emergence of the author, the claim (p. 116) that acknowledging authorship only became common after the col-lected folio editions of Jonson (1616) and Shakespeare (1623)—as if the dozens of London printers and publishers involved in printing plays had suddenly taken those editions as allowing them to disclose authorship, not having done so earlier. However, having made this claim, unambiguously enough, it suddenly seemed too definite and Masten characteristically qualified it, in a tortuous sequence of argument:

> I resist the notion that dramatic authorship becomes an accomplished fact with the publication of the Shakespeare folio in 1623 because such a construal often *assumes* that authorship is a desire in the minds of authors that pre-exists its articulation; the appearance of authorship in

the Ben Jonson and Shakespeare folios of 1616 and 1623 respectively is said to give voice to that which is always-already present, the *presumptive* human desire to possess what one has written. Authorship, in this paradigm, does not come into being so much as it is at long last given articulation. (p. 120; my italics)

Masten can be seen struggling to delay the author's *'emergence'* as long as possible, pooh-poohing any attempt to link his appearance with 'the category of the "individual"', which he mistakenly takes to be a modern category 'severed from history' (ibid.). The question arises again, who is guilty of misleading assumptions, and whose sense of history is correct.

Having tried out three possible explanations for 'the emergence of the author', Masten came up with a fourth, in terms of the collaborating dramatists' sexual orientations. Masten attempted to give a large role in the creation of Renaissance drama to what he called the 'homoerotic' impulse. Masten never defined this term, but I assume that he used it in the standard sense, when applied to 'activities, or works of literature, art or popular culture', namely 'expressive of or derived from homosexual affections'.[68] Given that every significant English dramatist from Marlowe to Shirley took part in a co-authorship, to claim that a 'homoerotic' impulse compelled them all into literary collaboration would be a massive, but ridiculous, claim, for which no historical evidence exists. In fact, Masten cited no historical evidence (apart from one discredited source, the anecdotalist John Aubrey), relying once again on literary–critical interpretation, especially the anachronistic sexualization of seventeenth-century language. Indeed, much of Masten's case rested on non-dramatic literature, an essay by Montaigne in English translation, hardly compelling evidence for dramatists working in the London theatre.

In a chapter entitled 'Between gentlemen: homoeroticism, collaboration, and the discourse of friendship' (pp. 28–62), Masten first discussed Richard Brathwait's treatise *The English Gentleman* (1630), a conventional account of male friendship in which he briefly claimed to find a 'homoeroticism' somehow related to '*textual* intercourse' (my italics). More portentously, Masten described Montaigne's essay 'Of Friendship' as 'a complex negotiation of the issues at the nexus of homoeroticism, male friendship, and collaboration' (p. 32). In this famous essay, 'De l'amitié' (I, xxviii), 'On affectionate relationship', as M. A. Screech translates it,[69] Montaigne attempted to define the friendship he had enjoyed with Etienne de la Boétie (1530–63), a law graduate and magistrate in the Parlement de Bordeaux, where Montaigne became his colleague in 1557. It was a 'loving-friendship', Montaigne writes, unique in its kind, having no likeness to 'those four ancient species of love . . . : the natural, the social, the hospitable and the erotic' (p. 207). Montaigne sets this relationship above those between father and son, brother and brother, and 'the passion men feel for women' (pp. 207–8), 'that fire' being 'rash, fickle, fluctuating and variable':

> To enjoy it is to lose it; its end is in the body and therefore subject to satiety. Friendship on the contrary is enjoyed in proportion to our desire: since it is a matter of the mind, with our souls

---

[68] Alan Bullock and Stephen Trombley (eds.), *The New Fontana Dictionary of Modern Thought*, 3rd edn. (London, 1999), p. 401.
[69] *The Essays of Michel de Montaigne*, trans. M. A. Screech (London, 1991), pp. 205–19; page references will be included in the text.

being purified by practising it, it can spring forth, be nourished and grow only when enjoyed. Far below such perfect friendship those fickle passions [for women] also once found a place in me . . . (p. 209)

Montaigne explicitly values the constancy and gentleness of 'the love of friends' above heterosexual passion, but also above homosexual love:

And that alternative licence of the Greeks is rightly abhorrent to our manners; moreover since as they practised it it required a great disparity of age and divergence of favours between the lovers, it did not correspond either to that perfect union and congruity which we are seeking here. (p. 210)

Montaigne summarizes some of the views discussed in Plato's *Symposium*, concluding dismissively that 'the only point we can concede to the Academy is that it was a love-affair which ended in friendship' (p. 211).

It is obvious to any responsive reader that the relationship that Montaigne describes between himself and de la Boétie was not physical, and that it involved souls, not bodies: 'In the friendship which I am talking about, souls are mingled and confounded in so universal a blending that they efface the seam which joins them together so that it cannot be found.' (The concept of 'soul', clearly enough, has not so much religious as moral and psychological connotations, what we would describe as 'personality'.) It was 'some inexplicable quintessence' of qualities, Montaigne writes, 'which, having captured my will, brought it to plunge into his and lose itself and which, having captured his will, brought it to plunge and lose itself in mine with an equal hunger and emulation' (p. 212). He and de la Boétie were so close,

our souls were yoked together in such unity, and contemplated each other with so ardent an affection, and with the same affection revealed each to each other right down to the very entrails, that not only did I know his mind as well as I knew my own but I would have entrusted myself to him with greater assurance than to myself. (p. 213)

In such a 'noble relationship' each friend 'is seeking the good of the other', both 'completely committed to each other, . . . guided by virtue and led by reason' (ibid.). Montaigne and de la Boétie attained an ideal coherence of interests, thoughts, beliefs: their unity was 'that of one soul in bodies twain' (p. 214), making them 'indivisible' (p. 215).

Anyone who has read, and understood Montaigne's essay on friendship will be disturbed by the twofold manœuvre by which Masten bent it to his thesis: first he sexualized the essay as an apologia for 'homoeroticism', then he took the friendship it celebrates as an instance of literary collaboration. Using Florio's translation, and seldom referring to the original French, Masten seized on individual words in order to give them an erotic sense. Montaigne writes that friendship, being 'a matter of the mind, with our souls being purified by practising it', can 'grow only when enjoyed', which Florio translates 'nor encreaseth but in jouissance'. Masten claimed that what he calls the 'language of jouissance and sexual "enjoying"' here undermines Montaigne's argument about the chaste nature of friendly love. He added a footnote conceding that *jouissance* 'apparently did not mean "orgasm" in either French or English at this time', but he 'nevertheless' claimed that in the 'context (in both French and English texts)' as in 'historical dictionaries . . . *jouissance/enjoying* signified sexually . . .' (p. 178 n. 17). But the context in Montaigne gives no such interpretative licence, is indeed quite explicit in distinguishing this kind of friendship from 'ces quatres especes anciennes: naturelle, sociale, hospitaliere, venerienne',[70] and in delimiting the semantic context of jouissance: 'L'amitié, au rebours, . . . ne prend accroissance qu'en la jouyssance comme estant *spirituelle*, et l'ame *s'affinant* par l'usage' (i. 186; my italics). Masten ignored Montaigne's unambiguous emphasis on '*spirituelle*' and '*s'affinant*', misreading for his own ends, as he does again with Montaigne's categorical rejection of Greek homosexuality as 'justement abhorrée par nos meurs' (i. 187), claiming that Montaigne finds 'sexual relations between men . . . incompatible with friendship not because they are sexual *per se* . . .' (Masten 1997, p. 34).

The anachronistic forcing of a modern, sexualized meaning into Montaigne's intense but chaste image of male friendship reached its climax in Masten's commentary on the passage I have quoted where Montaigne describes how the 'quinte essence de tout ce meslange, . . . ayant saisi toute ma volonté, l'amena se plonger et se perdre dans la sienne', and vice versa (i. 189). From the context it is clear that by 'volonté' Montaigne means *voluntas*, the power of self-determination in the present and future. Florio translates it as 'will', reasonably enough, and uses 'plunge' for 'plonger', 'loose' for 'perdre', both unexceptionable in their contexts. Masten, however, announcing that 'some linguistic excavation is necessary to recover [the] remarkable homoeroticism' of this passage, pointed out that 'will' could mean (*inter alia*) 'the male sex organ', and that 'plunge' 'meant "to put violently, thrust, or cast *into* (or *in*) a liquid, a penetrable substance, or a cavity" . . . Taken together, these significations suggest that the essay figures a mutual interpenetration in which each friend's "will" acts as desire, penetrator, and receptacle' (p. 35). 'Penetrator and penetrated are indistinguishable in this paradigm', he continued, and although 'the essay prohibits the "Greeke licence" of pederasty . . . it valorizes another, interpenetrating version of sex between men' (p. 36). This 'version' is presumably that of sex between consenting adults, in modern terms, a perfectly legitimate activity, of course—as Montaigne put it, 'It is not my concern to tell the world how to behave (plenty of others do that) but how I behave in it' (i. 193; trans. Screech, p. 216). But it has no justification in Montaigne's text, which explicitly rejects such behaviour. Masten's 'linguistic excavation' crassly ignored the non-physical connotations of Montaigne's idealized 'affectionate relationship', forcing on it an anachronistic and inappropriate meaning.

Masten did equal violence to Montaigne's text in taking the essay's 'source and subject' to be 'collaboration' (p. 33). Looking closely at Masten's text we find a repeated association of the terms 'friendship' and 'collaboration', at some point taking the second word to be equivalent to *literary* collaboration or co-authorship, a move made by insinuation, not argument. Masten wrote about 'the collaborative texture of this friendship'; 'the network of collaborative, friendly relations'; 'translation, collaboration and friendship intersect' (p. 33). The only evidence that Masten had for this reading was his report that Montaigne 'has "advised [him] selfe to borrow" and insert into his own book an essay ("Voluntary Servitude")' by Boétie. It seems that Masten

---

[70] Montaigne, *Les Essais*, ed. Pierre Villey, re-ed. V.-L. Saulnier, 3 vols. (Paris, 1968), i. 184; future page references incorporated into the text.

failed to notice that, although Montaigne had planned to include it, Boétie's *Discours de la servitude volontaire* 'had been exploited by Protestants as an anti-monarchical pamphlet, so he reluctantly omits it' (Screech, p. 218 n.), substituting for it twenty-nine sonnets by his friend (Villey, i. 196). It is true that Montaigne encouraged de la Boétie's essay-writing, and acted as his literary executor.[71] But otherwise Masten had as much warrant for calling their friendship a literary 'collaboration' as for describing it as 'homoerotic': that is, none at all.

By his own criteria, however, Masten believed that this literary–critical exercise, blind to Montaigne's meaning and value-system, had established a historical truth about 'English Renaissance culture' (p. 36), which allowed him to issue the ambitious 'contention that late sixteenth- and early seventeenth-century dramatic writing occurs within [the] context of a collaborative homoerotics' (p. 37). After utterly predictable readings of *The Two Gentlemen of Verona* (pp. 37–48) and *The Two Noble Kinsmen* (pp. 49–60) in terms of 'homosocial networks', a 'homosocial power structure', and 'the homosocial network of power' (Michel Foucault, thou art mighty yet), Masten reverted to his thesis with a new extension, characterizing 'collaboration in dramatic writing as a mode of homoerotic textual production existing *prior to and eventually alongside* the more familiar mode of single authorship . . .' (p. 60; my italics). This is another pseudo-historical statement involving questions of chronological priority, for which no evidence was given. Masten's utterances referred primarily to Beaumont and Fletcher, who are perhaps the figures he had in mind earlier, when he declared that 'identifying Renaissance figures as gay—"outing" them—seems the mildest of possible claims one might make on the basis of the evidence we will read . . .' (p. 7)—a frank enough declaration of his anachronistic approach, appropriating this topic for the contemporary gay agenda. Masten's evidence for classifying the dramatists' relationship as 'homoerotic' partly depended on the dubious anecdote recorded by John Aubrey that 'They lived together on the Banke side, not far from the Play-house, both batchelors; lay together; had one Wench in the house between them, which they did so admire; the same cloathes and cloake, &c. betweene them.'[72] Rather than evidence of homosexuality, Aubrey's snigger seems to describe an indiscriminate (or poverty-ridden) heterosexuality, the two writers sharing the same bed, clothes, and mistress. Disavowing any wish to describe the two writers as ' "gay" in our modern terms', Masten insisted that his interest was purely 'in the material facts of cohabit-ation'. However, despite these disclaimers he explicitly suggested that Aubrey's '&c.' may 'open further erotic possibilities' (p. 61), and recorded that 'men routinely shared beds in this culture, in ways that were often erotically charged' (p. 62). A wink is as good as a nudge. As for Aubrey, that notoriously salacious gossip, whose compilation of unverifiable anecdotes dates from the 1680s or so, long after the events he claims to

---

[71] For a helpful account see Donald M. Frame, *Montaigne: A Biography* (New York, 1965), ch. 5: 'La Boétie [1559–1563]', pp. 63–84. For a sensitive reading of this essay, 'le plus noble, le plus humain, le plus chaleureux de tous', see Hugo Friedrich, *Montaigne* (Paris, 1967; trans. R. Rovini from the second German edition, 1967), pp. 253–8. In Friedrich's words, 'chaque fois qu'il aborde ce sujet de l'amitié, il s'élève à une singulière noblesse de ton, à une légère exaltation, qui tranchent sur le style ordinaire des *Essais*' (p. 254). Friedrich also pointed to the remarkable transformation by which 'cet observateur ironique de l'humanité moyenne est si religieusement saisi de cette extraordinaire union des âmes qu'il joue avec l'idée qu'un décret du ciel les avait destinées l'un à l'autre, lui et son ami, longtemps avant leur rencontre' (p. 255).

[72] Oliver Lawson Dick (ed.), *Aubrey's Brief Lives* (Harmondsworth, 1962), p. 128.

describe, most historians treat him with great scepticism, and it is disappointing that Masten gave any credit to his insinuations.

But Masten added multiple insinuations on his own account when discussing the preliminary materials to the 1647 Folio, subjecting conventional poetic tributes to Beaumont and Fletcher—whose 'strange unimitable Intercourse | Transcends all rules'—to a heavy-handed sexualized reading. It is ironic, perhaps, that a writer who has so freely accused all who do not share his Foucault-derived theories as being 'anachronistic' should repeatedly make semantic interpretations which violate the historical record, or ignore the contextual evidence limiting any word's range of possible meanings. Here, although he knew that 'the *OED* does not record the word *intercourse* as referring to sexual activity . . . until late in the eighteenth century', Masten ignored history, since he needed the word to take on that meaning in order to prove his thesis of Beaumont and Fletcher's homoerotic collaboration, and he eagerly latched on to the fact that 'strange' could mean 'queer' (pp. 132–3). Reading these conventional (and usually uninspired) poetic tributes, Masten repeatedly forced innocent words to take on an ominously sexual meaning, including 'spirit', which 'often signified both "penis" and "semen" ' (p. 141)—the unfortunate poet who used it evidently meant 'spirit' in the sense of brain or intellectual capacity. A poet who writes 'I swell', describing some kind of vatic urge, can only mean 'phallic swelling' (ibid.). Masten predictably discovered 'sexual resonances [in] the terms "out-done" and "Most knowing" ' (p. 149).[73] Earlier (p. 1) Masten had quoted Aston Cokain's '1658 poem "*An Epitaph on Mr.* John Fletcher, *and Mr.* Philip Massinger, *who lie buried both in one Grave in* St Mary Overie's Church *in* Southwark":

> In the same Grave Fletcher was buried here
> Lies the Stage-Poet Philip Massinger:
> Playes did they write together, were great friends,
> And now one Grave includes them at their ends.

Some readers might wonder why Cokain could be so categorical that Massinger (died 1640) had requested that the grave of Fletcher (died 1625) should be broken open to preserve his remains, since no official documentary evidence records this.[74] Masten's eye, however, was on what he took to be 'the homoerotic meanings of Cokain's language', and he asked us to 'note the brief sodomitical resonances of the rhyme "friends" and "ends" ' (pp. 2–3). Here Masten's 'linguistic excavation' was not explicit, and innocent readers unversed in the art of insinuation may wonder just what

---

[73] One is only grateful that Masten did not linguistically excavate the metaphor used by the Chorus to *Henry V*, referring to 'Our bending Author' (p. 75)—which properly means 'bowing as to a superior'.

[74] Masten asserts that Cokain's account agrees with 'other bits' of evidence: 'both Fletcher and Massinger are recorded in the church registry as having been buried in the parish graveyard—Massinger for a fee of £2, the exorbitancy of which may reflect *his* desire (for he was buried last) to be interred with Fletcher in the church itself' (pp. 1–2; author's italics). Had Masten consulted the standard edition, Philip Edwards and Colin Gibson (eds.), *The Plays and Poems of Philip Massinger*, 5 vols. (Oxford, 1976), he would have found that 'the reason for the high fee for burial, two pounds, is simply that it was a regulation at Southwark to double the fee for a "stranger" ', as the church register described Massinger (his home was not in the parish), and that the church's account books 'say categorically' that Massinger was buried ' "in the church" ' (i, pp. xliii–xliv). See also D. Lawless, 'The Burial of Philip Massinger', *NQ* 216 (1971): 29–30.

'sodomitical resonances' Masten could hear: does 'ends' mean 'penises'? or 'anuses'? or 'orgasms'? or something else? One recalls Doll Tearsheet's complaint: 'God's light, these villains will make the word [captain] as odious as the word "occupy", which was an excellent good word before it was ill sorted' (2 *Henry IV*, 2.4.147–9).

Readers may react as they wish to this queering of the English language.[75] I observe that, once again, instead of producing any historical evidence for his claims that collaboration '*historically preceded . . . singular authorship*' (p. 132; his italics), or that the 1647 Folio marks in some way a 'distance from *the process of undifferentiated collaboration earlier in the century*' (p. 133; my italics), Masten relied on a literary–critical approach, what we might call 'close misreading'. As to just when the idea of the author emerged, or why, the book's concluding chapter leaves us none the wiser. Masten cited Margaret Cavendish's acknowledgement in 1662 that her husband wrote parts of her plays, and argued that it took place 'within the newly emergent discourse of companionate marriage', a 'startling' innovation, Masten believed, demonstrating 'the emergence of male–female collaboration *out of the prior discourse of homoerotic friendship* that informs the Beaumont and Fletcher volume' (p. 158; my italics). Once again, in what is now his fifth attempt to link the emergence of authorship with some other phenomenon, Masten attached too much significance to a single artefact: since this is probably the only instance of male–female collaboration in the seventeenth century we can hardly talk of an 'emergence'. (Masten's designation of 'companionate marriage' as also 'newly emergent' betrays his debts to Lawrence Stone.) A few pages later Masten tried to forge another historical link, describing Cavendish as 'the self-possessed, proto-bourgeois individual who accompanies the rise of authorship' (p. 161)—of all his 'explanations', this was the most vacuous. (It seems odd to describe the Duchess of Newcastle as 'proto-bourgeois'.) Still, we wonder what—according to Foucault's theory—caused the author to 'emerge'? Masten was careful not to ascribe any definite causes to the 'emergence of authorship': it happened 'in conjunction with . . . patriarchal absolutism' (p. 73); the 'authorial presenters . . . establish a space' for an author-figure to emerge (p. 75); the acknowledgement of co-authorship takes place 'within the . . . discourse of companionate marriage' (p. 158); it 'accompanies' proto-capitalism (p. 161). The proliferation of these accompanying phenomena, which itemize nothing so definite as an actual cause, shows that Masten had no real explanation for an event which, in his terms, ought not to have occurred, since Current Literary Theory has demonized the very notion of individual agency so often since the

---

[75] In recent years the wide spectrum of literary criticism has included a 'politicizing' strand, the term referring not to large-scale political activity within the state but to so-called 'identity politics', categories of race and gender where 'the identities in question are social constructions based on mythical portrayals of a collective past attached to symbols of ongoing subordination in the larger society' (Bullock and Trombley 1999, p. 414). Identity politics either practises the discourse of guilt, the injured minorities (blacks, women, gays) attaching blame to writers living and dead for their complicity in persecution, or it seeks in literature of the past justification for its own defining attitudes. Either way, the results are often extremely damaging to literary texts, which become distorted, forced into inappropriate and anachronistic categories. It remains a puzzle why political movements which are perfectly justified in the contemporary world—to stamp out racism, to win equal working conditions for women, to prevent the persecution of homosexuals—should have such a deleterious effect on literary texts and on the practice of literary criticism. For a penetrating analysis of this phenomenon see John M. Ellis, *Literature Lost: Social Agendas and the Corruption of the Humanities* (New Haven and London, 1997).

1960s as to make even its fleeting appearance too distasteful to contemplate. Indeed, Masten explicitly rebuked any writers—even Foucault himself—who betray signs of granting authors individuality or intentionality.[76]

Masten acknowledged that his 'observations are obviously indebted to Foucault's conceptual shift' (p. 27), and included himself among 'the many following Foucault' (p. 197 n. 41), but the debt seems to have paralysed his ability to think clearly, and blinded him to any phenomena other than those recognized by his Foucauldian thesis. Several of the passages that he cited to support it are in fact manifestations of completely different attitudes, those that I characterized earlier as tending to protect individual authors' moral rights to their own work. Masten cited the Bishop of Winton's prefatory remarks to King James's works as exemplifying the language of patriarchal absolutism. But the Bishop in fact expressed the concern of so many other writers in this period to establish an author's moral right to his work, declaring his willingness 'to labour much in the recovering those that have been lost; *to give . . . to every Booke the trew author*' (p. 72; my italics). Masten cited Aston Cokain's well-known epigram to the editors who published the 1647 Beaumont and Fletcher Folio and ascribed the plays solely to that duo, but he was blind to its real significance:

> In the large book of Playes you late did print
> (In Beaumont and in Fletchers name) why in't
> Did you not *justice? give to each his due?*
> For Beaumont (of those many) writ in few:
> And Massinger in other few; the Main
> Being sole Issues of sweet Fletchers brain.
>
> (p. 153; my italics)

That rebuke in fact proves the point I have been making, that, for writers in the sixteenth and seventeenth centuries, to acknowledge the activities of co-authors is simply an act of 'justice', to 'give to each his due', *suum cuique tribuere*, that key principle of Roman law. Another witness to this widespread moral commitment throughout the English Renaissance to distinguish *suus* from *alienus* is Margaret Cavendish's address to the readers of her collected *Playes* (1662), where she scrupulously recorded that her husband had in some instances added lustre to her pages (using the verb *illustrate* in the old sense of 'to make illustrious, to confer honour, distinction upon'):

> My lord was pleased to illustrate my Playes with some Scenes of his own Wit, to which I have set his name, that my Readers may know which are his, as not to Cozen them, in thinking they are mine. (p 158)

---

[76] Hesitantly, Masten announces that, despite his debt to Foucault, 'I would at the same time want to interrogate his imagination of a post-authorial "constraining figure", for it seems to register both a residue of intention left by the deceased author and a singularity . . .' (p. 27), neither of which he finds acceptable. The 'deceased author' is a Foucauldianism, of course, and does not refer to an actual writer. More confidently, Masten indicts one woman critic for 'her assumption that authorship in this period is an expression of already extant desires . . .' (p. 192 n. 81), and another for attributing 'to Jonson a transparent agency or self-selected authorial ideology' (p. 195 n. 23). But of all Renaissance authors, Jonson had perhaps the most robust sense of his own agency.

Masten interpreted Cokain's rebuke as expressing a 'familiar patriarchal rhetoric' (p. 153), and he took Cavendish's honest acknowledgement of her husband's occasional co-authorship to show that she was 'writing within a sexual or reproductive discourse' (p. 158). The relevance of these utterances to early modern sensitivities to plagiarism, or to authorship being wrongly claimed, has escaped him. But we have seen exactly the same compunctions about using another writer's work expressed by many English Renaissance authors cited here.

The defining weakness of Masten's work is that it is theory driven, a new form of locomotion owing nothing to historical scholarship. Although purporting to offer a historical account, it failed to examine the primary evidence for authorship, contained on plays' title-pages, in the Stationers' Register, in Henslowe's Diary, and in Sir Henry Herbert's licensing book. Simply to open these sources is to notice not just the presence of the author but his centrality, in creating the play-texts without which no theatrical production could take place. My all-too-brief attempt to characterize the general awareness, in this period, that authors wrote books, dedicated them to patrons, and sometimes stole from other authors, who would rightly feel aggrieved at such plagiarism, necessarily relied on printed evidence. But on most days in Elizabethan, Jacobean, and Caroline London playwrights could be seen moving from their lodgings to a theatre or other meeting-place, carrying ideas for a play, or a plot-outline, perhaps even one or two acts of a completed play. If they fall behind the due date, the theatre manager may even send a messenger to their lodgings, who sometimes finds a dramatist in the throes of composition, or waits half an hour until he has finished writing the sheet. The documents from which I quoted in Chapter 1 give a good sense of the immediacy of the composition process, and the all too real hazards that lay in wait for the careless: imprisonment for writing and performing a scabrous satire, for offending the King, or for failing to pay debts. Playwrights collaborating on a play must have regularly met to compare notes, discuss progress, make changes in their allotted share if the plot or characterization had taken a different direction. Quick workers, ready to take on several commissions simultaneously, even for different companies, these authors for the stage could earn a reasonable living and attain public recognition. Some of them were also actors in their own and other plays; others were sharers in the theatre company; a lucky few owned shares in the theatre building, and benefited from the company's takings. In emulating Foucault's abstract historiography, Masten never made contact with the dramatists, figures of flesh and blood busily earning their living by their pens. It is ironic that Masten's orientation, through a form of literary criticism subordinated to gay agendas, should have cut him off from the emphasis on the materiality of cultural processes also currently fashionable (but also subject to ideological distortion). The pioneer dramatists—Marlowe, Kyd, Greene, Peele, Shakespeare—all 'born in the decade 1555–66 and maturing in the 1580s', as Neil Carson observed, 'had demonstrated that playwriting could be a viable, even successful career'.[77] Their immediate successors, starting up in the 1590s—Heywood, Jonson, Marston, Dekker—not only achieved economic independence but helped the theatre acquire some intellectual and social respectability. Those in Shakespeare's company, the King's Men, also enjoyed a privileged status at court,

---

[77] N. Carson, *A Companion to Henslowe's Diary* (Cambridge, 1988), p. 54.

and were included in the official dispensation of cloth and other perquisites on state occasions, such as James's coronation.

If Masten had not been under Foucault's influence, and had trusted his own eyes, he could have found in the marvellous reference works by E. K. Chambers and G. E. Bentley detailed discussions of the life and work of more than 150 named dramatists.[78] In the Elizabethan theatre world the author had not just 'emerged', he had established himself as an independent agent, intellectually and economically. So much must be obvious to anyone with a smattering of historical awareness. Masten's pre-selection of texts to be 'linguistically excavated' ignored much relevant material familiar to students of Renaissance drama. Where he constructed a tendentious argument that 'the emergence of the author' was aided by the author-presenter figure in *Pericles* and later plays, many early Tudor plays had had presenters, and to find an author-figure on stage we need look no further than the 'Good' Quarto of *Hamlet* (1604):

> *Enter Hamlet, and three of the Players*
>
> *Ham.* Speake the speech I pray you as I pronounc'd it to you, trippingly on the tongue, but if you mouth it as many of our Players do, I had as live the towne cryer spoke my lines . . .
>
> . . . and let those that play your clownes speake no more then is set down for them . . .
>
> (3.2.1–4, 38–40)

Hamlet is as concerned as many other authors in this period must have been about what the actors might do to 'my lines', especially that the clown should not exceed what he has 'set down for them' to perform. We know that Elizabethan actors' contracts included a stipulation that they should 'attend all such rehearsall which shall the night before the rehearsall be given publickly out' (Carson 1988, p. 37), and when the author was one of the actors—as were Shakespeare, Heywood, Jonson, Nat Field, and others—he would surely have adjudicated on matters of meaning and interpretation.

To make this (by no means novel) suggestion is to apply the historical imagination to a material context for which much other information exists. Jeffrey Masten ignored relevant material and historical evidence, dismissing as 'anachronistic' the work of attribution scholars such as Cyrus Hoy, David Lake, and MacDonald Jackson.[79] Yet, as readers of this book will know, their work was based on an extensive first-hand knowledge of Elizabethan drama texts and the historical contexts (theatre production; printing-house practices) which affected the ways in which play-texts have come down to us, but without erasing the individuality of the dramatists involved. Masten's preoccupation with Foucauldian theory generated or encouraged a historical amnesia

---

[78] See *Eliz. S*, Book V, ch. 23, 'Playwrights' (iii. 201–518); *JCS*, 'Plays and Playwrights' (iii. 1–470; iv. 471–959; v. 961–1280).

[79] Masten criticized some of the leading modern attribution scholars on ideological grounds, rebuking Cyrus Hoy for 'his post-Enlightenment assumptions about authorship, textual property, and individuality of style' (p. 16), and for having 'distinctly modern notions of individuality and authorial property', displaying 'a historically inappropriate idea of the author' (p. 18). Hoy is also made guilty of providing 'the model and basis for extensive (and similarly compromised) work on Massinger, Middleton and others' by David Lake and MacDonald Jackson (p. 173 n. 31). In all such utterances, Masten remained sublimely unaware of his own 'distinctly modern notions', and his attempt to challenge Hoy's work (pp. 16–20) on scholarly terms was embarrassing in its failure to understand either the method or the principles involved.

which blotted out for him the large quantity of evidence enabling us to reconstruct actual authorship practices, and his wish to appropriate co-authorship to a modern gay agenda added another level of anachronism to his interpretation. The deficiencies of his approach are all too evident, but they may usefully remind us how anachronism distorts the past to suit the whims of the present.

Bibliography

1. PRIMARY WORKS

BATE, J. (1995) (ed.), Shakespeare, *Titus Andronicus*, New Arden Shakespeare (London).

BERTHOUD, J., and MASSAI, S. (2001) (eds.), Shakespeare, *Titus Andronicus*, New Penguin Shakespeare (London).

BROOKE, C. F. T. (1908) (ed.), *The Shakespeare Apocrypha: Being a Collection of Fourteen Plays which have been Ascribed to Shakespeare* (Oxford).

BULLOUGH, G. (1966) (ed.), *Narrative and Dramatic Sources of Shakespeare*, vi. *Other 'Classical' Plays* (London and New York).

DEL VECCHIO, D., and HAMMOND, A. (1998) (eds.), Shakespeare, *Pericles, Prince of Tyre* (Cambridge).

FOAKES, R. A. (1957) (ed.), Shakespeare, *Henry VIII* (London; rev. edn., 1962).

——and RICKERT, R. T. (1961) (eds.), *Henslowe's Diary* (Cambridge).

GABRIELI, V. and MELCHIORI, G. (1990) (eds.), *Sir Thomas More*, Revels edition (Manchester).

GREG, W. W. (1905), edition of *The Elder Brother*, in A. H. Bullen (ed.), *The Works of Francis Beaumont and John Fletcher*, Variorum edition (London) vol. ii.

——(1911) (ed.), *The Book of Sir Thomas More*, Malone Society (London); repr. with a supplementary introduction by Harold Jenkins (London, 1961, 1990).

HIBBARD, G. R. (1970) (ed.), *Timon of Athens*, New Penguin Shakespeare (Harmondsworth).

HOENIGER, F. D. (1963) (ed.), Shakespeare, *Pericles*, New Arden Shakespeare (London).

HUGHES, A. (1994) (ed.), Shakespeare, *Titus Andronicus* (Cambridge).

KLEIN, KARL (2001) (ed.), Shakespeare, *Timon of Athens*, New Cambridge Shakespeare (Cambridge).

LITTLEDALE, H. (1876) (ed.), *The Two Noble Kinsmen. Reprint of the Quarto, 1634* (London: The New Shakspere Society).

——(1885) (ed.), *The Two Noble Kinsmen. By William Shakspere and John Fletcher. Edited from the Quarto of 1634. Part II. General Introduction and List of Words* (London: The New Shakspere Society).

MCKERROW, R. B. (1905), edition of *The Spanish Curate* in A. H. Bullen (ed.), *The Works of Francis Beaumont and John Fletcher*, Variorum edition (London), vol. ii.

MCMULLAN, G. (2000) (ed.), Shakespeare and Fletcher, *King Henry VIII (All Is True)*, Arden Shakespeare, Third Series (London).

MARGESON, J. (1990) (ed.), Shakespeare, *Henry VIII* (Cambridge).

MAXWELL, J. C. (1957) (ed.), Shakespeare, *The Life of Timon of Athens* (Cambridge).

——(1961) (ed.), Shakespeare, *Titus Andronicus*, Arden Shakespeare (London, rev. edn.; 1st edn., 1953).

——(1962) (ed.), Shakespeare, *Henry VIII* (Cambridge; rev. edn., 1969).

OLIVER, H. J. (1959) (ed.), Shakespeare, *Timon of Athens*, New Arden Shakespeare (London; rev. edn. 1963).

PETTER, C. G. (1973) (ed.), George Chapman and Ben Jonson, *Eastward Ho!* (London).

POTTER, L. (1997) (ed.), Shakespeare, *The Two Noble Kinsmen*, New Arden Shakespeare (London).

PROUDFOOT, G. R. (1970) (ed.), Fletcher and Shakespeare, *The Two Noble Kinsmen* (London).

PROUTY, C. T. (1952–70) (ed.), *The Life and Works of George Peele*, 3 vols. (New Haven).

SISSON, C. J. (1954) (ed.), *William Shakespeare: The Complete Works* (London).

WAITH, E. M. (1984) (ed.), Shakespeare, *Titus Andronicus* (Oxford).

——(1989) (ed.), Shakespeare, *The Two Noble Kinsmen* (Oxford).

WILSON, J. D. (1948) (ed.), Shakespeare, *Titus Andronicus* (Cambridge).

2. SECONDARY WORKS

ADAMS, J. Q. (1945) 'The Author-Plot of an Early Seventeenth-Century Play', *Library*, 4th ser., 25: 17–27.

ALEXANDER, P. (1931) 'Conjectural History, or Shakespeare's *Henry VIII*', *Essays and Studies*, 16: 85–119.

BAKER, H. (1939) *Induction to Tragedy: A Study in a Development of Form in 'Gorboduc', 'The Spanish Tragedy' and 'Titus Andronicus'* (Baton Rouge, La.; New York, 1965).

BALD, R. C. (1931) 'Addition III of *Sir Thomas More*', *RES* 7: 67–9.

——(1949) '*The Booke of Sir Thomas More* and its Problems', *ShS* 2: 44–65.

BALDWIN, T. W. (1944) *William Shakspere's 'Small Latine and Lesse Greeke'*, 2 vols. (Urbana, Ill.; repr. 1966).

——(1959) 'The Work of Peele and Shakespeare on *Titus Andronicus*', in Baldwin, *On the Literary Genetics of Shakspere's Plays, 1592–1594* (Urbana, Ill.), pp. 402–20.

BARKER, R. H. (1945) 'The Authorship of *The Second Maiden's Tragedy* and *The Revenger's Tragedy*', *Shakespeare Association Bulletin*, 20: 51–62, 121–33.

——(1958) *Thomas Middleton* (New York).

BENTLEY, G. E. (1941–68) *The Jacobean and Caroline Stage*, 7 vols. (Oxford), abbreviated as *JCS*.

——(1948) 'Shakespeare and the Blackfriars Theatre', *ShS* 1: 38–50.

——(1986) *The Professions of Dramatist and Player in Shakespeare's Time 1590–1642* (Princeton).

BLAYNEY, P. (1972) '*The Booke of Sir Thomas Moore* Re-Examined', *SP* 69: 167–91.

BOLTON, J. S. G. (1929) 'The Authentic Text of *Titus Andronicus*', *PMLA* 44: 765–88.

——(1933) '*Titus Andronicus*: Shakespeare at Thirty', *SP* 30: 208–24.

BOWERS, F. (1989a) (ed.), *The Dramatic Works in the Beaumont and Fletcher Canon*, vii (Cambridge).

——(1989b) *Henry VIII*: 'Textual Introduction', in Bowers 1989a, pp. 3–20.

BOWERS, F. (*cont.*) (1989c) *The Two Noble Kinsmen*: 'Textual Introduction', in Bowers 1989a, pp. 147–68.

BOYD, B. (1995) 'Common Words in *Titus Andronicus*: The Presence of Peele', *NQ* 240: 300–7.

BOYLE, R. (1880–2) 'On Wilkins's Share in the Play Called Shakspere's *Pericles*', *TNSS* 8: 323–40.

——(1885) '*Henry VIII*: An Investigation into the Origin and Authorship of the Play', *TNSS* 11: 443–87.

BRADLEY, A. C. (1929) 'Scene-endings in Shakespeare and in *The Two Noble Kinsmen*', in Bradley, *A Miscellany* (London), pp. 218–24.

BRAINERD, B. (1979) 'Pronouns and Genre in Shakespeare's Drama', *CHum*, 13: 3–16.

——(1980) 'The Chronology of Shakespeare's Plays: A Statistical Study', *CHum*, 14: 221–30.

BRAUNMULLER, A. R. (1983) *George Peele* (Boston).

BYRNE, M. ST CLARE (1932) 'Bibliographic Clues in Collaborate Plays', *Library*, 4th ser., 13: 21–48.

CARSON, N. (1988) *A Companion to Henslowe's Diary* (Cambridge).

CHAMBERS, E. K. (1923) *The Elizabethan Stage*, 4 vols. (Oxford), abbreviated as *Eliz. S.*

——(1930) *William Shakespeare: A Study of Facts and Problems*, 2 vols. (Oxford).

CHAMBERS, R. W. (1931) 'Some Sequences of Thought in Shakespeare and in the 147 lines of *Sir Thomas More*', *MLR* 26: 251–80.

——(1939) 'Shakespeare and the Play of *More*', in Chambers, *Man's Unconquerable Mind* (London) pp. 204–49, 407–8; repr. 1952.

CLEMEN, W. (1961) *English Tragedy before Shakespeare: The Development of Dramatic Speech* (London); trans. T. S. Dorsch from *Die Tragödie vor Shakespeare: ihre Entwicklung im Spiegel der dramatischen Rede* (Heidelberg, 1955).

CRAIK, G. (1857) *English of Shakespeare, illustrated in a philological commentary on his 'Julius Caesar'* (London; rev. edns. 1859, 1864, etc.).

DAWSON, G. (1990) 'Shakespeare's Handwriting', *ShS* 42: 119–28.

DELIUS, N. (1867) 'Ueber Shakespeare's Timon of Athens', *ShJb* 2: 335–61.

——(1868) 'Ueber Shakespeare's Pericles, Prince of Tyre', *ShJb* 3: 175–204.

DORAN, M. (1954) *Endeavors of Art: A Study of Form in Elizabethan Drama* (Madison).

EGE, K. (1922) 'Shakespeares Anteil an *Henry VIII*', *ShJb* 58: 99–119.

——(1923) 'Der Anteil Shakespeare's an *The Two Noble Kinsmen*', *ShJb*, NS 1: 62–85.

ELLIOTT, W. E. Y., and VALENZA, R. J. (1996) 'And Then There Were None: Winnowing the Shakespeare Claimants', *CHum*, 30: 191–245.

ELLIS-FERMOR, UNA (1961) '*Timon of Athens*: An Unfinished Play', in Ellis-Fermor, *Shakespeare the Dramatist* (London), pp. 158–76; originally in *RES* 18 (1942): 270–83.

ERNE, L. (1998) 'Biography and Mythography: Rereading Chettle's Alleged Apology to Shakespeare', *ES* 79: 430–40.

FARNHAM, W. E. (1916) 'Colloquial Contractions in Beaumont, Fletcher, Massinger, and Shakespeare as a Test of Authorship', *PMLA* 31: 326–58.

FLEAY, F. G. (1874a) 'On Metrical Tests as applied to Dramatic Poetry. Part I. Shakespeare', *TNSS* 1: 1–16, 38–9 (a 'Postscript' correcting 'a numerical blunder'); repr. in Fleay 1876b, pp. 121–38.

——(1874b) 'On Metrical Tests as applied to Dramatic Poetry. Part II. Fletcher, Beaumont, Massinger', *TNSS* 1: 51–72; repr. in Fleay 1876b, pp. 151–70.

——(1874c) 'On the Authorship of *Timon of Athens*', *TNSS* 1: 130–51; repr. in Fleay 1876b, pp. 187–208.

——(1874d) 'Mr. Hickson's Division of *The Two Noble Kinsmen*, Confirmed by Metrical Tests', *TNSS* 1: 61*–64*; repr. in Fleay 1876b, pp. 172–4.

——(1876a) 'On the Play of *Pericles*', *TNSS* 3: 195–209; repr. in Fleay 1876b, pp. 209–23.

——(1876b) *Shakespeare Manual* (London).

FOSTER, D. (1989) *Elegy by W. S. A Study in Attribution* (Newark and London).

FRAZER, W. (1991) 'Henslowe's "ne" ', *NQ* 236: 34–5.

FURNIVALL, F. J. (1874a) 'Another Fresh Confirmation of Mr. Spedding's Division and Date of the Play of *Henry VIII*', *TNSS* 1: 24*.

——(1874b) 'Mr. Hickson's Division of *The Two Noble Kinsmen*, Confirmed by the Stopt-line Test', *TNSS* 1: 64*–65*.

GRAY, A. K. (1928) 'Shakespeare and *Titus Andronicus*', *SP* 25: 295–311.

GRAY, J. C. (1984) (ed.), *Mirror up to Shakespeare: Essays in Honour of G. R. Hibbard* (London and Toronto).

GREG, W. W. (1907) *Henslowe Papers: Being Documents Supplementary to Henslowe's Diary* (London).

——(1921) *Dramatic Documents from the Elizabethan Playhouses*, 2 vols. (Oxford).

——(1939–57) *A Bibliography of English Printed Drama to the Restoration*, 4 vols. (London).

——(1955) *The Shakespeare First Folio: Its Bibliographic and Textual History* (Oxford).

HARBAGE, A., rev. SCHOENBAUM, S. (1964) *Annals of English Drama 975–1642* (London; Supplements: 1966, 1970).

HART, A. (1934a) *Shakespeare and the Homilies: And Other Pieces of Research into the Elizabethan Drama* (Melbourne and London; repr. New York, 1970, 1977).

——(1934b) 'Shakespeare and the Vocabulary of *The Two Noble Kinsmen*', in Hart 1934a, pp. 242–56; from *RES* 10 (1934): 278–87.

——(1943a) 'The Vocabularies of Shakespeare's Plays', *RES* 19: 128–40.

——(1943b) 'The Growth of Shakespeare's Vocabulary', *RES* 19: 242–54.

HERDAN, G. (1965) 'Discussion of Mr. Morton's Paper', *Journal of the Royal Statistical Society*, Series A, 128: 229–31.

HICKSON, S. (1847) review essay on *The Two Noble Kinsmen*, *Westminster and Foreign Quarterly Review*, 92: 59–88; repr. as 'The Shares of Shakspere and Fletcher in *The Two Noble Kinsmen*', *TNSS* 1 (1874): 25*–61*.

——(1850) Letter to the Editor, *GM*, 178 (NS 34): 198; repr. as 'A Confirmation of Mr. Spedding's Paper on the Authorship of *Henry VIII*', in *TNSS* 1 (1874): 18*–20*.

HILL, R. F. (1957) 'The Composition of *Titus Andronicus*', *ShS* 10: 60–70.

HINMAN, C. (1963) *The Printing and Proof-Reading of the First Folio of Shakespeare*, 2 vols. (Oxford).

HOENIGER, F. D. (1982) 'Gower and Shakespeare in *Pericles*', *ShQ* 33: 461–79.

HOLDSWORTH, R. V. (1994) 'Middleton's Authorship of *A Yorkshire Tragedy*', *RES* 45: 1–25.

HONIGMANN, E. A. J. (1965) *The Stability of Shakespeare's Text* (London).

——(1990) '*Pericles*, Acts I and II: New Evidence for George Wilkins', *NQ* 215: 192–6.

HOPE, J. (1994) *The Authorship of Shakespeare's Plays: A Socio-Linguistic Study* (Cambridge).

HORNE, D. H. (1952) *The Life and Minor Works of George Peele* (New Haven), vol. i of C. T. Prouty (ed.), *The Life and Works of George Peele*, 3 vols. (New Haven, 1952–70).

HOWARD-HILL, T. H. (1989) (ed.), *Shakespeare and 'Sir Thomas More': Essays on the Play and its Shakespearian Interest* (Cambridge).

HOY, C. (1956) 'The Shares of Fletcher and his Collaborators in the Beaumont and Fletcher Canon (I)', *SB* 8: 129–46.

——(1957) 'The Shares of Fletcher and his Collaborators in the Beaumont and Fletcher Canon (II)', *SB* 9: 143–62.

——(1958) 'The Shares of Fletcher and his Collaborators in the Beaumont and Fletcher Canon (III)', *SB* 11: 85–106.

——(1959a) 'The Shares of Fletcher and his Collaborators in the Beaumont and Fletcher Canon (IV)', *SB* 12: 91–116.

——(1959b) 'Verbal Formulae in the Plays of Philip Massinger', *SP* 56 (1959): 600–18.

——(1960) 'The Shares of Fletcher and his Collaborators in the Beaumont and Fletcher Canon (V)', *SB* 13: 77–108.

——(1961) 'The Shares of Fletcher and his Collaborators in the Beaumont and Fletcher Canon (VI)', *SB* 14: 45–67.

——(1962) 'The Shares of Fletcher and his Collaborators in the Beaumont and Fletcher Canon (VII)', *SB* 15: 71–90.

——(1976) 'Critical and Aesthetic Problems of Collaboration in Renaissance Drama', *RORD* 19: 3–6.

——(1984) 'The Language of Fletcherian Tragicomedy', in Gray 1984, pp. 99–113.

HUNTER, G. K. (1984) 'Sources and Meanings in *Titus Andronicus*', in Gray 1984, pp. 171–88.

INGRAM, J. K. (1874) 'On the "Weak Endings" of Shakspere, With Some Account of the History of the Verse-Tests in General', *TNSS* 1: 442–64.

JACKSON, M. P. (1962) 'Affirmative Particles in *Henry VIII*', *NQ* 206: 372–4.

——(1971) 'A Non-Shakespearian Parallel to the Common Mispronunciation of *ergo* in Hand D of *Sir Thomas More*', *NQ* 216: 139.

——(1976) review of D. J. Lake, *The Canon of Thomas Middleton's Plays*, *JEGP* 75: 414–17.

——(1978) 'Linguistic Evidence for the Date of Shakespeare's Addition to "Sir Thomas More"', *NQ* 223: 154–6.

——(1979) *Studies in Attribution: Middleton and Shakespeare*, Jacobean Drama Studies, vol. 79 (Salzburg).

——(1981) 'Hand D of *Sir Thomas More*', *NQ* 226: 146.

——(1990) '*Pericles*, Acts I and II: New Evidence for George Wilkins', *NQ* 215: 192–6.

——(1991) 'George Wilkins and the First Two Acts of *Pericles*: New Evidence from Function Words', *LLC* 6: 155–63.

——(1993*a*) 'The Authorship of *Pericles*: The Evidence of Infinitives', *NQ* 238: 197–200.

——(1993*b*) 'Rhyming in *Pericles*: More Evidence of Dual Authorship', *SB* 46: 239–49.

——(1996) 'Stage Directions and Speech Headings in Act 1 of *Titus Andronicus* Q (1594): Shakespeare or Peele?', *SB* 49: 134–48.

——(1997*a*) 'Phrase Length in *Henry VIII*: Shakespeare and Fletcher', *NQ* 242: 75–80.

——(1997*b*) 'Shakespeare's Brothers and Peele's Brethren: *Titus Andronicus* Again', *NQ* 242: 494–5.

——(1998) 'Editing, Attribution Studies, and "Literature Online": A New Resource for Research in Renaissance Drama', *RORD* 37: 1–15.

——(1999) 'Medium and Message: Authors and Poetic Styles in *Pericles*', unpublished paper delivered to the Shakespeare Association of America, 1–3 Apr. 1999.

——(2002) 'Pause Patterns in Shakespeare's Verse: Canon and Chronology', *LLC* 16: 37–46.

——(unpublished), 'Some Thoughts on the "Shakespearian" Additions to *Sir Thomas More*, and on Carol Chillington's Study'.

JOHNSON, P. F. (1974) 'The Use of Statistics in the Analysis of the Characteristics of Pauline Writing', *New Testament Studies* 20: 92–100.

JONES, F. L. (1932) 'An Experiment with Massinger's Verse', *PMLA* 47: 727–40.

JOWETT, J. (1989) 'Henry Chettle and the Original Text of *Sir Thomas More*', in Howard-Hill 1989, pp. 131–49.

KENNY, A. (1982) *The Computation of Style: An Introduction to Statistics for Students of Literature and Humanities* (Oxford).

——(1986) *A Stylometric Study of the New Testament* (Oxford).

KNIGHT, C. (1849) *Studies of Shakspere* (London).

LAKE, D. J. (1969*a*) 'Rhymes in *Pericles*', *NQ* 214: 139–43.

——(1969*b*) ' "More" and "Mo(e)" in *Henry VIII*', *NQ* 214: 143–4.

——(1969*c*) 'Wilkins and *Pericles*—Vocabulary (1)', *NQ* 214: 288–91.

——(1970) 'The *Pericles* Candidates: Heywood, Rowley, Wilkins', *NQ* 215: 135–41.

——(1975) *The Canon of Thomas Middleton's Plays* (Cambridge).

——(1977) 'The Date of the "Sir Thomas More" additions by Dekker and Shakespeare', *NQ* 222: 114–16.

——(unpublished) 'Stylistic Variation in *Henry VIII* and *The Two Noble Kinsmen*' (typescript).

LANDSBERG, E. (1910) 'Der Stil in George Peeles sicheren und zweifelhaften dramatischen Werken', Ph.D. Diss. (Breslau).

LANGWORTHY, C. A. (1928) 'Verse–Sentence Patterns in English Poetry', *SP* 7: 283–98.

——(1931) 'A Verse–Sentence Analysis of Shakespeare's Plays', *PMLA* 46: 738–51.

LAW, R. A. (1957) 'Holinshed and *Henry the Eighth*', *Texas Studies in English*, 36: 3–11.

—— (1959) 'The Double Authorship of *Henry VIII*', *ShQ* 56: 471–88.

LEDGER, G. R. (1989) *Re-counting Plato: A Computer Analysis of Plato's Style* (Oxford).

LUCAS, E. V. (1904) (ed.), *The Works of Charles and Mary Lamb, iv. Dramatic Specimens and the Garrick Plays* (London).

McMANAWAY, J. G. (1950) 'Recent Studies in Shakespeare's Chronology', *ShS* 3: 22–33.

McMILLIN, S. (1987) *The Elizabethan Theatre and 'The Book of Sir Thomas More'* (Ithaca, NY).

McMULLAN, G. (1994) *The Politics of Unease in the Plays of John Fletcher* (Amherst, Mass.).

MAHOOD, M. M. (1957) *Shakespeare's Wordplay* (London).

MAXWELL, B. (1939) *Studies in Beaumont, Fletcher, and Massinger* (Chapel Hill, NC; repr. New York, 1966).

MAXWELL, J. C. (1950) 'Peele and Shakespeare: A Stylometric Test', *JEGP* 49: 557–61.

MELCHIORI, G. (1985) 'Hand D in *Sir Thomas More*: An Essay in Misinterpretation', *ShS* 38: 101–14.

MERRIAM, T. (1982) 'The Authorship of Sir Thomas More', *ALLC Bulletin*, 10: 1–7.

—— (1989) 'Taylor's Statistics in *A Textual Companion*', *NQ* 234: 341–2.

—— (1992) '*Pericles* I–II Revisited and Considerations Concerning Literary Medium [*sic*] as a Systematic Factor in Stylometry', *NQ* 237: 341–5.

METZ, G. H. (1985) 'Disputed Shakespearean Texts and Stylometric Analysis', *Text*, 2: 149–71.

MINCOFF, M. (1952) 'The Authorship of *The Two Noble Kinsmen*', *ES* 33: 97–115.

—— (1961) '*Henry VIII* and Fletcher', *ShQ* 12: 239–60.

—— (1976) *Shakespeare: The First Steps* (Sofia).

MORTON, A. Q. (1965) 'The Authorship of Greek Prose', *Journal of the Royal Statistical Society*, Series A, 128: 169–224; followed by a discussion, pp. 224–31.

—— (1978) *Literary Detection: How to Prove Authorship and Fraud in Literary Documents* (London).

—— (1984) 'Stylometry vs. "Stylometry"', *ShN* 34: 5.

—— (1986) 'Once: A Test of Authorship Based on Words which are not Repeated in the Sample', *LLC* 1: 1–8.

—— and McLEMAN, J. J. (1966) *Paul, the Man and the Myth* (London).

MOSTELLER, F., and WALLACE, D. L. (1964) *Inference and Disputed Authorship: The Federalist Papers* (Reading, Mass.).

MUIR, K. (1960) *Shakespeare as Collaborator* (London).

NEUMANN, K. J. (1990) *The Authenticity of the Pauline Epistles in the Light of Stylostatistical Analysis* (Atlanta, Ga.).

NICOLSON, M. H. (1922) 'The Authorship of *Henry the Eighth*', *PMLA* 37: 484–502.

NOSWORTHY, J. M. (1955) 'Shakespeare and *Sir Thomas More*', *RES* ns 6: 12–25.

NUTTALL, A. D. (1989) *Timon of Athens* (Hemel Hempstead).

OLIPHANT, E. H. C. (1919) 'Sir Thomas More', *JEGP* 18: 226–35.

—— (1926) 'The Authorship of *The Revenger's Tragedy*', *SP* 23: 157–68.

——(1927) *The Plays of Beaumont and Fletcher: An Attempt to Determine their Respective Shares and the Shares of Others* (New Haven; repr. New York, 1970).

ORAS, A. (1953) '"Extra Monosyllables" in *Henry VIII* and the Problem of Authorship', *JEGP* 52: 198–213.

——(1960) *Pause Patterns in Elizabethan and Jacobean Drama: An Experiment in Prosody*, University of Florida Monographs, no. 3 (Gainesville, Fla.).

PARROTT, T. M. (1919) 'Shakespeare's Revision of *Titus Andronicus*', *MLR* 14: 16–37.

PARTRIDGE, A. C. (1949) *The Problem of Henry VIII Re-opened* (Cambridge); revised as Partridge 1964*b*.

——(1964*a*) *Orthography in Shakespeare and Elizabethan Drama: A Study of Colloquial Contractions, Elision, Prosody and Punctuation* (London).

——(1964*b*) '*Henry VIII*: Linguistic Criteria for the Two Styles Apparent in the Play', in Partridge 1964*a*, pp. 141–63.

PIERCE, F. E. (1909) *The Collaboration of Webster and Dekker* (New Haven; repr. Hamden, Conn., 1972).

——(1912*a*) 'The Collaboration of Dekker and Ford (I): The Authorship of *The Sun's Darling*', *Anglia*, n. F. 34: 141–68.

——(1912*b*) 'The Collaboration of Dekker and Ford (II): The Authorship of *The Witch of Edmonton*', *Anglia*, n. F. 34: 289–312.

POLLARD, A. W. (1923) (ed.), *Shakespeare's Hand in The Play of Sir Thomas More* (Cambridge).

PRICE, H. T. (1943) 'The Authorship of *Titus Andronicus*', *JEGP* 42: 55–81.

PRIOR, R. (1972) 'The Life of George Wilkins', *ShS* 25: 137–52.

——(1976) 'George Wilkins and the Young Heir', *ShS* 29: 33–9.

RIBNER, I. (1957) *The English History Play in the Age of Shakespeare* (Princeton).

SAMPLEY, A. M. (1933) '"Verbal Tests" for Peele's Plays', *SP* 30: 473–96.

——(1936) 'Plot Structure in Peele's Plays as a Test of Authorship', *PMLA* 51: 689–701.

SARRAZIN, G. (1897) 'Wortechos bei Shakespeare, I', *ShJb* 33: 121–65.

——(1898) 'Wortechos bei Shakespeare, II', *ShJb* 34: 119–69.

SCHÄFER, J. (1973) *Shakespeares Stil. Germanisches und romanisches Vokabular* (Frankfurt).

SCHLUETER, J. (1999) 'Rereading the Peacham Drawing', *ShQ* 50: 171–84.

SCHOENBAUM, S. (1966) *Internal Evidence and Elizabethan Dramatic Authorship: An Essay in Literary History and Method* (London).

SENN, W. (1973) *Studies in the Dramatic Construction of Robert Greene and George Peele* (Berne).

SIMPSON, R. (1871) 'Are There Any Extant MSS. in Shakespeare's Handwriting?', *NQ*, 4th ser., 8 (July): 1–3.

SISSON, C. J. (1936) *Lost Plays of Shakespeare's Age* (Cambridge).

SMITH, M. W. A. (1985*a*) 'An Investigation of Morton's Method to Distinguish Elizabethan Playwrights', *Computers and the Humanities* 19: 3–21.

——(1985*b*) 'An Investigation of the Basis of Morton's Method for the Determination of Authorship', *Style*, 19: 341–68.

——(1987*a*) 'Hapax Legomena in Prescribed Positions: An Investigation of Recent Proposals to Resolve Problems of Authorship', *LLC* 2: 145–52.

SMITH, M. W. A. (*cont.*) (1987*b*) 'The Authorship of *Pericles*: New Evidence for Wilkins', *LLC* 2: 221–30.

—— (1988) 'The Authorship of Acts I and II of *Pericles*: A New Approach Using First Words of Speeches', *CHum*, 22: 23–41.

—— (1989*a*) 'Forensic Stylometry: A Theoretical Basis for Further Developments of Practical Methods', *Journal of the Forensic Science Society*, 29: 15–33.

—— (1989*b*) 'A Procedure to Determine Authorship Using Pairs of Consecutive Words: More Evidence for Wilkins's Participation in *Pericles*', *CHum* 23: 113–29.

—— (1989*c*) 'Function Words and the Authorship of *Pericles*', *NQ* 234: 333–6.

—— (1990) 'A Note on the Authorship of *Pericles*', *CHum* 24: 295–300.

—— (1991*a*) 'The Authorship of *Timon of Athens*', *Text* 5: 195–240.

—— (1991*b*) 'Statistical Inference in *A Textual Companion* to the Oxford Shakespeare', *NQ* 236: 73–8.

—— (1992*a*) 'Shakespeare, Stylometry and *Sir Thomas More*', *SP* 89: 434–44.

—— (1992*b*) 'The Problem of Acts I–II of *Pericles*', *NQ* 237: 346–55.

—— (1994) '*Sir Thomas More*, *Pericles*, and Stylometry', *NQ* 239: 55–8.

SPALDING, W. (1833) *A Letter on Shakspere's Authorship of 'The Two Noble Kinsmen'* (Edinburgh; repr. London, 1876).

SPEDDING, J. (1850*a*) 'Who Wrote Shakspere's *Henry VIII*?', *GM* 178, NS 34: 115–23; repr. as 'On the Several Shares of Shakespeare and Fletcher in the Play of *Henry VIII*', *TNSS* 1 (1874): 1*–18*.

—— (1850*b*) Letter to the Editor, *GM* 178, NS 34: 381–2.

SPENCER, T. (1939) '*The Two Noble Kinsmen*', *MP* 36: 255–76.

SPENCER, T. J. B. (1957) 'Shakespeare and the Elizabethan Romans', *ShS* 10: 27–38.

SPIKER, S. (1933) 'George Wilkins and the Authorship of *Pericles*', *SP* 30: 551–70.

SPURGEON, C. (1930) 'Imagery in the *Sir Thomas More* Fragment', *RES* 6: 257–70.

STEEVENS, G. (1780) Notes on *Pericles*, in E. Malone (ed.), *Supplement* to the 1778 edn. of Shakespeare by Johnson and Steevens (London).

STEVENSON, B. (1989) 'Adapting Hypothesis Testing to a Literary Problem', in R. G. Potter (ed.), *Literary Computing and Literary Criticism* (Philadelphia), pp. 63–74.

SYKES, H. D. (1919*a*) *Sidelights on Shakespeare* (Stratford-upon-Avon).

—— (1919*b*) '*King Henry VIII*', in Sykes 1919*a*, pp. 18–47.

—— (1919*c*) 'Wilkins and Shakespeare's *Pericles, Prince of Tyre*', in Sykes 1919*a*, pp. 143–203.

—— (1924) 'The Problem of *Timon of Athens*', *Sidelights on Elizabethan Drama* (Oxford), pp. 1–48; originally as essays in *NQ* 1921.

TARLINSKAJA, M. (1987) *Shakespeare's Verse: Iambic Pentameter and the Poet's Idiosyncrasies* (New York).

TAYLOR, G. (1987) 'The Canon and Chronology of Shakespeare's Plays', in Wells and Taylor 1987.

—— (1989) 'The Date and Auspices of the Additions to *Sir Thomas More*', in Howard-Hill 1989, pp. 101–30.

—— (1995) 'Shakespeare and Others: The Authorship of *Henry the Sixth, Part One*', *MRDE* 7: 145–205.

THOMAS, S. (1983) 'The Problem of *Pericles*', *ShQ* 34: 448–50.

THOMPSON, A. (1978) *Shakespeare's Chaucer: A Study in Literary Origins* (Liverpool).

——(1992) with T. L. Berger, A. R. Braunmuller, P. Edwards, and L. Potter, *Which Shakespeare? A User's Guide to Editions* (Milton Keynes and Philadelphia).

THOMSON, N. (1989) 'How to Read Articles which Depend on Statistics', *LLC* 4: 6–11.

THORNDIKE, A. H. (1901) *The Influence of Beaumont and Fletcher on Shakspere* (Worcester, Mass.; repr. New York, 1966).

TIMBERLAKE, P. W. (1931) *The Feminine Ending in English Blank Verse: A Study of its Use by Early Writers in the Measure and its Development in the Drama up to the Year 1595* (Menasha, Wis.).

TURNER, R. K. (1987) 'Collaborators at Work: The *Queen of Corinth* and The *Knight of Malta*', in B. Fabian and K. Tetzeli von Rosador (eds.), *Shakespeare: Text, Language, Criticism. Essays in Honour of Marvin Spevack* (Zurich), pp. 315–33.

VICKERS, B. (1968) *The Artistry of Shakespeare's Prose* (London; repr. 1979).

——(1974–81) (ed.), *Shakespeare: The Critical Heritage, 1693–1801*, 6 vols. (London and Boston), abbreviated as *CHS*.

——(1988) *In Defence of Rhetoric* (Oxford; 3rd edn., 1997).

——(1993a) 'Shakespearian Consolations', *Proceedings of the British Academy*, 82: 219–84.

——(1993b) *Appropriating Shakespeare: Contemporary Critical Quarrels* (New Haven and London).

——(1999) (ed.), *English Renaissance Literary Criticism*, Oxford.

——(2002) *'Counterfeiting' Shakespeare: Evidence, Authorship, and John Ford's Funerall Elegye* (Cambridge).

WAITH, E. M. (1952) *The Pattern of Tragicomedy in Beaumont and Fletcher* (New Haven; repr. Hamden, Conn., 1969).

WALLER, F. O. (1966) 'The Use of Linguistic Criteria in Determining the Copy and Dates for Shakespeare's Plays', in W. F. McNeir and T. N. Greenfield (eds.), *Pacific Coast Studies in Shakespeare* (Eugene, Ore.), pp. 1–19.

WEBER, H. (1812) 'Observations on the Participation of Shakespeare in *The Two Noble Kinsmen*', in Weber (ed.), *The Works of Beaumont and Fletcher*, 14 vols. (Edinburgh), xiii. 151–69.

WELLS, S. (1984) *Re-Editing Shakespeare for the Modern Reader* (Oxford).

——and TAYLOR, G., with J. JOWETT and W. MONTGOMERY (1987) *William Shakespeare: A Textual Companion* (Oxford), abbreviated as *TxC*.

WELLS, W. (1920) 'Timon of Athens', *NQ*, 12th ser., 6: 266–9.

WENTERSDORF, K. (1951) 'Shakespearean Chronology and the Metrical Tests', in W. Fischer and K. Wentersdorf (eds.), *Shakespeare-Studien. Festschrift für Heinrich Mutschmann* (Marburg), pp. 161–93.

——(1973) 'Linkages of Thought and Imagery in Shakespeare and *More*', *Modern Language Quarterly*, 34: 384–405.

WERSTINE, P. (1989) 'On the Compositors of *The Two Noble Kinsmen*', in C. H. Frey (ed.), *Shakespeare, Fletcher and 'The Two Noble Kinsmen'* (Columbia, Mo.), pp. 6–30.

WILLIAMS, C. B. (1970) *Style and Vocabulary: Numerical Studies* (London).

WILSON, J. D. (1923) 'Bibliographical Links between the Three Pages and the Good Quartos', in Pollard (1923), pp. 113–41.

WRIGHT, E. H. (1910) *The Authorship of Timon of Athens* (New York).

Index